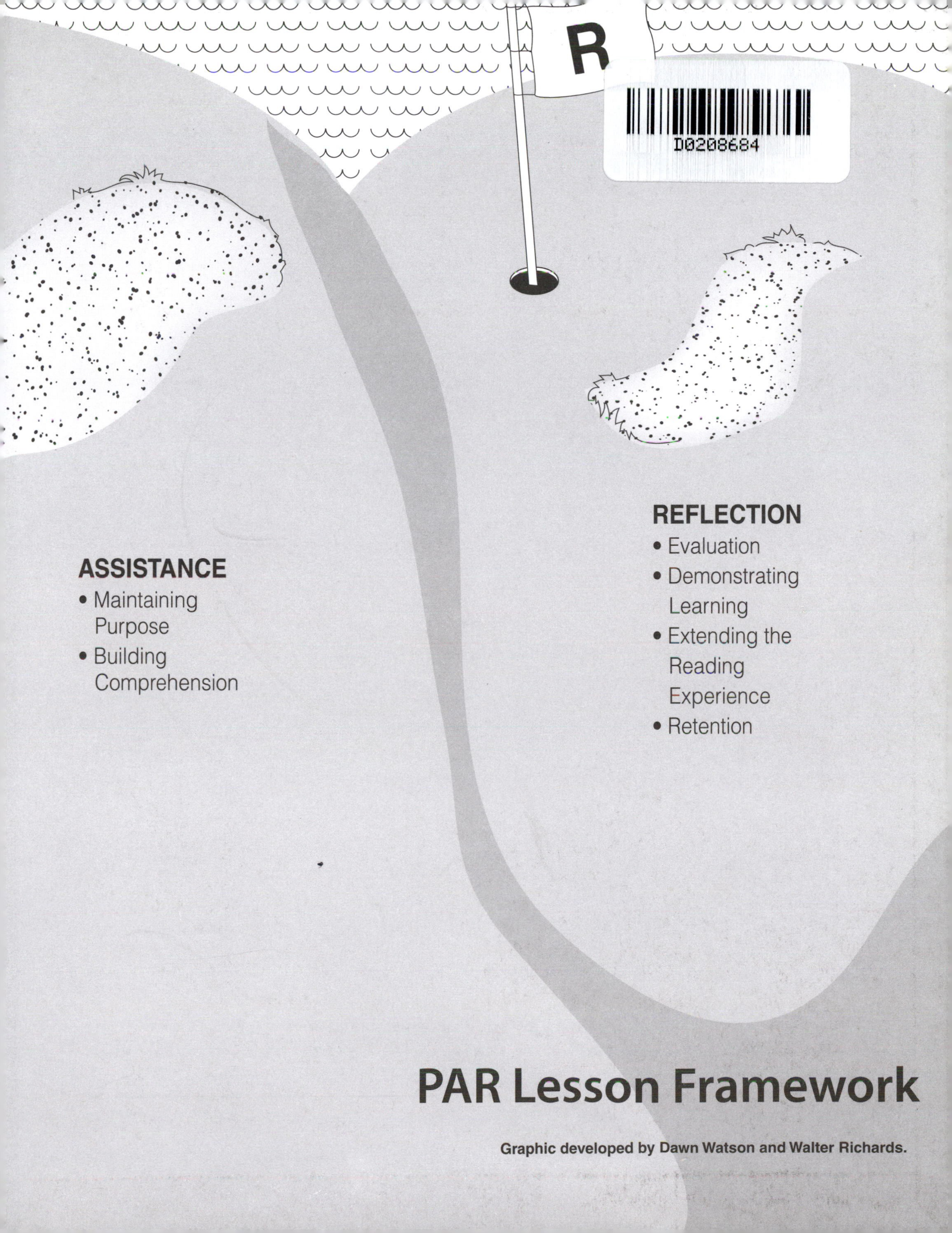

PAR Lesson Framework

Graphic developed by Dawn Watson and Walter Richards.

EIGHTH EDITION

Reading to Learn in the Content Areas

JUDY S. RICHARDSON

Professor Emerita, Virginia Commonwealth University

Professor, J. Sargeant Reynolds Community College

RAYMOND F. MORGAN

Professor Emeritus, Old Dominion University

CHARLENE E. FLEENER

Professor, Old Dominion University

WADSWORTH

CENGAGE Learning™

Australia • Brazil • Japan • Korea • Mexico • Singapore • Spain • United Kingdom • United States

WADSWORTH
CENGAGE Learning™

Reading to Learn in the Content Areas, Eighth Edition
Judy S. Richardson, Raymond F. Morgan, Charlene E. Fleener

Senior Publisher: Linda Schreiber-Ganster

Executive Editor: Mark Kerr

Associate Developmental Editor: Caitlin Cox

Assistant Editor: Genevieve Allen

Editorial Assistant: Greta Lindquist

Marketing Manager: Kara Kindstrom Parsons

Marketing Coordinator: Klaira Markenzon

Senior Marketing Communications Manager: Heather L. Baxley

Content Project Management: PreMediaGlobal

Design Director: Rob Hugel

Art Director: Jennifer Wahi

Print Buyer: Rebecca Cross

Rights Acquisitions Specialist (Image & Text): Roberta Broyer

Production Service: PreMediaGlobal

Text Designer: Brenda Carmichael

Photo Researcher: Scott Rosen

Text Researcher: Isabel Saraiva

Copy Editor: Danielle Shaw

Cover Designer: Bill Reuter/Reuter Design

Cover Image: Fotosearch Enhanced/ Royalty Free

Compositor: PreMediaGlobal

Library of Congress Control Number: 2011926141

ISBN-13: 978-1-111-30273-3

ISBN-10: 1-111-30273-1

Wadsworth
20 Davis Drive
Belmont, CA 94002-3098
USA

Cengage Learning is a leading provider of customized learning solutions with office locations around the globe, including Singapore, the United Kingdom, Australia, Mexico, Brazil, and Japan. Locate your local office at **www.cengage.com/global**

Cengage Learning products are represented in Canada by Nelson Education, Ltd.

For your course and learning solutions, visit **www.cengage.com/wadsworth**

Purchase any of our products at your local college store or at our preferred online store **www.cengagebrain.com**

Printed in the United States of America

1 2 3 4 5 6 7 15 14 13 12 11

In memory of Janice Kohler Richardson, a "book babe" and extraordinary middle school librarian, who died in August 2010.

Judy S. Richardson

In memory of my cherished cousin Bill Morgan, who was my brother in spirit, close confidant, and best golfing buddy.

Raymond F. Morgan

In memory of Doyle and LaVerne Emmert, true lifelong learners, readers, encouragers and dream makers: my parents.

Charlene E. Fleener

Contents

Preface xv

CHAPTER 1

Content Teachers and Content Literacy 1

Voices from the Classroom 2
Preparing to Read 2
Objectives 3

What Is the Role of Literacy in Content Classrooms? 3
Improved Instruction—Are We There Yet? 4
Twelve Principles for Effective Content Teachers 6

The Importance of Structure through a Lesson Framework 14

PAR: A Lesson Framework for Instruction 14

Four Lessons of PAR Used in Teaching Content 16
Example from a Primary Social Studies Lesson 16
Example from a Fifth Grade Art Class 18
Example from a Middle School Mathematics Lesson 19
Example from a High School Biology Class 20
Now Meet Four Students 23
At-risk Profile: JaNette 23
ESL Profile: Gustavo 23
Struggling Reader Profile: Mark 24
Special Education: Trinka 24

The Organization of This Text 24

One-Minute Summary 25
End-of-Chapter Activities 26

CHAPTER 2

Teaching in the Affective Domain 27

Voices from the Classroom 28
Preparing to Read 28
Objectives 29

Affect and Learning 29

Assessing Attitudes for Affective Teaching 31

Motivating Students to Learn 34

Conation as a Variable in Teaching Reading 36
Promoting Affect in Brain-Based Teaching 39
Fostering the Habit of Reading 40
Locus of Control and Reading 42
Questioning 43
Challenge Box: JaNette, the At-Risk Student 43
Using the PAR Lesson Framework to Develop Lesson Plans 45
One-Minute Summary 49
End-of-Chapter Activities 50

CHAPTER 3

Preparation for Learning 51

Voices from the Classroom 52
Preparing to Read 52
Objectives 52
The Importance of Determining Prior Knowledge 54
The Problem of Matching Reader with Text 55
Challenge Box: Gustavo, English as a Second Language Student 55
Schema Theory and Prior Knowledge 56
The Role Prior Knowledge Plays in Heightening Interest 57
Limited Prior Knowledge 59
Incorrect Prior Knowledge 60
Preparing the Learner through Building on Prior Knowledge 61
Prelearning Concept Check 61
Story Impressions 62
K-W-L Activity 63
What-I-Know Activity 64
Rewriting Text 64
Written Previews 68
Clarifying Thinking with Graphic Organizers 68
Anticipation Guides 71
Factstorming 73
PreP Strategy 74
Analogies 75
Final Thoughts 77
One-Minute Summary 77
End-of-Chapter Activities 77

CHAPTER 4

Assistance in Learning 79

Voices from the Classroom 80
Preparing to Read 80
Objectives 81
Providing Assistance in the Construction of Meaning 81
Improving Comprehension through the Use of Instructional Strategies 82

Constructivism and Reading 85
Comprehending Segments of Text 87
Directed Reading–Thinking Activity 87
Guided Reading Procedure 90
Reciprocal Teaching 93
Assisting Students in Learning Text Structure 93
Strategies for Comprehending Text Structure 94
Improving Comprehension through Questions and Questioning 100
Student-Generated Questions 101
Questioning Strategies 101
Strategy Repertoire 105
Challenge Box: Mark, The Struggling Reader 105
One-Minute Summary 106
End-of-Chapter Activities 106

CHAPTER 5

Learning through Reflection 107

Voices from the Classroom 108
Preparing to Read 108
Objectives 108
The Reflection Phase of Reading 108
Reflection Creates Autonomous Learners 109
Important Skills to Emphasize in the Reflection Phase of Reading 110
Reflecting through Cooperative Learning 116
Distinguishing Cooperative Learning from Group Work 117
Why Cooperative Learning Is Effective 118
PAR and Cooperative Learning 118
Strategies and Activities for Reflection in Reading 119
Brainstorming 119
Post-Graphic Organizers 120
Making Connections 122
Double-Entry Journals 123
Rallytable 123
Numbered Heads Together 123
Challenge Box: Gustavo, English as a Second Language Student 124
Paired Reading 124
Three-Step Interview 125
Repeated Readings and Text Lookbacks 125
Group Summarizations 126
Reflection Guides 126
Think–Pair–Share 127
Extended Anticipation Guides 128
ABOUT/POINT 128
Self-Generated Questions 130
Think-Alouds 130
One-Minute Summary 133
End-of-Chapter Activities 133

CHAPTER 6

Moving beyond the Traditional Textbook and Transmission Methods 134

Voices from the Classroom 135
Preparing to Read 135
Objectives 135

Why Textbooks Cannot Stand Alone 137
  Limitations of the Traditional Textbook 137

Using Multiple Resources in Addition to Textbooks 139
  Multimodal Text and Multitext 139
  Read-Alongs and Read-Alouds 139

Challenge Box: Mark, the struggling reader 140

Issues Related to Using Multiple Resources in the Classroom 142
  Setting the Environment 142
  Locating Materials and Resources 142

Using Literature in the Content Classroom 143
  Using and Selecting Trade Books 143
  Content Area Literature Circles 144
  Multimodal Literature Circles 146

Assessing the Readability of Textbooks and Resources 147
  Barriers to Comprehension and Learning 147
  How to Determine Readability of Textbooks and Resources 149

Assessing Students' Ability to Use Books 156
  The Cloze Procedure 156
  Using Cloze for Determining and Building Background Knowledge 157
  The Maze 161

Critical Literacy Applications for Multimodal Texts 162
  Interactive Reading 162
  Approaches to Reading Electronic Vs. Traditional Print 162

Cooperative Learning Beyond the Textbook 163
  Jigsaw 164
  Three-Step Interview 164

One-Minute Summary 165
End-of-Chapter Activities 166

CHAPTER 7

Teaching Vocabulary 167

Voices from the Classroom 168
Preparing to Read 168
Objectives 168

Content-Specific Vocabulary and Academic Vocabulary 169

A Closer Look at Word Knowledge 170

Preventing Vocabulary and School Failure 172
  Incidental Vocabulary Development 174
  Intentional Vocabulary Development 176

Vocabulary Instruction for Children with Learning Disabilities 176

Teaching Vocabulary in Preparation for Reading 179
  Word Inventories 179
  Graphic Organizers 180
  Possible Sentences 182

Teaching Vocabulary to Assist Students in Their Reading 183
  Context Clue Discovery 185
  Structural Analysis 187
  Vocabulary Podcasts 190
  Vocabulary Lists 191
  Organizational (Jot) Charts 191
  Using the Dictionary 192

Teaching Vocabulary as a Reflection Activity 193
  Semantic Feature Analysis 193
  Postgraphic Organizers 194
  Categorization 195
  Directed Reading–Thinking Activity Vocabulary Search 197
  A Vocabulary Study System 197
  Four-Column Organizer for Word Mastery 198
  Vocabulary Self-Collection Strategy 198
  Language Enrichment through Reflection 198

Challenge Box: Mark, the Struggling Reader 201

One-Minute Summary 210
End-of-Chapter Activities 210

CHAPTER 8

Writing to Learn in the Content Areas 212

Voices from the Classroom 213
Preparing to Read 213
Objectives 214

The Importance of Writing 214
  On-Demand Writing 216
  Authentic Writing 216

The Importance of the Reading–Writing Connection 219

Writing as a Product 222

Writing as a Process 223

Computers as Writing Tools 224

Writing and the PAR Framework 226
  The Preparation Phase of Writing 226
  The Assistance Phase of Writing 230
  The Reflection Phase of Writing 240

Writing for At-Risk and Struggling Readers 248

Challenge Box: Gustavo, English as a Second Language Student 250

One-Minute Summary 251
End-of-Chapter Activities 251

CHAPTER 9

Study Skills in the Electronic Age 253

Voices from the Classroom 254
Preparing to Read 254
Objectives 255

What Are Study Skills? 255
 Who Needs Study Skills? 256

A Brief History of Study Skills 257
 What Does This Brief History Tell Us about Study Skills? 259

Preparation for Study 260
 Assessments 260
 Homework, Study Conditions, and Time Management 261

Preparation Strategies and Activities 266
 Listening 266
 Locating and Selecting Information 268
 Previewing 271
 Following Directions 274

Assistance Strategies and Activities 275
 Interpreting Graphic Aids 275
 Organizing Information 276

Reflection Study Techniques 282
 Mnemonics 284
 Reading Flexibly 287
 Rate of Reading 288
 Skimming and Scanning 289
 Retention and Systems of Study 289
 Challenge Box: JaNette, the At-Risk Student 289

One-Minute Summary 291
End-of-Chapter Activities 292

CHAPTER 10

Technology in Today's Content Classrooms 293

Voices from the Classroom 294
Preparing to Read 294
Objectives 294

It's a Flat World 295

A Brief Explanation of Digital Literacy 297

Standards 298

Advantages of Digital Literacy 298

Technology for Classroom Use 300
 Word Processing and Other Production Applications 300
 Instructional Software 301
 Auditory Resources 303
 Electronic Books 303

Challenge Box: Trinka, a Student with Learning Disabilities 304
The Internet 304
A Hypertext Environment 306
Online Communication 306
Social Computing 307
Cautions about Digital Literacy 310
Ease of Use 310
Privacy Issues 311
Limited Teaching Capabilities 312
Availability of Resources 313
Technology in Your Classroom 314
One-Minute Summary 315
End-of-Chapter Activities 315

CHAPTER 11

Supporting Diverse Learners in Content Classrooms 317

Voices from the Classroom 318
Preparing to Read 318
Objectives 319
Diverse Learners 319
Students with Special Needs 320
Types of Students with Special Needs 320
Issues in Special Education 321
Teaching Students with Special Needs in the Content Classroom 323
At-Risk Students 324
Identifying and Helping At-Risk Students 325
Resilient Students 325
Students from Low-Socioeconomic Environments 327
Instructional Guidelines for Working with Students from Low-Socioeconomic Environments 328
Students with Low Self-esteem 329
Building Positive Relationships 329
Guidelines for Working with Students with Low Self-esteem 331
English as a Second Language Students 331
English Language Learners 333
School Programs for English Language Learners 335
Instructional Guidelines for Working with English Language Learner Students 335
Instructional Misconceptions about English Language Learner Students 337
Techniques That Work Well with English Language Learner Students 337
Reading Instruction for Struggling Students 340
Comprehension Monitoring 340
Differentiation for Struggling Learners 341
Steps for Content Teachers 343

Strategies for Struggling Readers 344
Additional Strategies for the Most Challenging Cases 347
Teaching Diverse Learners in the Content Classroom 351
One-Minute Summary 351
End-of-Chapter Activities 351

CHAPTER 12

Assessment and Evaluation Issues 353

Voices from the Classroom 354
Preparing to Read 354
Objectives 354
Teaching in an Age of Accountability 355
Key Concepts in Assessment and Evaluation 356
Standardized, Norm-Referenced Tests 357
Criterion-Referenced Tests 358
Evaluation in the Era of No Child Left Behind 359
No Child Left Behind and Evaluation Procedures 359
Experts Weigh In 360
Understanding High-Stakes Testing 361
How Are High-Stakes Tests Constructed and Used? 362
What Educators Can Do in the Age of Accountability 362
When Teachers Make Tests 364
The Role of Pop Quizzes 364
Traditional Teacher Assessments 366
Creating Effective Teacher-Made Tests 367
How to Improve the Design of Tests 369
Preparing and Assisting Students to Take Traditional Tests 370
Using Study Questions 370
Using Open Books or Notes 371
Nontraditional Ways to Assess 372
Graphic Organizers 373
Factstorming 375
Designing a Test with a Self-Rating 376
A Checklist for Designing a Test 377
Helping Students Become Test-Wise 378
Authentic Assessment 379
Developing Authentic Assessments 380
Portfolios as a Means of Authentic Assessment 381
Challenge Box: Trinka, a Student with Learning Disabilities 282
Getting Started with Authentic Assessment 385
One-Minute Summary 386
End-of-Chapter Activities 387

APPENDIX A

Assessing Attitudes toward Reading 389

APPENDIX B

Readability Information 403

References 408
Activity Contributors 455
Author Index 457
Subject Index 470

Preface

Reflections on the Eighth Edition

Since publishing the first edition of *Reading to Learn in the Content Areas* in 1990, we have held true to the belief that theory and research should guide teachers in selecting the most effective strategies. Our basic approach to content reading instruction has remained unchanged, but our knowledge of the field grows with each edition. We subscribe to learner-centered strategies for guiding students to become confident, independent learners. We continue to listen to and gain insight from our fellow learners: teachers, students, researchers, professors, and administrators.

We thank those of you who have weathered these editions with us and welcome those of you new to our text. We hope it will serve as a rich entry point for developing engaging and effective instruction for your students.

Who Should Read This Book?

This textbook is designed for those who want to teach students to learn and think deeply about subject matter. This book is for readers who have not really studied about reading, as well as for those who have studied how students learn to read, but not how they read to learn and think in subject areas. This book demonstrates how teachers can use reading, discussion, technology, and writing as ways to learn in any discipline.

Why Did We Write This Book?

We, the authors, enjoy reading about new topics and ideas. We consider learning a pleasurable opportunity to increase our knowledge. But we recognize that not everyone thinks of reading and learning as enjoyable experiences. This is often because their own learning history contains negative associations of uninspiring and ineffective instruction. No one wants learning to be dull or uncomfortable. Effective instruction encourages curiosity, inquiry, and investigation; the confidence to read and discover; and ultimately lifelong learning. This belief has served as impetus for us to continue building our own understanding and to remain in the teaching profession for more than 30 years.

We believe in what we teach. We realize that all serious learning must be put in perspective. We want to share our joy of reading, thinking, and learning with students of all ages. We have ideas to share with you.

Teacher preparation has been criticized. Some say teachers are too focused on testing and not able to teach their students to think critically or to teach students to complete complex tasks required to advance in college or the workplace. Some critics say teachers learn too much content and not enough methodology. Other critics say the opposite. Many critics say teachers have learned to teach content rather than to teach students the content.

This textbook represents an ongoing effort to find positive solutions to the criticisms just cited. We believe that if teachers learn to appreciate the world of their students, including the language and resources their students bring into the academic world, they will begin to design content lessons that engage their students. When teachers learn to apply a simple instructional framework and teach strategically by using activities that demonstrate how reading can be a tool for learning, many of our classroom challenges can be successfully met.

Special Features of This Textbook

1. Reader involvement is important in this textbook. Each chapter is introduced with a vignette (*Voices from the Classroom*) and questions inviting the reader to consider how he or she might respond to challenges and situations related to chapter content. These lend relevance, interest, and applications for chapter concepts.
2. We believe that readers need to be prepared to read, need some assistance to understand, and need to be guided to reflect on their reading. So we ask readers to engage in all three stages as they read each chapter of this textbook. We introduce new terms first with an activity and then within the text in boldface with explanation; we maintain informality to keep our readers comfortable and interested. We endeavor to be reader friendly.
3. We take a balanced approach, a realistic and practical treatment of reading and methodology issues, theory, research, and historical perspective. We emphasize the effect of the past on the present.
4. We address teachers of primary through secondary grades because learning content starts long before middle school. We look at reading in the classroom as a natural tool for learning, no matter what the grade level or content area. We provide examples that show how teachers can construct lessons and use a variety of activities that work at different levels and in different content areas.
5. We have designed an instructional framework, one that reflects current thought but is uniquely ours: PAR (Preparation, Assistance, and Reflection). We explain it, compare it, and apply it consistently throughout the book, as well as on the front and end sheets.
6. We endeavor to be considerate of our readers by organizing and demonstrating the information that we present. You can expect to find a graphic organizer at the beginning of each chapter; the *Preparing to Read* section that starts each chapter builds reader background and provides objectives; a one-minute summary (for the streamlined reader) is always provided; and Assistance as well as Reflection activities provide chapter closure. Throughout each chapter, Margin Notes are interspersed to add emphasis, to provoke thought beyond the page, or to invite the reader to visit our website for additional resources and information. Icons are included in the margins throughout the chapters to flag information of specific interest related to technology, diversity, writing, principles for learning, websites, and cooperative learning.

7. Visual literacy is featured in this textbook. We use many visuals because visual literacy is the first literacy. One important visual is the PAR Cross-Reference Guide in the end sheets at the back of the book, which identifies specific activities for different content areas and grade levels.
8. We believe that literacy is a basic and essential tool for learning. Reading and the other language arts work together. Just as students listen and discuss to learn, so do they read and write to learn. We integrate the communicative arts. When an activity is presented, we explore with the reader how that activity facilitates or encourages discussion, reading, and writing. As well, literacy comes in many forms, including resources beyond the textbook (e.g., multimodal resources, cooperative learning).
9. Ours is a strategy-based approach. When readers learn about a new activity, they should understand that activity as a strategic means to aid learning. We present the activity as a way to enhance instruction and help teachers see how this activity can be both an instructional strategy and a learner strategy.
10. Ours is a theory-based approach. When readers learn about a new activity, they should understand how it reflects sound instruction and why that is so.
11. This textbook contains several often neglected topics including the role of affective domain in teaching (Chapter 2), resources beyond the textbook (Chapter 6), and study skills and tools in the electronic age (Chapter 9).

New to This Edition

We are delighted to welcome four contributing authors to this edition, Dr. Joan Rhodes, Dr. Valerie Robnoldt, Dr. Yaoying Xu, and Dr. William Muth. Dr. Rhodes made significant changes to Chapters 10 and 12, the technology and assessment chapters. Dr. Robnoldt lent her expertise to revising and updating Chapters 3 and 8 to offer new ideas for preparation and current trends in writing to learn. Dr. Xu, well recognized for her work in the field of special education, revised and augmented the special education section in Chapter 11, the diversity chapter. Dr. Muth provided insight for the new principles in Chapter 1 about student discourse patterns and their impact on discourse in an academic setting.

This edition reflects the influence of diversity and technology on reading to learn and think throughout the text to include many critical thinking margin notes, links to websites, suggestions for software, and examples of technology use and techniques effective for diverse learners. Students can go to CengageBrain.com to access this text's Education CourseMate website, where they can access an integrated e-book and other useful study tools and resources, including quizzes, flashcards, videos, software suggestions, related links, and PAR examples for each chapter. The authors and Cengage Learning affirm that the website URLs referenced herein were accurate at the time of printing. However, because of the fluid nature of the Internet, we cannot guarantee their accuracy for the life of the edition. For product information and technology assistance, contact Cengage Learning Customer & Sales Support (800-354-9706 or cengage.com/support).

A new feature of this edition is the introduction of the "Challenge Box," which presents profiles and special challenges for four diverse learners that are threaded throughout the book. All four learners are described in Chapter 1, and are revisited in various chapters to consider interventions and strategies important for instruction to address each of their particular needs. These provide opportunities for reflection and connection to real learners in the classroom.

Another new feature for the eighth edition is the "Tech App." These are suggestions in brief for appropriate and timely technology applications within day-to-day instruction. They are integrated with the content of each chapter and offer ideas that will excite and engage students in active learning of core content concepts.

In this edition, we have updated and revised all of the chapters from the seventh edition. Chapter 1 presents four examples of the PAR Lesson Framework, from primary through secondary level, showing how technology and literature can be part of good content lessons. At the suggestion of both students and reviewers, we have moved our chapter on the role of affect in learning to Chapter 2. The PAR framework is presented in Chapters 3, 4, and 5 and demonstrated throughout the rest of the chapters.

Chapters 9 (vocabulary) and 10 (writing) have been extensively revised. Current research and professional resources have been incorporated in the revision. We have endeavored to maintain a theory-to-practice balance. Visuals continue to play an important part in expressing our ideas: cartoons, diagrams, and examples are provided throughout. All chapters have been revised to include new ideas, activities, and references. Activity examples have been purposefully selected to provide a balance across content areas and levels.

Organization of This Book

The first five chapters are foundational. Chapter 1 discusses research and principles of content area instruction. In it you will discover our philosophy of teaching. It also presents a capsule view of the PAR Lesson Framework for instruction and how it works in three different types of classrooms. Chapter 2 discusses the affective domain of teaching, a topic crucial to learning but so often neglected. Chapters 3, 4, and 5 are PAR Lesson Framework chapters. Chapter 3 demonstrates how to determine reader background and prepare readers to study content material. Chapter 4 is an assistance chapter, demonstrating why and how to provide an appropriate instructional context to develop comprehension. Chapter 5 considers the role of reflection that stresses how to help readers think critically about, extend, and demonstrate their knowledge of their reading.

Chapters 6 through 10 demonstrate how PAR works. We show how multiple resources, vocabulary, writing, study skills, and technology can be used in all phases of the PAR framework. Chapter 6 presents the importance of learning with multiple resources. Chapter 7 and 8 describe activities and strategies for effective vocabulary and writing instruction in a variety of content and classroom settings.

Chapter 9 explains study skills techniques along with the use of associated electronic tools. Chapter 10 extends the technology discussion to include additional ideas and examples for innovative instructional use in today's classrooms. Chapter 11 explores considerations and techniques found effective for use with diverse learners. Chapter 12 considers the role of assessment and evaluation as it influences classroom teachers.

Instructor's Manual

The Instructor's Manual summarizes each chapter's main points with bulleted lists and displays the authors' graphic organizers and the vocabulary list and accompanying activity for each chapter. Test questions are provided for each chapter, including multiple-choice and short-answer items. Suggestions for relevant websites and article searches are also provided. A special section contains recommendations about grouping possible assignments for the course. The Instructor's Manual is available on the book's Education CourseMate website at www.cengagebrain.com.

CourseMate

Cengage Learning's Education CourseMate brings course concepts to life with interactive learning, study, and exam preparation tools that support the printed textbook. CourseMate includes an integrated eBook, quizzes, TeachSource Video Cases, web links, and exercises related to InfoTrac articles. Access to Education CourseMate includes access to InfoTrac® College Edition, an Online Research and Learning Center featuring over 20 million full-text articles from nearly 6,000 journals. The accompanying instructor website offers access to password-protected resources such as an electronic version of the instructor's manual with test bank.

Acknowledgments

We extend thanks to the colleagues who encouraged us and aided and abetted us in this endeavor. We appreciate the comments of our students and instructors who used the seventh edition of the textbook and provided useful suggestions.

We acknowledge gratefully the contributions of the reviewers, who gave us such excellent suggestions throughout the writing of this textbook: Janette Lada, Kean University; Andrea Sledge, Central Washington University; Kelly Farmer, Augusta State University; Paula Selvester, California State University, Chico.

We wish to thank our developmental editor, Lynne Lipkind, for her expert guidance to help us further develop our own understanding of the art and science of good writing. We also thank Pradhiba Kannaiyan, our production manager. Special thanks go to all of the teachers who agreed to let us showcase their lessons and activities (please refer to the Contributor List at the end of this book); to Ms. Kimberley Cossey, who assisted with the Reference List; and to Ms. Nancy Williams, who reviewed many videos to help us select the best ones to accompany chapters in this book.

CHAPTER 1

Content Teachers and Content Literacy

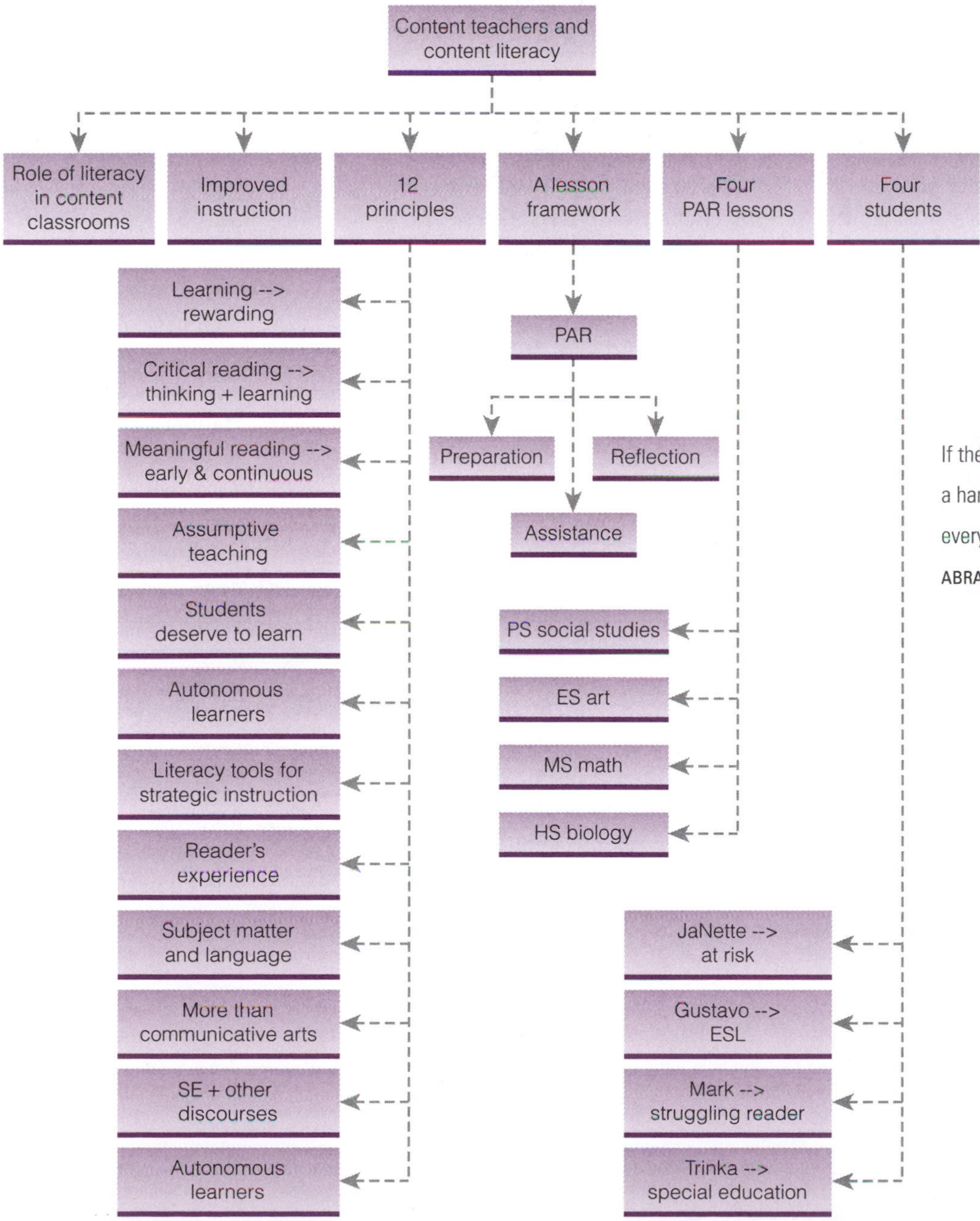

If the only tool you have is a hammer, you tend to treat everything as if it were a nail.

ABRAHAM MASLOW

VOICES FROM THE CLASSROOM

It is the first class meeting for a course titled "Reading in the Content Areas." Students gather in the classroom before the instructor has arrived. Some are teachers, having rushed to get to class; they are already tired from a day of instruction, interaction with their own students, driving to get to this class, and finding parking. Others are prospective teachers—either preparing to teach as a first career or entering teaching as a second career.

One turns to another and says, "Well, I'm here, but this course is just another big waste of time."

The other responds, "I have to take this course to get certified. I can't figure out why."

A third chimes in, "But my adviser said this is a really good course and will help me with good classroom ideas."

"Well," says a fourth, "we will see about that."

What do you think? Why are you reading this textbook? What do you think this text and the course for which it is assigned reading will be like? Are you feeling resentful or dubious?

PREPARING TO READ

1. How do you currently help your students study for deep understanding in your content area? Do they discuss, read, and write about the content? Make a list of all the ways you guide—or plan to guide—your students. How many of these ways include active participation, demonstration, problem solving, student involvement, assessment of success, and self-initiative?
2. Following is a list of terms used in this chapter. Some may be familiar to you in a general context, but in this chapter, they may be used in unfamiliar ways. Rate your knowledge by placing a plus sign (+) in front of those you are certain you know, a check mark (✓) in front of those you have some knowledge about, and a zero (0) in front of those you don't know. Be ready to locate these items in the chapter and pay special attention to their meanings. Decide how you can arrange the terms in four or five groupings and give each group an appropriate label. There may be several ways to group them, so there is no single right answer. Be ready to explain your selections. Next, using a piece of paper, make a three-column organizer with the following headings: Terms, Predicted Definitions, and Chapter Definitions. Select 10 terms with which you are least familiar, record them in your organizer, and predict how they might be defined for this chapter. As you read the chapter, verify your predictions and rewrite your definitions as necessary.

_______ NAEP
_______ student-centered approach
_______ communicative arts (language arts)
_______ visual literacy
_______ new literacies
_______ Standard English SE
_______ local discourse
_______ code switching
_______ literacy tool
_______ assumptive teaching
_______ dependent learners
_______ incomplete thinking
_______ autonomous learners
_______ strategic learning
_______ framework
_______ PAR Lesson Framework
_______ preparation step
_______ assistance step
_______ reflection step

OBJECTIVES

As you read this chapter, focus your attention on the following objectives. You will

1. Summarize some recent history about research and views of education.
2. Explain why there is a need to improve instruction in schools today.
3. Explain 12 principles for content reading instruction and understand the importance of each.
4. Describe the steps and use of the PAR Lesson Framework and the importance of using a framework when teaching.
5. Identify the characteristics of an effective teacher.
6. Read examples of the PAR Framework used at the primary, elementary, middle, and high school levels.
7. Meet four learners who represent some of the diverse students you may meet in your own classrooms.
8. Use this textbook in an organized manner with attention to technology applications and differentiation for student needs.

What Is the Role of Literacy in Content Classrooms?

Many teachers wonder why they should complete a course in content reading instruction. After all, when teaching content, they are not teaching reading—or are they? Content teachers teach a subject, not how to read. But within the subject, students will encounter many new words or words used in new ways. They will have to read with understanding and study effectively to learn that subject. So, literacy is a major tool for learning any subject. Literacy skills help us learn how to learn. Literacy is a tool that must be used in every classroom, at every grade level, and in every school to provide the application and practice necessary for students to become effective learners. Think of literacy as vocabulary, comprehension, and study skills. Try substituting "literacy" or "learning" for "reading." Then the course title might become "Teaching for Learning in the Content Areas" or "Instruction in the Content Areas" or "Teaching for Literacy in the Content Areas."

In the past several years, public comment, research, and assessment results have led to concerns about and criticism of our educational system. Some critics claim that students are not learning important factual information, are unable to think critically, and cannot apply skills in the real worlds of work and college. This textbook represents an effort to help teachers and administrators find positive, effective solutions to these criticisms.

Improved Instruction—Are We There Yet?

A major factor in how we measure educational progress is the **National Assessment of Educational Progress (NAEP),** a test authorized by Congress in 1969. The NAEP's mission is to collect, analyze, and present reliable information about student knowledge and practice of that knowledge. The NAEP is administered at grades 4, 8, and 12 to both public and nonpublic students in core subjects. During the last third of the 20th century, many politicians and educators wrote about a crisis in education. They cited evidence that achievement levels were declining in our nation's schools. Test gains on the NAEP had fluctuated only slightly; national results (National Center for Educational Statistics, 2003) for fourth and eighth graders from 1970 to 2003 had shown a decline (although it was slight from 2002 to 2003). In the new century, results seem to show a slight increase. NAEP long-term comparisons in reading (2010) indicate that American students have performed somewhat better in recent testing than in 1971. All age levels and white, black, and Hispanic students alike have improved from the 1971 NAEP tests (from 1975 for Hispanics); gains range from 4 to 12 points.

Please visit the Education CourseMate website at **www.cengagebrain.com** to find links to NAEP progress reports over the past several years or perform a Web search using the term "NAEP" to locate the results.

To find out what the public thinks about progress in education, Phi Delta Kappa conducts a poll every year. The 2009 Phi Delta Kappa (PDK)/Gallup Poll (Rose & Gallup, 2009), the 41st annual poll, reported that the public believed that schools are less effective than they used to be. Respondents blame a lack of funding and indicate a need for better teachers, more emphasis on technology, and more parental support. Most people polled opposed recommendations at the national level to relaxing teacher education and certification plans. Wilson, commenting in the 41st PDK/Gallup report (Bushaw & McNee, 2009), indicated that "teachers are professionals who should have skills and abilities to teach" (p. 15). In contrast, the results of the 39th PDK poll (2007) assigned schools their highest ratings in 39 years. At that time, the public thought that schools were placing the appropriate amount of emphasis on science and math but that they needed to devote more time to other subjects. The 38th Phi Delta Kappa/Gallup Poll (Rose & Gallup, 2006) found that 47 percent of the public said the curriculum needed to be changed—up from 31 percent in 1979. This report indicated that rather than confining itself to the basics, the curriculum should include a wide variety of courses.

Please visit the Education CourseMate website at **www.cengagebrain.com** to find a link to the online version of the Phi Delta Kappa/Gallup Poll.

Many educators think that instruction and teaching have improved in recent years. Some researchers (Bracey, 1997; McQuillan, 1998; Whittington, 1991) believe that children in the United States are reading as well now as they did in past generations—and maybe even better. David Berliner, a prominent psychologist interested in education, maintained in 2001 that posturing about poor schools and instruction has caused us to waste money, harm already effective school programs, and add to the declining morale among teachers. Berliner commented that schools are far better than many reports claim and are doing as good a job of educating our youth as has ever been done in our history. He believes the educational system produces good results in most instances. According to Berliner, problems that exist result from poverty, dysfunctional families, and poor health care. Bracey, commenting within the 41st PDK report (Bushaw & McNee, 2009), agrees with Berliner, commenting that the public "never hears anything positive about the nation's schools and [hasn't] since the years just before Sputnik in 1957" (p. 11).

The debate continues about whether American instruction is improving; we do not seem to be there yet. A number of past reports and books—still quoted often—have portrayed our nation's schools as being in crisis, questioning the practices and core beliefs of our entire educational system (Bloom, 1987; Hirsch, 1987). Some teachers believe that students are experiencing difficulty with higher-level reading and writing skills such as thinking critically, drawing inferences, and applying what they read. This opinion is supported by research and writing about deep and surface structure comprehension. For instance, Holschuh (2000) found that high performers use more deep-level and specific strategies and seem to know when to use the most appropriate strategies. Learning requires a **student-centered approach** that includes an emphasis on the literacy students bring to school as much as on what the school wants them to leave with (Pitcher, Martinez, Dicembre, Fewster, & McCormick, 2010). Relying on skills-centered instruction, as a test emphasis tends to do, leaves little time for a student-centered orientation. Simpson and Nist (2000) caution that strategic learning requires mature and complex knowledge, such as task understanding, the ability to generalize, and cognitive and metacognitive processing.

The political response to test results and public opinion about whether "we are there yet" changes often. During the decade of 2000, the result was No Child Left Behind, a federal response to improving education. During the early Obama years, the result was Race to the Top. Both initiatives, in different ways, sought to improve education by designing and implementing rigorous standards and high-quality assessments. Please visit the Education CourseMate website at **www.cengagebrain.com** to find links to these initiatives.

Gettinger and Seibert (2002) contribute a significant perspective about academic competence by identifying four clusters of study skills: (1) repetition-based, (2) procedural, (3) cognitive-based, and (4) metacognitive. Study skills, according to these authors, contribute to learning because they are cognitive skills and processes for effective learning, requiring that we locate, organize, synthesize, remember, and then use information learned. These concerns about deep thinking and self-regulated learning—which may clash with a current emphasis on testing—are discussed in subsequent chapters.

The "Information Age" (Frand, 2000) has "flattened" (Friedman, 2006) the world, starting with the breakdown of the physical and symbolic barrier of the Berlin Wall and then continuing worldwide with the interactivity and productivity of the Internet. We now have new communities without geographic borders, industries that work over physical distance, and information obtained almost instantly. Pedagogy has subsequently undergone radical change in the past several years. We are in an age of technological innovations (Kleiner & Lewis, 2003), accountability (Johnson & Johnson, 2002; Stewart, 2004), high-stakes testing (Afflerbach, 2002; Berliner, 2008; Worthy & Hoffman, 2000), and standards for learning (Valencia & Wixson, 1999). These innovations and issues cross school divisions, states, and nations. Literacy has gained a level of attention far greater than in past generations. It is no longer enough to focus on literacy only at the beginning reader level or in elementary schools. Educators recognize that literacy permeates learning at all ages and in every classroom.

Please visit the Education CourseMate website at **www.cengagebrain.com** to find a link to the National Education Standards for the major subject areas.

Questions and concerns remain, though. The adoption of state and national standards may lead to too much emphasis on testing and not enough on learning content (Berliner, 2008; Berube, 2004). Emphasis on the "new" literacy, specifically technology, may alter teacher training for better or worse (Henderson & Scheffler, 2004). Boyd (2004, p. 105) expresses this new direction: "We are living in what the Chinese call 'interesting times.' Already facing difficult times, public education—and the arts as well—are in real danger of a confluence of forces that could form a 'perfect storm.'"

The concerns suggest that teachers need more information and training to teach higher levels of language and literacy. But often, teachers do not have this exposure even though they expect students in their classes to be fluent in processing reading material, making inferences, and reading critically. Teachers assume that students will be able to express their understanding of material orally and on tests. They also expect that students will possess a certain amount of knowledge and want to read to learn. This is assumptive teaching, described later in this chapter as Principle 9. Such assumptive teaching creates a difficult instructional dilemma.

Twelve Principles for Effective Content Teachers

In the next section, we present 12 guiding principles for facilitating literacy as a tool for learning in content areas. These principles are grounded in theory and supported by research. Sometimes theory is presented in isolation from its application, but teachers asking for "what works" are also asking why a particular technique works so that they can replicate it in optimal circumstances. Teachers know that imposing an activity on students in the wrong circumstances can produce a teaching disaster. No activity has much merit aside from the construct underlying it (Hayes, Stahl, & Simpson, 1991). The 12 principles presented here link the theoretical with good practice in content area instruction.

1. Learning is influenced by the reader's personal store of experience and knowledge. Successful learning depends on numerous factors. The learner's store of knowledge and experience certainly contributes, as does the learner's attitude toward reading. Many people may share the same experience, read the same book, or hear the same lecture, but thinking and learning differ from individual to individual because of what each person brings to the experience. Individuals relate to a common body of knowledge in different ways because of what they already know—or don't know. Converting to the metric system, for example, will probably be difficult for learners who were taught measurements in inches, feet, and miles. Similarly, understanding conflicts in another nation can be difficult when learners do not know the climate, geography, and history of that nation. If learners cannot find relevance in a subject, they are likely to ignore it. Thus, teachers must become aware of their students' previous knowledge of and experiences with a particular concept in content subjects.

2. We learn through language. Subject matter and language are inextricably bound. Language generally comprises listening, speaking, reading, and writing, traditionally called **communicative or language arts.** Kellogg (1972) describes the communicative arts as blocks that build on one another. One cannot use one communicative art without also using another. This integration occurs with greater facility as children practice each literacy skill. Yet school environments are often artificial rather than natural when teachers talk and students listen so much of the time that little response and interaction can take place. In reviewing the 51 articles about content reading published in *The Reading Teacher* from 1969 to 1991, Armbruster (1992) noted the "emphasis on the importance of integrating writing and reading in content instruction." It is our premise that students can learn better if they spend more time practicing all the language arts in their content subjects. Subject matter and language are inextricably bound. The main concern for the subject matter teacher, however, is teaching content. In 1965, Nila Banton Smith reminded readers that the term *primer* did not originally mean "first book to read," as it does today; rather, it referred to the contents of a book as being primary, or foremost. Today the content of a subject is still primary for teachers, as it should be. But using the communicative arts as a major learning tool creates a positive combination for enhancing critical thinking and learning. For example, Richardson (2004) describes several successful content lessons designed by content teachers that incorporate language arts and technology. The communicative arts are essential to teaching content area subjects, and teachers should encourage students' use of all the communicative arts as effective thinking and learning tools. As we present activities in this book, we often identify how they facilitate the use of language to enhance content learning. Chapter 8 addresses the role of writing in particular.

3. Literacy in the 21st century is more than the traditional communicative arts. Although listening, speaking, reading, and writing have been considered the basic communicative arts, sometimes communication occurs most easily through nonverbal, visual literacy. For instance, a picture of a pie divided into pieces may convey the concept of fractions more effectively than a page of explanation. Chauvin (2003) notes, "The fact that we are visual beings before we become linguistic beings is sometimes forgotten" (p. 126).

Visual literacy is the first and most pervasive literacy (Avgerinou & Ericson, 2002; Stokes, 2002). Sinatra's classic model (1986) of literacy development suggests the interactive relationship of visual literacy with the oral and written literacies (Figure 1.1). Visual literacy conveys emotion through such means as illustration and art. Visual literary precedes listening and helps build experiences necessary to thinking and learning. It is action oriented; the scribbles that young children call writing are a manifestation of visual literacy. Teachers know that when they use visual aids such as graphs, charts, and pictures, they ensure and reinforce learning for many students. An alternative approach is offered for those who excel in visual but not traditional literacy. Because visual literacy has implications for the affective aspects of instruction, it is discussed further in Chapter 2. Many activities presented in this book, such as the Graphic Organizers that begin chapters and the comic strips, capitalize on visual literacy.

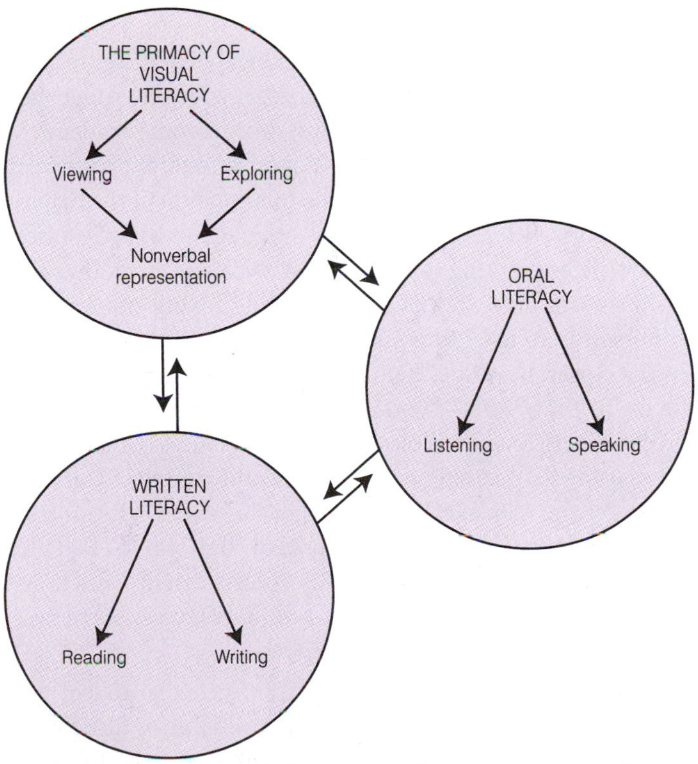

FIGURE 1.1

Stage Three of Literacy Development: Visual Literacy and Its Interactive Relationship with the Oral and Written Languages

From R. Sinatra, *Visual Literacy Connections to Thinking, Reading, and Writing,* 1986. Courtesy of Charles C. Thomas, Publisher, Springfield, Illinois.

The term **new literacies** (Luke, 2000) has been used often to describe how the communicative arts are applied in the electronic environment. This term is discussed in depth in Chapter 10. The electronic environment has changed how we use listening, speaking, reading, and writing so much that the term "new literacies" alerts us to consider them as almost different experiences. In fact, some lament (Pressler, 2006) that writing has changed so much with the advent of computers that penmanship is becoming a lost art. As keyboards replace pens, manuscript has become an exercise in block letters. Journalists find they cannot "live" without their electronic modes of communication, as discussed in the experiment conducted for a week by eight *Washington Post* reporters who unplugged themselves from the Web (Fisher, 2010). Technology is changing how people function in society (Friedman, 2006), and technological literacy must be part of content instruction to ensure that students are adequately prepared for the future (Reinking, 1997).

Please visit the Education CourseMate website at **www.cengagebrain.com** to find a link to the online articles "The Handwriting Is on the Wall" and "Unplugged."

4. Most language users are equipped with more than one version of their language; ideally they will use a version that suits the circumstances. **Standard English** (SE) is the language used in textbooks written for English-speaking countries, but SE is not the only variation of language out there! According to Crystal (2004), a noted scholar of English structure, not enough attention is given to other forms of English. And use of one form of language may send a powerful tacit identity message for kids with non-mainstream dialects—that they are inferior. Gee (2000), however, stresses the value of social language in learning content. He points out that students create "identity kits" (2001) that define how they communicate with others. Students possess and use multiple forms of their language in their time away from school. Many students are so immersed in the language of their surroundings that using SE during assigned textbook reading feels almost like working with a foreign language. In fact, SE may be a barrier to acquiring the message of the text.

Some students are adept at changing from **local discourses** to academic ones **(code switching),** but other learners—especially those whose home languages and dialects are most different from SE—may have the hardest time learning academic ways of speaking. Their understanding of content material is compromised not because they cannot *comprehend* but because they cannot *relate* to the presentation of the material in SE.

Selecting from different versions of language to express oneself is much like selecting an article of clothing (Crystal, 2004). We put on clothes that will fit the occasion. Evening attire may work at a formal wedding but not at an informal summer picnic. If a person is so used to wearing jeans and a T-shirt that evening clothes are not even in the closet, how does he or she prepare for an evening party? One choice: Go buy the outfit that "suits" the occasion. Another choice could be not to attend that party. When confronted with text in SE, what choice would students who are not accustomed to using SE make? Possibly, they would read the SE carefully, spending the time it takes to get the message. Students who "do school" (Bean, 2001) would do just that. But other students would more likely skip that "party." For teachers, accepting that there are many "languages for learning" means discovering how to connect textbook language to more meaningful out-of-school language. Activity 1.1 demonstrates an assignment that links two versions of English.

Please visit the Education CourseMate website at **www.cengagebrain.com** to find a link to the Janelle Monae podcast (skip to about 4 minutes in).

5. The discourse of one content discipline may be different than that of another. Although good instruction is similar in many ways from discipline to discipline, there are differences in application. Moje (2008) argues that subject areas "become subcultures . . . with their own ways of knowing, doing and believing" (p. 99). Lemke (2004) points

ACTIVITY 1.1 Example of Student Discourse and Matched Material

Who are the students in this class? Twelfth graders in an English class in a high-risk school. When asked what subjects are easiest, one student responded, "The ones I study for." When asked what those subjects were, he replied, "almost nothing." When asked if they like to read, two-thirds said yes, but "it has to hold my interest." Among materials they listed as reading were magazines, Facebook, and Yahoo!News. Music they liked included rhythm and blues, rap, jazz, country, and anything but country.

What is the topic? Discovering language features in literature

What is the activity objective? Explain how imagery and figures of speech (personification, simile, metaphor) appeal to the reader's senses and experience.

What is the material? (1) A song with a variation of English not found in the textbook explanations, selected to connect with the language students use, the music they like, and the literacy experiences they encounter daily and (2) A textbook explanation of figures of speech and literary examples.

PROCEDURES

1. Listen to the song "Sincerely Jane" by Janelle Monae (from her *Funky Otherworldly Sounds* album). This song contains many of the language structures that help us read critically.
2. Identify at least *two* of these language features:
   - Simile, metaphor
   - Connotation = a suggested meaning of a word
   - Denotation = a dictionary meaning of a word
   - Personification = human characteristics given to inanimate object
   - Understatement
   - Hyperbole = exaggeration
   - Irony = an unexpected twist
   - Figures of speech = comparisons, as in a simile or metaphor; differ from literal meaning (e.g., "I'm stuffed")
3. Explain how you think Ms. Monae uses these features to make her point.
4. Now look in the text and read the definitions for the language features a second time. Write definitions in your own words.

Did this activity work? The teacher thought so.

STUDENT RESPONSES

"The language features are irony & hyperbole. I think that Ms Monae uses the features that she does to get her message through to whomever is listening to her music. She expresses herself and her musiq in such a unique way. I like when she said "What good is love if it burns bright, and explodes in flames". I took that as if she was comparing the love the world has to fire. I believe she was tryna make the statement that the world needs more love and we shouldn't treat people the way we do."

The personification was by trying to make the French horns cry, the strings plead, and her voice touch people hearts. She also uses contrast in her song when she says "your cousins are round'here selling' dope while they're daddies, your uncle is walking round' strung out . . ." and she uses contrast also when she says "Spending money on spinners but wont pay college loans."

ACTIVITY 1.2 Identifying Discourse Tools in Different Disciplines

Consider the list of terms below. Match each with a content area in which you think the term would be useful as an instructional tool. Which ones fit the literacy needed for science, math, history, English, foreign language, music, art, health, physical education, and so on? Why?

Music	Symbols	Talk	Actions	Art
Activity	Numbers	Equipment	Pantomime	Drawings
Scribbles	Reports	Summaries	Poems	Graphs
Questions	Gestures	Sound files	Dance	Pads of paper
Notebooks	Themes	Pictures	Books	Diagrams
Scrap paper	Web searches	Calculators	Dictionaries	PowerPoints
Smart phones	Routines	Podcasts	Journals	Magazines

out that science begins with questions, so inquiry skills are important. A calculator would be a **literacy "tool"** in science or math. Numbers, diagrams, and scribbles are valuable literacy resources. Mathematicians point out that numbers and equations are a language that crosses the borders of other languages. In history or English, one might start with completed accounts or stories and then evaluate their impact. An electronic dictionary would be a "literacy tool." Versions of language may also be valued differently. Comparing two accounts of one historical event often culminates in a new written account in SE. Comparing two experiments often culminates in another experiment written in equations or procedures. Physics and math may find a non-SE version of language somewhat problematic or irrelevant. Creative writing class may celebrate out-of-school language. In any discipline, critical thinking is imperative, and literacy skills are used. But literacy conditions differ.

The authors are grateful to William Muth, who provided advice in the presentation of Principles 4 and 5.

6. Learning should be a rewarding experience. Learning in content subjects should be satisfying. People avoid doing what is not interesting or rewarding in some personal way. Students avoid reading in content subjects if they find it uninteresting, unrewarding, or lacking in meaning (Daisey, 2010). In out-of-school discourse, children often select content (nonfiction) books to read just as readily as fiction. If teachers can provide a relevant reading environment in content subjects, learning will surely improve. Because we think this principle is so important, we devote Chapter 2 to the affective dimension of learning in the content areas.

Pleasurable feelings about learning will lead to successful learning and to more reading. Teachers like to teach students who have good learning habits. This cannot happen simply because teachers tell, or even implore, students to read, learn, and study. Morrison, Jacobs, and Swinyard (1999) documented that teachers who read can better motivate students to read and that teachers who read for personal pleasure report using recommended literacy practices in their classrooms significantly more often than do teachers who report less personal reading. Teachers should share newspaper articles about a content subject or a book they have read that relates to a topic at hand. Modeling is a form of visual literacy. When teachers model reading visually, they are using one communicative art to promote another.

Good readers read because it gives them pleasure and they do it well; consequently, they get practice in reading and become better at it. However, the research on Striving Readers (Ayers & Miller, 2009) provides evidence that many poor readers get so discouraged that they lose the will or desire to read and thus to succeed. In a series of questionnaires we administered over a four-year period to incoming college students, we found a consistent correlation between those who chose not to read and those who perceived that they had poor reading and study habits. The Striving Readers research stresses the need for effective strategies that can make a difference in literacy and learning for those who struggle to read even after the elementary years. It seems clear that teachers need to give more attention to bolstering students' will to learn (Fleener et al., 2000) and their skills to do so. Content teachers are not trained to teach reading skills, but they can provide support for struggling readers by asking reading specialists for help and providing strategic instruction that engages all learners—even struggling readers—in rewarding learning experiences

7. The practice of critical reading enables better thinking and learning to occur. Reading is an active, thinking-related process. Yet students often lack critical thinking skills. It is not that students are incapable of critical thinking; they just have not practiced it. In the section about the need for improved instruction, several studies were mentioned that support this principle (Barnett, 2000; Gettinger & Seibert, 2002; Holschuh, 2000; Pitcher, Martinez, Dicembre, Fewster, & McCormick, 2010; Simpson & Nist, 2000). By using tools of literacy and being immersed in a thinking climate, students can practice these skills.

Special note: We recognize that reading for facts (the literal level) is often a prerequisite step toward critical reading. We are not disregarding the importance of factual reading. A reader who understands material at a factual level and can interpret what is read is more likely to be a successful critical reader. However, many students who are unable to recall names or dates can predict and infer. It is probably because teachers realize the necessity of literal reading that so much classroom time is spent on literal recall of reading material to the detriment of higher-level thinking and reading comprehension.

8. Meaningful reading should start early and continue throughout life. From the first grade on, learning content material is part of most school curricula. Many schools now introduce science, math, and social studies material in kindergarten. Because most children are still learning to read in the early grades, reading to learn may not be used as often as visualizing, listening, and speaking to learn. However, both reading and writing to learn are being advocated more frequently for children in the early grades. By the same reasoning, learning about content subjects continues far beyond high school. Content information bombards people daily as they listen to the radio and watch television, read newspapers, and surf the Internet on their computers. The basic difference here is that learners can structure the environment and choose what to learn and what to avoid. The adults whom teachers meet daily will attest that they continue to enjoy and learn about topics that interested them in school. Teachers develop lifelong learners by introducing them to reading for learning's sake at an early age.

9. Teachers need to refrain from assumptive teaching. Herber (1978) used the term **assumptive teaching** to describe what teachers do when they unconsciously take for granted that students know how to read and to learn and have the motivation and interest to do so. Teachers may picture that all students have plentiful reading resources and supportive home environments. Teachers may incorrectly assume that students can switch codes or versions of discourse readily from out-of-school to in-school experiences. Unfortunately, these assumptions are not always true.

Some assumptive teaching is necessary. Teachers cannot start all over again every year in a content subject. They may need to assume that a particular skill or concept was covered the year before, but it is crucial to find the point of familiarity with a concept. Content area teachers should be certain about what they are assuming their students already know. By learning to determine and build on students' backgrounds, teachers can avoid assumptive teaching.

10. All students, no matter at what level of literacy or learning challenges, deserve instruction in content subjects that enables them to learn. The "average" student is an elusive creature. Teachers teach students who are gifted, have learning disabilities, and physical disabilities, as well as students who speak English as a second language, struggle with reading, and are at risk of failure—to list just a few heterogeneous students. All students in content classrooms deserve instruction that helps them to learn. Chapter 11 presents information about diverse students and suggests how to instruct them in meaningful ways within the content classroom. In this chapter, we present four diverse learners whom the readers will follow throughout the text, considering their learning needs as they pertain to each chapter. By engaging all learners using research-based strategies, teachers support students as they practice and become strategic and proficient learners. Teachers can teach in ways that students prefer for learning, as brain-based learning and instruction stresses. Chapter 2 covers this topic fully.

11. Content reading instruction enables students to become autonomous learners. Dependent learners wait for a teacher to tell them what a word is, what the right answer is, and what to do next. Such learners are disabled intellectually. When they need to function independently, they will not know how to do so. To become independent learners, students need to practice a study system to make learning easier. The PAR (preparation, assistance, and reflection) Lesson Framework, explained in this chapter and used as the basis for this textbook, is a system that can help a teacher show students how to become autonomous learners. The teacher first models PAR and then gradually weans students to independent use of PAR. The four examples presented in this chapter illustrate such independent learning.

Dependent students often use **incomplete thinking.** They skip important steps in learning. Edward de Bono (1976) used the term *two-finger thinking* to explain this shortcutting of steps. According to de Bono, two-finger thinking is analogous to two-finger piano playing. A person who plays the piano with only two fingers uses fewer resources than are available. This is fine for playing "Chopsticks" but not suitable for Chopin. In the same way, two-finger thinking uses only part of the brain to perceive and comprehend important reading material. Inadequate use of resources can cause trouble when complex learning skills are required. For instance, two-finger thinking might work on an easy math word problem but not for a difficult one.

Teachers may inadvertently foster two-finger thinking and enable dependence when they abandon a textbook because it seems too hard for their students. Teachers who give students all the answers or hand out the notes already organized in the teacher's style bypass opportunities for students to learn how to find answers or take notes. Schools may perpetuate an environment in which students are excused from learning and avoid responsibility. The goal of teaching is to move students from being dependent on teachers to being independent in their learning habits—that is, to make them **autonomous learners.** According to Barnett (2000), the more a person feels in control of his or her comprehension, the more self-regulated about learning he or she will be. But it is not fair to expect that students can become autonomous in thinking and learning without the benefit of instruction. Teachers at any grade level or of any subject area can assist students in this transfer of responsibility when they balance the students' level of proficiency and the content to be studied.

12. Teachers should use literacy "tools" that enable students to learn content material strategically. This principle is the sum of the former. Teachers need knowledge and skills—new tools (notice Maslow's quote that begins this chapter)—that match new ways of teaching. Yet some teachers have only one tool: the lecture. That is simply not adequate. Although many of *us* sat through classes in elementary school, middle school, high school, or college in which the teacher used only the lecture, students today have new expectations.

Teachers must incorporate the full spectrum of communication into their instruction. One new tool is to use students' discourse in instruction. Another is using real-world material as well as textbooks. Technological literacy and visual literacy are two important and pervasive forms of literacy that teachers must emphasize with students. Research in the past two decades has shown that the most effective and long-lasting learning occurs when learners of any age are active in the process of evaluating their learning. Therefore, teachers need to know how to engage their students in literacy activities that motivate them to learn (Gambrell, 1996; Guthrie, 2000, 2004). Activities such as those presented in this textbook can be great tools as long as they are strategically chosen to suit the needs of the students and the topic being studied. Strategies for instruction and learning are very effective when they are linked to the previous principles. A strategy is simply a way of doing that creates a learning environment. It is a "grand design" that points the way to achieving a goal. Teachers provide inspired instruction when they guide students by showing them how to learn strategically. **Strategic instruction** uses the methods that are most efficient and effective to suit the learning situation. A strategy for content teachers, for example, could be helping students set purposes for learning. An activity is a task or organized procedure that can culminate in achieving the grand design. An activity that could help students become strategic in setting purposes is a Written Preview (see Chapter 3) or a Directed Reading-Thinking Activity (DR-TA) (see Chapter 4). The activity selected must match a set of conditions that help formulate a successful lesson.

As you read this textbook and find activities that you would like to use in your classrooms, use the checklist (Activity 1.3) to be sure the activity not only works for you in your content teaching but is also strategic and applies the principles of good teaching.

Please visit the Education CourseMate website at **www.cengagebrain.com** to find suggested formats for designing a lesson plan.

ACTIVITY 1.3 A Checklist for Strategic Teaching

_____ Engages reader's prior knowledge

_____ Uses communication skills

_____ Respects and uses students' discourse patterns

_____ Provides for satisfaction with learning

_____ Enhances critical reading and problem solving

_____ Enhances readers' autonomy and self-initiative

_____ Uses active involvement and participation and social interaction

_____ Provides feedback to students

To use tools effectively, content teachers must have an essential understanding of the content and a logical sequence for teaching the topics. Most states in the United States have developed sets of standards for each discipline. Also, there is a movement toward national standards (No Child Left Behind; Race to the Top). Voluntary national educational standards are also available to help teachers. In the section "Reflecting on Your Reading" that follows each chapter in this textbook, we suggest some standards for consideration.

Please visit the Education CourseMate website at **www.cengagebrain.com** to find links to voluntary national education standards.

The Importance of Structure through a Lesson Framework

Many mental operations are necessary in reading. For instance, one must sort out relevant from irrelevant information. In addition, learners must be able to summarize information, draw inferences from the text, generate their own questions to be answered about the topic, and monitor their comprehension as they read (Guthrie, 2004). Students require a well-prepared teacher's structured guidance in learning to adequately perform these mental operations and develop better habits of thinking and reading. This is what a lesson **framework** provides.

A framework is the structure around which anything is stretched. It is the systematic arrangement of the basic parts of something. Furthermore, it can represent an organized plan condensed to a series of steps, usually represented by keywords. Such a framework becomes a model for finishing a task. It must be complete and clearly explain all parts of the task.

The framework becomes an aid to learning and a way to activate students to learn. An instructional framework that identifies successful components of a content lesson facilitates the relationships among reading, thinking, and learning. Frameworks for content reading instruction are historically grounded (Herber, 1978; Singer & Donlan, 1985; Vaughan & Estes, 1986) and formulate instruction in a complete and structured way. The most popular content reading frameworks include three basic assumptions:

1. The learner must be ready to learn, and the teacher must prepare the learner for this beforehand.
2. The learner must be guided through the learning so that comprehension can be developed during the lesson.
3. The learner should review what has been learned. As part of this step, the teacher must provide after-reading opportunities to help students retain the learning.

If these basic steps are taught explicitly and repeated consistently in the instructional sequence, the learner begins to use them independently of the teacher in a self-instructional (autonomous) manner. It does not matter what keywords are used in a framework as long as they stimulate recall of the steps incorporated in the framework and use words that help teachers adhere to the framework's structure.

PAR: A Lesson Framework for Instruction

PAR stands for "preparation, assistance, and reflection." The **PAR Lesson Framework** is a framework for content reading instruction (Figure 1.2). PAR is similar to other content instructional frameworks. We coined the acronym *PAR* to develop an association

FIGURE 1.2

The PAR Lesson Framework

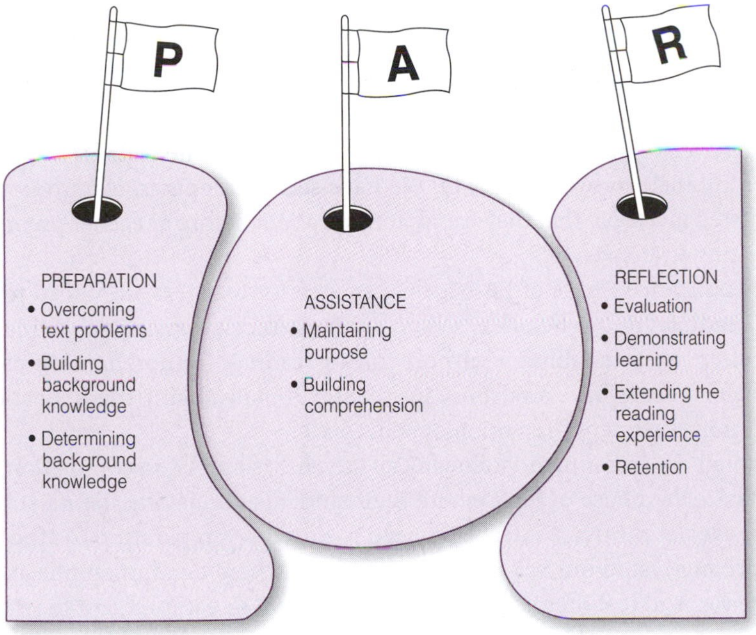

Developed by Dawn Watson and Walter Richards.

with the golf term *par,* which refers to the completion of a hole or holes by taking only the allotted number of strokes—not exceeding the limit. Golfers usually feel pleased when they achieve par for a course. Likewise, teachers who consistently use PAR to underpin their instruction will be pleased because students will be more meaningfully engaged in their learning. As a byproduct, discipline problems that grow from inattention and boredom will decline considerably.

In the **preparation step,** teachers need to consider text problems and students' background knowledge. Sometimes students have incorrect or insufficient background knowledge, which hinders purposeful and successful learning. The teacher needs to choose preparation activities that will strategically build a conceptual base of understanding for students. The preparation step motivates students to want to learn.

After motivation is heightened in the preparation step, the teacher moves to the **assistance step,** which provides an instructional context for the lesson. This is a crucial step to help students better comprehend the passage. Teachers often prepare and motivate students but then tell them to read a passage on their own without guidance. But students need assistance as they read to maintain purpose and build comprehension. The teacher needs to choose assistance activities that will strategically help students construct knowledge. The assistance step provides students with ways to respond actively as they read.

In the **reflection step,** teachers provide extension, enrichment, and critical thinking opportunities. Careful reflection by students is not the same as answering questions either posed by the teacher or listed at the end of the chapter. True reflection occurs when students ask themselves tough questions. (What did I learn from this reading? Was it appropriate for me? Do I believe what the author said? Is this reading material worth retaining?) When students truly reflect on their reading, they retain the material longer and at greater depth.

Using the PAR Lesson Framework improves a teacher's ability both to teach the subject and to monitor the reading comprehension of students; however, each phase of PAR is also notable for distinct contributions to the learning environment. As we mentioned earlier, careful preparation for reading enhances students' desire and motivation to learn. In the Preparation Phase, the teacher gets students to *want* to read by awakening their natural curiosity. We have seen students in classrooms become very interested in a topic that they cared nothing about before a teacher prepared them with activating strategies.

The Assistance Phase of PAR is the key area for teachers who need to improve students' reading comprehension. When students receive assistance while reading, they are better able to establish a purpose for the reading. Comprehension usually improves when students have a purpose for reading. Finally, using the Reflection Phase of PAR reinforces students' retention of concepts.

Although we recommend following all the phases of PAR to completion, teachers can emphasize the phase of PAR where their students are having the most difficulty. If students are not motivated, teachers need to do more preparation for the lesson. If students are motivated but not comprehending, teachers need to emphasize the Assistance Phase. And if students are motivated and seem to comprehend the reading but fail to retain the material, then teachers need to place more emphasis on the Reflection Phase. The key for the teacher is consistently to model all the PAR steps with the understanding that students will, through such guided practice, improve their understanding significantly.

The following sections present four examples of content-specific lessons that illustrate use of the PAR Framework. They provide a sense of how this simple structure can improve any teacher's delivery of content. The PAR Framework can help both novice and experienced teachers to become more effective in the classroom.

Four Lessons of PAR Used in Teaching Content

To show that PAR easily accommodates any content area of instruction at any grade level, we chose four lessons—primary, upper elementary, middle, and high school—to illustrate its adaptable nature. All four teachers in these examples use the same framework to lead their learners in a structured and well-paced lesson before, during, and after reading about the assigned subject. They have selected strategies that guide students to learn the content effectively, and they have implemented appropriate activities for the lesson topic, the students, and the situation. These examples provide only an overview; directions for constructing activities are given in succeeding chapters, where the activities are presented in a larger context. The examples demonstrate how literacy can be incorporated into content lessons. They help address recent concerns about the reading achievement levels of students at all ages and grade levels.

View the video of Mark Diacopoulos on the Education CourseMate website at **www.cengagebrain.com** to see how a teacher integrates all phases of PAR while using writing, group work, and critical thinking skills to engage his students in learning about the Articles of the Confederation.

Example from a Primary Social Studies Lesson

Ms. Alex Seeley, a first grade teacher, incorporated literature into her lesson about school and classroom rules. The lesson would be taught at the start of the school year, when first graders are beginning to understand school and classroom expectations, as well as how to be good citizens. She chose the book *David Goes to School* (by David Shannon, Blue Sky Press, New York, 1999). It is about a little boy who is in school but does not seem to understand any of the rules. The book is funny and silly, but it makes students think about the poor choices David is making and how his choices impact everyone around him, as well as himself. Seeley coordinated her lesson with her state standards for first grade civics and English:

The student will apply the traits of a good citizen by:

- Focusing on fair play, exhibiting good sportsmanship, helping others, and treating others with respect.
- Recognizing the purpose of rules and practicing self-control; working hard in school.
- Taking responsibility for one's own actions; valuing honesty and truthfulness in oneself and others.
- The student will continue to expand and use listening and speaking vocabularies.
- The student will use meaning clues and language structure to expand vocabulary when reading.

To *prepare* her students, she would present this lesson after having spent several days discussing the rules. To highlight literacy, she would read the title and author of the book and show the children the cover art. By asking students to predict what the book might be about, she would promote discussion and engagement. The children would look at the pictures in the book (picture walk) to make further predictions about David's school experience. During this prereading phase, the children would be demonstrating their prior knowledge of rules.

To *assist* her students, the teacher would read the story with expression. Next she would present a cause/effect chart (on a chart, chalkboard, or computer screen) to note what David did and how it affected him and the other children (Activity 1.4). Then the class would discuss what would happen if David were in their class and how his behavior would make the children feel. Also, they would comment on how David should be acting. The teacher would write the rule that goes along with what David did wrong. Then she would ask the children to present other rules that would benefit the class. With each rule, they would be asked to explain why it is necessary. The children might even role-play some of these good versus bad behaviors.

To help children *reflect,* the teacher would give each child a piece of drawing paper folded in half. On one side, they would draw a sad face at the top with a picture below of David breaking a school rule. On the other side of the paper, they would draw a happy face and a picture of David following that rule. Underneath each picture drawn they would write a sentence about the picture. (If a software program such as *Inspiration* and computers are available, the lesson could incorporate technology as another learning tool.) After, the students would share their pictures and make a class book to

ACTIVITY 1.4 Cause/Effect Chart: What David Did

Cause	Effect	Rule
David did not wait his turn.	Other children had to wait longer.	Everyone gets a turn when we all wait for our turn.
David pushed another child.	Someone got hurt.	No pushing—respect each other.

show their families. The teacher would include a letter to parents, explaining how the children made the book and requesting that families read the book carefully together to review the rules.

This lesson for young children is about a content subject and uses material that meets state standards for instruction. It also includes several literacy and reading-to-learn strategies such as predicting, determining cause and effect, and writing to learn as it follows the PAR format.

Example from a Fifth Grade Art Class

Ms. Tenembaum taught a lesson incorporating art and poetry using the popular children's poetry book *Falling Up* by Shel Silverstein (1996). She selected the poem *A Closet Full of Shoes* (p. 118). The poem includes many different types of shoes along with their materials, purposes, and descriptions. She coordinated her lesson with her state's standards for fifth grade visual arts:

> The student will use the elements of art—line, shape, form, color, value, texture, and space—to express ideas, images, and emotions.
>
> The student will develop ideas for works of art by brainstorming, conducting research, and making preliminary sketches.

She supplemented these standards with her own objectives:

- The learner will understand how the poem is used to develop ideas for an art project.
- The learner will create a drawing of the shoe that he or she has designed.

To *prepare* her students, she gathered the children in a circle and asked them to look at their classmates' shoes. The children then described the shoes, including their colors and materials. Then she encouraged them to listen carefully to the poem to discover how shoes are described, what they are made of, and why they think the author wrote this poem. Reading the poem was also a part of her preparation in this lesson.

To *assist* her students, Ms. Tenembaum organized the class into small groups at art tables, each group with a copy of *A Closet Full of Shoes* and a jot chart to prompt the organization of the activity and the poem's meaning. She explained that a jot chart is used to organize information and identified the heading in each column, pointing out that the first line was already provided and then asking the class to help her fill in the next line (Activity 1.5). She also projected a copy of this jot chart in the front of the classroom so she could guide them as they completed their group charts. She had the students reread the poem with their groups to identify the materials, purposes, and descriptions of the shoes represented in the poem. Then she asked them to fill in the other lines on the chart in their groups. She walked around to help. After groups had completed their charts, she collected the copies of the poem and asked students to think about a shoe they would like to design. She showed them shoes that other students had designed in the past.

To help her students reflect, Ms. Tenembaum gave each student a piece of 9 × 12 paper. They designed a shoe using the elements of art—line, shape, form, color, value, texture, and space—as inspired by the poem. Finally, Ms. Tenembaum asked the students to show group members their individual designs and explain how their shoes might be described in the Silverstein poem. Students liked being able to create their own shoes. They liked showing off these shoes to others in the class.

ACTIVITY 1.5 *A Closet Full of Shoes* Jot Chart

Name of Shoe	Purpose	Material	Description
Working shoes	Work	Leather, steel	Working shoes are made of leather and have laces and steel toes.

The shoe you will design goes right here.

This lesson for upper elementary children meets state standards for instruction. It also includes several literacy strategies such as listening with purpose, social interaction to learn, and visual literacy to create a piece of art.

Example from a Middle School Mathematics Lesson

Mr. Michael Tewksbury, a middle school mathematics teacher, designed a lesson to teach the difference between ratios and fractions. He had found that many students cannot differentiate between what they learn about fractions and ratios. However, from a practical and conceptual standpoint, the two are quite different—all ratios are fractions, but not all fractions are ratios. A ratio is a comparison between two quantities. A key developmental milestone is the ability of a student to begin to think of a ratio as a distinct entity, different from the two measures that make it up. Recalling a book he had read to his 5-year-old son, he selected it as the basis for this lesson (*If You Hopped Like a Frog* by David M. Schwartz, Scholastic Press, New York, 1999). This picture book highlights the amazing abilities of animals by showing what children could accomplish if they were capable of taking on the speed, strength, and size of certain animals. After the story, the book provides a detailed section that delivers proof of the outlandish claims found in the first 24 pages. These two aspects of the book make it an attractive preliminary instructional activity on ratios. For instance, "If you hopped like a frog . . . you could jump from home plate to first base in one mighty leap!"

Mr. Tewksbury *prepared* his students with a brief overview about ratios and the course of study for the unit using a What-I-Know Activity (WIKA) about ratios. He asked the students to list what they already knew about ratios and what they needed to know. The list could be reviewed for follow-up and additions at the end of the lesson. The teacher also used this preparation activity to assess and build background knowledge.

After the WIKA activity, Mr. Tewksbury read *If You Hopped Like a Frog*. As Mr. Tewkesbury read the first 25 pages, he encouraged student interaction. This helped introduce important mathematical concepts, consistent with his state's standards:

- The student will identify representations of a given percent and describe orally and in writing the equivalence relationships among fractions, decimals, and percents.
- The student will describe and compare two sets of data using ratios and will use appropriate notations, such as *a/b*, *a* to *b*, and *a:b*.
- The student will compare and order whole numbers, fractions, and decimals using concrete materials, drawings or pictures, and mathematical symbols.

For *assistance,* students selected one of the comparisons made in the book and brainstormed a number of ideas about how this comparison could be visually represented (numerically, graphically, or any way they chose). After the discussion, the teacher shared all 12 sets of actual ratio information detailed at the end of the picture book. Students incorporated this information into their WIKA. Next students were assigned to work in groups of three to find and develop an original animal/personal comparison. To determine specific examples, students needed to research statistics and facts from one of several Internet sites.

After identifying their comparison and facts, students designed visuals to represent their ratios and wrote explanations describing what their representations meant and why they selected particular representation methods. When students had completed the written portion of this task, each group shared its findings, explanations, and justifications. The teacher's primary objectives during this *assistance* activity were to assess student understanding, clarify misunderstandings, maintain a focus of relevant discussion, and build comprehension of relationships and ratios. The process of focusing discussion and building comprehension was accomplished largely by providing divergent questions aimed at helping students develop a conceptual understanding of ratios.

For *reflection,* students returned to the WIKA. This served as a review and preparation for the next lesson about ratios. The specific items reviewed included what they knew, what they still wanted to know, and what they found interesting and important. This lesson was meant to help students independently formulate their own working conceptual framework and connections for ratios. They did this while using literacy as a learning tool.

Example from a High School Biology Class

Ms. Plott taught tenth graders a lesson about cells structures and functions. She relied on the textbook *Biology: Concepts and Connections* (4th ed., 2003) and the chapter "A Tour of the Cell."

She expected that after her lesson, the students would be able to:

- Participate in a discussion about their understanding of the terms before reading the text.
- Assess their prior knowledge of cell structures and functions.
- Prepare themselves for the textbook chapter.

- Understand how to compare cell structures and functions of prokaryotic, plant, and animal cells.
- Identify text structure while comparing cell structures and functions.
- Understand the difference between prokaryotic and eukaryotic cells.
- Participate in a class discussion about cell structures and functions.
- Identify at least five organelles and their general function.
- Identify at least three organelles and their specific functions.
- Summarize the meaning of the chapter by developing a model of the information.

To *prepare* her students, she used a prelearning concept guide (Activity 1.6). She chose this activity because it would expose the students to key vocabulary words used in the chapter and to find out how much the students already knew about the topic. She explained that there were some difficult terms in the chapter that might be unfamiliar to them. The students then turned to a partner to check their answers. Students received support and reinforcement from a partner so they would be more likely to partake openly in the class discussion. After the paired sharing, a class discussion took place so she could find out how many students knew the meaning of the words, were familiar with them, or didn't know the meanings.

During the *Assistance* Phase, the class read the chapter individually. When everyone had completed the reading, they went back to the key terms as a class and determined if their prior knowledge of the words was correct. They thoroughly reviewed the terms that were the most difficult to comprehend. Then Ms. Plott collected the guide so she could assess each student's preliminary understanding of the subject. Next, she gave each student an organizational jot chart so they could apply what they had just learned (Activity 1.7). She had several purposes for using this organizational jot chart. By having the students fill in the table as they referred back to what they had read, they would understand how to identify text structure. The chart showed comparisons of the material, which would assist readers in recognizing and organizing the pertinent information and reinforce independent reading. The organizational chart

ACTIVITY 1.6 Prelearning Concept Guide for *A Tour of the Cell*

Before reading: The terms that follow appear in the next chapter. Rate your knowledge by placing a plus sign (+) in front of those you are sure you know, a minus sign (-) in front of those you have some knowledge about, and a zero (0) in front of those you don't know.

______ Prokaryotic cells

______ Eukaryotic cells

______ ATP

______ Cytoplasm

______ Nucleus

______ Organelles

______ DNA

______ Chloroplasts

When you read the next chapter in your textbook, pay attention to the meaning of these words. This assignment will not be graded; however, I will collect it at the end of class to determine your level of understanding.

ACTIVITY 1.7 Jot Chart for Cell Structures and Functions

Fill in the chart while reading the textbook chapter. It will help you understand the information presented in the chapter.*

CELL STRUCTURES AND FUNCTIONS

Cell Organelle	General Function	Specific Function	Type of Cell (Prokaryotic, Plant, and/or Animal)
Nucleus			
Nucleoid region			
Ribosomes			
Rough ER			

*This example provides only the first few rows of the entire jot chart.

would not only help construct meaning, but the completed form would also provide an effective study guide.

After the students had completed the chart, she divided the class into groups of four. The students within each group compared their organizational charts, filling in any blanks and coming to a consensus if there were discrepancies. They had approximately 10 minutes to complete this step. Ms. Plott then conducted a class discussion to review the answers. She added information and explained incorrect information. At the end of the class, she summarized the main points of the chapter with a PowerPoint® presentation in order to reinforce what the class had learned and to promote the storage of this information into long-term memory. She did not collect the organizational jot chart, because the students needed to use it as a study guide.

For *reflection,* the class was divided into groups of three, and Ms. Plott explained how to develop a graphic organizer. The groups decided among themselves what form the graphic organizer should take. The students then reviewed the text silently, gathering information to be included in the group's graphic presentation. After each member of the group had gathered the information they wished to include, the group decided how to organize the information in a model. The groups then presented their finished products to the class.

Ms. Plott decided on a post-graphic organizer. For students to complete the graphic organizer, they needed to be able to think critically about the text reading and to focus their understanding. They needed to convert complex ideas into a holistic graphic display that summarized the meaning of the reading. Biology includes copious information, so it is often hard for students to visualize the material. Creating a visual image makes it easier for the students to see the relationships among the various types of cells and cell structures. Meaningful reflection also helps students to retain the information.

At the end of this lesson, students had read their chapter once and reviewed it twice. They had responded to three types of organizing activities that demonstrated strategically how to pay attention to important vocabulary and to construct knowledge. They also left the lesson with study material.

Please visit the Education CourseMate website at **www.cengagebrain.com** to find other examples of PAR lesson plans for secondary health and physical education.

CHALLENGE BOX

Now Meet Four Students

We are introducing you to four learners who represent some of the diverse students you may meet in your own classrooms. The profiles are based on real students, but none of the profiles represents a single, specific person. You will see one of these students featured in several of the chapters of this book. When you encounter them, you will be encouraged to think about how the chapter information might apply for this student's needs. In Chapter 11, you will learn more about what the professional literature indicates about these diverse students.

At-Risk Profile: JaNette

JaNette is in eleventh grade at an urban high school. She lives in a housing project with her two older brothers, her older sister (who, at 19 years old, has two children), and her mother (who is seldom home because she works two jobs). Opportunities to get illegal drugs are rampant, but JaNette has avoided the drug scene thus far. She does not care for school except as a place to hang out with friends outside of class. No one reads in her home—there is no time for that. When Janette graduates, she will be the first in her family to do so.

Although her attitude is defensive, JaNette is very capable. She learned to read easily and liked primary school. Her grades fluctuate, sometimes in a downward spiral but sometimes soaring. If she gets interested in a subject, she will pursue it. JaNette often expresses her frustration with remarks such as: "I hate this book" or "I'm not gonna do this sh-t." However, she is determined to find a vocation and earn a good salary.

One teacher tries to foster Janette's interests and encourages her to "bounce back" from her anger and disappointments. This teacher asked students to read the essay "On Honoring Blackness" by Henry Louis Gates (1995) and listen to a podcast in which LeBron James talks about being poor before becoming a great basketball player. The teacher then asked students to respond by writing about what they thought defined their own cultural identity. JaNette wrote:

> What defines my cultural identity would be my religion, my family, and my friends. I grew up in a what they call ghetto neighborhood so I thought my background was like slang talking, being bad and hanging out with people that had a bad influence on me. I don't know if I am half of anything, every time I asked my mom she say I am all black but my grandma is half Indian. I am proud of being African American like that essay Gates. I can relate to the podcast LeBron James because I have a really rough childhood growing up. Like one point of time all we had to eat was noodles, one point we didn't have a lot of money it was hard and stressful for all of us. We were always moving, switching schools and everything. I also can relate because finishing high school is my way out of the roughness I went through, I want to be able to not go through what I went through when I was younger but I still want to keep my cultural background going.

English as a Second Language Profile: Gustavo

Gustavo is 13 years old and in seventh grade. His parents and older sister are from Mexico; they are undocumented immigrants living in the United States. His mother works as a maid and his father is a construction worker. He and his three younger siblings are U.S. citizens and are eligible for Medicaid, so his parents are able to get them the medical care they need. He is more likely to have eyeglasses or other important aids that can impact his learning because his parents do not have to pay for treatment out of pocket. His father has been deported once and sometimes talks about going back to Mexico when times are tough for the family. Because living in the United States is all that Gustavo has known, this uncertainty causes him stress.

Similar to the majority of U.S. English as a second language (ESL) students, Gustavo was born in the United States, yet English is his second language. Spanish is the only language spoken in his home. Gustavo didn't go to preschool. The elementary school he attended had Title I status, and ESL students made up 30 percent of the school's population, mostly from Spanish-speaking countries; the school was able to have three full-time ESL teachers, so he received a lot of attention. Although he was able to communicate in English by the end of kindergarten, he repeated the year to catch up. He was exited from ESL services at the end of fifth grade, so now he is considered a former limited English proficient (FLEP) student.

Although he struggled early in school, Gustavo is now doing very well academically. He passed all of his state's standardized tests while in middle school. Although he is bilingual, Gustavo cannot read or write in Spanish; he has been accepted into a summer program that focuses on developing and enhancing the literacy and math skills of ESL students in both English and Spanish. This program also supports students in realizing their dreams of going to college. Gustavo hopes to become a doctor.

(continued)

Struggling Reader Profile: Mark

Mark was quite excited to begin his first year in Washington Middle School. Although he knows that reading and writing are somewhat difficult for him, he is confident in his abilities to learn science and math. Science is his favorite subject. He is really curious and intrigued by mysteries in nature. In elementary school, he enjoyed the hands-on projects and experiments, and he typically earned good grades on the illustrations and models he used for his graded presentations. He spent considerable time viewing video clips on the Internet to learn more about the topic of the week or unit. He managed to earn average grades in science while in elementary school because he had adapted and learned to compensate for his struggles with reading the textbook by becoming a keen listener and paying close attention to visual aids that supported the lessons. Because science was so interesting, he was willing to push hard—memorizing vocabulary words, reading very slowly and trying to pronounce each word letter by letter, and paying very close attention. He compensated for poor reading skills with auditory skills.

He grew accustomed to gleaning key points and information from in-class lectures, chapter sections read aloud in class, video supports, visual computer supports, and group discussions. He was able to remember enough to pass multiple-choice and matching exams and to adequately complete assignments that entailed more illustrations and labeling than substantive writing. His parents helped with homework by reading the instructions and passages aloud to Mark. His grades in subjects other than science were low Cs or Ds. He began to dislike those subjects because they did not seem worth the effort to him. Sometimes he zoned out altogether and then became defensive if his teacher called attention to his daydreaming during class.

His listening and speaking vocabulary is appropriate for the content taught in a sixth grade classroom, but his reading and writing vocabulary is well below the standard needed for success. He is not prepared for a middle school science classroom and certainly not for his other classes.

Special Education Profile: Trinka

Trinka has a learning disability, although she is intellectually very capable of working at higher grade levels. She entered third grade after several years of moving from school to school because of her father's work. She had the benefit of a strong preschool program with a focus on mastering the alphabet, basic sounds, and name writing. After this fairly academic program, she moved into a school system that valued a developmental approach to early learning experiences. Such an approach was helpful for Trinka because she could go at her own pace and produce acceptable academic work without a lot of pressure or frustration. However, by the time she reached second grade, in her third school, she was in need of additional support. Her classroom teacher and parents wanted to ensure that Trinka had the benefit of consistent instructional support as she prepared for her next move.

Trinka's academic testing in third grade indicated that she would need additional assistance with tasks that required short- and long-term memory work. When she began third grade in her new classroom, her teachers were well prepared for collaborating to support Trinka's learning. She was able to participate in a Title I reading class, a small group focusing on phonemic awareness, a small group for students with learning disabilities, and the regular literacy instruction program.

These experiences, plus the hours at home that her parents dedicated to ensuring that she mastered the nightly homework and understood the day's work, really helped Trinka to keep up. As she prepares for fourth grade, Trinka and her teachers are feeling more secure about her ability to succeed in content area course work that requires remembering facts and main ideas. Although she is keeping pace with her class, she could do even better; however, Trinka often becomes frustrated with the time she must spend to learn what others seem to grasp so easily.

The Organization of This Text

The 12 principles presented earlier are an integral part of the discussion in every chapter of this book. The first six chapters are foundation chapters; they present the basic theory and rationale for the approach used in this text. Chapter 2 describes how to create an affective learning climate. Chapters 3 to 5 develop the idea of PAR. Applications for teachers are provided, as well as examples from several content areas and grade levels. Chapter 6 presents ways to teach with multiple resources beyond the traditional textbook. Chapters 7 to 9 discuss how PAR works with vocabulary, writing, and study skills. Chapter 10 expands upon the chapter-relevant tech applications throughout the book to demonstrate the possibilities for integrating technology in content classrooms. Chapter 11 describes different types of learners teachers might find in content classrooms and ways to help them. Chapter 11 will also reintroduce and reconsider the four diverse learners presented in this chapter. Chapter 12 presents information about the trend for accountability and evaluation for students in content classrooms through standardized testing.

Each chapter presents the PAR steps by asking readers to prepare themselves to read at the start of the chapter; by providing tools to assist students in their reading; and by fostering reflection on their comprehension at the end of the chapter. Furthermore, we highlight at the end of each chapter standards relevant for content instruction. We feature a technology application in each chapter. Icons highlight writing, cooperative grouping, diversity, and technology.

We recommend that you, the reader, select a subject topic to aid you in creating practice activities. The topic should be one that you are currently teaching or may use in the future as you teach. The books you select will be resources for completing some of the assignments given at the end of each chapter. After completing this textbook, you should be able to analyze any resource or textbook to determine if it is suitable for learners; to evaluate its effective qualities; and to decide if it will allow you to apply the PAR Lesson Framework, its study skills and vocabulary aids, and its attention to different learners. In addition, you should be able to construct activities that help you teach content through a reading-to-learn approach.

When teachers use the PAR Lesson Framework, they facilitate improvement in students' thinking ability. This type of teacher intervention and guidance is a necessary step in improving cognitive ability. In 1983, Pearson and Tierney assessed the instructional paradigm most used by teachers. They found that the key elements of instruction included the use of many practice materials; little explanation of cognitive tasks; little interaction with students about the nature of specific tasks; and strong emphasis on one correct answer, with teachers supplying answers when students remained confused. Not surprisingly, Pearson and Tierney concluded that such a paradigm was ineffective. We have had much experience since that time observing the teaching that takes place in schools. We find the same practices prevalent today that Pearson and Tierney observed. Applying the PAR Lesson Framework to teach specific strategies and skills will help improve how teachers teach. Use of this framework will make teachers more effective in content area classrooms.

ONE-MINUTE SUMMARY

This chapter provides a short historical overview of the status of education and reading in the late 20th and early 21st centuries. It also cites studies of researchers who have documented the many achievements of our educational system. We briefly introduce ways of teaching a discipline with literacy tools, and we cultivate an awareness of what students bring to the classroom. Next, we summarize our beliefs about reading to learn and provide the foundation for the textbook by describing 12 core principles for content reading instruction. The goal of good content reading instruction is to aid students in becoming autonomous learners in the classroom. Well-planned reading instruction can prevent students from skipping important parts of a lesson, thus alleviating incomplete thinking by learners. We explain our consistent system that encourages readers to practice PAR as they read this textbook. PAR provides a way to overcome incomplete thinking and poor student learning by offering a structured plan for teachers to deliver content in an effective and organized manner. Finally, we provide four examples of the use of the PAR Lesson Framework to demonstrate how teachers can meet the needs of their students in content instruction at several levels of education from kindergarten through adulthood.

END-OF-CHAPTER ACTIVITIES

Assisting Comprehension

1. Look at the list you made at the beginning of this chapter of all the ways you guide—or plan to guide—your students. Add to this list and respond again to this question: How many of these ways include active participation, demonstration, problem solving, student involvement, assessment of success, and self-initiative?
2. Reconsider the 10 terms you selected from the list at the start of this chapter. Create an explanation in your own words for each one and teach them to someone else.

Reflecting on Your Reading

1. Your content organization (e.g., National Council of Teachers of Mathematics, National Council of Teachers of English, National Council for the Social Studies, National Science Teachers Association, International Reading Association) has most likely developed a set of standards that identify the performance criteria relevant to classroom teachers. Standards usually delineate elements of foundational knowledge that a classroom teacher should possess. Locate and become familiar with what the organization recommends. For instance, teachers should:
    - know foundational theories related to practices and materials they use in the classroom.
    - recognize historical antecedents to contemporary methods and materials.
    - articulate how their teaching practices relate to current research.
2. How did this chapter address these elements? How does being informed about these elements aid in content instruction?

CHAPTER 2

Teaching in the Affective Domain

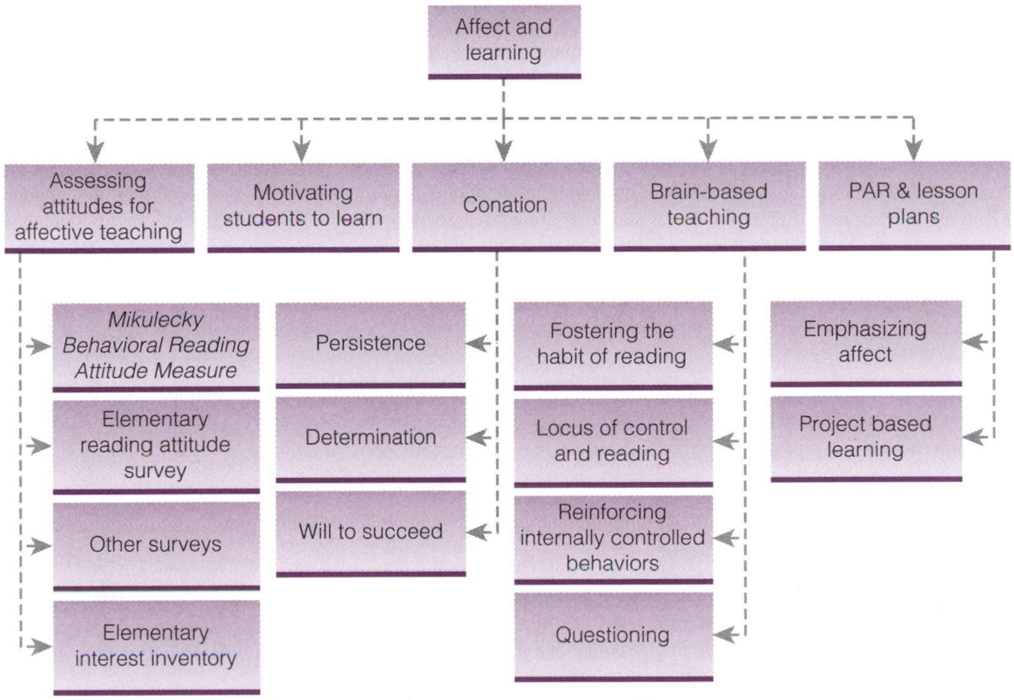

> The three indispensables of genius are understanding, feeling, and perseverance.
>
> ANONYMOUS

VOICES FROM THE CLASSROOM

Mr. Bardgardner hardly ever smiled. He told his history class that he would not tolerate bad behavior and he was there only to teach them history, not to deal with their problems or any feelings of frustration they might be experiencing about school. And indeed, he taught his class by strictly adhering to the facts as outlined in the textbook in a straight lecture format. His favorite line in class was "As the book points out . . ." followed by the recitation of a fact noted from the text. The students were bored by his lectures and flat personality, and they especially did not like his humorless and tough teaching style. His tests were, of course, directly from the book. Predictably, he had a test every two weeks on the contents of the book chapters, and he always had a review two days before the test.

The only fun the class had was a classroom pool, unknown to the teacher, that all students took part in each week. Everyone put one dollar in the pool and guessed how many times Mr. Bardgardner said, "As the book points out . . ." that week. The student with the correct guess won all the money for the week. Mr. Bardgardner never guessed that all the rapt attention the students were showing him in his lectures was really anticipation of a possible win in the pool. Attention was especially riveted toward the end of the week.

Do you think the above description is fiction? No, this was an actual class observed by one of the authors (the teacher's real name is not used) and described by one of the students. Where is the fun, the attention to the affective domain (feelings) in the above description, except when the students seemed forced to make their own fun in a decidedly underhanded way? Have you ever been involved in a class devoid of feeling such as this one? If so, try to remember how it felt.

PREPARING TO READ

1. Following is a list of terms used in this chapter. Some may be familiar to you in a general context but used in unfamiliar ways in this chapter. Rate your knowledge by placing a plus sign (+) in front of those you are certain you know, a check mark (√) in front of those you have some knowledge of, and a zero (0) in front of those you don't know. Be ready to locate them in the chapter and pay special attention to their meanings.

   _______ affective domain
   _______ attitude
   _______ motivation
   _______ conation
   _______ brain-based learning
   _______ locus of control
   _______ internal locus of control
   _______ questioning in the affective domain
   _______ differentiation of instruction
   _______ project-based learning

2. Match the words in the left column with their definitions in the right column:

   1. affective domain
   2. attitude
   3. brain-based learning theory
   4. locus of control
   5. internal locus of control

   a. The disposition, temperament, or feeling one has about something or someone
   b. Accepting responsibility for one's own behavior
   d. The way someone explains his or her successes and failures affects learning.
   e. The domain of learning dealing with feelings and emotions
   f. The perceived control one has over a condition or situation
   g. A theory that the brain is modular and as such helps form and shape certain kinds of learning behaviors

OBJECTIVES

As you read this chapter, focus your attention on the following objectives. You will

1. Describe what is meant by the *affective domain of teaching.*
2. Explain why affect is important to reading.
3. Discuss the importance of attitudes in teaching.
4. Discuss the importance of conative factors in reading.
5. Describe what constitutes a brain-based approach to learning.
6. Explain the importance of attitude tests.
7. List several examples of attitude tests and surveys.
8. Define the *locus of control* and its importance for content area instruction.
9. Show how you could incorporate affective strategies in a content area curriculum.
10. Show how you could use the PAR Lesson Framework in making lesson plans.
11. Explain how to differentiate instruction in the content classroom.
12. Describe project-based lesson plans.

"SOON AS YOU LEARN TO READ, JOEY, THE WHOLE WORLD'S AGAINST YOU."

Dennis the Menace © Hank Kercham Enterprises. North American Syndicate.

Affect and Learning

The Voices from the Classroom section described a class almost entirely devoid of feelings. There was no attention to the attitudes displayed by the students. There was only a dogged quest for retrieval of the facts of history. This was so even though we know research (Cardoso, 2003) shows that students can learn best when they care about the subject matter. This chapter deals with the **affective domain** of learning as it applies to reading. The term *affect* (from the Latin *affectus*, which means to afflict or touch) refers to a response to a stimulus that causes feelings or emotions. Affective constructs, such as feelings, emotions, attitudes, self-concepts, values, self-esteem, and locus of control, connote slightly different meanings but all influence a student's ability to learn.

Students from kindergarten to twelfth grade "dwell" in the affective domain—that is, their lives are often ruled by strong feelings and emotions, and they often exhibit very positive or very negative attitudes toward their school environment. Conversely, teachers seem to concentrate solely on student achievement and the cognitive development of students as the criteria for success (Sherry, Cronje, Rauscher, & Obermeyer, 2005). Despite research (Belfiore, Auld & Lee, 2005) showing that large numbers of students in urban school districts are failing to reach their potential because of reading difficulties, as well as evidence (Maatta, Dobb, & Ostland, 2006) that attention to the affective domain is essential in learning, especially for second language learners, teachers often neglect the affective domain.

The challenge of teaching affect in the content classroom stems from the type of interaction among students and teachers. Students and teachers are physically in the same classroom, but they have very different needs. Whereas teachers are driven to impart knowledge and assist students in their learning, students tend to focus on discovering how their learning relates to people and everyday events. Thus, real communication does not always occur in classrooms where the focus is only on content. Throughout this book, we assert that it is teachers' job to get students to think more clearly. Some students can be lazy thinkers, and others have not been trained to think. However, we also contend that teachers need to pay more attention to the affective domain—to make learning more interesting by making classes more fun, functional, and rewarding, and to value what students have to say (Demetriou & Wilson, 2010). We as teachers are unlikely to reach students cognitively if we do not reach them affectively. We devote this chapter to engaging students through good affective teaching, presenting both theory and practice (strategies) to enhance the teaching of affect in content classrooms.

For decades, researchers (Bandura, 1986, 1997; Dechant, 1970) have been writing about the importance of the social aspects of learning. New research by Padmala and Pessou (2010) confirms the importance of motivation in the learning environment. Because so many of the reports, such as the annual Phi Delta Kappan polls, emphasize the lack of student achievement, research on such affective variables as attitude and self-concept has waned. Initiatives and reform efforts have resulted in rigorous national standards, and specific performance measures have been mandated for students in many states. Despite research showing that affective variables have an important connection to outcome performance measures such as memory and recall (Hager & Gable, 1993; Wolfe, 2001), studies examining affective variables have been largely absent from funding proposals. Van Valkenburg and Holden (2004) have written that "every cognitive behavior has an affective counterpart" (p. 347) and that every cognitive approach is concerned with as much affection as cognition.

Please visit the Education CourseMate website at **www.cengagebrain.com** to view the video with Chapter 2 and see how affect works to engage students in learning. The real-world math project motivates students to take responsibility for running the school store.

The most outward manifestation of the affective domain is **attitude**—the mental disposition one exhibits toward others. For a long time, educators have known that student attitude is a critical variable in reading achievement (Purves & Bech, 1972; Walberg & Tsai, 1985). Frank Smith (1988) notes that the emotional response to reading "is the primary reason most readers read, and probably the primary reason most nonreaders do not read" (p. 177). M. Cecil Smith (1990) found, in a longitudinal study, that reading attitudes tend to be stable over time from childhood through adulthood, adding to the notion that poor attitudes (or good attitudes) toward reading are inculcated early in schooling and tend to remain stable throughout life. However, Wolfe and Antinarella (1997) maintain that teachers can win over and inspire students by developing in them attitudes and dispositions for learning that cause them to honor, respect, and value themselves and others.

ACTIVITY 2.1 Student Comments in the Affective Domain

Here are some actual statements from students that overtly demonstrate the speakers' attitudes toward the subjects they are learning. Think about Principles 4 and 5 in Chapter 1 as you read these comments. Can you identify the attitude corresponding to each statement?

Why are we doing this?
This is so stupid.
I didn't learn nothing.
All we ever do in this class is read and write.
The Odyssey was kinda cool.

I never read that deep into a story before, but I thought the contradictions were interesting. Odysseus was a hero, but he cheated on Penelope and killed a lot of people. It tells me something about the people that wrote this story.

I guess blood and killing were as popular then as they are now.

Researchers such as Maurer and Davidson (1999) call for teachers not to ignore the affective domain and what they call the "power of the heart" when using new technologies in the classroom for teaching the skills of literacy. Because students today are accustomed to using technology regularly in their lives outside school and because they may see literacy differently than their teachers do (Gee, 2000), instruction that incorporates technology in academics can be highly motivating.

Teachers can easily identify student attitudes, which students telegraph though their remarks (Activity 2.1).

Assessing the overall attitudes of all students in the class requires more precision than offhand comments, of course. The next section provides some excellent tests for use in attitudinal assessment in the affective domain.

Assessing Attitudes for Affective Teaching

The *Mikulecky Behavioral Reading Attitude Measure* (Mikulecky, Shanklin, & Caverly, 1979) for older students (Activity 2.2) and the *Elementary Reading Attitude Survey* (McKenna & Kear, 1990) for early elementary grade students (Activity 2.3) were designed to cover a broad range of affective interest and developmental stages. These tests can be given as pretests and again after several months as posttests to determine whether students' attitudes have changed significantly. Activity 2.2 provides only a few example statements.

Appendix A provides the entire Mikulecky test, keys for interpreting these two surveys, and technical information about their construction and validation.

By finding out what students like to do in their spare time, teachers can ensure a more positive atmosphere in the classroom while keeping in mind the goals and perceived needs of the lesson, To this end, teachers can create general-interest inventories such as the one shown for middle school and high school in Activity 2.4 and the one for early elementary school in Activity 2.5.

Through the use of an inventory, a high school English teacher asked her eleventh graders to indicate what types of writing experiences they liked best. She discovered that they enjoyed writing personal messages but disliked writing essays. The curriculum expectation was that all students would learn and practice writing persuasive essays. While teaching "Sinners in the Hands of an Angry God" by Jonathan Edwards,

ACTIVITY 2.2 Mikulecky Behavioral Reading Attitude Measure: Some Example Items

Example:

You receive a book for a holiday present. You start the book but decide to stop halfway through.

Very unlike me   1   2   3   4   5   Very like me

1. You walk into the office of a doctor or dentist and notice that there are magazines set out.

Very unlike me   1   2   3   4   5   Very like me

2. People have made jokes about your reading in unusual circumstances or situations.

Very unlike me   1   2   3   4   5   Very like me

3. You are in a shopping center you've been to several times when someone asks where books and magazines are sold. You are able to tell the person.

Very unlike me   1   2   3   4   5   Very like me

4. You feel very uncomfortable because emergencies have kept you away from reading for a couple of days.

Very unlike me   1   2   3   4   5   Very like me

ACTIVITY 2.3 Elementary Reading Attitude Survey

1. How do you feel when you read a book on a rainy Saturday?

2. How do you feel when you read a book in school during free time?

3. How do you feel about reading for fun at home?

4. How do you feel about getting a book as a present?

5. How do you feel about spending free time reading?

6. How do you feel about starting a new book?

7. How do you feel about reading during summer vacation?

8. How do you feel about reading instead of playing?

9. How do you feel about going to a bookstore?

10. How do you feel about reading different kinds of books?

11. How do you feel when the teacher asks you questions about what you read?

12. How do you feel about doing reading workbook pages and worksheets?

13. How do you feel about reading in school?

14. How do you feel about reading your school books?

15. How do you feel about learning from a book?

16. How do you feel when it's time for reading class?

17. How do you feel about the stories you read in reading class?

18. How do you feel when you read out loud in class?

19. How do you feel about using a dictionary?

20. How do you feel about taking a reading test?

ACTIVITY 2.4 Student Survey for Middle and High School

Name ______________________________

What name do you prefer to be called?______________

Your usual grade in Math _____ Social Studies _____ English _____ Science _____

Grade you plan to earn this year: Math _____ Social Studies _____ English _____ Science _____

Complete the paragraph about you:

My favorite subject: ______________________________ My least favorite: ______________________________.

What percentage of your grades should come from tests? ______________.

In what other ways do you want to earn grades? ______________________________.

If you could change one thing about yourself, what would it be? ______________________________.

And one thing about school? ______________________________.

I like to read because ______________________________. My favorite book is ______________________________.

How many hours a day do you watch television? ______________.

Who watches TV with you? ______________ Your favorite TV program?

What kind of music do you like? ______________.

Do you use a computer? ______________. How many hours a day? ______________.

Circle all the words that describe you:

healthy	quiet	good sport	lazy
dependable	likable	hard worker	lonely
honest	determined	cooperative	artistic
worthless	nervous	shy	clean, neat appearance
sense of humor	quick-tempered	easily upset	easily discouraged
a winner	cheerful	good leader	
forgetful	easygoing	friendly	

My favorite hobby is ______________________________. My favorite sport is ______________________________.

At home, it is fun to ______________________________.

Ten years from now, I would like to be ______________________________.

Things I do well are ______________________________.

What I dislike about classes are ______________________________.

What I dislike about teachers are ______________________________.

Sports I play: ______________________________. Clubs I belong to: ______________________________.

My hero in life is ______________________________ because ______________________________.

the teacher talked about this sermon as an example of a persuasive essay. She then asked the students to relate their own experiences in trying to convince someone of something important to them and to estimate how successful their efforts had been. After developing a list of successful persuasion strategies, she told the students to write a persuasive essay in message form to a real person, trying to persuade that person about an important issue. The teacher allowed the students to choose the form of the letter (e.g., email, blog). The assignment was a huge success.

ACTIVITY 2.5 Elementary Interest Inventory

My name is ____________.

I am happy because ____________.

My family likes that I am ____________.

I am good at ____________.

I get unhappy when ____________.

I think reading is ____________.

If I could be another person, it would be ____________.

My favorite book is ____________.

My favorite thing to do is to ____________.

My favorite subject in school is ____________.

You can describe me as (circle one)

happy sad bored shy friendly

My hero is ____________ because ____________.

My favorite time at school is ____________ because ____________.

I enjoy reading because ____________.

Refer to Songs and Raps (Chapter 9), which explains how students' music preferences were used to create a rap song about economics.

The assessment instruments provided above enable teachers to determine attitudes and interests of their students. Using them will help teachers design effective instruction that is sensitive to their students as individuals. When teachers show students that they are interested in them as people, significant changes can occur in student behavior. The next section presents ways to use the assessment results.

Motivating Students to Learn

Good literature can be used to teach affect. Please visit the Education CourseMate website at **www.cengagebrain.com** to find Cyberstacks, a giant searchable database of literature that can be used to incorporate the affective domain.

Affective bonds can be strengthened for students when teachers assist students during lessons by designing tasks that influence children's **motivation**. To get students motivated to read, teachers first need to listen actively to their students. Teachers need to concentrate on what students are saying and reply to their comments, not formulate in advance a stock reply. Also, whenever possible, teachers need to make learning fun and rewarding. They can do this by keeping reading assignments manageable and encouraging students to read on their own. Yoon (2002) found that providing time for students to choose reading material improved students' attitudes toward reading. Teachers also can have students take part in frequent group sharing experiences. It is important for teachers always to speak well of reading and learning and to be readers who share the books they are reading.

To promote affect, teachers should bring good literature into class whenever possible, especially in content area classrooms. Bottomley and colleagues (1999) found that a literature-based approach to reading and writing had a greater effect on intermediate-age children's affective orientations toward literacy than did the regular reading routine. Purkey and Novak (1984) suggest that teachers can change student attitudes by making classrooms more affectively inviting. They outline four levels of invitation that directly affect student learning. Figure 2.1 shows Purkey's four levels, from intentionally disinviting to intentionally inviting. The authors stress that at the highest level, teachers must consciously work to make students believe that they are part of a learning community. Teachers must further be aware that students want to learn and that each day, teachers must nurture that innate desire and quest for knowledge.

Classroom arrangements can facilitate or hinder an affective climate. Classrooms where all students face forward and are always in straight rows convey the message

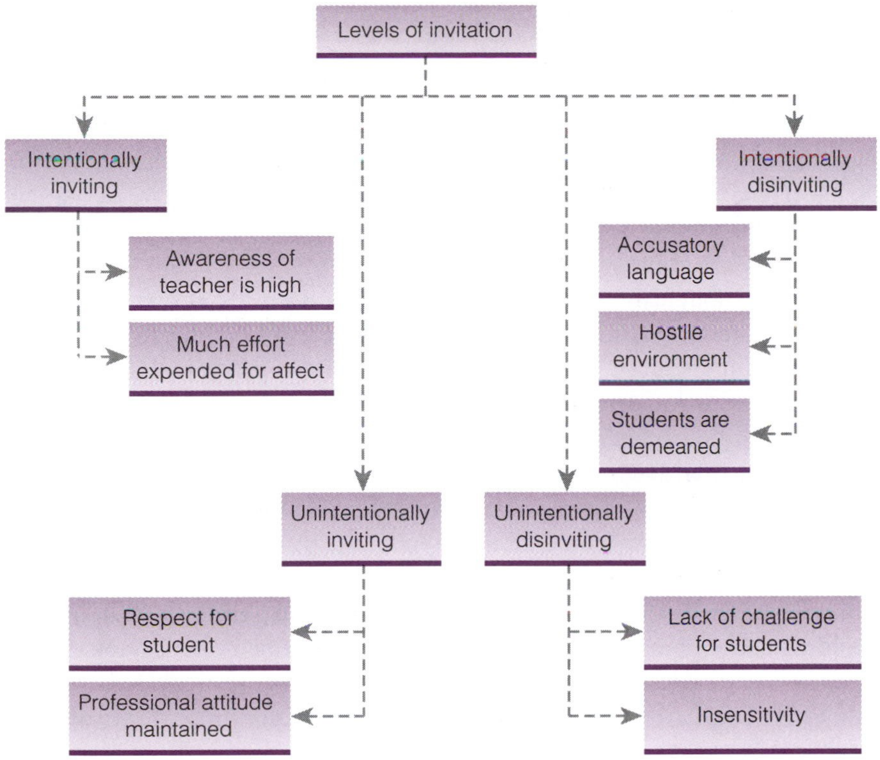

FIGURE 2.1

Purkey's Four Levels of Invitation

From W. W. Purkey and J. M. Novak, *Inviting School Success* (1984). Adapted with permission of Wadsworth, a Division of Thomson Learning.

that lecture and teacher control produce learning. To engage all students in learning, teachers must redefine the classroom climate (Kowalski, 1995).

Van Valkenburg and Holden (2004) suggest that the following activities can also improve student attitudes and effectively motivate students to learn:

- Keeping student journals about experiences
- Developing student portfolios of learning experiences
- Incorporating volunteerism into class assignments
- Using learning contracts with measurable desired results
- Adding a value component to each syllabus

Note this possibility for an effective classroom: A seminar approach (Strong, 1995) calls for long tables with all learners seated facing one another for intensive discussion. If such tables are not available, teachers and students might move several desks together to create the same effect. Group work calls for small clusters of chairs in several parts of a room.

Researchers (Fisher & Berliner, 1985; Palmer, 1998) have stressed the importance of creating a positive classroom climate. Teachers should provide a climate that says, "I am never going to give up on you; I believe in you." Many famous people did poorly in school—Albert Einstein, Woodrow Wilson, Thomas Edison, George Bernard Shaw, Pablo Picasso, William Butler Yeats, Henry Ford, and Benjamin Franklin. Paul Harvey (Aurandt, 1983) relates how Charles Schulz struggled with rejection in school for years and was a "loser" in school, yet he created *Peanuts,* one of the most popular comic strips. School settings should foster growth rather than hinder it. Most importantly, teachers must value inquiry, problem solving, and reasoning. By keeping an open mind and letting students take part in open-ended discussions, teachers make a statement about the true art of teaching through motivation that all students cannot ignore or misinterpret.

Another way to motivate students is for the teacher to develop a checklist for student self-assessment on certain affective variables. Such a checklist may make students more cognizant of their feelings, attitudes, and motivation to learn. It could be used once a week or at the beginning of a unit of instruction.

Conation as a Variable in Teaching Reading

Most educators have discussed learning only in terms of cognition. However, there are other factors in learning, such as energy, persistence, and will to learn, that can be defined as conative variables in learning. **Conation** focuses on individual will and desire to learn in conjunction with a student's determination not to give up until achieving success. That is, knowing is inextricably connected to an act of overt determination on the part of the learner.

Even though the term *conation* has been used for almost 200 years in psychological literature, it is a fairly obscure term, and few educators and researchers have incorporated it in discussions of affect. Emerson White, in his 1886 textbook, was the first to discuss the importance of the "energy of the senses, the intensity of the emotions and desires, and the energy and constancy of the will" (p. 92). Many years later, Paris, Lipson, and Wixson (1983) were among the first modern researchers to affirm the importance of intrinsic motivation and determination in a student's ability to become an independent learner. They noted that becoming a good reader requires both the skills of reading and the will to learn in increasingly complex educational environments. In 1986, Glasser addressed the importance of children caring about learning and their own achievement in his book *Control Theory in the Classroom*. More recent research (Wang & Guthrie, 2004) has corroborated what Paris, Lipson, and Wixson found about the importance of intrinsic motivation in reading comprehension.

Researchers (Cooter, 1994; Sullo, 2007) have urged educators to address the importance of conative components of learning. These researchers maintain that conative aspects of human behavior are necessary for a student to function cognitively and gain the intrinsic motivation necessary to learn.

The textbook *Strategies That Promote Student Engagement* (Gholar & Riggs, 2009) cites as the essential attributes of conation belief courage, energy, commitment, conviction, and change. In an environment that stresses conation, Gholar and Riggs maintain that these attributes provide a framework for teaching conation. The authors postulate that belief brings courage, which in turn gives a person the energy to perform. Such energy allows one to commit to goals and all four attributes together—belief, courage, energy, and commitment—strengthen one's resolve or conviction to succeed. From this conviction, motivation comes to change both internally and externally. Teachers should try to instill these essential attributes in their students so meaningful learning can take place.

In an earlier textbook, Gholar and Riggs (2004) say that conation can be stressed through (1) activities and strategies that give students choices in the learning experience, (2) pretend situations in which students learn self-efficacy by being challenged to succeed in difficult encounters, and (3) activities that ask students to decide whether a real or imagined historical or fictional character exhibits good or bad intentions.

Fleener and associates (2000) propose that conation be treated as a viable component of the reading development of children. They suggest a model of literacy development that integrates conation, cognition, affect, and social environment as connecting domains that interact to enable successful teaching and learning. These researchers propose that successful literacy development happens when teachers stress affect and conation and demonstrate the value of inquiry, sharing, and curiosity about learning

ACTIVITY 2.6 Affective Domain Checklist for Student Self-Assessment

Check which of these four levels applies to you.

I feel this way . . .	Always	Most of the time	Sometimes	Never
Determination: I am determined to learn. I care about learning. I must get better in this class. I am clear in my goals for this class. I take responsibility for my learning.				
Fair treatment of others: I play fair. I accept defeat and do not complain. I do not gloat in victory. Everyone needs to be treated fairly.				
My self-control in class: People are always bothering me. People make fun of me. I control my fate in this class. People do not bother me much. The teacher is unfair in this class. What I say matters in this class.				
How I communicate with fellow students: I listen to others. I interact well with other students. I want other students to do well. I encourage others. I am respectful of all my peers.				
How I treat my teacher: I respect what my teacher tells me. I respond positively to instruction. I daydream when the teacher talks. I ask for clarification from the teacher.				

Adapted from Gallo, A. M. (2003). Assessing the Affective Domain. *The Journal of Physical Education, Recreation and Dance.* 74(4), 44–49.

within a social context. The four key contexts in which these social attributes occur are the child, the teacher, the text, and the task. Table 2.1 lists the key attributes of learning that these researchers believe important for each of the four contexts.

Teachers can address conation by using study guides that emphasize the affective domain. In English courses, for instance, statements can describe a main character as willful, determined, or courageous. The statements in Activities 2.7 and 2.8 can be recast to emphasize conative factors within reading in other content areas.

The guide shown in Activity 2.7 could be used in a high school English or language arts class.

TABLE 2.1 Factors Contributing to Teaching and Learning Success

Child	Teacher	Text	Task
Quality of prior knowledge The learner's prior knowledge may be clear and factual or unclear and represent false knowledge.	**Quality of time on task** Teachers must develop caring relationships with children in completing the task.	**Perception of difficulty** Students cannot perceive the book in a negative way as being too difficult to comprehend.	**Interest** Tasks must be interesting to students.
Task-intrinsic motivation The child's readiness to perform an activity is a goal in itself.	**Modeling the value of thought processes** Teachers must value thinking and discussion as tools to develop the thought processes of children.	**Aesthetics** Texts must be appropriate for the audience, with pleasing formats.	**Appropriateness** Tasks must be appropriate to the intellectual, psychological, social, and moral development of students.
Insight Reflective awareness comes through cooperative interchange among students.	**Fostering curiosity** Teachers must believe that inquisitiveness and curiosity are most important in the learning process.	**Good writing** Subjects must come alive through the author's use of good writing.	**Cohesive context** Students must perceive that the task assigned makes sense in relation to what is read.
Perception of self as a reader Children must see themselves as generators of information, not passive receptors of knowledge.			**Perception of difficulty** Students cannot perceive the task in a negative way, such as being too difficult to perform.
Will to succeed Persistence and internal locus of control must be present.			**Will to succeed** Internal locus of control and a desire to be competitive with others or oneself—that is, persistence must be operational.

From Fleener, C., Hager, J., Morgan, R. F., & Childress, M. (2000). The integration of conation, cognition, affect, and social environment in literacy development. In P. Linder, W. M. Linek, E. G. Sturtevant, & J. Dugan (Eds.), *Literacy at a New Horizon: 22nd Yearbook of the College Reading Association.* Used with permission of the College Reading Association.

ACTIVITY 2.7 Middle and High School English

STUDY GUIDE EMPHASIZING CONATION

For *A Child Called It* by *Dave Pelzer*

Name ______________________ **Date** ______________ **Bell** ______________

Before reading: In the space to the left of each statement, place a check mark (✓) if you agree or think the statement is true.

During or after reading: Revise your answers. You may have to "read between the lines." Under each statement, note the page, column, and paragraph(s) where you find information to support your choice.

1. _____ Mothers always protect their children.
2. _____ The ending of a story can be in the last chapter or in the first chapter.
3. _____ Abusive parents use ordinary household items as weapons.
4. _____ Most abused children ultimately rebel and are violent with their parents.
5. _____ Abused children lose their self-respect and self-worth.
6. _____ Most abused children grow up to be abusers of their own children.
7. _____ It is the responsibility of each one of us to make sure child abuse does not occur.

ACTIVITY 2.8 Study Guide for High School: From the Article "Getting Into Painting"

Before reading: In the space to the left of each statement, place a check mark (✓) if you agree or think the statement is true.

During or after reading: Add new check marks or cross through those about which you have changed your mind.

_____ **1.** Reading a painting is like reading a book.

_____ **2.** Careers related to painting are limited to the fine arts.

_____ **3.** Art, from prehistory to the present, has reflected what was most important to the culture that created the art.

_____ **4.** I don't think I have the energy it takes to paint.

_____ **5.** Painting is just too difficult. It is hard to find enough time to devote to it.

_____ **6.** There are not many jobs to be had that require decorative painting.

Promoting Affect in Brain-Based Teaching

It might surprise you to know that the interconnections in a human brain outnumber all possible connections on the Internet by a large margin. The brain is tremendously complex, and science is just beginning to discover how this marvelous organ operates. Because of advances in functional magnetic resonance imaging (MRI), researchers have been able to pinpoint more precisely how the brain functions (Pink, 2005). Increasingly, educators are relying on **brain-based learning** theory to take advantage of a growing body of knowledge that neurologists are uncovering about how humans learn (Palombo, 2000). The newest imaging technology, such as MRI and positron emission tomography (PET), has shown us how the brain is structured in an incredible network of approximately 100 billion neurons, each connected to thousands of other neurons to form more connections than there are atoms in the entire universe. Sylwester (1994) describes the brain as modular, with separate components learning over time to combine information to form complex cognitive environments. Sylwester maintains that the brain is powerfully shaped by genetics, development, and experiences. The brain works to shape the nature of our experiences and is active in formulating the culture in which we live. In *Reading in the Brain* (2009), Stanislas Dehaene postulates that the neuronal networks of the brain are literally "recycled" for reading. In effect, literacy changes the brain so that it can invent and transmit cultural objects and concepts. Like Dehaene, Willis (2009) describes the brain as *plastic,* in that it can change over time with the growth of nerve fibers. Extended practice in reading can further the growth of such neural networks. Padmala and Pessoa (2010) postulate that cognitive and motivational signals actually interact in the brain when a person is reading. Dehaene describes the brain as a parallel processor that performs many functions simultaneously, making all meaningful learning complex and nonlinear. Many researchers (Diamond & Hopson, 1998; Sylwester, 1995; Weiss, 2000) assert that the brain is constantly in search of meaning. Green (1999) has asserted that "learning is enhanced by combining a rich environment with complex

Activity 2.8 is a guide for a fine arts class on painting at the high school level.

Please visit the Education CourseMate website at **www.cengagebrain.com** to locate several websites about brain research.

and meaningful challenges. Isolated pieces of information unrelated to what makes sense to a student [are] resisted by the brain" (p. 685).

All of this research supports the importance of conative factors in reading and learning. The human brain did not develop because of evolutionary needs for rote memory; manipulation of symbols; or tight, sequential structures or work systems; yet these activities constitute the main concerns of schooling. If a learner already knows something about a topic, then a logical, sequential, and fragmented presentation may serve well enough to transfer some new information about that topic to an appropriate retrieval area of the brain. But if a learner is not already familiar with a topic, this kind of presentation produces consistently poor learning results. Friedman (2006) warns that jobs of the future will go to people who can master new challenges, as opposed to the routine, and to those who can "synthesize the big picture rather than analyzing a single component" (p. 307). He calls for schools to heighten students' abilities to use the right hemispheres of their brains for increased intuitive, creative, empathetic thinking rather than emphasizing only left-hemisphere thinking, which deals with linear, logical, analytical thinking.

Focusing on what brain research is telling us about how students learn (Diamond & Hopson, 1998; Friedman, 2006; Lowery, 1998;Wolfe & Brandt, 1998), we believe the following guidelines are important to teaching:

To increase student motivation, Forget (2004) asks teachers to value student responses, use cooperative learning, combine challenge with support, establish relevance, make learning concrete and immediately important, measure success in more than one way, model expected behavior, be enthusiastic, call on students by their preferred names, and use a variety of activities. Which approaches do you incorporate in your teaching?

1. Students remember structured and meaningful material best (Jensen, 1998).
2. The classroom should always be a rich environment in which students interact so they can make sense of what they are learning.
3. Opportunities to talk and move around are important for heightened brain activity.
4. Pressures (and threats) should be held to a minimum.
5. Because the brain is essentially curious, learning must be a process of active construction by the learner, whereby students relate what they learn to what they already know. Intuitive learning should be stressed as much as step-by-step logic.
6. Learning is strongly influenced by emotion, so increasing positive emotion leads to enhanced retention.

Teachers need to learn the importance of brain-based learning. Please visit the Education CourseMate website at **www.cengagebrain.com** and find the 21st Century Learning Initiative website to locate information on brain-based research.

By taking advantage of what we now know about the way the human brain functions, we should create in our classrooms an environment in which all students can perform at their highest potential and develop patterns that will carry them through life as successful learners. In an affective environment that facilitates optimal use of the higher brain functions, students are empowered to become effective, self-motivated learners.

Fostering the Habit of Reading

In many classrooms, students individually and collectively avoid reading whenever possible. Students often listen to the teacher or to peers to glean information that will appear on tests. To combat this resistance to reading, teachers must be careful to design instruction that includes interesting reading as a crucial component. When students are presented with technology, they may "discover" reading to learn with new zeal.

It may be more enticing to read on an iPod or a smart phone than in a paper text. The content of the material remains the same, but the literacy environment seems more similar to the world students experience.

TECH APP

Suggested In-Class Activity for SmartPhones

To discover learning on the go: Send a text message to a classmate on a topic covered in class.

Time commitment: Minimal!

Why do it? To explain information learned in a compact message using familiar technology.

Values: Using writing to learn; using familiar and contemporary discourse; learning with familiar devices; creativity

Martin and Martin (2001) suggest a number of strategies for fostering reading habits in students who struggle to read effectively and efficiently. First, they maintain that students should progress at a pace that is comfortable enough to bring success. Many inefficient readers are rushed to finish exercises, and this only brings more frustration. To help in monitoring pace, teachers can give struggling students small, manageable portions of reading so students can stay focused. Martin and Martin (1989) also endorse the idea of acting as a coach to motivate students to acquire a habit of reading. Another important component is the motivational aspect of reading. Teachers should emphasize the emotional qualities of a passage, making the reading more personal and relevant to the student. Finally, they recommend that student self-checks (as shown in Activity 2.6) be used often to give students more responsibility and more of a stake in the activities.

Please visit the Education CourseMate website at **www.cengagebrain.com** and go to the New Horizons website to locate strategies that foster the habit of reading.

No chapter on the importance of the affective domain in reading would be complete without a discussion of the particular problem of boys and literacy. Researchers (Sommers, 2000) documented that boys have far more problems in school than girls. Young and Brozo (2001) have gathered alarming statistics on literacy and learning for boys. Some findings indicate that boys are more violent than girls, get in trouble with the law with much greater frequency, have much more trouble with alcohol and drug abuse than girls, and are far more likely to commit suicide. Perhaps the most surprising statistic is that boys experience far greater reading problems than girls. Boys are also three to five times more likely to be diagnosed with attention deficit disorder (ADD) and learning disabilities, as well as 50 percent more likely to be retained in school. In addition, far more boys drop out of school than girls. These facts are so disconcerting that Brozo, who asserts that boys "are fast becoming the culturally and academically disposesessed" (p. 318), calls the plight of boys in U.S. schools a national crisis.

There is no easy remedy, but educators must find solutions to foster the habit of reading in boys. Most boys still do not view reading as masculine. Teachers must find ways to make reading a more acceptable pastime for boys. A first step might be for teachers to discuss with male students the books that interest them. Then teachers, whenever possible, need to supply boys with readable, high-interest books.

Locus of Control and Reading

The term *locus of control* is often used interchangeably with *self-efficacy*. However, the meaning of these terms is not the same. Whereas self-efficacy deals with a feeling of acting competently, locus of control deals with a perception of control by outside agents (Spector & O'Connell, 1994).

Locus of control, based on Rotter's (1966) social learning theory, refers to a person's belief that life events can be controlled. People with an **internal locus of control** accept responsibility for the consequences of their own behavior. In addition, internally controlled people are much more likely to change their behavior after reinforcement than are individuals who do not have an internal locus of control. Those with an **external locus of control** blame fate, chance, other individuals, or task difficulty for their successes and failures. An external locus of control has been found to be related to poor attitude in the workplace (Duvdevany & Rimmerman, 1996). The concept of locus of control helps teachers understand certain behaviors in the classroom.

Morgan and Culver (1978) have proposed certain guidelines to help teachers emphasize internally controlled behaviors in their classrooms. First, teachers need to minimize anxiety about possible failure by building patterns of success for each student. Table 2.2 shows how this can be accomplished.

As a variant of the journal idea, students can make a "blame list" to indicate whether positive and negative events that happen to them are their own fault or the fault of others. These activities rely on the use of writing, thus integrating another communicative art into affective education. Please visit the Education CourseMate website at **www.cengagebrain.com** and find the Wordsmith website and the KidSpace website, where students can use writing and learn words that will help them gain a more internal locus of control.

Teachers also can adopt strategies that foster self-direction and internal motivation. For instance, students can write the class conduct rules and start their own class traditions, thus reinforcing the importance of both the group and the individuals in the group. Activities that rely on listening and speaking can be implemented even in the early grades. Teachers could let students work collaboratively with their teachers to create rubrics for projects and assignments. Another excellent activity for older students is an "internal-external" journal in which students record recent personal events. Student writers can explain whether the events were orchestrated and controlled by someone other than themselves and, if so, whether these externally controlled events frustrated them.

One of the most important classroom strategies for helping students develop an internal locus of control is to have them practice decision making whenever possible. Study guides and worksheets can be designed so that individuals and groups are asked to reason and react to hypothetical situations in which they need to make decisions. Group consensus in decision making about a possible conclusion to a story can be a powerful way to promote self-awareness and self-worth and to teach about relationships with others. Finally, teachers can stress affect by having students describe their emotions through drawings or pictures instead of through words. For instance, students could draw a picture of the planet Earth with people holding hands to describe unity and kindness. These kinds of exercises are very powerful and motivate students in their development of an internal locus of control.

TABLE 2.2 Guidelines for Emphasizing an Internal Locus of Control

1. Developing a realistic reward system of praise for work completed. The system of rewards can be kept simple with a contractual arrangement specifying a sequence of graduated, attainable tasks.
2. Stressing the concept of task mastery in grading students. Grading is stressful to students who are external in their thinking.
3. Deemphasizing the concept of time. This allows students unlimited time to complete and master certain tasks.
4. Encouraging school guidance staff to counsel students toward realistic life goals. Externally controlled people often have unrealistic aspirations or no aspirations at all.

CHALLENGE BOX: JaNette, the At-Risk Student

SITUATION: The challenge of working with JaNette will be formidable. JaNette lives generally in a world where her feelings matter most. She expresses herself freely and often negatively. She does not respond well to the cognitive world of academics. She is not familiar with the discourse used in school settings.

What can teachers do to help JaNette become an affective learner?

Her teachers need to understand that JaNette may be defensive, but she has potential and deserves understanding. JaNette needs to realize she has value as an individual. She needs to experience the social aspects of learning. She would most likely prefer a classroom where desks can be moved for group work or for a seminar or debate setup.

JaNette would benefit from assignments that help her connect her out-of-school world to academics. Because JaNette sees no models of reading at home, it is imperative that her teachers have many books, magazines, and other materials about their subjects around the classroom so she can pick them up and see what she likes. Her teacher could use materials beyond the traditional text (see Chapter 6) to inspire her and connect her to the subject.

Activities like the guides shown in this chapter would allow JaNette to express her own opinions, ask questions, and connect her knowledge to her feelings while learning content. This type of activity would encourage JaNette to respect her own voice but to also read and consider academic material.

JaNette practices an internal locus of control to follow her goals in life, but she needs teacher guidance to move from an external locus of control in academic situations. By practising conation in coursework, she will have a better chance at developing the qualities required for that high-paying job she wants in her future. She has begun to respect herself but needs to be rewarded for good work and encouraged to develop a positive, less defensive attitude. To that end, she might benefit from completing an attitude or interest inventory and then analyzing the answers herself. From the inventory, her teacher could learn what activities, songs, television programs, and technology she enjoys.

Questioning

Questioning in the affective domain is an important activity for teachers. Such questioning enables teachers to unlock students' emotions, attitudes, and knowledge (Jones, Morgan, & Tonelson, 1992). For example, students who are examining the problems faced by Abraham Lincoln when he was president of the United States might be asked to consider their own feelings about these problems; they are connecting their knowledge and feelings. Activity 2.9 shows possible small group questions for a science class on horticulture.

The questions in Activity 2.9 can be transcribed to the computer as the nucleus of a WebQuest. See Chapter 10 for details.

The GATOR (gaining acceptance toward reading) system can improve instruction by allowing the teacher to ask more reflective questions. To help gain student acceptance of reading, the teacher announces that students—and the teacher—must base all questions and responses on "feeling." The entire lesson is taught with questions such as these:

How did that make you feel?

Why is this lesson important?

How did you feel about the main character?

Why would you have done or not done what the main character did?

Why is this chapter important?

Why do you like what you just read?

GATOR also can be used when students are working in small groups. Students are asked to discuss only emotion-laden questions. An example of the GATOR technique using *The Lightning Thief* by Rick Riordan can be seen in Activity 2.10.

ACTIVITY 2.9 Sample Questions for a Horticultural Experience: The Science of Growing and Nurturing a Garden in Grade 3 Science

INTRODUCTORY TASK

To the students from the teacher: We are going to a new school and have no one to plant and maintain our flower gardens for the year. We are being asked to produce and maintain the flower gardens to make the school more beautiful. A local store has agreed to donate the materials needed to grow the garden. Are you ready to help?

Students will be divided into four horticultural teams. Each team will have a specific role. The roles will be defined as:

Soil investigators
Weather interpreters and predictors
Flower fanciers
Survivors

The tables below give questions to be answered by the teams.

QUESTIONS FOR THE SOIL INVESTIGATORS	**QUESTIONS FOR THE FLOWER FANCIERS**
What types of soil do flowers grow in? What types of soil are in our area? What needs to be done to prepare our soil for planting?	What are some flowers that will do well in our area? When and where do they grow? What is a perennial flower? What is an annual flower? Will perennials or annuals grow best in our area?
QUESTIONS FOR THE WEATHER INTERPRETERS AND PREDICTORS	**QUESTIONS FOR THE SURVIVORS**
What is the weather like in our area? Is the weather in our area favorable for flower growth? What will the weather probably be like for the next week? What will it be like for the next month?	What is a plant? What is a flower? What is the plant life cycle? What does a flower need to grow? What does a flower need to sustain life?

ACTIVITY 2.10 GATOR on *The Lightning Thief* by Rick Riordan

Appropriate for Middle School English and Language Arts

This book is the first in the *Percy Jackson and the Olympians* series.

- Do you think Percy is smart? Do you think his grades in school matter?
- Would you like to have a friend like Percy even though he's always in trouble?
- Do you think you'd want to embark on a quest like Percy did even if you knew you might not survive? What's appealing about a challenge of that type?
- Did you agree with the choice Percy made to leave his mother in the Underworld? Could you have done that?
- Have you ever had a friend as loyal as Grover or Annabeth? How was he or she like they are?
- Were you surprised that Luke seemed to be? Have you ever had to change your mind about someone whom you considered a friend?

Using the PAR Lesson Framework to Develop Lesson Plans

The PAR Lesson Framework described in Chapter 1 provides a consistent mode for delivery of learning. It does this by dividing the lesson into a series of distinct steps to be accomplished by both the student and the teacher. The students as well as the teacher should know these steps. It is not "guess-what-is-on-the-teacher's-mind time," which seems to be the prevailing mode of delivering instruction in many schools. Instead, the distinct steps provide a way to accomplish the learning and to get students to think at higher levels of cognition. Finally, the PAR Lesson Framework facilitates the relationship among reading, thinking, and writing, all while there is no appreciable loss of "content time" in the lesson.

Incorporate affective domain in your lesson plans. Please visit the Education CourseMate website at **www.cengagebrain.com** and go to the Outta Ray's Head website to see examples.

In examining each of the three steps of PAR, we see distinct mental operations being performed by both the teacher and the students. In the preparation step, teachers determine and build background knowledge and thereby motivate students to learn. In the assistance step, the students gain a purpose for reading and develop their comprehension as they read. Finally, in the reflection step, the teacher determines how much was learned by the students, and the reading experience is extended and retention of the material is improved.

Teachers can develop entire lesson plans using the PAR Lesson Framework as the centerpiece of the plan and making certain the plan has strategies that emphasize the affective domain. We end the chapter with two such lesson plans that make good use of affect and maintain the structure of PAR. The first lesson plan, presented as Activity 2.11, is meant for a middle or high school government class. It is very organized and thorough, with appropriate objectives and strategies for use in the affective domain. Notice how the teacher pays attention to **differentiation of instruction** by having students do different activities in different groups. These activities can range from difficult to easy and can be tailored to students with differing needs and abilities. Also, look for the affective component in each of the three groups in Activity 2.11.

A second example of making a lesson plan to include affective strategies also represents an example of **project-based learning.** In such an activity, students read and study about a subject—in this case, Native American tribes—and then complete a project. In this lesson plan, developed as part of the Teaching American History Grant for the Hampton Public Schools in Hampton, Virginia, students make a classroom quilt for display after studying the similarities and differences among three Native American tribes. They draw on small quilt squares after reading, researching photographs and drawings, and taking part in compare-and-contrast worksheets. This is a marvelous way to bring the affective domain into teaching; students get involved in the hands-on project and enjoy the learning process; both cognition and affect are cultivated. Activity 2.12 shows the lesson plan used in teaching the lesson.

ACTIVITY 2.11 PAR Lesson Plan on Ancient Greece and Rome

PART I: INTRODUCTION, RATIONALE, AND OVERVIEW

Students will understand and apply knowledge relating to ancient Greece and Rome regarding the government, the architecture of the time period, and the Olympic Games.

Students will be able to relate present-day government, government building architecture, and sports, to everyday life and choices that are made by each student as a citizen of the United States.

PART II: FOR EACH LESSON—GOALS AND OBJECTIVES, MATERIALS, LESSON CONTENT, AND INSTRUCTIONAL STRATEGIES AND ACTIVITIES

The student will:

- Make a conscious vote on a decision while understanding direct and representative democracy.
- Understand the implications of that decision to vote and how it affects one's life personally and through society.
- Be able to identify and describe the various forms of architecture from ancient Greece and Rome and how they are incorporated in our society today.
- Be able to describe various sporting events that occurred at the Olympics in the Greek era.
- Learn which sports are played in the Olympics today.

Students will work in groups of three: Government, Architecture, and the Olympics. Each group will review, learn, and create a project.

		Affective component
Government Group (A)	**1.** Have students brainstorm about what they know about Greece and its government. **2.** Review that between 500 and 323 BC, the Greek culture thrived. This was considered the classical period. **3.** Discuss the meaning of the word *democracy* and how it relates to citizenship and society. **4.** Create a bubble diagram with your group to present to the class.	When students discuss the word *democracy* in relation to society and citizenship, the group could incorporate the "feeling" of being able to vote and of being a good citizen and what that entails. This is where pictures help, along with the bubble diagram. Students can draw these ideas or feelings to show how they feel about society and being good citizens.
Architecture Group (B)	**1.** Discuss the word *architecture* as a class. **2.** Review styles of architecture from ancient Greece and Rome. **3.** Students are given a picture and description of the Parthenon. **4.** Students will look at a picture of the Lincoln Memorial. **5.** Students will construct a two-column poster to compare and contrast the Parthenon and the Lincoln Memorial.	The two-column poster can include the affect of the people who built the two different structures. The Parthenon and the Lincoln Memorial represent two very different time periods. The students can either draw or describe in writing how each particular society felt about building that structure. Why was it important to them at that particular time in history? Students can be directed to use expressive words such as *powerful, proud, dedicated.*

Olympics Group (C)	1. Students will brainstorm on what they know about the Olympic Games. 2. Students will visit websites to help them learn history about the Olympic Games. 3. Students will explore and take notes from what they have learned in the computer lab. 4. Student will create a Flip booklet of the Olympic Games. The items will include Title Page, Table of Contents, Past Sports, Present-Day Sports, and Pictures/Drawings.	The concept that people's emotions are often "written on their faces" can be taught. While viewing the Internet on the importance of the first Olympic Games, students can write what emotions they think Olympians experienced based on facial expressions that students see in their research. Then from that information, students can include the descriptive words in the pictures and drawings section of their flip booklet.

Materials

Use construction paper, poster board, markers, rulers, and access to the Internet, or adapt for electronic flipbook.

PART III: ASSESSMENT

	1	2	3
Participation	Students exhibit minimal effort while in groups.	Students present average effort while in groups.	Students present full participation and exhibit learning.
Creativity	Minimal creativity is put forth by the individual.	Students offers more than two ideas to the group effort.	Student is fully engaged and offers three or more ideas to the group.
Presentation	The student does not speak at all or offer any information regarding the project.	The student speaks but not clearly and with disorganized thoughts.	The student speaks clearly, makes eye contact, and offers information to the class.

PART IV: UNIT REFLECTION

Each group presents its work as a unit in front of the class (to educate their classmates). After each group has presented, a class discussion will be held on each topic for review. Discussion questions will include:

- What are the important aspects that the Greeks and Romans contributed to our society, both governmentally and architecturally?
- How do the present-day Olympics compare with the Olympics of the past?
- How would the ancient Olympics be viewed by our society today?

PART V: MECHANICS AND FORM

This lesson plan incorporates brainstorming, creating a bubble diagram, using vocabulary, describing pictures, and applying technology. Also, oral language is involved when the students present their work to the class.

PART VI: ATTENTION TO AFFECT

If we were to coach teachers regarding this lesson plan, we would tell them to be involved, not only with the history that this lesson presents but also to be interactive with the students. Go back in time, investigate, research, and remember! The lesson involves history, the arts, and sports. What could better get the students into affect—to feel the emotion of the times? If the students see that the teacher is excited, the students will enjoy and be involved in the lesson plan!

Adapted from a lesson plan developed by Meredith Young.

ACTIVITY 2.12 Native American Tribes Quilt Project for Second Grade

The quilt focuses on three First American tribal groups. This student-created quilt incorporates:

- Studying similarities and differences among Native American tribes, focusing on occupation, transportation, obtaining food, climate, and housing
- Comparing and contrasting Eastern Woodland Indians (Powhatan), the Plains (Lakota), and the Southwestern (Pueblo) tribes
- Recognizing contributions made by First Americans

The printed words framing the pictures in the quilt are taken from, "The Times They Are A-Changing," written by Bob Dylan (Columbia Records, 1964). Dylan's words connect the idea of a changing world to *every* era of America's history and the fact that we cannot alter the inevitable changes that occur in our history—the overarching theme of this Teaching American History Grant.

OVERARCHING BENEFITS OF THE PROJECT

Conceptualizing the idea that the United States has different climates, terrain, and food is difficult for many children. By using comparison charts, students are able to visualize methods of survival and the myriad ways people adapt to their environment. (These skills can be incorporated in the science classroom and the study of animal and plant habitats.)

LEARNING STYLES INCORPORATED IN THE QUILT

AUDITORY

Reading and telling stories about each of the three tribes emphasized, how homes were constructed; how they gathered, grew, and hunted for food; and their work styles and methods of transportation.

VISUAL

- Using websites, text, and trade books, students located archival photographs and historical drawings depicting the First Americans' livelihoods and incorporated them into quilt squares.

CREATIVE ACTIVITIES FEATURING AFFECT

- Students created their own drawings for the quilt after classroom discussion.
- Students completed compare and contrast activities and incorporated them into quilt pieces.
- Students researched and located photographs and drawings and incorporated then into quilt squares.
- Students completed comparison charts that allowed them to understand and use application techniques when describing similarities and differences among tribal groups.

State-Level Learning Objectives Incorporated in the Quilt

"Compare the lives and contributions of American Indians (First Americans), with emphasis on the Powhatan—Eastern Woodlands, the Lakota-Plains and Pueblo-Southwest."

- "Regions/Climate/Environment of eastern Woodlands, Plains, & Southwest"

Developed by Teachers Sandy Robinson, Barnedia Durrah Bassette, and Gail Running Hawk, Hampton City Schools, Hampton, Virginia.

This project was inspired by our participation in the Teaching American History Grant: *Communication & Citizenship in a Changing World: The Collision, Conflict & Cooperation of Cultures Throughout American History.*

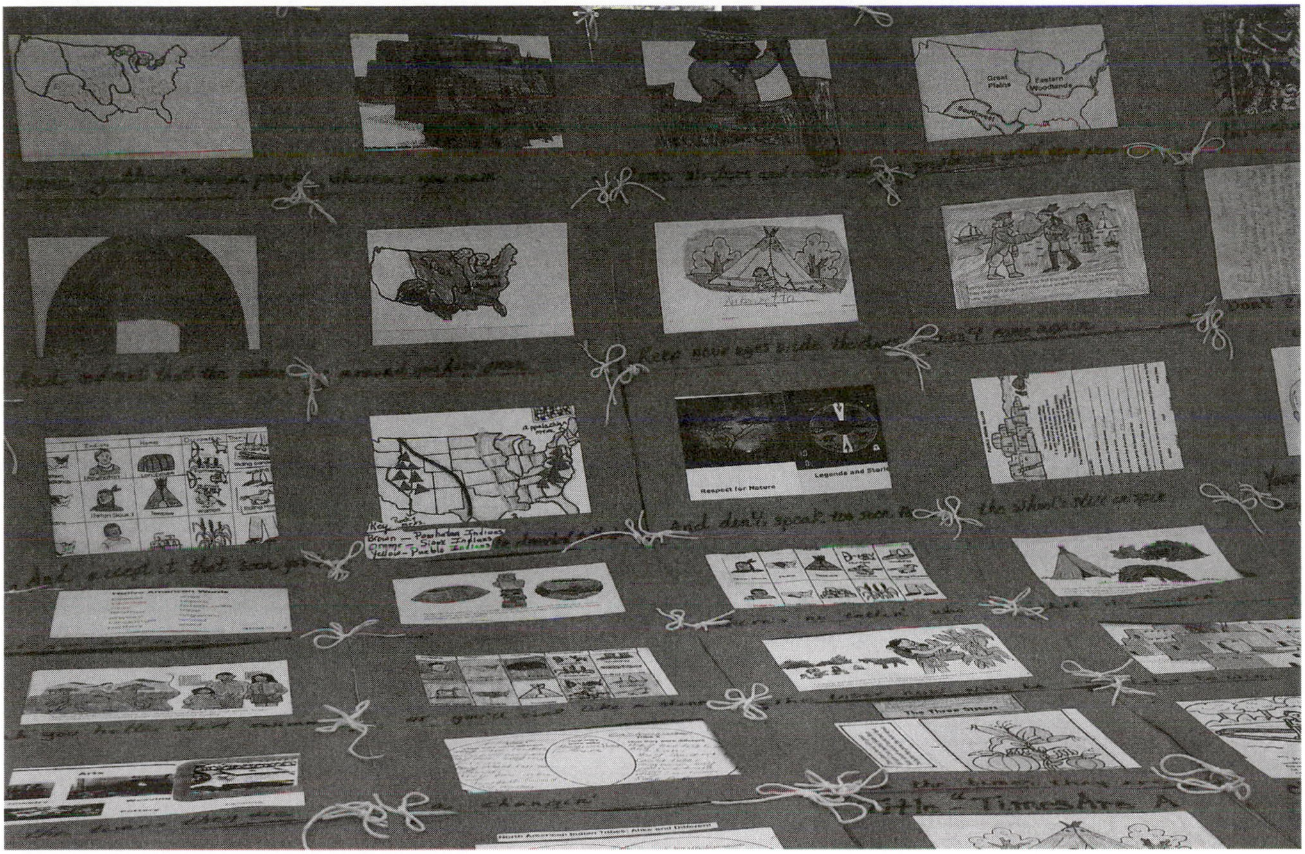

Courtesy of the author.

ONE-MINUTE SUMMARY

In this chapter, we stressed how important the affective domain—attitudes, emotions, interests, attributions, and conative factors—is for content area teaching. Student attitude tests and surveys, general-interest inventories, and a student checklist were presented to guide and motivate students and change attitudes about learning. The chapter addressed conation as a construct, as well as the importance of will and determination in the pursuit of academics. A brain-based approach to teaching and learning can heighten students' brain activity, thereby helping students overcome threats and pressures.

A positive classroom environment helps students feel capable of learning and becoming successful. One way to create such a setting is to foster the habit of reading in class and as a lifelong activity. Strategies that help create an internal locus of control were provided to improve learning and achievement.

We also described questioning in the affective domain and a strategy called GATOR, which helps students focus on affect as they read. Finally, we showed detailed lesson plans using the PAR Lesson Framework as a foundation, and we explained how to make lesson plans that result in student projects. Throughout the chapter, we reminded teachers to bring about lasting achievement by paying attention to both the cognitive and affective domains of learning. Classroom teachers who stress affect in their teaching of cognitive skills and course content will enjoy much greater success than those who omit such emphasis from their classrooms.

END-OF-CHAPTER ACTIVITIES

Assisting Comprehension

1. Why should you stress affect in your classroom? List some strategies for emphasizing affect.
2. Why is it important for teachers to know about locus of control? What are some teaching methods that can help students gain a more internal locus of control?
3. What is conation? How can knowing about it make you a better teacher?

Reflecting on Your Reading

1. Your content organization (e.g., National Council of Teachers of Mathethmatics, National Council of Teachers of English, National Council for the Social Studies, National Science Teachers Association, International Reading Association) has most likely developed a set of standards that identify the performance criteria relevant to classroom teachers. Standards usually delineate elements of foundational knowledge that a classroom teacher should possess. Locate and become familiar with what the organization recommends. For instance, teachers should:
   - Display positive dispositions toward reading.
   - Motivate students to become lifelong readers.
2. How did this chapter address these elements? How does being informed about these elements aid in content instruction?

CHAPTER 3

Preparation for Learning

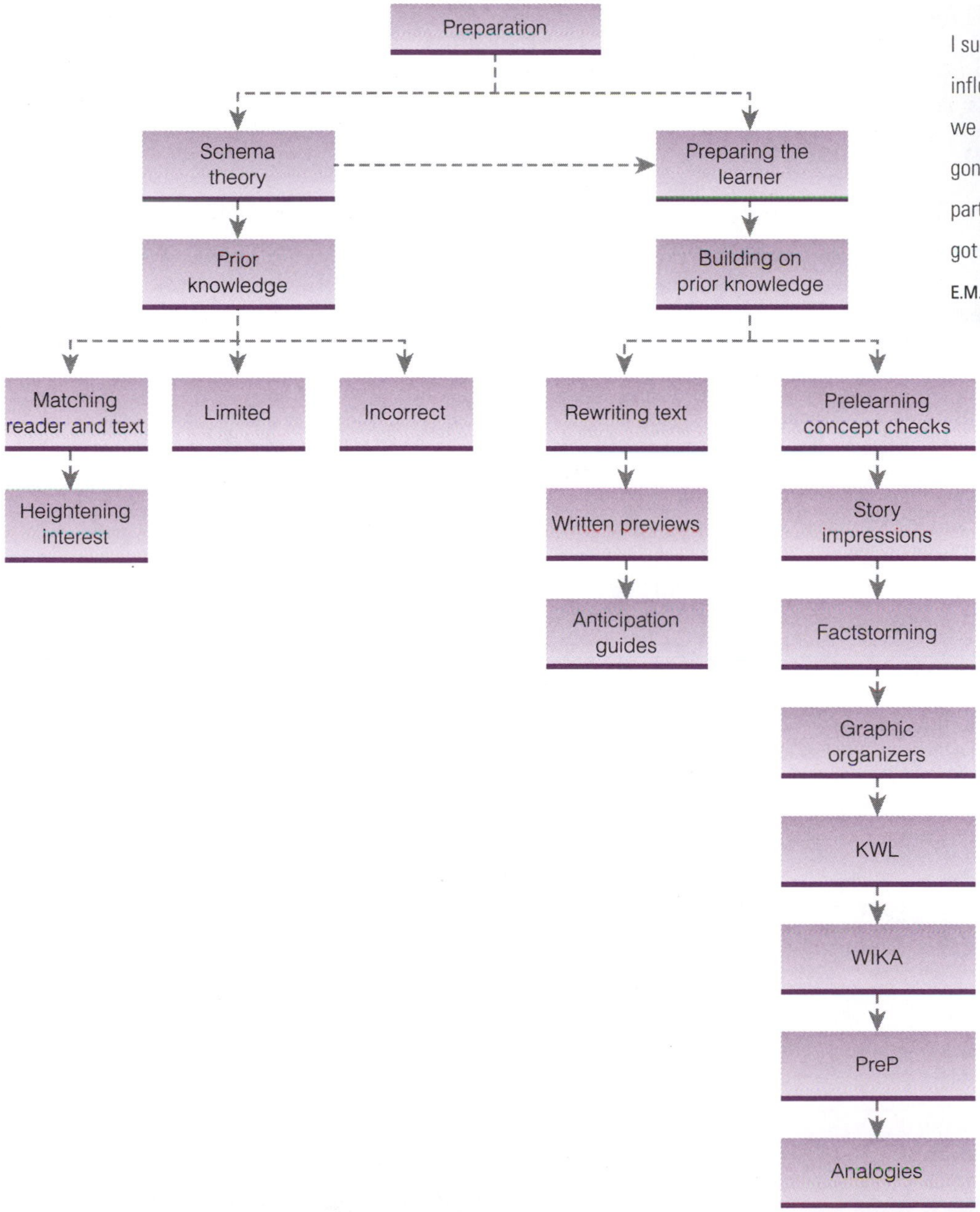

> I suggest that the only books that influence us are those for which we are ready, and which have gone a little farther down our particular path than we have yet got ourselves
>
> E.M. FORSTER

VOICES FROM THE CLASSROOM: MIDDLE SCHOOL CLASS PROBLEM

At the front of the classroom in an inner-city middle school stands a first-year seventh grade social studies teacher, Ms. Coleman. The class is beginning a unit on the causes and effects of American involvement in World War II. The teacher asks a question that she expects her students will be able to answer with ease: "What do you know about Pearl Harbor?" The students look at each other with unsure expressions. Finally, Monique, the student with the best grades, says hesitantly, "Is it a woman's name?"

Ms. Coleman tries to hide her surprise that her brightest student is so far off the mark. She thinks to herself, "Now what do I do? Obviously, my students have no prior knowledge about Pearl Harbor, which means they probably don't know much about World War II." She readjusts her next statement and says, "I understand why you might think that Pearl Harbor is a woman's name, but that's not quite right. Let's turn to page 215 in our textbooks and start reading about Pearl Harbor." The class proceeds to read the chapter on how the attack on Pearl Harbor led the United States to enter World War II, with each student taking a turn reading aloud a paragraph or two depending on their strength as a reader.

Have you ever observed a class with students who have limited or no prior knowledge of certain topics? More of these classes exist than you might believe. What could the teacher have done to build their prior knowledge in preparation for reading the chapter?

PREPARING TO READ

1. a. What is the importance of prior knowledge in reading comprehension?
   b. How does a teacher determine students' prior knowledge?
   c. How can teachers overcome students' misconceptions about a topic?
   d. Are there strategies a teacher can use to prepare students to read?

How would you answer? This chapter will help you answer these key questions.

2. Predict which of the following three meanings is most similar to the term:

schema
a. A devious person
b. Thinking done after reading
c. One's mental blueprint for constructing reality

Cognitive dissonance
a. Inconsistency of one's thoughts
b. Display of feelings and emotions
c. Being mad at someone

Graphic organizers
a. Written outlines of a chapter
b. Realistic depictions in paragraph form
c. Visual representations that show relationships among concepts

Anticipation guide
a. A prereading study guide that teaches literacy
b. A teacher who guides students orally through a lesson
c. A written guide used after reading to improve comprehension

Analogies
a. Pointing out differences among concepts
b. Comparisons among familiar and less familiar concepts
c. Analog timepieces

OBJECTIVES

As you read this chapter, focus your attention on the following purposes. You will:

1. Explain the importance of assessing and building on students' prior knowledge.
2. Explain why it is sometimes difficult to build on students' prior knowledge.
3. Identify pertinent research that supports the concepts of schema theory and prior knowledge.
4. Adapt texts for the needs of your students.
5. Use several activities that help build the match between readers and the reading materials.
6. Make decisions to build prior knowledge while using text materials to guide readers appropriately.

Few would deny the importance of literacy in today's fast-paced world. But beyond teaching basic literacy in the early elementary school years, most schools do not place a high priority on developing literacy skills for future success in the academic and business worlds. Based on 2009 National Assessment of Educational Progress (NAEP) scores, 33 percent of fourth graders and 25 percent of eighth graders are reading below the Basic level (Aud, Hussar, Planty, Snyder, Bianco, Fox, Frohlich, Kemp, & Drake, 2010). Based on 2007 NAEP scores, 27 percent of twelfth graders are reading below the Basic level (Planty, Hussar, Snyder, Kena, KewalRamani, Kemp, Bianco, & Dinkes, 2009). Although fourth and eighth graders have made progress in reading since the early 1990s (and eighth graders increased by one point from 2007 to 2009), reading scores have declined for twelfth graders. The authors of this book maintain that many students are having difficulty in reading because they are not receiving the right reading experiences in school. Research has found that elementary (Edmunds & Bauserman, 2006) and middle school students (Ivey & Broaddus, 2001) indicate that they would like to read texts in school that are personally interesting to them. Most of the time, students are asked to answer end-of-chapter comprehension questions or to fill in endless worksheets. In addition, most in-class reading is oral reading with one student reading the text aloud and all other students listening, as in this chapter's opening scenario. With such boring exercises, it is no wonder that students do not like to read textbooks and try to avoid such reading at all costs (Maria & Junge, 1993; McKeown, Bede, & Worthy, 1992; Purcell-Gates, Degener, Jacobson, & Soler, 2002).

This chapter was significantly revised and updated by Valerie J. Robnolt, Ph.D., Associate Professor in the Department of Teaching and learning, School of Education at Virginia Commonwealth University.

Please visit the Education CourseMate website at **www.cengagebrain.com** to find a link to the report, *The Condition of Education 2010* (NCES 2010-028) for an analysis of 4th and 8th grade NAEP results and *The Condition of Education 2009* (NCES 2009-081) for an analysis of 12th grade NAEP results.

We are in this unenviable state because students are simply not motivated to read. This trend begins in elementary school, particularly with boys. In a study conducted with third graders, Marinek and Gambrell (2010) found that the low value boys place on reading activities is related to their low motivation to read; girls favor and value reading significantly more than boys. Pitcher and colleagues (2007) found that adolescent girls valued reading more than boys, and the value girls place on reading increases as they progress through the grades; the opposite happens for boys. Significant differences were also found among ethnic groups; African American and Afro/Indo-Trini adolescents valued reading more than whites or adolescents of other ethnic groups. Sturtevant and Kim (2010) surveyed and interviewed middle school English language learners (ELLs) and found no significant differences between the value that boys and girls place on reading; however, they found that beginning-level ELL students valued reading more than intermediate and advanced ELL students. Not surprisingly, the students found science and social studies textbooks difficult.

View the video to see how this middle school social studies teacher prepares students to learn. He motivates them by connecting new knowledge to hip-hop and other aspects of adolescent culture.

Students don't become motivated when they read books they don't find interesting or when they do exercises they find dull. To motivate students, they need to be taught to think about a topic before beginning to read. Teachers need to determine students' prior knowledge and to build on that knowledge in order to frame a lesson in a proper learning context. What students learn is greatly determined by the knowledge they bring to the lesson (Byrnes, 1995; McDonald & Stevenson, 1998). This is even true when students are reading information online (Schmar-Dobler, 2003). They are able to use their prior knowledge, as well as their understanding of both traditional paper-based text structures and website structures, to better comprehend what they are reading (Coiro & Dobler, 2007).

Recall principle 1 in Chapter 1 that *learning is influenced by the reader's personal store of experience and knowledge.*

The Preparation Phase of learning is much like practicing for a basketball game. Playing the game takes up the smallest amount of time; the greatest amount of time is spent in workouts, strategy sessions, game film viewing, and concentrated practice—all intended to ensure success in the game itself. After the game, more time is spent analyzing what occurred on the court and then preparation for the next game. Players ask: "Why did we do well in this game?" or "Why didn't we do well?" Similarly, a proficient reader must prepare before plunging into reading. He or she spends time getting ready or preparing to read by determining and building background. Good comprehension is a natural result just as playing a game successfully is the natural result of practice. Teachers who are aware of this phenomenon and help students in the preparation stage of reading are like good coaches. The teacher, similar to the coach, is there at every step to assist and encourage students as they work through lessons. Students who realize that preparation for reading is like basketball practice will reap the benefits of higher achievement and better grades.

In this chapter, we discuss the importance of determining prior knowledge in preparing learners to read. In addition, we explain how teachers can build on limited stores of student knowledge to allow students to learn and better retain information while reading.

The Importance of Determining Prior Knowledge

Many studies have shown the importance of prior knowledge in reading (Alexander & Murphy, 1998; Hmelo, Nagarajan, & Day, 2000; Muller-Kalthoff & Moller, 2003; Verkoeijen, Rikers, & Schmidt, 2005). Within this context, researchers (Reynolds, Sinatra, & Jetton, 1996) have placed a strong emphasis on the social construction of knowledge and the idea that students working together have to combine shared knowledge to complete a task. Students with considerable prior knowledge of a subject can use strategies to problem solve more effectively than those with little prior knowledge (Alexander & Judy, 1998). Learners with rich prior knowledge can also focus on what is important in a learning task, but those with inadequate prior knowledge often search unproductively because they cannot distinguish between relevant and irrelevant material. Research (Coiro & Dobler, 2007; Last, O'Donnell, & Kelly, 2001; McDonald & Stevenson, 1998; Muller-Kalthoff & Moller, 2003; Schmar-Dobler, 2003) has indicated that prior knowledge plays an important role in how well students perform computer research. Lawless, Brown, Mills, and Mayall (2003) focused on students using their prior knowledge when navigating hypertext. Hogan, Natasi, and Pressley (2000) studied the processes involved in eighth grade students' construction of shared understanding. They determined the prior knowledge of groups of students about a science topic and then examined which groups improved significantly in knowledge and why. Prior knowledge was found to be very important in how well a group finally understood the topic; furthermore, the most successful groups agreed with, confirmed, and accepted others' ideas.

Researchers also have found that students with little prior knowledge of a topic are unable to formulate learning goals adequately (Last, O'Donnell, & Kelly, 2001) and often have trouble asking questions concerning the material (Choi, Land, & Turgeon, 2005; Miyake & Norman, 1979). For all of these reasons, teachers must be able to determine the prior knowledge of their students about any topic to be studied. They also need to make it clear to their students that "reading is more than extracting meaning from text and that the reader's perspective shapes what is understood" (Olson & Truxaw, 2009, p. 428). In other words, teachers must be adept at seeing instruction through the eyes of their students. As Ball and Cohen (1999, p. 8) have noted, teachers

CHALLENGE BOX

Gustavo, the English as a Second Language Student

SITUATION: Although Gustavo was born in the United States, English is his second language, and only Spanish is spoken in his home. He was exited from English as a second language (ESL) services after fifth grade, so he no longer receives language support in school. He is doing well in school, so his teachers sometimes forget that English is his second language.

How could a teacher use Gustavo's background knowledge to support his learning?

It's important for teachers to find out the background knowledge and experiences that all students bring to the classroom. Some teachers assume that students from ESL families do not have prior knowledge when in fact they have a wealth of cultural and linguistic experiences. The teacher can demonstrate and explain how Gustavo's experiences and culture are similar and different from the concepts being taught. Building connections helps develop understanding and relevance. Graphic organizers, pictures, and charts can all be useful in making these connections visible.

How could a teacher use Gustavo's background knowledge to support the learning of his classmates?

The teacher must first develop an environment that encourages sharing ideas without fear of criticism. During class discussions before reading, Gustavo can offer authentic details about his culture that cannot be found in textbooks. This can be particularly meaningful in social studies when the class is learning about other cultures or when they are reading a story set in Mexico, for instance. Gustavo can provide vivid details about food, music, holidays, family life, and other aspects of living in Mexico.

Twentieth-century U.S. immigration is covered in many middle school social studies classrooms. Inviting ESL students like Gustavo to share family stories of coming to the United States can build context for understanding the experience of immigrants. He can explain the difficulties of trying to learn math, science, and social studies while having to learn to speak, read, and write in English. Hearing Gustavo's story can help native English-speaking students understand their classmate's experience and, more broadly, the immigrant experience.

need to view students as "more capable of thinking and reasoning, and less as blank slates who lack knowledge." Borko and Putnam (1996) have said that acquainting teachers with the content area thinking of children should become an important component of teacher preparation programs. Cantrell, Burns, and Callaway (2009) surveyed secondary teachers and found that continuing professional development needs to address the incorporation of literacy skills and strategies in content area teaching, specifically to learn ways to support students who struggle with literacy. Researchers (Olson & Truxaw, 2009; Thompson, 2008) also found that teachers need to understand their students' literacy practices, both in and out of school.

The Problem of Matching Reader with Text

Good readers feel comfortable with how they read. They usually browse before starting to read because they want to see how familiar they will be with the material. They take note of how much they already know about the topic, how interested they are in it, and what strategies they might use to read the material. Basically, good readers do three critical things:

1. **Good readers size up the material.** They ask: Is it easy to follow? Is the content clear? Do I have a purpose for reading?
2. **Good readers assess the relative difficulty of a text.** They ask: Is it easy to read, like a story (narrative style)? Is it somewhat more difficult, like a newspaper article (journalistic style)? Or is it challenging to read, like many textbooks

For more in-depth information, see Mesmer's book *Tools for Matching Readers to Texts: Research-Based Practices* (2008).

(expository style with many new facts and concepts)? At what speed should I read this text? Should I take notes as I read?

3. **Good readers chart a course** and consequently feel more confident than a reader who opens a book and plunges into a text.

Mature, proficient readers often make assessments about the subject and difficulty of a reading almost automatically and unconsciously. Poor readers are not proficient readers, and they do few or no self-assessments. Many students are not well matched to texts and often can neither recognize words efficiently nor comprehend the material (Mesmer, 2005). More recently, Mesmer (2010) found that young readers improved their reading rate, thus recognizing words more quickly, "within highly repetitive, 'predictable' books with high numbers of high frequency words" (p. 36). Pitcher and Fang (2007) explain that "[it] is critical that teachers develop an awareness of and become knowledgeable about the various factors that influence text difficulty and text quality" (p. 51).

Think about your teaching. Are you matching students with texts? Look for additional information on readability measures and text matching in Chapter 6.

Achieving a good match between readers and texts makes sense. Studies are seeking a better way to match students to appropriate texts through quantitative measures of readability (Walpole, Hayes, & Robnolt, 2006). Until matching procedures are perfected, however, teachers remain on their own in dealing with the extensive variability between the ability levels of students in content area classrooms. The most important way a teacher can succeed in a classroom with a wide variation in reading ability is to plan each lesson to allow adequate preparation time to introduce the lesson and determine and build on prior knowledge. Teachers need to prepare readers through discussion and use of the strategies explained in this chapter. Teachers and readers who ignore this step neglect a crucial part of the overall process of reading.

Schema Theory and Prior Knowledge

Often, students' prior knowledge is not adequate to make necessary connections in learning content material. Some students create mental representations or images of new information that relate to knowledge structures that already exist in their memory (Nuthall, 1999). Schnotz and Kürschner (2008) found that the types of visuals readers use when learning can have an impact on the mental models they create and their learning outcomes. Psychologists stress that learning new information depends on relating the new to something already known. To make sense of the world, the learner attempts to relate new information to previously learned information by drawing a **schema** (plural *schemata*), or mental blueprint, of the way in which reality is constructed. Rumelhart (1980, 2004) stresses that schemata, which may be likened to diagrams or drawings stored in the brain, are fundamental to all information processing. Often, our diagrams are incomplete, but we create fuller pictures as more information is found to complete them.

A person's schemata can be thought of as the sum of knowledge and information one has accumulated and the information a learner acquires about a topic that is organized cognitively into the framework.

Gestalt psychologists probably introduced the term *schema* in the 1930s (Anderson & Pearson, 1984). Bartlett (1932) used the term to explain how information that has been learned is stored in the brain and, with repeated use, becomes part of a system of integrated knowledge. Bartlett contended that learners chunk knowledge in an organized fashion by connecting a new segment to what they already know. Only by so doing can a learner move the new chunk of information from short-term memory to long-term memory. Bartlett asserted that the process of memory retrieval involves reconstruction, which is brought about by the frameworks that people already possess.

Learning occurs in a process of planning and building information in the brain. In his classic work, *Understanding Reading,* Smith (1994) explains that just seeing words or even saying words is fairly superficial. Connecting the intent of the words to what is already stored in one's schemata is real reading.

Memory is both selective and interpretive, involving both construction and reconstruction, and therefore can sometimes be inexact (Butler & McManus, 1998, p. 35).

Schema theory is mostly accepted today as a bona fide theory of how children learn. It has been criticized for its vagueness and lack of a clear definition (Sadoski, Paivio, & Goetz, 1991) and for its lack of empirical verifiability (Beers, 1987), but schema theory can help teachers understand how children think as they prepare students to read an assignment. Sousa (2005) describes three ways schema theory can be useful to teachers as they structure their lessons. Sousa maintains that students might need to have a teacher help them add new information to their already existing and fairly stable schema. Sometimes, however, teachers might have to help students alter their existing schema to come into line with new learning in a reading assignment. Finally, Sousa posits that sometimes teachers must help students completely restructure or replace their prior knowledge with new schema. As an example of the second Sousa directive, one middle school mathematics teacher created a discovery activity designed to build her students' background by helping them see relationships between what they already knew and what they were about to learn. She was preparing them for a unit on the properties of quadrilaterals, showing them how to use what they already knew about parallel lines, perpendicular lines, and angles. This activity (Activity 3.1) exemplifies the concept of building prior knowledge by connecting the known to the new while making the content interesting.

Chapter 9 presents information about how the brain chunks information on memory training, and Chapter 2 explores the affective domain of learning.

The Role Prior Knowledge Plays in Heightening Interest

One of our reading professors recounted a story about a little girl who goes to the library and asks for a book about penguins. Excited by this small child's search for information, the librarian offers her a large volume about penguins. The child takes the hefty book home and returns it the next day. "How did you like that book?" the librarian eagerly asks. "To tell you the truth," the girl replies, "this book tells more about penguins than I want to know." A similar situation occurs when teachers misinterpret a little interest as a lot and thus do not match a reader with a suitable text.

ACTIVITY 3.1 Activity to Discover Prior Knowledge

WHAT'S IN A SHAPE? THE PROPERTIES OF QUADRILATERALS

The procedure is as follows:

1. Introduce students to a new chapter by having them read one page of the chapter.
2. Ask students to point out examples of the different types of quadrilaterals using pictures on pages in the chapter—squares, rectangles, parallelograms, trapezoids, rhombuses.
3. Have students sit with a partner; give each pair a compass, protractor, ruler, and worksheet.
4. Read the worksheet directions aloud: "Find as many true properties about quadrilaterals as possible. Draw lines, measure with a ruler and a protractor, and use a compass to assist in making conjectures. List at least four conjectures for each type of quadrilateral."
5. After partners have finished their work, discuss the conjectures as a class. Create a master list and have the class agree or disagree with each conjecture.
6. State that as the students read the chapter, conjectures will be verified by information in the chapter. They can put a check next to the items that they verified.

Developed by Jeannette Rosenberg.

The discussion on the affective domain of learning in Chapter 2 offers suggestions for determining interests and attitudes, as well as activities to stimulate positive feelings.

Students' lack of schema can also reduce interest. Notice the protagonist in the comic reproduced on this page. The character reads the first step for making an angel food cake. She expects the verb *separate* to mean "set or keep apart." In her schema, the verb *separate* does not include a picture for "detach," so she puts each egg in a different location rather than detaching the egg whites from the yolks. If she were in a home economics class, the teacher would need to help her build a more sophisticated schema.

Drum (1985) found that fourth grade science and social studies texts that were equal in vocabulary frequency, syntactic complexity, and overall structure were not equally easy for the study's fourth graders to read. Prior knowledge seemed to play a significant part in making the social studies texts easy for these students. Rupley and Slough (2010) explain that students may encounter words in a science textbook that they know in a general context, but these meanings may conflict with their scientific meanings, thus causing confusion or misconceptions. In other words, no matter how well-written material is, if readers do not possess background knowledge or interest in the reading material, they will find it hard to read.

The reader has a primary problem when there are deficiencies in prior knowledge and a lack of interest in reading. The author does not cause the problem, just as one cannot fault the author of the angel food cake recipe because the protagonist in the comic does not know the meaning of the verb *separate* in that context. The responsibility belongs to both the reader and the teacher to overcome any problems with prior knowledge and lack of interest.

If learners cannot find relevance in a selection, they are likely to ignore it. Thus, teachers must become aware of their students' knowledge about and experiences with a particular topic in order to build on that knowledge. Discovering whether students have developed any schemata can help a teacher generate content reading lessons that are directed, meaningful, and highly personal. For example, going from an easy text to a more difficult one can build and strengthen schemata. Gallagher (1995) had much success pairing adolescent literature with adult literature by "bridging" (Brown & Stephens, 1995). Studying the theme of the power of love in Harper Lee's novel *To Kill a Mockingbird* made it easier for students to grasp that same theme in Nathaniel Hawthorne's *The House of the Seven Gables*.

Even the most proficient reader can experience difficulty in understanding and thinking about a subject when there is lack of interest in the topic. Studies indicate that interest in a topic plays a very important role in students' comprehension (Lin, Zabrucky, & Moore, 1997; Schumm, Mangrum, Gordon, & Doucette, 1992; Wade & Adams, 1990). When asked to address textbook issues, 41 percent of teenage respondents commented that they would "include topics in their textbooks that would interest them" (Lester & Cheek, 1997, p. 288).

Cognitive dissonance causes unclear and disorganized thinking on the part of students.

If teachers recognize that their students bring little interest or negative attitudes to content material, they can use many activities to stimulate interest and appreciation for the subject. A teacher who assumes that students are interested in a subject is likely to be disappointed in students' reactions to it. For example, students often experience psychological tension when new information clashes with their previously acquired knowledge. This situation can be seen as a form of **cognitive dissonance**, defined by

Harris and Hodges (1995, p. 34) as "a motivational state of tension resulting from an inconsistency in one's attitudes, beliefs, perceived behaviors, etc." When students experience cognitive dissonance, they may lose interest and assume a negative attitude. Sternberg (1997) calls for teachers to make material presented in class relevant and practical for students. Teachers need to show students that their knowledge applies to the real world. Sternberg says that doing this makes students more interested in topics and results in better learning experiences. Furthermore, Brozo and Flynt (2008) explain that teachers can build students' self-efficacy by generating interest in new information they will learn in the classroom. In the next two sections, we discuss the two problems with prior knowledge: Students often have limited or incorrect prior knowledge. Both situations present great challenges for content area teachers.

Think about how tapping into and building background knowledge can be a positive experience for you and your students.

Limited Prior Knowledge

Students usually have some prior knowledge about most topics. The students in the scenario at the beginning of the chapter probably had some ideas about World War II. Even if readers know little about specific content, they may understand a related concept. For instance, fifth graders may not know much about the Pilgrims, but some may know what it's like to be uprooted and have to relocate to a strange place. Such students would have some background that the teacher could use in introducing the reading.

See the picture book *I Hate English!* (Levine, 1995), in which Mei Mei moves from Hong Kong to Chinatown in New York City.

Don't assume that your ELL students lack background knowledge on topics you cover. Similar to your other students, they come to your class with prior experiences.

The following dialogue about golf illustrates how difficult it is to understand material when one has limited background in a subject:

> "Do I deserve a mulligan?" asked Bob.
>
> "No, but don't take a drop," said Al. "Use a hand-mashie, then fly the bogey high to the carpet and maybe you'll get a gimme within the leather."
>
> "You're right," said Bob. "I'll cover the flag for a birdie and at least get a ginsberg if I'm not stymied."
>
> (From Morgan, Meeks, Schollaert, & Paul, 1986, pp. 2–3.)

Unless you are a golfer, reading this dialogue might be an exercise in pronouncing the words rather than in understanding the text. Try to answer the following questions about the passage:

1. Does Al think Bob deserves a mulligan?
   a. Yes.
   b. No.
   c. Maybe.
2. What does Al think Bob should do?
   a. Catch a gimme.
   b. Take a drop.
   c. Use a hand-mashie.
   d. Fly a kite.
3. What does Bob decide to do?
   a. Cover the flag.
   b. Take a drop.
   c. Birdie-up.
4. How can Bob get a birdie?
   a. By getting stymied.
   b. By getting a ginsberg.
   c. By covering the flag.

The answers are *b, c, a,* and *c.* The test was factual in nature. You probably scored 100 percent because you were able to look back at the passage and find the facts.

But you were simply decoding the sounds and using the syntax or structure of the passage. Many researchers maintain that this is what students often do when they read unfamiliar material (Opitz & Rasinski, 2008; Worthy & Broaddus, 2002).

Even though you may have decoded the passage and scored well, do you really know what this passage is about? To comprehend it fully, you need broad prior knowledge about golf. For instance, what is a mulligan? What is a birdie? Readers who don't know golf may try to create meaning for these words by calling on their store of information. Likewise, many students can answer rote questions after a reading without really understanding the passage. The following translation shows how paraphrasing by using more familiar language—more likely to be present in one's background—makes the passage meaningful:

1. "Do I deserve a mulligan?" asked Bob. Bob was asking if he deserved a second shot without a penalty.
2. "No, but don't take a drop," said Al. "Use a hand-mashie, then fly the bogey high to the carpet and maybe you'll get a gimme within the leather." Al said no but warned Bob not to take the option of moving his ball from a difficult location and dropping it at a better spot, which could cost him a penalty stroke. Another (but illegal) move is to kick the ball out of trouble with his foot (a "foot-mashie" or "hand-mashie"). He then might be able to hit the ball with a high trajectory to the green, or "carpet" (where the hole is). If Bob were to get the ball within 18 inches of the hole, or cup ("leather"), he would be able to pick up his ball and give himself one stroke (a "gimme") rather than having to actually putt the ball.
3. "You're right," said Bob. "I'll cover the flag for a birdie and at least get a ginsberg if I'm not stymied." Bob said that he would try to hit the ball close to the hole for a chance at a "birdie" (one stroke under par). If he reached the green, he could lay up his putt to the hole ("get a ginsberg"). In earlier days, golfers did not mark their balls, so they could get stymied by another ball—that is, have to shoot around the ball of another player. Bob was being facetious here; in modern golf, a player cannot get stymied by another player's ball on the green.

Can you think of some other topic that someone has discussed or you have read about where you had limited knowledge, as might have occurred in the golf passage here?

Incorrect Prior Knowledge

Sometimes readers have incorrect knowledge about material they will study. Grace Hamlin, a teacher, wrote this "telegram" to illustrate how incorrect knowledge can influence one's reading:

won trip for two st. matthew's island pack small bag meet at airport 9 am tomorrow.

Readers who "know" that islands are tropical, have a warm climate, and are surrounded by beaches for swimming and sunbathing will pack a suitcase with sunglasses, shorts, bathing suits, and suntan lotion. St. Matthew's Island, however, is off the coast of Alaska, where the average temperature is 37 degrees. Incorrect knowledge in this case will impede comprehension. Similarly, readers who "know" that the dinosaurs were destroyed by other animals will have difficulty reading and understanding a theory proposing that dinosaurs were destroyed by the consequences of a giant meteor.

Maria and MacGinitie (1987) discuss the difference between having correct, although insufficient, prior knowledge and having incorrect prior knowledge. They conclude that students are less likely to overcome a problem of incorrect knowledge because the new information conflicts with their supposed knowledge; this produces cognitive dissonance. In this situation, it is essential to build students' knowledge because the students who try to refute the material as they read will find it most unreadable.

Preparing the Learner through Building on Prior Knowledge

Preparation is the major factor in building on students' prior knowledge and in improving the quality of their interaction with a text. Many activities can help teachers and students prepare for texts. In the rest of this chapter, we describe a number of activities that prepare readers by building on prior knowledge. All of these activities should help students with limited or faulty prior knowledge.

The activities in this chapter represent possibilities but are not an exhaustive list. Can you design other effective tasks for your students or adapt them to meet the diverse needs of your students?

Prelearning Concept Check

One way to give students a sense of responsibility and a feel for the reading to come is through the use of prelearning concept checks. These simple lists of important terms in a reading are easy to construct and use, and they serve two purposes: (1) they expose students to key vocabulary in the reading and (2) they allow the teacher to find out how much students know about a topic. Students can be asked to rate what they know about the topic, from "know a lot about the concept" to "know very little about the concept." Students can also return to the list after completing the reading to check their knowledge. These checklists give students with limited prior knowledge a chance to consider what they know about key vocabulary in the new learning and to talk about the terms in groups or as a whole class. This textbook opens each chapter with a prelearning concept check to clarify vocabulary terms and to help you prepare for the chapter. Activity 3.2 is a prelearning concept check for an elementary civics class on taking part in a court hearing.

ACTIVITY 3.2 Prelearning Concept Check

TAKING PART IN A COURT HEARING

Following is a list of terms used in this chapter. Some may be familiar to you in a general context, but in this chapter, they may be used in unfamiliar ways. Rate your knowledge by placing a plus sign (+) for those you are sure you know, a check mark (✓) for those you have some knowledge about, and a zero (0) for those you don't know. Later, you will locate the terms in the chapter, paying special attention to their meanings.

______ defendant	______ witnesses
______ plaintiff	______ opening statement
______ jury	______ direct examination
______ judge	______ cross-examination
______ attorneys	______ closing statement

Story Impressions

Story impressions are similar to prelearning concept checks in that both activities provide a list of words that come from the text that a student will be reading. However, story impressions invite a student to use important terms, phrases, and concepts in a text to write a coherent prediction about what the text might be about (for narrative) or what they might learn (for nonfiction) (Buehl, 2009; McGinley & Denner, 1987).

When creating a story impression, the teacher must read through the text and decide what terms, phrases, and concepts to present in the order in which they appear in the text. When the text has a narrative structure, the terms should support the key story elements, such as the main character's name or distinguishing characteristic, the setting, the problem, basic events, the solution, and the theme (Activity 3.3). For nonfiction texts, the teacher should choose terms about which

ACTIVITY 3.3 Story Impression for the Narrative Story, *Sir Cumference and the First Round Table: A Math Adventure,* by Cindy Neuschwander (1997)

Camelot

⇩

King Arthur and his Knights

⇩

Shape of Table

⇩

Cannot Communicate

⇩

Square, Diamond, Oval

⇩

Fallen Tree

⇩

New Table

⇩

Peace in the Land

Sample prediction using the words from the Story Impression:

There was a famous land called *Camelot* where *King Arthur and his knights* lived. One day, they were meeting, but the *shape of the table* was a triangle, and there wasn't enough room for all of them to sit, so they said, "We *cannot communicate*." King Arthur's trusted knight, Sir Cumference, found a *square* table, a *diamond* table, and an *oval* table, but King Arthur and his Knights had a problem hearing each other because they were at different tables. After the meeting, Sir Cumference was riding his horse home when he saw a *fallen tree*. He thought, "We could cut a table from this tree." The *new round table* was perfect for all of the men to sit around, so they were able to talk to each other and have *peace in the land*.

ACTIVITY 3.4 Story Impression for the Nonfiction Text, *The Moon,* by Seymour Simon (2003)

Craters

⇩

Phases

⇩

Space Program

⇩

Gravity

⇩

No Air

⇩

Temperature

⇩

Flatlands

⇩

Moonquakes

Sample prediction (what you might learn by reading the book) based on the Story Impression:

I hope I can travel to the moon some day! When I go, I will see lots of *craters*. I'll know that the *phases* of the moon are making the ocean tides happen back on Earth. When I travel to the moon, I'll be part of the *space program*, and I will wear a space suit that will help me with the *gravity* on the moon that is less than on Earth and with breathing because there's *no air* on the moon. I think the *temperature* will be really cold because there isn't any air. Thank goodness my space suit will keep me warm! It will be exciting if I can go to the *flatlands* and feel *moonquakes* on my visit. I can't wait to blast off to the moon!

students have some knowledge but also select terms that "will reflect new learning for many students" (Buehl, 2009, p. 162). When first encountering story impressions, students benefit from working in groups to write predictions with the terms. As students become more comfortable writing story impressions, they can write them independently.

See Activity 3.3 for one narrative example and Activity 3.4 for one nonfiction example.

After students have written their story impressions, have them share them with the class. Then as students read the text, they can compare their writing with what actually appears in the text, thus heightening engagement with the reading.

K-W-L Activity

You learned that tapping into and developing prior knowledge is a key component of preparation for reading. A useful activity for finding out what students already know about content to be studied is K-W-L (Heller, 1986; Ogle, 1986). The *K* stands for what students know, or *think* they know, before they begin to read. The teacher asks students to state facts they know in the first of three columns. The *W* stands for what students

Please visit the Education CourseMate website at **www.cengagebrain.com** for the link to Reading Quest, a website that has many graphic organizers, including a K-W-L Chart.

want to know or think they will learn. When students tell the teacher this information, the teacher can determine what they think is important about the material and on what they may need to focus instruction so the students are successful readers. These responses are recorded in the middle column. The *L* stands for what was learned. After reading, the students correct misunderstandings and add information they learned to the third column; they compare and match what they knew with what they wanted to learn or thought they would learn with what they did learn.

This activity not only helps the teacher and students determine prior knowledge; it also models an appropriate reflection strategy after reading has occurred. Carr and Ogle (1987) developed the K-W-L Plus to expand on the reflection aspect of the activity to include summarization and/or creating a graphic representation of the acquired information. By adding these components, the students are able to synthesize what they learned more deeply and effectively (Activity 3.5).

What-I-Know Activity

An alternative to K-W-L is the What-I-Know Activity (WIKA). This type of activity better reflects the terminology and steps of the PAR (preparation, assistance, and reflection) Lesson Framework. To use this activity (Activity 3.6), students indicate their prior knowledge under the "What I Already Know" column. Next they formulate questions to explore "What I'd Like to Know." If students are encouraged to add to their own list after listening to and learning from class discussion, they build background by using other students' knowledge, adding to that column. Another way to complete this column is to make questions of the subheadings in the material. During and after the reading, students record information they learned in the "What I Know Now" column. Completing the "What I'd Still Like to Know" column encourages the development of both comprehension and reflective thinking. The class discussion and recording of associations integrate the communicative arts.

Activity 3.6 represents the results of a WIKA produced by a reader of a chapter about the basic telephone system. The reader already knows some information, and she uses her knowledge to create questions based on the subheadings in order to complete the second column. In the third column, she answers the questions posed in column two. In the fourth column, she indicates the gaps in her knowledge.

Rewriting Text

When students have a difficult time comprehending text, teachers can try the strategy of rewriting text in an easier form. Research has shown that text structure and organization, word familiarity, cohesion, and sentence length can influence reading comprehension (Meyer, 2003). Rewriting can address some or all of these problems and can help prepare students before introducing them to the original material. By using rewritten material to introduce text, teachers can simplify writing styles and clarify concepts that students may have difficulty understanding. However, in returning to the original text, teachers will still be using required materials, and students will receive the message that the text material is important.

Siedow and Hasselbring (1984) found that when eighth grade social studies material was rewritten to a lower readability level, the comprehension of poor readers improved. Currie (1990) rewrote text by shortening sentences, replacing unfamiliar words, changing metaphors to more literal phrases, and clarifying. Teachers using

ACTIVITY 3.5 K-W-L Plus in a Middle School German Class on Oktoberfest

Germany's Festival: Oktoberfest

Title: *Steadwell Books World Tour: Germany*

Author: Christopher Mitten (2002)

What We Know	What We Want to Know	What We Learned
• Oktoberfest started in Germany, but it is now celebrated all over the world. • Many tourists visit Oktoberfest.	• Does Oktoberfest start in October? • Where is the largest Oktoberfest celebration? • Why and when was it started? • How long does it last? • What happens at Oktoberfest?	• Oktoberfest starts on a Saturday in September and ends on the first Sunday in October. • The original and largest celebration takes place in Munich. • It started in 1810 when the people of Munich celebrated a royal wedding. • It lasts for 16 days every year. • Oktoberfest starts with a parade, bands, and music. People enjoy eating, drinking, singing, and dancing. There are also carnival rides and roller coasters. • Some people are dressed in traditional German clothing (Lederhosen), and there is traditional German food (bratwurst and pretzels).

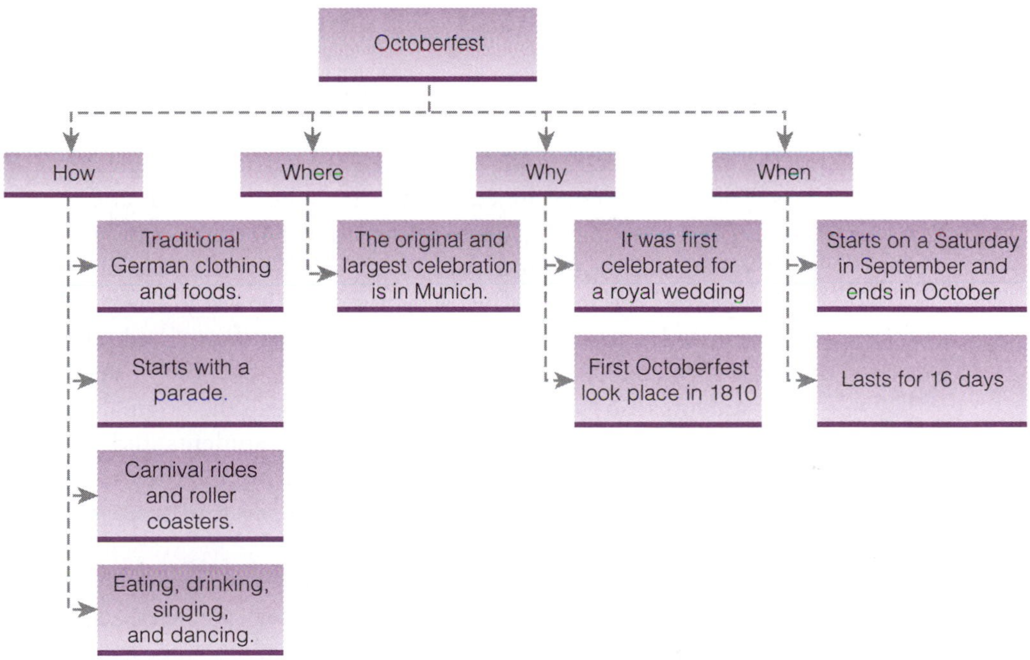

Developed by Laura Hoffmeister.

these materials reported that students, whether high or low achievers, significantly improved their grades. Beck and associates (1991) revised a fifth grade social studies text to create a more casual and explanatory style and then compared students who read the original version with those who read the revised version. Students who read

The semantic map in Activity 3.5 was created using Inspiration.

ACTIVITY 3.6 What-I-Know Activity

Before Reading		During Reading	After Reading	
What I Already Know	**What I'd Like to Know**	**Interesting or Important Concepts from My Reading**	**What I Know Now**	**What I'd Still Like to Know**
The telephone works by electricity.	How does electricity make the phone work?	Electrical circuits	A circuit is completed.	I need a simpler book about this topic!
You shouldn't use the phone in a lightning storm.	Why shouldn't you use the phone in a storm?	Electricity travels, and current jumps.	The current might jump—electricity might be conducted beyond the normal current by lightning.	A clearer explanation about telephones and lightning.
I can hear another voice and speak in return.	What is the role of vibration in carrying sound from one place to another?	There is a diaphragm in my telephone!	Sound vibrates and causes changes in air pressure. When air pressure hits the diaphragm, it vibrates again, reconstructing the original sound.	I need to be able to explain the diaphragm.

This technique can be particularly beneficial to struggling readers and ELL students.

the revised version recalled and explained the events better and answered more questions correctly.

The assignment to revise Virginia Woolf's essay "Professions for Women" (1966) illustrates rewriting (Activity 3.7). Rewriting this essay was a desperate move. The teacher had assigned the essay to stimulate the writing of a high school senior English class. The students interpreted Woolf's metaphoric angel literally and thought that Woolf had a ghost looking over her shoulder. They also could not understand why Woolf mentioned buying an expensive cat. Woolf's writing was not at fault; the readers did not possess the appropriate background for the essay. The students' backgrounds did not include the metaphors or experiences that Woolf had selected, and they did not know how to relate to her allusions.

Students read the rewrite first; then they read the original essay and compared the two versions. The results were satisfactory. Students understood the concepts Woolf was conveying, and as an unexpected bonus, they realized that Woolf's essay was far superior to the rewrite. As a preparation strategy, rewriting proved successful.

Rewriting can lower the readability level, sometimes significantly. The basic idea is to simplify words so that there are fewer syllables, sentences, and clauses. In the case of Woolf's essay, the original was found to be at a ninth grade level and the rewrite at a seventh grade level. Sometimes a revision does not lower the readability level but does clarify difficult material. The goal should be to present necessary material in an understandable form as a prelude to reading the original, not to show a change in a readability formula.

The reading levels were calculated using the Fry Readability Formula explained in Chapter 6.

Similar to so many activities, rewriting can be used at every step of the PAR Lesson Framework. If a rewrite is used in place of original material, then it is no longer being used to prepare the reader. One teacher rewrote portions of the Georgia Juvenile Court Code because the code (measured at a fourteenth grade level) was too hard for

ACTIVITY 3.7 A Rewrite of "Professions for Women" (Excerpt)

I was asked to speak to you about women as professionals and tell you about what has happened to me. This is difficult because my experiences in my job as a writer may not be that outstanding.

There have been many famous women writers before me who have learned and shown me the best way to succeed at writing. Because of their reputations, families today accept women who become writers. They know that they won't have to pay a lot of money for writing equipment or courses!

My story is this. I wrote regularly every day, then submitted an article to a newspaper. The article was accepted, I got paid; I became a journalist. However, I did not act like a struggling writer who spends her hard-earned money on household needs; I bought a Persian cat.

My article was a book review. I had trouble writing it and other reviews because something nagged at me. I felt that because I am a woman, I should be "feminine": have sympathy, be charming, unselfish, keep the family peaceful, sacrifice, and be very pure. When I began to write, this is what women were supposed to be like, and every family taught its girls to be this way. So when I started to write criticisms of a famous man's novel, all of the things I had learned about being a woman got in the way of my writing critically instead of writing just nice things. This problem was like a ghost whispering in my ear. I called this problem ghost "The Angel in the House" because it was always there, in my "house," telling me to be nice rather than truthful.

I got rid of this problem. I realized that being nice is not always the most important thing. Also, I had inherited some money, so I felt I didn't have to do what others expected of me in order to earn a living! I had to get rid of this obsession with being feminine rather than being truthful in order to write clearly. I killed my problem ghost before it could kill my true thoughts and reactions. This is really hard to do because "feminine" ideas creep up on you before you realize that what you're writing is not a true criticism but something you were raised to believe. It took a long time to realize what was my idea and what was society's idea about what I should write.

Readability, as measured by the Fry formula:
Original: ninth grade; rewrite: seventh grade

tenth graders to understand. The rewrite (to the seventh grade level) enabled students to read with attention to the main points. Rewriting can also be used as a reflective reading technique. A teacher might ask students to think about the material and try to rewrite it for younger students. In this way, students gain writing practice and demonstrate their learning, and an integration of the communicative arts takes place. Rewriting can also be a useful tool for at-risk readers who need to learn the same content as classmates but have difficulty reading at their level.

Please visit the Education CourseMate website at **www.cengagebrain.com** to find a link to the complete version of "Professions for Women" by Virginia Woolf.

The biggest drawback to rewriting is the time it takes. One teacher spent four hours rewriting a 15-page social studies selection. The Woolf rewrite took two hours. A teacher's time is precious, and he or she should weigh options carefully in attempting to overcome text-based problems. If rewriting is the best choice, we suggest these steps:

1. Read and restate the ideas in your own words.
2. Identify the concepts that are especially important for students to know.
3. Keep rewrites short and to the point.
4. Explain difficult concepts in the rewrite. Reformulate difficult words into already known words.
5. Make sentences short and use the active voice whenever possible.
6. Underline specialized vocabulary to make difficult words visible.

Written Previews

Graves, Prenn, and Cooke (1985) suggest that teachers write brief previews of material for students to read. These previews—especially valuable for difficult material—provide a reference point and offer students a way to organize new information. A written preview should be fairly short and is usually read aloud to the class before silent reading of the original material. Teachers can use information gained from their own previewing of material to write a preview. In writing previews, a teacher can follow these steps:

1. Select a situation familiar to the students and relevant to the topic. Describe the situation and pose questions that will enhance interest in the topic.
2. If the material demands background knowledge that students do not have, include the information.
3. Provide a synopsis of the material.
4. Provide directions for reading the material to facilitate comprehension.

Activity 3.8 is a written preview constructed by a high school government teacher about a section of the chapter called "Why Is Government Necessary?" The teacher includes questions at the end to heighten student interest.

Written previews are less time consuming than rewrites, and they heighten student achievement and interest by building on readers' prior knowledge and clarifying the structure of a text.

Graphic organizers are particularly useful for struggling readers and those with learning disabilities (Bos & Vaughn, 2002; DiCecco & Gleason, 2002).

Clarifying Thinking with Graphic Organizers

Many students have difficulty reading and interpreting expository text (Bryant et al, 2000). **Graphic organizers** visually represent relationships among concepts, thoughts, and ideas. They are also called *concept maps*, *story maps*, *advance organizers*, *story webs*,

ACTIVITY 3.8 Written Preview for "Why Is Government Necessary?"

HIGH SCHOOL GOVERNMENT CLASS

Have you ever been involved in a situation where an authority figure forced you to participate in an action that you would not have been involved in otherwise? How about an organized team or an academic club? For example, I recall a situation in my life when I was named captain of the football team and then told by the coach that my first task as captain was to do all within my power to force one particular young man to quit the team. Even though the player was a great running back, the coach did not like him. He was using his governing authority to get someone to do what he couldn't bring himself to do. I refused to help the coach, and he came down very hard on me. We had heated discussions about it, and when I would not compromise, the player stayed with the team. To this day, I feel that the extra work I had to do to overcome this problem contributed to my getting a football scholarship and gaining my undergraduate degree.

How do you handle conflicts that arise over leadership, loyalty, and duty? How do you respond when you do not agree with those in authority (those who are governing you)? How comfortable are you in a situation where you feel your voice and opinion have no value, and you are at the mercy of the "authorities"? How do you resolve personal conflicts and disagreements with authority figures?

Developed by Travis Sturgill.

or *semantic maps* (Callison, 2003). Similar to written previews, graphic organizers help the reader prepare for reading by presenting a pictorial road map of the text. Promoting *visual literacy*—the ability to interpret visual and hierarchical information—a graphic organizer asks a reader to interpret a concise, comprehensive, and compact visual aid. Forget (2004) notes that teachers help make reading easier for students through the use of graphic organizers because they show complex interrelationships.

A graphic organizer appears at the beginning of each chapter in this textbook to help readers see the relationships among the concepts and the key terms in the chapter through a visual representation of its content.

One type of graphic organizer that is normally used in the Preparation Phase before reading is constructed in the form of a hierarchical diagram of words, sometimes described as a *tree diagram*. Teachers construct these graphic organizers before the reading to display information for students; students (or by teachers and students together) construct them in the Assistance and Reflection Phases of the lesson. Activity 3.9 shows a graphic organizer in the form of a tree diagram of cloud formations for an elementary science class.

A number of studies (Lambiotte & Dansereau, 1992; Rakes, Rakes, & Smith, 1995) support the use of graphic organizers and displays to aid in organizing students' thoughts. Shapiro (1999) found that such overviews also help learning during hypermedia lessons. When readers understand the relationships among concepts in a selection, they can begin to connect the new relationships to their previous knowledge. Robinson's (1998) review of 16 studies on graphic organizers indicates that they facilitate memory for text. This outcome is most likely because they connect schemata and help students see connections between the new and the known.

Teachers usually find graphic organizers challenging to prepare but very much worth the effort. To construct one, follow these steps:

1. Identify the superordinate, or major, concept; identify all supporting concepts.
2. List all key terms from the material that reflect the identified concepts.

ACTIVITY 3.9 Graphic Organizer of Cloud Formations for an Elementary Science

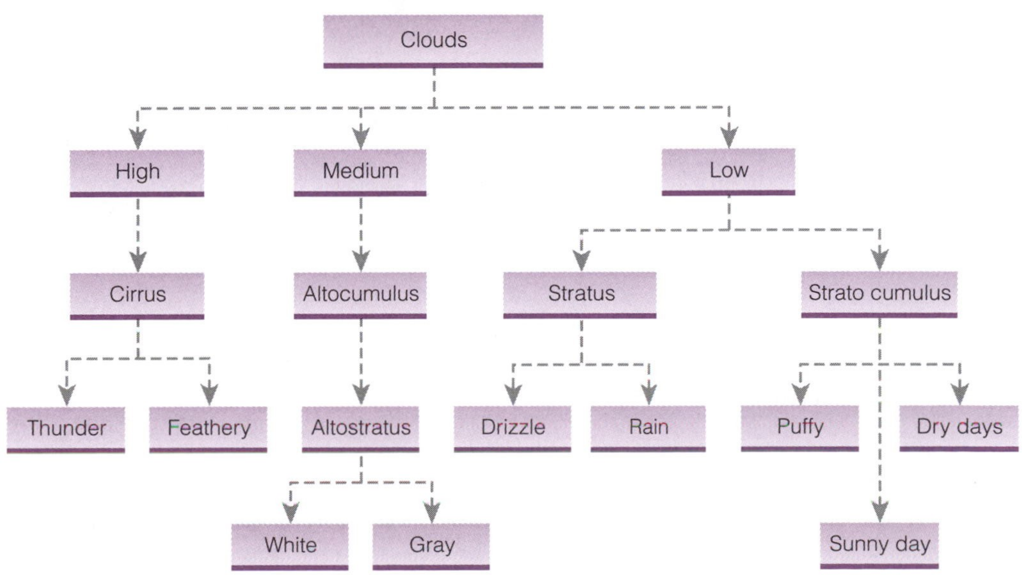

3. Connect the terms to show the relationships among concepts.
4. To show relationships between concepts, add terms from previous lessons or terms that are likely part of students' prior knowledge.
5. Construct a diagram showing these connections to introduce the reading.

When developing a graphic organizer, you do not have to include every word that might be new to readers. Including words that students already know is useful when these words represent key concepts—familiarity will aid understanding. Teachers should explain to students why they prepared the graphic organizer as they did, noting the relationships. This presentation should include a discussion to which students can contribute what they know about the terms as well as what they predict they will be learning. Students should keep the organizer available for reference while reading so they can refer to it as they encounter the terms.

After reading, students can use the graphic organizer to check comprehension or to reflect on their learning. Thus, the graphic organizer can be useful at each of the PAR steps and promote integration of the communicative arts. Activity 3.10 is a graphic organizer for elementary social studies.

ACTIVITY 3.10 Graphic Organizer for Elementary Social Studies Lesson About Jamestown

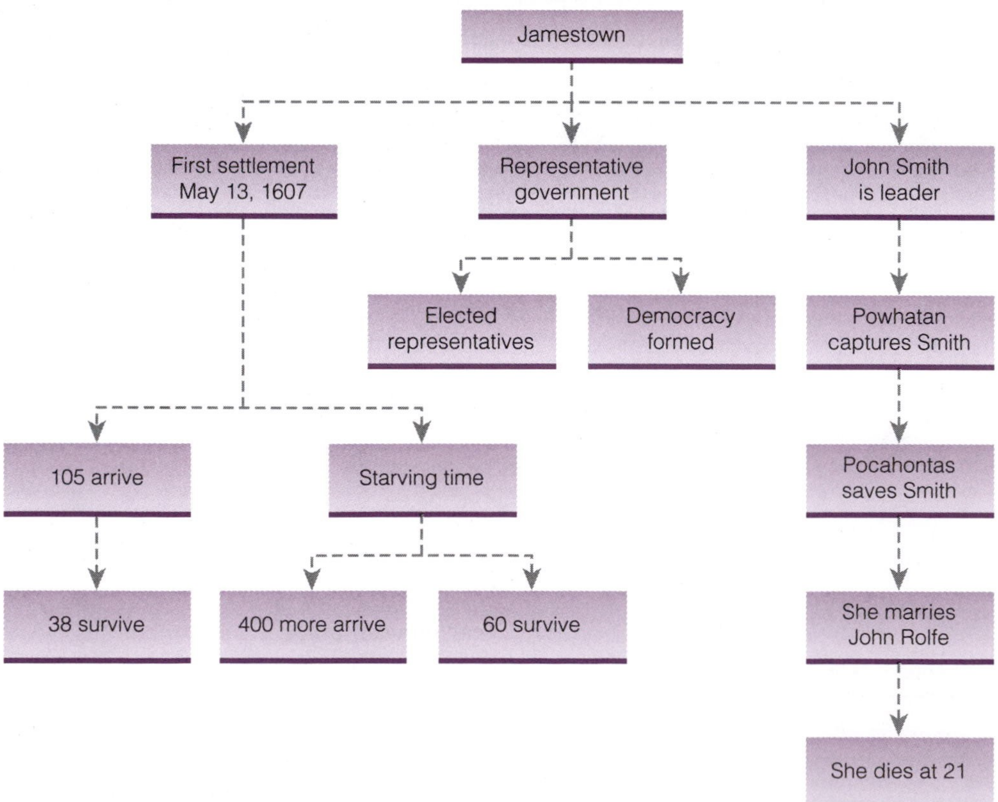

TECH APP

Creating Graphic Representations

There are many digital tools that can be used to create graphic representations of information that students are learning:

- **Inspiration/Kidspiration** is available online as a free trial. Schools can purchase site licenses so all teachers can have unlimited access to the software.
- **Microsoft Word** provides tools, including shapes, clip art, and pictures, as well the ability to make charts.
- **PowerPoint** provides similar tools as Microsoft Word to use clip art and pictures and to create charts and graphs.

Anticipation Guides

An **anticipation guide**, sometimes called a reaction guide or prediction guide, is a prereading strategy that teaches both content and literacy along with reading skills appropriate for all learners (Kozen, Murray, & Windell, 2006). Students react to statements prepared by the teacher. In doing so, students anticipate, or predict, what the content will be. After students have made their decisions about the statements, they have a purpose for thoughtful reading because of curiosity about their predictions. In this way, the guide assists learners while they read. In the Reflection Phase of the lesson, student group and teacher-led discussions attempt to come to final consensus on the answers. Conner (2003) notes that some statements should be true/false ones, but others should be vague enough to provoke disagreement and "challenge students' beliefs about the topic" (p. 1). Statements that are intentionally vague will arouse curiosity and discussion but might not lead to consensus. Anticipation guides are valuable because (1) students exposed to anticipation guides tend to become interested and participate in lively discussion, which motivates reading; (2) many students enjoy argument, and a well-structured anticipation guide leaves enough room for doubt about topics to generate healthy debate; and (3) students need to learn to predict outcomes of their reading, which this strategy teaches students to do.

Suppose a high school vocational education teacher has introduced the term *high amperages* to an unenthusiastic group of automobile mechanics students. In fact, no one is sure what the term means. In discussing the larger concept of automobile batteries, it becomes apparent that students think they know about batteries but lack a schema for important terms such as *amperage*, *conductance*, *plates*, and *voltage regulation*. To overcome misconceptions about how a battery operates, the teacher prepares an anticipation guide (Activity 3.11). As groups of students discuss the guide, they talk about their prior knowledge and begin to formulate more precise knowledge.

Anticipation guides involve students in discussion and reading and can also ask students to respond in writing to the statements. Furthermore, Yopp and Yopp (2010) suggest integrating technology by using an electronic response system so students respond through individual transmitters. The handheld remote control devices that they use to convey their responses are often called "clickers." Teachers can poll their students for answers to the anticipation guide questions. This allows teachers to pool the responses and display group data. Teachers can have students refer to the guide as they read, which enhances comprehension. If students return to the guide after reading to clarify or rethink previous positions, they apply every phase of PAR throughout the process. Anticipation guides are excellent for developing critical thinking and cultural understanding, and both teachers and students report that they like using them.

ACTIVITY 3.11 Anticipation Guide: Automobile Batteries

Before reading the pages in the text: In the space to the left of each statement, place a check mark (✓) if you agree or think the statement is true.

______ **1.** An automobile battery is, in many ways, like a long flashlight with several D-cell batteries inside.

______ **2.** The amount of current and voltage a battery can produce is probably related to the actual size of the battery.

______ **3.** The chemical liquid in a battery is a conductor that allows electrons to leave one type of plate in the battery and move toward another type of plate.

______ **4.** The plates inside a battery are soft and squishy and must be separated by a nonconductive material.

______ **5.** When you are driving down the road, you are actually charging your battery by increasing the number of electrons in the liquid inside the battery.

______ **6.** When buying a battery, it is better to spend a few extra dollars; you should keep in mind the saying that "You get what you pay for."

______ **7.** A battery that has both high amperages and a long reserve capacity probably has more plates inside it than a battery of lesser capacity.

______ **8.** The liquid inside a battery can disappear.

During or after reading: Add new check marks or cross through those about which you have changed your mind. Keep in mind that this is not like a traditional worksheet. You may have to put on your "thinking caps" and read between the lines. Use the space under each statement to note the page(s), column(s), and paragraph(s) where you find information to support your thinking.

Developed by Mark Forget. Used with permission.

Making an anticipation guide takes some thought but becomes easier with practice. Here are the basic steps for constructing an anticipation guide:

1. Read the passage and identify the major concepts to be learned in the lesson.
2. Decide which concepts are most important to tap into student background and beliefs.
3. Write three to six statements about these concepts. The statements should reflect the students' background and be thought provoking. Choose statements that might make students disagree. General statements, rather than statements that are too specific, work best. Well-known quotations and idioms are successful.
4. Use some statements that are intuitively appealing to students but that the text will prove incorrect. Write statements that require students to interpret large segments of text to focus on comprehension.
5. Make your statements more readable than the text.
6. Project the guide or distribute worksheets with space for responses. Give clear directions.
7. Conduct class discussion based on your concept statements. Students must support their responses—yes and no are not acceptable answers—by arguing based on their experiences and explaining any positions they take. Students should be asked to "think like lawyers" to argue their points.
8. After reading with the guide, students work in small groups to come to consensus on the answers. The teacher reconvenes the class to discuss group answers. Students discuss what they have learned, and the teacher clarifies any concepts that are still unclear to bring closure to the lesson.

9. The teacher may take the opportunity to review and reinforce the skill of predicting. The teacher may point out that readers in any subject area can make predictions to make a reading more interesting by setting a purpose for reading.

Activities 3.12, 3.13, and 3.14 are anticipation guides constructed by teachers of primary science, geometry, and elementary English classes, respectively. There is no right way to create a guide. Enterprising teachers develop anticipation guides that reflect sound instructional principles and research every day.

Factstorming

Factstorming is an excellent activity to determine students' prior knowledge and to build background. The whole class can participate at once as the activity proceeds from a single generative question. Factstorming is similar to brainstorming but focuses on facts and associations pertinent to the topic; brainstorming focuses on problem solving. The teacher asks students to say anything they can think of about the topic to be read (e.g., "Tell anything you know about the country of Egypt and the region known as North Africa."). The teacher projects student responses so the group can discuss them.

ACTIVITY 3.12 Anticipation/Prediction Guide for Primary Science

Directions: Read these statements to yourself as I read them aloud. If you agree with a statement, be ready to explain why. We will check all statements we agree with in the prereading column. Then we will read to see if we should change our minds.

PREDICTION GUIDE FOR MAMMALS

Before — After

________  are mammals. ________

________  are mammals. ________

________ All mammals have four . ________

________  are mammals. ________

________ Some mammals can . ________

ACTIVITY 3.13 Geometry

PREDICTION GUIDE: PROVING THEOREMS ABOUT ANGLES

Before reading, place a check mark (✓) next to the statements you think will be verifiable in the reading on pages 35–39. Then, during or after the reading, make changes to reflect new opinions. Be prepared to defend your interpretation with specific reference to the text. Note pages, paragraphs, or diagrams you are referring to in order to support your position.

______ **1.** Congruent angles have the same number of degrees in them.

______ **2.** The ways that runways point at airports differ from one airport to another.

______ **3.** Two supplementary angles always add up to the same number of degrees.

______ **4.** Proving theorems about angles is easy; it just requires using common sense.

______ **5.** Any two-column proof can also be written in paragraph form.

______ **6.** The term *complementary angle* is similar to the term *supplementary angle*.

______ **7.** If Jennifer had three pieces of pizza and Shenika had four pieces, then Jennifer consumed fewer calories than Shenika did.

Developed by Mark Forget. Used with permission.

ACTIVITY 3.14 Elementary Language Arts and Social Studies Connection

Anticipation guide: Reading *Pink and Say* by Patricia Polacco (1994)

Before reading: In the space to the left of each statement, place a check mark (✓) if you agree or think the statement is true.

______ **1.** Say, the white boy on the cover, is teaching Pink, the African American boy, to read.

______ **2.** Fighting in a war would be exhilarating.

______ **3.** It's possible to become like family with someone of another race.

______ **4.** A woman who isn't your mother can comfort you and make you feel better.

______ **5.** There are people on both sides of a war who are good and bad.

______ **6.** Sometimes feeling scared can be brave.

During or after reading: Add new check marks or cross through those about which you have changed your mind. This is not a traditional worksheet. You may have to put on your "thinking caps" and read between the lines. Note the page(s) and paragraph(s) where you find information to support your thinking.

PREP STRATEGY

A sophisticated version of factstorming is PreP, a prereading plan (Langer, 1981). PreP has three phases:

1. Initial associations with the concept, as in factstorming.
2. **Reflections on the initial concept,** when students are asked to explain why they thought of a particular response, thus building awareness of their prior knowledge and associations.
3. **Reformulation of knowledge,** when new ideas learned during the first two phases are articulated.

ACTIVITY 3.15 PreP with Categorization Health Education Class

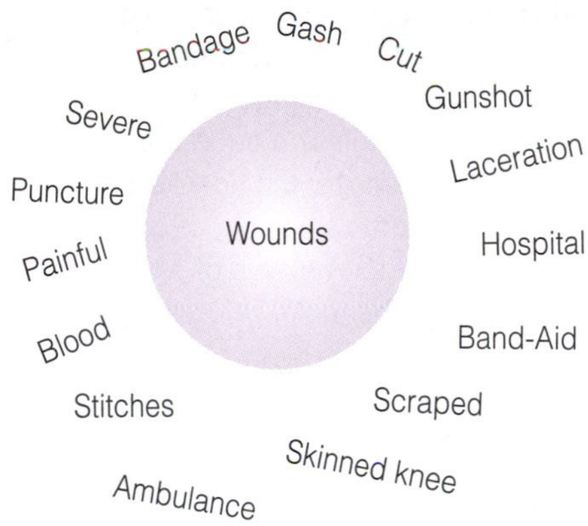

Categories:

Health facilities   Types of wounds   Reasons wounds happened

PreP helps ascertain prior knowledge and also builds background. Its steps encourage the reader to use prior knowledge by listening carefully to others' opinions. The teacher can correct misperceptions in a nonthreatening way with whole-group discussion as a supportive environment for expression. Listening, speaking, and reading all take place in a PreP activity. In Activity 3.15, students generate words from the main topic *wounds* in a health education class. They categorize the words they have generated during the PreP into three general categories: health facilities, types, and reasons it happened. Students then use the categories to guide their reading.

Analogies

Students can make comparisons between familiar and less familiar concepts by the use of **analogies**. Similar to previews, analogies begin with a connection point to the reader's background. However, whereas analogies carry out a comparison, previews focus more directly on the material to be read.

Analogies are excellent tools for content reading teachers because they are simple to create and highly relevant for students. Researchers (Glynn, 1997; Yanowitz, 2001) have found that analogies are a successful strategy for content area teachers, especially in science classes. The teacher can present them in oral or written form as an informal introduction to content material. Analogies actively engage students in listening and speaking, and if students are encouraged to write their own analogies after reading certain material, then analogies become useful reflection and writing activities. The example in Activity 3.16 was developed by a third grade teacher.

Analogies are powerful tools to use in reading, as the story below demonstrates.

When a high school junior resisted reading a history chapter that explained the circumstances leading to the American Revolution, his parent tried this analogy: "Suppose," the parent suggested, "that your parents decided to go to Europe for six months, leaving you on your own at home. You would have the car and access to money; you would be able to make all your own decisions. What would your reaction be?" As you might imagine, the high school junior thought this would be an excellent arrangement. "However," the parent continued, "we would return home and take charge once more. We would want our car back, and you would have to ask for permission to do the things you'd been doing freely. Now how would you feel?" The teenager did not like this turn of events. "Would you still love us?" the parent inquired, assuming, of course, that teenagers do love their parents even though they have funny ways of showing it.

"Well, yes," the junior reluctantly agreed. "But I'd be insulted, and family life wouldn't be the same."

"Exactly," agreed the parent. "That's the way it was with the British and their American colonies. The British had to attend to problems in Europe and in their own government. They let the American colonists have free rein for a while. Then they turned their attention back to the Americans. But the Americans didn't appreciate the intervention after this period of time. Many of them still 'loved' the British, but they deeply resented the renewed control. While you're reading this chapter, you might want to keep in mind your own reactions to this hypothetical situation and compare those feelings to the reactions of the colonists." Much later in the month, this teenager grudgingly reported to his parent that the chapter had turned out to be "pretty easy to read" because he understood the circumstances better than for most of the other chapters in the book.

ACTIVITY 3.16 Analogy

Goal: To enable students to connect new knowledge with existing knowledge.
Materials: Paper, pencils

DIRECTIONS

1. Read the following paragraphs as a primer for small-group discussion comparing cars with bodies.
   - "Your body is very similar to a car. You may have been told to 'rev up your engine' one time. When a car revs up, it begins to go."
   - "A car needs many different substances to keep it running well. It might need oil for the parts and air for the filters, as you would need oil for your joints or air for your lungs."
   - "Actually, there are many other things that a car and your body have in common. A car needs gasoline to make it go. What do you need?"
2. Divide the students into small groups and let them list on paper the ways that cars and bodies are similar. Some suggestions that you will be looking for are:

   Fats, oil
   Protein, gasoline
   Carbohydrates, spark plugs
   Vitamins, fuel additives, super grade gasoline
   Minerals, paint, rustproofers
   Air, air conditioning
   Muscles, wheels
   Heart, engine

3. After 15 or 20 minutes, have students share the group information. Write the analogies on the board. Ask for comments or clarifications.

Adapted from an idea by Kathy Feltus.

This on-the-spot analogy was simple enough to construct. The adult understood several characteristics of 16-year-old students and applied them to building an analogy that would hook the reader to the content material. The informal analogy was a simple preparation strategy. It worked because the reading took on new meaning for the student. His comprehension was enhanced—so much so that he admitted it to a parent!

Final Thoughts

Remember that preparing students to determine and build on prior knowledge before reading is a worthy goal but not always easy to achieve. This is true precisely because students are so special and unique, enigmatic, and often refreshingly unscripted in their thoughts and habits. One of the authors was visiting a first grade class in which the teacher was getting students to ask questions about the lesson. The author asked the class, "Who made the first American flag?" None of the 14 students seemed to know, and nobody ventured a guess. Ten minutes later, the visiting author said good-bye and started to leave. A small, red-faced, smiling boy, seated in the front, ran up, tugged on the pants of the visitor, and whispered almost inaudibly, "Betsy Ross."

ONE-MINUTE SUMMARY

This chapter has noted the importance of students' prior knowledge in reading and the necessity of building on prior knowledge throughout reading lessons. Careful preparation by teachers may help to overcome both students' limited or incorrect prior knowledge about a topic and their lack of interest in the topic. We described the problem of mismatches between readers and texts and how teachers must overcome such mismatches through strategies that better prepare students for reading.

We discussed many activities—some developed by classroom teachers—for building on students' prior knowledge in reading. Although textbook material sometimes needs adaptation, it should not be eliminated from the curriculum. Preparation activities can promote reading, writing, speaking, and listening. We emphasized that how a teacher uses an activity is more important than rigorous adherence to prescribed steps, and we included variations of activities that demonstrated the creativity of the teachers who constructed them. In this chapter, we described strategies to prepare the learner, such as prelearning concept checks, rewriting, written previews, graphic organizers, anticipation guides, factstorming, PreP, and analogies.

END-OF-CHAPTER ACTIVITIES

Assisting Comprehension

1. Look over these four questions we asked at the beginning of the chapter:

   a. What is the importance of prior knowledge in reading comprehension?

   b. How does a teacher determine students' prior knowledge?

   c. How can teachers overcome students' misconceptions about a topic?

   d. Are there strategies a teacher can use to prepare students to read?

   Are you better able to answer these questions now, after having read the chapter? Formulate answers to all four questions to help you remember this chapter.

2. Select a chapter from a content area textbook. Using the following questions as a guide, reflect on what your text offers to help you build on your students' prior knowledge:

   a. What aids are provided in the text chapter to help you build on students' prior knowledge?

   b. Is there a chapter preview or summary that students could build on?

   c. Are there any statements, such as those identifying objectives, that could be used in an anticipation guide?

d. Is there a graphic organizer?

e. Are these aids suitable for your students?

f. Are these aids sufficient for your students?

g. Should you construct aids to extend students' prior knowledge? What type(s)?

Reflecting on Your Reading

1. To help you remember the main content of this chapter, write a 30-word summary of the chapter. Compare it with the graphic organizer at the beginning of the chapter to see how many of the main concepts you were able to remember.
2. Your content organization (e.g., National Council of Teachers of Math, National Council of Teachers of English, National Council for the Social Studies, National Science Teachers Association, International Reading Association) has most likely developed a set of standards that identify the performance criteria relevant to classroom teachers. Standards usually delineate elements of foundational knowledge that a classroom teacher should possess. Locate and become familiar with what the organization recommends. For instance, teachers should:
   - Know and explain research and theories supporting the importance of prior knowledge and background for developing new concepts.
   - Use a variety of strategies to build background knowledge.
   - Use student interests and cultural and linguistic backgrounds to make connections to new concepts.
3. Try to formulate a coherent vision and purpose statement about why building on prior knowledge is the most important aspect of preparing learners. This vision and purpose statement should include goals you can articulate to others in the teaching profession.

CHAPTER 4

Assistance in Learning

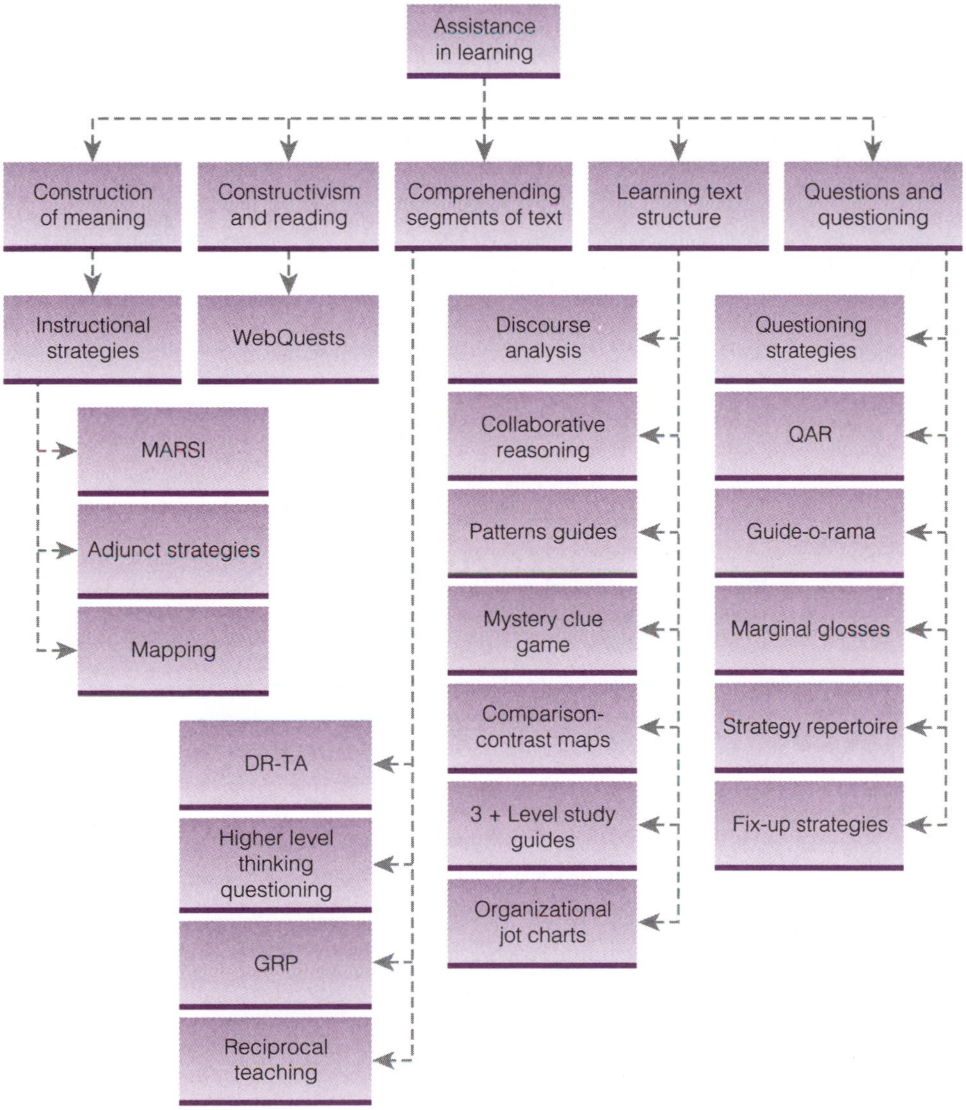

It is the supreme art of the teacher to awaken joy in creative expression and knowledge.

ALBERT EINSTEIN

VOICES FROM THE CLASSROOM

Ms. Ludisch was a dedicated teacher. No one could deny that. She had more than 25 years experience in teaching, mostly in the field of foreign languages. She was a no-nonsense type of teacher, was often terse with students, and expected a high level of achievement. One semester, she gave all 17 students in her class a failing grade for a six-week session; she was adamant that the students were lazy and just didn't want to learn French. She berated the students often.

The principal called her to his office to discuss student and parent complaints, as well as rumors circulating in the school. Ms. Ludisch was extremely upset and explained that she had standards that had to be met and that she wasn't changing her teaching practices or grading policy for anyone. All 17 of these "trifling" students, as she expressed it, would fail for the year if they didn't significantly improve their work habits. She would not change!

If you guessed that this was a fictitious class, you would be wrong. This was a real class. Is Ms. Ludisch providing enough support and assistance to get students "over the hard parts" in foreign language lessons? This chapter discusses critical ways to assist students to improve comprehension and thereby raise student achievement.

PREPARING TO READ

1. Can you predict what this chapter on "assisting comprehension" will be about? How and why would we help a student to comprehend?
2. Following is a list of terms used in this chapter. Some may be familiar to you in a general context, but in this chapter, they may be used in unfamiliar ways. Rate your knowledge by placing a plus sign (+) for those you are certain you know, a check (✓) for those you have some knowledge of, and a zero (0) for those you don't know. Be ready to locate them in the chapter and pay special attention to their meanings.

    _______ adjunct strategies
    _______ mapping
    _______ constructivism
    _______ segments of text
    _______ reciprocal teaching
    _______ structure of text
    _______ discourse analysis
    _______ collaborative reasoning
    _______ question-answer relationship
    _______ fix-up strategies

3. Match the words in the left column with their definitions in the right column:

    1. Adjunct strategies
    2. Constructivism
    3. Segments of text
    4. Structure of text
    5. Discourse analysis
    6. Metacognition

    a. The act of thinking about one's own thought patterns
    b. Small sections of subcategories of texts
    c. Strategies used to assist someone in reading
    d. How paragraphs are arranged and ordered in a textbook
    e. The study and identification of organizational structure in written material
    f. Active construction of meaning by the learner

OBJECTIVES

As you read this chapter, focus your attention on the following purposes. You will:

1. Identify why helping students to read is so important.
2. Describe why students have reading difficulties in content area subjects.
3. Describe the importance of adjunct strategies for teaching reading comprehension.
4. Identify constructivism, constructivist learning, and the theory underlying the construct.
5. Identify how to help students construct meaning while reading.
6. Identify strategies for teaching short segments of text.
7. Describe the importance of teaching the structure of text.
8. Describe strategies for teaching the structure of text.
9. Identify how to use questioning strategies to teach comprehension.
10. Describe fix-up strategies to improve comprehension in reading.

Shoe. Reprinted with permission of Tribune Media Services.

Shoe-New Business MacNelly. Distributed by King Features Syndicate.

Providing Assistance in the Construction of Meaning

An important aspect of any classroom is time spent reading in class during which teachers can assist students to learn the material. Lawrence and colleagues (2009) found that when teachers provided in-class time for students to read and discuss text with peers, students were more engaged in the learning and felt more able to interact with the text on meaningful levels. Yet Pilonieta (2010) found that most reading materials are not set up to provide comprehension strategy instruction during the reading lesson. Teachers must learn the important skill of strategic assistance for successful comprehension. An important step in the PAR (preparation, assistance, and reflection) Lesson Framework is the Assistance Phase in which students develop and deepen their understanding of any learning activity. Consider this chapter's opening scenario; teachers such as Ms. Ludisch might motivate students in the Preparation Phase of PAR but then provide little or no guidance to students as they learn.

Teachers need to know that reading is more than a basic skill. Mature readers take part in a complex process that is analytic, interactive, constructive, and strategic (Guthrie, Schafer, Von Secker, & Alban, 2000; Lederer, 2000). Fluent readers are independent readers who sample text, predict, confirm hypotheses, and self-correct quickly (Schoenbach, Greenleaf, Cziko, & Hurwitz, 1999). In addition, apprehension and reflection are requisites of comprehension. A reader must apprehend and ponder the significance of the content. This analysis must be active, generating strategies that aid the reader while reading and in future reading. Mature readers must also set their own purposes for reading, maintain meaning over time, cope with the complexities of text, draw inferences, and respond critically to an author's meaning (Whitehead, 1994).

Other important factors determine how much a student comprehends. Both novice and expert readers use existing knowledge to construct meaning from text. That is, a reader's world knowledge and specific knowledge of a topic play a crucial role in the comprehension process (Ozuru, Dempsey, & McNamara, 2009). In addition, not all readers will interpret the same reading material in the same way. Differences in background knowledge and experiences can cause different interpretations and even lead to invalid interpretations of text (Pressley, 2002). Motivation and emotions, discussed in Chapter 2, seem to play pivotal roles for students who have reading difficulties (Sideridis, Mouzaki, Simos, & Protopapas, 2006). Hall (2007) explains that motivation plays a significant role in struggling readers' ability to comprehend text. In one study, this researcher found that poorly performing students refused to take part in certain classroom reading activities when such activities compromised an image of success that the students were trying to project to their peers.

Chapter 2 discusses the pivotal role motivation plays in reading comprehension.

It should be noted that a mature reader's ability to use strategies in a coordinated fashion does not necessarily develop because teachers provide students with opportunities to read, such as oral classroom reading. Students benefit most from being taught comprehension strategies that are based on sound research (Neufeld, 2005). Morrison and Wlodarczyk (2009) maintain that even young students can benefit from comprehension strategy instruction that emphasizes higher order thinking skills. Teaching such strategies and reinforcing them over time help students learn in a self-regulated fashion.

Improving Comprehension through the Use of Instructional Strategies

To find out about students' awareness of reading and perceived use of reading strategies for learning, a teacher might rely on a test such as the *Metacognitive Awareness of Reading Strategies Inventory (MARSI)* by Mokhtari and Reichard (2002), which uses a self-report instrument. Activity 4.1 shows some of the test questions along with the Likert scale used. The entire test can be found in the appendix.

Strong evidence suggests that students can be taught comprehension strategies; such instruction is an excellent way to improve understanding of authentic texts (Duke & Pearson, 2002; Kropiewnicki, 2006). Unfortunately, much research also shows that comprehension instruction is often not occurring in content area classrooms (Neufeld, 2005; Pressley, 2002a; Pressley, Wharton-McDonald, Hampson, & Echevarria, 1998). Pressley (2002b) and his colleagues found that students were given opportunities to practice comprehension strategies but were not explicitly taught why it was important to use them. It is the instructor's role to teach students comprehension strategies as well as text information (Elder & Paul, 2009).

After giving the MARSI, teachers can pick strategies for instruction that coincide with problem areas students have noted on the test. For instance, if students say they do not use context clues to learn new words (item 19 on the MARSI), the teacher can teach the important skill of context clue discovery (see Chapter 7 about vocabulary). A number of the strategies we cover in this chapter, such as directed reading instruction and questioning strategies, are important for covering many of the potential problem areas in comprehension noted on the MARSI.

ACTIVITY 4.1 Metacognitive Awareness of Reading Strategies Inventory

All items graded on a 1 to 5 Likert scale:

1. I never or almost never do this.
2. I do this only occasionally.
3. I sometimes do this (about 50 percent of the time).
4. I usually do this.
5. I always or almost always do this.

   a. I have a purpose in mind when I read.
   b. I take notes while reading to help me understand what I read.
   c. I think about what I know to help me understand what I read.
   d. I preview the text to see what it is about before I read it.
   e. When text becomes difficult, I read aloud to help me understand what I read.
   f. I try to guess the meaning of unknown words or phrases.

From Mokhtari, K., & Reichard, C. A. (2002). Assessing students' metacognitive awareness of reading strategies. *Journal of Educational Psychology*, 94(2), 249–259. Used with permission.

The MARSI is used to help teachers design reading comprehension instruction that meets the needs of students who are having comprehension difficulties because of their lack of sophistication with using authentic textbook material. Remember also that MARSI results will help students better self-monitor their own reading behaviors. Chang (2010) found that students who adopt a self-monitoring strategy performed better academically and generally were positively motivated.

To reinforce learning during the Assistance Phase, teachers need to use **adjunct strategies** (strategies during reading) often. For instance, **mapping** is one activity that demonstrates the adjunct strategy of organizing information into major and subordinate ideas (Al khawaldeh, Salem, & Alolaimat, 2010). This activity, sometimes called *concept mapping,* provides a way for both the teacher and student to remember and organize key elements of knowledge (Romance & Vitale, 1997). Furthermore, mapping can assist readers in understanding concept relationships and thereby avoid fragmented or simple rote learning outcomes (Romance & Vitale, 1999). Mapping can also be done on a computer. Liu, Chen, and Chang (2010) found that a computer-assisted concept mapping strategy had significant benefit for reading of low-achieving students. Mapping has become a very popular activity for helping readers develop comprehension. Just as travelers use a map to find their way, readers can use a diagram that shows the route to understanding a passage, and they themselves can make maps to show their understanding.

Chapter 10 discusses software programs that help students learn the skill of mapping. For instance, Inspiration is a software program that helps teachers create maps. Please visit the Education CourseMate website at **www.cengagebrain.com** for a link to a website with many sample graphic organizers and maps.

Mapping can also introduce a topic before any reading takes place. In such a case, the teacher probably has already made the map or is relying on students' prior knowledge to construct the map; thus, the strategy is to use prior knowledge to prepare the readers.

The primary purpose of mapping is to visually portray the relationships of major and supporting ideas. Because maps encourage students to refer to the reading material and engage in interactive learning, reading educators recognize their value in assisting comprehension. Mapping can be used to teach vocabulary and to introduce outlining and note taking, and also functions as a study aid (see Chapter 7 on vocabulary and Chapter 9 on study skills).

Mapping also can aid reading reflection. After the map is made, it becomes a study aid. The following are suggestions for developing a map:

1. Identify the main idea of the passage. (Sometimes just a topic or a question may stimulate map generation.) Write the main idea anywhere on the page, leaving room for other information to be written around it.
2. Circle the main idea.
3. Identify subordinate categories, which may be chapter subheadings.
4. Connect the subordinate categories to the main idea.
5. Show supporting details.
6. Connect supporting details to the idea or category they support.
7. Connect all notes to other notes in a way that makes sense.

Although mapping a whole chapter may be time consuming, mapping sections may help readers understand the relationship between the superordinate (major idea) and the subordinate (minor ideas).

Maps engage readers as they read, reread, and study; and they demonstrate the hierarchical nature of exposition. After teachers have mapped several times, students will become proficient at making their own maps. Because a map is a diagram of information, it is a visual learning aid. Adding drawings to the map will often stimulate learning, especially for younger readers. Such visual reinforcement capitalizes on visual literacy and right brain functions. Activity 4.2 shows a map about "managing stress" from a high school health education class.

TECH APP

Email an Expert

Discovery Learning: Students in small groups make a map on a topic in history class and send it as an email attachment to a director of a museum. Students ask for a reply in the form of a critique of how well they constructed the map.

Time Commitment: Moderate. No more than one hour.

Why Do It? This use of technology enhances critical thinking skills, promotes group problem solving, and stimulates writing.

Values: In addition to the skills mentioned, students learn to get assistance from an expert as a natural course of learning.

Using mapping integrates all the communicative arts. Class discussion, which requires students to listen to one another and speak about the topic, must take place for the map to be developed. Reading is the source of the information mapped, and teachers can incorporate writing by asking students to use the map as a frame of reference for writing about the reading topic. For instance, students could be assigned to write a six-paragraph essay about the parts of a computer as generated from a map. A health education teacher who wants students to write a report could have them use a map similar to the one in Activity 4.2. Students could refer to both primary and secondary sources to find out more about each portion of the map.

ACTIVITY 4.2 Mapping Activity for High School Health Education Class

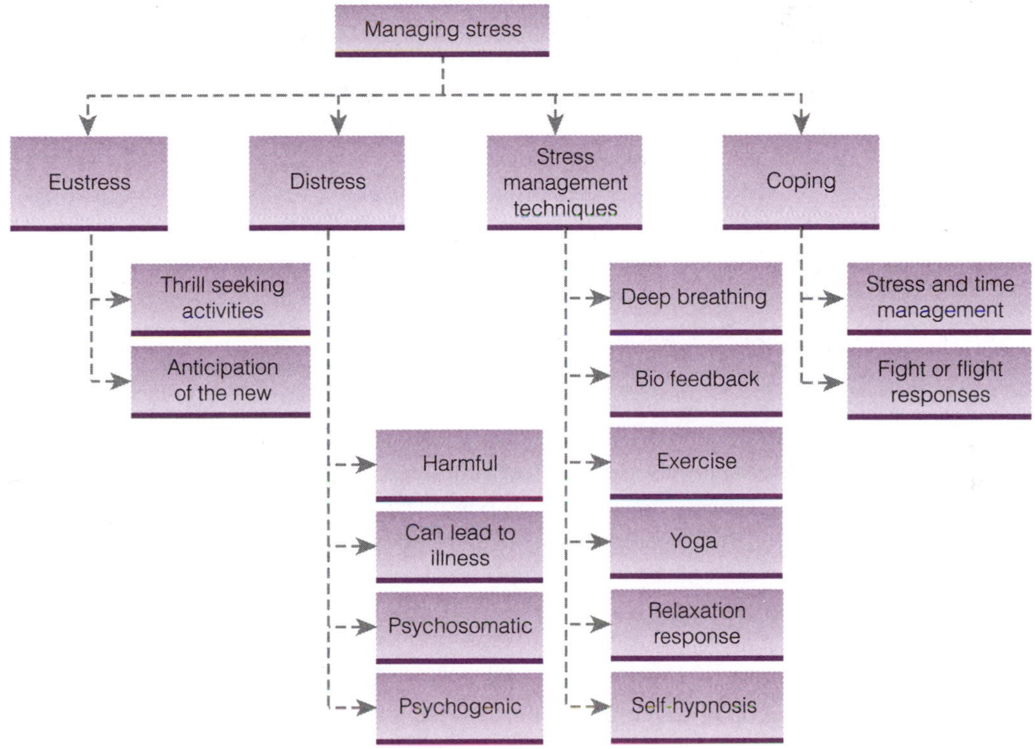

Constructivism and Reading

When students can make sense of their learning by developing a knowledge base or constructing their own purposes for reading a selection and developing tasks on their own that demonstrate their learning, they are constructing meaning. That is, knowledge is not passively received but is actively constructed by the learners on the basis of prior knowledge, attitudes, and values. This process is called **constructivism.** The constructivist theory of learning emphasizes the important role of the learner in literacy tasks, allowing readers to feel comfortable with learning because they are so fully integrated in putting it all together. In constructivist theory, students are asked through active consideration and assimilation to internalize material and reshape or transform information into thought that makes sense in their world (Brooks & Brooks, 1993). Constructivism emphasizes a student's ability to solve practical, real-life problems. The teacher's role in this theory is to assemble required resources and act as a guide or facilitator for students to formulate their own goals and learn by themselves (Inan, Lowther, Ross, & Strahl, 2010).

To see how questioning, constructivism and inquiry learning can be activated, view the video of a middle school science teacher in action at the Education CourseMate website at **www.cengagebrain.com.**

In a constructivist environment, students must be encouraged to use higher order thinking skills to find meaning in classroom experiences. Teachers do not stress the "one correct answer" to every question, with that answer being the one supplied by the teacher. Student questioning must be encouraged, and in certain situations, teachers

Look for WebQuests that teachers have constructed and WebQuest templates online; please visit the Education CourseMate website at **www.cengagebrain.com** to find some links.

In a constructivist classroom, less time will be spent in drill and rote exercise routines. Consider how a debate can facilitate constructivist thinking by watching the video of a high school social studies class on the Education CourseMate website at **www.cengagebrain.com**.

In addition, research suggests that constructivist learning is useful for improving interactivity in online learning (Rudestam & Schoenholtz-Read, 2002). Please visit the Education CourseMate website at **www.cengagebrain.com** to find:

- Reading materials on constructivist learning
- The ThinkQuest website, with examples of student-created websites

Constructivist theory remains only a theory (Dewey, Piaget, & Vygotsky); there is still no strong research to prove its efficacy (Green & Gredler, 2002; Vermette et al, 2001). Proponents of constructivism do not even agree on what makes for good constructivist teaching (Ali, 2004). What is your sense of its efficacy based on your experience as a learner and teacher?

should accept a variety of possible interpretations. Constructivism requires more than factual recall to questions and factual recall-type tests as the central proof that learning has taken place in their classrooms. Liaw (2004) has noted how Web-based learning, with such popular strategies as distance learning, interactive multimedia, graphic displays, and WebQuests, can be used innovatively to teach constructivist learning. Web-based learning environments can provide an excellent opportunity for the teacher to act as a facilitator to help students discover from their own background knowledge any new learning that must take place.

Constructivist learning can take place at any level of education. An example occurred when three professors who were located in different states shared insights about online instruction through a threaded discussion (Richardson, Fleener, & Thistlethwaite, 2004). By talking with each other online, each built new understandings and applications of what a threaded discussion could add to their courses. Another example was a threaded discussion among students from different schools, who all took a virtual tour of Jamestown and viewed the Werowicomoco exhibit. Then they "conversed" to build understanding of the importance of different cultures in colonial history using cooperative learning in an electronic environment. Chapter 10 provides more information about Web-based learning.

Teachers should consider seven pedagogical goals needed for classroom teachers to implement constructivism (Honebein, 1996):

1. Give students knowledge of the learning process.
2. Provide students with experience appreciating multiple perspectives.
3. Make learning realistic and relevant.
4. Encourage ownership and voice in the learning process.
5. Provide a social context for learning.
6. Encourage use of multiple modes of representation.
7. Encourage learners' self-awareness.

Dalgarno (2001) has noted that constructivism is emerging as a significant learning theory that emphasizes a student-centered approach to learning. In a constructivist model, teachers do not transmit knowledge to passive learners; instead, learners build information from the assistance that teachers provide (Weaver, 1994). The reader must actively construct meaning by relating new material to the known using reasoning and developing concepts.

By discovering what learners do as they read and how they constantly strive to construct meaning while reading, we can design strategies for assistance that enhance their learning. This can be illustrated by an encounter one of the authors had in helping an elementary school youngster read a history passage about log cabins. The boy could not say the two words *oil lamp* as he read the passage orally. Throughout the reading, he was not given the pronunciation of these two words. After the reading, the boy was asked several questions to help him recall the story, including one concerning what kind of lighting was used in the log cabin. The child quickly answered, "Oh, they had an oil lamp." This child was thinking as he read, trying to piece together the clues. He was processing what he knew were unknown data. When he reached the stage of retelling the story, he realized that he did know; he had successfully put the clues together. If the teacher had interpreted as a final product his failure to pronounce the words while he was reading, he would have thought the boy did not know the words.

In fact, all along the boy was constructing meaning. Ultimately, his processing led to a correct understanding. As this experience illustrates, we must give our students every chance to process information, thus discovering meaning as they read, before we measure their understanding.

Comprehending Segments of Text

Authors usually organize text by dividing it into meaningful sections or segments. These are usually signified by subheadings. Readers must pay attention to these **segments of text** to gain information and focus on important information. Teachers can use strategies that provide directed readings using small segments of text. Two important strategies for doing this are explained next: the Directed Reading–Thinking Activity and the Guided Reading Procedure.

Directed Reading–Thinking Activity

The Directed Reading–Thinking Activity (DR-TA) helps students understand that each segment of text can help them figure out the next segment. The teacher must decide in advance how to segment the material for a DR-TA. The organization of the material is the key factor affecting this segmentation. Studies by Stahl (2008) and El-Koumy (2006) have shown that the DR-TA is beneficial in teaching referential and inferential learning. Because the text is divided into smaller portions, students can focus on the process of responding to higher order questions (Fisher & Frey, 2008). As advocated by Stauffer (1969a), the DR-TA has three basic steps: predicting, reading, and proving. Predicting involves asking readers to use not only what they already know but also whatever they can learn from a quick preview of the material to predict what the material is going to be about. Because students can be encouraged to predict aloud and to justify their predictions, the DR-TA offers a lively listening and speaking opportunity within a social context.

After students make overall predictions, teachers encourage readers to make predictions about specific portions of text and then to read the appropriate portions to confirm or alter the predictions. How would this approach affect the tone of the classroom and students' attitude toward learning?

The key aspect of the DR-TA is predicting outcomes. Predicting prepares the reader for comprehension but cannot stand alone. Students reflect aloud on predictions before going on to read another segment. If teachers are worried that students will be reticent to make predictions, they can use a simple prediction guide, shown as Activity 4.3. Students predict in the left column and write what actually happened in the right column. This step can show the teacher whether the student is actively predicting and taking part in the process. The teacher guides the DR-TA process, making sure that each student is actively involved in understanding each segment before continuing to the next. The DR-TA is important because it teaches the correct reading process: predicting, reading, and proving that the reading has occurred. Also, the DR-TA uses all three phases of the PAR Lesson Framework.

Figures 4.1 and 4.2 outline the DR-TA steps to apply to fiction and nonfiction material, respectively. Note that step 2 in the fiction DR-TA requests that readers read to find out whether the predictions they made were accurate. Step 4 in the nonfiction DR-TA requests that readers read to find the answers to questions they have generated, and step 5 calls on students to think critically by defending responses. These steps focus on purposeful reading; they are the foundation for a successful DR-TA. A teacher must decide in advance how to segment the material for a DR-TA. The organization of the material is the key factor affecting this segmentation.

ACTIVITY 4.3 Directed Reading–Thinking Activity Prediction Guide

My Prediction	What Really Happened

FIGURE 4.1

DR–TA for Fiction

1. Previewing
   Preread: Title
   Pictures
   Subtitles
   Introduction (if story is long enough)
   Close book and make hypotheses: What do you think will happen?
   Why do you think that? (What gives you the clue?)
2. Verifying
   Read: To find whether predictions were right
3. Reflecting on reading
   Developing comprehension by
   Checking on individual and group hypotheses
   Staying with or redefining hypotheses

The prediction step of the DR-TA builds purpose for reading. When readers are asked what they think might happen next and then read to verify their prediction, they are being encouraged to read purposefully. Readers become very excited about this predictive involvement in their own reading. Often, they share their predictions orally before the individual reading occurs. This activity incorporates listening and speaking. If students are asked to write on the prediction guide what they predict during various

FIGURE 4.2

DR–TA for Nonfiction

1. Previewing
   Study: Title
   Introduction
   Subtitles
   Pictures
   Charts
   Maps
   Graphs
   Summary or conclusion
   End-of-chapter questions
2. Decision making
   What is known after previewing?
   What do we need to learn?
3. Writing
   Writing specific questions students need to learn
4. Reading
   Finding the answers to students' written questions
5. Reflecting on the reading by
   Determining answers to students' questions
   Having students defend their inferences by referring to text
   Finding out what we still need to know

portions of the reading and then review those written predictions at the end of the DR-TA, they use writing to determine purpose within the DR-TA.

Often, students are quite imaginative when formulating predictions about fiction but do not carry this enthusiasm into nonfiction material. The reason for this difference may be that they are not predicting the nonfiction outcome in the same way they do for fiction. The procedure for nonfiction DR-TAs is to survey, question, and then read for answers. The result, without proper preparation, can be similar to just "doing the questions at the end of the chapter." This defeats the purpose of the DR-TA, which is to allow students to create their own purpose in reading. One way we have found to help students write higher level questions is through use of the "higher level questioning bookmark," adapted from one developed by the Maryland State Department of Education and shown as Activity 4.4.

Students keep and use this bookmark with each nonfiction reading to remind them of creative and interesting prediction questions. The bookmark can teach students to see the importance of asking probing questions that tap higher levels of thought. How else might you use this in your teaching? Please visit the Education CourseMate website at **www.cengagebrain.com** for more ideas on teaching higher level thinking.

In Activity 4.5, we present the DR-TA steps in an elementary lesson through the use of a What-I-Know Activity (WIKA, introduced in Chapter 3). In this WIKA, students are given a four-column sheet and are asked to fill it in as they go through the reading. In the first two columns, before reading, students discuss what they already know about the topic after completing the preview and formulate questions to be answered in the reading. In the third column, they use the time during and directly after the reading to answer the questions they generated. They place questions they can't answer in the fourth column called "What I'd Still Like to Know."

One point to note when adhering to the DR-TA process in fiction is that the predictions themselves show whether the students are adequately comprehending the story. The postreading Reflection Phase enables the teacher to have students do higher level thinking in evaluating whether they liked the story. Such evaluation and concomitant critical thinking are needed for students to truly understand and appreciate a story.

The DR-TA teaches higher level thinking. When asking students to predict, one is teaching convergent inference. When asking students to tell why they liked or disliked a story or asking them to do a creative follow-up activity, one is teaching divergent inference.

ACTIVITY 4.4 Higher Level Questioning Bookmark

QUESTION MARK: QUESTIONING FOR QUALITY THINKING

Knowledge: Identification and recall of information
Who, what, when, where, how ______________?
Describe ______________

Comprehension: Organization and selection of facts and ideas
Retell ______________ in your own words. What is the main idea of ______________?

Application: Use of facts, rules, and principles.
How is it an example of ______________?
How is it related to ______________?
Why is it significant ______________?

Analysis: Separation of a whole into component parts
What are the parts or features of ______________?
Classify according to ______________
Outline/diagram/web ______________
How does ______________ compare/contrast with ______________?
What evidence can you list for ______________?

Synthesis: Combination of ideas to form a new whole
What would you predict/infer from ______________?
What ideas can you add to ______________?
How would you create/design a new ______________?
What might happen if you combined ______________ with ______________?
What solutions would you suggest for ______________?

Evaluation: Development of opinions, judgments, or decisions
Do you agree ______________?
What do you think about ______________?
What is the most important ______________?
Prioritize ______________
How would you decide about ______________?
What criteria would you use to assess ______________?

Maryland State Department of Education; adapted by Mark Forget.

Cruse (2007) found that teachers gained a better perspective on their teaching and drew new insights into the reading process when they used DR-TA lessons. The DR-TA is also compatible with the constructivist theory discussed earlier in this chapter. What good readers do as they read is predict and speculate, read to confirm, and stop reading and carry on a mental discussion of what they understand. Students are very active during reading. Through using the prediction process, the material is divided into manageable units. DR-TAs provide a vehicle for figuring out content as the reading occurs; they emphasize reading as a constructive process rather than a measurement of comprehension. The DR-TA uses all the phases of the PAR Lesson Framework. The teacher does not have to worry about whether he or she is preparing and assisting students because this is an integral part of the strategy. The DR-TA is a powerful tool. A teacher who uses the DR-TA method implements all phases of the PAR Lesson Framework.

Guided Reading Procedure

The Guided Reading Procedure (GRP), developed by Manzo in 1975, offers an excellent way to teach students to gather and organize information around main ideas. GRP uses brainstorming to collect information as accurately as possible and then rereading to correct misinformation and fill in conceptual gaps. The second reading is impor-

ACTIVITY 4.5 DR-TA Responses for First-Grade Science Class on Recycling Using a What-I-Know Activity

THIS WAS A LESSON FOR TIGER CUBS (CUB SCOUTS) ON RECYCLING

What I Already Know	What I Want to Know	What I Know Now	What I'd Still Like to Know
Some things have to be thrown away, and some things can be recycled.	How come some kinds of paper can be recycled but not every kind?	Paper that has wax on it, such as boxes for frozen foods, can't be recycled because of the wax.	
Different things can be recycled, such as glass and cans.		Most shiny paper can't be recycled because of wax.	
Some paper can be recycled, and some can't.		Pizza boxes can't be recycled because they are greasy. Probably other greasy things can't be recycled as well.	
There's a special container for recycling.	What happens to the stuff when it gets there?	Paper can be wet down and squished (squooshed?) into pulp to make new paper.	
A different truck, not the garbage truck, picks up recycling.			
	What do the little numbers on things mean?	People have to sort out our recycling.	
		The numbers tell us what kind of material the thing is made of. Different places take different numbered things for recycling.	
	Who decides what can be recycled?		Who decides what can be recycled?
	Where does the recycling truck take our stuff?		Where does the recycling truck take our stuff?
	What happens to glass and cans that we put in recycling?		What happens to glass and cans that we put in recycling?

tant because it heightens motivation—students read to prove that their statements are correct or disprove fellow students' statements. Students' purpose and focus intensify during this second reading segment. According to researchers Colwell and associates (1986), GRP is a very effective teacher-directed technique. It can be used to help students become more independent in their thinking and studying. Following are the steps teachers use to apply the guided reading procedure:

1. Prepare the students for the lesson by clarifying key concepts about the reading; assess students' background knowledge. The teacher may ask students to explain vocabulary terms or make predictions concerning concepts inherent to the reading.
2. Assign a selection of appropriate length and ask students to remember all they can about the reading. Manzo (1975) gives these general guidelines for passage

length: primary students—90 words, 3 minutes; elementary students—500 words, 5 minutes; middle school students—900 words, 7 minutes; high school students—2,000 words, 10 minutes.

3. After the students have completed the reading assignment, have them close the book and relate everything they know about the material they just read. Then list statements for the entire class to see without editing. Whenever possible, assign two students to act as class recorders so you can focus on monitoring and guiding the class discussion.
4. Direct students to look for inconsistencies and misinformation, first through discussion and then through a second reading of the material. Work with students after the second reading to change all statements to make them true before proceeding to the creation of categories.
5. Create major categories for the passage. If reading a narrative, help students organize and categorize concepts into a loose outline. For nonfiction, students can put information into two, three, or four categories and title each category. Then place gathered statements under the newly created categories.
6. To strengthen short-term recall, test students on the reading.

The main differences between the GRP and the DR-TA is that in the GRP, there are no initial student predictions of outcomes; also, unlike the DR-TA, the GRP reading is timed, and there is a second reading of the passage.

Activity 4.6 lists students' facts and concepts while taking part in a guided reading procedure on welding metallurgy. Students write statements they decide reflect the content and then check those statements during a second reading. Last, they organize the statements. In this manner, students create their own categories of learning as an aid to comprehension.

ACTIVITY 4.6 High School Welding Metallurgy

Part 1: Statements from students after first reading.

1. Chemical properties have a big influence on welding.
2. Heat is not a big factor in welding.
3. In hypoeutectoid mixtures, it is not necessary to use much steel.
4. All metals at some time form crystals.
5. The strength of a weld is most affected by its physical properties.
6. It is important to weld high carbon steels in a different manner than that of low carbon steels.
7. Oxygen must be prevented from contaminating the molten metal.
8. Steel is made of both carbon and iron.
9. There are generally three types of crystalline patterns.
10. These patterns are called space lattices.

Part 2: After students read a second time and reconsider statements, they group the facts listed in Part 1 under one of the three categories below.

Material Properties	Metal Structure	Carbon in Steel

Reciprocal Teaching

Palincsar and Brown (1986) describe a strategy to promote independent learning from a text. In this strategy, called **reciprocal teaching,** students and teachers establish a dialogue and work together in comprehending text. At the heart of reciprocal teaching are four shared goals: prediction, summarization, questioning, and clarification. First, the teacher assigns a paragraph. Then the teacher summarizes the paragraph and asks students several questions about it. The teacher then clarifies any misconceptions or difficult concepts. Finally, the students predict in writing what will be discussed in the next paragraph or segment. When the next cycle begins, students (listeners) reverse roles and become the modelers.

Studies (Alfassi, Weiss, & Lifshitz, 2009; Halberstam, 2009; Sporer, Brunstein, & Kieschke, 2009) have shown that reciprocal teaching provides assistance to students as they read and significantly improves achievement in both regular classrooms and with students with disabilities. This strategy uses small segments of reading; thus, struggling readers are not overwhelmed by too much reading. It is a highly structured method that incorporates all the language arts—listening, writing, reading, and speaking.

According to Palincsar and Brown (1986), this technique succeeds with small and large groups, in peer tutoring, in science instruction, and in teaching listening comprehension.

Reciprocal teaching has been successfully adapted and used with English language learners (Klingner & Vaughn, 1996). Explicit explanations of language needed for each role (predictor, summarizer, questioner, and clarifier) are provided as roles are demonstrated. Cue cards having language prompts are used for practicing each role and as students work in small groups (Harper & de Jong, 2004). In this way, linguistic skills are scaffolded as reading skills and critical thinking are developed.

Assisting Students in Learning Text Structure

Steven King (2002), in his book *On Writing*, says that the basic unit of writing is the paragraph. It is certainly true that after children learn the basics of reading, most print language they encounter will be in paragraph form. Research evidence suggests that the **structure of text**—how paragraphs are arranged and ordered—can affect the reading comprehension of students (Goldman & Rakestraw, 2000). Evidence also suggests that students who are taught text structure will use this knowledge to improve their writing and reading comprehension (Williams et al, 2009). The five most prevalent organizational formations of text are sequential or chronological order, analysis, cause and effect, comparison and contrast, and analogy or example. In chronological order, a logical order or sequence is given. In analysis, an important idea is investigated by studying the parts of the idea to the whole. In cause and effect, an event is given as the effect and theories are presented as causes of the event. In comparison and contrast, a writer seeks to highlight similarities and differences between facts, events, or abstract concepts. Sometimes a writer uses a specifically given example to explain a topic or concept.

Often, more than one structure is apparent in a single section of text. A writer may analyze means of a comparison and contrast. A writer may show cause and effect accompanied by example. Different structures may dominate at different grade levels and in different subjects. Table 4.1 gives examples of the text structures of some content area subjects.

The study and identification of organizational structure in written material, as well as student and teacher verbal interaction and reaction to text structure, are called **discourse analysis.** Gee (1996) has noted that students use discourses such as networking, talking, and interacting to learn about the world. Chinn, Anderson, & Waggoner (2001) include in discourse analysis such behaviors as teacher and student turn taking in discussions, questions, decision-making authority, and control of the topic of discussion. Waggoner, Chinn, Yi, and Anderson (1995) recommend the use of a technique called **collaborative reasoning,** which was found to be better than recitations

TABLE 4.1 Some Organizational Structures Used Frequently in Content Area Textbooks

Science	Math	Social Studies	English	Health
Sequence	Sequence	Cause and effect	Cause and effect	Compare and contrast
Cause and effect	Analysis	Example	Compare and contrast	Cause and effect
Compare and contrast	Example	Analysis	Example	
			Sequence or chronological	

The collaborative reasoning strategy has been effective in teaching critical reading and thinking. Comprehension is improved through this form of strategic instruction.

in improving student engagement and in teaching higher level thinking. Collaborative reasoning is an approach for discussion in any content area that is intended to stimulate critical thinking. After reading a selection, the teacher poses a central question that is worded so students take a position for or against the question. Students discuss the question and must defend the position they take. In this manner, students collaboratively construct arguments through a complex network of reasoning and through shared evidence (Chinn & Anderson, 1998). After prompting the discussion with the central question, the teacher acts only as a moderator and mostly stays out of the discussion. Students are encouraged to weigh evidence offered and decide whether to maintain or change their original positions.

Strategic instruction shows readers how to identify text structure (Garner & Gillingham, 1987). Overall comprehension of the text is enhanced for the readers. One simple activity to raise awareness of organization is to have students peruse the table of contents of a textbook and ask, "How did the author organize this writing? What overall structure of organization do you see in the table of contents?" Also, a teacher may simply ask students to identify the text structure used in a chapter, a section, or even a paragraph. Teachers can devise activities to assist readers in identifying structures, as we explain in the next section. When readers learn to recognize text structure and the relationships between large and small ideas and concepts, they take a major step toward independence in reading.

Strategies for Comprehending Text Structure

When the teacher uses activities to boost understanding of text structure, reading to learn is much easier (Kirkpatrick & Klein, 2009). Activities help students and create an interesting learning environment. Here we present some of our favorites.

MYSTERY CLUE GAME

The group mystery clue game is designed to help readers understand sequence. It works well when it is important for students to understand a sequence of events. The idea for this activity comes from *Turn-ons* (Smuin, 1978); we have adapted it to fit content materials.

1. To construct a mystery clue game, the teacher first studies the sequence of events in the material and writes clear, specific clue cards for each event. More than one card may be made for each clue.
2. The teacher divides the class into small groups and gives each group member at least one clue card. Each group can have one complete set of cards,

but each group member is responsible for his or her own cards within that set.

3. No student may show a card to another member of the group, but students can read cards aloud or paraphrase so that all group members know what is on each card. In this way, students who are poor readers will still be encouraged to try to read and to participate.
4. Each group of students must use the clues the teacher gives them to solve the mystery. For example, they must find the murderer, solve the equation, or find the chemical formula. There is usually a time limit.
5. A group scribe reports the group's solution to the whole class.
6. Students are instructed to read the material to find out which group came closest to solving the mystery.

This cooperative activity promotes oral language as well as reading, and it works well in most content areas. For instance, science teachers can write clues about doing an experiment, mathematics teachers can write clues for deriving a formula, and social studies teachers can write clues to sequencing historical events. The goal of the activity is for students to approximate the sequence of events before reading and then read with the purpose of checking their predictions. It is not necessary for students to memorize specific details. As they read, they will recall the clues they were given and construct meaning.

Activity 4.7 is a mystery clue game for a French lesson to help students master the Paris Metro. Students in small groups have to read (translate) the 10 clue cards (without referring to their textbooks) and put the cards in the correct chronological order. In doing so, students learn the logical steps in taking the Paris Metro and grasp the relationships from the Metro essay, the grammar, and the vocabulary presented in the French textbook.

Please visit the Education CourseMate website at **www.cengagebrain.com** for a link to the Great Cities Universities video of Kenya Brown teaching a mystery clue game: Select Secondary Modules/ Module Four/Video.

PATTERN GUIDES

Pattern guides (Herber, 1978) are most useful in helping students recognize a predominant structure such as cause and effect or compare and contrast. To construct them, the teacher locates the pattern, chooses the major ideas to be stressed, and designs the pattern-oriented guide.

Pattern guides can help students see causal relationships. Students need to learn to distinguish cause and effect when reading text materials, especially in social studies, science, and vocational education. Simply asking students to search for causes is often unsuccessful; students tend to neglect—or worse, misunderstand and misuse—this pattern without the teacher's intervention, support, and patience. Moreover, finding causal relationships is difficult because the cause of an event or situation may not be known or may not be traceable. Even so, students should endeavor to distinguish cause and effect for practice in the thinking it affords. Activity 4.8 provides an example of a cause-and-effect guide for middle and high school English.

Teachers can also encourage students to make comparison–contrast maps such as the one shown as Activity 4.9. These graphic organizers or concept maps stress similarities and differences, in this case comparing brown recluse spiders with black widow spiders. Teachers may help students by constructing some of the map to get them started. Or teachers can talk students through the map and in this way build the map with the students. Such maps provide excellent ways to teach patterns of organization inherent in print material.

ACTIVITY 4.7 Mystery Clue Game for A French Lesson

Luc et Jérome veulent aller au Louvre pour apprendre quelque chose pour leur cours d'art.

A la bouche du métro ils regardent le plan et ils comprennent qu'il faut prendre une correspondance.

Ils prennent la direction Porte de Clignancourt et ils prennent une autre correspondance aux Halles.

Bon! Ils sont là!

Après le musée, ils font des achats.

Ils n'ont pas de voiture. C'est trop loin—ils ne peuvent pas aller à pied ou prendre leurs vélos.

Le taxi est trop cher, ainsi ils veulent prendre le métro.

Ils vont au métro—c'est la station Maubert-Mutualité.

Ils achètent deux tickets.

D'abord, ils prennent la direction Boulogne–Pont de St Cloud, et ils changent à Odéon. Ils prennent la direction Pont de Neuilly. Ils descendent au Louvre.

Ils entrent dans le Louvre où ils voient la Joconde (Mona Lisa) et la Vénus de Milo.

ENGLISH TRANSLATION IN CHRONOLOGICAL ORDER

1. Luke and Jeremy want to go to the Louvre to learn something for their art class.
2. They don't have a car. It is too far—they can't walk or take their bikes. A taxi costs too much, so they want to take the Metro.
3. At the Metro entrance, they look at the map, and they understand that they will have to transfer to another line on the Metro.
4. They go into the Metro station "Maubert-Mutualité." They buy two tickets.
5. First, they take the "Boulogne–Pont de Saint Cloud" direction, and they change at "Odéon."
6. They take the "Porte de Clignancourt" direction, and they make another change at "Les Halles."
7. They take the "Pont de Neuilly" direction. They get off at the "Louvre."
8. Good! They are there.
9. They enter the Louvre, where they see the *Mona Lisa* and the *Venus de Milo*.
10. After the museum, they do some shopping.

Adapted from an activity by Laura Clevinger.

ACTIVITY 4.8 Cause-and-Effect Study Guide Middle and High School

Someone's Hiding on Alcatraz Island

by Eve Bunting

Match the causes with the effects by putting the letter for the cause in the appropriately numbered blank.

Effects

_______ 1. Danny decided to leave the island early.

_______ 2. Alcatraz was not used as a prison after 1963.

_______ 3. The lady on crutches got tired and decided to go back to the boat.

_______ 4. The Outlaws have targeted Danny.

_______ 5. The Outlaws are a dangerous gang.

_______ 6. The Outlaws come to Alcatraz Island to find Danny.

Causes

a. Danny turns in the mugger, not knowing his brother was an Outlaw.

b. A gang member mugs an old lady, and Danny witnesses it.

c. Danny rescued her.

d. Officials were afraid prisoners would dig their way out.

e. Danny knows he will have to be clever to survive.

f. Danny can't leave because the gang stalks him on the island.

ACTIVITY 4.9 Similarities and Differences Map: Brown Recluse and Black Widow Spiders Elementary Science

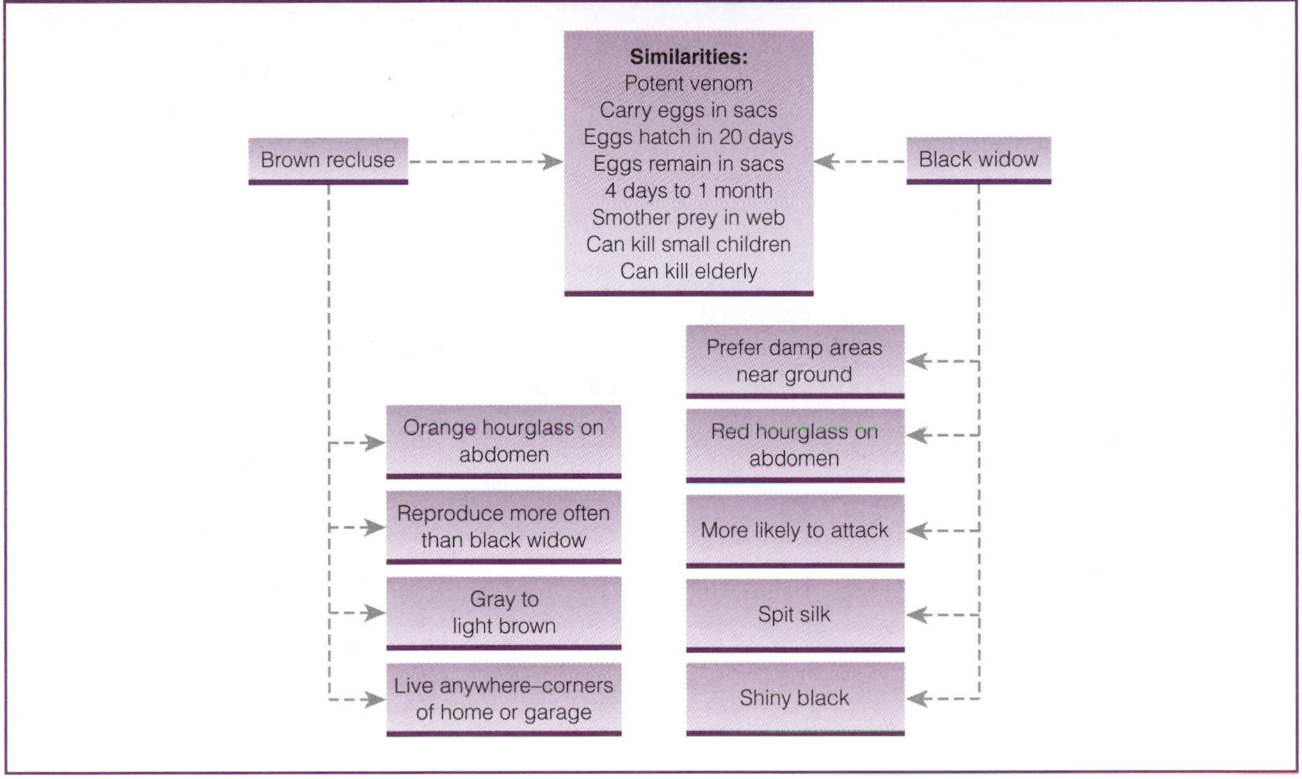

3+ LEVEL STUDY GUIDES

An excellent tool to teach comprehension is the three-level study guide developed by Herber (1978). The guide is an effort to connect and integrate three distinct levels of comprehension through the use of a series of statements designed for student reaction. The guide aids students in discerning the interconnectedness of literal, inferential, and applied learning.

Here are the steps in making the guide:

1. Begin with making level 2 of the guide (interpretive level). Five or six statements are ideal. At this level the teacher asks, "What are the main ideas and concepts I want to teach?" List them in statements that will be certain to elicit the interest of the students. Teachers can put "The author means . . ." in front of each statement to ensure that the statements truly belong in the interpretive level.
2. Go back and use the facts that support the interpretations you wrote in step 1. Teachers can put "The author says . . ." in front of each statement to ensure that the statements truly belong in the factual level. Then add "distracters"—statements that are untrue. When finished, you should have five or six statements at this level.

Add a fourth level to the 3+ level study guide to teach original Internet research on the topic. When students read a passage and react to the three-level guide, they often become interested in the topic. With this heightened interest, it is a natural progression for them to conduct research on the topic. An example of a 3+ level guide is given in Activity 4.10 for a high school English class on the poem "The Road Not Taken," by Robert Frost.

ACTIVITY 4.10 High School English 3+ Level Study Guide

ON "THE ROAD NOT TAKEN," BY ROBERT FROST

Instructions: After reading the poem, check those statements with which you agree. Be prepared to discuss why you chose the statements you did and to refer to the poem to defend your answers.

I. Check the statements of fact in the poem.

_______ **1.** The narrator had come to a fork in the road.

_______ **2.** Only one of the roads was well used when the narrator arrived at the fork.

_______ **3.** The horse did not understand why they were stopping.

_______ **4.** Both roads had the same amount of use by others in the past.

_______ **5.** The poem took place in summer.

II. Check the statements that are possible interpretations of the poem.

_______ **1.** One can always go back and start over in life.

_______ **2.** A person may always wonder whether choices made were the best choices.

_______ **3.** The narrator is pleased by the choices he has made in life.

_______ **4.** What appears simple is often complex.

_______ **5.** Knowing oneself is a lifetime endeavor.

III. Check statements that show how this poem has application to our own lives.

_______ **1.** Life is a journey with no clear destination.

_______ **2.** Hindsight is always 20/20.

_______ **3.** Like a poem, life should begin in delight and end in wisdom.

_______ **4.** Following the crowd may be easy in the short term, but in the long run, this may prove foolhardy.

IV. Determine which of the following statements are true:

_______ **1.** Frost graduated from Harvard University.

_______ **2.** Frost taught at the high school level for six years.

_______ **3.** Frost was an English professor at Dartmouth College for 22 years.

Follow-up Questions

1. Frost went to England early in his life. Why was this trip so important in his development as a writer and poet?

2. Was Frost ever accorded any accolades or awards in his lifetime?

Please visit the Education CourseMate website at **www.cengagebrain.com** for a link to the source of statements in Activity 4.10, Section IV.

3. As a final step, the teacher can ask, "What universal truths are depicted in this reading?" General statements of application are listed in the third level, the applied level of the guide. Teachers can put "We can use . . ." in front of each statement to ensure that the statements truly belong in the application level.
4. Finally, add student directions to the guide.

ORGANIZATIONAL (JOT) CHARTS

Jot charts organize text information by showing comparisons and contrasts. Students complete a matrix as a way to see how ideas are alike and different. Jot charts are relatively simple to construct and can be used at any grade level and in any content area. The teacher usually sets up the matrix and encourages students to fill it in as they read. In this way, students understand the relationships and build meaning as they read.

When completed, jot charts become a good study aid. When groups of students fill in jot charts, the social aspects of learning are also included in the activity. We present an example of a jot chart for middle school mathematics as Activity 4.11 on mathematical formulas.

ACTIVITY 4.11 Jot Chart: Formulas

	Shape	Picture	Perimeter/Surface area	Area/ Volume
2-dimensional	Circle	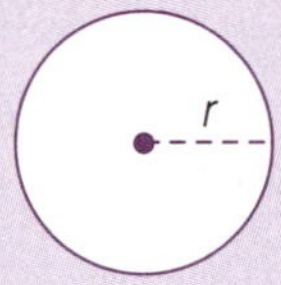	$2\pi r$	πr^2
	Triangle	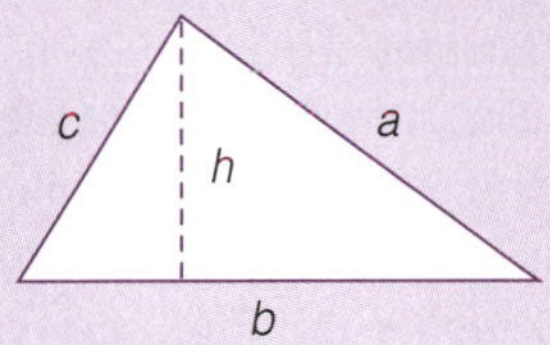	$a + b + c$	$^1/_2\ bh$
	Square		$4x$	x^2
	Rectangle		$2l + 2w$	lw
3-dimensional			Surface area	Volume
	Cone	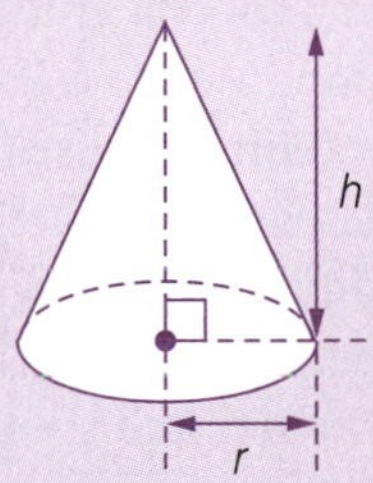	$\pi rh + \pi r^2$	$^1/_3\ \pi r^2 h$
	Rectangular box	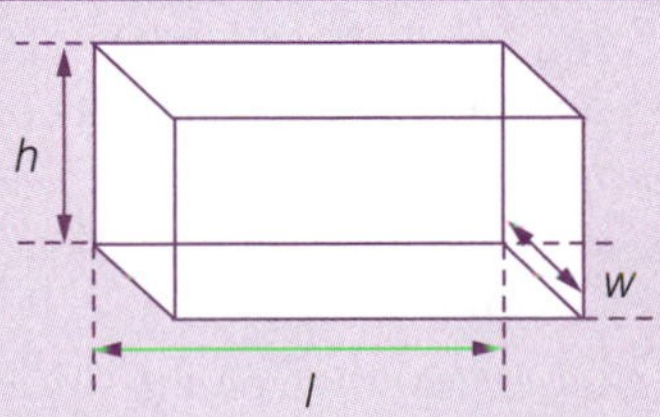	$2(lw) +$ $2(lh) +$ $2(hw) =$ surface area	lwh

Developed by Serena Marshall.

Improving Comprehension through Questions and Questioning

Many researchers believe that dialogue between teachers and students should be the most important medium for teaching and learning (Hillocks, 2002; Langer, 2001). The best dialogue may come in the form of teacher–student questions. Classroom questioning strategies and questioning instruction can help with memory for what was read, can improve students' information-finding abilities, and can lead to more in-depth processing of text (McKeown & Beck, 2003). Parker and Hurry (2007) found that even though teachers used questioning, they did not explain to students the importance of questions and did not encourage students to generate their own questions.

Studies show that when asking questions of students, teachers give longer response time to higher achievers than to lower achieving students. What effect could such a practice have in the classroom?

When questioning works, it works well. Studies show that the most effective teachers encourage higher level thinking through questioning techniques (Taylor, Pressley, & Pearson, 2002; Zucker, et al, 2010). Questions can help teachers know whether students understand text and can guide readers to consider many aspects of material. Question-generated discussions help create meaning for readers (Alvermann, O'Brien, & Dillon, 1990; Barton, 1995). Questions are excellent probes.

Sternberg (1994) argues that the ability to ask good questions and to know how to answer them is the most essential part of intelligence. Well-considered questions are essential to guide students' thinking and reasoning abilities (Marashio, 1995). Often, however, questioning does not work well because teachers fall into the common trap of writing questions that focus on literal comprehension. Research (Zucker et al, 2010) shows that teachers are asking inferential questions more than literal questions. This is a good sign. Getting little practice in answering higher level questions leaves students ill equipped to think critically. Elementary students are trapped into expecting only literal questions; secondary students have the experience of mostly answering recall questions. Research shows, however, that when instructional strategies are altered so that the focus is on inferences, critical thinking, and main ideas, students respond with improved recall and greater understanding (Hansen, 1981; Hansen & Pearson, 1983; Raphael, 1984). Cooter, Joseph, and Flynt (1986) were able to show that third and fourth graders who were asked no literal questions in a five-month period performed significantly better than a control group on inferential comprehension and just as well on literal comprehension. Menke and Pressley (1994) encourage teachers and their students to use *why* questions because their use greatly increases factual memory.

Another trap that teachers sometimes fall into is misjudging the difficulty of the questions they are asking or failing to match questions to students' abilities. Generally, questions are simplest when students must recognize and locate answers in a text rather than close their books and try to recall the same information. Easy questions also include those asked during or shortly after reading, questions that have only one or two parts, oral questions rather than written ones, and those that allow students to choose an answer from among several alternatives. Some questions should be asked in the simplest manner but others in more challenging ways. Teachers need to consider the difficulty of their questions and their students' abilities to answer them.

A final trap that often snares teachers is focusing more on the questions asked and the responses they expect than on the students' actual responses. Too often, teachers expect one response and do not consider an alternative. As Dillon (1983) remarks, we should "stress the nature of questions rather than their frequency and pace, and the type of student response rather than the type of teacher question" (p. 8). Students' answers tell a lot about their understanding of the topic. We need to listen for answers that let us know how well we are assisting the development of comprehension.

Student-Generated Questions

When students are encouraged to generate their own questions, they develop higher level understanding (Bintz & Williams, 2005; Meyer, 2010). D. L. Van Blerkom and colleagues (2006) found that students who read and generated questions comprehended authentic text better than those who read and took notes or read and highlighted. Ciardello (1998) argues that the process of asking questions helps students to focus on and learn content, as well as develop cognitive strategies that will help them understand new and challenging material. Ciardello describes a technique called TeachQuest in which the teacher guides students through a series of steps to identify and classify divergent-thinking questions. The goal is for students to generate their own divergent-thinking questions.

Crapse (1995) reports that "Through the experience of honest questioning, I have observed students celebrating their own insights and solutions to problems posed" (p. 390). Students can also develop their own questions using the "higher level questioning bookmark" discussed earlier in this chapter and shown in Activity 4.4. How would you create divergent-thinking questions as a model for your students?

Questioning Strategies

THE QUESTION–ANSWER RELATIONSHIP

Raphael (2005) has studied and applied a questioning technique called **question–answer relationship (QAR)**. This has been found to be a practical way to teach students how to formulate questions at different levels of cognition (Mesmer & Hutchins, 2002; Raphael & Au, 2005). Kinneburgh and Shaw (2009) found that instructing students in how to use QARs with a science text increased students' reading comprehension. QAR is a four-level taxonomy: (1) right there, (2) think and search, (3) the author and you, and (4) on your own. The best way to introduce QAR is with a visual aid showing the QAR relationship. Figure 4.3 shows one teacher's illustrated introduction to QAR. After introducing QAR, the teacher uses a short passage to demonstrate how QAR is applied. To model the use of QAR, the teacher provides, labels, and answers at least one question at each QAR level. The teacher then moves gradually to having students answer questions and identifying the QAR for themselves. At various times throughout the school year, the teacher should refer to QAR. Activity 4.12 lists QAR questions and answers for an early elementary social studies lesson on the ecosystem and the environment.

Because QAR is a straightforward procedure that is easily implemented, quickly beneficial to students, and useful at any grade and in any content area, we encourage content teachers to use it in their instruction. QAR has been proven to increase students' comprehension more than several other questioning strategies (Jenkins & Lawler, 1990). QAR fosters listening, speaking, and reading, and if students write their own questions, it also offers opportunities for writing. Raphael and Au (2005) recommend QAR as being especially helpful in schools with diverse populations. They maintain that it helps students with poor reading skills while at the same time teaching higher level thinking skills.

Teachers view QARs as a way to organize reading instruction on comprehension and comprehension strategy learning. Why might this be? How could you incorporate it to address a bilingual student or to offer an interesting writing prompt?

GUIDE-O-RAMAS AND MARGINAL GLOSSES

A guide-o-rama (Cunningham & Shablak, 1975) alerts the reader to notice certain information in a reading passage. The teacher creates directions for these passages and encourages students to use the directions as they read. For instance, if the teacher sees the word *perverse* used in an unusual way, he might write: "On page 13, second

FIGURE 4.3

Introduction to QAR

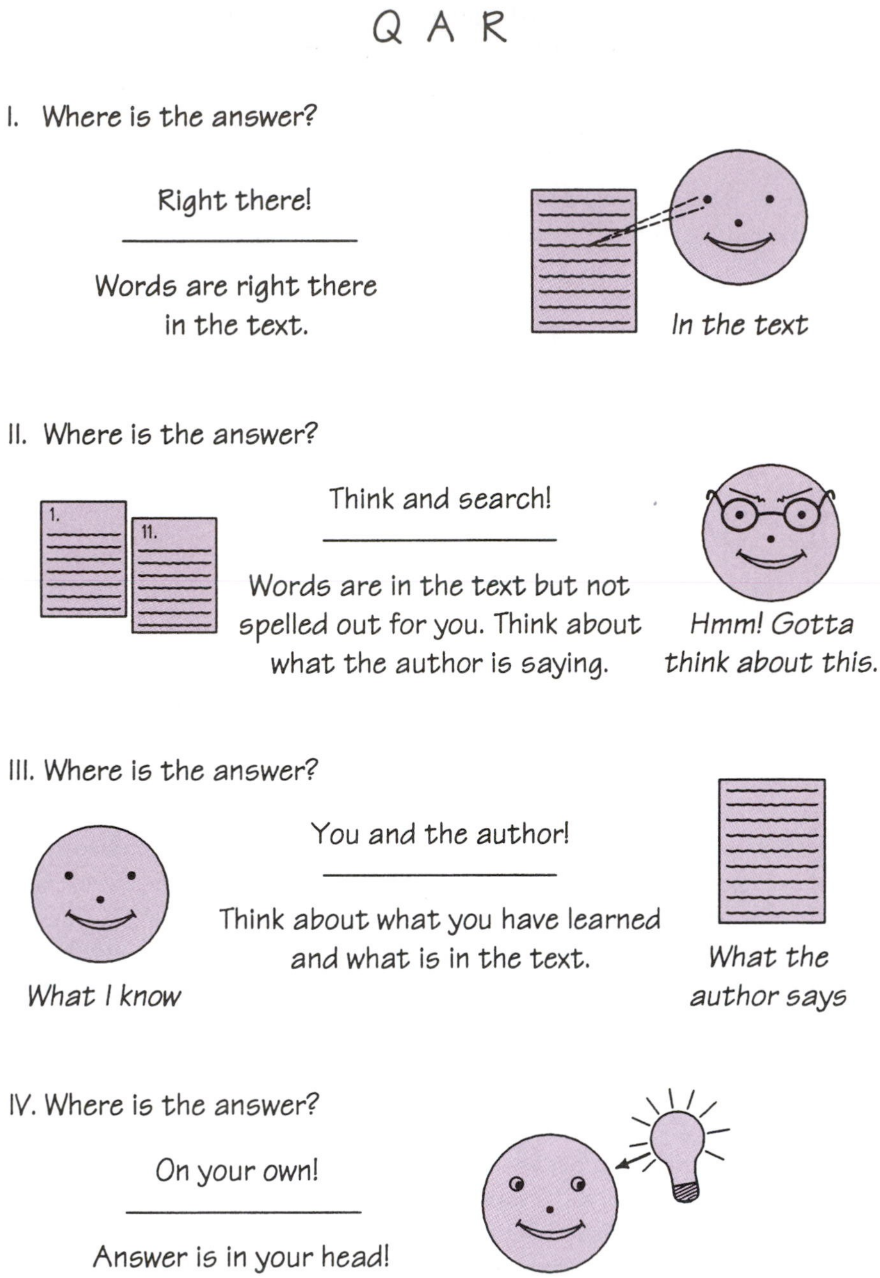

paragraph, third line, the word *perverse* is used a little differently from what you'd expect. Pay attention to the meaning." A teacher provides several directions such as this for readers to refer to as they read conventionally or electronically.

Marginal glosses (Singer & Donlan, 1985) are often found in content textbooks. Glosses are comments that authors make to their readers as asides, sometimes in the margin of the page. Because the comments are intended to help readers understand the passage, they assist readers in developing comprehension. Teachers can write their own marginal glosses, conventionally or in electronic format, if texts do not include them or if additional ones are needed. They are easily inserted into electronic text or can be printed to match the conventional text. Also, a guide-o-rama can be designed as a gloss.

Readers have a panoramic view of the reading—hence the name *guide-o-rama*. We hope you notice that we are using such glosses (notes to the reader) throughout our textbook!

ACTIVITY 4.12 Question–Answer Relationship for Early Elementary Study of People of the Ecosystem

Question 1: Right there!

What is found in abundance in the shallow water along the riverbanks of the Mattaponi River?

Answer

Many species of waterfowl such as the Great White Heron and the American Bald Eagle.

Question 2: Think and search!

Why does the author think the American Bald Eagle is important to the tribe?

Answer

The American Bald Eagle is a symbol for America. Tribal members believe the eagle carries messages for the tribe to God.

Question 3: You and the author!

How have the Mattaponi Indians helped to maintain a healthy river system?

Answer

The tribe has helped to preserve the marshes. They respect and preserve the waterfowl, and they maintain a reservation hatchery to introduce fish into the ecosystem and thus maintain balance in nature

Question 4: On your own!

The passage describes muskrats in detail. They live on the banks of the Mattaponi River. Can you name another animal similar to the muskrat, but larger, that also has webbed feet and lives along the streams and rivers?

Answer

The students can research other river animals and discover that the animal in question is the beaver.

QAR constructed after reading from a passage in *Powhatans: Past and Present*, edited by Angela L. Daniel ("Silver Star").

Here are some suggestions for making marginal glosses:

1. Fold a sheet of paper next to the margin of a text.
2. Identify the book page at the top of the master copy and line up numbers beside the teacher remarks and notes.
3. Write the marginal notes on the sheet of paper.
4. Duplicate and give students copies of these notes to match to text pages for use as students read.

Marginal glosses and guide-o-ramas are like having the teacher go home with the students and look over their shoulders as they read, guiding their reading attention. These strategies can help students use features of texts as well as help teachers facilitate comprehension by questioning. We suggest that the teacher select either very difficult portions of text to gloss, or beginning portions, when the reading may be tougher. Making guide-o-ramas or glosses for use throughout a text would be time consuming. However, it is worth the time to provide assistance in developing comprehension of challenging reading. Activity 4.13 shows a gloss for high school earth science.

Strategy Repertoire

Striving readers often do not realize that reading calls upon them to know what to do at a given point with the text they are reading (Gee, 1996). Consider the difficulties that Mark, our struggling reader, has with not knowing strategies to use in his reading. Even if a student like Mark knows he should take action, he is hampered by his limited repertoire of strategies to comprehend material. Proficient readers use such strategies

ACTIVITY 4.13 Marginal Gloss for High School Earth Science

How can I use this information?	Place on top edge at p.____ in binding.
	Complete this side first.
1. Vocabulary word ________________ Definition in your own words: (Use the picture for help, if needed.)	Part I: What do I know?
2. What do you think *mass* is?	Topic heading:
	Vocabulary word:
3. Why do you think ice floats in water?	Using words, give the density formula:
4. Why do you think the average Earth density is greater than the average density of the Earth's crust?	Recall: Volume = length × width × height 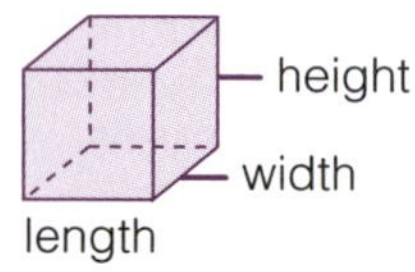 Average Earth density (include units):
5. Given a rock with a mass of 550g and a density of 2.75 g/cm^3, calculate the volume of the rock.	Average density of Earth's crust (include units):
	Recall from Chapter 1 two (2) materials found in the Earth's core: 1.
	2.
6. Bring a rock to class tomorrow—no larger than an egg!	
7. What brand-name product has used density of the product in its advertising?	

Developed by Nancy S. Smith.

deliberately and flexibly, adapting them to fit a variety of reading situations. When used for resolving comprehension difficulties, these are often referred to as **fix-up strategies**. When struggling readers encounter difficulty with text, their response may be to "shut down," stop, or give up because the text is too difficult. Proficient readers, in contrast, are aware of specific strategies—such as visual imagery, self-questioning, and rereading—that can be used to fix up or resolve the comprehension difficulty (Activity 4.14).

CHALLENGE BOX

Mark, Struggling Reader

Mark faces many challenges in comprehending text in his content classes. Although he likes science and math and puts forth more effort in those classes, he reads slowly and laboriously. He compensates for poor reading skills by listening carefully, relying on visuals and the Internet for basic information. He has begun to "zone out" in classes as the expectations get higher.

What techniques can a teacher use in the classroom to assist a struggling student like Mark learn at his potential?

First, to keep Mark from losing interest and daydreaming so much, teachers need to make certain they keep him active doing activities he enjoys. To keep him tuned in, a teacher might create a classroom calendar of assignments to help him maintain good organizational skills. Online programs that feature virtual field trips can be a catalyst to spark Mark's interest in learning. Please visit the Education CourseMate website at **www.cengagebrain.com;** teachers can find online resources to help a struggling student like Mark, including a free teacher-constructed and -maintained calendar for classroom assignments and a website that creates virtual field trips for students.

How can the teacher assist Mark in improving his skills?

The DR-TA and the WIKA will help Mark manage his reading. As he improves his ability to make predictions, his comprehension will improve. Mark and the teacher (or another student) can work together at Reciprocal Reading so he can better comprehend text and feel less discouraged. Breaking the reading into small component parts can make it easier for Mark to comprehend reading material. The GRP will point him in the right direction, and three-level study guides will divide the comprehension process into three distinct areas for him.

Listening activities, such as podcasts, will encourage Mark to use his listening ability and word knowledge. He then can transcribe his thoughts in a writing activity, critiquing the reading and telling what he remembers from the reading.

ACTIVITY 4.14 Fix-Up Strategies: Elementary Mathematics

VISUALIZATION

Visualize a tree house that you and your friends would like to build.

How would you measure it? In yards? In feet? In inches?

How big would it be? How would you measure it?

Name some objects that are 1 inch long.

Name some objects that are 1 foot long.

Think about some objects that are one yard long.

Think about something that is one mile long.

SELF-QUESTIONING

What are the standard units of length?

Why do I need to know them?

Why do we measure in fractions?

What if we couldn't measure in fractions?

REREADING

I will read and study the problem again, focusing on determining what "congruent" means as it applies to triangles. Read the problem again to get the overall idea.

The fix-up list in Activity 4.14 is especially effective with struggling readers, but teachers will also find numerous other activities that can be effective in each chapter of this text. Can you think of other activities that you have learned from reading this textbook?

Research suggests that whereas proficient readers spontaneously use fix-up strategies, struggling readers do not—even though they can and do use fix-up strategies under teacher direction (Gambrell & Bales, 1986). Kletzein (1991) investigated students' self-reports of strategies when reading different kinds of materials. He found little difference in the strategies used by good and poor readers, but good readers were more flexible and persistent. Poor readers did not seem to know when to use appropriate strategies. In fact, the most important goal of reading instruction for struggling readers may be to develop the ability to use strategies to enhance comprehension (Winograd & Paris, 1988). Embedding strategy instruction within content is an efficient way to help struggling readers in content classrooms (Hinchman et al, 2004). To do so, teachers must have a repertoire from which to draw.

ONE-MINUTE SUMMARY

This chapter has described activities to be used in the Assistance Phase of the PAR Lesson Framework. To understand text, students must construct meaning by using their prior knowledge when encountering new information. To facilitate comprehension, students need to be taught to be active seekers of knowledge and to use constructivist principles of learning. We discuss constructivist theory and how it relates to better student achievement in the classroom. Mapping techniques are described that help enhance constructivist learning.

In this chapter, we introduce strategies that enable students to better read segments of text, such as the DR-TA, the GRP, and reciprocal teaching. We explain the importance of students' understanding of text structure and present three strategies—pattern guides, three-level study guides, and organizational (jot) charts—that help students discover and relate to text structure. We also discuss questioning strategies as important for assisting comprehension in reading. We explain teacher questioning and student-generated questions, as well as describing. Other questioning strategies, such as guide-o-ramas and marginal glosses, can help students to better understand reading materials. Finally, we suggest fix-up strategies to help students build a reading strategy repertoire.

END-OF-CHAPTER ACTIVITIES

Assisting Comprehension

1. Discuss some good ideas for activities to teach comprehension to your students.
2. Should teachers stress constructivism and constructivist learning strategies in their classrooms? Why or why not?
3. What questioning strategies can you now use more effectively?

Reflecting on Your Reading

4. Your content organization (e.g., National Council of Teachers of Mathematics, National Council of Teachers of English, National Council for the Social Studies, National Science Teachers Association, International Reading Association) has most likely developed a set of standards that identify the performance criteria relevant to classroom teachers. Standards usually delineate elements of foundational knowledge that a classroom teacher should possess for teaching reading comprehension. Locate and become familiar with what the organization recommends. Many strategies and activities described in the chapter can be used to assist students in comprehension. Which do you think will be most useful in the classroom? Explain your response. Also, do you think any of the strategies can be used for computer-based instruction?

CHAPTER 5

Learning through Reflection

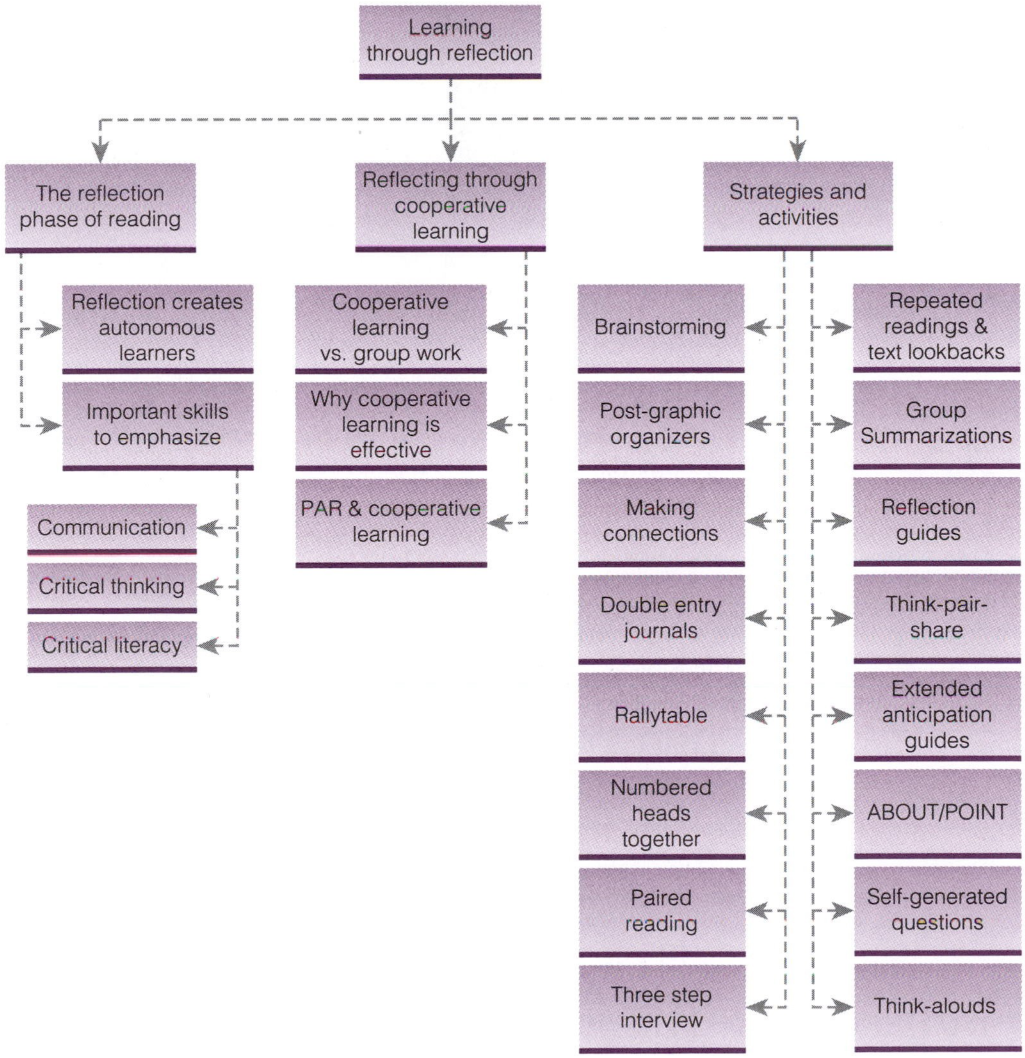

> Nothing is particularly hard if you divide it into small jobs.
>
> **HENRY FORD**

VOICES FROM THE CLASSROOM

A father tried to console his 7-year-old son after the boy came home from school distraught and crying. The boy blurted out that the teacher would never let him finish any work or project he started. "I know I could do a good job if she would just let me finish. But we always have to get to a new thing in a hurry," said the boy. This is the lament of many students, who are always feeling the pressure of finishing an activity under tight, even repressive, time constraints. Teachers also feel time constraints. They wonder how they can find the time to teach strategically and still teach content when state-mandated tests seem to constrain their instruction. The "hurry up and learn" concept of teaching doesn't take into account that learning takes time. To truly learn something, students need time to dissect, analyze, and reflect on new material.

PREPARING TO READ

1. Why is it important to reflect on learning after we finish reading a passage?
2. What is your definition of critical thinking? As you read and find out about critical thinking in this chapter, compare your definition of the construct with that of the authors.
3. Following is a list of terms used in this chapter. Some may be familiar to you in a general context, but in this chapter, they may be used in unfamiliar ways. Rate your knowledge by placing a plus sign (+) before those you are sure that you know, a check mark (✓) before those you have some knowledge about, and a zero (0) before those you don't know. Be ready to locate them in the chapter and pay special attention to their meanings.

_______ reflective thinking
_______ autonomous learners
_______ comprehension monitoring
_______ critical literacy
_______ brainstorming
_______ post-graphic organizers
_______ text lookbacks
_______ extended anticipation guides
_______ student-generated questions
_______ think-alouds

OBJECTIVES

As you read this chapter, focus your attention on the following objectives. You will:

1. Explain why it is important to help students become autonomous learners.
2. Describe why good communication skills are an asset in reading
3. Explain why it is important for students to monitor their own comprehension as they read.
4. Identify critical thinking skills that are important in reflection.
5. Evaluate a number of strategies that help foster reflective thinking and decide which will work best in your classroom.
6. Explain the factors that distinguish cooperative learning from working in groups.
7. Select and use some cooperative learning techniques to teach reading in the content areas.

The Reflection Phase of Reading

Can the first grader in the Voices from the Classroom realize his potential when he rushes through activity after activity in his daily work? To learn, students need to be in a relaxed atmosphere where they have time to reflect on the assignment. Purmensky (2006) has said that true reflection turns experience into learning. The third step in the PAR (preparation, assistance, and reflection) Lesson Framework is reflection, which takes place after reading has been completed. Many agree that postreading reflective strategies are crucial for comprehension beyond the literal level (Christensen, 2002; Massey & Heafner, 2004). But reflective thinking, for most students, does not develop naturally without teacher intervention to actively promote this skill in students (Tompkins, 2002).

Whereas the Preparation Phase of lessons helps motivate students and the Assistance Phase helps build comprehension, the Reflection Phase helps clarify thinking and focus understanding. In this phase, students learn better how to retain information. Full understanding cannot be achieved until students reflect in a meaningful way about their learning. Although teachers may guide students by providing instructional support, the students' role is crucial at this stage.

A number of positive changes occur when students are directed through the Reflection Phase. First, students think more in depth about what they have learned and have yet to learn about the lesson. Much has been written about the necessity of such **reflective thinking** in the reading process. John Dewey is considered to be the first educator who introduced the term *reflective thought* into the literature (Shermis, 1999). He considered reflective thinking to be careful thought persisting toward an objective of coming closer to the truth (Dewey, 1933). A second positive change of reflective thinking is that it helps students retain material they have read. The more students reflect, the longer they will remember information, and the more likely they will be to use the knowledge in further learning. A third positive aspect is that reflection provides a demonstration of one's learning through a system of informal evaluation. Teachers can use the Reflection Phase to assess what students did and did not comprehend. In this chapter, we discuss all these aspects of reflection.

Time → Reflective thought → Retention of material → Further learning

When teachers take the necessary time to guide students in reflective thought, students will learn more and assume more responsibility for their learning. How might you rethink in-class and out-of-class time to ensure that this important step takes place?

Reflection Creates Autonomous Learners

Researchers Baker, Luo, and Hung (2007) have noted that simply providing students with literature does not guarantee their interest, comprehension, or retention. These authors maintain that students do not become reflective without carefully organized instruction. Students need to practice reading behaviors that take the form of discussion, debate, lab application, writing, reorganizing, rehearsal, and other similar activities that let students process ideas and contemplate complex interactions concerning schemata and knowledge (Forget, 2004). After reading, students should think about new information, process ideas, and make sense of what they have read. This continual practice in reflection helps students become **autonomous learners** (self-regulated learners). Such students are not restricted in their learning because they know how to read for meaning, study, take appropriate notes, and organize information. All teachers should teach to make all students autonomous learners, but this does not always occur.

A major goal of education is to create autonomous learners, as discussed in principle 11, Chapter 1.

An example of the importance of autonomous learning can be found in Stephen King's *The Body* (1982). This story illustrates how cooperative study and will power can produce reflective readers who think critically and persevere in the face of intimidation. Gordon and Chris decide, after their experience finding a body near the train tracks and facing off with a gang of older boys, that they will escape their lonely and dangerous conditions by studying hard and achieving academic success. Chris refuses to stay in the "shop courses" even though the guidance counselor advises he do so. They study together for hours at a time, depending only on each other and their own fortitude. Both graduate near the top of their class and go on to college.

In this chapter, we teach important ways to help students become autonomous learners. Keep a list of the techniques as you read. Which ones seem most important?

Students can best become autonomous learners by monitoring their own comprehension as they read. **Comprehension monitoring**—keeping mental track of one's own learning—can take place when students demonstrate their comprehension through pausing, analyzing, recalling, and retelling of information in their own words. Good readers are adept at comprehension monitoring, but poor readers seem to lose track of their reading and to have no particular strategies for comprehending (Kolic-Vehovec, & Bajanski, 2007). Researchers (Van der Schoot et al, 2009) have noted that students who are good at monitoring comprehension resolve any word ambiguity much better than poor comprehenders. Research (Winne & Perry, 2000; Zimmerman & Schunk, 2001) has reiterated the critical importance of comprehension monitoring to effective study, and some research (Wiley, Griffin, & Thiede, 2005) suggests that the kinds of expository texts used may be a critical factor in comprehension monitoring. Kolic-Vehovec and Bajsanski (2006) found that comprehension monitoring strategies were effective in grades five through eight. Strategies that will aid students in monitoring their own comprehension are presented later in this chapter.

Important Skills to Emphasize in the Reflection Phase of Reading

COMMUNICATION SKILLS

Students must learn to communicate effectively if they are going to think and reflect after they read. More than any other phase of learning, reflective learning depends on informative communication. Researchers (Duffy & Hoffman, 1999; Villaune, 2000) have asserted that the key to successful teaching of communicative arts is the training of independent and spirited teachers who understand that their job is to use methods and materials in ways that accommodate student needs. Such teachers realize that just as students read to learn, they listen, speak, and write to learn—and that students use all of the communicative arts to make sense of the world. As Summers (2006) states, listening and speaking reflectively about reading reinforces that learning in a social context is imperative.

Oppenheimer (2003) illustrated the importance of learning as communication by describing a team of American researchers who journeyed to Japan in the late 1990s to investigate why Japanese children ranked near the top of all countries in standardized achievement tests at that time. What they found surprised them. Instead of classes steeped in memorization and rote learning, the researchers found classes in which students were engaged in "active exploration, argument, analysis, and reflection" (p. 360). Furthermore, they found that Japanese students didn't rush from topic to topic (as in the United States) but worked in depth on discrete problems, examining some questions for weeks at a time. Oppenheimer noted how much the classroom environment in Japan was at odds with Americans' notions of what happens in Japanese schools. And it appears that Japanese schools, with the highest achieving students in the world, were conducting classes that are compatible with the guidelines called for by the National Council of Teachers of English.

In an Australian study, Gillies and Boyle (2006) found that teachers need training to use communication skills in promoting student thinking and to scaffold student learning. They trained teachers specifically to challenge student perspectives, ask more cognitive questions that allowed students to monitor their own comprehension, and provide scaffolds for student learning. They found that students modeled many types of discourse used by the teachers in the study, and the group communication skills that were used contributed to the students' sense of security in learning.

Teachers must realize that the key element of the Reflection Phase of the PAR Lesson Framework is the type of communication described in this section. All of the communicative arts are present in some form in good communication, as stated in principle 2 in chapter 1.

CRITICAL THINKING

Critical thinking as an important dimension of learning is emphasized in textbooks and in the research literature. Research has shown the importance of critical thinking in changing students' misconceptions in a learning environment (Kowalski & Taylor, 2004). Educators have emphasized, however, that such critical thinking takes time and a sustained mental effort—a fact that is sometimes lost on those in charge of setting curriculum in our rushed, test-driven classroom environments (Jaimes, 2005). Most educators tend to agree about the benefits of teaching critical thinking. Law and Kaufhold (2009) found that students who engaged in regular activities that promote the development of critical thinking skills performed higher on tasks of higher order thinking. But even though there is agreement that some elements of critical thinking need to be taught across the curriculum, the concept itself remains so vague that educators are not certain about its meaning, about the best ways for classroom teachers to teach it, or even about whether it can be taught. After examining a textbook that contained practice examples in teaching critical thinking, a teacher once remarked, "It was a good book, but it really didn't contain much critical thinking." This comment underscores the subjective nature of the concept.

Two views of critical thinking are prevalent in the reading literature: narrow mastery versus all-encompassing + inductive.

The literature generally supports two interpretations of critical thinking. One is a narrow definition of critical thinking as the mastery and use of certain skills necessary for the assessment of statements. These skills take the same form as logic or deduction and may include judging the acceptability of authority statements, judging contradictory statements, and judging whether a conclusion follows necessarily from its premises (Beyer, 1983). A more encompassing definition includes these skills as well as inductive types of skills, such as hypothesis testing, proposition generation, and creative argument (Sternberg & Baron, 1985). Clark (1999) offers a definition that is more in line with this latter view of the construct. Clark says that such reflective and critical thinking "is thinking for an extended period by linking recent experiences to earlier ones in order to promote a more complex and interrelated mental schema" (p.1). We agree with this latter, more inclusive definition and emphasize critical thinking in this broader sense throughout this text.

As we have said, everyone agrees that one of the most important ways to emphasize reflection in reading is to ask students to think critically about what they read. Hynd (1999) encourages teachers to teach critical thinking by exposing middle and high school students to historical documents and multiple texts. This is now a much easier undertaking because many primary source documents are available on the Internet. In this way, students can read different or even opposing views and begin to think like historians. As students experience the process that historians use in researching and writing about history, they may be able to apply this thinking process to other subjects as well. Students have to consider the sources of information and when they were published to determine how to use them as resources. Authentic materials also demonstrate to students that discourse takes many forms and formats, depending on the time and situation. Thus, Hynd's research provides early support for use of many forms of discourse (see principles 4 and 5 of Chapter 1), as advocated by Crystal (2003) and Moje (2008). Thinking like a researcher enables students to think critically. By reinforcing the reading experience through critical thinking, teachers can challenge students to think about content material in new ways.

Too often, however, classroom teachers, especially at the elementary level, shy away from teaching critical thinking. One reason for this is that there is no clear definition of the construct. Another reason is that teachers mistakenly believe that *critical* means to find fault and emphasize the negative. Also, critical thinking is a difficult construct to measure through teacher-made tests, and critical thinking skills are not mandated for minimum competence in many subjects. Teachers are not well-trained in the skill of test construction in general, much less in testing for critical thinking. In addition, some teachers have the notion that at-risk learners are not capable of critical thinking. Finally, teachers often say that they do not have adequate time to plan instruction in critical thinking and lack appropriate materials and books to teach it properly. Despite these perceived obstacles, teaching critical thinking should not be neglected at any grade level. This important ability leads to greater success in academic subjects and will be useful to students after graduation. In short, critical thinking is a skill that will aid students in all facets of life.

The topic of evaluating critical thinking on test is addressed in Chapter 12.

We can clarify our view of critical thinking by studying what happens when this skill is put to use. Two of the most outward manifestations of critical thinking are problem solving and decision making. Research (Montague & Applegate, 2000) attests to the importance of problem-solving skills in content area subjects. Critical thinking leads to problem solving, which in turn leads to effective decision making. Students who use critical thinking are more effective thinkers; both their creative and contemplative abilities improve. We offer the following steps that teachers can use in helping students engage in problem solving:

1. **Gather ideas and information.** Students brainstorm to generate enough information to begin defining the problem. They can play a "reading detective" game or do research to gather information from all possible sources.
2. **Define the problem.** Students recognize the need to resolve a situation that has no apparent solution. They should be asked to clarify the nature of the task and completely describe the situation in writing.
3. **Form tentative conclusions.** This is a creative phase in which students suggest possible solutions from available data.
4. **Test conclusions.** Students discuss in groups which conclusions work best as solutions to the problem. Poor choices are eliminated until workable solutions remain. Students may also establish criteria for evaluating outcomes.
5. **Make a decision.** Students select one of the remaining solutions and give reasons for their choice.

Teachers can then construct study guides, such as the one in Activity 5.1, that provide cognitive activities to assist students in using these problem-solving steps. It is especially important to start these types of activities in early elementary classrooms because unsophisticated learners seldom let their minds journey across stories to think about possible similarities.

Group decision making can also be taught through the use of a group-and-label technique. The teacher begins by writing the topic on the board and telling the students that they will be reviewing important terminology. Then students volunteer any terms they can think of that fall under the topic heading. The teacher may ask leading questions or even eliminate this step by preparing a list in advance (on the board, on a worksheet, in a word processing file, on BlackBoard). Students reorganize the list into smaller lists of items that have something in common and give each of these sublists a label. Students may work individually or in small groups to reorganize and label the words. Activity 5.2 shows how grouping and labeling might work for a second grade social studies unit on communities.

ACTIVITY 5.1 Critical Thinking Guide: Problem Solving

- A problem arises.
- Why do we need to solve the problem?

Ways to Solve Problem	Reasons for Choosing Method
Method 1	Positive outcomes Negative outcomes
Method 2	Positive outcomes Negative outcomes
Method 3	Positive outcomes Negative outcomes
Best way to solve problem	Reasons for choosing to solve problem in this manner

Adapted from a decision-making model by J. McTighe and F. T. Lyman, Jr. (1988), Cueing thinking in the classroom: The promise of theory-embedded tools. *Educational Leadership* 45(7), 18–24.

ACTIVITY 5.2 Group-and-Label Technique: Second Grade Social Studies

The students will be asked to read *Berkeley: Life on the James River Plantations in Colonial Days. A Book to Read and Color* by Mary Bell and Elva Mapp.

From a jumbled list of words taken from the text, the students will be asked to divide the words into five groups, according to their similarities. The teacher will project these groups of words on the board. The students will label the groups. These labels will be projected by the teacher as titles for the groups of words.

The five groups:

Leaders	Plantations	Household Activities	Occupations	Colonial Activities

Words to be grouped:

Thanksgiving	Berkeley	making brick
cutting lumber	Plantation school	stableyard pets
Westover	John Carter	Shirley
Carter's Grove	John Rolfe	Mount Vernon
tobacco growing	shipyard	seine netting
blacksmith	tannery	grist mill
Colonel Benjamin Harrison	warming pan	fox hunting
steeple chasing	John Hancock	Cornwallis
Anne Carter	William Henry Harrison	Taps
General McClellan	Benedict Arnold	Elizabeth Harrison

Duke and Pearson (2002) list the attributes of good readers, and almost all of them involve the types of critical thinking that we describe. These researchers say that good readers:

- Are active readers.
- Have clear, established goals in mind.
- Constantly evaluate whether the reading is meeting their goals.
- Look over the text to determine text structure.
- Frequently make predictions.
- Read selectively, making decisions about what to read carefully, what to read quickly, what not to read, and what to reread.
- Construct meaning as they read.
- Revise and question meanings while reading.
- Determine meanings of unfamiliar words and concepts as they read.
- Draw from and use prior knowledge before and during reading.
- Monitor their understanding of the text.
- React emotionally and intellectually to text by evaluating the value and quality of the reading.
- Read disparate texts differently.
- Understand settings and characters in a narrative.
- Summarize what they have read in expository text.
- Process text even after they complete a reading.
- See reading as a consuming, continuous, and complex activity.
- Get satisfaction from reading and view it as productive.

Which one of the attributes of good readers do you consider the most essential in your content area?

Please visit the Education CourseMate website at **www.cengagebrain.com** and view several websites that list online books for teaching critical thinking in the broad sense discussed here.

All of these reading behaviors include critical thinking in its broader sense. Remember that students think critically when they monitor comprehension, determine text structure, read selectively, revise and construct the meanings of words and concepts, use prior knowledge to evaluate and analyze text, concern themselves with the value of what is being read, summarize text, and in general regard reading as a satisfying and complex activity.

Students in kindergarten through twelfth grade are seldom taught to reflect and solve problems except in published programs on thinking or in "critical thinking" sections of basal reading materials. But teachers do not need published "thinking" programs, and they cannot depend on textbooks to teach critical thinking skills. They must integrate their own critical thinking lessons with those of the textbooks they are using. For example, to teach critical thinking, teachers might present study guides that emphasize critical thinking and then have small groups of students practice a problem-solving exercise. In this manner, students can be taught critical thinking in a concrete context of carefully guided thinking. Studies indicate that, especially in early adolescence, formal reasoning and thinking can best be taught through teachers' use of guided prompts such as graphic overviews and study guides, which help students structure their thinking (Arlin, 1984). More recent studies (Dixon, Cassady, Cross, & Williams, 2005) show that the use of computers can improve critical thinking, especially for boys. Through guided prompts and use of computers (see Chapter 9 on study skills and Chapter 10 on technology), teachers are scheduling time to model intelligent and thoughtful behavior in the classroom by emphasizing critical thinking during class sessions.

Please visit the Education CourseMate website at **www.cengagebrain.com** to find links to virtual field trips for many content subjects.

TECH APP

Virtual Field Trips to Vicariously Experience Important Content

What is Done? Students discover in a personal way something they cannot experience in person, such as the cultural and political atmosphere of ancient Rome, by visiting a website that takes them on a virtual trip through Rome. Students can then understand the impact of an issue or event. For instance, after "visiting" ancient Rome, they understand how this majestic and grand civilization eventually crumbled both internally and externally.

Time Commitment: Approximately a 2-hour assignment

Why Do It? Honing critical thinking skills is an important activity in any content area subject.

Values: Critical thinking skills enhanced; cooperative learning in groups discussing what they have seen and heard; computer skills enhanced; financially expedient!

CRITICAL LITERACY

Another related skill is **critical literacy**. Critical literacy deals with analytical reading, or reading between and beyond the lines. The number of resources and writings now available at "the touch of a finger" stirs a sense of urgency to encourage students to become active readers rather than passive recipients of randomly discovered text (Devoogd, 2006; Knickerbocker & Rycik, 2006; Molden, 2007). Meyer (2010) believes that it is essential for teachers to address issues of social justice and equity in their social studies classrooms. She asserts that the curriculum should center on five themes for developing a democratic classroom: teaching multiple perspectives, finding authentic voice, studying social barriers, finding one's identity, and recognizing a call to service. Marshall and Klein (2009) call for teachers and prospective teachers to be trained in the effective use of primary sources, how to lead classroom role-play, and how to lead and set up student civic debates. Meller, Richardson, and Hatch (2009) call for teachers to be trained in using read-alouds in first grade classrooms.

Chapter 6 discusses read-alouds at greater length.

McLaughlin and Devoogd (2004) believe that students taught critical literacy learn a greater breadth of understanding when they are taught to consider and question the authors' purposes and stances for writing. The idea is not to encourage skepticism but to give students tools for investigating and becoming informed, rather than gullible, readers. When students critically examine a text, they think about the author's motivation for writing it; consider how the reader is being persuaded to understand ideas through emphasis, de-emphasis, facts, and opinions; and recognize that the author has one perspective but that other perspectives might exist. McLaughlin and Devoogd offer several strategies for making connections and detecting bias. *Juxtapositioning* is one such strategy, in which learners compare and contrast two texts having opposing perspectives. In so doing, viewpoints can be clarified, thus helping the reader come to a deeper and greater understanding for forming his or her own perspective.

Think again about principles 4 and 5 in Chapter 1; apply these principles to what you are reading in this chapter. How can newspapers, magazines, advertisements, and the Internet be used to teach critical literacy?

Reflecting through Cooperative Learning

Studies show that cooperative learning benefits students by getting them more actively involved (Slavin, 1995; Yang, Yeh, & Wong, 2010). Also, researchers have found that students not only feel more engaged but also perceive that their learning task is more important when working in a small group rather than during large-group instruction (Peterson & Miller, 2004). When students are ready to take ownership of their learning, it helps to consider other classmates' critical reflection on a topic, which cooperative learning provides. Cooperative learning has been found to be both an effective instructional method (Johnson, Johnson, & Stanne, 2000; Madrid, Canas, & Ortega-Medina, 2007; Rohrbeck, Ginsburg-Block, Fantuzzo, & Miller, 2003; Roser & Keehn, 2002; Slavin, 1996) and a successful way to enhance social and academic development among children (Boaler, 2006; Deen, Bailey, & Parker, 2001; Johnson & Johnson, 2003; Slavin, 2000). The end product of cooperative learning is collaboration and joint ownership.

Slavin (1991) reviewed 60 studies that contrasted the achievement outcomes of cooperative learning and traditional methods in elementary and secondary schools. His conclusions were as follows:

1. Cooperative learning improves student achievement. The groups must have two important features: group goals and individual accountability.
2. When students of different racial or ethnic backgrounds work together toward a common goal, they gain liking and respect for one another. Cooperative learning improves social acceptance of mainstreamed students by their classmates and increases friendships among students in general.
3. Other outcomes include gains in self-esteem, time on task, attendance, and ability to work effectively with others.

Cooperative learning is often a strategy used at the Reflection Phase of PAR because application of content and critical thinking occur.

In contrast, some studies show that collaboration doesn't always happen in cooperative groups (Blumenfeld, Marx, Soloway, & Krajcik, 1997). Success of the groups depends, in large measure, on the cohesiveness of students in the group, individual students' willingness to complete the task, and whether the task is considered worthwhile (Leonard & McElroy, 2000). Students with special needs may not benefit if certain aspects important to their participation are not monitored (McMaster & Fuchs, 2002, 2005). If well-meaning or impatient group members complete tasks for their less able peers, they remove the opportunity for those children to make contributions. Care must be taken to assign tasks with appropriate levels of difficulty so all learners can provide input important to meeting group goals. Each student must be held accountable for participating and learning.

Students can work cooperatively on a computer to perform tasks asked for in WebQuests. These are discussed in Chapter 10. Please visit the Education CourseMate website at **www.cengagebrain.com** to find several sites that offer themes in WebQuests.

Mastropieri and her colleagues (1998) studied the effects of cooperative learning during a seven-week science unit among three classes of fourth graders. Cooperative learning was used in one of the classes, and within that class, there were five learners with special needs. These learners were placed in groups with classmates known to work well with peers having special needs. Students in the cooperative learning class outperformed those in the two comparison classes on posttests, and those with disabilities scored near the average in their own class and above average of the comparison classes.

Cooperative groups can also allow students to develop leadership skills. Teachers need to allow time for homogeneous groupings on specific topics and for specific purposes. Hancock (2004) found that students who work together appear to have a higher regard for school and for the subjects they are studying and are more confident and self-assured. As a result, both motivation and achievement improve.

The value of cooperative grouping for gifted students has been questioned because research suggests that these students benefit more from working in homogeneous groups. See Chapter 11 for further discussion of this topic.

Distinguishing Cooperative Learning from Group Work

Cooperative learning is more than grouping students together to work. It is predicated on the ideas that small groups of students work together to accomplish shared goals and that each group member accepts responsibility for helping fellow group members learn. Teams are formed and ground rules established so students understand the basic principles:

1. **Positive interdependence:** Group success is positively correlated with the success of individuals within the group. Members of the group must understand that they are in the project together and that by taking responsibility for their parts and helping each other, they all gain.
2. **Individual accountability:** Each group member is responsible for his or her role or task and will ultimately have to demonstrate his or her understanding and learning. So although students can work as a team to learn the skills, concepts, or information, the teacher may choose to formally grade only individual assignments.
3. **Equal participation:** Turn allocation or division of labor can be used to structure group tasks so that each contributes and no one receives a "free ride."
4. **Simultaneous interaction:** Tasks are structured so that everyone is working at the same time. This is quite unlike most classroom structures, in which one student at a time may be called on to perform while all the others sit and listen (Kagan, 1994).

Do you think the acronym PIES helps students remember cooperative learning elements?

Another feature that distinguishes cooperative learning from group work is the development and use of interpersonal and social skills that contribute to positive interaction among students. Students learn the skill of working together as they discuss what and how material can best be learned. However, teachers cannot assume that students have the social skills to work productively as a group. Helping students realize and understand appropriate comments, questions, tones, and behaviors that contribute to learning is important. Taking time to explicitly teach and scaffold these skills is well worth the effort. For younger students, this may involve demonstrations and role playing. Having older students decide the ground rules as a class (usually no more than five) and posting them as reminders works well.

Upon completion of a task or project, students can set new team goals for future cooperative work. McKeachie (2002) makes these four points concerning ways to improve what he calls "peer learning":

1. Have students discuss what makes a group effective and why it is valuable to work together as a team.
2. Make sure students know exactly what the task is. To check on this, have students report on the nature of the task and what all the parameters are.
3. Move around the room a great deal to monitor the groups and make certain students are on the right course.
4. Help students develop the skills necessary for effectively working together.

Why Cooperative Learning Is Effective

Weinstein (1987) suggests that cooperative learning strategies are successful in aiding comprehension and retention because they fall into one or more of what she calls "categories of learning strategies"—processes and methods useful in acquiring and retrieving information. Weinstein proposes five categories of learning strategies:

1. **Rehearsal strategies:** The technique discussed in this chapter is think–pair–share.
2. **Elaboration strategies:** Techniques discussed in this chapter include paired reading and three-step interview.
3. **Organizational strategies:** The technique discussed in this chapter is the postgraphic organizer.
4. **Comprehension-monitoring strategies:** Techniques discussed in this chapter include rallytable and numbered heads together.
5. **Affective strategies:** Techniques discussed in this chapter include paired reading and discussion about the positive rewards of learning in groups.

To see an example of cooperative learning through use of the jigsaw activity (explained fully in chapter 6) in an elementary school lesson about the Olympics, view the video on the Education CourseMate website at **www.cengagebrain.com.**

In underscoring the importance of cooperative learning, we wish to reemphasize a point made frequently throughout this book: Learning is difficult in a hurried, pressured classroom environment. Recall the first grader in VOICES who said that the teacher never let him finish assignments. Jeremy Rifkin, in his book *Time Wars* (1987), argues that we appear to be trapped in our own technology. Rifkin maintains that the constant pressure to become more efficient causes Americans to believe that they do not have enough time to get things done. This pressure, which permeates classrooms, is detrimental because all types of classroom effort succeed best in a calm, unhurried atmosphere in which students are free to explore ideas, develop creativity, solve problems, and be thoughtful and reflective.

PAR and Cooperative Learning

Teachers should realize that group process is a multifaceted experience and is not limited to time spent by students working in groups. There are actually three phases of good group process:

Phase I: Individual phase; key concept—commitment

Phase II: Group work; key concept—consensus

Phase III: Teacher-led discussion; key concept—arbitration/mediation

In the individual phase, individual students should commit to something, usually written, to be shared later with the group. In this individual phase of the lesson, the teacher attempts to get a *commitment* from the students. This can be difficult because students today often do not wish to commit to anything; they sometimes prefer not to get involved in classroom activities. However, a sense of involvement is crucial to successful group interaction. Lack of commitment is the reason so much group work degenerates, with students getting away from the subject to be discussed or the problem to be solved. Rarely will commitment be generated by teacher assignment and threat or reward of a grade. Students need to be invested in their learning, and a commitment accomplishes that (Leki, 2001).

The second phase involves the actual work to be done in groups. The key word here is *consensus*. In the group phase, the students should share what they have done individually and arrive at a consensus, whenever possible, on the best possible answer. The teacher provides much assistance in this phase by moving from group to group to help students with areas of difficulty and to make sure groups stay on topic.

In the third phase, involving reflection, the teacher may lead a discussion with the groups—an exercise in *arbitration*. The teacher acts as a judge or a mediator to resolve difficult points of the lesson on which students could not come to consensus. Also, in this phase, groups may give reports to the whole class on their findings.

Teachers often express frustration with the results of group work. One solution is to have students role play different scenarios in which certain members of a group might sabotage the group effort. When students consider for themselves possible obstacles to the success of their group work and possible solutions, they become more productive in groups. Swafford (1995) describes a technique she uses with college students. Groups are given one of three scenarios in which one person in a group is not participating at all, underparticipating, or overparticipating. By discussing these problems and acting out solutions for the rest of the class, everyone experiences the process of commitment, consensus, and arbitration in a friendly atmosphere.

Learning is enhanced when cooperative learning teams are emphasized in content teaching (Abrami, Chambers, d'Apollonia, Farrell, & DeSimone, 1992; Johnson & Johnson, 1987; Meloth & Deering, 1992; Vermette, Harper, & DiMillo, 2004). Australian researchers Gillies and Ashman (1998) trained first and third grade students in formal and informal collaboration techniques during 10 social studies units. These students learned more content while in cooperative teams and thereby improved decision making. The study points to the benefit of teaching young children to learn cooperatively and use decision-making techniques. Roser and Keehn (2002), in a study of student collaboration and inquiry during a social studies unit on the Texas revolution, found that student knowledge increased significantly. Misconceptions decreased, and a positive motivation effect was found as well.

Please visit the Education CourseMate website at **www .cengagebrain.com** to find links to websites that provide additional ideas and example lesson plans. Also, review some of the video clips at CengageBrain to see aspects of cooperative learning in action.

Strategies and Activities for Reflection in Reading

Brainstorming

Group interaction and discussion on a topic to reach consensus or solve a problem, called **brainstorming,** offers an important way for students to use reflective thinking in the content classroom. Erten and Karakas (2007) found that brainstorming helped students perform better on inferential and evaluative comprehension questions. Brainstorming needs to take place with what Lotan (2003) calls "group-worthy" tasks for students to perform. Lotan says such tasks should

- Be open-ended and require complex problem solving.
- Provide students with multiple entry points to the task.
- Provide students with multiple opportunities to show intellectual competence.
- Deal with intellectually important content.
- Require positive interdependence.
- Include clear criteria for the evaluation of the group's product.

FIGURE 5.1

Ready Reading Reference Bookmark

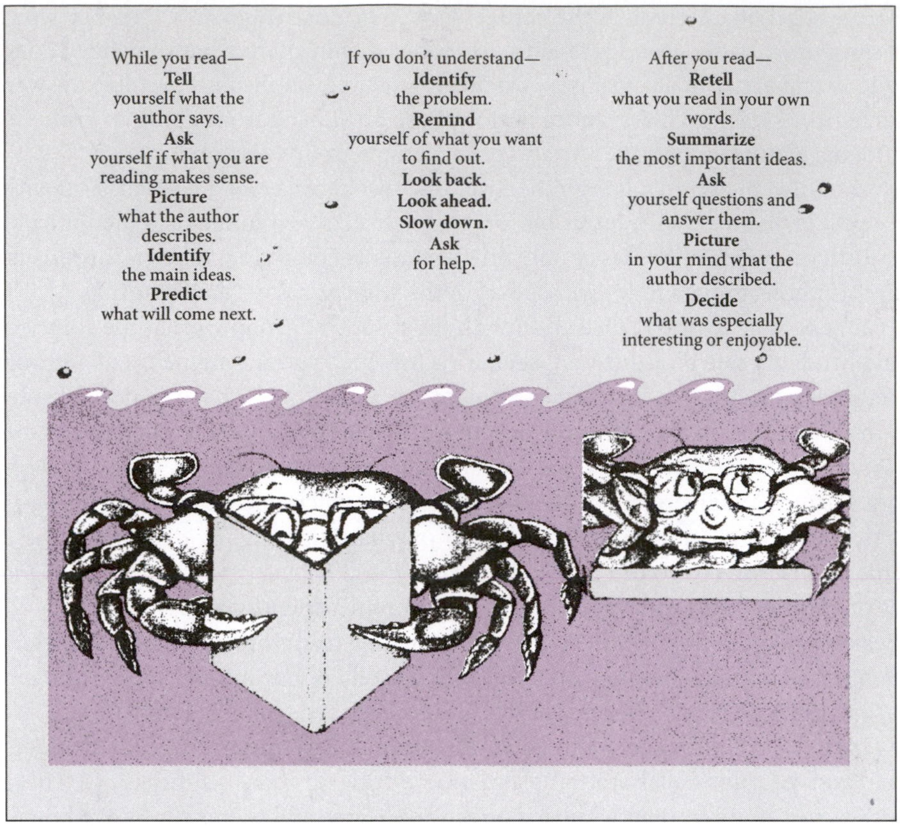

Reprinted with permission from Maryland State Department of Education.

An especially productive brainstorming session is one in which small groups of students list as many possible alternative solutions to a problem as they can. Group captains are chosen to report findings to the entire class. The teacher lists on the chalkboard alternatives that the students deem worthy. Discussion then centers on how to narrow the choices to one or two and why the final choices are the best ones. An important consideration is the size of the brainstorming group. Five-person groups seem to work best (Gillies & Boyle, 2006); however, three- and four-person groups are also effective. The most vocal students tend to dominate groups of six students or more.

The "Ready Reading Reference Bookmark" (Figure 5.1) developed by Kapinus (1986) can be used to get students ready to brainstorm after reading a passage. In the section "After You Read," students can use brainstorming to perform the five thinking operations called for retelling, summarizing, asking, picturing, and deciding. Students also can brainstorm the "While You Read" and "If You Don't Understand" operations at other points in the lesson—before reading, for example, or after reading specific sections.

Post-Graphic Organizers

Students benefit from working cooperatively to construct their own graphic displays to summarize meaning retained from a text reading. These visual images are an easier way for students to show relationships that are often too difficult to visualize mentally. A graphic representation can present a holistic picture of the text reading, creating concrete images of complex ideas and concepts. When students make graphic representations after the reading, these are called **post-graphic organizers**.

ACTIVITY 5.3 Post-Graphic Organizer from an Elementary Science Class

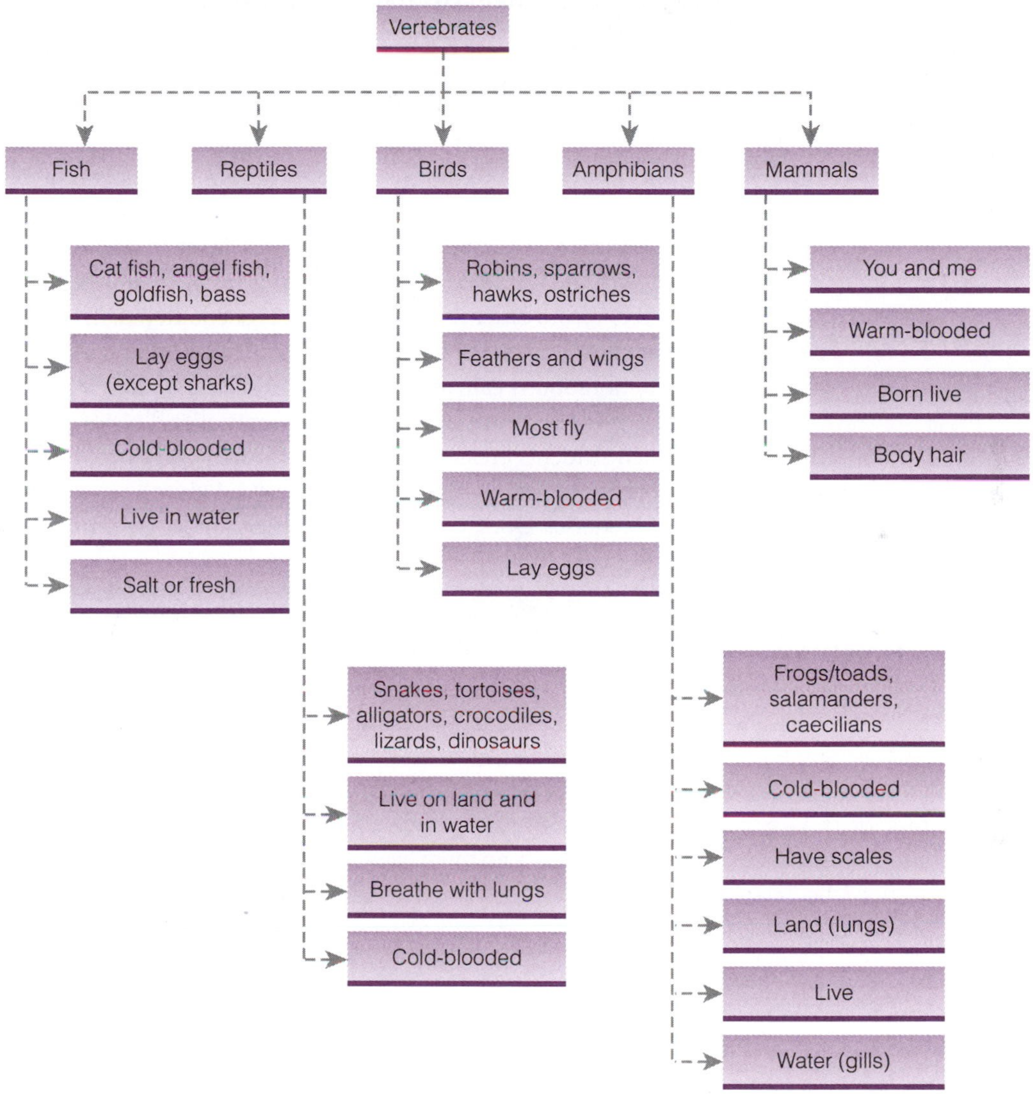

Designing post-graphic organizers represents another reflection activity that students of all ages enjoy.

We recommend the following steps to help students produce their own graphic organizers to create purpose for reading and to help one another construct meaning from the text:

1. Students preview the reading to determine the structure and main ideas.
2. Students work in small groups to decide what form the graphic organizer should take.
3. Students read the text silently, gathering information to be included in the group's graphic representation.

4. Groups meet to discuss the organization of the information each member has gathered. Each group makes a large model to present to the class.
5. Groups present their finished products to the class.

Making Connections

One way for students to reflect on the reading is through the making connections strategy (Harvey and Goudvis, 2000). In this strategy, to gain understanding of text, readers make three types of notations about quotes they encounter. For the first notation, called text-to-self, the readers draw on personal experiences, feelings, and their store of knowledge to connect with the text. Text-to-text notations let the reader tell how the quote is similar to or different from other texts the reader has encountered. In text-to-self, the student can compare plots, characters, various themes, and similar concepts encountered. The third type of notation is called the text-to-world connection. Students write about how the quote from the text is related to current events, world history, or famous people in the news. When students create these three categories, they become more interested in the text and comprehension is enhanced. Activity 5.4 gives an example of connecting with a speech of Frederick Douglass, studied in a high school government class.

ACTIVITY 5.4 Connections Chart

Quote from Text	My Thoughts	Type of Connection
The fact is, ladies and gentlemen, the distance between this platform and the slave plantation, from which I escaped, is considerable—and the difficulties to be overcome in getting from the latter to the former, are by no means slight (p. 526).	I can't even imagine how much suffering and loss Frederick Douglass went through to rise to the great heights he did. What steel resolve he must have had.	Text-to-self
Oppression makes a wise man mad. Your fathers were wise men, and if they did not go mad, they became restive under this treatment. They felt themselves the victims of grievous wrongs, wholly incurable in their colonial capacity. With brave men there is always a remedy for oppression (p. 529).	This reminds me of books and articles I have read about other great African American leaders like Booker T. Washington and Maya Angelou. They were all incredibly strong in their resolve to help their fellow human beings.	Text-to-text
	He was talking about the colonists here and how they were brave to go against England, their mother country. It takes great bravery to right the wrongs of oppression.	Text-to-self
	This speech reminds me of Martin Luther King and how he became a champion of his people and was the leader in the civil rights movement.	Text-to-world

From speech by Frederick Douglass, Rochester, NY, July 5, 1852.
From the text *American Speeches,* edited by Ted Widmer.

Double-Entry Journals

Researchers (Kaplan et al., 2007) have noted that journal writing leads to more reflective writing, especially when the journals are shared over e-mails. The double-entry journal is a writing activity that can be used for students to keep a record of their responses to reading (Blachowicz & Ogle, 2001). Students engaged with text through reading and writing experiences gain better comprehension of text. Similar to making connections (see Activity 5.4), students react to a quote in the text in a thought-provoking way. They reflect on their reading through a reaction piece that captures insights and observations. The double-entry journal promotes in-depth reflection of reading by encouraging learners to go beyond just making connections (L'Allier & Elish-Piper, 2007). Activity 5.5 provides an example of the Double-Entry Journal, with reactions to a text on Indians in the early American West.

Rallytable

For a rallytable (Kagan, 1994), an open-ended question or problem is posed. Students get in pairs, and each pair passes one piece of paper back and forth. Each time the paper is received, the student writes an answer until time is called. Pairs then share and compare answers. Teams can categorize and illustrate their responses using a graphic organizer.

Numbered Heads Together

This activity (Kagan, 1994) is most often used for prior knowledge assessment or review before an exam. When it used for review, it functions as a reflection activity. Students in teams of four count off so that each has a different number. The teacher

ACTIVITY 5.5 Double-Entry Journal for a High School History Class, Based on Ned Blackhawk's Book *Violence Over the Land: Indians and Empires in the Early American West* (2006), Cambridge: Harvard University Press

Quotes	**Thoughts and Reactions**
The narrative of American history, it argues, has failed to gauge the violence that remade much of the continent before U.S. expansion . . . this work suggests that American history is considered a place of comfort, not of pain; a realm of achievement rather than one of indigenous trauma (p. 1).	This quote is disturbing to me. The main idea of this book is stated here. That is, that we gloss over history and see it as a nostalgic voyage into the pristine past instead of the way it really was: many factions of people alternately participating in times of raging conflict and healthy cooperation.
Many American intellectuals who have sojourned in the region have looked askance at these Native peoples, since their wage labor and poverty have often conflicted with others' received knowledge of Indians. As in much of U.S. history, encounters with contemporary Native people tend to disturb others' expectations, and Indians remain among the least understood Americans (p. 272).	The saga of the Indian people continues to this day. They are misunderstood, but also, because of their long suffering, are a people who are not easy to get to know. Many of them—not all—are not talkative with people of other cultures. They are not readily accepting of other cultures, either. The Indian dilemma is a difficult one to grasp and more difficult to solve.

CHALLENGE BOX

Gustavo, English as a Second Language Student

Introduction: Although he struggled early in school, Gustavo is now doing very well academically. He has passed all of his state's standardized tests while in middle school. He is bilingual but cannot read or write in Spanish, so he has been accepted into a summer program that focuses on developing and enhancing the literacy and math skills of English as a second language (ESL) students in both English and Spanish. He hopes to do well and go to college to become a doctor.

How can the school do a better job of helping Gustavo with reflection?

Gustavo seems to be bright. He has overcome, and continues to overcome, much adversity. He is doing well academically and has high aspirations for the future. The school should continue the summer program into the regular academic year, whereby he can improve his literacy and math skills in both English and Spanish. The school should provide counseling to help relieve Gustavo's stress about his fears of deportation and his father's taking him back to Mexico.

How can the school give Gustavo practice at the type of thinking that he will be experiencing in the medical field?

As much as possible, Gustavo needs to be encouraged to take academically challenging courses to prepare him for the medical field. He needs practice in higher level thinking skills used by personnel in the medical field. To that end, he would be helped significantly in improving his critical literacy by practice with critical thinking strategies outlined in this chapter such as double-entry journals, self generated questions, and think-alouds. Double-entry journals would give him practice at self-assessment in learning. Such assessment is similar to the type of diagnostic thinking often used in the medical profession. When he practices self-generated questions, Gustavo is practicing prediction and inference testing that is so crucial in formal thought. Think-alouds probably would help Gustavo the most. Through think-alouds, Gustavo can hone his skills at making hypotheses, linking prior knowledge with information in the text, and making visualizations to help with problem solving.

gives a question or problem and a time limit for reaching a solution. All four students work together to determine an answer and make sure that everyone on their team knows the answer or a series of answers if the question has several parts. The teacher then randomly calls a number from 1 to 4. All students with that number raise their hands, and the teacher calls on one of them. Two variations on this activity can increase participation. First, allowing think time before working together gives struggling students a better chance to arrive at an answer. Another variation is to provide white boards or slates for teams to record answers that can be held up simultaneously by the team members from each team when their numbers are called.

Paired Reading

An activity that works well with middle school and secondary students is paired reading, developed by Larson and Dansereau (1986). Students begin by reading a short assignment and then divide into pairs. One partner is designated a "recaller," and the other is a "listener." The recaller retells the passage from memory; the listener interrupts only to ask for clarification. Then the listener corrects ideas summarized incorrectly and adds important ideas from the text material that the recaller did not mention. During the time the listener is clarifying, the recaller also can add clarification. In this manner, the two students work together to reconstruct as much as possible of what they read. The pair can use drawings, pictures, and diagrams to facilitate understanding of the material. Students alternate the roles of recaller and listener after each reading segment, which may number four or five during one class period. Wood (1987) notes that paired reading succeeds because it is based on research in metacognition, which suggests that without sufficient practice, some students have difficulty monitoring their own comprehension. Paired reading is also based on elaboration strategy, which, according to Weinstein (1987), helps students learn new concepts by drawing on their prior experiences. Because so much recalling, summarizing and clarifying occur with this activity, it is useful for both assistance and reflection.

Three-Step Interview

Another multipurpose activity designed for groups of four but adaptable for other group sizes is the three-step interview (Kagan, 1994). A question or topic is proposed for interviews. In groups of four, members partner for the first step. Partner one interviews partner two. For the second step, partner two interviews partner one. Finally, each of the four team members shares knowledge with his or her group. This activity is useful for exploring prior knowledge, making predictions, or sharing personal connections related to a topic in the Preparation Phase of a lesson. It may also follow a lesson or unit in the Reflection Phase to examine knowledge gained, lesson applications, or remaining questions. Affective as well as cognitive aspects of the objectives being taught can be explored. This activity provides a structure for role-playing when students consider how a character in a story might respond or how positions or viewpoints of historical figures might shape their answers. Or they might consider how different people from various professions can use a particular mathematical formula, procedure, or operation.

Repeated Readings and Text Lookbacks

Research on repeated readings—students in pairs reading and rereading text orally—has shown that such oral reading activities improve oral reading, fluency, and comprehension (Devault & Joseph, 2004; Yurick, Robinson, Cartledge, Lo, & Evans, 2006). We believe that it is just as important for students to repeat reading passages silently to improve reading comprehension. Both oral and silent repeated readings get students to look back over text to gain comprehension—a practice we believe strongly will improve comprehension. Some years ago, Garner and colleagues (1985) discussed the importance of reexamining text—backtracking, or **text lookbacks**—in overcoming memory difficulties. The researchers found evidence that both children and adults fail to use this activity even though recent research (Schisler, Joseph, Konrad & Alber-Morgan, 2010) shows that reinspection of text makes a significant difference in students' ability to comprehend.

Many students believe it is wrong to reread a passage they have read one time. However, meaningful rereading leads very quickly to benefits—for the detection of important information and the opportunity for reflection. What constitutes meaningfulness? How does a reader know if rereading is productive? How does a teacher know whether it's fruitful to encourage or require it for a given passage?

Richardson (2010) suggests several rereading steps to help students make connections, remember, and apply important information. If the instructor decides the material might be challenging but is essential in the course, he or she might read the text to the students as they follow along in their own copies (first reading). Second and third readings could emphasize visuals and word meanings. Then small groups can read smaller sections of text to identify specific information. In this manner, teachers can lead students through a difficult material with instruction and multiple encounters.

Ruth Strang, the great reading educator, once remarked that she was disappointed when she entered a school library and found students reading for long periods without looking up to reflect on what they were reading and not glancing back over material during their study. We maintain that readers should be taught the following: how to use text lookbacks (teachers should lead the class in oral reading lookback activities), when to use text lookbacks (when a question calls for information from the text), and where to use text lookbacks (where skimming or scanning will help one to find the portion of the text that should be read carefully). Next, readers should practice rereading for answers to questions asked after the reading is completed. Lookbacks are necessary when readers realize that they didn't understand all of what they read. Good readers evaluate their reading and decide whether to look back. But poor readers rarely have this skill, so deliberate text lookbacks will give them greatly needed practice in this aspect of critical thinking.

Teachers should use the lookback activity after a reading by working in groups to clarify confusing points. For instance, students in a social studies class can reinspect a chapter about Athens as a democracy to find out why, in the supposedly strong democracy of Athens, there were so many slaves and so few citizens. Students can then write a group summary of what the text says about the positive and negative aspects of Athenian democracy. What types of lookbacks might you do in your content area?

Group Summarizations

When students work in groups to summarize reading assignments, they are practicing a skill that will be beneficial in their daily classroom experiences. Summarizing involves judging the importance of ideas, working to condense what is known, and producing a product orally or in writing. A study by Friend (2001) found that student summaries were improved when students looked for ideas in the text that were repeated a number of times and tried to write summaries by generalizing—that is, keeping the gist of the passage uppermost in their minds. Skilled readers know how to summarize, whereas unskilled readers almost always lack this ability. To learn to write effective summaries, students can work in groups and use the following six rules, suggested by Brown and Day (1983):

1. Delete all unnecessary material.
2. Delete redundancies.
3. Substitute a major term for a list of items.
4. Use a superordinate term for a list of actions.
5. Select topic sentences from ones provided in the text.
6. Construct topic sentences when they are not provided explicitly in the text.

Chapter 8 describes group summarizing, which can be accomplished through the use of the GIST "Generating Interactions between Schemata and Text" (Cunningham, 1982). Students can work in small groups to make group GISTs and can share them with the entire class. The GIST procedure provides an excellent way to teach needed summarization skills.

One way to have students summarize in groups is for group members to develop a concept map (discussed in Chapter 4) based on the ideas they believe to be important in a chapter or a portion of a chapter. Groups can share their mapping exercises on the board, and discussion can center on why groups chose different concepts to map.

Reflection Guides

Teachers can construct a study guide to be used as an aid in reflection. Similar to the anticipation guide (discussed in Chapter 3) that is used before reading in the Preparation Phase, the reflection guide provides students a chance to work in groups, analyze, and make decisions about the reading they just completed. Students are given the guide after reading and use the guide to jump-start discussion on the passage. Activity 5.6 is

ACTIVITY 5.6 Reflection Guide on Pastels for a Middle School Fine Arts Class

After reading the selection, check the statements you believe to be accurate. Then be prepared to get in groups and discuss your choices with others.

_____ **1.** Pastels are sticks of ground pigment mixed with chalk.

_____ **2.** Paints can be mixed on a palette to blend colors, and you can blend pastels the same way.

_____ **3.** Whenever you have small fragments of pastels, you should recycle them instead of throwing them away.

_____ **4.** You can make your own pastels; it's easy to do.

_____ **5.** You can buy pastels in several hundred colors.

_____ **6.** When comparing painting with oils or pastels, there are more similarities than differences between the two.

_____ **7.** Although pastels have been used for thousands of years, one famous modern artist really advanced the medium to the level of complexity it has achieved today.

_____ **8.** With pastels, layers are applied to get a blending effect, and you sometimes paint with your fingers or other tools.

_____ **9.** Some pastels are harder than others, and there is a reason why an artist would choose one over the other.

presented as a reflection guide for a middle school level class in fine arts on the use of pastels in painting.

Think–Pair–Share

Think–Pair–Share (McTighe & Lyman, 1988) is a reading activity that stresses reflective thinking and cooperative learning. The activity starts with a prompt given by the teacher to probe students' thoughts about reading material. In mathematics, it might be a question such as, "How do you find the absolute value of a number?" In science, it might be, "How can we tell if an oxidation number of an atom is positive?" Students are asked to take some time to think about the question and then to write down an answer. Next students form pairs and discuss their answers. During this phase, students help each other to improve their own answers and work to formulate joint answers to these questions. Finally, in the sharing phase, the teacher brings the students together to obtain input from the entire class in discussing the topic. Then all students read to see if the text is helpful in answering the question.

Irvin and colleagues (Irvin, Buehl, & Klemp, 2007) cite this activity as being particularly good for teaching reflective thinking, saying that it allows "time for thought and reaction as well as providing for a fuller, richer, and more thoughtful discussion" (p. 51). This activity is effective because it can be modified to teach other skills like prediction, summarization, visualization, and elaboration. The key to Think–Pair–Share's effectiveness is that students have peers help them decipher tough questions about text. In addition, by transcribing learning into their own words, students use comprehension monitoring in their reflection about the text. Activity 5.7 is an example of a Think–Pair–Share activity in a high school history class on the Holocaust.

ACTIVITY 5.7 Think–Pair–Share in High School History on the Holocaust

Objectives: Students will:

- Evaluate their understanding of the Holocaust and the importance of the event.
- Gain knowledge about World War II, Adolf Hitler's power and position in Germany, and the Holocaust.

Think—Pair—Share will be divided into three parts.

1. **Thinking phase, questions as prompts:** What makes you you? How would you feel if someone blamed you for something you didn't do? Project information about Jewish families. Segue to Hitler, the Nazis, and why the Germans were mad at the Treaty of Versailles and how this led to World War II.
2. **Students work in pairs:** Activity projected at the beginning of class will be revisited. Students will also discuss the questions provided by the teacher. Students will discuss what may have happened to the Jewish people in concentration camps and how they may have felt about being separated from their friends and loved ones. While in groups, teacher will ask students: "Who has an example of how the Jewish people may have felt? Discouraged, humiliated, or angry? If you didn't use those adjectives, what were your descriptions?"

Additional group work: Students will divide a sheet of construction paper into three sections, labeling the section "World War II," "Hitler," and "Holocaust." In each section, students will discuss and then list five facts they learned in past readings from class and from their background knowledge without using their notes. Sample answers are provided.

World War II	Hitler	Holocaust
Germany	Leader	Jewish People
Anger	Mean	Death

3. **Sharing phase:** The teacher brings the students together to get input from the entire class. The three-part fact sheet is used for whole-class discussion. Then all students attempt to answer the questions that were posed.

Adapted from an activity by Shante Asprey.

Extended Anticipation Guides

Another activity that can foster reflective thinking is the **extended anticipation guide** (Duffelmeyer & Baum, 1992). As you learned in Chapter 3, anticipation guides can help students predict outcomes. The extended anticipation guides can also spark discussion in the Reflection Phase of learning. The guides reinforce or verify information students have learned, enabling them to modify their predictions and to take into account new insights and information. Activity 5.8 includes both an anticipation guide for high school students to complete individually before reading *Flowers for Algernon* and an extended anticipation guide to be completed by students individually or working in groups after reading.

ABOUT/POINT

Teachers are always looking for a simple yet effective way to teach students how to grasp the main idea of a paragraph and how to recognize subordinate detail. The ABOUT/POINT activity represents an easy way that students can learn to think reflectively about relationships in a paragraph. In this activity, the students concentrate on "what the passage is about" and what "main points" are covered in the reading. Simple study guides can be given to students to help them categorize the passage in this manner. In kindergarten and first grade, teachers can use this technique as a listening and speaking

ACTIVITY 5.8 Anticipation Guide and Extended Anticipation Guide for High School English

PART I: ANTICIPATION GUIDE

Instructions: Before you begin reading this section of *Flowers for Algernon* (pp. 150–180), read the statements below. If you agree with a statement, check the Agree column. If you disagree with the statement, check the Disagree column. Be ready to explain or defend your choices in class discussion.

Agree	Disagree	Statement
		_____ **1.** No matter how intelligent a person is, that person's success as a human being depends on how she or he relates to her- or himself.
		_____ **2.** Charlie is beginning to behave like Algernon.
		_____ **3.** Algernon is beginning to behave like Charlie.
		_____ **4.** Charlie may eventually be sent to Warren, a home for severely disabled persons.
		_____ **5.** Most normal people do not have the time or the desire to help mentally challenged people.
		_____ **6.** People often use other people to satisfy their own needs.
		_____ **7.** Charlie's work in psychology is similar in some ways to Algernon's work with mazes.
		_____ **8.** The life experiences of most human beings are somewhat like being in a giant maze.

PART II: EXTENDED ANTICIPATION GUIDE

Instructions: Now that you have read *Flowers For Algernon,* complete this section in groups. If you believe your reading supports your choices in Part I, check the "Support" column below. If the information you read does *not* support your choice in Part I, check the "No Support" column and write a reason why the statement cannot be supported in the third column. Keep your reasons brief and in your own words.

Support	No Support	Reason for No Support (in your own words)
1.		
2.		
3.		
4.		
5.		
6.		
7.		
8.		

aid after reading a story aloud to students. The student identifies the sun as the source of light and heat. In the upper elementary and middle school grades, students can work in groups to recall information from more than one paragraph of content material. To use the ABOUT/POINT activity in this larger context, teachers ask students to reread a passage and then to decide in groups what the passage is "about" and what "points" (details) support their response. Activity 5.9 presents an ABOUT/POINT on maintaining and caring for your teeth in elementary health education.

ACTIVITY 5.9 ABOUT/POINT Study Sheet

THE CARE AND MAINTENANCE OF YOUR TEETH

This reading is ABOUT:

- How to care for and maintain good hygiene for your teeth.

And the POINTS are:

- You can get holes in your teeth by not brushing.
- Plaque and tartar can do great harm to your teeth.
- Plaque combines with a common food substance to form acid that can eat away at the enamel of your teeth.
- Fluoride applied to your teeth can reduce your chances of having cavities.

Self-Generated Questions

Students seem to improve their understanding of texts when they generate their own questions either before or after reading. This activity, also called **student-generated questions**, succeeds because it shows students a strategy to monitor their understanding. Researchers (Van Blerkom, Van Blerkom, & Bertsch, 2006) asked 100 college students to participate in an experiment in which students were randomly assigned to one of four groups: reading and copying, reading and highlighting, reading and taking notes, and reading and generating questions. Students who generated questions achieved better than two of the other three groups on a 20-item multiple-choice test about the reading material. In a much earlier study, MacDonald (1986) found that groups instructed in methods for asking questions had comprehension scores higher than the scores of groups without this training. Activity 5.10 presents questions developed from an elementary science class.

ACTIVITY 5.10 Student-Generated Questions: The Prehistoric Mammoth

Was a mammoth an elephant?
How big was the mammoth?
When did they live on the earth? How long ago?
Did the mammoth have tusks?
The caption under the picture calls them "woolly" mammoths.
Why are they called "woolly" mammoths?
How many mammoth fossils have been found?
Where did the mammoth live? Which continents?
Why did they die out?

Think-Alouds

A think-aloud is an activity in which a reader orally "thinks through" a reading by verbalizing his or her thought processes about the passage at any given time. In a think-aloud, a reader may stop and reflect on the thinking he or she is doing to understand the text. Readers may describe visualizations and how prior knowledge is affecting their reading. A think-aloud is a way to have students examine their own thinking (Oster, 2001). First developed by Davey (1983), this procedure represents a modeling technique to help students improve their comprehension. Research on the benefits of think-alouds has shown that they are particularly effective as a diagnostic tool to assess students' ability to use inferences as they read (Laing & Kamhi, 2002). A more recent study by Hanna (2009) found that an experimental group using read-alouds and think-alouds performed better on multiple-choice comprehension measures than did the control group that used independent reading. When students can think aloud, they improve their reflection and demonstrate their reflection abilities on tests.

Please visit the Education CourseMate website at **www.cengagebrain.com** to find a link to a website that describes online books available for students and teachers to study and perform think-alouds.

At first, a teacher needs to show students how think-alouds work. To carry out a think-aloud, the teacher models the kinds of strategies a skilled reader uses during reading and points out specifically how he or she resolves a comprehension problem. The teacher models these reading comprehension techniques, although not necessarily all in one session:

1. Forming hypotheses about a text's meaning before beginning to read
2. Producing mental images (spontaneously organizing information)
3. Linking prior knowledge with a new topic
4. Drawing inferences from the reading
5. Reading ahead, rereading, restating, and summarizing paragraphs
6. Using context clues to decipher meanings of words and phrases
7. Using strategies to monitor comprehension
8. Identifying active ways to "fix" comprehension problems

Think-alouds help students realize that text should make sense and that readers use both information from the text and prior knowledge to construct meaning. Teachers can make predictions and show how to develop a hypothesis; describe the visual images that come to mind; share analogies and otherwise link new knowledge to prior knowledge; discuss confusing points or problems; and demonstrate fix-up strategies such as rereading, reading ahead to clarify a confusing point, and figuring out word meanings from context. After the teacher models think-aloud a few times, students can work with partners to practice think-alouds, taking turns in reading orally and sharing thoughts.

Activity 5.11 is an example of a teacher's think-aloud in a high school history class. The teacher is thinking aloud about a letter sent from James Madison in 1781 in reply to an evangelist's request to speak at an Anglican church.

Block and Israel (2004) explain an excellent activity that pairs students for practice in think-alouds, which they call the Peer Think-Aloud Game. The teacher writes think-aloud activities on flashcards (the researchers have a list of their own, but the think-aloud activities we just listed could be used), and the students place the flash cards face up so both students can see the activities. Then one student begins to read orally from the text. The student stops reading and performs one of the think-aloud activities when he or she gets to a point at which this is possible. After completing the think-aloud, the student holds up the flashcard naming the activities just completed. If the listening partner agrees that the think-aloud has been completed, the first student gets a point. Then the students switch roles, and the game continues in rotation. Block and Israel recommend practicing only certain designated think-aloud activities in a

Using think-alouds is an excellent way to teach the thinking process to students. How would they help Gustavo, the young student described in this chapter? How could they also be useful for JaNette, Mark, or Trinka?

ACTIVITY 5.11 Think-Aloud in High School History

EXCERPT OF A LETTER FROM JAMES MADISON, 1781

(The actual letter is printed; the italics represent what the teacher is thinking.
Parentheses show the thought processes.)

Letter from James Madison, 1781

For want of opportunity and leisure, I have delayed till now answering your letter relative to your preaching in the Pine Stake Church. When the Vestry met, I forgot to mention your request to them, as I promised you, till it broke up. Then I informed the members present what you required of them; Who, as the case was new and unprecedented, thought it had better remain as it then stood less the members of the Church should be alarmed that their rights and privileges were in danger of being unjustifiably disposed of.

(There is another paragraph to the letter that is not reproduced here)

I am, Sir, your humble Servant
James Madison
August 23, 1781

I am predicting that this is a letter from one of the colonial Founding Fathers, James Madison, to an evangelist preacher's request to speak at Madison's Anglican Church (prediction). *But as I start to read, it I remembered that Madison lived well into the 19th century* (prior knowledge) *and would probably have been too young to be an elder of a church at the time of this letter. I am guessing the author is one of Madison's older kin. Maybe it was his father or an uncle* (prediction).

When the Vestry met, I forgot to mention your request to them

What is a Vestry? I picture (imaging) *a group of very old men who run the church. From the context, I would guess Vestry means the leaders of the church* (context clues). *Why would Madison forget to mention this man's request until the very end of the meeting? Could it have been on purpose* (inference)? *Perhaps evangelical preachers would not be welcomed in the staid, old Anglican Church, I am guessing* (prediction). *So maybe he conveniently forgot* (inference)?

The Vestry . . . though it had better remain as it then stood less the parishioners of the church should be alarmed that their rights and privileges were in danger. . . .

Why would the members of the church feel in danger of losing their rights and privileges? Could it be they would fear any influence coming from outside the Anglican Church (inference)?

I think overall (monitoring comprehension) *this letter is a not-so-subtle rebuke of evangelicals of the time and is an attempt to keep the "status quo"—keeping things as they are—on the part of the leaders of one Anglican Church in colonial times. I do know that evangelical preachers at that time were making big inroads in the colonies and were drawing crowds wherever they went* (prior knowledge). *Maybe the Anglican Church feared this* (inference).

session. Students can let the teacher know which activities they need more practice with and which need to be retaught.

The think-aloud activity can become an excellent reflective study technique. To extend the Peer Think-Aloud Game, teachers can give the paired students a checklist to self-evaluate their progress, as shown in Activity 5.12. Such a checklist can be used from early elementary school through high school.

ACTIVITY 5.12 Think-Aloud Checklist for All Grade Levels

HOW AM I DOING ON MY THINK-ALOUDS?

Think-Aloud Checklist	Not Often	Sometimes	Often	Always
Made predictions				
Formed mind pictures				
Used comparisons				
Used prior knowledge				
Drew inferences from the reading				
Read ahead or reread				
Monitored comprehension				
Used fix-up strategies				
Summarized the paragraph or passage				

ONE-MINUTE SUMMARY

This chapter has described activities and strategies to be used in the Reflection Phase of the PAR Lesson Framework for improving comprehension and retention. We discussed the importance of using good communication skills to work toward making students autonomous learners. We also discussed ways to help students monitor their own comprehension as they read and while reflecting on the reading. We discussed the importance of critical thinking and defined the important construct of critical literacy. Cooperative learning was presented as a powerful tool for teaching content, social skills, and critical thinking. The chapter spelled out the differences between cooperative learning and working in groups. Retention of content is enhanced when cooperative strategies are used and opportunities are provided for students to practice, under a teacher's guidance, five important categories of reflective learning: rehearsal, elaboration, organizational thinking, comprehension monitoring, and affective thinking. Cooperative learning requires an atmosphere of serious purpose, confidence, assistance, and above all, commitment to disciplined inquiry and study. In this chapter, we presented a stylized three-step procedure for group process to help cooperative groups function better.

The second half of the chapter describes 16 strategies to teach communication, critical thinking, critical literacy, and cooperative learning. The chapter focused both on teacher-generated and -guided strategies such as making connections, text lookbacks, and think-alouds; and student-generated strategies such as brainstorming, double-entry journals, and self-generated questions.

END-OF-CHAPTER ACTIVITIES

Assisting Comprehension

1. The chapter emphasized that teachers need to help students become autonomous learners. What does autonomy have to do with reflection?
2. Writing is an especially good way to promote reflection. Describe in writing some strategies discussed in this chapter that will be beneficial to your students.
3. Strategies and activities described in this chapter feature teachers' use of small-group instruction and cooperative learning. Which strategies will be most useful for individual and whole-class learning activities for diverse learners? Which strategies could be used for computer-based instruction?

Reflecting on Your Reading

1. Your content organization (e.g., National Council of Teachers of Mathematics, National Council of Teachers of English, National Council for the Social Studies, National Science Teachers Association, International Reading Association) has most likely mandated that teachers use appropriate grouping options, such as individual, small-group, whole-class, and computer-based grouping plans. Classroom teachers are asked to model and use scaffolding procedures so that students learn to work effectively in groups. What is the best grouping plan for you? Describe strategies from this chapter that you feel would suit your grouping plan needs as a teacher.

CHAPTER 6

Moving beyond the Traditional Textbook and Transmission Methods

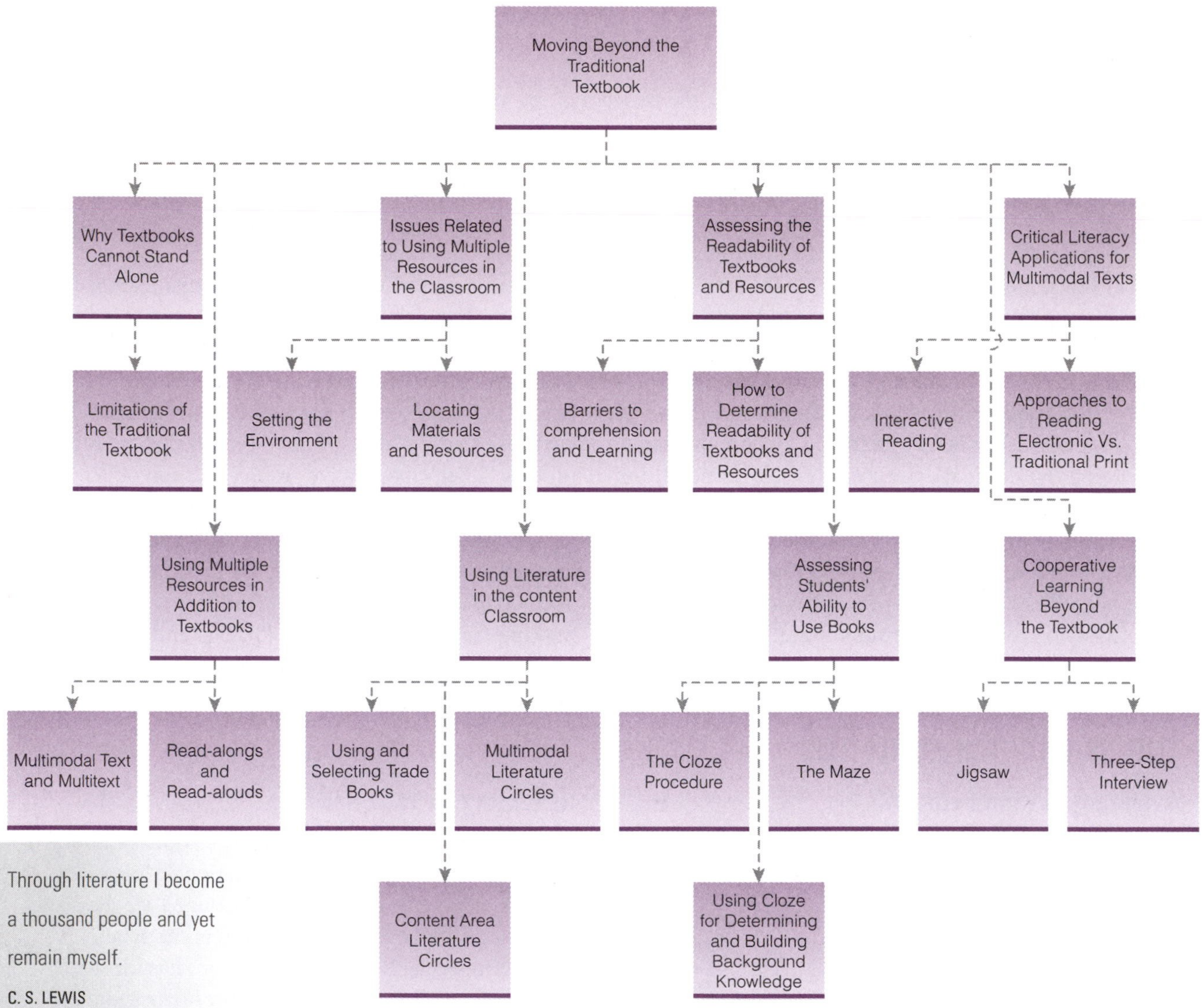

Through literature I become a thousand people and yet remain myself.

C. S. LEWIS

We are each of us angels with only one wing, and we can only fly by embracing one another.

LUCIANO DE CRESCENZO

VOICES FROM THE CLASSROOM

Ms. Carson is an energetic and innovative fourth grade teacher in her second year at Urban Elementary. She is about to plan a science unit about hurricanes and tornadoes. She wants her students to understand the differences between the two storm types, the principles behind their formation, and safety tips and information for dealing with each. She also hopes to find some way to use the same topic to develop math, social studies, and reading lessons.

Her class of 25 includes three students reading well below grade level and four reading well above grade level. Three of her students—Jorge, Maria, and Juan—are English language learners (ELLs). Although Ms. Carson's school is located on the Atlantic coastline, many of her students have never experienced a hurricane. Only four pages in her 2003 science textbook are devoted to the topic. She wants to locate some resources that may help, and she wants to use some peer grouping strategies during instruction.

Where might she find appropriate resources, and what special considerations must she make to provide for the needs of all her students? How can she use the same topic to teach the other disciplines? Answer these questions before reading this chapter; then revisit them following the reading to decide if you need to modify your responses.

PREPARING TO READ

1. Do the textbooks provided for the courses you teach work for all of your students? Why or why not? How do you select materials and resources that will address mandated standards and competencies but go beyond those limits to consider and connect with student interests, cultures, and personal lives? As you read this chapter, think about how you can use its information when selecting textbooks and other content materials, including technology resources and non-print media.
2. How do you go beyond traditional print text to engage your students in interactive social and cultural learning experiences?
3. While reading this chapter, look for ways to assist students in developing habits for evaluating and selecting various text forms as they learn how to make decisions and accept responsibility for their own learning.
4. Following is a list of terms used in this chapter. Some may be familiar to you in a general context, but in this chapter, they may be used in unfamiliar ways. Rate your knowledge by placing a plus sign (+) for those you are sure that you know, a check mark (✓) for those you have some knowledge about, and a zero (0) for those you don't know. Be ready to locate them in the chapter and pay special attention to their meanings.

_______ multitext
_______ multimodal text
_______ trade books
_______ readability
_______ inconsiderate discourse
_______ textual coherence
_______ dumbed-down text
_______ rule of thumb
_______ readability formulas
_______ Lexile Framework
_______ cloze
_______ jigsaw

OBJECTIVES

As you read this chapter, focus your attention on the following objectives.

1. Explain why a textbook cannot stand alone as the only classroom text for reading.
2. Discuss the importance of using multiple resources in classrooms.
3. Explain and describe the importance of including technology and non-print media in your instruction.
4. Select appropriate and relevant content resources to complement textbooks, heighten interest, and deepen understanding.
5. Compare the use of readability measures, book leveling, and Lexiles for matching learners with reading materials.
6. Learn the benefits and techniques of read-alouds for young children and adolescents.
7. Describe the role of critical literacy for instruction with texts beyond the textbook.

Shoe-New Business MacNelly. Distributed by King Features Syndicate.

Chapter 10 discusses these and other technologies in detail.

Reading in today's content classrooms cannot be limited to course textbooks. The near obsession with communication and the exchange of ideas in this age of information have dramatically changed the speed and ways of making meaning. People communicate using **multimodal** platforms, including live (person-to-person), paper (e.g., note, magazine, book), and electronic (texting, email, Internet) interactions (Anstey & Bull, 2006). To ignore the broader definition of text and especially electronic and non-print media leads to the proverbial "head in the sand" problem. These new forms of communicating are so popular with our students and important for negotiating their life worlds (Sweeny, 2007) that it behooves us to consider ways to use these tools to enhance learning and understanding. As the New London Group (1996) pointed out, globalization and changes in the workplace make it necessary to prepare students for their futures by including various technologies, listening and oral communication skills, critical analysis, and higher order thinking skills in the curriculum. Literacy is being redefined to recognize the growing types of texts such as podcasts, interactive videos, blogs, and primary and secondary source information available on various websites (Leu, 2000; Richardson, 2004).

Coiro (2003) maintains that such a combination prepares students for the new literacies, including cultural and linguistic contexts (Leu, Kinzer, Coiro, & Commack, 2004) that will increasingly define their futures.

- Cultural context is the customs, traditions, and life experiences that help to shape one's view and understanding of the world.
- Linguistic context is the language, dialects, and colloquialisms that are critical to communication.

To prepare students to be educated citizens in the 21st century, teachers must include the understanding of how to, and the ability to, critically negotiate the meaning of text in numerous forms and media. Leu and colleagues (2004) recommend using Internet activities and resources with print versions of children's literature to expand the response to reading in new and more powerful ways. Because understanding these new text formats requires cognitive processing that is both similar to and different from reading traditional texts, researchers (Leu, Kinzer, Coiro, & Commack, 2004; Olson & Truxaw, 2009; Tyner, 1998; Wilson, 2008) have postulated that it is more important than ever to learn how meaning is created in both traditional textbooks and the new technologies. To this end, Anstey & Bull (2006) identify a number of critical thinking questions that teachers need to consider when dealing with alternative texts.

How do these critical thinking questions relate to Principles 4 and 5 from Chapter 1?

4. Most language users are equipped with more than one version of their language; ideally, they will use a version that suits the circumstances.
5. The discourse of one content discipline may be different than that of another.

1. Who produced the text?
2. What is the purpose of the text?
3. Who is the text produced for?
4. Of what relevance is the text?
5. Why is the topic being written about?
6. From whose perspective is the text constructed?

7. Are there other possible constructions from different points of view?
8. Whose interests are being served by the text?
9. Who is excluded or included in the text? Why?
10. What assumptions about the potential audiences of the text have been made?
11. Are there particular attitudes, values, and ideologies that are foregrounded in the text?
12. Are there certan discourses that are valued?
13. Who is silenced or marginalized by the text?
14. Who is empowered by the text?
15. Are any stereotypes represented or challenged?
16. How might the text be transformed or reconstructed? (p. 106)

These questions are equally relevant for more traditional texts.

Textbooks are still the most frequently used teaching resources along with handouts and manipulatives (e.g., those used in mathematics). However, many teachers are diverging from the old norm and choosing books and readings apart from, or in addition to, the designated or assigned textbooks. Research (Guthrie, 2004) supports the idea that students are more motivated when textbooks and readings are interesting. The North Central Regional Educational Laboratory (NCREL) (2005) explains that when students are interested and engaged, they "can succeed even in less-than-optimal environments" (p. 6). Often, this engagement results from making connections that relate to their own life experiences.

This chapter has several purposes: to validate the use of books and multimodal texts apart from the traditional textbook, explain ways of determining how readable any chosen text is, and provide guidelines for helping students select and read materials critically. Much of this chapter's content represents the teacher's first step in the PAR (preparation, assistance, and reflection) Lesson Framework: preparing learners. Without planning for appropriate resources to teach content, teachers and students will not be prepared to use the vast information resources now available for supporting rich learning experiences. Although we are not advocating that teachers abandon traditional textbooks, they certainly need to explore other print and non-print options for reading. Anstey and Bull (2006) aptly state that traditional print literacy remains essential for learning but that it is not sufficient for preparing students of the 21st century for their futures. Dove (1998) suggests that the availability and accessibility of multiple resources allow teachers many options for instruction in diverse classrooms, and he states that "the one-textbook approach is no longer viable" (p. 29).

Please visit the Education CourseMate website at **www.cengagebrain.com** to find links to the NCREL reports on using student engagement to improve adolescent literacy, or perform a Web search using the term "NCREL reports" to locate these results.

Why Textbooks Cannot Stand Alone

Limitations of the Traditional Textbook

Learning today is often "disjointed and piecemeal" (Jetton & Alexander, 2000). Total reliance on textbooks as the single resource for learners contributes to this limited approach. The strength of a textbook is that it can provide within one source a breadth of information, or overview, covering a range of grade- or course-specific topics.

But inherent in this strength is a problem: the inability (because of space issues) to provide the depth to pique student curiosity or to make concepts and content memorable. Similar to encyclopedias, textbooks present an overview of selected topics rather than in-depth information. They are often condensed, secondary sources in which much of the story behind a topic is omitted and the original author's enthusiasm and style are not apparent.

Hiebert (1999) makes an analogy between a variety of reading resources and a balanced diet. Someone using only one type of reading material may not receive all the nutrients needed to nourish the reading experience—or, we add, balanced knowledge about a content area.

Generally, when teachers assign homework to guide students to learn more about a topic, they want students to research multiple resources. However, teachers are often frustrated when students submit papers and projects for which the only resource was an encyclopedia or Wikipedia. Teachers prefer that students read widely about a topic, especially primary sources (original records, documents, or artifacts) rather than secondary sources (a summary or analysis of an event by someone not present when the event occurred). But by using textbooks as the single classroom resource, teachers model a single-resource approach, and learners tend to imitate this. Because textbooks condense information, their treatment of subject matter can be dry and boring. Textbook information should be complemented with a multiplicity of resources, including trade books, fiction with content information, magazines, newspapers, Internet resources and websites, video clips, and computer software (Atkinson, Matusevich, & Huber, 2009; Guillaume, 1998; Myers & Savage, 2005).

As far back as 1970, textbooks have been criticized for their conceptual density (Hurd, 1970). Textbooks' challenging technical vocabulary (Atkinson, Matusevich, & Huber, 2009) and bland presentation of facts are continuing criticisms. Lack of text coherence and use of uneven writing make reading a textbook even more difficult. It is not easy, especially for struggling readers, to make the shift from reading stories, or narrative style, to reading for information in expository text.

Teachers may sometimes use old or outdated textbooks containing information that does not reflect factual and conceptual changes in the field of study. The National Education Association (NEA) (2002) found that one-third of teachers reported using textbooks that were 10 or more years old. While teaching in the 1980s, the fourth grade science text a teacher was issued predicted, "Someday we may put a man on the moon," well after those first historic steps were taken in 1969. Living at a time when televisions were rolled into classrooms so classes could watch space launches, these students got quite a chuckle. This type of problem lends to disinterest, devaluing text, and exposure to incorrect information (Hunter, 2006; Villano, 2005).

Refer to Chapter 11 for information on the power of stories, visuals, and alternative perspectives for enhancing learning for struggling readers and ELLs.

Recall the profiles in Chapter 1 for JaNette, Gustavo, Mark, and Trinka. Think about these students' needs and situations as you read this chapter. Consider which ideas and strategies could work or be adapted for each of them, and take notes. Create a graphic organizer to illustrate your findings and ideas.

The traditional notion of using one textbook for all classroom assignments limits student success. Villano (2005) recommends that textbooks be used as a *guide* for curriculum rather than *becoming* the curriculum. Of some concern is the matter that textbooks may not appropriately address the standards or competencies required (Demski, 2009) or the flexibility for connecting to the cultures and diversity represented in a particular classroom. Thus, teachers must locate outside resources to assist with the teaching of objectives not addressed within the textbooks students are issued. To add to the problem, the NEA (2002) found that one of every six teachers reported not having enough textbooks to issue one to each student. The problem is even more pronounced among urban schools and schools with high populations of students from low-socioeconomic (SES) homes, creating what appears to be an economic divide. For various reasons, students from low-SES environments frequently struggle with reading. Struggling readers and ELL students often need resources beyond the textbook to add interest and facilitate understanding.

Using Multiple Resources in Addition to Textbooks

The American student population is growing ever more diverse. It is not unusual for a classroom to include a half dozen nationalities and cultures or for students to speak several languages. There is growing concern that teachers in all content subjects must be adept at offering reading choices that reflect students' interests, cultures, and customs (see Chapter 11 for more on diverse learners). A multimodal, **multitext** approach is necessary.

Multimodal Text and Multitext

Multimodal texts incorporate visual, auditory, spoken, and nonverbal cues for understanding and learning through the use of various technologies (Anstey & Bull, 2006, p. 102). Understanding basic concepts remains important for learning a discipline, but doing so is no longer sufficient. It is important to move beyond a narrow definition of mastery of science, social studies, mathematics, and other content areas as the organized accumulation of facts and information a student memorizes (Atkinson, Matusevich, & Huber, 2009; Yager, Yager, & Lim, 2006). Mastery learning must also include the ability to evaluate and synthesize information for problem solving and discovering meaning both in and outside school walls (Juel, Hebard, Haubner, & Moran, 2010; Myers & Savage, 2005). This type of learning necessarily involves the student in decision making to process linear, nonlinear, interactive, or dynamic texts.

Jewitt (2008) contends that no one mode is used exclusively to make meaning. Instead, several modalities have distinct contributions that lead to understanding, which are particularly helpful when working with second language learners. Kenner's (2004) ethnographic research on writing illustrates how the use of direction, space, and graphic markings assist in the understanding and meaning making of young bilingual students. Ajayi (2009) found that ". . . multimodal/multiliteracies pedagogy could foster critical literacy practices by offering ESL students opportunities to create new identities and challenge discursive practices that marginalize them" (p. 594).

Addressing challenges faced by diverse learners must be integral to lesson preparation in all disciplines and not regarded as an add-on. Refer to Chapter 11 for additional information on and resources for working with English as a second language (ESL) students

Refer to Chapter 1 to refresh your memory on Mark, the struggling middle school student. Carefully read the Challenge Box and make notes about Mark's learning difficulties.

Read-Alongs and Read-Alouds

How can the resources we have discussed be used to support, augment, and move beyond textbooks? Excerpts of literature, such as read-alouds and read-alongs, are good ways to start. Literature and technology can be easily incorporated into existing instruction with no major restructuring of lessons. The teacher can collect and use excerpts of literature as adjuncts to the content being taught. Two plans of action are read-alongs and read-alouds. Using **read-alongs**, the teacher shares an excerpt with students, who read the piece individually, in small groups, or with the teacher. Using **read-alouds**, the teacher generally reads the excerpt, story, or article to the entire class. Teachers need to be on the lookout for passages of literature that illustrate concepts in their fields of study. Over time, teachers can compile a collection of examples. Many book lists are annotated and organized by topic and grade. Content teachers should start a personal database of literature selections to augment a content topic. As they come across an appropriate excerpt, they can enter it into the database along

Please visit the Education CourseMate website at **www.cengagebrain.com** to find links to various professional associations:

- National Council for the Social Studies
- International Reading Association
- National Science Teachers Association
- National Council of Teachers of Mathematics
- American Library Association

CHALLENGE BOX

Mark, the Struggling Reader

SITUATION: Mark can read but not easily and not well. It requires a great deal of effort for him to get through a passage. However, he loves science, works well with hands-on projects, and favors learning via the Internet and video media.

What can teachers do to help him develop both his knowledge and skill levels in reading and other content areas? What do his teachers need to know and understand about him?

It is important not to ignore his reading difficulties, but it is *just as* important to use the adaptations he has made for learning to build reading skills. Read-alouds and read-along strategies would work well to help Mark make text-to-reader connections while building his understanding of the content. It is important for his teacher to make explicit some of the strategies that she is using while reading to make transparent the thought processes and steps necessary for success. Graphic aides and other visual resources (as discussed in Chapters 3 to 5) can provide needed support and repetition for Mark as he learns.

How might multimodal and multitext materials, readability formulas, and Lexile scores support his learning?

Multimodal activities can enhance and build conceptual understanding while encouraging Mark to take the lead on developing materials for use in presentations and projects. Cooperative learning group strategies described in Chapter 5 and later in Chapter 6 would provide opportunities for Mark to use his strengths while observing and discussing methods and ways other group members are learning. Literature circles focusing on content topics and integrating two or more disciplines could help him see the important connections among science and reading, mathematics, social studies, and other areas in real-world applications. His teachers could use Lexile scales to assist him in locating reading materials on topics of study that would challenge but not frustrate him. Mark has a great deal of potential, and the use of multitexts and multimodal materials beyond the textbook should build and assist him in making substantial growth.

with suggestions for its use. Many professional organizations publish annual lists of literature selections appropriate for supplementing or enriching studies and concept development among students.

Read-alouds sometimes work more effectively than read-alongs, at least initially, because the teacher can stimulate interest and observe how much attention is given to the excerpt. Read-alouds have been shown to be effective in engaging students in learning (Ariail & Albright, 2006; Erickson, 1996; Palmer & Stewart, 2005; Richardson, 1995a, 2000a; Villano, 2005). Besides promoting a love of reading and modeling fluent reading, teachers cite several reasons for reading aloud. Enhancing understanding, developing interest, demystifying text structures, and reinforcing concepts and content have all been listed as important reasons (Ariail & Albright, 2006). Reading aloud carefully selected passages and stories can build needed background and schemata for greater concept development, thus letting students learn content before having to negotiate texts for themselves (Villano, 2005).

While teaching a high school reading improvement class some years ago, one student in particular was adamant that the teacher read aloud a portion of the day's reading for the students before they began reading for themselves. When asked why this was so important to him, he responded, "When you read to us, then I know how it is supposed to sound in my head when I read so that I can understand it." Reading aloud can encourage those who can read but choose not to read (aliterate individuals) to gain new or renewed interest in reading (Lesesne, 2001). However, teachers seem to

ACTIVITY 6.1 Cultural Fairy Tales, Myths, and Legends (Middle School and High School Social Studies and History)

PRIMARY LESSON OBJECTIVES

Students will:

1. Listen to and discuss Japanese fairy tales, myths, and legends.
2. Identify aspects of Japanese culture found in fairy tales, myths, and legends.
3. Read Japanese fairy tales, myths, and legends.
4. Compose a fairy tale, myth, or legend that appropriately depicts aspects of Japanese culture.

PROCEDURES

- Teacher reads aloud a Japanese myth, legend, or fairy tale followed by a discussion connecting historical and cultural merit with story characteristics. Books used: *Myths and Legends of Japan* by F. Hadland Davis and *Japanese Fairy Tales* by Yei Theodora Ozaki.
- Students independently read selected fairy tales, myths, and legends from Japan and then discuss their readings in small groups. Discussions focus on historical and cultural merit.
- Students visit a Scholastic website to learn about the genre and to read about how to write a myth, legend, or fairy tale. Please visit the Education CourseMate website at **www.cengagebrain.com** to find the Scholastic site.
- Each student writes his or her own myth, legend, or fairy tale that illustrates specific cultural traits and historical connections. Students prepare and present their compositions to include complementary PowerPoint, iPod, or video components.

abandon this practice by the time students start middle school even though students of all ages enjoy and learn from it (Fisher, Flood, Lapp, & Frey, 2004; Richardson, 1994).

A social studies teacher for a ninth grade honors class tried read-alouds to help her students understand myths, legends, and fairy tales from different cultures. After listening to read-alouds, students were expected to read stories from Eastern and Western cultures and then write their own myths. Although good work is expected from honors students, the enthusiasm with which these students participated was greater than usual for this unit. See an example of this type of activity in Activity 6.1.

In science, one teacher found a website that described the very expensive error in calculations made when the Mars *Climate Orbiter* was sent into space. It never reached its target because one set of scientists calculated using kilometers and the other group used miles. This site provided the perfect read-along "hook" to entice the students into real-world reasons to study metric measurement systems.

Please visit the Education CourseMate website at **www.cengagebrain.com** to find information on the Mars *Climate Orbiter*.

Another science excerpt can be drawn from Robert C. O'Brien's novel *Mrs. Frisby and the Rats of NIMH* (1971), in which a science experiment works better than expected. Here the scientists divide rats and mice into three groups—control, experimental A, and experimental B—and then inject serums and conduct experiments. The serum works so well for experimental A that those rats and mice escape and set up their own society. Because this excerpt is several pages long—a whole chapter plus part of another—it might best be shared through students reading silently and then discussing what constitutes experimental design.

See Chapter 17 ("A Lesson in Reading") and Chapter 18 ("The Air Ducts") in *Mrs. Frisby and the Rats of NIMH* (1971).

The reading of short passages followed by thoughtful, lively discussion is a way to introduce a topic and provoke curiosity and wonder. Barry (2010) explains that when the stage and protocol for discussion are set within an environment that respects diversity and multiple perspectives, students learn to think deeply and respond thoughtfully and are considerate of other viewpoints. The framework she describes is based on the Touchstone Discussion Project that grew out of St. John's College in

Refer to the *Journal of Adolescent and Adult Literacy* for the "Read It Aloud" column for literature excerpts and instructional uses for read-alouds (Richardson, 1994–1997).

Please visit the Education CourseMate website at **www.cengagebrain.com** to find a link to:

- The Reference and User services Association (for information and links to primary source documents).
- The Touchstones Discussion Project.

Annapolis, Maryland. Developed as a natural outgrowth of the Great Books program, the project encourages dialogue that includes the common reading of a text, sharing of ideas and questions, active listening, openness to and respect for ideas of others, and willingness to change. Discussions are based on paintings, photographs, or brief readings that relate to poignant topics and content. Passages may be excerpts of longer primary source documents. Barry likens the difference between primary text and a textbook to "the difference between fresh and canned peas" (p. 44).

Issues Related to Using Multiple Resources in the Classroom

Setting the Environment

The physical environment in a classroom can facilitate the use of literature and technology to support the textbook; the way a classroom is arranged affects the climate for learning and teaching (Kowalski, 1995). The availability of books, opportunities not only to read but also to choose what to read (Corcoran & Mamalakis, 2009; Gambrell, 1995), peer-led discussion groups (Gambrell, 2004), and an environment that builds trust and respect (Patrick, Ryan, & Kaplan, 2007) appear to motivate both good and poor readers. A classroom arranged to entice readers meets these criteria. When teachers provide bookshelves with literature, folders with newspaper clippings, magazines on racks, and baskets of books about topics being studied, students will be as enticed as any learners who browse in bookstores or libraries and feel the itch to pick up a book. A designated quiet reading spot is a friendly, encouraging touch. If possible, no fewer than five computers should be available in the classroom so students have easy access when they need to participate in threaded discussions or classroom blogs, create written products, develop presentations, enter data, send or receive email, or find information on the Internet.

Locating Materials and Resources

Locating and obtaining trade books, magazines, newspapers, and even computers may be less difficult than it might seem. Some possibilities include:

- Parent organizations raising money for purchases
- Libraries lending books for extended classroom use
- Local businesses donating materials or offering small grants
- Teachers using bonus points from book club orders to get additional materials
- Schools purchasing mobile labs or common labs

Chapter 11 addresses the use of multicultural literature and effective strategies.

As teachers integrate more literature in their content teaching, they should include multicultural literature. Bieger (1995) describes a four-level hierarchical framework for teaching multicultural literature: (1) looking at the contributions of people from other cultures; (2) adding information about other cultures to the curriculum; (3) changing the curriculum to help students see different cultures from new perspectives; and (4) identifying as well as proposing solutions to social problems that occur in multicultural environments. Lawrence (2007) advocates the use of cultural stories for helping students of all cultures connect science content and different cultural perspectives. Multicultural literature is more widely accepted and used in school today, but the manner in which it is implemented ranges from additive or contribution approaches to assisting students in forming deep understandings and respect for cultural differences and similarities that serve to transform their perspectives.

Look for discussion and examples of writing activities and learning logs in Chapter 8 and postgraphic organizers and other visuals in Chapters 5, 7, and 8.

Supporting textbooks with literature and technology enhances teachers' abilities to distinguish between the relevant information that textbooks offer and any incorrect, outdated, or abbreviated information that they may present. Teachers need to know how to encourage students to respond to supplemental texts through writing, discussions in response groups, and even art and drama renderings. Exemplary programs do this all the time. Lafayette Township School in New Jersey was granted the International Reading Association Exemplary Reading Program award (Mahler, 1995) for integrating instruction in numerous ways—for example, by organizing a fair at which middle school students read about the Renaissance, wrote stories, built inventions inspired by Leonardo da Vinci, staged a play, and coordinated activities to teach students in the lower grades about the Middle Ages. Alvarez and Rodriguez (1995) describe a project called "Explorers of the Universe," in which high school students learned not only subject matter but also how to think and ask questions as a result of searching in teams for information beyond the classroom textbooks. As part of the project, one group of students began to correspond with two astronomers via telecommunications.

Please visit the Education CourseMate website at **www.cengagebrain.com** for a link to the Explorers of the Universe site.

As you view this video notice the ways two teachers from different disciplines (social studies and English) work together to use literature and a variety of resources and strategies that cross disciplines. Students are guided to use the connections to gain a greater understanding of both disciplines.

Using Literature in the Content Classroom

Using and Selecting Trade Books

Harvey and Goudvis (2007) report that almost 5,500 children's trade books were published in 2005 alone. **Trade books** are books that are considered to be in general use, such as books borrowed from a library or bought at the local bookstore, rather than textbooks bought and studied as a major course resource. Most trade books are written in either a journalistic or a narrative style; they are interesting resources but are not specifically intended as instructional tools. Informational texts and texts that include a combination of narrative and factual components, such as Wright-Frierson's (1998) *An Island Scrapbook,* offer rich opportunities for concept connections that are both interesting and relevant.

Certainly, the familiar story structure found in fiction or historical fiction adds interest and aids comprehension when connections are made to concepts being studied. Students are often drawn to nonfiction as well because of their curiosity about nature and the ways things work (Palmer & Stewart, 2003, 2005; Pappas, 1991). Two decades ago, Guzzetti, Kowalinski, and McGowan (1992) conducted research that confirmed how using trade books improves the affective domain of learning for students; the researchers were impressed "with students' enthusiasm for self-selection of 'real books'" (p. 115).

A classic study by Calfee (1987) noted that trade books offer causal relationships between concepts and provide a framework in which students can answer their own questions about the reading.

Although narrative has long been the main genre in use for primary aged students, Pappas's (1993) classic study questioned that practice and introduced the value of including expository text in the early grades. Duke's (2000, 2003) seminal research with first grade students has shown that young learners can effectively process and appreciate informational texts. As more quality books and materials have become available for young students, even emergent readers can find choices that appeal to their interests. Texts written at a variety of levels make it easier for teachers to find supplemental materials to support and enhance the curriculum.

Consult the reference section for articles containing complete copies of rubrics for evaluating science by Atkinson, Matusevich, and Huber (2009) and mathematics by Hunsader (2004). If your content is not science or math, how would you reword the questions to suit your content?

Not all trade books are created equal, so consider your selections carefully. Atkinson, Matusevich, and Huber (2009) developed and tested a rubric for identifying appropriate trade books for science instruction. To integrate key aspects recognized by experts in the field, they identified three critical questions for selecting quality trade books:

1. Does the book have substantial science content (scientists at work or scientific information)?
2. Is the science content (text, scale, vocabulary, and graphics) accurate?
3. Is the science content current? (p. 491)

Look for Joseph's (2008) complete article, "Beyond the textbook: Studying Roswell in the social studies classroom." *The Social Studies,* 99(3), 132–134.

Their rubric is an adaptation of Hunsader's (2004) model for evaluating mathematics trade books. In each case, books were rated for both qualities of literacy and content.

One of the primary advantages of using trade books with various content areas is the provision of real-world context and application for sometimes abstract and unfamiliar concepts (Hunsader, 2004). Teaching points situated in meaningful context helps students recognize the utility of the information for their own lives. "When students are captivated by a particular text, in a specific situation, with a host of environmental supports, they are enjoying a moment of situational interest" (Guthrie, Hoa, Wigfield, Tonks, & Perencevich, 2006, p. 2). Guthrie and his colleagues (2004, 2006) find evidence that situational interest, although not sufficient alone, can work together with other practices to increase long-term motivation for engaging with text.

Joseph (2008) developed a unit on Roswell for his social studies class to take them beyond the textbook to explore an age-old mystery in history. He included lessons to demonstrate the natural cross-curricular connections the topic presented for study. One lesson in that unit included the creation of a Venn diagram with interlocking circles for science, history, and English. Students were to fill in areas of study related to Roswell (e.g., UFOs, space travel, national security, solar system) that the disciplines would have in common. This could easily be adapted for many topics and disciplines. Inspiration Software, a visual learning tool for developing graphic organizers, would be a natural technology complement for this activity. See Activity 6.2 for a tree diagram example using communicable diseases as the unit topic.

Richardson (2000a) shows teachers how to present lessons that integrate literature with content topics. When teachers bring complementary reading selections to their students, they can help revitalize instruction by opening new avenues for students and teacher alike. Literature serves to cross the boundaries that seem to exist among content areas to demonstrate how skill sets used for each are similar. Predicting, making inferences, drawing conclusions, recognizing details and main ideas, identifying patterns, and problem solving are just a few that are commonly shared by all content areas. Joseph (2008) suggests using a well-known graphic organizer, the Venn diagram, to assist students in recognizing the crossover and overlapping connections a topic may have across the disciplines.

Please visit the Education CourseMate website at **www.cengagebrain.com** to find websites for cross-curricular units and lesson plans focusing on the environment, health, and diseases.

Content Area Literature Circles

Literature circles and book clubs are research based (Daniels, 1994; Lantendresse, 2004; Raphael, Florio-Ruane, & George, 2004; Sandmann & Gruhler, 2007) and widely accepted for reading instruction. Initially, fiction was the genre of choice for these small-group based strategies, but nonfiction has now been used with good success as well (Miller, Straits, Kucan, Trathen, & Dass, 2007; Straits & Nichols, 2006). Typically, the teacher introduces the book selections to the class, groups choose the book they will read, each group member is given or selects a role, roles are rotated as the book is read, regular discussions are held within the group, and a culminating project or

ACTIVITY 6.2 Communicable Diseases: Cross-curricular Connections (Middle School and High School)

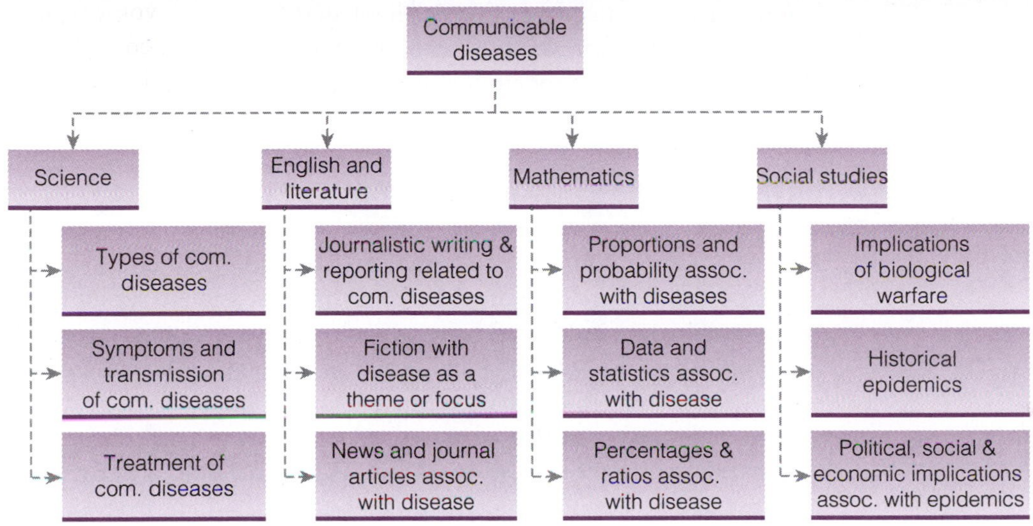

presentation is given. Literature circles are highly interactive and are appropriate for a myriad of topics and concepts. Straits and Nichols (2006) found that situating literature circles within science classes rates as a student favorite and encourages rich and lively discussion. These can be structured around a theme or topic or around a specific text or book.

With a topic as the focal point, a variety of texts can be used allowing for different reading levels. In text-based circles, all members read the same book. However, a possible alternative might be to have half of the members read an informational text and the other half read a fictional account that connects to the topic of the informational text. In any case, one of the primary tenets of literature circles is student choice, so although the teacher may bring in several sets from which the groups may choose, the selection is theirs. This gives them "buy-in" and heightens interest.

Typically, each group member has a specific task. Roles can be adapted or created to fit the text or the content. Straits and Nichols (2006) recommend tasks for use with science texts that could be modified for use with other content areas; these tasks include *science translator* (collects important words in the reading and records where each word is found in the text along with a brief definition), *science biographer* (finds and shares information about notable people connected to the topic), *fact finder* (goes beyond information in the text to find more detail and interesting related facts), and *everyday life connector* (finds examples, applications, and uses in everyday life that relate to the topic or text under study). Each circle presents a culminating project to demonstrate concepts learned. These may take the form of performances, videotapes, interviews, rewritten stories, or news broadcasts.

Daniels (1994), well known for his work with literature circles, offered the following tasks for beginning groups:

- Discussion director
- Illustrator
- Summarizer
- Passage master

To learn more and to see an instructional plan for Textmasters, please visit the Education CourseMate website at **www.cengagebrain.com** to find a link to ReadWriteThink, a website supported by the International Reading Association and the National Council of Teachers of English.

Considering the published success of literature circles (Miller, Straits, Kucan, Trathen, & Dass, 2007; Stein & Beed, 2004) and motivational factors typically associated with them, Wilfong (2009) decided to use a similar structure with textbooks as the focal reading material for an action research project she and a middle school teacher created and piloted. The structure, termed Textmasters, is a program for using literature circles with textbooks. Students have roles and presentations are given just as in literature circles, and the format essentially gives new life to textbook reading.

Multimodal Literature Circles

Technology applications should not be an add-on but rather a natural outgrowth of instruction and learning. Thompson (2008) had the vision to see multimodal literature circles as a logical and beneficial approach for adolescents to make use of tools for communication they use on a daily basis as a means for learning. She stressed that *multimodal* includes more than technology in that there are many other media forms besides traditional print that are effective for conveying ideas. She also wanted to help students recognize the overlap of disciplines within a unit of study, so she provided a structure that would allow students to view a concept or topic from various perspectives as well as from their own life experiences. Students were tasked with reading a text with each member of the group approaching the reading, discussion, and product with a different mindset based upon their roles. Students were encouraged to think about and include a variety of text types in their products and discussions rather than limiting themselves to traditional print text. Before meeting and discussing the text as a group, they were to first read the text for themselves and respond with their roles in mind using a blog.

TECH APP

Suggested Technology for Multimodal Literature Circles

Story Mapper: PowerPoint, Inspiration software

Discussion Director: Blackboard, discussion boards, blogs, social networking (Twitter, Facebook)

Artful Artist: Music recording software, iPods, photo software, video software or Flip camera, Internet clips or pictures

Investigator: Online research tools, Flip cameras

The primary text for this assignment was *Keesha's House* by Helen Frost. Using poetry, the work describes six teens dealing with issues of poverty, abuse, pregnancy, and other struggles and their search for safety and security. One investigator researched safe houses in the immediate area to find out what a teen should do in his or her community to get help. The product this student chose to illustrate her findings was a virtual poster providing critical information for locating help. A student having the role of story mapper created a game involving decision making that directed and changed the pathways and intersections of the teens' lives as they found their way to Keesha's house. Multimodal literature circles give students alternative ways to access and convey information for learning while developing an understanding of subtleties and differences each mode brings to the meaning.

Assessing the Readability of Textbooks and Resources

Barriers to Comprehension and Learning

This chapter so far has stressed the importance of using multiple resources instead of relying entirely on a textbook to convey content information. Too often teachers organize their instruction around the textbook rather than around the topic. Materials being considered by a teacher need to undergo thorough examination to determine what the textbook (or other supplementary content material) has to offer—but also to assess possible barriers to comprehension and learning. One common barrier is the reading level of the text. Considering readability when selecting texts and materials can be one useful way of determining the appropriate match of materials to students within a classroom. If the match is not a good one for the target readers, the teacher must consider finding materials that better match student background and expertise. Doing otherwise puts readers at a disadvantage.

With the standards movement and textbooks that are not a good match for required standards, teachers have had to seek out supplemental resources, so the focus on textbook only will need to change.

What is this notion of readability, and how does a teacher determine a readability match? Simply stated, **readability** is the match between reader and text. Readability suggests that content is clear, well expressed, and suited to the reader. It is an exploration of what characteristics within the reader and within the text will create a successful marriage. By examining readability, teachers can appropriately prepare readers to learn. Professional judgment is essential in determining readability; no score or formula can do more than help teachers understand that problems may arise with reading material. Too many factors are involved for teachers to settle for simple solutions. For instance, careful thought about grammar and its complexity is necessary when considering why students find written material more difficult than oral discussion of a topic. Unsworth (1999) discusses how English writing "packs" many content words into expository text—many more than in the spoken form. One can determine the lexical or grammatical density of a piece of writing by using Halladay's (1994) formula, which divides the number of lexical items by the number of clauses. Unsworth notes that this technique requires a functional grammatical perspective on English.

Another practice that has gained acceptance and popularity in elementary schools is that of using leveled texts. Various guidelines and leveling systems are used to organize and package sets of books targeting readers at specific levels. Other factors such as text formatting, content, predictability, and literary features that go beyond those generally included in readability formulas are criteria often used in determining these levels. This can be a useful tool for classroom teachers but when used to excess can be a concern (Dzaldov & Peterson, 2005). Dzaldov and Peterson found that "teachers' familiarity with their students' backgrounds, interests, and sociocultural identities is at least as important in identifying appropriate books for students as are lists based on book, print, language, and literary uniformity" (p. 228).

Recall Principle 1 in Chapter 1: *Learning is influenced by the reader's personal store of experience and knowledge.* Remind yourself why this is so important!

INCONSIDERATE DISCOURSE

"Your ring adjusters will shape to fit you right by following these simple steps." Wait a minute! Are the "ring adjusters" going to follow some simple steps? As this is written, the subjects, *ring adjusters,* are going to follow simple steps. Doesn't the author mean the reader is supposed to follow simple steps? And will the ring adjusters change shape to fit the reader, or fit the ring, or help the ring fit the reader? The author has written

Recall Principle 4 in Chapter 1: *Most language users are equipped with more than one version of their language; ideally, they will use a version that suits the circumstances.* How many readers abandon or postpone mastery of a new software program because its documentation is poorly written or presented? How many parents are frustrated when they find poorly written instructions for assembling toys?

a clumsy sentence in which the relationships between subject, verb, and direct object are confused.

Readers need to work extra hard to understand the meaning of text passages such as these. When confronted with such careless text, the reader must make a decision. Too often students decide that the text is simply not worth the energy. Similarly, some content material, particularly that found in textbooks, may be poorly written and therefore place unnecessary stress on a reader. If this is the case, teachers must identify the difficulties in the material to help readers expend the least energy for the greatest gain.

Poorly written material is recognizable because of its loose organization, lack of a discernible style, incorrect syntax, and incoherent passages. Armbruster and Anderson (1984) coined the term "**inconsiderate discourse**" several years ago to describe such material. College students indicated in a survey (Smith, 1992) that textbooks are generally boring because passages are too long, the writing style is hard to follow, graphics don't seem to relate to text, and information is either too detailed or repetitive. High school students who were asked to rate their textbooks and indicate how often they read and studied them said that they used mathematics texts most often followed by social studies, science, and English texts. However, they reported the text they liked *least* was the mathematics text because it was "hard to understand, boring, not specific enough, and poorly arranged" (Lester & Cheek, 1997, p. 285).

Textbooks are changing to include more images, features, and layouts that will appeal to students in contemporary society (Bezemer & Kress, 2008). They are designed to make use of technology, websites, and a variety of resources. Walpole (1999) found that newer science texts are more enticing to readers. She compared science textbooks for third graders written in 1992 and 1995 and found significant improvements in format, organization, text coherence, and illustrations. These factors all enter the mix that makes texts considerate or inconsiderate, coherent or incoherent.

TEXTUAL COHERENCE

For a text to be readable, it must exhibit **textual coherence** (Beck & McKeown, 1988), another term that has "stuck" in the file over time. Textual coherence—the clear presentation of material to facilitate comprehension—can be divided into two categories: global coherence and local coherence.

Global coherence refers to the big picture. Major ideas should span the entire text so readers are made aware of the global nature of the material and can follow the ideas without becoming confused. The way a text is structured can ensure global coherence. For example, the organization of ideas according to logical patterns, such as clear sequences of cause and effect, aids global comprehension. The style of text is also significant. A narrative style is usually easiest for readers followed by a more journalistic style. Hardest to read is exposition. It is confusing when a writer mixes exposition and narrative style but doesn't cue the reader. "This is a story about" or "The following description explains" provides clear cues to the style of text to follow. The frequent use of one style also helps the reader recognize and understand the structure of a text. Of course, the content of the material and how well the author matches it to its structure are also important for global coherence.

Local coherence involves the many kinds of aids that connect ideas at the more immediate, or local, level. These aids include cues within sentences—phrases or clauses, for example—between sentences or within paragraphs. When an author clearly identifies the subject and then uses a pronoun to refer to that subject, coherence is much greater than when the pronoun referent is vague and the reader is forced to guess to whom or what the author may be referring. Consider these passages, which Lederer (1987, p. 156) quotes as an example of text ambiguity:

> Guilt, vengeance, and bitterness can be emotionally destructive to you and your children. You must get rid of them.
>
> After Governor Baldwin watched the lion perform, he was taken to Main Street and fed 25 pounds of raw meat in front of the Cross Keys Theater.

Another type of poorly written text is that in which the author oversimplifies the context. Former Secretary of Education Terrell Bell (Toch, 1984) expressed concern over such textbooks, calling them "dumbed down." In **dumbed-down text**, global coherence may be so simplified that the author can't do justice to the content, and local coherence may be absent because there isn't enough complexity to the text. When important points and intricacies are missing, the reader loses both content and cues. To determine whether textual coherence is a problem, students are often the best resource.

How to Determine Readability of Textbooks and Resources

CHECKLISTS

One way to determine the readability of text material is to use a checklist in judging its overall strengths and weaknesses. Bader's (1987) textbook analysis chart (Figure 6.1) has always helped teachers by including and identifying several areas of concern, and lists specific items for teacher evaluation. The user is encouraged to summarize the textbook's strengths and weaknesses after completing the checklist and then to decide the implications of the summary for teaching the material evaluated.

The Bader analysis encourages teachers to consider several factors that contribute to readability. Whereas the category "linguistic factors," for example, describes word difficulty in six ways, a readability formula considers only the length of a word. Whereas the "writing style" category considers four measures of style, a readability formula considers only sentence length. The four other categories are not considered at all in a formula. "Conceptual factors" and "organizational factors" include criteria that many authors identify as having a crucial effect on text difficulty. In addition, the teacher is asked to think about "learning aids" because such aids can make otherwise difficult material easier for students to handle. This category also gives teachers direction in how to guide the reading of otherwise difficult material. For instance, visual aids often make difficult material readable. Because features such as typography, format, illustrations, and book appearance can enhance meaning in a text, Bader includes these items in her last category.

Be cautious when using checklists. First, no single checklist can cover all teaching factors. In addition, checklists must be general and rarely cover instructional content. But armed with tools such as those presented in this chapter, and with some knowledge of why determining the difficulty of reading material is important, teachers can proceed wisely.

THE RULE OF THUMB

A quick, reader-centered way to determine readability is to teach students to use the **rule of thumb** (Veatch, 1968). Younger students are told to select a book they want to read and to open to a middle page. If they spot an unknown word while reading that

FIGURE 6.1 Bader's Textbook Analysis Chart

+	✓	–		
Excellent/ Evident Throughout	Average/ Somewhat Evident	Poor/ Not Evident		

Book Title ______________________

Publisher ______________________

Grade Level ______________________

Content Area ______________________

+	✓	–	**Linguistic Factors**	*Comments*
______	______	______	This book is generally appropriate to intended grade level(s) according to ______ formula.	______________
______	______	______	Linguistic patterns are suitable to most populations and fit intended level(s).	______________
______	______	______	Vocabulary choice and control are suitable.	______________
______	______	______	New vocabulary is highlighted, italicized, in boldface type, or underlined.	______________
______	______	______	New vocabulary is defined in context.	______________
______	______	______	New vocabulary is defined in margin guides, glossary, or beginning or end of chapter.	______________
			Conceptual Factors	
______	______	______	The conceptual level is generally appropriate to intended grade level(s).	______________
______	______	______	Concepts are presented deductively.	______________
______	______	______	Concepts are presented inductively.	______________
______	______	______	Major ideas are highlighted, italicized, in boldface type, or underlined.	______________
______	______	______	Appropriate assumptions are made regarding prior level of concepts.	______________
______	______	______	New concepts are sufficiently developed through examples, illustrations, or redundancy.	______________ ______________
______	______	______	Sexual, racial, economic, cultural, and political bias are absent.	______________
			Organizational Factors	
______	______	______	Units, chapters, table of contents, and index present clear, logical development of subject.	______________
______	______	______	Chapters of instructional segments contain headings and subheadings that aid comprehension of subject.	______________
______	______	______	Introductory, definitional, illustrative, and summary paragraphs/sections are used as necessary.	______________
______	______	______	Topic sentences of paragraphs are clearly identifiable or easily inferred.	______________
______	______	______	Each chapter/section/unit contains a well-written summary or overview.	______________

FIGURE 6.1 (Continued)

+ Excellent/ Evident Throughout	✓ Average/ Somewhat Evident	− Poor/ Not Evident		*Comments*
Writing Style				
______	______	______	Ideas are expressed clearly and directly.	______
______	______	______	Word choice is appropriate.	______
______	______	______	Tone and manner of expression are appealing to intended readers.	______
______	______	______	Mechanics are correct.	______
Learning Aids				
______	______	______	Questions/tasks are appropriate to conceptual development of intended age/grade level(s).	______
______	______	______	Questions/tasks span levels of reasoning: literal, interpretive, critical, values clarification, and problem-solving.	______
______	______	______	Questions/tasks can be used as reading guides.	______
______	______	______	Suitable supplementary readings are suggested.	______
______	______	______	The book is clear and convenient to use.	______
______	______	______	Helpful ideas are presented for conceptual development.	______
______	______	______	Alternative instructional suggestions are given for poor readers, slow-learning students, and advanced students.	______
______	______	______	The book contains objectives, management plans, evaluation guidelines, and tests of satisfactory quality.	______
______	______	______	Supplementary aids are available.	______
Binding / Printing / Format / Illustrations				
______	______	______	Book size is appropriate.	______
______	______	______	Cover, binding, and paper are appropriate.	______
______	______	______	Typeface is appropriate.	______
______	______	______	Format is appropriate.	______
______	______	______	Pictures, charts, and graphs are appealing.	______
______	______	______	Illustrations aid comprehension of text.	______
______	______	______	Illustrations are free of sexual, social, or cultural bias.	______
Summary				
______	______	______	Totals	______

The strengths are:

The weaknesses are:

As a teacher, I will need to:

Original text analysis chart by Dr. Lois Bader, Michigan State University. Used with permission of Lois Bader.

page, they press a thumb on the table. For each hard word, they press down another finger. If they press down five or more fingers by the time they finish the page, the book may be too hard. Three or fewer fingers indicate a more reasonable challenge. No fingers means the book might be very easy. Older students can determine readability by using two hands and closing their fingers into fists. One closed fist indicates that the book is just right, two closed fists may indicate difficulty, and only one or two closed fingers may indicate easy material.

Of course, students should read the chosen book even if it appears to be too easy or too hard if that is their wish. The rule of thumb is not scientific and is intended only to help readers make decisions. It is not intended to discourage a reader from trying any book. Its value is that it encourages the reader to be responsible for determining difficulty. This involvement of the reader promotes independence.

READABILITY FORMULAS

Readability formulas are frequently used for determining the difficulty of material. They are fairly reliable starting measures for making instructional decisions about texts. Readability formulas are a narrow measure of readability.

A quick first look at material to spot potential problems with difficulty can be accomplished by using a readability formula. Because formulas identify a certain grade level of difficulty, they are used most often to report information about textbook difficulty in terms of reading-level scores. A formula can be helpful when a prediction of difficulty is necessary, such as when a textbook adoption committee considers several texts but cannot try out the book with real students. Similarly, a formula may be useful and efficient when a teacher wants to assess the difficulty of several materials that students are to read on their own in the library. A readability formula offers a fairly quick measure and can be used independently of student interaction. However, teachers must not rely on the grade level obtained as an exact measure; it is only a predictor.

HOW READABILITY FORMULAS WORK

The Lexile Framework developed in the mid-1980s is based on the words found in textbooks. It is designed to measure both a student's reading ability and the difficulty level of a text using the same numeric scale. More detailed information can be found in the next section of this chapter.

A readability formula would score the first sentence as more difficult, but would it be more difficult for children to comprehend?

Over the years, reading researchers have developed and statistically validated many readability formulas. Some are cumbersome in that they necessitate checking long lists of words. Over several decades, the formula approach has evolved somewhat. Both the Dale and Chall (1948) and the Spache (1953) measure "word familiarity"—that is, whether students should be expected to know a word within a given passage—by relying on lengthy word lists. Mosenthal and Kirsch (1998) developed a comprehensive measure that focuses on the structure and density that create complexity. Their measure demonstrates that difficulty in reading a document may be due more to the document's complexity than to the reader's abilities.

Essentially, two measurements are used for almost all of these formulas: sentence difficulty and word difficulty. The underlying assumption is that longer sentences and words create harder material. Usually, this assumption holds true; sometimes, however, it does not. For instance, in William Faulkner's novel *The Sound and the Fury,* several sentences are as much as one and a half pages long, and most readers would agree that the length of Faulkner's sentences makes challenging reading. But could one say that because Ernest Hemingway's sentences are shorter, his material is easier to read? In these cases, one reads to understand style and theme, and sentence length is of little importance. Compare these two sentences: "The children played on the playground with the elephant." "We reneged on all prior briefs."

The syntactical structure of sentences probably deserves more attention than it receives in readability formulas. For example, sentences in the active voice may be easier to understand than those in the passive voice. Readability formulas do not measure with such sensitivity. Also, word length may be a fairly accurate indicator of difficulty. Just as short sentences seem easier to read, short words generally also seem easier on a reader. First graders recognize many one-syllable words. But *elephant* might be an easier word for young readers than *the*. *Elephant* may be longer, but it's a lot easier to picture an *elephant* than to picture *the!* Because visualizing words facilitates comprehension, the longer word is easier in this case. Few readers wish to encounter a lot of long words all at once, but they will be bored by too many short ones. Given these qualifiers, the way most readability formulas measure reading material is common, if not common sense. A few formulas remain popular because they are easy to apply and seem reliable. We describe the Fry readability formula and the SMOG formula in Appendix B.

THE LEXILE FRAMEWORK

In recent years, many school systems have adopted the use of the Lexile Framework® (Lennon & Burdick, 2004). It is an adaptation of readability measures but has the added benefit of including both reader ability and text difficulty on the same scale, as a means to match a reader with an appropriate text. Most standardized reading tests have the capability of providing student reading scores in Lexiles. This removes some of the inconsistency that may be experienced with leveled texts because criteria for determining levels vary so much that one method may yield a different level than another. Notice the variation across the measures for *When Hitler Stole Pink Rabbit* (Kerr, 2009) and *The Old Man and the Sea* (Hemmingway, 1996) in Table 6.1. They have the same Lexile score but quite different recommended grade levels and Fry scores. Additionally, there may be a wide range of difficulty levels associated with one grade level, as you will also see in Table 6.1.

TABLE 6.1 A Comparison of Recommended Books and Readability Scores

Author and Book	Recommended Grade	Fry Readability Score	Lexile Score
Patricia Polacco, *Chicken Sunday*	Second	Second	650L
Paula Danziger, *Amber Brown is Not a Crayon*	Third	Fifth	720L
Richard and Florence Atwater, *Mr. Popper's Penguins*	Third	Sixth	910L
Louis Sachar, *Holes*	Fifth	Seventh	660L
Mildred Taylor, *Roll of Thunder, Hear My Cry*	Fifth	Eighth	920L
Judith Kerr, *When Hitler Stole Pink Rabbit*	Seventh	Sixth	940L
Karen Cushman, *The Midwife's Apprentice*	Seventh	Eighth	1240L
Sandra Cisneros, *The House on Mango Street*	Ninth	Sixth	870L
J. R. R. Tolkien, *The Hobbit*	Ninth	Seventh	1000L
Olive Ann Burns, *Cold Sassy Tree*	Tenth	Fifth	930L
Ernest Hemingway, *The Old Man and the Sea*	Eleventh	Eighth	940L
J. D. Salinger, *Catcher in the Rye*	Eleventh	Sixth	790L
Jane Austen, *Sense and Sensibility*	Twelfth	Eleventh	1180L
H. G. Wells, *The War of the Worlds*	Twelfth	Tenth	1100L

One of the primary advantages to Lexile scores is the use of the same scale for measuring student ability and text difficulty; this can offer a more precise manner of matching readers with texts. Another clear advantage to Lexile scores is that they do not look like grade levels, so this minimizes stigma attached to grade level texts (e.g., third grade reader, fourth grade reader). Lexile scores range from 0L to 2000L with each Lexile unit "calibrated to represent equal intervals of difficulty" (Westby, 2008, p. 9). About 200 units represent each grade, but with the wide range of reading abilities found within the typical classroom, Lexiles for a classroom of students will overlap the grades. A student's score indicates a range of 50 above and 100 below on the Lexile scale. When students are matched with texts using their Lexile measure, they should have a 75% comprehension rate; this would be challenging but not frustrating.

Most schools and school systems provide students a list of recommended books from which to select summer reading or even reading during the school year. Take a look at a comparison of books recommended for students in various grade levels along with Fry Readability scores and the Lexile scores for those books. Clearly, books recommended for students in a common grade are not all written at the same level of difficulty, nor will all students within that grade have equal ability to read those books. Just because a book has vocabulary and sentence length thought to be suitable for a certain student does not mean the content and concept development are appropriate for that student. *Catcher in the Rye* (Salinger, 2001) is one case in point. Book selection and choice involve a great deal more than vocabulary and sentence length.

However, because in actuality the trade books identified with a particular grade level may vary considerably in difficulty level, knowing the Lexile score may help avoid the stigma struggling students often experience while offering appropriate matches for them. For example, one fourth grader could be reading *Tales of a Fourth Grade Nothing* (Blume, 1991) (470L), and another could be reading *From the Mixed Up Files of Mrs. Basil E. Frankweiler* (Konigsburg, 2002) (700L) with both books typically considered fourth grade material.

Textbook and trade book publishers are increasingly providing teachers with Lexile information so they can make selections for their students. Similar to readability formula scores, Lexile scores are based primarily on semantics (word difficulty) and syntax (grammar and sentence structure). The Lexile Framework® is one way to measure a student's reading ability, but it is not a method or program for teaching reading.

SMOG, FRY, AND FLESCH-KINCAID READABILITY FORMULAS

Try calculating readability of a passage in a textbook using both the Fry and the SMOG to see the difference in the results. Remember, the Fry is used for determining instructional reading level, and the SMOG is for finding independent reading level.

For **independent-level reading**—material that students will read on their own with 90 percent or more comprehension—the McLaughlin's (1969) SMOG formula may be used. Directions for using it and the Fry Readability Formula are presented in Appendix B. In choosing between Fry and SMOG, remember that these two formulas are used for different purposes and that the readability scores they yield are interpreted differently. The Fry formula measures the readability of material used in an instructional setting. Because the teacher explains difficult words and sentences, the Fry score is based on students understanding 65 to 75 percent of the material at a given grade level. The SMOG formula is intended to measure the readability of material that a teacher will *not* be teaching, such as material that the teacher has suggested a student use independently. Because the teacher will *not* be explaining difficult words and sentences, the SMOG score is based on students understanding 90 to 100 percent of the material. If Fry and SMOG scores were calculated on the same material, the Fry score probably would be lower.

Word processing programs such as Microsoft Word provide readability statistics for any document being processed. The statistics provide the Flesch-Kincaid grade level, which measures readability based on the average number of syllables per word and the average number of words per sentence. The score is reported as a grade level similar to the Fry grade-level score. Some programs provide various measures with which to compare the Flesch-Kincaid grade-level scores. By typing a few passages into a computer and using these readability measures, you can get a feel for the readability of text without counting words and syllables.

Microsoft versions as well as Mac and PC differences make accessing readability features different. Consult the "Help" information to find specific steps.

CAUTIONS ABOUT READABILITY FORMULAS

In recent literature, professionals warn teachers of the limitations of readability formulas. Formula estimates represent a limited number of factors that can be counted without consideration of student interest or background that are not easily quantified. Most formulas do not provide a scale that measures both student performance and text difficulty. Consequently, this adds to the difficulty of matching students with appropriate texts (Walpole, Hayes, & Robnolt, 2006). Readability formulas are not precise determiners of the difficulty of material; they merely predict how difficult material might be for readers.

1. **A readability formula gives a grade-level score, which is not a very specific measure of difficulty because grade level can be so ambiguous.** Cadenhead (1987) describes this ambiguity as the "metaphor of reading level" and claims that it is a major problem of readability formulas. What does *17th grade level* mean when applied to a topic such as "electrical attraction of dielectric insulation" without consideration of the reader's interests, background, and knowledge? A grade-level readability score gives teachers a start in their considerations of text difficulty—not a complete picture.
2. **The lengths of sentences and words are convenient and credible indicators of readability and fit neatly into a formula but are not comprehensive measures.** The various factors that make a text coherent are difficult to quantify. Remember that readability formulas cannot get at the depth of the ideas inherent in a text. One cannot compute such factors in a simple mathematical formula.
3. **Measures of word and sentence length are sometimes not the most accurate indicators of difficulty.** We refer readers to noted author E. B. White's (1951) essay "Calculating Machine," which recounts White's reaction when he received a "reading-ease calculator" developed by General Motors and based on the Flesch Reading Ease Formula. "Communication by the written word," writes White, "is a subtler (and more beautiful) thing than Dr. Flesch and General Motors imagine" (p. 166). His point is well taken: It is dangerous to reduce language to such simplistic evaluation. Additionally, background of experience and cultural differences can assist or hinder when reading new material. Reading a text describing space travel and research may prove less challenging for students living in a community of people employed primarily

by the National Aeronautics and Space Administration. Reading difficulty may be increased as ELL students struggle with the added challenges presented by figurative language and language structures unlike those of their native languages.

4. **The fewer the sections of material measured, the less consistent and reliable the resulting score is likely to be.** Even three sections may be too few. If three or fewer sections are measured, a teacher should be cautious about accepting the results. We include the Fry Short Formula in Appendix B, which should be used only when material contains fewer than 100 words, such as in books for young readers. However, almost always in such a case, the teacher can assess readability efficiently by relying on checklists and professional judgment.

The concept of readability and the efficacy of readability formulas stir much controversy. Although formulas can tell us some things, they yield levels based on the percentage of readers who have performed well at those levels and as such tell us a lot less than we want to know. We maintain that formulas provide only one measure and should be used with checklists and commonsense criteria to judge the readability of a text for a group of students.

Assessing Students' Ability to Use Books

Several activities can help teachers assess students' comprehension of text and general background knowledge. Using relevant materials, the teacher can construct cloze and maze passages that can serve as guides for students to learn how to think about texts both before and during the reading.

The Cloze Procedure

The cloze procedure offers an interactive way to assess the match between readers and texts. The term **cloze**, first used by Wilson Taylor in 1953, reflects the gestalt principle of closure, or "the tendency to perceive things as wholes, even if parts are missing" (Harris & Hodges, 1995, p. 33). In the cloze procedure, a passage is cut up so that students can fill it in. The premise is that readers rely on prior knowledge and use of context as they close, or complete, the cut-up passage. Ebbinghaus (1908), in the late 1800s, used a modified form of closure when he conducted his verbal learning and retention studies (described in Chapter 9).

When Taylor designed the cloze procedure, as we now use it, his purpose was to determine the readability of material for different readers. In the strict format that Taylor designed (random cloze), the teacher first chooses a passage of 250 or more words. Then words are deleted at regular intervals—every 5th, 10th, or *n*th (any predetermined number) word. The beginning and ending sentences remain intact. Blanks replace the deleted words, and no clues other than the context of the material are provided to the reader, who must fill in those blanks. The cloze procedure can be useful at any grade level if the pattern of deletions is sensitive to the students' familiarity with language. We generally recommend that every tenth word be deleted for primary students because young students need more clues than older, more proficient readers with greater reading experience. Every fifth word should be deleted for older students (fourth grade and above) because they have had more experience with reading and using context.

Using Cloze for Determining and Building Background Knowledge

By using a cloze test, a teacher can find out whether students have prior knowledge about upcoming material and are able to adapt to the author's style. The readers demonstrate their prior knowledge because they have to apply it when choosing the best words to insert in a cut-up passage. Their background knowledge helps them fill in gaps; their prior knowledge of language also helps them make good choices. If students complete the cloze with ease, they achieve an *independent-level score,* indicating that they can read the material on their own. If they can adapt when the teacher provides instruction about the material, they achieve an *instructional-level score.* A *frustration-level score* indicates that the material is difficult for readers to understand even with instruction.

Because the purpose of the cloze procedure is to help a teacher quickly see whether students have adequate background knowledge and understand the language clues used in the material in question, scoring should be rapid and efficient. When cloze is used to determine prior knowledge, students are not expected to see the cloze exercise again, and the teacher should not use it as a teaching tool. When cloze is used in this way, exact word replacement is the most efficient scoring procedure. In Taylor's presentation of cloze, only the exact word that was deleted is counted as a correct answer, and research (Bormouth, 1969) indicates that the exact word score is the most valid. Because only exact answers are counted, a score of 40 to 60 percent correct is acceptable. Although scoring seems stringent, the criteria for achieving an instructional level of readability are quite relaxed to compensate for inadequate prior knowledge and the synonym factor.

Recall a mention of modified cloze in Chapter 3. Directions for constructing a cloze test to determine readers' background knowledge and comprehension can be found in Appendix B.

EXAMPLES OF CLOZE TO DETERMINE BACKGROUND KNOWLEDGE

An English teacher of eleventh graders in a school that was new to her wondered how the students might perform with a textbook that was also new to her and what accommodations she might need to make. These students had been labeled "high ability," but she knew that labels often do not indicate true performance. So she developed a cloze on a 300-word passage from the introduction to the textbook. The passage compared the origins of early American literature to people landing on the moon: Both were adventures and initial explorations of a new era. Would her students have sufficient background to understand this analogy? Would they have enough language skill to read this and ensuing passages with facility?

Try to create a cloze activity for assessing students' background knowledge of a topic in a textbook used in one of the classes you teach.

She administered the cloze during the first week of school before issuing textbooks so she could anticipate difficulties from the outset. Students were instructed to do their best to fill in the words they thought would fit as a way to help the teacher get to know them better; the teacher assured them that they would not be graded. She

ACTIVITY 6.3 Cloze for Elementary Social Studies

A VISIT TO ST. PETERSBURG, RUSSIA

St. Petersburg was first called Lovingood. It is on the delta of the Neva River. __1__ is at the eastern end of the Gulf of __2__. The city is built on both bodies of the __3__ and on islands in the river. It is the __4__ largest city in Russia. The city is a major __5__. St. Petersburg is famous for its elaborate palaces and __6__. One of the city's most visited attractions is the __7__ Palace. It was the winter home of the Czars __8__ the 1917 Russian Revolution. The Hermitage is a museum. __9__ has a great art collection. Visitors to St. Petersburg __10__ its beauty and history. It is a majestic city.

ANSWER KEY

1. It; **2.** Finland; **3.** Neva; **4.** second; **5.** seaport; **6.** churches; **7.** Winter; **8.** before; **9.** It; **10.** love

never returned the cloze to the students; the exercise was for diagnosis, not instruction. She scored it using the exact-word criterion. In this way, she was able to develop a quick profile for 55 students in two sections. One student scored at the independent level; two scored at the frustration level. She decided that with proper guidance, the majority of students would bring adequate knowledge to the textbook. She made a note to watch the two students who scored poorly, as well as the high scorer.

What might the teacher do with this information to differentiate appropriately and to address these students' needs?

As the first weeks passed, she learned that one of the low-scoring students came from an abusive home and could not concentrate on academics even though he was capable. The other low scorer was unhappy to have been placed in a high-ability class because all she wanted to do was play in the band and coast through school. The teacher was able to find appropriate help for each of them. The high scorer continued to perform almost flawlessly on the assignments during the beginning weeks of school. The teacher discovered that this student was new to the school but had been in advanced classes in her previous school. Within the first three weeks, the teacher was able to recommend that the student be placed in an advanced class; the cloze results provided supporting documentation. The teacher might have missed an opportunity to help these three students had she not administered the cloze. Helpful diagnostic information was learned from an activity that took little time: It was administered to 55 students in 15 minutes.

Note two examples of cloze activities:

- Activity 6.3 is a cloze for an elementary level social studies chapter.
- Activity 6.4 is an example of a cloze for high school reading from a technology textbook.

Caution: A cloze procedure can reveal what students already know about a subject and can indicate whether the material is appropriate. The better students do, the more they probably know about the topic. If most students fall in the frustration level, the material is inappropriate because they may not bring enough background to it. Ashby-Davis (1985) warns, however, that a cloze procedure is not like the usual reading that students do. Reading speed, eye movements, and use of context are likely to be different when reading a cloze. Therefore, a cloze may be a helpful indicator of a student's background in a particular topic but it is not a reliable measure of a student's specific reading skills.

USING CLOZE TO BUILD ON BACKGROUND KNOWLEDGE

When a cloze is used for instructional purposes instead of for assessment, the range of possible cloze constructions increases. Instead of exact replacement of vocabulary,

ACTIVITY 6.4 Cloze for Secondary Vocational Education

STUDENT DIRECTIONS

Below is a passage taken from your technology textbook. Some of the words the author wrote have been deleted. Your job is to write in the blank the word that you *think* the author might have used in the same space. Your choices will help me get to know you as readers of this textbook. Good luck, and do your best!

CONSTRUCTION OF THE SMALL GASOLINE ENGINE

The internal combustion engine is classified as a *heat* engine; its power is produced by burning a fuel. The energy stored in __1__ fuel is released when __2__ is burned. *Internal combustion* __3__ that the fuel is __4__ inside the engine itself. __5__ most common fuel is __6__. If gasoline is to __7__ inside the engine, there __8__ be oxygen present to __9__ the combustion. Therefore, the __10__ needs to be a __11__ of gasoline and air. __12__ ignited, a fuel mixture __13__ gasoline and air burns __14__; it almost explodes. The __15__ is designed to harness __16__ energy.

The engine contains __17__ cylindrical area commonly called __18__ *cylinder* that is open __19__ both ends. The top __20__ the cylinder is covered __21__ a tightly bolted-down plate __22__ the *cylinder head*. The __23__ contains a *piston*, which __24__ a cylindrical part that __25__ the cylinder with little __26__. The piston is free __27__ slide up and down __28__ the cylinder. The air/fuel __29__ is brought into the __30__, then the piston moves __31__ and compresses it into __32__ small space called the __33__ chamber. The *combustion chamber* is __34__ area where the fuel __35__ burned; it usually consists __36__ a cavity in the __37__ head and perhaps the __38__ part of the cylinder. __39__ the fuel is ignited __40__ burns, tremendous pressure builds __41__. This pressure forces the __42__ back down the cylinder; __43__ the untamed energy of __44__ is harnessed to become __45__ mechanical energy. The basic __46__ within the engine is __47__ of the piston sliding __48__ and down the cylinder, __49__ *reciprocating* motion.

There are __50__ many problems, however. How can the up-and-down motion of the piston be converted into useful rotary motion? How can exhaust gases be removed? How can new fuel mixture be brought into the combustion chamber? Studying the engine's basic parts can help answer these questions.

ANSWERS

1. the; **2.** it; **3.** means; **4.** burned; **5.** The; **6.** gasoline; **7.** burn; **8.** must; **9.** support; **10.** fuel; **11.** mixture; **12.** When; **13.** of; **14.** rapidly; **15.** engine; **16.** this; **17.** a; **18.** the; **19.** at; **20.** of; **21.** with; **22.** called; **23.** cylinder; **24.** is; **25.** fits; **26.** clearance; **27.** to; **28.** within; **29.** mixture; **30.** cylinder; **31.** up; **32.** a; **33.** combustion; **34.** the; **35.** is; **36.** of; **37.** cylinder; **38.** uppermost; **39.** When; **40.** and; **41.** up; **42.** piston; **43.** thus; **44.** combustion; **45.** useful; **46.** motion; **47.** that; **48.** up; **49.** a; **50.** still

synonyms can be considered. In constructing an instructional cloze, the teacher leaves beginning and ending sentences intact, but the deletions can serve different instructional purposes. For example, the teacher may delete all of a specific part of speech (rational cloze), such as the verbs or adjectives, and then ask students to predict what part of speech the deleted words must be. An instructional cloze can also include clues. For example, in Activity 6.5, the teacher deleted important terms about the making of the cell and provided a diagram of an animal cell. Clues from the reading help give a student the answers. At the same time, the student gets visual clues in the drawing to help in decision making.

ACTIVITY 6.5 Cloze for Building on Prior Knowledge (Middle School)

CLOZE ACTIVITY ON CELLS

Cells are made of smaller parts that do certain jobs. Look at the animal cell on the next page. It is about 1,600 times larger than the actual size of the cell. Notice the cell has a large (1) ___ floating in cytoplasm.

The cell has an outer covering called the (2) _____ _____ The cell membrane lets nutrients, water, and other materials in and out of the cell. The inside of the cell is filled with cytoplasm—a clear, jellylike material. Cytoplasm is mostly water, but it also contains dissolved nutrients and cell parts called (3) ___.

The organelles in the cytoplasm have different jobs. Some organelles help make proteins in the cell. Others release energy from nutrients. The saclike organelles in the picture—called (4) ___ —store nutrients, water, and wastes. Find the nucleus in the cell. The nucleus is a large organelle. It has a membrane that surrounds a mesh of structures called chromosomes. The chromosomes are made of (5) ___ —deoxyribonucleic acid. The chromosomes contain instructions that control all the cell's activities. For example, chromosomes control how fast the cell grows and when the cell reproduces.

Different kinds of organisms have different numbers of chromosomes in their cells. Most of your cells have 46 chromosomes. A crayfish has 200 chromosomes in most of its cells, while a sunflower has 17 chromosomes in most of its cells.

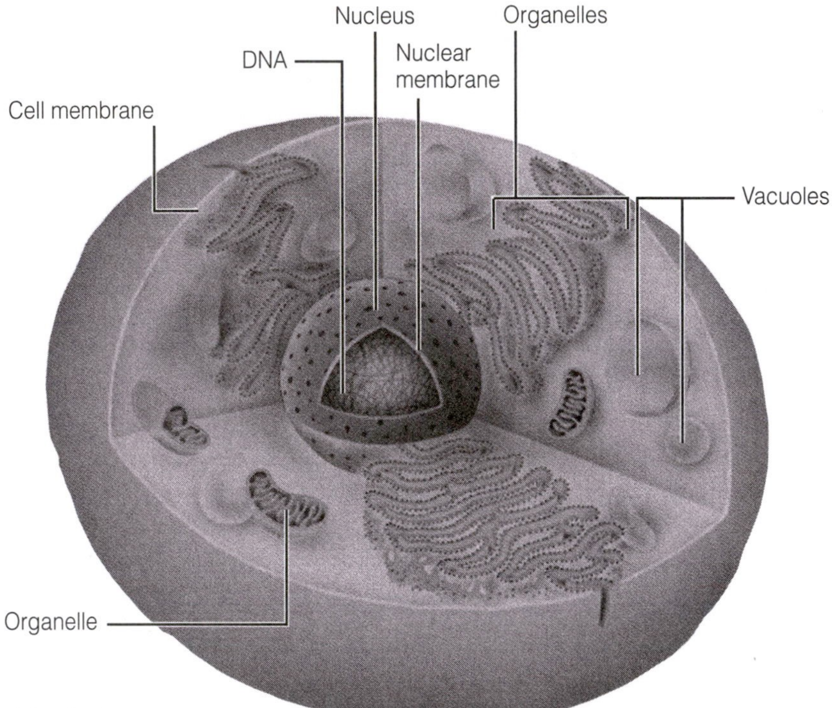

Animal cell

Whatever the design, an instructional cloze can help teachers learn what their students already know and, along with discussion of the choices made, build their knowledge of the material. Steinman (2002), who uses cloze for instruction with ELL students, emphasizes the importance of selecting passages that are both interesting and relevant to keep students engaged and focused. Discussion should whet readers' appetites for the reading material that follows, thus giving students a purpose for reading and assisting their comprehension of the material. Because discussing the students' choices is an obvious part of the activity when it is used for instruction, cloze also fosters listening and speaking opportunities. Although word choices are limited to single-word entries, some writing occurs as well.

Some teachers find cloze useful as a technique for reflection. Such an interactive cloze procedure is explained in the Chapter 7 discussion of vocabulary.

The Maze

A strategy similar to cloze but easier for students to respond to is a **maze** (Guthrie, Burnam, Caplan, & Seifert, 1974), which is especially useful for ascertaining students' prior knowledge and understanding of a subject. The teacher selects a passage of 100 to 120 words from a representative part of the textbook and deletes every fifth or tenth word. The students are then given three choices: (1) the correct word, (2) a grammatically similar but incorrect word, and (3) a distracter, which is a grammatically different and incorrect word. Because a maze is easier for students to complete than a cloze, the scoring criteria are more stringent. A maze is a bit harder to construct than a cloze because the teacher must provide three choices for each deleted word; nevertheless, many teachers prefer it. Activity 6.6 shows a maze for primary science material.

What are the differences between a cloze and a maze, and what are the benefits and disadvantages of each?

ACTIVITY 6.6 A Maze for Primary Science Students

WHAT CAN MAKE THINGS MOVE?

Air can make things move. It can make a toy frog jump. Squeezing pushes {art / are / air} through a tube.

Air fills the legs under the {frog. / fig. / from.} The legs push the frog to make it jump. {And / Air / At} can make a horn blow.

Squeezing pushes air through {the / them / tug} horn. Then the horn makes a sound.

Moving air {also / as / ago} makes this party blower work. Moving air is a {poor. / push. / pin.}

Wind is moving air. Wind can fill the sails {of / on / or} a boat and push it across the water.

Wind {cane / coat / can} push a pinwheel and turn a windmill. Water can {made / make / mask} things move, too.

Water can make a water wheel {turn. / torn. / told.} It can also push people and things.

Developed by Marvette Darby.

Similar to a cloze, a maze builds background as it reveals it. Because choices are given, students who lack prior knowledge have some material to react to. This interaction promotes the use of partial associations. Many teachers prefer a maze to a cloze for building background because it is less threatening to students and better promotes discussion. From the maze, students can move right into reading the whole material, practicing the use of context clues.

Critical Literacy Applications for Multimodal Texts

Interactive Reading

Wray (1994) describes the roles of text author, student, and teacher as interactive. He encourages students to consider the author's role in clarifying meaning through text. This can be done only when teachers support students in becoming critics rather than remaining passive recipients. As students thoughtfully examine texts while making decisions and taking action, knowledge and its application go beyond the classroom walls. Lent (2006) reminds us that when students reach high school, they often become disengaged from learning and may look upon it as something they are *made* to do rather than as something beneficial and enjoyable:

> For students to become engaged in learning a subject, they must be both immersed in it and intrigued by it—and they must believe that their new learning has relevance to their lives. Consider why adults think critically: to solve a problem, satisfy curiosity, or increase knowledge. Rarely do we dig into learning just for the purpose of passing a test. (p. 69)

The process of recording, editing, and rerecording episodes for a podcast project can help students understand ways information can be manipulated and socially constructed.

Building on the introduction to critical literacy in Chapter 5, teachers must consider that students are able to access and use a greater variety of texts and text sources than ever before. Many of these texts are not reviewed, regulated, or monitored for accuracy or bias. Students need to understand that published text (printed, electronic, broadcast) is not necessarily accurate or neutral (Anstey & Bull, 2006; Gainer, 2010; Vasquez, 2010). Teachers can help raise awareness levels to help students recognize that texts are consciously constructed to inform and shape the ideas, attitudes, and actions of the reader. Students must learn to read various forms of text with an eye toward author intentions and purpose, the authenticity and authority of the source, and facts in evidence and those left unsaid. A multiliterate person must be "a problem solver and strategic thinker, that is an active and informed citizen" (Anstey & Bull, 2006, p. 23).

Approaches to Reading Electronic Vs. Traditional Print

Developing the skill and practice of questioning and investigating texts and finding more than one source for verification in order to make informed decisions is a life skill. Students must understand that traditional print and the many things they read on the Web are all written by an author or authors who write with perspectives, values, and viewpoints that shape the writing and the reader's understanding. Students approach traditional and electronic texts with very different mindsets, strategies, and beliefs, and that perceived textual authority influences how adolescents read

(Olson & Truxaw, 2009). Olson and Truxaw found that students tend to trust traditional texts and routinely read them linearly and carefully.

Students in the same study (Olson & Truxaw, 2009) approached online selections quite differently. Some students scanned sites quickly, judging site credibility based on the structure and type of site. They discounted blogs and dismissed sites that were difficult to navigate. Some students went directly to sites of well-respected organizations, searched for keywords, and read only portions they considered relevant for their investigation. Still others went to the first site on the list provided by the search engine. Skill levels for searching and analyzing were not equal among students, and facility with traditional text did not translate to facility with online resources. Reading electronic text analytically includes making selections about which links to explore more deeply; reading traditional text carefully doesn't involve the same level of deep thinking and decision making. Consequently, students were more likely to analyze online text than to read traditional print resources critically.

Soares and Wood (2010) suggest a series of questions that may be used to examine text critically:

1. What does the author want us to know?
2. What different interpretations are possible?
3. What kind of person with what interests and values wrote this text?
4. What view of the world is this text presenting?
5. How is power used, and what effect does power have on others?
6. Whose voice is missing, and what alternate ways can texts be presented to give voice to the silenced? (p. 488)

What might you do in the classroom to connect the curriculum to students' life experiences?

The pressure to prepare students for passing standards assessments has in some cases limited the scope of the curriculum, the use of resources, and the range of pedagogical approaches. In fact, there are frequently options for moving beyond the constraints while addressing the standards and requirements within a system. Teachers need ways to have a more inclusive curriculum, sources, and strategies for providing students with life and community connections to bring the element of relevance to the classroom. These types of connections make the learning experiences long lasting. Cordova and Mattiesen (2010) argue that teachers who use life connections "are guiding students to navigate the cultural expectations and demands embedded within the official curriculum, by honoring their own lived experiences as resources for academic learning" (p. 456).

Cooperative Learning Beyond the Textbook

One way of engaging students in social interaction and problem solving experiences similar to those in their life worlds is to involve them in collaborative and cooperative learning endeavors.

You learned about a variety of cooperative learning strategies in Chapter 5.
In Chapter 11, you will find cooperative strategies that work well with diverse learners.

However, it is important to address some particular aspects of cooperative learning for use with texts beyond the textbook. Ozkan (2010) proposes that an Internet-based environment offers an excellent venue for using cooperative learning strategies for building community and enriching learning both synchronously and asynchronously. He contends that cooperative learning has some distinct advantages for use with Web-based education. Certainly, it provides easy access and means of

Students enjoy using electronic devices and Web tools to enhance projects and add to their learning experience. For example:

- Flip cameras: video clips and photographs
- Podcasts: sound bites and interviews
- Skype: video dialoging
- PowerPoint: presentations with key points and pictures
- Inspiration software: graphic organizers

exchanging ideas and information in both real and delayed timeframes. However, consideration must be given to students who do not have the advantage of home computers, Internet service, and other electronic devices. Some schools may offer support, and many public libraries have computers available for the public use at no charge. Two cooperative learning strategies that students can work within to use electronic tools at school and home are jigsaw and three-step interviews.

Jigsaw

Aronson (1978) describes a cooperative learning strategy called **jigsaw**, named for its resemblance to a jigsaw puzzle. In this strategy, each student in a five- or six-member group is given unique information about a topic that the group is studying. After reading their material, the students meet in "expert groups" with their counterparts from other groups to discuss and master the information. In a variation called jigsaw II (Slavin, 1980), all students are first given common information. Then student "experts" teach more specific topics to the group. Students take tests individually, and team scores are posted by the teacher.

Jigsaw uses two distinct grouping patterns: heterogeneous study groups and homogeneous discussion groups. Study groups are arranged heterogeneously by ability or age level to learn about subtopics. The purpose of the study groups is to allow each member to become expert in a particular topic in common with other group members. Discussion groups are arranged homogeneously by ability or age level to discuss the different subtopics that members studied in their study groups. The purpose of the discussion groups is to allow each member to share his or her expertise with others who share a common perspective.

The number of members in each discussion group must equal or exceed the number of study groups. This is to ensure that at least one discussion group member is in each study group. For example, a class of 22 students might be divided into three groups by reading ability to form homogeneous discussion groups. Discussion groups would then count off by fours to establish the heterogeneous study groups, thus ensuring equal representation of the reading groups in each study group.

Each study group is assigned one of the subtopics to research, dividing the available materials and informational resources among its members. After each member completes his or her assignment, the study group meets for a sharing session. Each member teaches the other members what he or she learned about the subtopic, so that all members become experts on the assigned subtopic. They bring the results of their study back to the discussion group for sharing with students who have become experts on other subtopics. In this way, all students have the opportunity to do a small amount of research, present their findings, and listen to and learn from other students. See Activity 6.7 for an example.

Three-Step Interview

The three-step interview is a multipurpose, critical thinking strategy designed for groups of four but adaptable for other group sizes (Kagan, 1994). The teacher proposes a topic or starting questions for interviews. In groups of four, members partner for the first step. Partner one interviews partner two. For the second step,

ACTIVITY 6.7 The Life of the Native American

HOMOGENEOUS GROUPS		
Above Level	**On Level**	**Below Level**
1. Sue	4.Terrique	1. Carlos
2. Ramon	1. John	2. Lisa
3. Malique	2. Terrell	3. Jesse
4. Shannon	3. Carol	4. Carmen
1. LaShawn	4. Erica	1. Luke
2. Robert	1. Jim	2. Monique
3. Heather	2. DaQuan	
	3. Raquel	
	4. Maria	

THE LIFE OF THE NATIVE AMERICAN—HETEROGENEOUS GROUPS—STUDY GROUPS			
Traditions, Myths, and Legends	**Occupations and Products**	**Lifestyles**	**Origin and History**
1. Sue	2. Ramon	3. Malique	4. Shannon
1. LaShawn	2. Robert	3. Heather	4.Terrique
1. John	2. Terrell	3. Carol	4. Erica
1. Jim	2. DaQuan	3. Raquel	4. Maria
1. Carlos	2. Lisa	3. Jesse	4. Carmen
1. Luke	2. Monique		

Homogeneous groups → Heterogeneous groups → Homogeneous groups

partner two interviews partner one. Finally, each of the four team members shares with his or her group what he or she learned. For a group of three, two students may team to interview one each time so that all three are interviewed and hear all responses. Flip cameras and podcasts offer interesting and natural ways of including technology and multimodal methods with this strategy. This strategy is useful for exploring prior knowledge, making predictions, or sharing personal connections related to a topic in the preparation phase of a lesson. It may also follow a lesson or unit in the reflection phase to examine knowledge gained, lesson applications, or remaining questions.

Use this strategy to provide a structure for (1) role playing a character's response; (2) responding from the perspective of a historical figure; and (3) explaining how people from various professions can use a particular mathematical formula, procedure, or operation.

ONE-MINUTE SUMMARY

This chapter has addressed the importance of going beyond the traditional textbook and traditional instruction models in the content classroom. Textbooks can no longer stand alone; multiple resources are necessary to aid learning. There are numerous ways to supplement traditional textbooks; this chapter suggested multiple resources and solutions for issues that may arise.

Teachers must consider several factors when selecting textbooks, trade books, and electronic resources to ensure an appropriate match for students. Multimodal and multitext media offer numerous ways to include verbal, special, auditory, and visual platforms for optimal learning experiences. Given the variety of electronic devices, Internet resources, and easy accessibility students have to electronic materials, it is imperative that they understand and are able to use critical literacy strategies for evaluating texts from a variety of sources.

When making text selections, readability formulas can be useful beginning points for finding appropriate reading level materials for the range of levels present in today's classrooms. Care must be taken when using these measures as they do not account for the conceptual density of the material or the maturity, background knowledge, or cultural understanding that each student brings to the reading.

END-OF-CHAPTER ACTIVITIES

Assisting Comprehension

1. How would you explain to your principal the importance of using resources beyond the textbook and what resources would you consider most critical to instruction for the students you teach or will teach?
2. Think about why it is important to use both a readability formula or Lexile scale and a cloze procedure with your students to get an accurate measure of how readable any text is for your students. Why do the two go together? Which do you feel better about—readability formulas or cloze? Why?
3. In what ways is critical literacy instruction important for instruction in your teaching field?

Reflecting on Your Reading

1. Your content organization (e.g., National Council of Teachers of Math, National Council of Teachers of English, National Council for the Social Studies, National Science Teachers Association, International Reading Association) has most likely developed a set of standards that identify the performance criteria relevant to classroom teachers. Standards usually delineate elements of foundational knowledge that a classroom teacher should possess. Locate and become familiar with what the organization recommends. For instance, teachers should:
   - Use a wide variety and range of curriculum materials and approaches for instruction to include technology-based practices in the classroom.
   - Select curriculum materials to accommodate the developmental, cultural, and linguistic differences of students.
2. Reflect on how this chapter has helped you think about using multiple resources in curriculum development. Ask yourself two central questions: In what ways did this chapter help you plan to use a range of curriculum materials? In what ways will this chapter help you select resources that accommodate the developmental, cultural, and learning differences in your students?
3. List ways in which you might change the daily operations of your class to incorporate some or all of the techniques and technology applications described in this chapter.

CHAPTER 7

Teaching Vocabulary

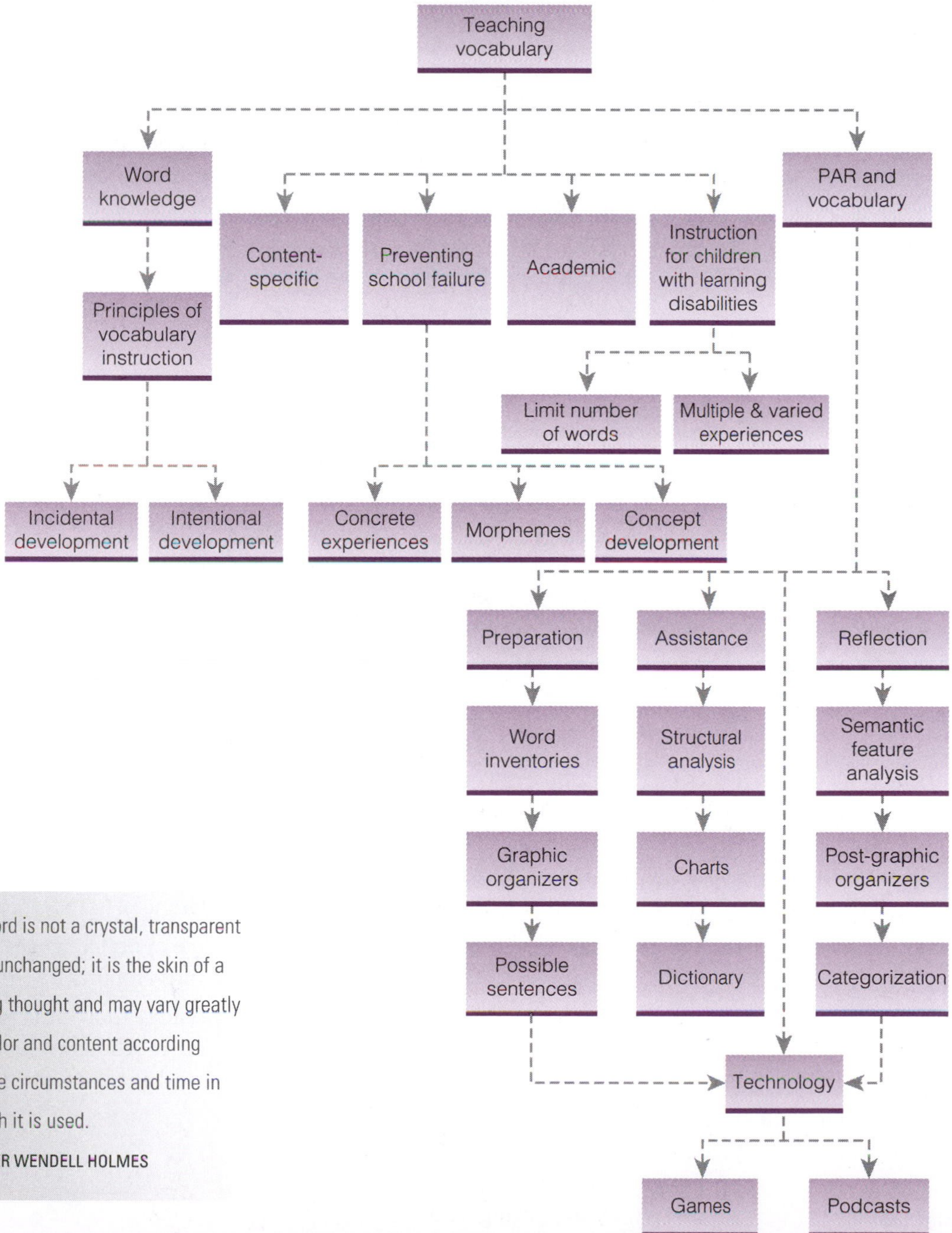

A word is not a crystal, transparent and unchanged; it is the skin of a living thought and may vary greatly in color and content according to the circumstances and time in which it is used.

OLIVER WENDELL HOLMES

VOICES FROM THE CLASSROOM

Ms. Carson is eager to start a new unit in her first period eighth grade mathematics class. She has been teaching for seven years and knows her content well. She believes vocabulary is important for her students to understand in order for them to be able to master the concepts she teaches, so she consistently presents and makes assignments for each instructional unit in the same way. The following is her approach.

"I hope you had a great weekend and are ready to start fresh with our new unit on probability and statistics. I've listed the vocabulary terms we will focus on for this study. You know the drill: Copy the terms, write the definitions, and write a sentence using each appropriately. Some of them will be a little difficult for now. Give it your best effort. Are there any questions?"

Why is this approach to vocabulary study so common? Is it appropriate? Why or why not? How has this worked for you as a student?

PREPARING TO READ

1. What do you remember about how you were taught vocabulary? Are your memories and associations pleasant or painful? List some ways in which you think content area teachers can get students more interested in finding out the meanings of unfamiliar words. As you read the chapter, consider how your ideas can be added to or blended with those presented in the chapter to make vocabulary study appealing as a lifelong habit for your students.
2. Following is a list of terms used in this chapter. Some may be familiar to you in a general context, but in this chapter, they may be used in unfamiliar ways. Rate your knowledge by placing a plus sign (+) for those you are sure you know, a check mark (✓) for those you have some knowledge about, and a zero (0) for those you don't know. Be ready to locate them in the chapter and pay special attention to their meanings.

_______ content-specific vocabulary
_______ academic vocabulary
_______ contextual knowledge
_______ incidental vocabulary development
_______ intentional vocabulary development
_______ conceptual base of understanding
_______ morphology
_______ free morphemes
_______ bound morphemes
_______ categorization
_______ closed word sort
_______ open word sort
_______ TOAST
_______ keyword strategy
_______ magic squares
_______ vocabulary illustrations

OBJECTIVES

As you read this chapter, focus your attention on the following objectives.

1. Explain the importance of vocabulary in reading comprehension.
2. Explain the underlying theory and research for vocabulary development in content areas.
3. Describe the four necessary mental operations for mastering new vocabulary.
4. Explain and apply the four guiding principles for vocabulary instruction.
5. Describe the various aspects of incidental and intentional vocabulary development.
6. Compare academic vocabulary and content-specific vocabulary and the importance each holds for academic success.
7. Use teaching strategies to increase a student's conceptual understanding of words.
8. Identify research-based practices to include strategies and activities for teaching vocabulary before, during, and after reading.
9. Learn a wide range of vocabulary enrichment activities that address developmental, cultural, and linguistic differences.
10. Explain the role of oral language in vocabulary development.
11. Identify technology tools and applications for vocabulary development and enrichment.

In 1839, Edward George Bulwer Lytton wrote, "Beneath the rule of men entirely great, the pen is mightier than the sword." The words of language convey the essence of thoughts, ideas, musings, and emotions. Having a command of language—and specifically the vocabulary within that language—puts power in the hands of learners. A strong vocabulary equips students to actively participate in society as educated citizens and informed consumers.

For years, studies and experts have agreed that a good understanding of the vocabulary in a story or passage is critical for reading comprehension (Blachowicz & Fisher, 2000, 2006; Davis, 1944, 1968; Dunn, Bonner, & Huske, 2007; Farstrup & Samuels, 2008; Graves, 2006a, 2009; McKeown & Beck, 2004; Pressley, 2002c; Snow, Burns, & Griffin, 1998). In its well-recognized report, The National Reading Panel (NRP; National Institute of Child Health and Human Development, 2000) identified vocabulary instruction as one of the five key areas necessary for successful reading among children in the early grades. Given the heavy concept load and academic terms students must learn in each subject area, vocabulary development is at least as important for middle and high school students. Should content teachers accept responsibility for vocabulary instruction? Bravo and Cervetti (2008) argue that understanding the words is critical for grasping deeper meaning, and that "learning the language of the content area is as important as learning the content itself" (p. 130).

Content-Specific Vocabulary and Academic Vocabulary

Two types of vocabulary are of particular importance for general and content area instruction, content-specific vocabulary and academic vocabulary. **Content-specific vocabulary** relates to terms that are critical, yet specific, to a particular discipline or unit of study. These are the terms commonly targeted for instruction prior to reading a textbook chapter. For example, content-specific terms that might be used in a fitness unit are *aerobic capacity*, *flexibility*, *skinfold measurement*, and *body mass index*. Although one of the example terms (*flexibility*) may be somewhat familiar to students, the context is likely new to them. The term *scale* is used across several disciplines but holds considerably different meaning depending on the context: music, science, mathematics, or physical education. Content-specific terms for in-depth study must be selected judiciously based on students' prior knowledge, purpose of the lesson or unit, and need for clearly understanding the unit or lesson.

How might you support academic vocabulary development for struggling second language learners?

Academic vocabulary encompasses a set of terms often found among expository texts and formal presentations or speeches but which is not unique to any content or academic discipline (Coxhead, 2000; Lesaux et al., 2010). These terms (e.g., *assess, analyze, sector, significant, function*) are rarely found in narrative text or used in everyday conversation, but they are important for gaining full understanding of expository text. Unfamiliarity with academic vocabulary may impede learning, especially for struggling or second language learners (Hiebert & Lubliner, 2008). Coxhead developed an empirically based list, the Academic Word List (AWL), of 570 commonly found word families cutting across 25 or more subject areas. The General Service List (GSL) developed by West (1953) is composed of the most useful word families in the English language. "Taken together, the first 2,000 words in West's GLS and the word families in the AWL account for approximately 86% of the Academic Corpus" (Coxhead, 2000, p. 213).

Please visit the Education CourseMate website at **www.cengagebrain.com** to access the AWL website housed in the University of Victoria at Wellington or perform a Web search for AWL.

Please visit the Education CourseMate website at **www.cengagebrain.com** to find a link to Word Generation, a highly successful program with a focus on infusing academic vocabulary instruction into curricula for middle school students, or perform a Web search.

Do you think the use of electronic devices adds to students' communication skills? Do you think that the use of these devices could interfere with students' understanding of formal register when reading and use of formal register when writing?

Most of these words on the AWL have rich morphological families—at least 76% have three or more words in their families. "Analyses have shown that more than one third of the words in academic texts are Spanish-English cognates" (Nash, 1997) and that "knowledge of cognates enhances reading comprehension achievement" (Nagy, Garcia, Durgunoglu, & Hancin-Bhatt, 1993; see also Hiebert & Lubliner, 2008, p. 115). All things considered, attention to AWL for vocabulary instruction for many students, particularly struggling learners and English language learners (ELLs), has the potential to raise achievement levels across curricula. A current study used AWL for improving achievement levels of urban middle school students. "These study findings highlight the promise of improving academic vocabulary instruction as a key ingredient in increasing opportunities to learn for students in urban middle schools" (Lesaux, Kieffer, Faller, & Kelley, 2010, p. 223).

Vocabulary scores on standardized tests of students entering college have declined over the past few years (Manzo, Manzo, & Thomas, 2006). Electronic devices and technology, among other influences, have made forms of abbreviated language popular. Students are using acronyms and a less formal register of conversation in all types of written communication. Manzo and colleagues explain that a wider acceptance of "coarse" language within daily life and the media, along with the well-intentioned use of simpler terms to explain concepts, may contribute to vocabulary decline. One challenge, then, is to find advantageous ways to connect, include, and effectively integrate new technologies in instruction while helping students recognize the importance of acquiring and appropriately using academic vocabulary at both elementary and secondary levels.

This chapter explores what it means to know a word, how vocabulary develops, how many and what types of words are important for learning, and the principles and strategies important for vocabulary instruction.

A Closer Look at Word Knowledge

More than a half century ago, Davis (1944) and Thurstone (1946) wrote that knowledge of word meanings is one of the most important factors in reading comprehension. Simply stated, if readers do not know the meanings of most words in a passage, they will be unable to understand the passage. Struggling readers and second language learners are at a disadvantage because of their limited vocabulary knowledge as they try to make sense of the content they are expected to master (Beck & McKeown, 2007; Helman, 2008; Lesaux, Kieffer, Kelley, 2010; Manyak & Bauer, 2009). But what constitutes word knowledge?

It is generally agreed that readers can "know" a word, but each person may relate it to a different experience. Consider the sentence "John took a plane," for example. A young child reading it might imagine playing with a toy, a high school student might imagine a scene in an airport, and an adult who is a carpenter might imagine a carpenter's tool. Word knowledge is not static, but rather dynamic—changing and growing over time as a learner experiences, hears, and reads a word in a variety of places and circumstances. Knowing a word involves more than identification and pronunciation. Lesaux et al. (2010) characterize vocabulary knowledge as "multidimensional and complex in nature" (p. 197). Besides matching definition with context, deeper word knowledge involves developing an understanding of connections and relationships to other words and concepts that add to the learning load. Becoming familiar with changes in form that may occur as the word is used in different ways adds yet another dimension. Consider the word *locate.*

- Mr. Kinsey couldn't *locate* his car keys.
- The decision was made to *locate* the meeting in the Town Center Building.
- When Karen took the job as State Senator, she had to make plans to *relocate.*
- The *location* of the receptacle made a difference in the outcome of the experiment.

Nagy and Scott (2000) identify five facets of the intricate nature of word knowledge as:

1. **Incrementality:** levels of word knowledge develop over time
2. **Polysemy:** multiple meanings associated with a word (e.g., *record player, set a record*)
3. **Multidimentionality:** many different types of knowledge to be learned about a word (e.g., *meaning, connotation, denotation, register, morphology*)
4. **Interrelatedness:** connections are made between or among words (e.g., *weather, storms, hurricanes, forecast, umbrella, raincoat, cancelled meeting*)
5. **Heterogeneity:** word type, purpose, and prior knowledge influence word knowledge required (*the* versus *telephone* versus *sanction*)

We may think of word knowledge as being similar to coming to know a person; the process involves a continuum (Dale, 1965; Pierce & Fontaine, 2009; Stahl, 1999). For instance, initially a word is a *stranger*, one we have not seen or heard before. Then that word becomes an *acquaintance*; we have seen or heard it and know a little about it. As our depth of understanding grows and we become confident using the word in a variety of contexts, it takes on the status of *friend.*

Developing these levels of word knowledge typically takes time, exposure, active engagement, and experience, but not all words need to be learned to an in-depth level. Targeting words for a lesson or unit involves several factors that contribute to instructional emphasis and learning intensity. Graves (2009) identifies seven different tasks and considerations:

1. Learning a basic oral vocabulary
2. Learning to read known words
3. Learning new words representing known concepts
4. Learning new words representing new concepts
5. Learning new meanings for known words
6. Clarifying and enriching the meanings of known words
7. Moving words into students' expressive vocabularies (pp. 17–18)

When students have little or no understanding of a concept, teachers need to either provide learning opportunities to develop students' understanding or postpone instruction until students learn the prerequisite knowledge. Teachers need ways to determine when to spend time on vocabulary. If they find that students already know a concept and words associated with it, time spent on vocabulary will be wasted. If they assume that students know something that they do not know, not spending time on vocabulary will hinder the lesson.

Polysemous (multi-meaning) words require a mindset for associating a new meaning with a familiar word. Notice Calvin's confusion when considering the term *peck*. The meaning of *peck* in a math context is quite different from its meaning in a social context. Making distinctions among shades of meaning found among words involves additional skill. Understanding that *short* and *succinct* connote slightly different meanings requires thought precision. Helping students develop comfort and confidence with these skills and use of sophisticated words is the task involved in making the transition from oral and reading (receptive) vocabulary use to written and spoken (productive) vocabulary. Each of these tasks requires different thought processes and amounts of effort depending on prior knowledge and experience, as well as the linguistic facility of each student.

Preventing Vocabulary and School Failure

Often, a mismatch occurs between school expectations and students' achievement, especially in the case of struggling readers. This is true despite a plethora of compensatory educational programs designed to reduce the conceptual and language deficits of culturally disadvantaged and minority children (Bryant, Goodwin, Bryant, & Higgins, 2003; Jitendra, Edwards, Sacks, & Jacobson, 2004; Moats, 2001). These children are often taught vocabulary through rote exercises that require dictionary definitions of extensive numbers of technical and specialized terms. In a typical exercise, as in Voices from the Classroom for this chapter, the teacher informs students that before reading the chapter they must find, look up in the dictionary, and define 30 words from the chapter. It's no wonder reading is often thought of as decidedly dull by students who have to perform such rote tasks! This method of teaching vocabulary and concepts is product oriented; the rote production of the written word is the product. Rather than in-depth or thoughtful word exploration, what occurs is "considerable mentioning and assigning and little actual teaching" (Scott, Jamieson-Noel, & Asselin, 2003, p. 14). Such vocabulary exercises are used even though most disadvantaged students, at-risk populations, and generally poor readers use action words in much of their communication (e.g., "he gone"); they use processes to facilitate information rather than memorizing an extensive written vocabulary. This prescriptive approach has been described by researchers (Irvin, 1990; Ryder & Graves, 1994; Scott, Jamison-Noel, & Asselin, 2003) as minimally effective, resulting in temporary retention of material, student disengagement, and little student understanding of text.

Jitendra, Edwards, Sacks, and Jacobson (2004) attest to the effectiveness of interventions and direct instruction that go beyond definitional learning for vocabulary growth among students with learning disabilities. Several researchers (Biemiller, 2001; Blachowiz, Fisher, Ogle, & Watts-Taffe, 2006; Manzo & Manzo, 2008; Stahl & Shiel, 1999) state that direct instruction of carefully selected vocabulary is needed by and appropriate for most students. Selecting a root word or morpheme for instruction can unlock many words: teaching *print* shows the connections among *printer*, *printed*, and *imprint*.

Nagy and Scott (2000) describe true word knowledge as applied knowledge: "being able to do things with it: to recognize it in connected speech or in print, to access its meaning, to pronounce it—and to be able to do these things within a fraction of a second" (p. 273). Unlike the "definition only" method of learning vocabulary, the teacher should start with concrete experiences in order to instill concepts and words. Consider this story:

> A 9-year-old was visiting a theme park with his parents. They walked past a ride named "Ribbault's Adventure." Although the father pronounced the ride's name, the boy kept asking when they would get a chance to ride "Rabbit's Adventure." In exasperation, the father turned to the mother and asked, "Why can't he remember the name of the ride?" The mother pointed out that the boy had read *Alice in Wonderland* and *Peter Rabbit* and had picked a name that was close in looks and sounds to "Ribbault's Adventure." "Perhaps," she suggested, "when he gets on the ride, he will call it what it is."
>
> Sure enough, the guide on Ribbault's Adventure explained who Ribbault was. And when the boy exited the ride, he remarked, "That was fun. I'd like to ride Ribbault's Adventure again before we go home."

Jean Ribbault (sometimes spelled Ribault) was a French naval officer who explored the Florida and Carolina coastline in the late 1500s.

When this child first heard the term, he tried to fit it into what he knew (schema), which to some degree worked because he understood about adventures; however, *Ribbault* was a new term for a new concept. After the concept was explained, giving him a point of reference, he was able to "get it" and say the term correctly. Full-concept learning of vocabulary, according to Simpson (1987), requires four mental operations: (1) recognizing and generating critical attributes—both examples and nonexamples—of a concept; (2) seeing relationships between the concept to be learned and what is already known; (3) applying the concept to a variety of contexts; and (4) generating new contexts for the learned concept. The first of the four operations can be developed by asking students to exclude a concept from a list of concepts to which it does not belong. Note the following:

Muezzin   mosque   minaret   *mangrove*

Also, students can brainstorm attributes and nonattributes of a given concept, as shown in Activity 7.1

Students can better understand relationships (operation 2) by brainstorming about targeted vocabulary concepts and then writing possible definitions. For mental operation 3, students can apply what they know about a vocabulary concept by being exposed to the word in different contexts. Stahl (1983) calls this teaching comprehension through developing **contextual knowledge**.

ACTIVITY 7.1 Concept Learning: Middle School World History

Use the textbook to brainstorm attributes and nonattributes of *nationalism.*

Attributes		Non-attributes
Honor	Imperialism	Maturity
Pride	Prestige	Democracy
Superiority	Force	Cooperation
Wealth	Fascism	Isolationism
Power		Equality

Students can learn how to generate new contexts for a learned vocabulary term (operation 4) by creating new sentences using previously learned concepts. To encourage frequent practice at this task, Simpson (1987) recommends a technique called *paired-word sentence generation:* Two words are given, and students are asked to write a sentence demonstrating the relationships between them. Possible examples are *method–analysis, genes–environment, graph–plot,* and *juvenile delinquency–recession.* A sentence for *juvenile delinquency–recession* might be: "Incidents of juvenile delinquency occur more frequently during a recession."

Word knowledge results from both incidental and intentional learning experiences. Considerable word knowledge is developed naturally through exposure and daily living through incidental experiences. It is not necessary to teach every word that becomes part of an individual's store of knowledge (Beck, McKeown, & Kucan, 2002; Biemiller, 2001; Brabham & Villaume, 2002). Creating an environment for encouraging language play, inquiry, and discovery in addition to planning explicit instruction provides a means for positively influencing vocabulary acquisition to include both intentional and incidental learning pathways.

Incidental Vocabulary Development

Incidental vocabulary development occurs through conversation, word play (e.g., puns, rhymes, or jingles), exposure to spoken words from a variety of sources (e.g., television, radio, and video), and reading. Our earliest experiences with language are exposures to spoken words as parents and caregivers respond to our needs. Language development begins as a spontaneous and natural process as we listen, experiment, approximate, and put our understanding into practice. Through incidental experiences, words are initially categorized and filed away in the mind based on personal connections and conceptions. Naive understandings may occur until explicit and intentional instruction clarifies and realigns faulty reasoning. For instance, young children believe that the sun actually "comes up" before learning the full meaning of planetary movements and distinctions between revolving and rotating.

As children are read stories and literature steeped in rich vocabulary, the initial and repeated exposure to language beyond daily conversation adds to their personal vocabulary growth. Cunningham and Stanovich (1998) found in their study examining vocabulary used in sources of spoken and written language that rare or "rich" words are more frequently found in children's literature than in adult conversation except for that which may occur in courtroom testimony. In contrast, Biemiller and Boote (2006) note that during preschool and primary grade instruction, emphasis is typically on word recognition and decoding with little attention given to word meaning. Teachers in their study indicated reluctance to spend as much as 30 minutes a day on vocabulary instruction. Although decoding is critical to reading, being able to recognize and pronounce a word does not ensure its understanding. Devoting time and instruction to conceptual understanding of vocabulary terms should be considered as important for young readers as for their older counterparts (Padak, 2006). Given that many children begin school with limited vocabularies, inattention to concept development can set them up for academic disadvantages that are difficult to overcome (Hart & Risley, 2003). Biemiller and Boote's study provided evidence that primary grade, or preliterate, vocabulary instruction using repeated oral readings along with explanations and reviews of substantial numbers of words can improve vocabulary acquisition among young learners. They contend that teaching appropriate word meanings "at a successful rate, and during the three primary years, could result in a child learning 1,000 to 1,500 additional word meanings. This would be enough to significantly improve the vocabulary of children with initially low vocabularies" (p. 55). Vocabulary becomes a bridge to greater understanding when children understand that:

1. Words are labels for things (Padak, 2006).
2. Words are critical for understanding sentences and passages (Kamil & Hiebert, 2005).

When children begin reading on their own, they can take greater responsibility for building their vocabulary. With modeling and scaffolded instruction, they can learn to question unfamiliar words in the text and use root meanings and contextual clues. Evidence suggests that wide and extended independent reading experiences further contribute to vocabulary growth (National Institute of Child Health and Human Development, 2000; Tekmen & Daloglu, 2006). Although language begins with listening and speaking experiences and moves and develops into reading and writing, all four channels contribute to our continued growth as literate individuals. In their study of building "meaning vocabulary" in the primary grades, Biemiller and Boote (2006) provided evidence that limited oral vocabularies among children in early grades predict limited reading comprehension later in their schooling experiences.

Read about Pulido's (2004) study of the role of culture in incidental vocabulary development in *The Reading Matrix*. This study provides insight about the impact of culture and background knowledge on the development and retention of unfamiliar vocabulary encountered naturally while reading a passage.

Children from low-socioeconomic status (SES) groups—and those whose first language is not English—generally have less well-developed oral vocabularies that typically do not increase at rates great enough to approach the levels of their more affluent and linguistically advantaged peers. Graves (2009) cited a number of studies to explain that linguistically advantaged first graders enter school and later complete their high school education with approximately twice as many words as their linguistically disadvantaged peers. August & Shanahan (2006) in the report of the National Literacy Panel on Language Minority Children and Youth reported finding a positive correlation between oral language proficiency in English and reading comprehension in English. However, study results (Beck & McKeown, 2007; Shanahan & Beck, 2006) have provided positive evidence that efforts to build oral language and vocabulary development can serve to begin narrowing the gaps. Low-SES children can experience a significant degree of success in learning even sophisticated words in their oral vocabularies at an early age (Beck & McKeown, 2007). Activities that encourage classroom talk, including discussion, project work, role playing, storytelling, and

Please visit the Education CourseMate website at **www.cengagebrain.com** to find a link to the Executive Summary of the Report of the National Literacy Panel on Language Minority Children and Youth for additional details on their findings or perform a Web search.

drama, are important for continued vocabulary development and are not reserved exclusively for young children.

View this elementary classroom of struggling readers to see explicit strategies for intentional vocabulary development. Strategies are made visible so that students know what to do when reading independently.

What if such ideal incidental learning has not been done and students lack these rich vocabulary experiences? Francis and Simpson (2003) found that one way of improving secondary and college students' vocabulary knowledge is to actively involve them in oral expression activities. Daily classroom conversations with new vocabulary allow students to try out and understand appropriate use of the terms they are learning. Graves (2006a) stresses the introduction of "meaty and somewhat academic topics" (p. 5) for discussion to ensure sophisticated and rich vocabulary development results.

Intentional Vocabulary Development

Making time to develop full word knowledge for **intentional vocabulary development** for depth and breadth of concept understanding is beneficial (Francis & Simpson, 2003; Nagy & Scott, 2000). Research supports practices that help students connect new vocabulary to known vocabulary and concepts. Francis and Simpson found that when teachers engaged students in explicit discussions identifying synonyms, antonyms, connotations, and nuances of the language, students were helped to clarify misunderstandings and were redirected to improve their reading comprehension.

Through direct instruction teachers may think aloud, model, and provide opportunities for practice and clarification to scaffold strategies and techniques for independent word learning. Interactive strategies in which students work together focusing on semantic connections using semantic maps, semantic feature analysis, and word sorts have been identified in the research as effective means for vocabulary development (Blachowicz & Fisher, 2000). The personal components of vocabulary learning that research supports include involving students in selecting words for study as well as choosing the strategies that work best for independent reading. Finally, instruction should go beyond introducing words prior to reading, the most common practice found in classrooms (Scott, Jamieson-Noel, & Asselin, 2003). Graves (2006b) advocates a four-part, long-term vocabulary program that includes "providing rich and varied language experiences, teaching individual words, teaching word-learning strategies, and fostering word consciousness" (p. 1). Vocabulary instruction, similar to comprehension and skills instruction, needs to be addressed before, during, and after the reading of text, providing repeated and reflective experiences with the words targeted for study.

Vocabulary Instruction for Children with Learning Disabilities

To help students learning words for which they seem to have no prior experiences or concepts, teachers need to present concepts in a very concrete manner through direct and purposeful experiences followed by varied and repeated exposures (Bryant, Goodwin, Bryant, & Higgins, 2003; Jitendra, Edwards, Sacks, & Jacobson, 2004; Moats, 2001). Bryant and colleagues (2003) found in their review of the research on vocabulary instruction for students with learning disabilities a clear need for explicit, systematic instruction that includes opportunities for word manipulation, planned intervention, and personal connections and associations. It is especially important for instruction to include word examination that provides a means for deeper processing and retention at the word meaning level.

When teaching students with learning disabilities, the number of words for study should be limited to those most needed, and multiple and varied exposures are critical. Productive approaches such as creating semantic maps or manipulating word parts (affixes and roots) make the most of word learning and may even accelerate the process and help future learning (Snow, 2002). When hands-on experiences are not possible, students need "activities of observation," such as field trips, demonstrations, graphics, and visuals, to build a knowledge base for learning. Attention should be given to building and enriching oral language and basic concepts of study in an environment that encourages focused classroom talk and word play. "Just as a house needs a strong foundation, so reading comprehension depends on a strong base of oral language and concept development" (Blachowicz & Fisher, 2003, p. 67). A reader's background knowledge is important in determining how much vocabulary he or she will understand and absorb. Effective readers consider their own background when trying to solve for unknown words encountered in a text. A former student told the story of her 6-year-old son trying to figure out the word *Kentucky* in a book he was reading. He asked for her help but explained that he knew the word had something to do with chicken. He apparently was drawing from his own experience with takeout food.

Look for virtual field trips on the Internet. Please visit the Education CourseMate website at **www.cengagebrain.com** to find some example links for virtual field trips or perform a Web search.

Students with broad understandings of the world will have an easier time learning vocabulary because of their experience. This view has been substantiated in the research literature for decades (Ausubel, 1968; Blachowicz & Fisher, 2003; Carr & Wixson, 1986; Drevno et al, 1994; Graves, 1985; Henry, 1974). For instance, students who have toured historic Philadelphia can relate to a passage about the influence of the Constitution more easily than can those lacking such firsthand experience. Teachers who follow this view emphasize building on background knowledge in all phases of the PAR (preparation, assistance, and reflection) Lesson Framework. For example, a teacher might ask students what they know about small loan agencies in a business mathematics lesson about small loans. She might carefully present new vocabulary such as *collateral*, *passbook savings*, *debt*, and *consolidation loans*. At each phase of the lesson, she would try to identify how much students already know about the topic. In this manner, the teacher can help build students' general background knowledge as well as vocabulary knowledge.

This chapter has addressed ways to help students establish a **conceptual base of understanding**—an underlying knowledge of subject matter—with which to expand vocabulary knowledge. Vocabulary instruction can be beneficial in increasing the base of knowledge at any phase of a lesson. Teachers need to make their own vocabulary lessons that will aid students before, during, and after reading. They cannot rely on vocabulary exercises in textbook manuals because these mostly stress teaching vocabulary before reading in the "definition only" method mentioned earlier. Teachers' manuals may also target words already known to students or select words not particularly useful beyond the text selection. Nor can teachers rely on assuming students will read freely in class or at home; this is important to vocabulary development but not sufficient for large vocabulary growth (Carver, 1994; Cunningham & Stanovich, 1998). Students struggling with reading either cannot or do not independently read the volume of material necessary to make a significant difference in their vocabulary growth (Baker, Simmons, & Kame'enui, 1998).

Flanigan and Greenwood (2007) designed a system to address in a specific way the consideration of students, objectives, word levels, strategies, and lesson placement for selecting words for study. Using the work of both Graves (2000) and McKeown and Beck (1988), they categorized words as follows:

Level 1: Critical "before" words

Level 2: "Foot-in-the-door" words

Level 3: Critical "after" words

Level 4: Words not to teach (p. 228)

Some level 4 words may be highlighted by the publisher, but there is usually no need to take time to address these. However, do not assume that struggling learners or ELL students understand these.

The teacher needs to read the text to decide the importance and purpose of the passage for addressing instructional goals. Words are selected based on their importance for understanding the concepts in the lesson. Figure 7.1 illustrates the timing, level of understanding, and amount of instructional time recommended for each level.

The PAR Framework works for vocabulary just as for other aspects of reading and learning. Strategies need to be used for the preparation, assistance, and reflection stages. The amount of time and type of strategies used for each stage vary depending on the lesson goals and student backgrounds. This three-step approach supports the specialized type of language development needed for students to come to full word understanding of the academic and content-specific vocabulary necessary for study and life application. Content area learning involves gaining a clear understanding of sets of terms that are critical to new concept development. Because concepts often build on one another, gaining a clear understanding of basic terms is important for later learning and advanced study. For example, students need to be able to understand, remember, and use the terms from basic mathematics as they move into algebra and geometry.

FIGURE 7.1

The Four-level Framework developed by Flanigan & Greenwood (2007, p. 230)

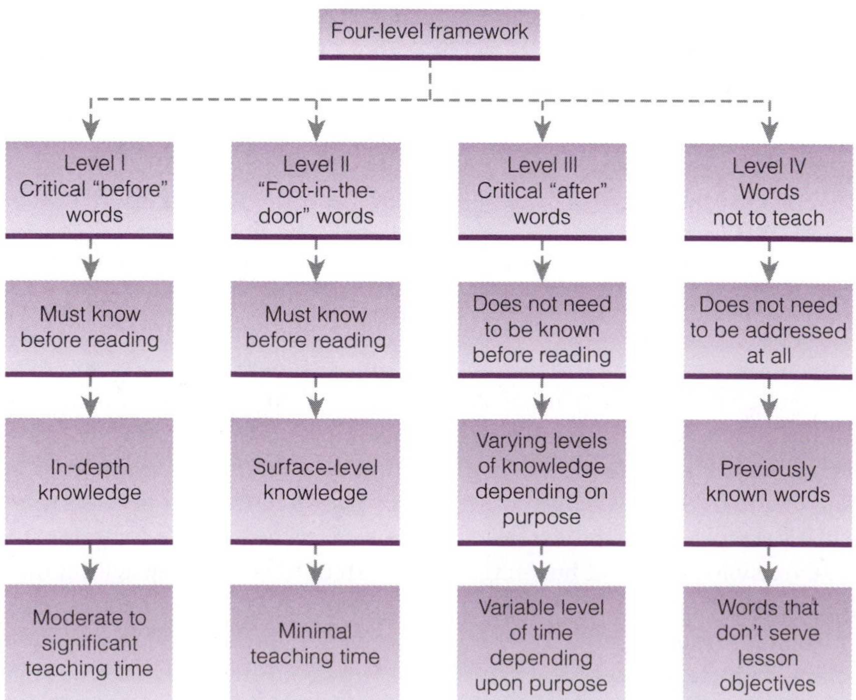

The rest of this chapter describes research-based practices and strategies for developing vocabulary that you can use before, during, or shortly after reading. They also can work as follow-up activities (the next day) after reading. We describe how teachers can use the strategies to teach vocabulary through activities that are meaningful to students.

Teaching Vocabulary in Preparation for Reading

Vocabulary instruction before reading improves student comprehension regardless of a student's reading ability (Flanagan & Greenwood, 2007; Graves, 2000; McKeown & Beck, 1988). Teaching vocabulary before reading involves not so much the teacher "teaching" the terms as the students exploring and attempting to make sense of them before beginning the reading. As strategic learners, students need to recognize whether a link exists between words in the content material and their own knowledge.

Word Inventories

Included in this book as self-inventories, word inventories are often at the start of each chapter. This activity encourages readers to assess their own prior knowledge and rate themselves. Although teachers can use such ratings to instruct, readers are in charge of their own assessment of conceptual knowledge. Activity 7.2 is an example of a word inventory developed for elementary school students.

ACTIVITY 7.2 Word Inventory in Elementary English

Directions: Use the happy faces to tell how well you know these words. This isn't a test, and you won't be graded. Remember: You aren't supposed to know all the words.

I know it!

I think I've seen or heard it.

I don't know it.

_____ **1.** Blanket
_____ **2.** Question
_____ **3.** Straight
_____ **4.** Constantly
_____ **5.** Treacherous
_____ **6.** Friend
_____ **7.** Burrowed
_____ **8.** Forever
_____ **9.** Muckraker
_____ **10.** Shadow
_____ **11.** Believe
_____ **12.** Television

Developed by Terry Bryce.

Graphic Organizers

Please visit the Education CourseMate website at **www.cengagebrain.com** to find links to a variety of sites offering graphic organizers and interactive tools for creating graphic organizers.

Reviews of graphic organizer research (Armbruster, 1992; Dunston, 1992; Egan, 1999; Rice, 1992) conclude that graphic organizers significantly aid students in remembering text. Graphic organizers can be an effective strategy for getting students on the same wavelength as the teacher in understanding the direction a lesson is taking. The teacher interacts with students by displaying a diagram and discussing why it is arranged in a particular way.

One of the most popular types of graphic organizers, a semantic map, effectively depicts the interrelationships and hierarchies of concepts in a lesson. Research (Bos & Anders, 1990) demonstrates the effectiveness of semantic mapping for increasing reading comprehension and vocabulary learning. Mapping was introduced in Chapter 4 as a way to develop comprehension. A semantic map can be used as a prereading or postreading exercise. To use semantic mapping before reading, follow these steps:

Extension of #3: Have students rank the words or categorize them from "most important" to "least important." This activity may help students see that all words in the lesson are not equally important and that information needs to be categorized.

1. Select an important word from the reading assignment.
2. Ask students to think of as many related words and key concepts as possible that will help in understanding the keyword.
3. Project the words that students identify on the board.
4. Organize the words into a diagram like the one in Activity 7.3.

ACTIVITY 7.3 Semantic Map in Elementary Language Arts

ROTTWEILERS

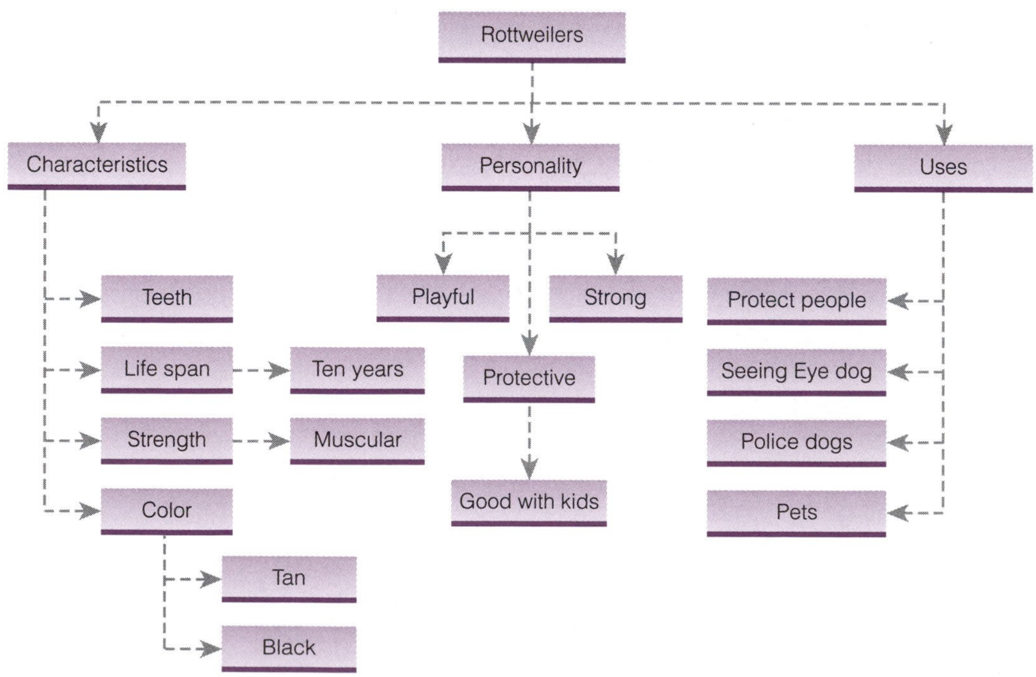

ACTIVITY 7.4 Semantic Map in Spanish

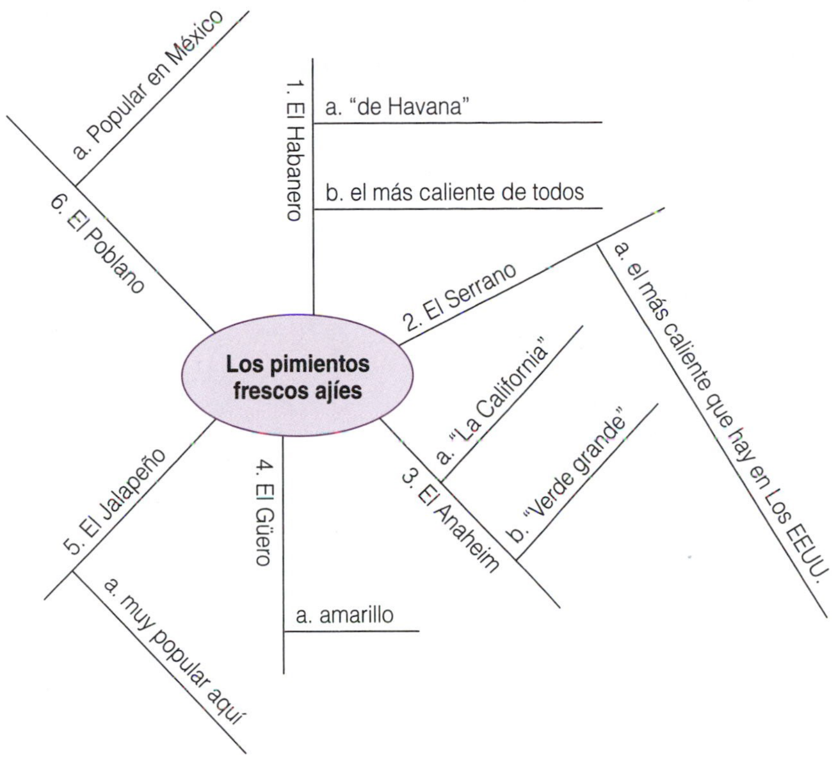

Developed by Brian Littman.

Software such as Inspiration and Kidspiration may fit seamlessly into a lesson using features such as Rapid Fire to create graphic organizers with visual elements and vocabulary connections. The teacher may select a target word from the lesson and have students contribute words they associate with it. Initial organizers can then be reorganized as students recognize groupings, headings, and subheadings. Activity 7.4 shows a variation of a semantic map. In this activity, the Spanish teacher helped students learn about types of chili peppers.

Using the semantic map as their base, Schwartz and Raphael (1985) designed a word map. To begin, the teacher or student places the keyword in the center of the page and boxes it. Next, a definition and lists of examples and properties are put in boxes or circles and organized around the keyword. This process guides students in their understanding from concrete examples to abstract definitions and concepts. Activity 7.5 is a word map for the key word *metaphor.* Activity 7.6 presents a type of word map that is sometimes called a *spider map* because the graphic organizer resembles a spider's web. This activity is from an early elementary lesson on the benefits of music. Both semantic maps and word maps are excellent ways of getting students to clarify their thinking before reading an assignment.

Please visit the Education CourseMate website at **www.cengagebrain.com** to look for a link for Inspiration online. Try out an interactive presentation or demonstration using graphic organizers. Download a trial version of *Inspiration* to learn more about the product's capabilities.

ACTIVITY 7.5 Word Map for the Keyword Metaphor

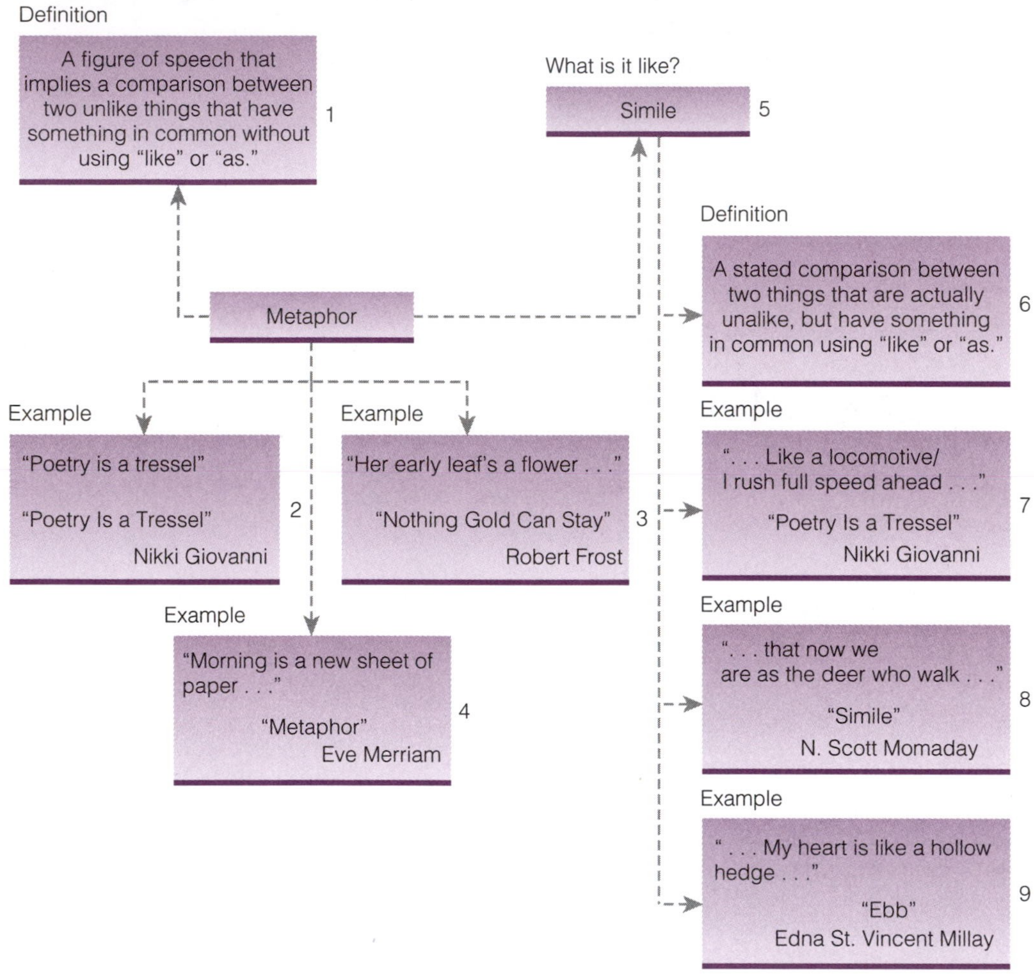

EXTRA CREDIT

Why is this handout titled "Word Map Simile"?

Because it compares a metaphor to a simile and uses "like" or "as."

Developed by Tara Furges.

Possible Sentences

Ideally, students write their real sentences beside possible sentences. Unfortunately, chart paper does not allow space for this arrangement.

Possible sentences (Moore & Arthur, 1981) is an activity that combines vocabulary and prediction. It is designed to acquaint students with new vocabulary that they will encounter in their reading and guide them as they attempt to verify the accuracy of the statements they generate. Additionally, it arouses curiosity about the passage. This activity is best used when unfamiliar vocabulary is mixed with familiar terminology. The teacher might give students a worksheet such as the one shown in Activity 7.7. Teachers pick between five and eight vocabulary terms, such as those from elementary science in Activity 7.7.

ACTIVITY 7.6 Concept Map: The Benefits of Music

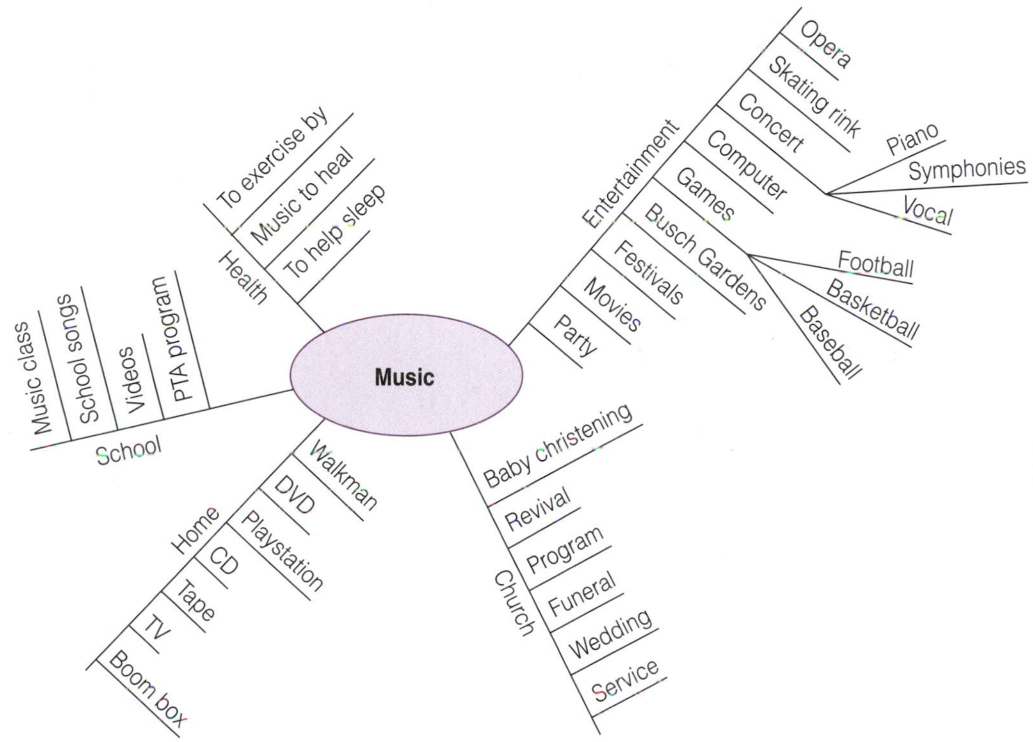

Developed by Audra Jones and her students.

For each term, students write a possible sentence on the left side of the worksheet. Then during reading, they look for the real meaning of the term and write this meaning in a sentence. In doing so, students create a mnemonic, with the possible sentence cuing them to the real meaning of the word. This is a simple but powerful strategy for learning words. Research attests to the advantage of using such mnemonic devices to learn vocabulary (Levin, Levin, Glassman, & Nordwall, 1992; Moore & Surber, 1992; Scruggs, Mastropier, Brigham, & Sullivan, 1992). Mnemonic devices are discussed later in this chapter and in detail in Chapter 9.

Mnemonics are rhymes, catchy phrases, acronyms, or even hand motions that can support memory of lists, important points, or other information.

Teaching Vocabulary to Assist Students in Their Reading

Students need to be assisted in all content areas and at every grade level in interpreting unfamiliar words. Teachers cannot "protect" students from words by teaching every difficult term they will encounter, but they do need to help students understand words that clarify text. Encouraging students to develop word consciousness (Graves, 2000) may help them bring unfamiliar words that interfere

Vocabulary Connections (Iwiki, 1992) challenges students to use a term to describe a situation in a book or chapter that they are reading. In mathematics, for example, the term *conversion* may be used with *product volumes* in one chapter and comparative international money values in another chapter. How could students do this in your content area?

ACTIVITY 7.7 Possible Sentences: Elementary Science

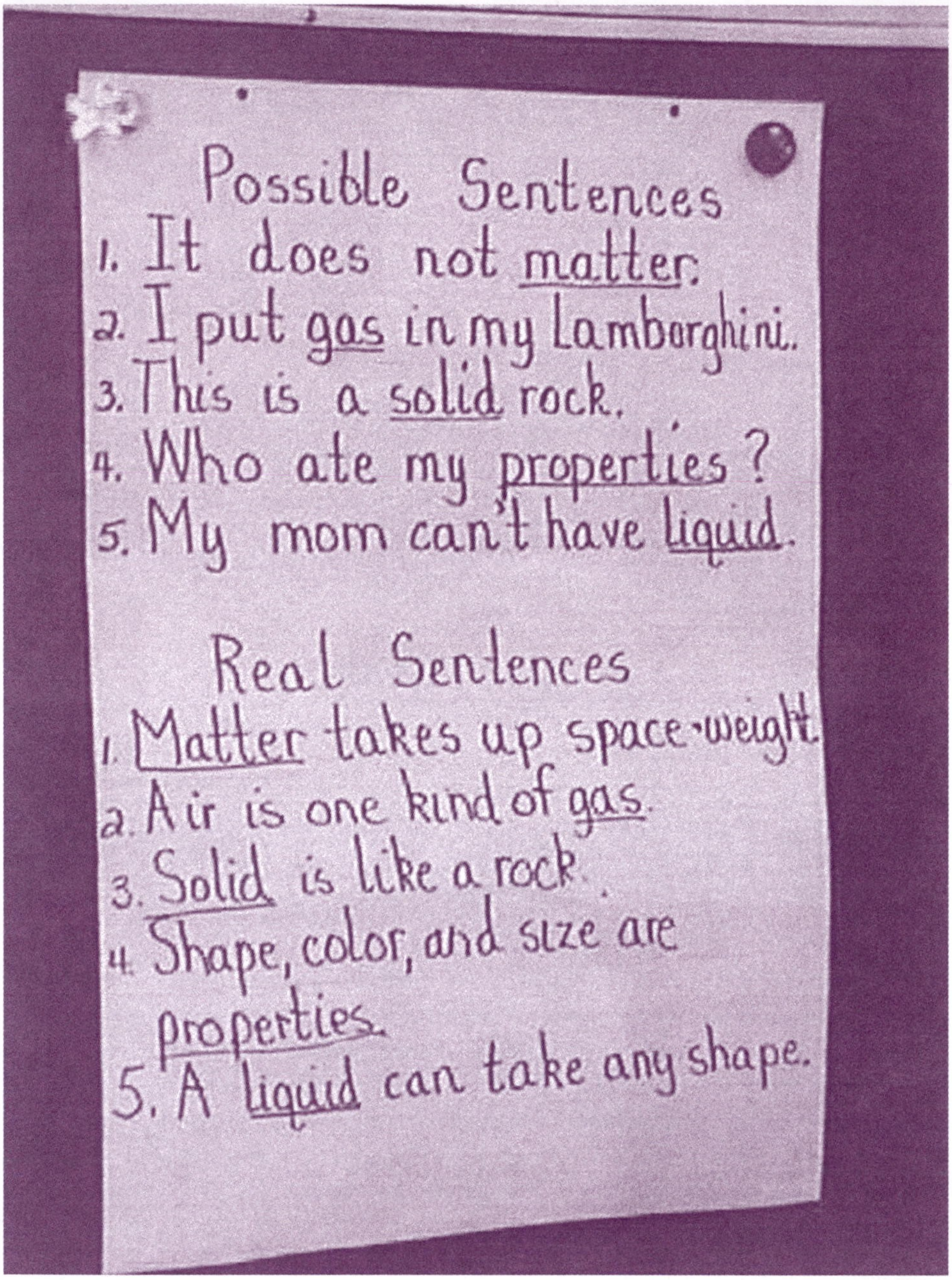

Courtesy of the author.

Developed by Suzanne McDaniel.

with their understanding of the text to the forefront. Noticing new or unknown words is the first step in being proactive and taking responsibility for unlocking their meanings. Using sticky notes, highlighting tape, or flags to mark difficult or interesting words in the text engages the reader in actively attending to and identifying words for further consideration.

Leading students to become independent strategists when encountering unknown vocabulary can begin as early as third or fourth grade with attention to context clues, **morphology**, and understanding appropriate use of dictionaries and reference sources (Blachowicz, Fisher, Ogle, & Watts-Taffe, 2006; Edwards, Font, Baumann, & Boland, 2004; Graves, 2004, 2006b). Even though context is not foolproof, it can often provide a beginning point. The order of words in a sentence offers syntactic clues that can help students determine if an unfamiliar word is an action, a thing, or a description. Semantic clues can provide information in the form of examples, definitions, synonyms, antonyms, or descriptions. Students can be taught to recognize the various kinds of context clues as well as how to read ahead and use the clues to predict, infer, and reason out meanings. They also need to understand that context can sometimes be insufficient or even misleading. Other factors need to be considered to ensure accurate comprehension.

Refer to Chapter 9 for a discussion of study skills and for suggested uses of resources that can enhance vocabulary in online environments.

Several excellent techniques for assisting readers to engage in vocabulary development are described in the sections to follow. In addition, a discussion of how and when to use a dictionary, thesaurus, and online resources provides guidance for achieving independent vocabulary acquisition.

Context Clue Discovery

To begin to understand the importance of "concepts in context," think of any word in isolation; then try to define it. Take, for example, the word *run*. It is not difficult to give a synonym for the word, but it does not have a clear meaning until it is placed in a context. First thoughts may be of the most common definition, "to move with haste," but "to be or campaign as a candidate for election," "to publish, print, or make copies," or even "to cause the stitches in a garment to unravel" would have been equally accurate. A precise meaning cannot be determined until *run* is seen in context. One way to help students recognize the importance of context to meaning is to do a brief word association activity (Activity 7.8) with them. Have them number a sheet of paper

ACTIVITY 7.8 Word Association Activity

Word	Possible Definition	Possible Definition
1. Record	Musical disk	Data or information
2. Tie	Clothing for neck	Interlocking
3. Mouse	Furry animal	Computer device
4. Bad	Not good	Good
5. Story	A tale	Building level
6. Column	Newspaper story	Stone pillar
7. Break	Tear up	Brief relaxing period
8. Cell	Jail	Body part
9. Bank	Building for money	Land next to river
10. Bill	Bird part	Money owed

from 1 to 10 and write a one- or two-word definition or association that comes to mind when words are called out. Select words that clearly have multiple meanings and words for which the students probably know two or three of the meanings.

Students often use context clues to help determine word meanings. Sometimes, however, students are unsuccessful at using context clues because they lack a systematic strategy for figuring out unknown words. To help students develop the ability to use context to discover the meaning of unfamiliar words, teachers can discuss specific clues that they should look for in text.

DEFINITIONS

Authors often define a word in the sentence in which it first appears. This technique is used frequently in textbooks when an author introduces terminology. Note the following example:

> The *peltier effect* is the production of heat at the junction of two metals on the passage of a current.

SIGNAL WORDS

Some of the most frequently used signal words are *for example, this way, such as, especially, like, in (the way) that,* and *such.*

Certain words or phrases may signal the reader that a word or a term is about to be explained or that an example will be presented.

> Martin Luther King was more than just a leader in America *in that* he was recognized worldwide.

DIRECT EXPLANATIONS

Often, authors provide an explanation of an unfamiliar term. This technique is used frequently in difficult technical writing.

> Mead emphasized that the mind is a social product; indeed, one of the most important achievements of socialization is the development of *cognitive abilities*—intellectual capacities such as perceiving, remembering, reasoning, calculating, and believing.

SYNONYMS

A complex term may be followed by a simpler, more commonly understood word, even though the words may not be perfect synonyms. Again, the author is attempting to give the reader an explanation or definition—in this instance, by using a comparison. In the following example, *obscure* is explained by comparison to the word *unintelligible.*

> The lecture was so *obscure* that the students labeled it *unintelligible.*

ANTONYMS

An author may define or explain a term by contrasting it with words of opposite meaning:

> The young swimmer did not have the *perseverance* of her older teammates and *quit* at the halfway point in the race.

INFERENCES

Students can often infer the meaning of an unfamiliar word from the mood and tone of the selection. In this case, meaning must be deduced through a combination of the author's use of mood, tone, and imagery and the reader's background knowledge and experience. The author thus paints a picture of meaning rather than concretely

1. *Definitions:* An *extemporaneous* speech is one that is given on the spot without prior preparation.
2. *Signal words:* There are several forms of *precipitation* such as rain, sleet, snow, and hail.
3. *Direct explanations:* Carl was *despondent,* making him feel so downhearted that he didn't want to participate in anything.
4. *Synonyms:* When we looked into the jar, we saw the *larva* stage, or worm, of the beetle we were studying.
5. *Antonyms:* Tamara was quite *gregarious* while her sister Mary was very shy.
6. *Inferences:* It was a good thing the locksmith only charged a *nominal* fee to unlock John's car because he only had only a few dollars.

FIGURE 7.2

Context Clue Types and Examples

defining or explaining a word within the text. In the passage that follows, the meaning of *scarcely* and *brandishing* are not made clear. The reader must infer the meaning from the mood and tone of the paragraph and from his or her personal experience with thunderstorms.

> The rain driving hard against the back of the house, was *scarcely* sprinkling here. But it whooped windily through the great beech tree on the lawn, *brandishing* branches, tearing off twigs (from *Storm in the Night,* by Mary Stolz. New York: Harper Trophy, 1988).

Students can use context clue strategies to unlock the meaning of unfamiliar terms. Therefore, it is a good idea to have these six clues (with explanations and sample sentences) posted at points around the classroom or on handouts to be kept in students' work folders (Figure 7.2).

Structural Analysis

Even if students practice and remember the strategy, context clues sometimes are not of much help in decoding unfamiliar words (Blachowicz & Fisher, 2000; Nagy & Stahl, 2000). For example, readers probably would have trouble guessing the meaning of the following italicized term from context clues: They put a *lien* on our house. Using context clues alone would give readers no idea at all of the meaning of *lien.*

When a student is working alone, it can potentially be more helpful to use structural analysis, also known as morphemic analysis, along with contextual analysis to derive meaning. Instruction in morphology to learn word parts in the form of roots and affixes can be an advantage serving to unlock numerous words across disciplines (Baumann, 2005; Baumann, Edwards, Boland, Olejnik, & Kame'enui, 2003). More than half of all English words originated from Greek or Latin (Padak, Newton, Rasinski, & Newton, 2008). The features and patterns provide a consistent base for unlocking many words—not only in English but also in other languages—that have similar origins and thus share many cognates. Many terms in the sciences have Greek or Latin roots. The potential that morphology offers as a means to build vocabulary makes it a strong tool for classroom instruction and for developing student independence. Morphology is like the next level of "word families" (e.g., hat, fat, cat, rat) commonly used for instruction in the early grades. However, morphology has added value in that roots share not only pronunciation but also meaning (e.g., biology, biography, biosphere, biophysics, biopsy). Generally, students are ready for using structural analysis to assist them in understanding unknown terms by the time they enter fourth grade (Edwards, Font, Baumann, & Boland, 2004; Graves, 2006a, 2006b; White, Sowell, & Yanagihara, 1989). Baumann and his colleagues (2002, 2003) have found empirical evidence that instruction and practice in using contextual and structural analysis together can improve independent vocabulary acquisition. Kieffer and Lesaux (2007) found in their study of fourth and fifth graders that morphology (the study of word parts) and vocabulary development have a reciprocal relationship. As students develop a greater understanding of morphology, their vocabularies increase; students with larger vocabularies tend to better understand morphology.

Please visit the Education CourseMate website at **www.cengagebrain.com** to find links to websites that offer lists of roots and affixes.

Structural analysis provides a way to examine words looking for roots and affixes as keys to unlocking word meanings. Roots (the most basic word parts) and affixes (prefixes and suffixes) are all morphemes. Morphemes are the smallest meaning-bearing units that make up words. In the word *unlock*, there are two morphemes, *un* and *lock*. A **morpheme** can be **free** to stand alone like *lock* or **bound** like *un* (needing to be joined to another morpheme).

As few as 20 prefixes with consistent meanings and spellings are used in 97 percent of words containing prefixes found in texts and instructional materials commonly used in school (White, Sowell, & Yanagihara, 1989). Knowing *un, re, in,* and *dis* gives students a key to the meanings of more than 1,500 words (Cunningham, 2006). Beyond prefixes, it is useful to teach commonly used suffixes, especially derivational suffixes such as *less (regardless)* and *able (affordable)* because of their effect on meaning. Inflectional suffixes, often referred to as inflections, alter word forms but do not change the essential meanings of the roots. In the case of nouns, *cat* becomes *cats.* Verbs may change as *hop, hops, hopping,* and *hopped.* Greek and Latin roots can be effectively introduced as they become important to learning content-specific and specialized terminology. Edwards and colleagues (2004) suggest four guidelines for teaching morphemic analysis:

1. *Provide explicit instruction in how morphemic analysis works.* This includes modeling and practicing breaking words apart and putting them back together for the purpose of locating meaningful clues.
2. *Use word families to promote vocabulary growth.* Learning to recognize word families may help students make connections from common to less common derivations of a word.
3. *Promote independent use of morphemic analysis.* Encouraging and challenging students to build their repertoire through recording words with common affixes and roots in their vocabulary journals or notebooks can enhance independent vocabulary growth.
4. *Enhance students' awareness that morphemic analysis does not always work.* Word part meanings are not always consistent, and meanings of isolated parts when combined do not always produce true meanings of words (pp. 164–166).

When combining structural analysis and contextual analysis, the vocabulary rule strategy (Edwards, Font, Baumann, & Boland, 2004) of using a whole–part–whole sequence is recommended. Students first read and make use of context, then consider the word parts of the key word(s), and finally put it all together again in the context of the passage. With explanations, modeling, and think-alouds, students can begin to adopt combinations of structural and contextual analysis strategies for continuing to develop mental habits that increase vocabulary understanding.

FIGURE 7.3 Biheaded, Trilegged Hydrosaur

Semantic maps make good vehicles for illustrating morphological relationships. Kidspiration and Inspiration, the well-developed software tools for creating semantic maps, provide a way to include picture examples along with words and word parts being studied. Word sorts also work well for assisting students as they develop their understanding of words that share common morphemes. When working with young students, an activity called Affix Animals offers a playful way to experiment with prefixes and suffixes. Students are given a list of number and characteristic affixes from which they may choose to draw, create, and appropriately name an imaginary animal (Figure 7.3).

DISSECT

This mnemonic, created by Deshler and Schumacher (1988), provides a ready reminder of several factors that help determine a word's meaning. When modeled and practiced, this may be a helpful tool for independent reading:

Discover the word's context.

Isolate the prefix.

Separate the suffix.

Say the stem or root word.

Examine the stem or root word.

Check with someone.

Try the dictionary.

WORD ATTACK PARADIGMS

Aguiar and Brady (1991) suggest that vocabulary deficits of less skilled readers stem from difficulty in establishing accurate phonological representations for new words. Their research points to the importance of structural analysis and the following strategy, called a *word attack paradigm,* to help students recognize words. In this activity students are given a card with a series of steps to aid them in deciphering new words they encounter in reading. Such a paradigm might look like this:

1. Figure out the word from the meaning of the sentence. The word must make sense in the sentence.
2. Take off the ending of the word. Certain endings, such as *s, d, r, es, ed, er, est, al,* or *ing,* may be enough to make the word look "new."
3. Break the word into syllables. Don't be afraid to try two or three ways to break the word. Look for familiar prefixes, suffixes, and root words.
4. Sound out the word. Try to break the word into syllables several times, sounding it out each time. Do you know a word that begins with the same letters? Do you know a word that ends the same way? Put them together.
5. Look in the glossary if there is one in the back of the book.
6. Ask a friend in class or the teacher. No one should be ashamed of asking for help.
7. As a last resort, find the definition of the word in the dictionary.

Why should dictionaries be the last source a student consults? Why do teachers so often advise students to use it first?

Dictionaries should be the last source one uses in figuring out the meaning of a word—after all sources are exhausted. Unfortunately, teachers (and parents) often tell students to use the dictionary as a first option in discovering the meaning of words. A word attack paradigm gives students a way to attempt newly found words without resorting to a dictionary. Students should keep the paradigm in their folders, or a large one can be posted on the wall by the teacher.

Vocabulary Podcasts

The use of auditory tools for reinforcing instruction is not a new phenomenon, but the tools for recording and transmitting are quite different from the old devices and are popular among children, adolescents, and adults alike. Putman and Kingsley (2009) wanted to know if podcasts held promise for increasing science vocabulary development among their fifth grade students. Students were randomly selected from each of three classes to be given access to podcasts. All students received the same in-class instruction. Before beginning the unit, students were pretested on words being considered for study. Words were selected based on pretest results in conjunction with importance for good conceptual understanding of the science content. Words were introduced and discussed in class to arrive at common definitions. Demonstrations and in-depth small group strategies were used to give exposure and practice with the terms.

The songs and ideas for these podcasts were prepared to appeal to fifth graders. Please visit the Education CourseMate website at **www.cengagebrain.com** to find links to podcasts designed for older second language learners and information for creating instructional podcasts.

Using a blog, teachers explained how podcasts could be downloaded. Parents and students were provided instructions for listening to podcasts one or more times each week as a review. Students in the treatment group were allowed time at school to listen but only during a lab time or when regular work was completed. Students receiving podcasts scored significantly higher on tests of vocabulary understanding at the end of the unit than their peers in the control group. Putman and Kingsley (2009) offered the following pointers for creating podcasts for use in instruction:

1. Don't rely on traditional definitions. Use your own or have students develop their own and use them.
2. Include information that shows the words in context. Periodically read portions of text that include the targeted vocabulary word.

3. Don't just lecture. Keep the tone light so the podcasts feel like a conversation.
4. Make them interactive. Students should have to stop the podcast periodically to complete a brief activity.
5. Make them fun. Students will not listen to the podcasts if they are not interesting or motivating, so add sound effects or an occasional joke (p.106).

TECH APP

Designing a Vocabulary Podcast

1. Create an interesting beginning using music, a jingle, or an intriguing lead.
2. Review 10 or fewer terms with student-friendly definitions.
3. Ask the listener to make a personal connection to the word; jot down the connection.
4. Read aloud a short and engaging text that uses the words in appropriate context.
5. Pose questions for recalling definitions or thinking of examples, non-examples, or attributes associated with the terms.
6. Provide clues to help the student figure out the "mystery" words.
7. Conclude with a review.

Vocabulary Lists

Encourage students to make vocabulary lists of new terms they have mastered, whether by context clue discovery, structural analysis, or the word attack paradigm. Students may keep such lists in notebooks, on file cards, or in Word files. If they use cards, first they can write a word and its dictionary pronunciation on the front side. Then on the back they can write the sentence in which the word was found and the dictionary definition. Periodically, students can share their vocabulary terms with one another: One student calls out the term, and another gives the definition and uses the word in a sentence. In this manner, students make a habit of working with words to expand their content vocabulary. Activity 7.9 is an example of a vocabulary list.

Organizational (Jot) Charts

Students can compare and contrast words using organizational (jot) charts, as described in Chapter 4. For instance, a Spanish teacher had third-year students chart command words so they could see at a glance on one simple chart the relationship of the three

ACTIVITY 7.9 Beginning Vocabulary List (Elementary Level)

Word	Page	Possible Definition	Verified Definition
Dwelling	132	Living area	A place where people live
Fossil	133	To harden or make like stone	The remains, trace, or impression of an animal or plant that lived long ago

ACTIVITY 7.10 Los Mandatos Regulares

Key	Tú		Ud.		Uds.	
afirmativo hablar comer escribir	**-ar** **-er,ir**	habla- come escribe	**-ar** **-er,ir**	hable coma escriba	**-ar** **-er,ir**	hablen coman escriban
irregulares	decir-di hacer-haz ir-ve poner-pon	salir-sal ser-se´ tener-ten venir-ven	dar-de´ estar-este´ ir-vaya saber-sepa	ser-sea	dar-den estareste´n ir-vayan saber-sepan	ser-sean
escribir **negativo** hablar comer	**-ar** **-er,ir**	no hables no comas no escribas	**-ar** **-er,ir**	no hable no coma no escriba	**-ar** **-er,ir**	No hablen No coman No escriban
irregulares	**dar-** **ir-** **estar-** **ser-**	no des no vayas no este´s no seas	dar- estar- ir- saber- ser-	no de´ no este´ no vaya no sepa no sea	dar- estar- ir- saber- ser-	No den No este´n no vayan no sepan no sean

Developed by Heather Hemstreet.

types of commands in negative and affirmative statements. Activity 7.10 shows the chart. Students can do this by using the "create table" tool in their word processing program.

Using the Dictionary

Dictionary use is most often associated with writing definitions and sentences using a set of assigned words. Although this exercise may provide some exposure and focus on selected words, it is not particularly useful for building and encouraging vocabulary development. However, dictionaries are valuable tools and sources of much more than definitions when students know how and when to use them as resources. When a person asks for a word meaning, he or she is not typically expecting a dictionary definition as a reply and may not appreciate being told to "look it up in the dictionary." A more common response is a description, an example, or even an analogous connection offered in explanation. Although formal definitions are not often used in conversation or many forms of writing, they can help people learn the meanings of words.

Create an activity to engage students in exploring the pronunciation key, guide words, word origins, and parts of speech. Help students see the value in these features for developing independence as "wordsmiths."

PIQUING STUDENTS' INTEREST

Blachowicz and Fisher (2006) describe **Piquing Students' Interest**, a strategy developed by Smith (1983) for raising student awareness of the many pieces of information a dictionary entry may give about a word. In small groups, students are given copies of a dictionary page and are challenged to list as many different pieces of information as they can find that the dictionary entry gives for a word specified by the teacher. The teacher may first share how many he or she found as a target or incentive. After 10 minutes, students share their findings and compare them with the teacher's. This can provide an opening for discussion and exploration of elements with which students are less familiar.

THE DICTIONARY GAME

Koeze (1990) developed a classic activity that challenges students to predict words that might be found in the definition of a selected term. One person in the group selects a term, such as *amphibian*. Starting with the person to the left, each student in a small group of three to five gives a word that has a good possibility of being in the dictionary definition. Duplications, articles, and prepositions are not allowed. When play returns to the person who selected the term, he or she gives a word and then looks up the term (in this case, *amphibian*) in the dictionary to verify predictions. Points are awarded for correct predictions, and play continues with the person to the left. This activity offers an interesting way to review and affirm understanding during or after completion of a unit of study.

Thesauruses, foreign language dictionaries, and specialized dictionaries and reference tools can be found on the Internet. These can be great sources of interest and may include animation and sound dimensions not available in other formats.

Teaching Vocabulary as a Reflection Activity

Considerable research shows the benefits of teaching vocabulary before reading (Carney, Anderson, Blackburn, & Blessing, 1984; Medo & Ryder, 1993). However, an intriguing finding emerges consistently from reading research: It can be as beneficial—or more so—to teach vocabulary after reading (Mealey & Konopak, 1990; Memory, 1990). The conventional wisdom has been that vocabulary is best taught before reading. In fact, the more students are asked to discuss, brainstorm, and think about what they have learned, the more they comprehend and retain the material. Thus, the reflection phase of vocabulary development holds much promise in helping students thoroughly grasp the meaning of difficult terms in their reading. In this section, we offer a number of strategies for reflection that are best carried out by small groups of students.

Semantic Feature Analysis

Semantic feature analysis (Pittleman, Heimlich, Berglund, & French, 1991) is a technique for helping a student understand deeper meanings and nuances of language. To accomplish the analysis, the teacher projects a matrix with a vertical list of terms and asks students to help choose the features that will be written across the top of the matrix. Students then complete the matrix with a plus sign (+) for features that apply to each word. Students should do this analysis after reading the lesson, after having used a technique such as the guided reading procedure or the directed reading–thinking activity (see Chapter 4). Activity 7.11 shows a semantic feature analysis used in a science class about energy.

The power of semantic feature analysis lies in the structure that engages students in thinking deeply about fine gradations of meaning concerning vocabulary terms and stating whether a term is affiliated always, sometimes, or never with a given concept or feature. With some low achievers, teachers will need to fill out both the vocabulary terms and features beforehand. Students should be allowed in groups to (1) brainstorm

This technique was originally suggested as both a prereading activity and a postreading activity. Students seem to do better with semantic features after they have completed a reading and have established a conceptual base of knowledge about the passage.

ACTIVITY 7.11 Grid for Semantic Feature Analysis

Topic: ______ Energy (Chapter 11)

Directions: Mark those features that apply to each vocabulary term.

A = the vocabulary term always applies to the feature
S = the vocabulary term sometimes applies to the feature
N = the vocabulary term never applies to the feature Energy (Chapter 11)

Features

Vocabulary Terms	Renewable resource	Nonrenewable resource	Fossil fuels—direct use	Nuclear material	Naturally occurs	Manmade materials	Conservable	Pro-environment	Pollutant
Uranium^{235}									
Hydrogen									
Biomass									
Geothermal energy									
Hydroelectricity									
Wind energy									
Passive solar heating									
Active solar heating									
Deuterium + Tritium									
Oil									
Coal									
Natural gas									

Developed by Wendy Barcroft.

words in the reading that they find difficult and (2) find the major concepts that they are learning in the chapter (the features). Eventually, students can both create and fill out the matrix themselves.

Postgraphic Organizers

Please visit the Education CourseMate website at **www.cengagebrain.com** to access some of the many graphic organizer sites online.

Earlier in this chapter, we discussed how students could help construct their own graphic organizers before reading to learn new vocabulary terms and to attempt to construct a hierarchical pattern of organization. To enhance concept development, students can return to these organizers after reading. Chapter 5 described postgraphic organizers for use in the reflection phase of learning. Here we present a variation

ACTIVITY 7.12 Elementary Units of Measure for Length, Area, and Capacity

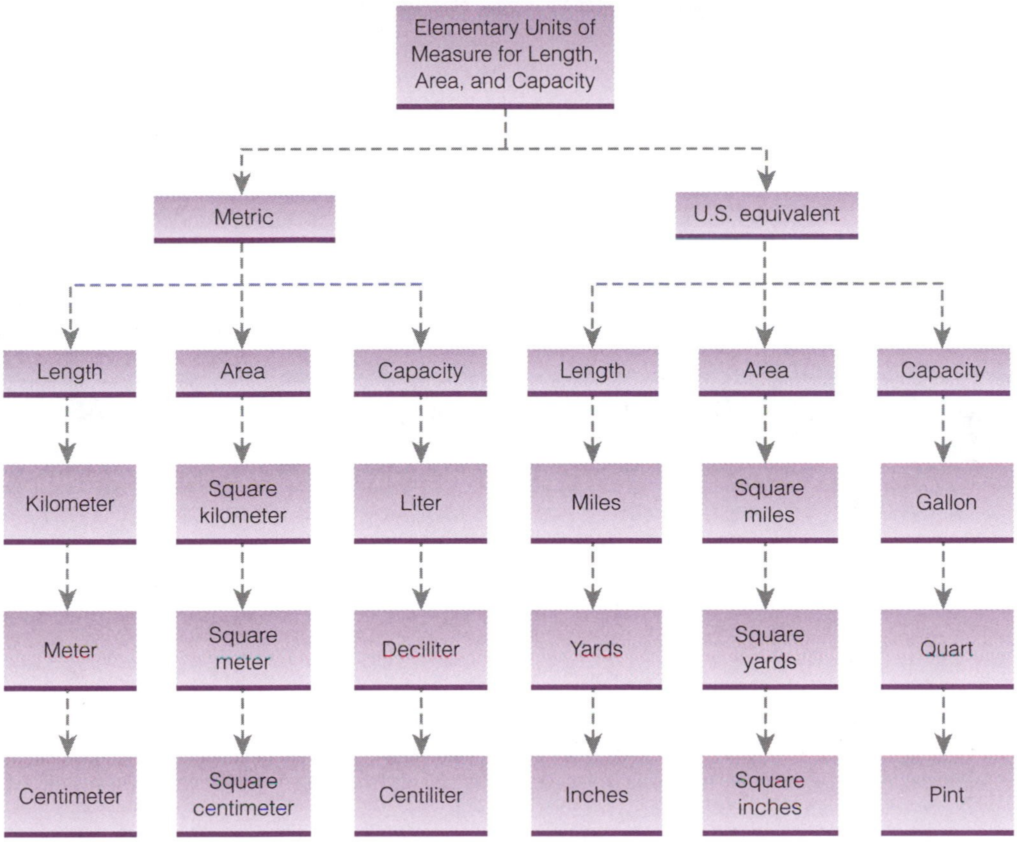

specifically for vocabulary. Students can construct a postgraphic organizer directly after the reading. Activity 7.12 shows an example of an elementary mathematics postgraphic organizer used after a basic unit about measurement.

Categorization

One of the best ways for students to learn relationships of concepts after a reading is through a categorization activity. **Categorization** is the act of assigning something to a class, a group, or a division. Categorization can be accomplished through a word relationship activity that begins with the teacher suggesting a topic and asking students to supply words that describe the topic. The teacher may supplement the words given by the students or skim the text to find more words. If students' abilities or backgrounds are limited, the teacher can provide a list. Activity 7.13 is a list of body systems that was developed by a science teacher.

Students organize the list of words into smaller lists of items that have something in common, as shown in Activity 7.13. It is best during this phase for students to work in small groups to categorize and label the words. The groups explain their categories and labels to the entire class; then the whole class tries to reach a consensus on what the correct labels are and where the particular words belong. During this final phase, the teacher needs to act as a guide to make certain that discussion and labeling are being channeled in the proper direction. It is also essential that students be allowed to provide a rationale for their decisions.

The focus on explanation and discussion in this activity makes it an excellent strategy for teaching difficult vocabulary, concept development, and critical thinking, especially because much learning depends on students' ability to create meaningful categories of information. Practiced in a relaxed and purposeful atmosphere, this activity can be an excellent tool for helping students develop concepts, improve comprehension, and retain information. Gillett and Temple (1983) call this type of categorization activity a word sort. In a **closed word sort**, students are given the categories in advance.

ACTIVITY 7.13 Categorization Exercise: Body Systems

Below are three categories that describe functioning systems in the human body—the digestive, respiratory, and circulatory systems.

DIGESTIVE	RESPIRATORY	CIRCULATORY

Place each of the following vocabulary terms in the correct category:

aorta	gastric juice	trachea
esophagus	diaphragm	flatus
ulcer	lung	artery
atrium	salivary gland	asthma
pneumonia	angina pectoris	hypertension
bronchi	ventricle	peristaltic waves

Answers:

DIGESTIVE	RESPIRATORY	CIRCULATORY
ulcer	asthma	aorta
gastric juice	pneumonia	atrium
salivary glands	bronchi	angina pectoris
flatus	diaphragm	ventricle
peristaltic waves	lung	artery
esophagus	trachea	hypertension

Developed by Kim Blowe.

This teaches classification and deductive reasoning. In an **open word sort**, students have to group words as concepts and title their relationships. This teaches inference, or reading between the lines, which is an important concept for students to learn at any age.

Directed Reading–Thinking Activity Vocabulary Search

When doing a Directed Reading–Thinking Activity (DR-TA) in a content area classroom, the teacher can ask students to jot down difficult vocabulary terms. The student lists are given to the teacher without student names, and these terms become the words to be studied after the DR-TA or at the beginning of the next class period. The teacher first teaches word recognition by using a "word families" phonics approach to sound out words. If a word is *expressive*, for example, the teacher asks for other words in the same word family (e.g., *express*, *expression*, *press*, *pressure*). Students work through the word family to sound out the word, thereby achieving word recognition.

Next comes a skimming and scanning exercise. The teacher begins by saying, "Find the word *expressive*. Tell the page, column, and paragraph number where you found it and read the paragraph aloud." The teacher assists students in learning the meaning of the word using the context of the story or chapter. This word search approach teaches word recognition, speed reading, and comprehension through the use of context clues. The teacher selects words for study that may impede clear understanding of the passage.

A Vocabulary Study System

Dana and Rodriguez (1992) proposed a vocabulary study system using the acronym **TOAST** that has been more effective for learning vocabulary than other selected study methods. The steps in this vocabulary study technique are as follows:

T: Test. Students self-test to determine which vocabulary terms they cannot spell, define, or use in sentences.

O: Organize. Students organize these words into semantically related groups; arrange words into categories by structure or function, such as words that sound alike or are the same part of speech; and categorize words as somewhat familiar or completely unfamiliar.

A: Anchor. Students "anchor" the words in memory by using a keyword method (assigning a picture and a caption to a vocabulary term), tape recording definitions, creating mnemonic devices, or mixing the words on cards and ordering them from difficult to easy.

S: Say. Students review the words by calling out the spellings, definitions, and uses in sentences to another student. The first review session begins 5 to 10 minutes after initial study and is followed at intervals by several more.

T: Test. Immediately after each review, students self-administer a posttest in which they spell, define, and use in context all the vocabulary terms with which they originally had difficulty. The response mode may be oral, written, or silent thought. TOAST encompasses all aspects of PAR, and we recommend this vocabulary study system from early elementary grades through high school as a good method for getting students actively involved in the study of words.

Please visit the Education CourseMate website at **www.cengagebrain.com** to find a link to Building a Better Vocabulary. It offers tips, games, and clear explanations for building a strong vocabulary base.

Four-Column Organizer for Word Mastery

Four-column organizers can be particularly useful for struggling learners or ELL students because it provides assistance with definitions while encouraging personal and visual connections.

In Activity 7.14, the words and definitions are provided to ensure that students are learning a context-appropriate meaning and to allow students time to engage in thoughtful, interactive pursuits.

A less complex and scaffolded system for vocabulary study is described by Leno and Dougherty (2007). A middle school teacher, Mandy Panzer, created a graphic organizer to be used as both an interactive guide and a study tool for vocabulary in her science classes. Three columns with the headings *Word, Definition, and Knowledge Connection* are on the front of the handout. The words to be studied and their definitions are filled in when the students receive the handout. In the *Knowledge Connection* column, students are directed to write in an example or connection to an in- or out-of-class activity, lab, or experience related to each term. On the back of the paper, there is a column labeled *Visual*, so that the column can eventually be folded over to cover the *Definition* and the *Knowledge Connection* columns. Students create a sketch or visual reminder that represents the meaning of each term in the *Visual* column.

This strategy is quite similar to Subjective Approach to Vocabulary (SAV) developed by Manzo (1983). The teacher projects the word and explains the meaning, providing students with an objective definition to write in their journals. The teacher then invites students to share a personal connection or experience that relates to the word. Students then record one or more subjective meanings for the word in their journals.

Vocabulary Self-Collection Strategy

The VSS allows students to generate the vocabulary list based on interest. The teacher can set it up as a cooperative assignment: Each group member brings in an interesting word. Members of the group work together to identify the appropriate definition for each word and to choose a final list to present for the class to study.

Another effective strategy for use after reading is the vocabulary self-collection strategy (VSS) (Haggard, 1986). The VSS is a cooperative vocabulary activity that allows both teachers and students to share words they wish to learn and remember. The strategy begins after students read an assignment. Each member of the class, including the teacher, is asked to bring a word that is perceived as important for the class to learn. Words usually come from the content area textbook but may also come from what students have heard within or outside the classroom. Students share their words in class, defining and elaborating on the presented words as the teacher writes them on the chalkboard. Then as a whole class, students decide which words are most important and should be learned by the class. The students record the chosen words in vocabulary notebooks. Class discussions ensue in which students use the words in purposeful sentences.

Chase and Dufflemeyer (1990) have designed an adaptation of the VSS for English classes that they call *vocab-lit strategy.* To begin this strategy, the teacher introduces a new vocabulary term; in a journal, the students write the term, the sentence where it is found, and a note about whether the student is acquainted with the word. Then students can work as a group to define the word and write sentences telling how the word is used in a story. As the story progresses and students get familiar with the technique, they can offer words and define and use them in this manner.

Language Enrichment through Reflection

Students find many of the activities described in this chapter so enjoyable that their interest in words is heightened. In this section, emphasizing word play, we offer additional techniques that will help students experience the pleasure of

ACTIVITY 7.14 Four-Column Organizer for Word Mastery

Water Pollutants (front side of handout)		
Word	**Definition**	**Knowledge Connection**
Sediment Pollution	Insoluble particles from rock or soil moved by water or wind that harms plant or animal life	Mud from the coal mining site flowing into the river
Nutrient Pollution	The infusion of too many nutrients into bodies of water that can cause excessive growth of algae	Discharge from Joey's old boat goes into the bay
Toxic Pollution	Harmful chemicals released into water sources	Video of the gulf oil spill
Pathogen Pollution	An organism, usually bacteria, that can cause disease or death that is released into the environment	Recall of tainted eggs bought in the supermarket
Thermal Pollution	Hot water runoff from industrial and power plants	News story on t.v. about the hot water runoff from the local power plant

	Water Pollutants (back side of handout)	
		Visual
		 MiloVad/Shutterstock.com
		 Gary Blakeley/Shutterstock.com
		 Cheryl Casey/Shutterstock.com
		 CrackerClips/Shutterstock.com
		 Kletr/Shutterstock.com

(continues)

ACTIVITY 7.14 (Continued)

Water Pollutants (back folded over front)	
Visual	**Knowledge Connection**
 MiloVad/Shutterstock.com	Mud from the coal mining site flowing into the river
 Gary Blakeley/ Shutterstock.com	Discharge from Joey's old boat goes into the bay
 Cheryl Casey/ Shutterstock.com	Video of the gulf oil spill
 CrackerClips/ Shutterstock.com	Recall of tainted eggs bought in the supermarket
 Kletr/Shutterstock.com	News story on t.v. about the hot water runoff from the local power plant

working with words. Specifically, we present eight techniques: imaging through keywords, word analogies, magic squares, vocabulary illustrations, vocabulary bingo, word bubbles, odd word out, and word inquiry.

USE OF KEYWORDS AND IMAGING

Probably no type of mnemonic device has been researched more thoroughly than the **keyword strategy** as an aid in learning new vocabulary terms. Much research over the past several decades has demonstrated the usefulness of this activity (Levin, Levin, Glassman, & Nordwall, 1992; McGivern & Levin, 1983; Zhang & Schumm, 2000). Atkinson (1975) described the keyword method as a two-stage strategy. First, the learner imagines a concrete and easily remembered word that sounds similar to the word to be learned. Next, an image is remembered that cues the learner to the

CHALLENGE BOX

Mark, the Struggling Reader

Think again about Mark, the struggling middle school reader.

SITUATION: One of Mark's greatest challenges is reading and understanding content-specific and academic vocabulary in his textbooks. Textbook language is not like language used in conversation, and many of the terms he encounters represent new ideas and concepts for him. Sometimes words that he knows do not make sense when he reads them in his textbook.

What should Mark's teachers consider when selecting vocabulary to help him make strides in word and concept development?

Teachers need to keep in mind the goals and objectives for the lessons and units when making decisions about vocabulary development for Mark. His teachers should select a small number of words that are critical for understanding the key ideas and concepts so Mark will not become overwhelmed or discouraged. High-utility words will build his vocabulary across all subject areas. These include academic vocabulary and words with common Greek or Latin roots. It will also empower Mark to ask him to choose two or three words from the readings that he would like to know. He may need extended direct instruction, including definitions and rich context, to develop deep understanding. Varied opportunities to hear and use the terms in discussion and writing will provide the repetition for solidifying his learning. Explicit lessons featuring polysemous (multiple-meaning) words could help Mark resolve the confusion he experiences when known words just don't seem to fit the passage. A balance of direct instruction and strategies for independent word learning will help Mark build his understanding and confidence to approach unknown words "head on."

What strategies and technology connections could Mark's teachers use to interest and encourage him?

The PAR Framework will give Mark's teachers the structure and means to introduce, build, and reinforce vocabulary understanding throughout a unit of study. Teachers could use graphic organizers, posters, podcasts, video clips, and computer vocabulary games to introduce, assist, and provide structure for reflection on his understanding. Strategies like the Four-Column Organizer for Word Mastery and SAV offer hands-on engagement with definitions, opportunities to make personal connections, and the benefit of creating a visual prompt to trigger memory and understanding. Vocabulary Illustrations combine visual connections with written explanations. Mark can also benefit from opportunities to discuss terms with team members in cooperative group projects. Hearing others' perspectives may challenge or affirm his own understanding. Mark's teachers have many options to provide structured and engaging methods for helping him succeed while equipping him with tools that will help him learn vocabulary and concepts beyond their classrooms.

keyword and then, of course, to the word to be learned. As an example, imagine someone trying to remember the term *tryptophan* in a class about nutrition. The keyword would be *fan.* The image that would be conjured up would be of an attic. Someone trips over a *fan* and falls in the attic: He tripped the *fan* in the attic (hence *tryptophan*). It should be noted that although keywords have been shown to be effective, they do not work for all students and may not work with certain words. Also, some studies have found keyword gains in vocabulary growth to be temporary—sometimes the learned words stay with students as little as one week before fading. As with all mnemonic strategies, it is best to get students to make their own images rather than having keyword images dictated by the teacher. We included this strategy here because it has been shown to be effective in teaching vocabulary terms. A more thorough discussion of mnemonics can be found in Chapter 9.

WORD ANALOGIES

Word analogies are excellent for teaching higher level thinking. To do word analogies, students must be able to perceive relationships between what amounts to two sides of an equation. This may be critical thinking at its best in that the student is often forced

ACTIVITY 7.15 Word Analogies: Language Arts (Elementary Level)

1. Hot is to cold as day is to ______________.
   up night long
2. Dog is to cat as small is to ______________.
   little big short
3. Puppy is to ______________ as young is to old.
   playful dog kitten
4. ______________ is to white as on is to off.
   Red Black Door
5. Happy is to ______________ as stop is to go.
   glad sad frown
6. Slow is to ______________ as long is to short.
   silly happy fast

Developed by Colleen Kean.

to attempt various combinations of possible answers in solving the problem. At first, students may have difficulty with this concept; therefore, the teacher should practice with students and explain the equation used in analogies:

____________ is to ____________ as ____________ is to ____________.

or

____________:____________::____________:____________

For elementary students, teachers first spell out "is to . . . as" rather than using symbols. In addition, students say that analogies are easiest when the blank is in the fourth position, as in terms 1 and 2 in Activity 7.15, an early elementary activity in language arts. More difficult analogies can be constructed by varying the position of the blank, as in items 3 through 6.

MAGIC SQUARES

Any vocabulary activity can come alive through the use of magic squares, a technique that can be used at all levels—elementary, junior high, and high school. **Magic squares** are special arrangements of numbers that when added across, down, or diagonally always equal the same sum. Teachers can construct these vocabulary exercises by having students match a lettered column of words to a numbered column of definitions. Letters on each square of the grid match the lettered words. Students try to find the magic number by matching the correct word and definition and entering the number in the appropriate square or grid. Activity 7.16 gives explicit instructions for constructing magic squares. Activity 7.17 represents a magic square history lesson on Greece, Rome, and the ancient world taught in an early elementary classroom.

VOCABULARY ILLUSTRATIONS

Joe Antinarella, an English teacher at Tidewater Community College in Chesapeake, Virginia, developed a creative way to enrich students' study of vocabulary that he calls **vocabulary illustrations**. He has students first define a word on a piece of

ACTIVITY 7.16 Instructions for Making Magic Squares

1. Start with a range of numbers, such as 1 to 9 or 4 to 12, to fill 9 squares in a 3 3 3 magic square.
2. Add the first and last numbers: 1 + 9 = 10; 4 + 12 = 16.
3. Determine the midpoint and put that number in the middle of the square: Between 1 and 9, put 5; between 4 and 12, put 8.
4. Add the first and last numbers: 1 + 5 + 9 = 15.
5. Make combinations that add up to this magic square number and fill in the square.

8	1	6
3	5	7
4	9	2

As a shortcut to step 5, take the first number in your sequence, such as number 1; counting from that number, follow the directions below. In the diagram below, 1 is used as the first number.

1. Put the first number in the center of the top row.
2. Put the second number diagonally to the right; then place it in the corresponding position in the magic square.
3. Put the third number diagonally to the right; then place it in the corresponding position. Because you can't put the fourth number on the diagonal, you drop it below the third number.
4. Place the fifth number and then the sixth number on the diagonal.
5. You can't put the seventh number on the diagonal, so drop the seventh number down below the sixth.
6. Put the eighth number diagonally to the right and move to the corresponding position.
7. Put the ninth number diagonally to the right; then move it to the corresponding position below.

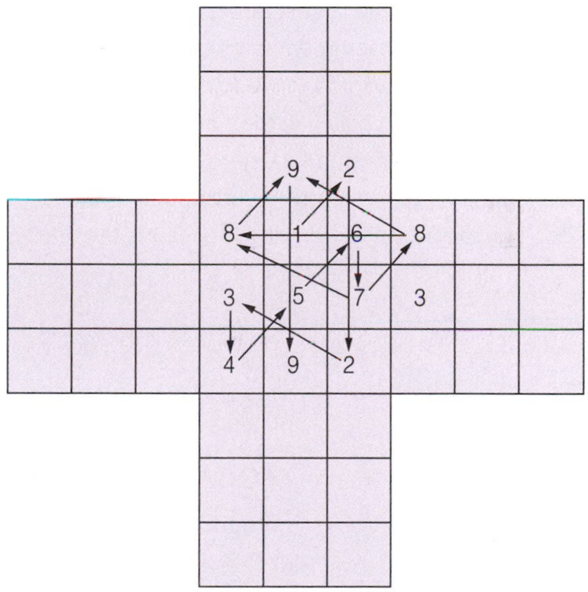

Variations on combinations:

672	294	438	618	492	834	276
159	753	951	753	357	159	951
834	618	276	294	816	672	438

drawing paper and then find a picture or make an original drawing that illustrates the concept. Below the picture, students use the term in a sentence that clarifies or goes along with what is happening in the picture or drawing. Activity 7.18 is a vocabulary illustration completed by a student in a primary language arts classroom. Activity 7.19 shows an example created by a student in a seventh grade English class. Finally, Activity 7.20 shows a vocabulary illustration of a first grade student in a science lesson.

ACTIVITY 7.17 Magic Squares: The Ancient World (Elementary Level)

Directions: Read each of the sentences below the magic square. Match the sentence to the correct word on the square. Put the number of the sentence in that box. If your answers are correct, the sum of the numbers when added across or down will be the same for each row.

Parthenon ______	Olympics ______	Slaves ______	______
Athens ______	Columns ______	Arches ______	______
Republic ______	Aqueduct ______	Rome ______	______
______	______	______	

1. The sporting event the Greeks invented to help train warriors.
2. This city ruled the largest empire in the world.
3. This city was the largest direct democracy in the world.
4. The type of government where citizens elect people to represent them.
5. The Greeks invented these to build temples and other important buildings.
6. These people could win their freedom by fighting in the Colosseum.
7. The Romans invented these to provide strong support for buildings.
8. The name of the temple built to honor the goddess Athena.
9. This carried water from the mountains to the city.

Developed by Ed Toscano.

VOCABULARY BINGO

Bingo is one of the most popular of all games. Playing vocabulary bingo lets teachers work with words in a relaxed atmosphere. The steps in playing vocabulary bingo are as follows:

1. Students make a "bingo" card from a list of vocabulary items. (The game works best with at least 20 words.) Students should be encouraged to select words at random to fill each square.
2. The teacher (or student reader) reads definitions of the words aloud, and the students cover the word that they believe matches the definition. (It's handy to have the definitions on 3- × 5-inch cards and to shuffle the cards between games.) The winner is the first person to cover a vertical, horizontal, or diagonal row.
3. Check the winner by rereading the definitions used. This step not only keeps everyone honest but also serves as reinforcement and provides an opportunity for students to ask questions.

ACTIVITY 7.18 Vocabulary Illustration: Elementary Language Arts

Courtesy of the author.

Developed by Barbara Wood.

ACTIVITY 7.19 Vocabulary Illustration: Seventh Grade English

Courtesy of the author.

Developed by Barbara Wood.

A sample bingo game in mathematics is shown in Activity 7.21.

Most students enjoy the competition of bingo and participate enthusiastically. It is an excellent game to play as a review in any content area. The constant repetition of the definitions can act as reinforcement for aural learners. For instance, in chemistry, students can make bingo cards with symbols of elements, and the names of the elements are called out. For a higher level, the caller can use other characteristics of elements such

ACTIVITY 7.20 Vocabulary Illustration: First Grade Science

Courtesy of the author.

Developed by Barbara Wood.

as atomic numbers or descriptions (e.g., "a silvery liquid at room temperature" or "used to fill balloons"). As a variation on Activity 7.21 in mathematics, the bingo cards can contain the pictures of the shapes, and the caller names the shapes.

WORD BUBBLES

The word bubble provides a good review of vocabulary. Students are given one clue to the word's meaning on a line below the bubble. Using this clue and the bank of words to be reviewed, they fill in the bubble and list other clues on the lines. Students are not limited to the word bank as they list new clues. Activity 7.22 is a sample word bubble for a third grade mathematics class.

ODD WORD OUT

Odd word out offers a way of considering similarities and differences among words and concepts as students try to determine which word does not belong and why. Students are given several groups of four words each. For each grouping, students select one

ACTIVITY 7.21 Shapes and Solids Bingo

Clues (also write on index cards)

Square—a shape with four equal sides and four right angles

Rectangle—a shape with four sides, two of them longer than the other two, and four right angles

Triangle—a shape with three sides

Circle—a round shape with no angles

Pentagon—a shape with five sides and five angles

Octagon—a shape with eight sides and eight angles

Trapezoid—a shape with four sides and four angles, which are not right angles

Cube—a solid with six equal square sides

Cylinder—a solid shaped like a can

Sphere—a solid shaped like a ball

Rectangular prism—a solid shaped like a box

Pyramid—a solid with sides shaped like triangles

Directions: Each student should prepare a bingo card with 25 spaces. Write each term twice to fill up 24 boxes. The extra box can be a "free" box in the middle. The teacher shuffles the index cards and reads the *clues only*. The students decide which term matches the clue and cover one space with a chip. If all the clues are read without reaching a "Bingo," the cards can be reshuffled before continuing.

Square	Rectangle	Octagon	Trapezoid	Pentagon
Triangle	Circle	Cube	Cylinder	Sphere
Cylinder	Sphere	FREE	Rectangle	Rectangular prism
Circle	Octagon	Square	Triangle	Trapezoid
Cube	Pentagon	Pyramid	Rectangular Prism	Pyramid

Developed by Mary Fagerland.

word that is different from the others and explain why they chose each word. Which word would you eliminate from each of the following sets?

- **A.** Cottage, blue, American, cheddar
- **B.** Rectangle, triangle, quadrilateral, parallelogram
- **C.** Lincoln, Ford, Johnson, Bush
- **D.** Condensation, evaporation, dehydration, precipitation

ACTIVITY 7.22 Word Bubble: Third Grade Mathematics

Directions: Use the measurement word clue under each bubble to help you place the correct word from the word column in a bubble (in the example, "inch" is the word in the bubble). Then look at the word column again to add two more clue words on the blank lines extending below each bubble.

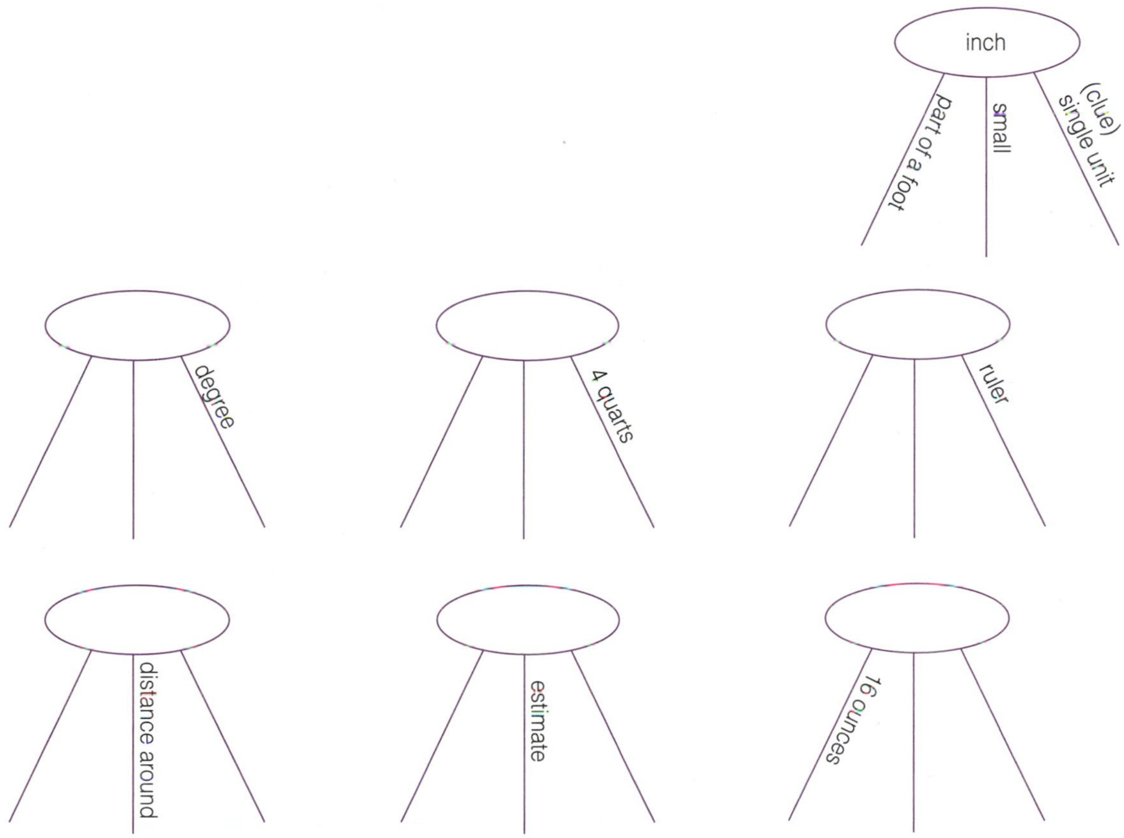

For extra credit, make your own word bubble game using words not found in this exercise.

Developed by Bessie Haskins.

As you can see, there may be more than one right answer. In set A, *blue* may be chosen as the only word that is a color, or *American* may be chosen as the only one that begins with a capital letter. You will probably think of other selections for that set with yet other justifications. Students must carefully consider various aspects and attributes of each word to make their selections and state their rationale.

Another version of *odd word out* created by Ur and Wright (1992) begins with six words, all purposefully selected from a broad category:

committee bills congress senator vote gavel

Students select one word that doesn't belong and state why. From the remaining words, students repeat the procedure. The steps are repeated until only two words are left. Students then decide on 10 ways the last two words are different.

WORD INQUIRY

Word inquiry uses the old 20 questions format. Ten to 15 words are randomly placed on a page or transparency. Students work in groups of two (partner A and partner B). Each selects a word and writes it on a slip of paper so that the partner will not see it. Partner A may then ask questions of partner B that can be answered with yes or no to determine the secret word. As questions are asked, a tally is kept. The one who figures out the secret word using the fewest questions is the winner. The activity encourages students to examine words closely in order to choose the kinds of questions that will narrow the field. Students can ask questions concerning prefixes, suffixes, word meanings, roots, compound words, parts of speech, and so on.

ONE-MINUTE SUMMARY

The central idea of this chapter is that students learn and grow intellectually when teachers spend time teaching vocabulary and vocabulary strategies that students may use independently to enrich their own understanding. Having a good understanding of most of the words in a text is necessary for optimal comprehension and fluency. Preparation strategies help elevate word consciousness, provide personal connections, and build background to aid in understanding. Teachers need to assist students with long-term aids and strategies to help them grasp the meaning of unfamiliar words they encounter. Often, however, it may be best to have students reflect on difficult vocabulary after reading when they have established a conceptual base of knowledge with which to learn. By reconsidering and reflecting on selected vocabulary, students get opportunities for in-depth vocabulary knowledge development for later reference as independent learners. This chapter presented numerous vocabulary strategies that can be used at all phases of the PAR Framework. Increasing vocabulary knowledge is key to producing richer, deeper reading experiences for students.

END-OF-CHAPTER ACTIVITIES

Assisting Comprehension

How well do you remember the following strategies? Place them in categories (preparation, assistance, reflection) on this organizational chart. Be ready to explain your choices to a peer.

	Categories		
	Preparation	**Assistance**	**Reflection**
Semantic map			
Graphic organizers			
Word bubbles			
Odd word out			
Structural analysis			
Vocabulary self-collection			
Keyword strategy			
Context clue discovery			
Word mapping			
Dissect			

	Categories		
	Preparation	Assistance	Reflection
Word analogies			
Word inquiry			
Magic squares			
Semantic feature analysis			
Vocabulary connections			
Vocabulary lists			
Vocabulary illustrations			
Postgraphic organizers			
Word attack paradigms			
Vocab-lit strategy			
Word inventories			
Possible sentences			
TOAST			
Categorization			
Organizational (jot) charts			
DR-TA			
Vocabulary search			
Vocabulary bingo			
Word sorts			

Reflecting on Your Reading

1. Your content organization (e.g., National Council of Teachers of Math, National Council of Teachers of English, National Council for the Social Studies, National Science Teachers Association, International Reading Association) has most likely developed a set of standards that identify the performance criteria relevant to classroom teachers. Standards usually delineate elements of foundational knowledge that a classroom teacher should possess. Locate and become familiar with the standards your content organization recommends that relate to principles presented in this chapter. For instance, teachers should:
   - Use a variety of evidenced-based instructional strategies to increase content and academic vocabulary development.
   - Use evidence-based instructional strategies that develop independence for learning vocabulary critical to concept and content knowledge development.
   - Use technology and other resources for vocabulary development and enrichment.
2. How does knowing about these elements inform and shape instruction in the content areas? Jot down points that you can explain to a fellow teacher or administrator.
3. Considering the developmental, cultural, and linguistic differences of the students in your classroom, select a vocabulary strategy for each stage of PAR and write a reflection explaining how you plan to use each strategy to meet the needs of your students.

CHAPTER 8
Writing to Learn in the Content Areas

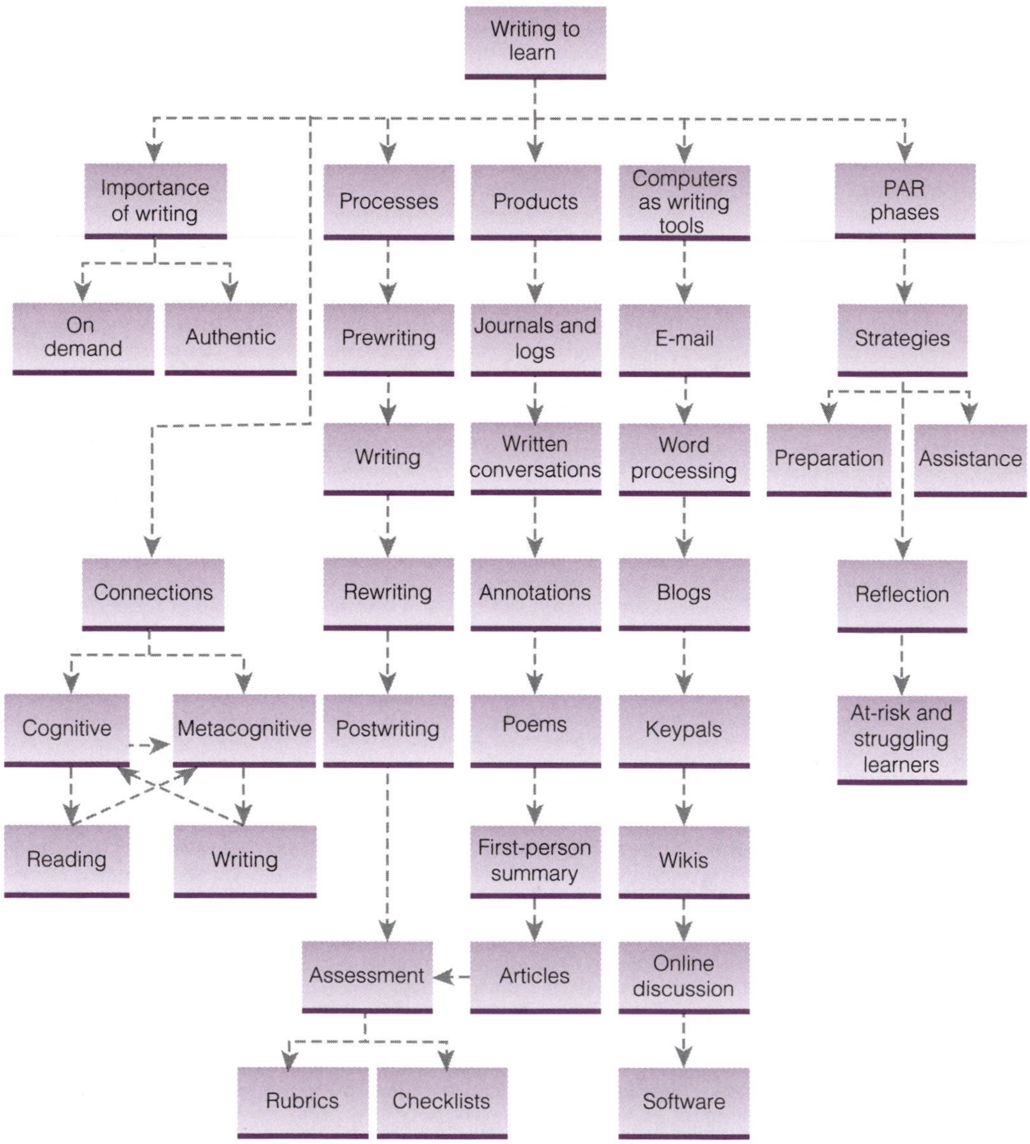

To read is to empower,
To empower is to write,
To write is to influence,
To influence is to change,
To change is to live.
JANE EVERSHED

VOICES FROM THE CLASSROOM

At Thomas Jefferson Middle School in a suburban school district, a multidisciplinary team of sixth grade teachers has been teaching together for about five years. The team has participated in professional development on how to incorporate writing in all their classes. This year they believe the students are really demonstrating their learning through their writing.

At a recent team meeting, Ms. Williams, the science teacher, shared that she received a note from Eddie's mother, who is normally very supportive of his teachers, expressing concern that the writing he's bringing home from her class has a lot of misspellings and punctuation and capitalization errors. The team discussed that this concern was brought up at several parent conferences recently. After further discussion, they decided they would send a newsletter to all the parents on the team and explain what the term "writing-to-learn" is and how it benefits their children. They would encourage parents to call or email them if they had questions. The team felt good about this plan and decided they would see how the parents responded.

Use a discussion web (instructions following) to consider the team's dilemma. Fold your paper into three parts or columns. In the center column, put the question, "Did the team make the right decision to continue to incorporate writing in the content areas?" In the right column, place the word "No" at the top. In the left column, place the word "Yes" at the top. In the right column, list reasons you can think of for responding "No." In the left column, list reasons you can think of for responding "Yes." Think of an equal number of reasons for each stance. After considering each side of the issue, write a conclusion or final response and your justification. Then reconsider this question after reading this chapter.

PREPARING TO READ

1. Anticipate what you will learn in this chapter by checking any of the following statements with which you agree. Be ready to explain your choices. After reading the chapter, return to decide whether you wish to reconsider any of your selections:

    ______ Writing is the most complex of the communicative arts.
    ______ Writing is often taught as a way of learning in the content areas.
    ______ Writing should not be taught to young children in kindergarten.
    ______ Elementary and college students may use metacognitive strategies to enhance their writing.
    ______ All writing should lead to a formal product or publication of the writing.
    ______ Computers help students improve their writing skills.
    ______ Writers may make major changes during the drafting stage.

2. Following is a list of terms used in this chapter. Some may be familiar to you in a general context, but in this chapter, they may be used in unfamiliar ways. Consider what you know about the terms and decide how you might sort them into logical groupings. Decide how the terms in each grouping are similar and make a descriptive label for each grouping. Be ready to explain the rationale for your choices.

    ______ on-demand writing
    ______ authentic writing
    ______ reading–writing connection
    ______ metacognitive
    ______ emergent literacy
    ______ process writing
    ______ write-alouds
    ______ cubing
    ______ brain writing
    ______ learning log
    ______ double-entry journal
    ______ annotating
    ______ REAP
    ______ biopoem
    ______ geopoem
    ______ first-person summary
    ______ RAFT
    ______ guided writing procedure
    ______ collaborative writing
    ______ C3B4Me
    ______ rubrics and checklists

OBJECTIVES

As you read this chapter, focus your attention on the following objectives.

1. Connect reading to learn and writing to learn.
2. Distinguish between the process of writing and the products of writing.
3. Explain how computers can aid students in learning to write.
4. Identify the stages of writing from prewriting through revision and publishing strategies.
5. Use strategies for preparing, assisting, and reflecting on writing.
6. Use writing as a complement to reading as a way to learn in the content areas.
7. Explain ways to grade students' writing.

The Importance of Writing

This chapter was significantly revised and updated by Valerie J. Robnolt, Ph.D., Associate Professor in the Department of Teaching and learning, School of Education at Virginia Commonwealth University.

Writing may be the most complex communication process within the communicative arts because of the ways it can be used to challenge and enhance thinking skills. "Like close reading, writing is thinking—perhaps in its most powerful and intense form" (Schmoker, 2007, p. 419). Writing is active involvement that allows students to explore subject matter. Knipper and Duggan (2006) explain that writing to learn is a "catalyst for further learning and meaning making" (p. 462). One can progress from a blank sheet to a page filled with statements about content learned, revelations about thoughts, and discoveries about oneself.

When writing is viewed as a way of discovering rather than as merely an avenue for testing knowledge, learning is the result. Brain research (Berninger & Winn, 2006; Davis, 1997) has provided evidence in the form of PET (positron emission tomography) scans that writing activates numerous areas of the brain with more intensity than other activities investigated. Writing challenges us to communicate, at the same time, with others and with ourselves. The advantage afforded by vocal timbre, facial expression, and gestures must be accounted for in written communication through careful word choice and organization (Houston, 2004). With the now daily use of computers, a new area of brain research indicates that there may be a difference in how writing develops depending on whether a pencil or a keyboard is used (Berninger & Winn, 2006).

Writing includes both process and product in various stages of development. So although writing is often assumed to be the responsibility of elementary school teachers or English teachers, it is related to learning in all areas of the curriculum as well as to learning as a life pursuit. "Along with reading comprehension, writing skill is a predictor of academic success and a basic requirement for participation in civic life and in the global economy" (Graham & Perin, 2007, p. 3). Budig (2006) found in his study involving survey data collected from human resource directors that being able to communicate effectively though writing is a highly valued skill necessary for employment and critical to promotion in fast-growing industries. Another survey (Gray, Emerson, & MacKay, 2005) asked employers of recent science graduates about their new employees' science writing skills; the employers indicated that students need to develop better writing skills in college.

Although some distinguish between learning to write and writing to learn, the two are intertwined. A writer has to develop an understanding of the skills, form, and function of writing, but without a purpose or focus, there is no meaning. Writing requires abstract thinking, synthesis, and the ability and skill to apply several discrete skills. Writing is more than the sum of the skills necessary for creating an interesting piece: Collecting and organizing thoughts to communicate ideas and feelings lead to understanding and learning. When putting pen to paper or fingers on a keyboard to create an expository or informational piece, the writer must ask several questions:

_____ What do reliable sources have to say?

_____ What evidence is there?

_____ What do I think?

_____ What do others think?

_____ What can I do to encourage my readers to think about the topic?

If the purpose is to create a narrative, the author must consider aspects of good storytelling:

1. Where will the story take place, and how will I help the reader see it as I do?
2. Who are the characters, and what parts do they play in the story?
3. How does the story begin?
4. What problems are to be resolved? How will they be resolved?
5. Is the story interesting? Does it make sense to me and to others?
6. Does the story have a message?

Whether writing an expository or narrative piece, there is much to be learned through writing.

Writing is a true complement to reading when it enables students to clarify and think critically about concepts they encounter in reading. Reading and writing are often taught separately even though research has found that writing can be used in every content area as an effective means of learning (Bangert-Drowns, Hurley, & Wilkinson, 2004; Brown, Phillips, & Stephens, 1992). For example, McDermott (2010) reports that writing letters, creating storybooks, and designing magazine articles improved his science students' scores on end-of unit assessments. Boyer (2006) includes similar writing activities in the social studies classroom but also encourages writing poetry to help students deepen their understanding of content. When reading and writing are taught as detached entities, students may adopt a superficial view of writing. Vacca (2002) submits that it is rare for students to consider writing a vehicle for exploring or interpreting concepts and ideas. Students can learn through direct instruction, modeling, and practice that writing can be a tool for learning. Teachers can demonstrate the process and enlist students in active discussion of the criteria and expectations for writing products. McKenna, Labbo, Reinking, and Zucker (2007) provide helpful hints on how to provide this support in a digital environment through the use of an LCD projector so teachers enhance their instruction by modeling and integrating technology.

Unfortunately, writing is not used often enough as a way of learning in the content areas. Teachers may be reluctant to teach writing for some of the same reasons they often feel reluctant to teach mathematics and science concepts. If content teachers see writing as primarily prescribed forms and structures to be taught rather than as a means to clarify, reinforce, and support concept learning, they may feel unqualified to incorporate it in their courses. A lack of confidence in their own writing abilities can contribute to frustration and uncertainty as they try to instruct their students. Although more needs to be done, writing programs and in-service training have increased with the emphasis and attention placed on writing scores and standardized testing in recent years. Salahu-Din, Persky, and Miller (2008) reported that there was an improvement in writing performance for eighth and twelfth graders between 2002 and 2007 with increases for whites,

Street and Stang (2009) found that almost half the teachers who participated in their study had negative concepts of themselves as writers. After intensive professional development through the National Writing Project, this number decreased to 12%. Would you benefit from professional development? Please visit the Education CourseMate website at **www.cengagebrain.com** to find links to professional development opportunities.

Please visit the Education CourseMate website at **www.cengagebrain.com** for a link to the report, *The Nation's Report Card: Writing 2007* (NCES 2008–468), for a more detailed analysis of progress in student writing performance.

blacks, and Asian-Pacific Islanders at both grade levels and increases for Hispanics at eighth grade but not at twelfth grade. However, a high percentage of students still score below the proficient level (i.e., 65% at eighth grade and 75% at twelfth grade).

On-Demand Writing

Teachers must avoid a reductionist approach to writing, which may occur when the only writing students do is **on-demand writing** for a given prompt in preparation for high-stakes testing. Because the consequences are great, teachers and administrators are often reluctant to go beyond narrow instructional practices targeting good test performance. However, Higgins, Miller, and Wegmann (2006) have asked: "Can best practices and demands of mandated testing truly coexist?" (p. 310). Research by Manzo (2001), Fletcher (2001), and Tchudi and Tchudi (1999) provides evidence that broader-based writing instruction that includes student choice, creativity, genre variety, feedback, and aspects of process writing and writing workshop yield higher scores on standardized tests than do more narrowly structured curriculum practices. Through professional development and collaborative discussions, teachers, administrators, and university partners can examine state literacy assessments in the context of developmentally appropriate and sound writing instruction to support "writing instruction, not destruction" (Brindley & Schneider, 2002, p. 339). This means raising awareness levels of all partners and working together to find solutions that support generative writing practices and give students the tools for success.

Setting aside or ignoring on-demand writing is not the solution. Helping students understand its purpose and proactive ways of approaching it can prepare them to do well in testing and real-life situations where this type of writing is important. Key questions and modeling can scaffold the process and help the learner gain confidence and develop a well-written response:

1. What is the prompt asking me to do? (Describe, explain, defend, compare, create?)
2. What do I know about the topic?
3. What do I need to say? (Points and details.)
4. In what order do I want to say it?
5. Have I stated my points clearly, logically, and with enough detail?
6. When I reread, is my grammar correct? Is my spelling accurate?

Authentic Writing

Research (Purcell-Gates, Degener, Jacobson, & Soler, 2002; Purcell-Gates, Duke, & Martineau, 2007) provides strong evidence for the potential impact of authentic reading and writing tasks on both adults' and elementary students' abilities to read and write in a variety of genres. Ray and her colleagues (Ray & Cleaveland, 2004; Ray & Glover, 2008) make a strong case that children in preschool and the primary grades are capable of constructing fully realized pieces of writing in different genres that are meaningful and have clear ideas. Such writing includes pictures and scribbles, which Vygotsky (1978b) describes as gestures that represent children's thoughts. Purcell-Gates and her colleagues found that students given "real" purposes for reading and writing beyond classroom assignments and for "real" audiences beyond a teacher made significant

FIGURE 8.1

Writing to Learn in Kindergarten

progress in both reading and writing. Authentic literacy, more particularly authentic tasks, can be defined in a variety of ways. Duke, Purcell-Gates, Hall, and Tower (2006) used an authenticity rating scale for differentiating levels when considering tasks for reading, writing, or listening (Figure 8.2). Traditional, nonauthentic writing tasks include completing worksheets, writing for a given prompt, book reports, reports about a topic, and the like. Authentic tasks include creating and distributing brochures for a local museum or upcoming community event; writing letters to community members,

FIGURE 8.2

Authenticity Rating Sheet

Brief description of activity, including (a) text students are reading, writing, or listening to, and (b) purpose of student's reading, writing, or listening:

____

____

____

____

Authenticity of purpose

Rating: 3 2 1

3 = This reading, writing, or listening-to-text purpose exists in the lives of people outside a classroom, or it is as authentic as the use of that genre for that purpose can be.

2 = This reading, writing, or listening-to-text purpose exists in the lives of people outside a classroom, but it differs in that for reading the impetus is less personal and for writing the audience is less compelling.

1 = This reading, writing, or listening-to-text purpose is identified by its absence of any purpose beyond school work. This takes different forms depending on the genre and process (reading or writing).

Authenticity of text

Rating: 3 2 1

3 = This text type occurs naturally in the lives of people outside a classroom. You can find it in bookstores or order it for home delivery. This category also includes texts that are written primarily for instructional purposes but that closely mimic the naturally occurring texts–the only difference being the publisher's audience.

2 = This text is written primarily for use in schools and, although it mimics to an extent the genre style, form, and purpose of those texts that do occur naturally outside school, it includes enough school "stuff" to be recognizable. This type would include texts that have comprehension questions, special vocabulary sections, and perhaps even "Checking What You Have Learned" sections. These texts are hybrid forms reflecting school and authentic genres in different combinations and emphases.

1 = This text would not occur anywhere except in a school or other teaching and learning contexts. It is written to teach skills and is used only for learning and practicing skills. You may be able to purchase these texts in stores but they reflect a skills-learning purpose.

Total authenticity rating: ________

Duke, Purcell-Gates, Hall, & Tower (2006), Authentic literacy activities for developing comprehension and writing. *The Reading Teacher,* 60(4), 344–345. Reprinted with permission of the International Reading Association.

Figure 8.1 shows examples of kindergartners' writings and pictures.

Please visit the Education CourseMate website at **www.cengagebrain.com** for a link to a teacher's blog on using websites, wikis, and blogs in the classroom.

organizations, or businesses related to topics of study; and writing a speech to be given to an outside club, group, or community meeting. Blogs, wikis, and podcasts, digital writing tools that allow for authentic, collaborative writing with a wide audience, have been found to increase students' engagement (Beach, Anson, Breuch, & Swiss, 2009; Boling, Castek, Zawilinski, Barton, & Nierlich, 2008). These studies' findings do not suggest replacing explicit instruction with authentic tasks but rather give evidence of value added by thoughtful and purposeful inclusion of meaningful experiences that cross over into daily life.

When students use writing as a means for learning as well as a tool to be learned, this dual purpose contributes to achievement in writing and content learning. Content gives students something to write about. Bintz and Shelton (2004) explained that the power of a writing strategy and the potential of the curriculum for assisting students' learning are directly related to the teacher's ability to merge the two harmoniously.

The Importance of the Reading–Writing Connection

Students need to write about what they are going to read about, and after reading, they need to use writing again as a culminating activity to clarify what they read. This write–read–write model is sometimes referred to as the **reading–writing connection.** In a longitudinal study of students in first through seventh grade, Abbott, Berninger, and Fayol (2010) found strong evidence that reading and writing are intricately connected. As students embrace this model, they use writing as a tool for learning content. Content teachers can emphasize writing as a way to learn. In their meta-analysis of the effects of school-based writing on learning, Bangert-Drowns, Hurley, and Wilkinson (2004) explained, "Students are more effective learners when they possess a rich arsenal of learning strategies, awareness of their strategies, knowledge of the contexts in which the strategies will be effective, and a willingness to apply their strategies" (p. 32).

Both cognitive and **metacognitive** strategies may help students learn as they engage in writing tasks. Weinstein and Mayer (1986) categorized cognitive strategies as rehearsal strategies, elaboration strategies, organization strategies, and comprehension-monitoring strategies. As students consider points raised during the planning and drafting stages of writing, they engage in repetition and rehearsal. Organization and elaboration strategies come into play while students order, reorder, and describe points related to their own understandings and backgrounds. Self-monitoring and reflection as well as peer review offer opportunities for using comprehension-monitoring strategies. Tracy, Reid, and Graham (2009) found that third grade students who were provided writing instruction through the Self-Regulated Strategy Development model were able to write stories that were "longer, schematically stronger (in terms of inclusion and quality of story parts), and qualitatively better" (p. 330) than students who were not instructed using this model. Finally, Bangert-Drowns and colleagues (2004) cite several studies supporting the power of metacognitive comprehension-monitoring strategies for improving learning among kindergarten through college populations. Metacognitive prompts and repetition of the process appeared to help students internalize the strategies as well as boost academic achievement (Bangert-Drowns et al, 2004). Conversely, reduced effects in achievement occurred with lengthy writing assignments. There were also reduced effects among the middle school students. Self-regulation strategies serve as a bridge to metacognitive strategies because they help students to be aware of their thinking as they are writing and give students a tool for determining their own use of strategies and for evaluating how well those strategies may work in each situation for future reference and use.

What may have caused reduced effects when writing assignments were longer? What do you think may be causing reduced effects for middle school students?

Children in the early grades are capable of writing reports about content subjects (Calkins, 1986; Ray & Cleaveland, 2004; Ray & Glover, 2008). Although these reports may contain inventive spelling and pictures that one might not expect to find in an older student's report, they reflect learning through language. Teachers are now encouraged to recognize this early reading and writing as a part of **emergent literacy** and to foster children's use of all of the communicative arts as early as possible in content subjects. Figure 8.3 contains two writing samples from a first grader. Both demonstrate learning

FIGURE 8.3

Writing to Learn in First Grade

Courtesy of the author.

Courtesy of the author.

(*continued*)

FIGURE 8.3

(continued)

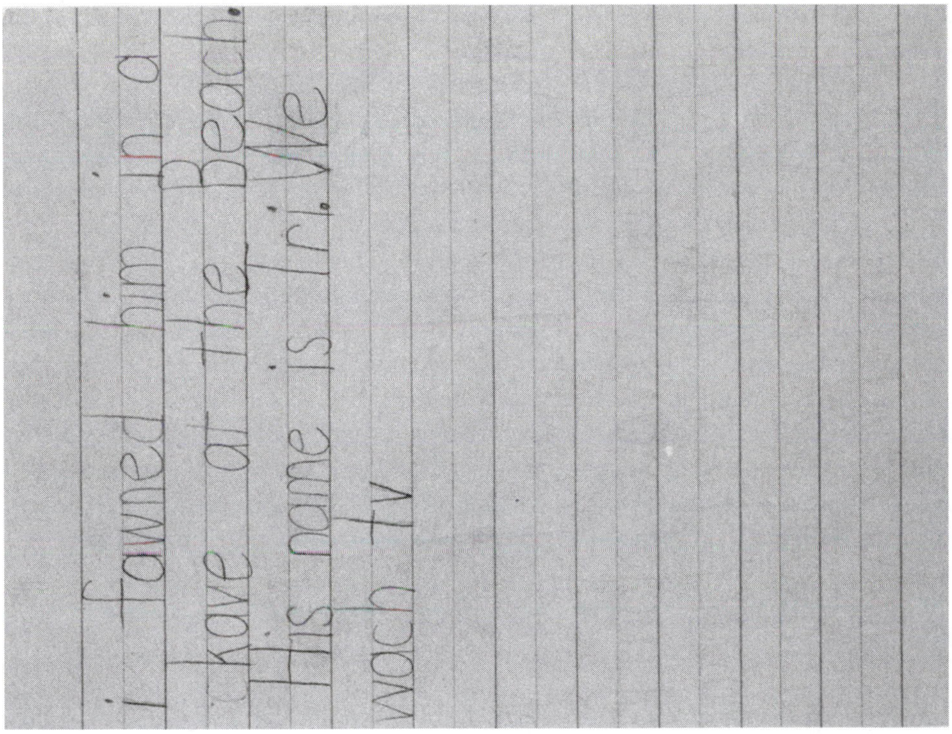

Courtesy of the author.

Courtesy of the author.

about science through writing. The teacher made comments about the content of the writing, not about the "invented" or "temporary" spellings.

Teachers should not underestimate the sophistication of thinking and the composition process young writers are capable of bringing to the experience of writing informational text. Read (2005), in her first grade study of informational text writing, created a writing workshop environment. She modeled and scaffolded thinking aloud, taking notes, reading, taking more notes, reading notes, and collaborating with students to create shared writings. Students then made their own topic selections. She paired them by topic for the purpose of creating a collaborative book. They were given considerable freedom to make choices and to work through the writing. Read discovered that, contrary to her expectations, students did not spend most of their time grappling with sentence-level issues. Nor were their products like mini-encyclopedia articles. Rather, these first graders, like older more experienced writers, could and did consider the need for creating interest, using good form, and critically reflecting and making adjustments throughout the writing process. The simple products were appropriate and indicated comprehension of both the content and the writing process.

Writing as a Product

Teachers often use the products of writing as a form of evaluation, such as evaluating a test essay or a research report. But teachers need to see products of writing not only as a versatile way of evaluating a student but also as a unique way to develop comprehension. For instance, as textbook writers, we learned more about our field of knowledge as we wrote this book. We discovered ways to express the information that we wanted to share with readers; before we drafted this text, we did not know all that we would write. In a similar way, readers learn as they read. Because both reading and writing can assist comprehension, it seems logical to use them in tandem when assisting readers. To support this idea, Montelongo, Herter, Ansaldo, and Hatter (2010) found with middle school students that using a cycle of introducing vocabulary words, identifying expository text structures, completing a fill-in-the-blanks activity that combined vocabulary and text structure, and summarizing the content led to students improving their abilities to find the main ideas of paragraphs.

Unfortunately, writing is not used often as an activity to help students understand content material (Knipper & Duggan, 2006; Pearce & Bader, 1984). However, teachers such as Miss K in *Ralph S. Mouse* by Beverly Cleary (1982) would turn anything into a writing project. When Miss K and her class discover that Ralph the mouse came to school with Ryan, she inspires the students to write about mice and later to write rejoinders to a newspaper article that contains misinformation about their projects. Many teachers, in contrast, seem to use writing activities that are mainly product oriented and graded. Products can take many forms, such as essays, poems, articles, journals, letters, and plays, to name a few.

Research shows, however, that writing doesn't always have to have an end product to be successful; that is, writing can be a powerful tool to assist comprehension (Von Glaserfeld, 1996). Writing requires the formation of an idea, or a cluster of ideas, generated from the writer's experiences, understanding, and imagination. It is a conscious shaping of the materials selected by the writer to be included in composition. In selecting what to include and remove, the student is using the elements of writing draftsmanship that he or she can manage.

A relationship exists between the process and the products of writing. Much process-oriented writing results in a formal product. The best products are generated when students are given opportunities for prewriting, writing, and revising. Not all writing leads to a formal product, but all writing can be a means of learning.

Writing as a Process

Graves (1983) and Calkins (1994) have been influential in getting teachers to view writing as a process that has as its components generating ideas, drafting, conferencing, and revising. Writers must think about a topic in a prewriting phase and develop a first draft from their initial thoughts. In the drafting phase, students think, change direction, organize, and reorganize their purposes. During this phase, students do not focus on such things as grammar and spelling or any other aspects of mechanics.

The 6+1 TRAIT® model supports process writing using "certain characteristics that make writing work: ideas, organization, voice, word choice, sentence fluency, conventions, and presentation" (Culham, 2003, p. 7). This framework allows teachers to share a vocabulary, based on the model, with their students to teach writing. Students can learn to use the vocabulary with other students. For example, Paquette (2009) conducted a study in which fourth graders tutored second graders on their writing using the 6+1 TRAIT® model. The fourth grade tutors significantly improved their writing through the experience, most likely because of using higher level thinking skills to teach the younger students.

Please visit the Education CourseMate website at **www.cengagebrain.com** for a link to a website on the 6+1 TRAIT® model.

Gone are the days when teachers asked students to write only one draft. Teachers often ask students to do revisions, which may include major reorganization of the material, additions and deletions, editorial changes, and formatting. The emphasis shifts to producing a product to be shared in the postwriting phase of the lesson.

The previous paragraphs describe **process writing**, whereby the student goes through many distinct phases in writing—from initial brainstorming of ideas to researching the topic and organizing information and ideas into a coherent piece of writing. A student working through this process may produce several drafts to clarify her or his message. An important part of this process is to have peers and others read drafts to help improve the writing. Activity 8.1 was developed by a primary science teacher to direct her students through the various phases of writing. **Write-alouds** (Cooper & Kiger, 2003) can make visible the thinking that forms each stage of writing, just as read-alouds help students understand the thinking that good readers use when reading. Using write-alouds, teachers can demonstrate thinking through the writing process on chart paper or using an LCD projector and laptop.

Although **rubrics** are typically used as instruments for assessment after an assignment, they can also provide focus, direction, and clarification for helping students understand what is important and what must be included for a successful product (Knipper & Duggan, 2006). If students are invited to participate in developing rubrics, it gives them opportunities to thoughtfully consider and negotiate elements important to the writing. Checklists highlight "must-have" components for an assignment and can provide point values for each component. Using rubrics and checklists consistently can help students understand expectations, develop a plan for writing, and monitor their progress from the beginning to the end of the process. Examples of checklists and rubrics are presented later in this chapter under "Grading Reflective Writing."

ACTIVITY 8.1 Stages in the Writing Process: Primary Science

I. PREWRITING

The teacher will show the book *Desert Voices*, written by Byrd Baylor and Peter Parnall, to the class.

"Byrd Baylor, who writes the words of the book, lives in the Southwest. I don't know which *particular* state in the southwestern portion of the United States. The title of this book has the word *desert* in it, and she has written another book called *The Desert Is Theirs*. If she lives in the Southwest and likes to write about deserts, could you guess a state where she *might* live?" (The students may remember that Arizona has desert land.)

"Peter Parnall illustrates the book. He lives on a farm in Maine with his wife and two children."

"If the title of the book is *Desert Voices*, who might be speaking? Who are the voices in the desert?" (Wait for responses.) "Byrd Baylor has written the words for 10 desert creatures as they tell us what it is like for the desert to be their home. I will read you what the jackrabbit and the rattlesnake have to say." (Teacher reads aloud.)

A. FACTSTORMING

The teacher will divide the class into small groups of four or five students. The teacher types on the computer the names of the other creatures who "speak" in *Desert Voices:* pack rat, spadefoot toad, cactus wren, desert tortoise, buzzard, lizard, coyote. (The tenth voice is called "desert person.")

B. THE ASSIGNMENT

"Each group must select one of these creatures or any other desert animal or plant that has been mentioned in our unit. Each group member should jot down on a piece of paper any ideas he or she has about this creature's feelings relating to living in the desert. You may want to think about the appearance of this creature or thing. Does it have any body parts or habitat specifically suited to the desert's environment? After you jot down your ideas, place your paper in the center of the table and choose another member's paper. Add some of your ideas to his or her paper. After you have written something on every other group member's page, your group as a whole should compile the *best* list of ideas. Then we will begin to write our individual drafts."

II. WRITING

The students work together to get the best list of ideas, and then they begin to write their rough drafts. As they write, they use the list of ideas generated by their group.

III. REWRITING

Students may work in pairs to edit and proofread each other's work. The child's partner would be from another "creature's" group.

IV. POSTWRITING

Oral presentations

Room displays

Compilation of compositions dealing with the same "voice" into book form

Note: This project would continue for several days. Even the group factstorming might require more than one day, especially if some reference work is necessary.

Developed by Kathryn Davis.

Computers as Writing Tools

Connect with a teacher you know when you set up keypals for your students, even as young as second grade. For the students' safety, be sure to use password-protected media when communicating.

Now that we are well established in the digital age and students are digital natives who use computers from an early age, teachers have a responsibility to integrate technology in their writing instruction. As a matter of fact, a growing body of research indicates that computer use improves student learning in general and student writing in particular (Russell & Abrams, 2004). As digital natives, students have their own email accounts to communicate with their grandparents and friends. Teachers can also encourage email use for instructional purposes, such as communicating with other students and even with authors of books they love and experts on topics in which they are interested.

Kinzer (2005) describes keypals as penpals who write emails instead of traditional letters. Silva, Meagher, Valenzuela, and Crenshaw (1996) found that students using such media progressed more quickly than students who were asked to use more traditional grammar practice and textbook readings. Williams (2005) suggests connecting what students do with instant messaging, such as changing their voice depending on the person with whom they are communicating, to the writing they are doing in school. Two advantages of using online communication are (1) students get responses much more quickly and (2) teachers connect students' outside of school literacies with what they do in school.

Word processing on the computer gives students an opportunity to improve their writing skills. Students can write drafts quickly, revise them easily, and save anything they have written. Studies (Bangert-Drowns, 1993; Cochran-Smith, 1991; Goldberg, Russell, & Cook, 2003) have shown that when computers are used for developing writing skills, students make more revisions during writing and before the final draft than those using paper and pencil. Students using computers for writing produced longer products and more often shared their writing with one another during the process. Overall, Goldberg, Russell, and Cook's (2003) meta-analysis of research on the effects of computers on student writing revealed significant positive results for both the quantity and quality of student writing when computers were used as tools for developing writing skills.

See Chapter 10 for other ways of integrating technology into your instruction.

Using computers as tools for writing is not just for older students. Van Leeuwen and Gabriel's (2007) study of computer use for writing with first graders indicated that even young authors enjoy and benefit from this tool. With these children, the quality of writing was comparable to paper-and-pencil products, but the products generally were shorter. More student-to-student interaction took place and was accepted as they asked one another for spelling and computer help. Students chose to use prewriting webs and plans less often, possibly because computers make editing a document a relatively easy process. Even though students used fewer planning aids, they did more reading and rereading while composing than they typically do with handwritten documents. Different tools and means of producing writing provide different types of opportunities and challenges for developing and enhancing writing techniques and strategies.

HOT blogging (Zawilinski, 2009) uses the class blog to help students build background knowledge, summarize what they read, and comment on their classmates' ideas about what they learned.

Networking systems and databases available to students can assist and even motivate them to perform the research necessary for their writing. Chamberlain (2005) encourages teachers to publish their students' writing on a class website, noting that only first names should be used to protect the students. When students assess information and write about their findings, they use real-world practices that increase their overall competence in writing. Teachers need to encourage students both at home and at school to use this tool. Many course-authoring programs enable teachers to produce websites so their students can participate in online threaded discussions. When students write about a topic to one another online and then read, consider, and reply within such a threaded discussion, they improve their writing skills in a digital format.

Interestingly, "across the nation, a higher percentage of teachers in urban locations and in lower-performing schools, . . . believe they have decreased instructional use of computers for writing because of the format of the state test" (Russell & Abrams, 2004, p. 1351). What are your concerns about this?

See Chapter 10 for more details and information about using technology for teaching reading and writing across the curriculum.

TECH APP

Technology Examples for Peer Writing

Online Discussions: Students participate with learners at a different grade level.

Wikis: Students collaborate with learners at another grade level using wikis to research topics for a writing assignment.

Blogs: Students write about personal issues in the context of literature, in online discussions using blogs.

Writing and the PAR Framework

Writing, just like reading, has phases that overlap, are recursive, and relate to the PAR (preparation, assistance, and reflection) Lesson Framework. The prewriting phase matches what happens before reading, which corresponds to what we have called *preparation.* The drafting, revising, and editing phases match what happens during reading, or *assistance.* The act of producing a product can be likened to the *reflection* phase of learning that occurs after reading. An important part of the reflection phase is the discussion among students about their writing. As students share their writing, they can explain their thought processes, and the listeners can provide feedback. Breaking down the writing process into several phases is advisable because this process is new to many students. Because the phases truly overlap as they do in reading, the process works seamlessly. The remainder of this chapter discusses strategies for teaching writing during each of these phases of the learning process.

In summary, excellent lessons using writing in the content areas often include:

1. Teacher demonstration and modeling.
2. Clear goals and expectations.
3. Guided practice.
4. Permission to make decisions and mistakes along the way.
5. Feedback from both peers and teachers.
6. An audience.
7. A purpose that goes beyond a classroom assignment.

The Preparation Phase of Writing

Writing may be commonly used across the curriculum as a culminating project or report to demonstrate learning and understanding. Writing prompts now routinely appear in subject area textbooks but generally as follow-up or extension activities. Teachers in various content areas confirm that they find few suggestions in their textbooks for using writing as a preparation activity. Because teachers rely on textbooks and teachers' manuals for the majority of their instruction, they may be missing a rich source of preparation through writing activities.

Refer to Chapter 3 for prereading activities: Anticipation Guides (Activities 3.11 to 3.14), Story Impressions (Activity 3.3 and 3.4), PreP (Activity 3.15), and What-I-Know Activities (Activity 3.6). All use writing to prepare students to read.

Beginning a lesson with writing invites students to explore what they know and to consider what they want to learn. Inquiry drives investigation and study. We often think of science as being inquiry based, we think of mathematics as problem solving, and we ponder mysteries and causes and effects underlying history. By recording, in some form, current understandings and expectations before launching into reading or lesson activities, students are guided to clarify thinking and plan the next steps in learning. In this section, we present numerous writing activities to use before reading to clarify students' thinking and spark interest in the material to be read.

CUBING

Cubing is an activity that prepares students as both writers and readers by having them think on six levels of cognition. Cowan and Cowan (1980) created cubing as a way to stimulate writing, especially when writers have a block and can't think of anything to write. The writer imagines a cube, puts one of the six tasks on each of the six sides, and

ACTIVITY 8.2 Cubing the Slope-Intercept Form of Linear Equations (High School Mathematics)

Describe: It is the equation of a line, and it has two variables. It is written with the *y*-variable all by itself on one side.

Compare: Compared to the standard form, $Ax + By = C$, it is easier to use to find the line.

Associate: It makes me think of the coordinate plane with the *X* and *Y* axis.

Analyze: It is $y = mx + b$. The *y* is a variable, and so is the *x*. The *m* tells the slope of the line (how steep it is). The slope, *m*, is the rise over run, the change in *y* over the change in *x*. The *b* tells where the line crosses the *y*-axis. It is called the *y*-intercept.

Apply: For the line written $y = mx + b$, which has a slope of *m* and a *y*-intercept at *b*, there are an infinite number of solutions for *x* and *y*. For each *x*, there is a *y*, and vice versa. An example is $y = 2x + 3$. The slope is 2, which means the rise in the *y*-value is 2 for every increase in the run of the *x*-value. The line crosses the *y*-axis at 3. So it looks like this:

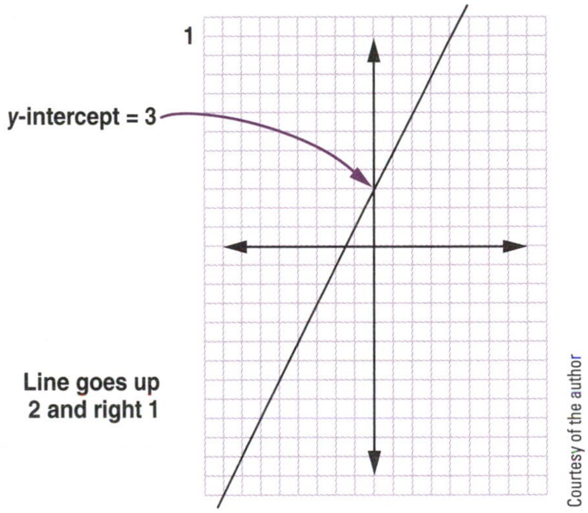

Argue: The slope-intercept form of writing linear equations is the easiest one to be able to see the line quickly. It is better than the standard form because you don't need to change the signs or anything to calculate the slope or intercept. I can just look at the equation and picture the line in my head.

Developed by Dr. Mark Forget.

considers each task for no more than five minutes. Because the writer considers all six sides, he or she has to look at a subject from a number of perspectives. When applied to reading (Vaughan & Estes, 1986), cubing can lead to purposeful reading and help develop reading comprehension. Activity 8.2 shows the use of cubing in a mathematics class about linear equations.

Making the cube is simple. Cover a square tissue box with construction paper and label each side or use the outline shown in Figure 8.4 to construct a cube from cardboard. The teacher may begin cubing by modeling the strategy for a simple construct such as a pencil. Then the teacher has students practice cubing for a concept that is in their sphere of prior knowledge. Finally, students practice cubing with difficult concepts

Playful options for making a cube:
- Material or foam
- Customizable blow-up cubes from teacher supply companies
- A beach ball (by writing on each color stripe)

FIGURE 8.4

Cubing: Making the Cube

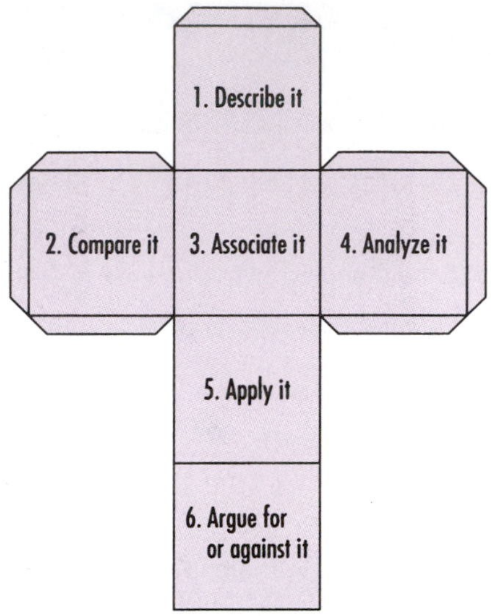

to help clarify thinking. A variation called *perspective cubing* (Whitehead, 1994) helps students consider concepts from perspectives other than their own. A number of teachers report excellent success with this approach. Students select a chart, map, graph, or picture in a textbook and then study and write about it from these six viewpoints:

Face 1—Space: What would it look like up close? What would it look like from a distance?

Face 2—Time: What do we think about it today? What will people think about it in 100 years? What did people think about it 100 years ago?

Face 3—Location: What does it look like from above? What does it look like from the side? What does it look like from below?

Face 4—Culture: What would the indigenous people (first settlers of this land) think about it? What would visitors from another country think about it?

Face 5—Talk: If it could talk, what might it say?

Face 6—Size: If it changed size, how would that change affect the way we might think about it?

BRAIN WRITING

A variation of factstorming called **brain writing** (Brown, Phillips, & Stephens, 1992) can help students generate ideas. Small groups of students respond to a topic, write down their ideas, and then exchange and add to one another's lists. While working in the brain-writing groups, students could do any of the following:

1. Predict and write down the definition of a new word in a chapter or what they think they might learn by reading the chapter.
2. Write what they think a visual aid is illustrating or could have to do with a topic.
3. Write how a new topic might fit with previous topics studied.
4. For mathematics, students could write about what they think a particular symbol might mean, what the possible steps for solving a problem could be, or why a particular unit of study is presented at a particular place in the text. For example, a fourth grade mathematics textbook starts the chapter on fractions with

a picture of a sectioned pizza, but no explanation is given. Elementary students could be asked to write why they think this illustration has been selected.

5. For science, students could write what they anticipate to be the steps in an experiment, what a formula will produce, what the composition of a substance is, or why certain conditions facilitate certain results.
6. For social studies, students could write about problems people might face when they move from one place to another or after they have settled in a new place (Pearce, 1987).
7. For English, students could write why a particular punctuation rule might be necessary. What would happen if we didn't use commas in our writing?

THREE WARM-UP WRITING ACTIVITIES

When students first enter the classroom, teachers can direct them to write as a warm-up to the intended instruction for the day. One activity is called a *quick write* because teachers ask students to jot down ideas and write for one or two minutes about the topic to be studied. Also, students can be asked to complete a *free write*—writing that takes somewhat longer to complete, usually from three to five minutes, to get students to write their perceptions of certain events or classroom operations without worrying about mechanics and correctness. The only rule is that when students put pencil to paper, they cannot stop until they are completely out of ideas or until the teacher calls an end to the free write. In this way, students are guaranteed to exhibit free associations of ideas. If students cannot sustain a free write over five minutes, teachers can start with an easier quick write for shorter practice and less frustration.

A third writing activity is *student-generated questions*. Students can be asked in small groups to write questions that they would like answered about a topic to be studied. As a variation, the questions can be about points, vocabulary, or concepts that students find unclear. Activity 8.3 presents a quick write from a high school English class. Activity 8.4 presents a free write from a high school geography class. Activity 8.5 presents student-generated questions from an elementary science class.

ACTIVITY 8.3 Quick Write on Mark Twain's *Huckleberry Finn*

I believe Mark Twain is one of the better writers of American literature. I actually read this book for my 11th grade lt. English class (which is a surprise because I rarely read the books we're assigned in English). I can see how the book was so controversial, being that the best character (I think) is black. He is very real and down to earth. The book is very easy to read and hard to put down. My only problem with it is when the character of Tom Sawyer comes in. I'm not very fond of this character. In fact I hate him. He just makes the story drag on, making me think "UGH! When is this going to end?!" Although I realize that he is only trying to make things more adventurous but I still find it very stupid. I was very angry in the end when Tom explains that Jim had been set free by Miss Watson and the whole escape plan was unnecessary. So much time wasted! I could have gone out with my friends instead of reading that stuff! Anyway, I think the book was done very well overall despite the Tom Sawyer character.

Dave N. Aznar

ACTIVITY 8.4 Free Writes in Geography

Students in a ninth grade geography class have been studying northern Eurasia (the former USSR). The teacher writes the following on the board:

communism v. market economy
autocracy v. democracy

and asks students to discuss these terms in their own groups of three. After a few minutes of small-group discussion, the teacher informs students that they will perform a free write as a prereading activity to prepare for the day's reading, the second chapter on northern Eurasia. The teacher reinforces the rules of free write, stating to students that when they begin writing, they may not stop for five minutes. Rather, they should rewrite the last phrase or sentence if they confront writer's block. The following are a few of the results. (They are reproduced with original student spelling and grammar.)

> Democracy is what we have in our country where the people have rights and freedoms. Autocracy is led by a couple of leaders and they own all the land. With a communist there is no freedom. The government does what it wants and there is no incentive to do well in life. The government gets the profits. Unlike with a democracy where the people keep the money that they make. So they want to do well in life and will work harder to make money and start new businesses. In communist countries the people must do whatever their government tells them to do and are not have the freedoms of other countries such as speech and religion. Russia was once communist and after they were no longer communist they became poor because they people weren't use to it and wanted a leader. They had the freedoms but didn't know what to do with it.

> I know that capitalism is when you have ownership and it is not shared with the government. You are able to be richer or poorer than other people. Communism is the complete opposite. Everything is owned and controlled by the government and you don't own anything you have. If you won a million dollars, you'd own 0% of it. Or if you've been working in a factory for 40 years you can never buy it. That's just the way it goes!!!!!!!!!!!!!!!!!!!!!!!
>
> ¡Yep!

> Capitalism is a government that is more right wing and communism is far left wing because of its government trying to take care of the people too much which causes no incentive for the people, but under capitalism people have different wages and therefore have an incentive to work hard.

> Capitalism is when the businesses are owned by people. It is also called a market economy. Communist is when the government makes people work and get all the money. Democracy is when the people of a country get to select a leader. Autocracy is when a person is put into power without an election. In my view capitalism and democracy are the 2 top keys to true power of the people.

Developed by Dr. Mark Forget.

The Assistance Phase of Writing

The drafting or assistance stage of writing is much like the assistance phase in reading. Writers begin to realize what they understand and have to say about a topic. The flow of thought is represented in the writer's draft as it is in the reader's discussion.

Gebhard (1983) suggests four principles for developing writing activities that assist comprehension. First, students need an audience other than the teacher (Gebhard, 1983; Purcell-Gates, Degener, Jacobson, & Soler, 2002; Purcell-Gates, Duke, & Martineau, 2007). Peers are a fine resource because they can provide supportive comments and suggestions. Often, students become much more active and committed to writing when the audience is someone other than the teacher. The use of peers as an

ACTIVITY 8.5 Student-Generated Questions in Elementary Science

Student-Generated Questions

1. What does the sun do for plants?
2. Do all plants have seeds, leaves, and flowers?
3. Can the sun harm some plants?
4. Which plants grow best in deserts?
5. What do you call plants that come back every year?
6. Which part of the plant makes the food?
7. Do all plants need the same things to grow?
8. What are the four things that all plants need?
9. Do people need the same four things?
10. Can we eat some plants?

Answers

1. The sun helps the plant make food.
2. Yes, all plants have seeds, leaves, and flowers.
3. Yes, some plants only like shade and filtered sun. (Filtered sun is sun that has something blocking some of its rays.)
4. Cacti grow best in deserts. They need very little water.
5. Perennials are plants that come back every year.
6. The leaves make the food by taking in the oxygen and sun.
7. No, some plants need more sunlight than others. Some need a lot of shade.
8. All plants need air, water, sunlight, and soil.
9. No, people do not need soil because we move around freely.
10. Yes, we can eat a lot of vegetables such as beans, tomatoes, and corn.

Developed by Susan W. Hamlin.

audience conveys the message that the process of writing is more important than the final product, which is the case when writing is an activity to assist comprehension. Writing for peers may eliminate the teacher's need to "grade" the writing at all. If the teacher does decide to grade, then the revision and editing of the paper mean that the teacher will see a polished product. Correction will take second place to content.

Second, the writing task needs to be of some importance to the student. Assigning a grade to the writing is not necessarily a motivating factor. Students need to be able to write about topics that interest them. The Foxfire books illustrate this principle of consequential writing well. Eliot Wigginton (1986) inspired his English students in Rabun Gap, Georgia, to write about the crafts and habits of their own community. In this way, he combined the subjects of English and social studies, using writing as the medium of instruction. This assignment itself was much more inspiring to students than receiving a grade. The audience consisted of their fellow students and their community. The work was collaborative, with many students planning and writing together to create a cultural history of their community. The result of their writing is the Foxfire books, whose success has been phenomenal.

The third and fourth principles suggest that writing assignments should be varied and should connect prior knowledge to new information, providing students with a creative challenge. Cubing, described earlier in this chapter, does this well. Another excellent activity to encourage this connection is the jot chart, introduced in Chapter 4 as a way to promote comprehension. Jot charts provide a matrix for learning by giving students an organizational guide—a series of boxes in which they can enter their thoughts about content areas as they read and thereby see the connections between what they already knew, what they need to find out, and—when the chart

Writing assignments that target low-level thinking and copying may invite students to plagiarize because of the ease and convenience of locating information on the Internet.

is completed—what they have learned. Instead of stating or reporting facts, teachers should challenge students to compare, analyze, or do something with information to encourage deep thought and discussion.

LEARNING LOGS

Teachers should request that students write regularly in a journal called a **learning log** under headings such as "Two new ideas I learned this week in science and how I can apply them to my life" or "How I felt about my progress in math class this week." These entries can be read by other students or by the teacher, but they should be valued for their introspective qualities and not graded. Richardson (1992a) found that such journal writing helps students work through problems they are having in learning material and verbalize concerns that the reader can respond to individually, also in written form. These types of activities tap the metacognitive aspects of learning to engage students in thinking about their own learning and the processes involved. Both a kindergarten study by Glaubman, Glaubman, and Ofir (1997) and a college study by McCrindle and Christensen (1995) found evidence of positive academic achievement when writing activities involving metacognitive thinking were used.

Learning logs are a relatively simple yet effective way to get all students to write in content area classes and stimulate thinking. Normally, students write in their logs every day, either in class or outside class. Students can be asked to write entries that persuade, describe personal experiences and responses to stimuli, give information, or are creative and spontaneous. Activity 8.6, a learning log from a high school science class, demonstrates how a log can document students' problem-solving abilities.

Another way of doing double-entry journals is using the left column for recording "What the Author Says" and the right column for "What You Say."

Another journal activity, the **double-entry journal** (Vaughan, 1990), is a log in which students write on the left side of the page about their prior knowledge of a topic. After reading, they enter comments about what they learned on the right side of the page. These comments might include drawings or questions.

A class log, or class notebook (Richardson, 1992a), is a combined writing and note-taking activity that encourages students to take responsibility for writing about class content. Sometimes called content journals, they provide a way for students to review and interpret information to be discussed in class. Students can write in the journals during class—for instance, while reading a passage or text. Students also can write in journals at home as a way to clarify their thinking.

WRITTEN CONVERSATION

Part of the learning that occurs as students engage in writing tasks involves social aspects of learning theory (Vygotsky, 1978a). Written conversation uses to advantage a mechanism students typically like to use to communicate on the sly. The very nature of the task provides active engagement for all students. Students work in pairs or triads to conduct a silent discussion. One sheet of paper and one pen or pencil is used to talk about a text, passage, or questions (Bintz & Shelton, 2004). Written conversation can be structured in a variety of ways to encourage idea and viewpoint exchange before, during, or after reading. Bintz and Shelton found in a study of written conversation among middle school students that the strategy encouraged students to really listen to one another, to take responsibility for their own participation and learning, and to take responsibility for supporting the learning of others. Different levels of participation and learning occurred based on partner satisfaction and compatibility. The data revealed several types of reading processes going on during written conversation: making a prediction, drawing an inference, making a personal connection, taking a position, asking a question, and

ACTIVITY 8.6 Hank's Learning Log: His Thinking Process with Bulbs and Batteries

The only preknowledge I brought to this activity was how to put batteries in a flashlight. Using that knowledge, I immediately put the two batteries together like this:

Then, I ignored the wires to see what would happen if I just placed the bulb on top of the battery, because that is how a flashlight seems to work. It didn't work.

One person in my group said, "Remember, it's a circuit." So I held the wires to either end of both batteries and twisted them together and touched the bottom of the bulb. That did not work either, so I untwisted the wire ends and touched the bottom of the bulb with them separate from each other, but simultaneously. However, the bulb would not light.

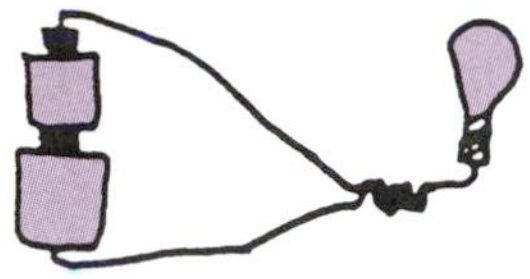

I had a lot of trouble holding everything together, so I reasoned that I probably only had to use one battery since a positive charge from one end and a negative charge at the other end was all that two (or more) batteries really amounted to. I thought that maybe the problem was that the circuit was broken because of all my fumbling around. I retried touching the ends of the wires to the bulb, but it still would not light.

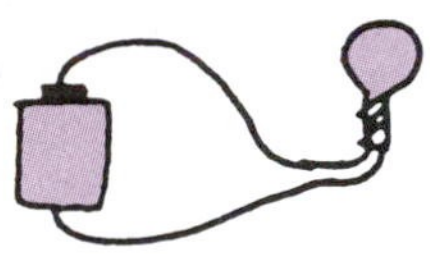

Then I remembered when I installed a new phone last year, I had to wrap the end of a wire around something that looked like a screw. So I tried wrapping the wire ends around the bulb. The bulb still would not light.

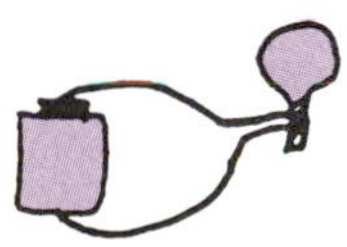

I unwrapped one of the wires from around the bulb, intending to try twisting it again with the end of the other wire and then wrapping that whole thing around the neck of the bulb. However, before I did that, I accidentally touched the end of that wire on the bottom of the bulb and I saw a very quick flicker. For a moment, I wasn't sure what I had done to make it work. Then I deliberately touched the bottom of the bulb again and got the bulb to light.

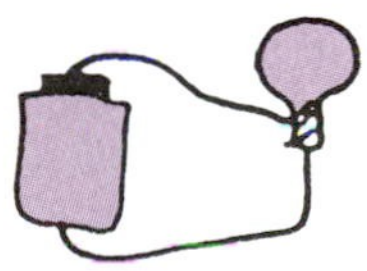

Next, I wondered if I could reverse the wrapping wire and the bottom-touching wire to make the bulb light up. The bulb lit up this way as well.

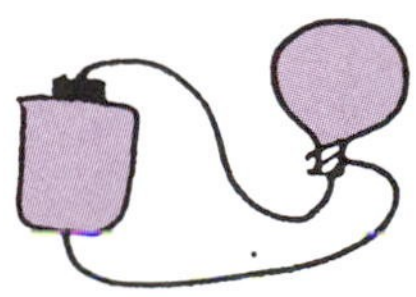

Next, I realized that my original "flashlight model" would work if I added a wire to complete the circuit, when working with my partner.

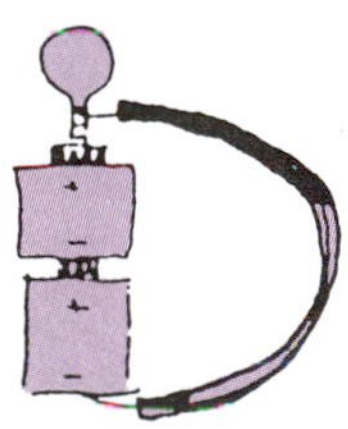

From Deal, D. (1998). Portfolios, learning logs, and eulogies: Using expressive writing in a science methods class. In Sturtevant, E. G., Dugan, J. A., Linder, P., & Linek, W. M. *Literacy and community: The twentieth yearbook of the College Reading Association*. Commerce, TX: Texas A&M University–Commerce. Used with permission.

detecting an anomaly. This writing strategy offers a means for engaging students in active processing and critical thinking as they read and write to learn.

Dialogue journals (Salcedo, 2009) are another type of written conversation that encourages writing. Traditionally, the student first writes in the journal about what he or she is learning, having trouble understanding, or anything related to class. The teacher responds to support the student through engagement in a written conversation. Rasinski and Padak (2009) suggest that parents use dialogue journals with their children as a way of communicating about many aspects of their lives, including what they are learning in school.

ANNOTATIONS

Students need frequent chances to practice critical thinking in their reading and writing. One way of providing these opportunities for older students—middle and secondary level—is through a system of annotation. **Annotating** (making notes about a reading) helps students think about their understanding of the material and enable them to get their reflections down in writing. One such system is **REAP** (read, encode, annotate, ponder), developed by Eanet and Manzo (1976). This procedure is designed to improve comprehension skills by helping students summarize material in their own words and develop writing as well as reading ability. The four steps in REAP are:

R—Reading to discover the author's ideas.

E—Encoding into your own language.

A—Annotating your interpretation of the author's ideas.

P—Pondering whether the text information is significant.

Students can write annotations on sticky notes so their ideas appear in the text near the information to which they are responding.

Creating annotations helps students increase their maturity and independence in reading. Although annotations may be submitted for grading—perhaps as homework or class grades—they are probably more valuable as written notes to facilitate understanding. Next we describe seven different annotation styles, which students can use singly or in combination:

1. A *heuristic* annotation is a statement, usually in the author's words, that suggests the ideas of the reading selection and provokes a response.
2. A *summary* annotation condenses the selection into a concise form. It includes no more or less than is necessary to convey adequately the development and relationship of the author's main ideas.
3. A *thesis annotation* is an incisive statement of the author's proposition, cutting directly to the heart of the matter.
4. A *question* annotation directs attention to the ideas the annotator considers most germane, determining the most significant issue at hand and then expressing this notation in question form.
5. A *critical* annotation is the annotator's response to the author's thesis, such as agreement, disagreement, or a combination of the two.
6. An *intention* annotation is a statement of the author's intention, plan, or purpose—as the student perceives it—in writing the selection.
7. A *motivation* annotation is a statement that attempts to speculate about the probable motive behind the author's writing, such as the author's belief system and perceptions.

POETRY

Poetry, as a genre, may be used to introduce a concept, raise a question, provoke thought, or sum up an idea. Poetry, just like science, mathematics, social studies, and other content areas, involves reasoning, understanding, and making connections to the world. At the same time, it provides a means for appreciating the power and subtleties found and expressed through words. Merging poetry with learning in content areas helps students develop basic understandings of principles and theories as well as experience how those understandings can be described and enjoyed through the senses, feelings, and beliefs (Howes, Hamilton, & Zaskoda, 2003). Dickson (2002) found that characteristics inherent in poetry, such as brevity, repetition, and rhythm, often help students see a concept or idea in a fresh new way. Several types of poetry and poetry adaptations are described in the paragraphs to follow.

A Brief Sampling of Poetry Books with Science, Social Studies, or Math Connections

Heller, R. (1983). *The reason for a flower.* New York, NY: Penguin Putnam Books.

Hopkins, L. B. (2001). *Marvelous math: A book of poems.* New York, NY: Simon & Schuster Children's Publishing.

Hopkins, L. B. (2000). *My America: A poetry atlas of the United States.* New York, NY: Simon & Schuster Children's Publishing.

Hopkins, L. B. (2002). *Spectacular science: A book of poems.* New York, NY: Simon & Schuster Children's Publishing.

Lewis, J. P. (2001). *A burst of firsts: Doers, shakers, and record breakers.* New York, NY: Dial Books.

Lewis, J. P. (2002). *A world of wonders: Geographic travels in verse and rhyme.* New York, NY: Dial Books.

Pollock, P. (2001). *When the moon is full: A lunar year.* Boston, MA: Little, Brown Young Readers.

Rice, D. L. (1997). *Lifetimes.* Nevada City, CA: Dawn Publications.

Sceizska, J. (1995). *Math curse.* New York, NY: Viking Books.

Sceizska, J. (2004). *Science verse.* New York, NY: Penguin USA Viking Children's Books.

Shields, C. D. (2002). *Brain juice: American history fresh squeezed: 41 thirst for knowledge quenching poems.* Brooklyn, NY: Handprint Books.

Shields, C. D. (2003). *Brain juice: Science fresh squeezed!* Brooklyn, NY: Handprint Books.

Whitman, W. (2004). *When I heard the learn'd astronomer.* New York, NY: Simon & Schuster Children's Publishing.

BIOPOEMS

The modified **biopoem** is a poem whose subject is the writer him or herself. Gere (1985, p. 222) provides the following pattern for writing biopoems:

Line 1: First name.

Line 2: Four traits that describe the author

Line 3: Relative of ("brother," "sister," "daughter," and so on)

Line 4: Lover of (list three things or people)

Line 5: Who feels (three items)

Line 6: Who needs (three items)

Line 7: Who fears (three items)

Line 8: Who gives (three items)

Line 9: Who would like to see (three items)

Line 10: Resident of

Line 11: Last name

An example of a biopoem written by an early elementary student is provided in Activity 8.7.

Similar to biopoems, pattern poems provide structure for capturing main ideas and details important to content or topics.

A biopoem can also be adapted to different subject matter, such as a historical figure in social studies. In Activity 8.8, a variation called a **geopoem** focuses on a country or region. A geopoem may include all or some of the following elements:

Line 1: City, state, or country name

Line 2: Four physical features that describe this place

ACTIVITY 8.7 Modified Biopoem

Andrea
who is blue-eyed, brown-haired and nice
relative of Aunt Kathy
lover of Mom, Aunt Kathy, and Louie (my dog)
who feels good, happy, and tired
who needs more chapter books, friends, and long nails
who fears snakes, mom dying, mom's lupus
who gives clothes, toys, and money
who would like to see Miley Cyrus, Lady Gaga, and Beyoncé
resident of Virginia Beach

Developed by Terry Bryce.

ACTIVITY 8.8 Geopoem: Elementary

Texas
Piney woods, rolling hills, grassy planes, and dry canyons
Fiestas, Octoberfests, Pow-Wows
Mexico's neighbor
Hot and dry or hot and wet
Home of the big open spaces, oil, and longhorn cattle
Battle of the Alamo, Juneteenth/Emancipation Proclamation, Southern hospitality
Rio Grande border, a hotbed of activity
Diamond of the Great Southwest!

Line 3: Three cultural features

Line 4: Neighbor of (bordering country or location)

Line 5: Climate (temperature and precipitation) description in a season

Line 6: Home of (three items, resources, landmarks, or famous people)

Line 7: Three events that have shaped this place

Line 8: Issues or problems present

Line 9: Country or region name

CINQUAINS

Another writing strategy similar to the biopoem is the **cinquain**. A cinquain (pronounced sin-kān) is a five-line poem with the following pattern:

Line 1: Noun or the subject of the poem

Line 2: Two words that describe the first line (adjectives)

Line 3: Three action words (verbs)

Line 4: Four words that convey a feeling

Line 5: A single word that refers back to the first line.

Students at all educational levels will enjoy this language enrichment activity. Cinquains require thought and concentration and can be tried in any content area. Activity 8.9 shows examples of cinquains written for middle and high school.

SEE WHAT I FOUND

This poetry pattern focuses on an object or concept critical to the area or topic being studied. Although the pattern is simple, it requires students to examine the object or idea critically "up close with new eyes." Activity 8.10 shows one example used during a simple machines unit and another for a stop sign that could be used in a social studies lesson.

ACTIVITY 8.9 Cinquain

Middle school: After reading of the Boston Tea Party

Boston Tea Party
aggressive, risky
planning, breaking, entering
done for American independence
risk taking

High school business: After reading from *Introduction to Business*

Central Processing Unit
active, electronic
sorting, comparing, calculating
control center of computer
CPU

ACTIVITY 8.10 See What I Found

See What I Found
A type of simple machine
Right there on my bicycle
Makes my bicycle roll
Gets me from home to school
Awesome!

See What I Found
A STOP sign
A red octagon on the street
A signal meaning halt
Necessary for preventing crashes
A shape for saving lives

Procedure

1. Think of an object or item of significance that was a part of the passage read.
2. Write the word or object you chose on the first line.
3. Tell something about it on the second line.
4. Tell where you might find it on the third line.
5. Tell what purpose(s) that object has on the fourth and fifth lines.
6. Say anything you would like about it on the sixth line.

This idea is particularly supportive of English language learners.

Teachers can use real objects, as well as pictures of objects, to provide concrete examples and models.

FIRST-PERSON SUMMARY

A **first-person summary** is an excellent writing activity in which students write about something in the first person as if they were part of the action, allowing them to process information by writing in their own words about a topic. Using the first person encourages the writer to become personally involved in the material. Teachers may be able to recognize and correct any deficiencies in students' understanding by reading their summaries. For instance, when studying photosynthesis in science, students might write first-person essays in which they take the part of a water molecule. They must explain how they get into a plant, where they journey in the plant, what happens once they reach the chloroplast, and so on. In this way, students gain a deeper understanding of the photosynthesis process, and teachers can identify problems students are encountering. This type of assignment can work with a topic such as "A Day in the Life of a New Irish Immigrant in 1835" or "A Day in the Life of a Blood Cell," as demonstrated in Activity 8.11.

Another approach to first-person summary may take the form of an interview script. Students may take on the role of reporter and create a script to include relevant questions and responses. Another variation is to have students write conversations related to what they are learning. They could write dialogue between two characters in the book they are reading; two scientists who have discoveries related to what they are learning in science; or two historical figures, such as Robert E. Lee and Ulysses S. Grant during the Civil War.

ACTIVITY 8.11 A Day in the Life of a Blood Cell

There I was, stuck on a boring day doing absolutely nothing. It was 1:32 in the afternoon. Agent 002 was in hot pursuit of the gangster known as Ned the Nucleus. Agent 0012 called me for backup because there was a shoot-out at the Cell Bank on 112 Membrane Street. I rode out there, but there was a backup in the bloodstream so I rode down the back way. Ned the Nucleus was threatening to blow the Cell Bank sky high. I snuck up and over the cell wall. I climbed up the Cell Bank with the help of Don the DNA. I went in and brought out Bob the Brain Cell. How could I be that stupid? Now Ned the Nucleus had a gun. He was shooting at the cops. What could we do?

I went back to the station and figured out a plan. I'd go in the bank disguised as a customer! He'd hold me hostage, then I'd hit him with my elbow and put him under arrest! I got into the building OK. Then I went up to the top floor. He had two other hostages. Their names were Rick the Red Blood Cell and Wally the White Blood Cell. He was arrested on the spot. I got promoted to Chief Lieutenant. Ned the Nucleus got 15–20 years and $500,000 cell bail. A very good lesson was learned today. Killing cells doesn't pay.

HEADLINE!

Ned the Nucleus Breaks Out of Jail!

So now I had to get him back in jail. I went to headquarters so I could get all of the information. Then it hit me like a Mike Tyson jab. Where else would he be than Ned's Night Club in downtown Los Nucleus? So I took the bloodstream down there. He wasn't there, but I got some useful information. They told me he was at the dock. On San Fran Cellular's finest dock, Cells Wharf. I pulled up in the bad neighborhood. I wasn't alone, though.

I had the help of Carl the Blood Clot and Priscilla the Spore. Ned the Nucleus was not alone; in fact, he had his whole gang there! I recognized some of their faces; they were Beau the Bruise, Cad the Cut, Rick the Red Blood Cell, and Wally the White Blood Cell, who had faked being a hostage at the bank. We called for backup and got out of there.

We missed the bullets shot at us and met the other cops at my house, where we had told them to go. We went back to the wharf with the SWAT team and the rest of the police squad. We had a stakeout. People shot at us from the water with their stun guns. Our snipers from the roof shot them. Then we had a shoot-out. But we had them surrounded, so they just gave up. I got a medal of honor and became head of the SWAT team and the police. But to me it was just another day in the life of a detective.

Written by Jon Morgan.

OTHER ASSISTING ACTIVITIES

Many writing activities can be practiced with students at the assistance phase of learning. Students can write out the steps they would follow to solve a math problem or complete an experiment. The teacher can ask students to speculate about what would happen if they altered one step. Students can also practice writing about mathematics problems through being asked to write questions about them: What is the sum of 15 and 30? The questions should reflect students' knowledge of the correct vocabulary and operations.

In a history class, students can be asked to rewrite a historic event by altering one cause or one effect. For example, using the saying, "If walls could talk. . ." students can write from the perspective of a historical structure describing the events and feelings experienced there during the time for which it is famous. Then students can contrast the way the event really happened with their invented version.

How can you envision using this activity with other content areas?

The Reflection Phase of Writing

A number of researchers (Atwell, 1987; Sanacore, 1998) maintain that the publication of writing is a natural motivation for writing. Atwell believes that teachers should support student publication efforts because students write better when they know someone will read their writing.

When writing is to be published or finished as a product, writers should be concerned with both content and form. Revision and editing are important steps in the writing process. Revision requires the writer to make decisions concerning content elaboration and organizational format to give the reader a clearly focused message. During revision, writers are still learning to express what they understand about the information, but they also are learning to be considerate of their audience by putting the writing in a consistent, organized format. During the editing stage, writers must attend to standard spelling, grammar, and mechanics to put the finishing touches on their work. After the writer has revised and edited his or her writing, an audience will read it and react in a formal way. Often, teachers confuse the evaluation stage with the drafting stage and expect students to produce writing that meets format considerations before or while they are writing to express content. This is a difficult task for even the most experienced student writers. Here is a rule of thumb to use when analyzing a student's piece of writing:

Fluency → Clarity → Correctness → Eloquence and style

Many students have poor handwriting, spelling, and grammar skills. In analyzing student writing, teachers first need to concentrate on the sincerity and fluency of the effort. Later they can ask for more clarity. Finally, the goal is to write correctly and with some style. Remember that for the student, motivation to write may come from the teacher, who follows this progression in grading and analyzing student writing.

RAFT (Vanderventer, 1979) offers one way for writers and their teachers to keep the appropriate audience in focus:

R stands for the role of the writer: What is the writer's role—reporter, observer, eyewitness?

A stands for audience: Who will be reading this writing—the teacher, other students, a parent, people in the community, an editor?

F stands for format: What is the best way to present this writing—in a letter, as an article, a report, a poem?

T stands for the topic: What is the subject of this writing—a famous mathematician, prehistoric cave dwellers, a reaction to a specific event?

RAFT is a flexible strategy that can be used at various stages within a unit of study. It also provides a means to address the needs of students who struggle as well as those who desire a challenge.

When teachers are clear about the purpose of the writing and students keep RAFT in mind, the product will be clearer and more focused. Students benefit from teachers modeling how to write a RAFT paper. Students can be included in the particulars of this strategy by volunteering suggestions for specific problems to be addressed. They can also share additional role, audience, and formatting possibilities. Students can also help establish criteria or a rubric needed for assessment.

Please visit the Education CourseMate website at **www.cengagebrain.com** links to RAFT examples and suggestions for use in content classrooms.

The strategy works well for controversial local, state, and national issues of concern such as those dealing with environment, social unrest, politics, or economic factors. One example focusing on global warming can be viewed in Activity 8.12. Groenke and Puckett (2006) describe several examples and ways of using RAFT within

ACTIVITY 8.12 RAFT: High School Students Write about Global Warming

The RAFT chart provides a few suggestions and possibilities that can be mixed and matched as needed.

Role	Audience	Format	Topic
Scientist	Scientific community	White paper or journal article	Global warming
Politician	Constituents	Letter	Environmental protection
Local citizen	CEO	Newspaper article or editorial	Global economy
High school student	Local community	Brochure or speech	Effects of global warming on the local community
Oil company CEO	Legislators	Interview	Global, state, and local economy
Journalist	Self	Journal or diary entry	Personal fears, hopes, and expectations concerning global warming

Using the chart above, write a RAFT paper with these guidelines:

Role: You are a concerned high school student who has just been made aware of the dangers and impact of global warming.

Audience: You believe it is your responsibility as a well-informed citizen to alert the community of the potential harm that is being done to the environment and what they as private citizens can do to reverse or at least help correct the problem.

Format: Choose one of the following:

- You are going to prepare and deliver a compelling speech to a local civic organization explaining the facts and what they as local citizens can do to help.
- You are going to design a brochure explaining the dangers of global warming and the steps that local citizens can take to help. The local newspaper has agreed, upon approval of your final brochure copy, to distribute it through local delivery.

Topic: Causes and Effects of Global Warming.

a science curriculum. An excellent example of criteria that can be used or adapted for assessment is provided as well.

ACTIVITIES FOR REFLECTIVE WRITING

A number of activities help students write reflectively with an end product as the outcome.

GUIDED WRITING PROCEDURE

The **guided writing procedure** (Smith & Bean, 1980) uses writing specifically to enhance comprehension. Because guided writing leads to a graded product, it is classified as a reflection activity; however, guided writing also involves the preparation and assistance steps. Smith and Bean give seven steps for its implementation, to be completed in two days. On the first day, the teacher (1) activates students' prior knowledge to facilitate prewriting, (2) has students factstorm and categorize their facts, (3) has students write two paragraphs using this organized list, and (4) has students read about the topic. On the second day, the teacher (5) has students check their drafts for functional writing concerns, (6) assigns rewriting based on functional needs and revision to incorporate the information from the reading, and (7) gives a quiz. Teachers can have students submit a rewritten paragraph as an alternative to taking a quiz. Activity 8.13 is an example of a modified guided writing procedure used by a middle school English teacher to help her students write limericks.

Students can type their limericks on the computer and use clip art to decorate them.

ACTIVITY 8.13 Guided Writing: Limericks

Strategy: The purpose of this activity is to extend the students' abilities to compose a poem. They will achieve this purpose in a guided writing exercise. I have students write poetry because they will understand poetry better after they have become poets. The exercise will begin with clustering, and from there, the students will be guided through their first and final drafts. Because this is a guided exercise, I will determine the students' background, build on that background, direct the study, and finally determine their comprehension. The extension of this activity is publishing these poems.

First step: Prewriting (determining background). The teacher writes the word *limerick* on the board and then draws a circle around it. He or she then asks the students to think about the characteristics of that word. As they give answers, the teacher writes them on lines extended from the main word. Then the teacher directs them to look at some limericks in the text.

Second step: Prewriting (building background). The limericks are read and studied for rhyme scheme and rhythm. The characteristics are listed as further subtopics of the main topic, "limericks."

Third step: Guiding the first draft (developing comprehension)

1. Tell the students that instead of writing limericks, they will be writing pigericks.
2. Pigericks are like limericks except they are always about pigs. They are short, have lines that rhyme, and contain a definite rhythm. Furthermore, they are humorous.
3. Pass out handouts on pigericks and show Arnold Lobel's book title *The Book of Pigericks.* Go over the poems, noticing the similarities between limericks and pigericks.
4. On the board or overhead, begin a line for a pigerick. Have the students continue brainstorming the remainder of the poem.
5. Assign the writing of a pigerick. Monitor.

Fourth step: Revising (reflection)

6. Have students exchange their poems and share suggestions.
7. Students then revise and rewrite onto large index cards. Then they illustrate their poems.
8. Post the finished products on the bulletin board.

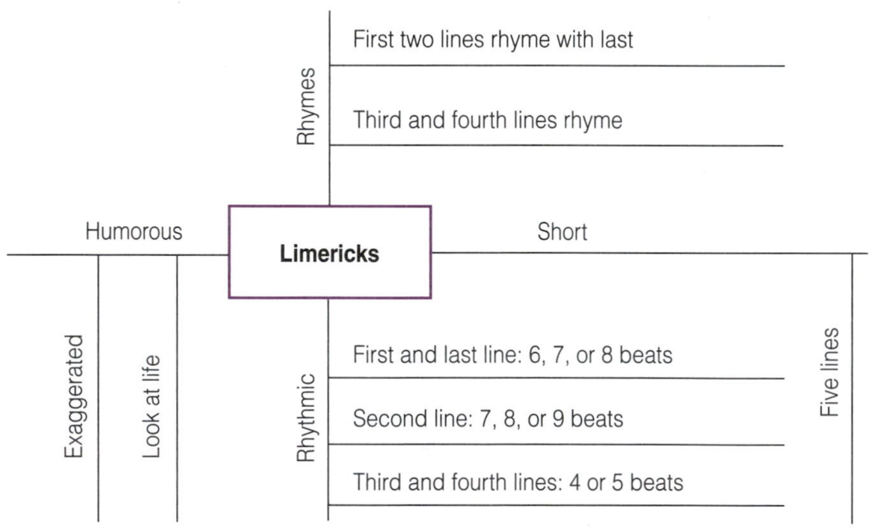

Students' Limericks

There was a giant pig named Moe Cork
Who acted on a stage in New York
Said he, "Of we three I am the greatest of thee
Because my head is made of more pork."

There once was a piggy named Lance,
Who wanted to do nothing but dance.
He danced every day,
In a very awkward way.
But that was okay for dancing Lance.

Developed by Frances Lively.

CONTENT-FOCUSED DRAMA

Cooter and Chilcoat (1991) describe how high school students can cooperatively study and perform content-focused melodramas to stimulate connections between what they know and what historical texts describe. Students pick a topic of interest within a unit of study and, in groups of five or six, develop a melodrama by writing the plot, developing characters, and making scenery. Students draft the writing in several stages: (1) the prewriting stage, in which they research the topic, organize facts, and develop characters (2) composing the initial draft of the script and (3) conferencing with the teacher to revise, edit, and polish the final script. The Readers' Theater format is motivating because students don't have to memorize a script to perform. They just have to practice reading their lines with expression.

COLLABORATIVE WRITING

We mentioned **collaborative writing** in connection with the Foxfire books, cited earlier as an example of making writing relevant and relating it to students' backgrounds. Collaborative writing is most effective in demonstrating to students the necessity of finished products that reflect consideration for the intended reader. When students work together, they are less intimidated by what they see as the immense tasks involved in thinking, drafting, revising, and evaluating. Brunwin (1989) organized the students in an entire elementary school to produce a historical account of their neighborhood. They developed questions, targeted the best people to ask, conducted and transcribed interviews, organized their material, and wrote a book to report their findings.

However, collaborative writing need not involve such large groups. One teacher divided her class into several groups. Each individual read an article and reacted to it independently. Then individuals brought their reactions to their assigned groups. Within each group, a common draft was produced using the individual reactions. Each group member then revised the draft and brought suggestions back to the group. Finally, the groups evaluated and rewrote the papers, which the teacher then graded. She discovered that students were able to demonstrate their knowledge of the content well while practicing good writing skills—and as a bonus, she received fewer papers to grade.

Students can provide editing and revising advice for each other using rubrics (Activities 8.15 and 8.16) or checklists (Activity 8.17) to help peers improve their final writing products.

C3B4ME

Yeager (1991) introduced **C3B4Me** (See Three Before Me) to remind students that they must carefully review and revise their writing for a grade. This can work well for collaborative as well as individual work to encourage students to assist one another in learning. As critical friends they can begin to understand how to give and take constructive criticism. For this strategy, students should remember to see three other helpers before submitting their work to the teacher. First the writer should think critically about his or her writing. Next the writer should confer with a peer, asking for specific advice about designated portions of the writing—not just "Do you like my work?" but "Do you think I have been clear enough in this section?" Last, the writer should be able to consult a "reading associate." Teachers can facilitate the revising and evaluating process by organizing the class into three types of associates. One type includes students who volunteer to be editors for other class members; they and the teacher should agree that they have this skill. The second type includes students who volunteer to illustrate others' written work. The third type helps writers find available editors and illustrators.

GIST

One strategy for teaching students to summarize text effectively is called GIST (Cunningham, 1982)—"**g**enerating **i**nteractions between **s**chemata and **t**ext." It has been found to improve students' reading comprehension and summary writing (Bean & Steenwyk, 1984). With GIST, teachers must model and guide after the reading stage of a lesson. The reader is interrupted and directed to record a summary of the material just read. Cunningham recommends the following steps:

1. Select a short passage in a chapter that has an important main idea. A passage containing from three to five paragraphs works best. Type the paragraphs on the computer.
2. Project using an LCD projector but display only the first paragraph. Open a document on the computer and type 20 blanks. Have students read the paragraph and instruct them to write a summary with 20 or fewer of their own words.
3. Have students generate a class summary on the computer in 30 or fewer words. Their individual summaries will function as guides for this process.
4. Reveal the next paragraph of the text and have students generate a summary of 30 or fewer words that encompasses both of the first two paragraphs.
5. Continue this procedure paragraph by paragraph until students have produced a GIST statement for the entire passage being taught. In time, they will be able to generate GIST statements for segments of text in a single step.

By restricting the length of students' GIST summaries, the teacher compels the students to use the three major strategies necessary for comprehension and retention of key ideas in any text. They must delete trivial information, select key ideas, and generalize in their own words (Kintch & Van Dijk, 1978). In this manner, GIST is beneficial for teaching reading and writing. Eventually, GIST can be constructed after the reading as a reflective activity, although one should practice with the strategy in both the assistance and the reflection phases of the lesson. Activity 8.14 is an example of a GIST done following the reading of a passage about hurricanes.

SHORT STATEMENTS

How could you adapt this strategy for solving a math problem?

Short pieces of writing can be quite motivational and provide a venue for exploring topics, synthesizing information, and expressing the most critical parts clearly and concisely. Yell (2002) describes the short statement strategy as a way for students to learn to express points and ideas precisely while using research techniques. Students explore a topic and write one, two, or even three "information-rich" paragraphs to describe their findings. A shorter task may appear less daunting to students—but it often requires as much or more reading, research, and thought as does a longer assignment to accomplish writing an effective, concise product. Yell describes the steps for using this strategy to

ACTIVITY 8.14 GIST: What Is a Hurricane?

Forming over warm waters in the Northern Hemisphere, this tropical storm has an "eye," 75+ mph counterclockwise winds, and flooding rains.

create a brief biography. First, students are asked to explain the action, idea, or event for which the person is known. Next, enough background information must be supplied to clarify the historical context. Writers must use action words. Finally, students must condense the information into five or fewer sentences per paragraph.

GRADING REFLECTIVE WRITING

Teachers sometimes question whether they should accept writing from students when it contains grammatical errors, misspellings, and other errors. "Surely seventh graders can write better than this!" they admonish. However, teachers must allow students to focus on one stage of writing at a time. The 6+1 TRAITS® model (Culham, 2003) includes rubrics for each trait on a five-point scale so teachers can focus on one aspect of the writing at a time. Spandel (2009) also has created rubrics on 4- and 6-point scales for each trait.

Errors are a normal part of learning, and they will occur in student writing. The amount and types of writing practice that students have had will determine their level of sophistication. If the pressure to focus on errors is eliminated during the prewriting and drafting stages, when the focus should be on content, then attention to errors can be greater during the revision and editing stages. If students have had prewriting and drafting opportunities, their revised writing will reflect both improved content and improved form.

As you view this video notice how the teacher makes peer editing a positive experience to build self-esteem among her students while improving their writing skills.

Teachers can guide students in their writing activities by making clear their expectations for the final product. Students should understand exactly what will be evaluated. Of course, the content of the writing is most important. But "content" is a vague criterion. To clarify expectations and grading criteria for students, a checklist or rubric may be developed. A **rubric** is an expectation guide that lists the qualities of a range of papers—from the strongest to the weakest (Activities 8.15 and 8.16). A rubric helps students, who can refer to it as they revise, as well as the teacher, who can refer to it during grading. Similarly, checklists are useful because they list the features the teacher expects to find in students' writing (Activity 8.17). Teachers can use a checklist to quickly rate the features of a written assignment, and students can check their papers against this list during revision. Teachers can hand out the rubric or checklist when giving the assignment. In this way, students know in advance what factors will be considered in their grade, and they have a chance to organize their writing accordingly.

As with reflective reading, students should be involved at the evaluation and publishing stages of writing. Even if the teacher gives the final grade—as the teacher does if students take a test to demonstrate learning after reading—students should have opportunities to evaluate their own writing before giving it to the teacher. Only when students know that their own analysis is a crucial part of the process will they take responsibility for it.

Another way to facilitate such realization and responsibility is to allow preview and revision opportunities. Teachers can let students turn in drafts of assigned writing early for early review at no cost to their grades. After receiving a graded writing assignment, students can be encouraged to rewrite the paper and receive an average of the first grade and second grades. Using a computer and word processing program helps students become more receptive to polishing their writing (Bangert-Drowns, 1993; Brown, Phillips, & Stephens, 1992; Cochran-Smith, 1991; Goldberg, Russell, & Cook, 2003). Writing a draft and then returning to it with a critical eye is much easier when the major work does not have to be recopied. Cronin, Meadows, and Sinatra (1990) found that secondary students who used a computer for writing assignments across the curriculum improved their writing ability, attaining 100 percent success on a standard written essay test.

Please visit the Education CourseMate website at **www.cengagebrain.com** for links to numerous sites that offer writing ideas that teachers can use, such as creating writing rubrics.

View this video to see how the teacher uses first person and draws upon multiple intelligences theory to help his students develop and improve their writing.

ACTIVITY 8.15 Rubric for Peer Editing

WRITER'S NAME: ______________________________ DATE: ____________

PEER EDITOR'S NAME: ______________________________ TITLE: ____________

The writer would like this peer editor to examine and provide feedback for the following:

Content and ideas: ______________________________

Organization: ______________________________

Mechanics: ______________________________

Questions the writer has for the peer editor:

RUBRICS THAT SERVE AS A GUIDE FOR EACH DOMAIN

Domain	**Needs Considerable Improvement 1**	**Needs Some Improvement 2**	**Well Done! 3**
Content and ideas			
• Focus	• Information is scattered and random with no clear focus.	• Information is organized well enough to make the focus apparent.	• Information is clear, logical, and well focused.
• Major points	• Few to no major points are included.	• Most major points are included.	• All major points are addressed, and additional points of interest are appropriately included.
• Support	• Main points that are included are not supported by details and evidence.	• Main points are supported by some details and evidence.	• All main points are well supported by details and evidence.
• Interest	• Writing is bland with facts or thoughts just stated one after the other; uninteresting.	• Writing is interesting enough to hold the attention of the reader.	• Writing interests the reader and encourages further investigation of the topic.
Organization			
• Introduction	• There is no clear introduction.	• An adequate introduction is provided.	• The introduction is interesting and encourages the reader to think about the topic and read on.
• Order	• Points are randomly addressed and bounce back and forth.	• Most points and paragraphs follow a logical sequence appropriate for the topic.	• Points are clearly ordered to avoid confusing the reader or the issues.
• Transition	• Writing moves abruptly from one point to another with no apparent connection.	• Enough transitions are used to provide good flow from one sentence, paragraph, or section to the next.	• Transitions move the reader seamlessly along from one sentence, paragraph, or section to the next.
• Conclusion	• The writing just stops with no conclusion provided.	• The conclusion is appropriate and logical.	• The conclusion is strong, well stated, and well supported.

ACTIVITY 8.15 (Continued)

Domain	Needs Considerable Improvement 1	Needs Some Improvement 2	Well Done! 3
Mechanics			
• Spelling	• There are numerous spelling errors.	• Most words are spelled correctly.	• There are no spelling errors.
• Sentence structure	• Several sentences are poorly constructed or are not complete.	• Sentences are complete and are constructed well enough to make the meaning clear.	• Sentences are well constructed and easy to understand.
• Language	• Formal language conventions are not maintained.	• Most language conventions are followed.	• Formal language conventions are used throughout.
• Punctuation	• Several punctuation errors are present.	• Few punctuation errors are found.	• There are no punctuation errors.

ACTIVITY 8.16 A Rubric for Grading

Paper topic: 1960s approaches to civil rights in the United States.

High-quality papers contain

An overview of civil rights or their lack during the 1960s, with three specific examples.

A statement defining civil disobedience, with three examples of how it was used and Martin Luther King's role.

At least one other approach to civil rights, with specific examples, and a comparison of this approach with King's civil disobedience that illustrates differences or similarities in at least two ways.

Good organization, well-developed arguments, few mechanical errors (sentence fragments, grammatical errors, spelling errors).

Medium-quality papers contain

An overview of civil rights during the 1960s, with two specific examples.

A statement defining civil disobedience, with two examples of its use and Martin Luther King's involvement.

One other approach to civil rights, with examples, and a comparison of it with King's civil disobedience by their differences.

Good organization, few mechanical errors, moderately developed arguments.

Lower quality papers contain

A general statement defining civil disobedience with reference to Martin Luther King's involvement and at least one example.

One other approach to civil rights and how it differs from civil disobedience.

Fair organization, some mechanical errors.

Lowest-quality papers contain

A general statement on who Martin Luther King was or a general statement on civil disobedience.

A general statement that not all blacks agreed with civil disobedience.

A list of points, poor organization, many mechanical errors.

From Pearce, D. L. (1983). Guidelines for the use and evaluation of writing in content classrooms. *Journal of Reading* 27(3), 212–218. Reprinted with permission of Daniel L. Pearce and the International Reading Association.

ACTIVITY 8.17 Writing Assignment Checklist

Content	Weak	Average	Strong
1. Clear and interesting topic or main idea.			
2. Topic appropriate to the assignment.			
3. Ideas and details support and develop the topic.			
4. Ideas stated clearly and developed fully.			
5. Good use of language.			
Form			
6. Introduction, body, and conclusion.			
7. Details arranged logically; appropriate to the topic.			
8. Coherent; paragraphs constructed well.			
Mechanics			
9. Grammar and usage.			
10. Spelling, capitalization, punctuation.			

Comments

Key

Strong—10 points
Average/strong—7 points
Average—5 points
Weak—3 points

Developed by Dianne Duncan.

Writing for At-Risk and Struggling Readers

What other types of learners do you think would have an easier time with narrative text?

Motivating poor readers and students at risk of failure requires techniques that engage them in both practical and creative writing. Teacher demonstrations, write-alouds, and scaffolding to build skills and understanding are important for developing the ability and confidence necessary for students to do well on their own. Students need to be given adequate time to write, opportunities to discuss questions and progress with their peers as well as with the teacher, and timely and appropriate feedback. A homework assignment in writing is often not successful with at-risk students because they may not be able to get answers to their questions or the support needed.

One teaching technique that has been used over time in all kinds of settings has been to tell anecdotes and stories that connect to the principles being taught. Isolated facts are easily forgotten, but facts woven into a story become memorable. Children with learning disabilities often have an easier time reading narrative text than expository text (Saenz & Fuchs, 2002). Readers understand narrative texts more easily because of the emotions and human qualities present in stories and the familiar structure. Hand (2006) has implemented a program called "History as Story" in her school system. This program is designed to guide students to research and use facts to create stories that will lead them to understand the significance of the facts. The information must come from reliable sources, such as websites that are proven trustworthy. Students weave stories based on facts, so there is less chance they will plagiarize and write encyclopedic-type reports.

Please visit the Education CourseMate website at **www.cengagebrain.com** for links with information on teaching students about plagiarism.

For struggling writers, pictures can prompt discussion, which in turn fuels a story or informational text. The class can discuss characters in a picture, and students can be asked what is happening in the picture, what may be about to happen, and what may have happened in the past. To accompany the picture, the teacher may construct partial sentences for the students to complete, such as these for a picture showing the signing of the Declaration of Independence:

1. The man in the picture is . . .
2. He is signing . . .
3. If I were at the signing, I would . . .
4. The men in the picture look . . .
5. There are no women in the picture because . . .
6. The men will soon be . . .

One purpose of using writing as a means of learning is to help struggling students read and think more clearly through awareness of their own ability to write. Research suggests that semiliterate students may have a writing vocabulary not exceeding 500 words (Tonjes & Zintz, 1981). Student understanding and confidence can be developed by starting small (with sentences), moving to paragraphs, and then organizing and elaborating to create comprehensive texts that reflect their learning. An overemphasis on mechanics is discouraging for struggling learners. Many students who fail have poor handwriting and are weak in spelling and grammar. Such students get discouraged when teachers find fault and dwell on their inadequacies. Teachers should tell these students that they will be graded on the sincerity and fluency of their efforts. Later teachers can ask for clearer student writing. Patience is the key when teaching students with these limitations. The goal is to produce students who write correctly and with some style.

Students at risk are generally characterized as passive learners who lack the ability to produce and monitor adequate reading behaviors (Harris & Graham, 1985; Torgensen & Licht, 1983). However, teachers can help them by first modeling and then providing support to use self-regulatory strategies so they are more thoughtful about their writing (Helsel & Greenberg, 2007). Writing that stresses discovery and active learning represents an excellent way for passive students to become active learners who are responsible for creating their own concepts and understanding their own thought process as they write. Such techniques can aid even children with a severely limited capacity to learn.

Zaragoza (1987) lists several fundamental elements of writing that, if followed, can help children identified as having learning disabilities or being at risk gain control and become more active and involved in their learning. She says students need a 30-minute block of "time to write" each day—a period devoted expressly to writing so they acquire the habit of writing. Zaragoza also calls for children to have considerable freedom in choosing topics to build self-confidence that what they say is important.

The aim of process writing is to foster a feeling of control in students so that they "learn that the influence of their choices extends beyond their work to the larger classroom environment" (p. 292). She also recommends that a revision be done after the first draft and that teachers edit this revised version. Later children can "publish" their work in the form of student-made books.

Research shows that poor readers have trouble identifying important ideas in a passage and have trouble using the rules for summarizing (Winograd, 1984). Summary writing can help students by allowing them to focus their thinking about the reading passage. The teacher can get these students to concentrate on the "big picture," or central theme, instead of getting caught up in minutiae. Zakaluk and Klassen (1992) report that Dan, a remedial ninth grader labeled as having a learning disability, was taught to use check marks while reading so he could identify important points. Then he used the check marks to write headings for an outline. By going back to the text, he found supporting details. Then he was able to write summary paragraphs about what he had learned.

A number of reading professionals and researchers have formulated rules for condensing major ideas in a text (Brown, Campione, & Day, 1981; Kintch & Van Dijk, 1978). Here are six classic rules all students generally should follow:

1. **Delete unnecessary detail.** With practice, students will become adept at separating important text information from minor facts and trivial statements.
2. **Delete redundant information.** Students should make lists and collapse information into broader categories of information as they notice redundancies.

CHALLENGE BOX

Gustavo, the English as a Second Language Student

SITUATION: You will remember that Gustavo was introduced in Chapter 1 and revisited in Chapter 3 describing ways that teachers can support his preparation to read in the content areas.

How might Gustavo's cultural background be used to support writing to learn in the content areas?

In Chapter 3, teachers were encouraged to tap into Gustavo's background knowledge and experiences, especially in relation to his family's experiences as immigrants. A meaningful way to build on Gustavo's experiences would be to ask him to create a graphic organizer to compare his family's immigration from Mexico with European immigrants' experiences when they came to the United States in the early to mid-twentieth century. The graphic organizer would serve as a planner for Gustavo's ideas before he writes an essay comparing these experiences. Writing his ideas will help him synthesize the information about European immigration and help him understand the similarities and differences that immigrants have when they come to a new country.

Describe a way the RAFT strategy could be used to encourage Gustavo to actively participate and write about his learning.

Life science is a focus of the science curriculum in many seventh grade classrooms. As Gustavo learns about organisms living in their ecosystems, he can write a RAFT paper (described in this chapter) from the point of view of an animal that he chooses (e.g., an elephant), describing its ecosystem (e.g., the African savannah), in the form of a letter to an audience of elementary children. In his RAFT paper, he would include important information about how the elephant gets food, water, and shelter in the African savannah while living with the other animals in that ecosystem. As with any writing that Gustavo completes, he should be encouraged to use the vocabulary that he is learning in his classes, especially cognates that connect English and Spanish etymology (see Chapter 7 for a discussion of vocabulary and Chapter 11 for a discussion of cognates).

3. **Use blanket terms.** Students should replace lists of smaller items of information with more encompassing terms.
4. **Select topic sentences; summarize paragraphs.** Often, paragraphs have easily identifiable topic sentences. Sometimes there is no discernible topic sentence, however, and students have to create their own topic sentence for the summary. Doing this can be difficult for poor readers. Much practice is needed for these students to feel successful at this difficult step.
5. **Write a first draft of a summary.** Students need to integrate information by making more general certain topic sentences, keywords, and phrases already compiled in steps 1 through 4. The first four steps prepare students to write the first draft of the summary.
6. **Revise the summary.** With the help of other students or the teacher, students should rework the summary to make it more readable. By doing so, students will get a clearer idea of the major points covered in the material.

ONE-MINUTE SUMMARY

This chapter described how to teach, emphasize, and apply writing across the content areas and at different grade levels. Writing to learn in various curricular areas gives students opportunities to rehearse, elaborate, and organize their thinking about the content while monitoring their understanding. Students concurrently practice and reinforce their writing skills and techniques. The chapter discussed the connections between reading and writing, as well as the importance of teaching writing in preschool and the earliest elementary grades. We differentiated between processes and products of writing and described a number of phases of writing across the curriculum. We provided ways to integrate technology with writing in the content areas to improve students' writing quality and quantity. To demonstrate how easily writing to learn can be incorporated into content instruction, we explained activities to promote writing at each phase of the PAR Lesson Framework. We included real classroom applications to show teachers how content writing works in action. Considerations and techniques for working with at-risk students were described. Writing is a skill, an art, and a tool that can be effectively used for learning in all curriculum areas.

END-OF-CHAPTER ACTIVITIES

Assisting Comprehension

1. Keep your own learning log to record your reactions as you use the writing strategies described in this chapter. Assess how each activity helps you teach the writing process. Practice writing in your log every day. Share the writing in your log with your students.
   a. Considering your own background of experience, training, and classroom practices, write three to five questions you have concerning the role, skills, approaches, and your feelings about the teaching of writing within content areas.
   b. How might you use technology and other resources to find appropriate answers to your questions?
   c. Now answer your questions using the resources and plan you selected for locating answers.
2. Try cubing. Write a short paragraph about this chapter on each of the following six sides of the cube:
   a. How would you describe this chapter?
   b. To what would you compare this chapter?
   c. What does this chapter make you think of?
   d. How would you analyze this chapter?
   e. Apply this chapter to your own life.
   f. Do you agree with the tenets of this chapter?
   g. Argue for or against writing to learn in the content areas. Do you favor writing as a product or process writing?

Reflecting on Your Reading

1. Your content organization (e.g., National Council of Teachers of Math, National Council of Teachers

of English, National Council for the Social Studies, National Science Teachers Association, International Reading Association) has most likely developed a set of standards that identify the performance criteria relevant to classroom teachers. Standards usually delineate elements of foundational knowledge that a classroom teacher should possess. Locate and become familiar with what the organization recommends. For instance, teachers should:

- Engage students in writing to describe, persuade, argue, and explain concepts and their applications.
- Involve students in analyzing and explaining observations in written form.
- Use a variety of strategies to engage students in articulating their ideas and understanding in written form.

2. How did this chapter address these elements? Select one topic in a content area you teach and describe one writing strategy for each: preparation, assistance, and reflection.
3. The following professional books provide excellent extension reading resources for finding out more about writing to learn in the content classrooms:

Blasingame, J., & Bushman, J. H. (2005). *Teaching writing in middle and secondary schools.* Upper Saddle River, NJ: Pearson Education.

Bright, R. (1995). *Writing instruction in the intermediate grades: What is said, what is done, what is understood.* Newark, DE: International Reading Association.

Bromley, K. (1993). *Journaling: Engagements in reading, writing, and thinking.* New York: Scholastic.

Culham, R. (2003). *6+1 traits of writing: The complete guide grades 3 and up.* New York: Scholastic Professional Books.

Duke, N.K., & Bennett-Armistead, V.S. (2003). *Reading & writing informational text in the primary grades: Research-based practices.* New York: Scholastic.

Graves, D. (1994). *A fresh look at writing.* Portsmouth, NH: Heinemann.

Houston, G. (2004). *How writing works: Imposing organizational structure within the writing process.* Boston: Pearson Education.

Irvin, J. L., Buehl, D. R., & Radcliffe, B. J. (2007). *Strategies to enhance literacy and learning in middle school content area classrooms,* (3rd ed.) Boston: Pearson Education.

Maxwell, R. (1996). *Writing across the curriculum in the middle and high schools.* Boston: Allyn and Bacon.

Olson, C. B. (2007). *The reading/writing connection: Strategies for teaching learning in the secondary classroom,* (2nd ed.) Boston: Pearson Education.

Routeman, R. (2004). *Writing essentials: Raising expectations and results while simplifying teaching.* Portsmouth, NH: Heinemann.

Scarborough, H. A. (Ed.). (2001). *Writing across the curriculum in secondary classrooms: Teaching from a diverse perspective.* Upper Saddle River, NJ: Pearson Education.

Spandel, V. (2008). *Creating writers through 6-trait writing assessment and instruction* (5th ed.). New York: Allyn & Bacon.

Wolfe, D., & Reising, R. (1983). *Writing for learning in the content areas.* Portland, ME: J. Weston Walch.

Wollman-Bonilla, J. (1991). *Response journals.* New York: Scholastic.

CHAPTER 9

Study Skills in the Electronic Age

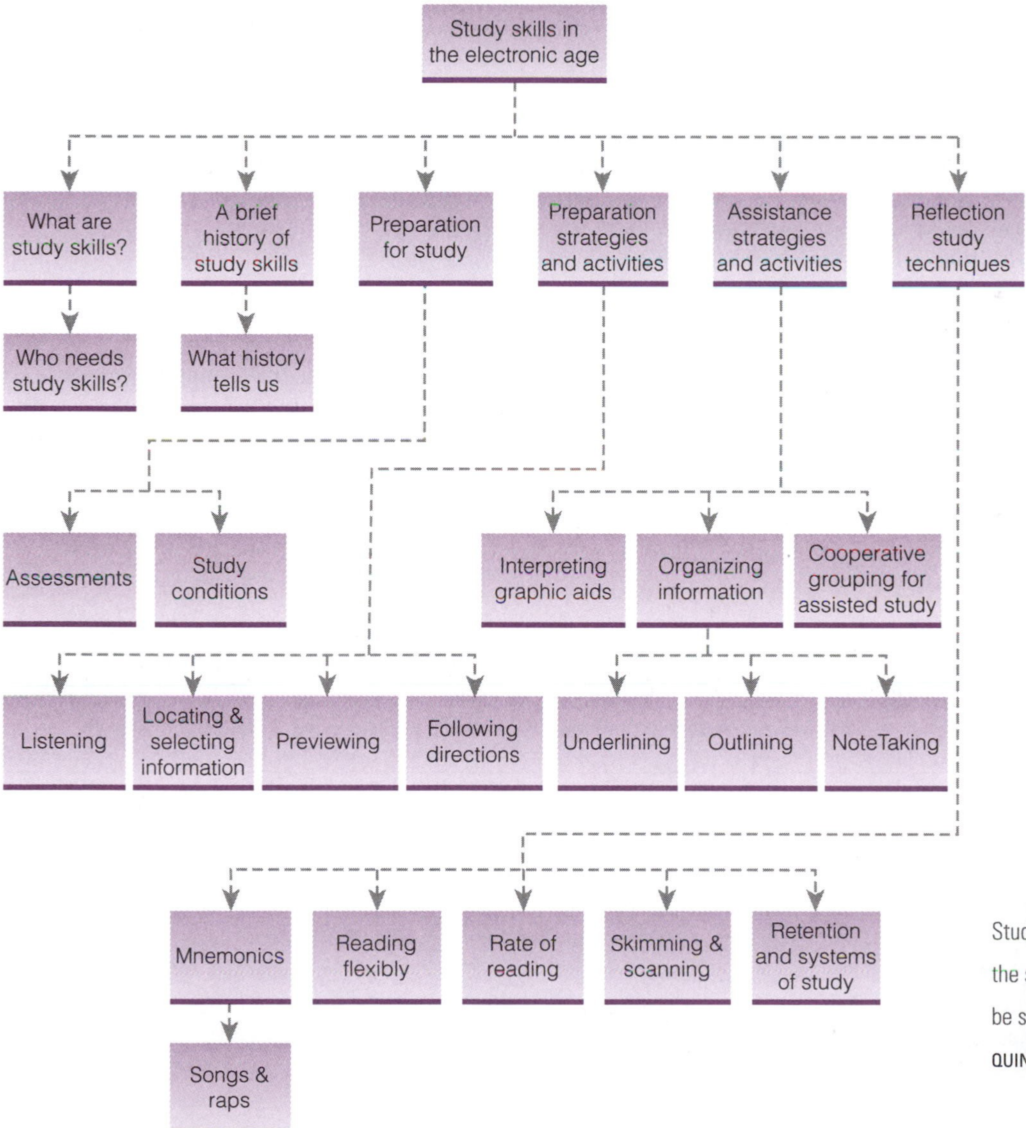

> Study depends on the goodwill of the student: a quality that cannot be secured by compulsion.
>
> QUINTILIAN (35–100 AD)

VOICES FROM THE CLASSROOM

Maria's fifth grade teacher assigned this: "Discuss three ways you use computers in your daily life and the advantages and disadvantages of using computers this way." Maria can present the information any way she chooses, but it needs to reflect her personality. Maria wishes the teacher had just told her exactly what uses to explain and the steps to follow. In school, the class has read about and practiced using the computer to read, find websites, browse, produce reports, organize information, communicate, and research . . . and now she must apply this information.

She would like to address the advantages of texting over emailing and to share her FBFKids (formerly FacebookforKids) page, but she worries that these uses may not be acceptable in school. She ultimately chooses *Wikipedia* as a way to discover basic information, *Googlekids* to locate resources, and *Inspiration* to create diagrams and outlines.

Her dad checks on her progress. He sees her huddled over the computer, frowning and hitting herself with a pencil. "Maria, it's almost your bedtime. Haven't you finished studying yet?"

"No," she replies. "This is harder and takes more time than reporting facts. I have to think about everything we learned, make and explain some choices, and decide how to report them."

"Well, bedtime is in 30 minutes, so you had better decide very soon," her father says.

In frustration, she takes her pencil in both hands and breaks it, throwing the two pieces across the room.

Should she make a diagram using *Inspiration*? Should she create a *PowerPoint*? Should she cut and paste from websites? Should she write a report? Would an outline be better? Maybe she could make a podcast. This is hard work.

Why is this task so hard for Maria? Would it have been better for her teacher to give more specific directions and fewer choices?

PREPARING TO READ

1. What study skills do you use? List them now and refer back to your list as you read this chapter. Do you teach study skills as you teach your subject? If so, list the study skills you teach. As you read, see how many of the study skills you teach are described in this chapter.
2. Following is a list of terms used in this chapter. Some may be familiar to you in a general context, but in this chapter, they may be used in unfamiliar ways. Try to match the words from the list to a study term in the table below. The examples should help you begin. Be ready to locate them in the chapter and pay special attention to their meanings.

A Theory about Study	A Study Activity	A Study Behavior	A Study Skill/ Category	A Term about Computer-based Study
Transmission vs. transaction	SQ3R	Creating mnemonics	Flexible reading	Podcast

_______ study behavior
_______ transmission versus transaction
_______ situated cognition
_______ self-regulation
_______ information literate
_______ time management
_______ podcasts
_______ time shifting
_______ Google Scholar
_______ Wikipedia
_______ previewing
_______ two-column note-taking system
_______ massed study
_______ the spacing effect
_______ mnemonics
_______ acronym
_______ flexible reading
_______ saccadic eye movements
_______ skimming
_______ scanning
_______ study system

OBJECTIVES

As you read this chapter, focus your attention on the following objectives.

1. Explain why study can be difficult for students.
2. Describe the importance of self-regulation and deep thinking in study.
3. Be able to assess students' perceptions of study skills and how they study.
4. Describe several categories of study skills and explain their place in the PAR Framework.
5. Describe several activities that lead students to effective study behaviors.
6. Identify ways to incorporate technology with study skills activities.
7. Be able to use the systems of study described in this chapter in your own classroom.
8. Explain the importance of developing students' ability to use study skills at all grade levels.

Studying requires the use of many literacy skills, especially metacognition—moving beyond the page to thinking about how to learn and remember. Deep reading and thinking, identifying main and supporting ideas, listening carefully, and writing are all required. Every concept presented in this textbook so far is part of the study process. Sedita (1997) compares the successful student to a carpenter who has learned to assemble his tool kit and then to use each tool efficiently and effectively to build a house.

The "ability to take responsibility for directing and improving one's own learning" (Allan & Clarke, 2007) is central to effective study. Study skills necessitate "independent carryover" (Marcell DeCleene & Juettner, 2010). But learners find it difficult to study responsibly, and some even face what Lehrer calls "paralysis by analysis." The neocortex, according to Lehrer (2010), is a "pretty feeble part of the brain" that can handle about seven choices at once. Learners may find that study tasks are difficult because they have many choices but do not know how to select the best tools for the job. Teachers can help by presenting effective strategies for study, but students must convert these strategies into individual **study behaviors** (Gettinger & Seibert, 2002; Lenz, Ellis, & Scanlon, 1996). Maria's teacher (from Voices from the Classroom) has taught her students many uses for computers and is now asking Maria to do some deep thinking and application. Maria must make choices, but she feels paralyzed by so much analysis!

Next, students must have a sense of autonomy and independence. Study skills require active decision making rather than prescriptive steps. Students must learn to implement strategies and activities teachers have presented (Marcell, DeCeleene, & Jettner, 2010) by personalizing the information. Also, learners need to feel free to use their own discourse as they study (Gee, 2001; Moje, 2002). Maria feels insecure about making her own choices; she would rather have a prescription even though doing the assignment her own way may be more rewarding. She does not feel confident to apply the assignment to her own world of computing; she thinks her preferences are not academic enough. Learners often become conflicted when they do not know which tool to use and how to be independent.

Lehrer's book, *How We Decide*, explains the role of the neocortex and limbic system in decision making. To learn more about being overwhelmed by choices, please visit the Education CourseMate website at **www.cengagebrain**.com for a link to a podcast about "analysis by paralysis" or perform a Web search using this term to locate the results.

What Are Study Skills?

Study skills are "self-regulated learning strategies" (Cubuku, 2007, p. 99). Harris and Hodges (1995) in the *Literacy Dictionary* define study skills as "a general term for those techniques and strategies that help a person read or listen for specific purposes with the intent to remember; commonly, following directions, locating, selecting, organizing, and retaining information, interpreting typographic and graphic aids, and reading flexibly" (p. 245). In 1984, Rogers defined *study skills* as the deliberate procedures (strategies) a learner uses to retain information. For instance, he noted that when studying, one reads more slowly and uses techniques such as underlining, note taking, rereading, and reading material aloud. Study skills are "comprehension under construction" according to Marcell, DeCeleene, and Jettner (2010).

Lists of study skills usually include listening and reading with attention, creating and understanding visual representations of information, previewing a text before reading, locating information, taking notes, and intending to learn. This list has remained consistent over several years. As far back as 1909, McMurry listed the following study skills: setting specific purposes for study, identifying supplemental information, organizing ideas, judging the worth of the material, memorizing, keeping an open attitude, and relying on self-direction in learning. Dechant (1970) organized study skills into five categories: dictionary, location and reference, use of graphics, use of library resources, and organization. In their history of content reading, Moore, Readance, and Rickelman (1983) concluded that study skills included organizing skills, such as note taking, underlining, outlining, and summarizing. Blai (1993) identified comprehension of main ideas, self-monitoring, physical setting, organization, goal setting, and pacing as crucial to effective studying.

Who Needs Study Skills?

Study skills instruction is especially crucial for those students in middle school who have attention deficit/hyperactivity disorder (ADHD) and who struggle with reading (Myer & Kelley, 2007). Chapter 11 provides information about these diverse learners and how you can anticipate this need in your classroom.

The obvious answer is everyone! However, the tendency is to forget or ignore study skills—or to assume someone else has taught them. Teachers often think that students don't understand the content when actually they are having problems with study skills. Students must learn to read content with a "critical eye" (Soars & Wood, 2010). Most teachers assume that middle schoolers have mastered study skills (Meneghetti, DeBern, & Cornold, 2007), but all educators at all levels need to teach study skills as part of their curriculum. Basic study skills should be introduced to children as early as the first grade (Strauss, 2003). "Kindergartners can do it too!" state Gregory and Cahill (2010). Kindergarten children learned to visualize, ask questions, infer and make connections when interacting with text. Students with learning disabilities need specific and extended attention to study skills from the primary level on (Sedita, 1999).

At-risk learners (discussed further in Chapter 11) often have poor study skills, which exacerbates their difficulties in an academic environment (Metcalfe, 2005). If they reach college without efficient study skills, they face a glaring problem. Community colleges debate the efficacy of intervention and study skills programs, usually weighing in on the side of aggressive intervention (Milligan, 2007; Simmons, 2006) to stem academic probation and attrition.

Students across the world need study skills (Cubukcu, 2007). Learners from different countries may prefer to use some study skills rather than others, but all students agree that a quiet atmosphere is optimal. Whereas Turkish students rely a great deal on listening, Dutch and Belgian students like to ask others for help and especially like cooperative groups for study. Cubukcu's findings have relevance for English language learner (ELL) in our schools. If study behaviors are viewed differently in other countries, children who have moved to this country may carry those preferences with them. They will also have the added challenge of accessing academic English while learning to study. The English they know may be more out-of-school than in-school oriented, which can cause marginalization within the school and an inability to study (Ma'ayan, 2010; Ogle & Correa-Kovtun, 2010).

Refer to Chapter 1 and apply what you are reading here about ELLs and study difficulties to Principle 4.

Students who have consistently performed well in academic situations may have learned early how to study and likely do not need the same amount of emphasis on study skills that many other students do (Proctor, Prevatt, Adams, Reaser, & Perscher, 2006). Those who achieve high scores on study skills and attitude inventories are, not surprisingly, the ones who have the highest grades (Crede´ & Kuncel, 2008). There is ample evidence in the literature, however, that most learners need a lot more attention to study skills than they receive.

A Brief History of Study Skills

Study skills seem to be underappreciated as a stand-alone topic in literacy journals (Richardson, Robnolt, & Rhodes, 2010). For instance, the list of "what's hot and what's not" in the *Journal of Adolescent and Adult Literacy* does not include study skills—and never has, since the first list in 1997. The terms on the "hot" list that come closest to mentioning study skills are "comprehension," "critical reading and writing," and "informational texts" (Cassidy, Valadez, Garrett, & Barrera, 2010). Sebasta's (1997) list of the "hot literacy topics" at International Reading Association conventions from the 1960s to the 1990s did not include study skills, either. Yet study skills may be the "premier practical attainment" (McBride, 1994, p. 461) of anything a student learns in school. Many articles about study skills appear in college journals about education, probably because college is when the impact of study on student success becomes very clear. For instance, Simmons (2006) found, from his survey of 254 students, that 81 percent reported that they did not receive any training or a class in how to study before entering community college. What has been the "press" about study skills over the years?

The topic of study skills was "hotter" a century ago than it is today. For instance, Moore, Readance, and Rickelman (1983) cite such works as that of Hall-Quest (*Supervised Study*, 1916) and Woodring and Flemming (*Directing Study of High School Pupils*, 1935). Consider these tenets from Huey (1908; 1968, pp. 6–7); they show his emphasis on study skills (the italics are ours) as an important area of study in reading:

- Reading should always be accomplished with a *purpose* in mind that is known to the student.
- *Study skills* such as *library skills* and *note taking* should be taught as early as possible in the elementary grades.
- In high school, students should be given free reign to read widely on subjects of interest. This is preferable to a focused and analytical *study* of a few texts and authors.

In 1937, Gray stated that "pupils should be trained to study effectively as they read" (p. 580). Gray considered topics such as reading to discover relationships, outlining, retention of material, and rate of reading. Strang wrote several texts and articles spanning four decades (1920 to 1960) about improving study in high school, such as "Another Attempt to Teach How to Study" (1928), "The Improvement of Reading in High School" (1937), and "Progress in the Teaching of Reading in High School and College" (1962). Study skills publications in the 1980s focused predominantly on college students. At that time, experts conducted significant studies of comprehension and retention to construct models of curriculum and instruction that would raise literacy to a high standard (Bereiter & Scardamalia, 1987). Langer (1986) reported that different study tasks caused different thinking patterns and learning for high school students.

The impact of motivation or affect on study was a predominant theme in the 1970s. In *Self-Directed Learning: A Guide for Learners and Teachers*, Knowles (1975) proposed that a learner should practice autonomy and inquiry, with guidance from the teacher. See Chapter 2 for more information about autonomy and motivation.

To see an example of transaction versus transmission and using critical thinking along with taking notes to facilitate study skills, view a video of a middle school science lesson on the Education CourseMate at **www.cengagebrain.com.**

In the 1990s, articles described new ways of perceiving literacy, especially studies about comprehension that are relevant to study skills. For instance, when Smith (1992) discussed reading as **transmission** versus reading as **transaction**, he found that students acknowledged being passive about reading and studying textbooks, often missing important clues. Waters and Waters (1992) stressed that there should be an underlying competence for study, especially the ability to think critically. Pressley and Afflerback (1995) identified these key study strategies: taking an overview before reading, looking for and paying great attention to important information, relating important points, activating prior knowledge, changing strategies when necessary, and monitoring and fixing inaccuracies.

These key strategies define the importance of metacognition and high literacy. Hattie, Biggs, and Purdie (1996) cautioned that study skills training needs to be conducted in the same context where the skill will be needed and used to promote learner active involvement and metacognition. In using the term ***situated cognition***, Hattie, Biggs, and Purdie tied their analysis of study skills to a new, more active, and grounded way of looking at comprehension in the 1990s. The use of new technology—specifically computers—stimulated a new need for study skills. Use of computers changed how students studied (Anderson-Inman, 1999a, 1999b). Stahl, Hynd, Britton, McNish, and Bosquet (1996) cautioned that students need specific instruction in the use of multiple resources when studying from multiple sources in history.

The theme of studying as part of the greater picture of comprehension and metacognition continued into the 2000s. Simpson and Nist (2000) cautioned that strategic learning requires mature and complex knowledge, such as task understanding, ability to generalize, and cognitive and metacognitive processing. Barnett (2000) used a more descriptive term, **self-regulation**, to emphasize the role of one's behavior and affect as well as cognitive awareness. According to Barnett, the more a person feels in control of his or her comprehension, the more self-regulated about study he or she should be. Students can be self-regulated only when they are motivated to be metacognitive and behave actively in their own learning (Young & Ley, 2001). Kitsantas (2002) found that those who performed best on tests regulated their study effectively. Cole and Goetz (2000) concluded from their study of under-prepared college students that a student must possess appropriate beliefs about learning and knowledge in order to be successful in school. This kind of knowledge is developed over time; it is not static. Holschuh (2001) found that high performers used more thoughtful and specific strategies and seemed to know when to use the most appropriate strategies.

What do the terms *metacognition, situated cognition, transaction,* and self-regulation have to do with study?

The "age of multiliteracies" (Turbill, 2002), when one reads text plus "color, sound, movement, and visual representations," continues into the twenty-first century. The "information handling skills" students need to take advantage of electronic information became a popular topic of discussion (Macdonald, Heap, & Mason, 2001; Slaouti, 2002). For instance, students have to evaluate the quality of online documents and websites, realizing the difference between citing and plagiarizing a source and understanding what copyright laws mean in the Web-based world (Goett & Foot, 2000). The term *new literacies* (Kist, 2000; Moje, 2000; Leu, Kinzer, Coiro, & Cammack, 2004; Moje, Ciechanowski, Kramer, Ellis, Carrillo, & Collazo, 2004) was coined to describe this electronic environment.

More experts are now emphasizing the importance of study skills for younger and older students alike, echoing the early twentieth century emphasis. Making information relevant to students at all grade levels increases their motivation to study (Frymier & Schulman, 1995). Most strategies and activities presented in this chapter can be adapted to suit students at every level. Table 9.2 shows where study strategies can be introduced in the curriculum.

What Does This Brief History Tell Us about Study Skills?

With the advent of discussion about metacognition, self-regulation, and constructivism, reading processes—including study skills—are now thought to be much more complex and important than any activities, programs, or simple discussions of motivation can account for. Applefield, Huber, and Moallem (2000) note that "there has been a paradigm shift in designed instruction: from behaviorism to cognitivism and now to constructivism" (p. 36). The search for a "perfect" study skills program or the "best" activities is probably fruitless. However, students need to be instructed in agreed-upon study skills and strategies and told about the "tried and true" behaviors and tactics for study that others have found successful. But ultimately, the learner must decide why to study and how to go about it.

Constructivism may be one of the most influential views of learning during the past two decades. This theory emphasizes a student-centered approach, whereby readers actively construct meaning by relating new material to the known using reasoning and developing concepts. See Chapter 4 for further discussion.

The age of multiliteracies is redefining study skills for emphasis in content area reading. Readers must now be **information literate** (Henderson & Scheffler, 2004)—that is, able to find and use information in any paper or electronic form. Web-based reading and study differ from paper-based study—sometimes producing less efficient study and resultant learning (Eveland & Dunwoody, 2002). Reinking (1997) made the point that although technology itself is neutral, the way we use it to learn enables learners to be more creative and engaged. A reader still must use comprehension, vocabulary, and study skills to construct meaning, but the behaviors students must use differ from those required in a paper-based environment. For instance, when reading from a textbook, one may write notes on index cards or sticky notes. When reading electronically, one may take notes by inserting remarks into a document in color or even by using track editing or footnoting.

To remain competitive in a global economy, students must know how to study in a different environment than they did in the last century. Web-based reading and study differ from paper-based study—sometimes producing less efficient study and resultant learning. How will you help learners adapt to computer-based study tactics?

Teachers can show students how to use technology as a study tool (Eveland & Dunwoody, 2002; Anderson-Inman, Knox-Quinn, & Szymanski, 1999). The "new literacies" research has shown us new strategies and activities. Content teachers now design WebQuests and treasure hunts to guide their students to content information that is informative and suitable on the Web. Hypertext lets students create their own quick references to word meanings. Software programs such as *Inspiration* facilitate study by helping students create graphic organizers and outlines.

As Gettinger and Seibert (2002) explained in their information-processing model, study skills require intensive reading and thinking; the more complex the strategy, the deeper the processing must be. Learners expend more energy in study when they use several tactics or behaviors. For instance, to study, one should read the information and then repeat the reading via note taking, highlighting, mapping, or other means of learning. Then one needs to organize that information by schematizing it. Next one needs to think about the information and how it is useful to the learning goal—perhaps by generating questions and linking answers from the organized notations. During all this study, the learner must plan, monitor, and assess how the study is progressing and when to alter a tactic for more effective and efficient study.

To rely on only demonstrations and lectures about study skills or to assume that students can practice such skills independently or that students will see their importance is unwise. Purdie and Hattie (1999) concluded that when students learn effective study behaviors and incorporate them into a meaningful approach to learning, they experience academic and affective results. Self-directed learning, as Sobrol (1997) noted, benefits most students.

When we consider the students of this millennium and the topics raised in a historical perspective, the possibilities for study that is refreshing, challenging, exciting, and learner controlled contribute to the makings of a crucial topic in the field of reading. Study is difficult and time consuming, and many students do not know how to apply themselves sufficiently to become productive learners. Onwuegbuzie, Slate, and Schwartz (2001) found that graduate students responded appropriately only 57.8 percent of the time to statements about their study skills. Simmons (2006) found that only 21 percent of his surveyed community college students felt they knew how to study very well. In public schools, a survey conducted in 2000 (American School Counseling Association) showed that 70 percent of teachers and 60 percent of guidance counselors polled say their students have poor study skills, but 50 percent of schools do not offer study skills courses, and only 11 percent of students in those schools take the study skills course.

Despite evidence that students who use a range of study skills achieve greater success in school (Purdie & Hattie, 1999) and that good study habits lead to academic success (Belzer, Miller, & Hoemake, 2003; Jones, Slate, & Marini, 1995), most teachers are unsure how to integrate study skills with content (Elliot, Foster, & Stinson, 2002; Jackson & Cunningham, 1994). What ideas can you find in this chapter for your students?

Research indicates that programs for study intervention offered outside of content classrooms can make a difference (Allan & Clarke, 2007; Milligan, 2007). However, some experts propose that study skills should be taught in content classrooms and applied in context (Soares & Wood, 2010). A compromise might be both a short, stand-alone course and embedding study skills (Allan & Clarke, 2007). This may be a very good alternative, but it may not be possible. Walker and Masterman (2006) point out that teachers often do not embrace someone else's program or integrate it in their own instruction. Whether or not a specific course is offered, teachers can help students by providing opportunities whereby studying leads to learning interesting information and where the payoff is worth the effort expended. For the remainder of this chapter, we will use the PAR (preparation, assistance, and reflection) Lesson Framework to present ideas that teachers can use to facilitate appropriate, self-regulated study skills.

Preparation for Study

Assessments

Just as with any other reading-to-learn task, one must prepare for study. To be prepared, learners must realize what they know and need to know. Therefore, an assessment of the reader's skills and strategies is an important first step. Most standardized achievement tests include subtests of study skills. However, these subtests are usually limited in scope, measuring students' knowledge of standard items such as reference skills; alphabetization; and the ability to read maps, charts, and graphs. Often neglected are important skills such as following directions, presenting reports, taking tests, taking notes, and training the memory. Unfortunately, most assessments are outdated; Rogers's 1984 informal checklist, for example, was intended to help teachers and students realize what they do while studying and what else they may need to do. In designing his checklist, he drew from Karlin's (1977) checklist and his own experiences, and organized his checklist into four basic categories: (1) study and reading comprehension skills, including interpreting graphic aids and following directions; (2) location skills, including varying reading rate and location of information; (3) retention, including remembering what is studied; and (4) organizing information.

The LASSI (Learning and Study Strategies Inventory) was published in 1988 (Weinstein, Zimmerman, & Palmer). This commercially published instrument is still used to evaluate learning and study strategies (Proctor, Prevatt, Adams, Reaser, & Perscher, 2006). Cubukcu (2007) used the LASSI for his research. It is a 76-item inventory that asks self-report questions about study. Eldredge (1990) developed the LASSI-HS, a high school version of the college-level LASSI.

None of these assessments reflects the current need for a way to assess what students actually do as they study. Similar to Hubbard and Simpson (2003), we recommend that assessments of study skills for today's students find out if the behaviors and tactics students create and use are task appropriate and sufficiently deep. Just asking students to complete a checklist won't discover students' personal theories about learning. Furthermore, assessments have to consider both paper and electronic study contexts, as well as what tactics a student would self-select to study in either environment.

One could also use the MARSI to assess study. To see the inventory, see Chapter 4, Activity 4.1, and Appendix A.

To address the need for a broader assessment of study skills, Rhodes, Robnolt, and Richardson (2005) created an inventory using categories of study in the Harris definition of study skills (1995) and Rogers's list of study skills (1984), as well as their findings from a historical look at study skills (Richardson, Robnolt, & Rhodes, 2010). The newest version of this study skills survey has 19 categories of study skills. The survey asks students to think about whether they use a skill, whether they use it with electronic or paper materials (or both), and how they use the skill. This assessment is intended for student self-reflection; it is best administered either over time or in an untimed session. Although a teacher can immediately see what skills students think they use by the ratings, we also encourage teachers to talk with students about how they use the skills. Only when teachers realize what students actually do to achieve a study skill will they know how to guide effective study. Activity 9.1 presents selected items from this inventory, as well as responses from three different community college students. The responses show how differently students perceive their strengths when in a computer or a print environment and what behaviors they use. Student a is bilingual; her first language is Russian. She is an a student. Student b is an older student, a grandfather returning to college. He is a B student. Student c is a reluctant learner who makes Cs but could do a lot better; she is a C student. She provided no descriptions of study behavior; this should be a "red flag" for the teacher, indicating that the student either does not know what he or she does or does not want to take time to explain—in either case, this may mean a study skills gap. Note that a study skills category is marked in bold, with the phase (P, A, or R) that applies best to the skill.

How can a teacher use a study skills checklist in content area instruction? What other ways can teachers find out what study skills their students use—or do not use?

Homework, Study Conditions, and Time Management

Before study starts, the environment and conditions for study should be optimal. Students attend to tasks better if they are taught to concentrate and think about what they are learning and to be responsible for their own learning. Study distracters can interfere significantly with learning information and completing assignments in a timely manner. Teachers can help students to fend off external distractors by suggesting these questions:

- Where will I study?
- What interruptions may interfere (the phone, instant messages, television, enticing websites)?
- Do I have what I need at hand, such as pencils, highlighters, sticky notes, Internet access, and necessary software?

ACTIVITY 9.1 Selected Example Items and Responses from 3 First-Year College Students: Study Skills for the Twenty-First Century

Please complete the following checklist and add your description of how you would accomplish these study skills. Answer the questions in *all* columns.

Study Skills/Strategies for Reading Electronic environments	How **competent do you feel** when you use this skill in a **digital** environment (the computer) to study.	**Study Behavior/Tactic** Please describe what you would do for each skill when using a **digital** environment (the computer) to study.
If I am studying in a **digital** (computer) environment, such as BlackBoard, the Internet, or reading text online, I can create a positive study environment.	Strong...fairly confident...weak Student a: fairly confident Student b: weak Student c: fairly confident	What do I do? (circle one or add your own): I make sure that there are few distractions I make sure that I have equipment at hand I plan time to study effectively I use my time effectively to study My own comments: Student a: I make sure I have equipment at hand. "Facebook is a huge distraction!" Student b: I make sure that there are few distractions—"put phone, tv, anything else off!" Student c: I make sure that there are few distractions. (No personal comment provided)
If I am studying in a **digital** (computer) environment, and I need to locate a resource, I can use the on-line library catalog at my school to locate what I need.	Strong...fairly confident...weak Student a: weak Student b: weak Student c: strong	What do I do? Explain how you make sure you are successful. Student a: Not my usual way because it is too confusing and time consuming. Try to use the research bar to make it easier. Student b: Don't know much about a computer or how to do this. Student c: (No personal comment provided)
If I am studying in a **digital** (computer) environment, I can change how fast I read when I want to find **only one piece of information.**	Strong...fairly confident...weak Student a: strong Student b: weak Student c: weak	What do I do? Explain how you make sure you are successful. Student a: "Control F, find it and quickly read it over." Student b: "I don't know how." Student c: (No personal comment provided)
Print environments	How **competent do you feel** when you use this skill in a **print** environment (paper) to study.	**Study Behavior/Tactic** Please describe what you would do for each skill when working in a **print** environment (paper) to study.
When I study in a **print** environment, I can to create a positive environment for study	Strong...fairly confident...weak Student a: strong Student b: strong Student c: fairly confident	What do I do? (circle one or add your own): I make sure that there are few distractions I make sure that I have equipment at hand I plan time to study effectively I use my time effectively to study Student a: I use my time effectively to study * Student b: I make sure that there are few distractions * Student c: (She made no selection from the list or any personal comment.) *No personal comment provided

(continued)

ACTIVITY 9.1 (*Continued*)

When I study in a **print** environment, I can find reference materials.	Strong…fairly confident…weak Student a: strong Student b: fairly confident Student c: fairly confident	What do I do? Explain how you make sure you are successful. Student a: "Books and libraries have more relevance info and reference materials." Student b: "Its at your hands—find it much more easier" Student c: (She made no personal comment.)
When I study in a **print** environment, I can change how fast I read when I want to find **only one piece of information.**	Strong…fairly confident…weak Student a: weak Student b: fairly confident Student c: fairly confident	What do I do? Explain how you make sure you are successful. Student a: "Time consuming. Can't always find one thing easy." Student b: "Somewhat. When I know were the part is around." Student c: (She made no personal comment.)

Developed by J. S. Richardson, J. Rhodes, and V. Robnolt (2004); updated by J. S. Richardson (2010). Used by permission

Teachers can help students to avoid internal distractors by suggesting these questions:

- Do I have a realistic study plan and enough time to study?
- Am I bringing unresolved issues to the study that might interfere with my concentration?

Teachers can help students to avoid physical distractors with these key questions:

- Have I had enough to eat to give me energy to study but not to weigh me down?
- Have I slept enough to be refreshed for study?

To see a fuller version of the Richardson Study Skills Survey, please visit the Education CourseMate website at **www.cengagebrain.com.**

Time management can also contribute to successful study conditions. **Time management** is effectively using one's time through prioritizing, planning, and adhering to a schedule (Francis-Smythe & Robertson, 1999; Nist-Olejjnik & Holschuh, 2009). Although research about time management is sparse (Trueman & Hartley, 1996), positive time management has been associated with higher achievement levels in students (Britton & Tesser, 1991; Suraya et al, 2007) and with improved self-evaluations of academic performance (Davidowitz & Schreiber, 2008; Macan et al, 1990). An effective technique for teaching time management is having students monitor themselves with self-evaluation logs. An activity that can be modified for different grade levels is "How I Spend My Time." Activity 9.2 shows excerpts from this activity with eleventh grade students (Richardson, 1997). First students estimate how they think they spend their time. The teacher keeps these estimates. Next students record how they use their time for a given period. For first or second graders, one day is enough—from waking up until bedtime. Recording can be completed with teacher supervision during the school day. Next, students examine their records and compare the activities in which they spent their time with their estimates of how they thought they would spend it. Results are often revealing and help

For upper elementary and middle school students, a week is an appropriate block of time. Students should keep records outside school hours, but the teacher might provide some class time for catching up. For high school and beyond, the block of time should be at least one week, with recording of all hours—even sleep—done outside class.

ACTIVITY 9.2 Time Management Example: How I Use My Time

Eleventh graders made a record of how they used their time for one week. Then they answered the following questions:

- How much time did I spend on study and recreation?
- How much more study time should I have in my schedule?
- Where can I find the study time?

The students wrote study goals such as: "I will study 10 more minutes each evening for English class." They all wrote rewards that they might receive if they achieved a goal, such as: "Because I studied wisely, I will probably get a better grade." A classmate had to sign the contract; a parent's signature was optional. Students were to consistently practice achieving their goals for one month. Here are some responses they recorded in their journals:

What was your time management objective?

K: I wanted to spend more of my time studying—more quality time, that is—and thus achieve a better understanding of the material.

J: I decided to increase preparation—for instance, for tests, quizzes, and essays.

E: My goal was to spend time studying and preparing for class.

Did you achieve this goal? Why or why not?

K: I was successful because I studied the material more extensively instead of just reading over it.

J: I did not achieve my goal because of my lack of will and lack of time for preparation.

E: Sort of. I did spend some more time but not enough.

What did you discover about managing your time for study in English?

K: I need to spend more time preparing for class instead of talking to friends on the phone. Also, I need to understand the material more fully.

J: I found out that I spend most of my time working. I spent at least 7 hours a day on school days and 16–19 hours on weekends working. The rest of my time went to being at school and some time—very little—sleeping.

E: I found that my priorities were not entirely in order. I previously would watch TV, eat dinner, and lie around before doing my homework. I now do my homework as soon as I get home, shower, and eat dinner, and then I take my leisure time. I sometimes study just before going to sleep as well.

Was this assignment helpful? Why or why not?

K: The assignment was helpful to me because the chart helped me to budget my time more wisely.

J: The assignment was helpful because it made me realize what I was doing and should be doing. I should spend more time on schoolwork, but at this time it is not possible.

E: This assignment was helpful because it allowed me to get somewhat of a schedule together in order to get things done. I seem to work much more efficiently now, and my grades have improved.

students see where they can make changes. Teachers who have conducted this study report that the assignment does not take much class time, and it leads to an increase in student responsibility.

For many students, changing the study environment at home might be difficult. Some children in inner cities have witnessed murders, dodged bullets, and gone to bed hungry on numerous occasions. Experimenting with study environments at home will not work under such conditions. However, arranging for the school or community to provide a study environment in another location might help—in the school after hours or in a local community center or place of worship, for example.

Helping students find the best behaviors for homework is part of study preparation. Homework also provides practice for study, so it can be thought of as spanning the PAR stages. Corno (in Bemnenutty, 2009) points out that homework has a significant impact on achievement only if the tasks are relevant and help students spend time practicing classroom topics. Homework can be a good motivator for learning and developing time management skills. Sadly, students often encounter homework that is too difficult or boring and not of any inherent interest to them. Elementary students seem to be more autonomous and interested in homework than middle school students. Katz, Kaplan, & Gueta (2010) found that underachieving middle school students wish their teachers would support them more, although they do not communicate this to the teachers. Teachers might be able to determine the level of commitment to homework by asking students to experiment: Do homework or study in their usual way for a specific period of time (dependent on the age of the students) and then in the teacher's way (using behaviors the teacher has suggested) for the same amount of time. While studying, students can note how much they accomplish. Usually, they discover by experimenting that at least some of the teacher's tips about a study environment really do help them study.

Because students study independently in the home, teachers may also want to assess what parents do to help their children study and compare the perceptions of parents and students about the study environment. Activity 9.3 provides example questions to ask kindergartners and first graders, but adaptations can be made for any grade level. Teachers who have compared parents' with students' responses have discovered a difference in perception between the two groups. Discussing such findings early in the school year with both students and parents can help establish positive study environments from the beginning of the school year.

When teachers can post a website that provides updated homework information, students or their parents can print the contents so that parents or tutors can help students with the assignments. Also, teachers can insert reminders onto Web calendars.

Teachers can challenge students to think about how they approach homework; are they similar to Maria in this chapter's opening scenario? Do they concentrate and finish tasks in a reasonable amount of time?

Gifted students usually complete tasks in school more quickly than others because they have strong cognitive skills; homework is an excellent opportunity for teachers to assign differentiated tasks that will challenge gifted students, such as projects, independent writing, and reports (Bembenutty, 2009).

Zits © Zits Partnership, King Features Syndicate.

ACTIVITY 9.3 Study Skills for Kindergarten and First Grade Students (sample questions)

SURVEY OF PARENTS

Please circle YES or NO for each statement.

YES	NO	My child has a special place to study. If so, where? ____________
YES	NO	My child watches television while completing homework.
YES	NO	I sometimes help my child with homework.

SURVEY OF STUDENTS

Circle the true sentences as you read them.
I have a special place to do my homework.
No one helps me with my homework.
I watch TV when I do my homework.

Preparation Strategies and Activities

The following strategies and activities are grounded in the preparation stage of study, but they can also be considered part of the assistance stage of study, depending on the circumstances.

Listening

The listening activities can be adapted for a computer environment as well. One could do *PowerPoint* presentations with the voice feature. Technology lets teachers use voice, either synchronously or asynchronously, in online teaching. Students can practice using listening skills in an online class that uses synchronous chats or voice with discussion threads.

This type of activity provides a means of study in a social context, which learners often find productive.

Listening is the foundation for all other study skills, and it can enhance learning in any classroom. Listening is a prerequisite for taking good notes from an oral presentation. In conjunction with teaching keywords and previewing, training in listening has been found to increase oral reading proficiency among low-achieving students (O'Donnell, Weber, & McLaughlin, 2003; Skinner, Cooper, & Cole, 1997). A classic activity is the directed listening technique (Gold, 1981) for motivating and guiding students to improve listening. Before the lesson, teachers ask students to listen for certain information in the presentation or in the oral reading. In this pre-presentation phase, students brainstorm areas of interest and questions to be answered. Teachers then deliver a presentation or read portions of a chapter from a textbook. In this way, students are trained to know what they must listen for and what they are expected to learn from listening.

As a variation, teachers can construct listening guides to point to parts of a lecture or oral reading that need to be emphasized. In this way, students are taught to listen more carefully for details and key points. Through such an active listening strategy, even primary students can be trained to be better listeners. Activity 9.4 presents such a listening guide for a high school class on the topic of genetics.

The authors of this book have designed "first step to note taking," which also promotes listening and purpose setting. One result of this technique is that it offers practice in group note-taking strategies. Thus, the "first step to note taking" is a listening

ACTIVITY 9.4 Listening Activity: Genetics

Listening Purpose: Listen for the three aspects of genetics.

Directions: As you listen to the lecture, circle all of the topics you hear discussed. Feel free to make notes about the subjects as you hear about them in the lecture.

Heredity	**DNA**	**Mutation**
Traits	Replication	Inbreeding
Genes	Proteins	Hybridization
Dominant	Chromosomes	Producing insulin
Recessive		Cloning
Genotype		
Homozygous		
Heterozygous		
Phenotype		

Note: After listening to the lecture, get together with several classmates and see if they circled the same words you did. Discuss the meanings of the words.

activity, a note-taking activity, and a cooperative grouping activity. The activity consists of five steps:

How could you modify Activity 9.4 for teacher-based instruction or for an independent student learning experience, depending on the ages of students?

1. The teacher or a student defines a listening purpose. If, for instance, the student is completing an activity for independent practice, he or she could listen to the evening news for the purpose of identifying the major stories and two significant details of each story.
2. Listening with a purpose commences. Students might listen to the teacher read, listen to the news on television, or listen to a tape recording, for example. No writing is allowed during the listening.
3. The students react by listing what they heard in relationship to the stated purpose. Responses are now recorded, but no modifications are made.
4. Students listen to the material again with their lists in sight. No writing is allowed during the listening. (If students listened to the evening news, then either a recording of that news broadcast or a later news show would provide an appropriate second listening.)
5. Individually or in small groups, students edit their lists—adding, deleting, or modifying information—and organize them into information following a logical pattern. They have now generated notes for study.

Students can organize the listening and note taking in two-column form, as shown in Activity 9.14.

Podcasts are popular with Internet users (see Chapter 10 for more information) because audio files allow students to practice listening skills; they can listen as many times as they need to before they are ready to proceed to the lesson. A device such as an iPod is portable and compact and is already used for numerous listening purposes. So listening to a podcast that lets students practice listening tactics for study is a great integration of modern technology with the academic world. Podcasts allow time shifting in learning—study at all times rather than only at the "homework" hour. Podcasts offer a new way to

Please visit the Education CourseMate website at **www.cengagebrain.com** to locate links for some podcasts, such as Grammar Girl for English or the Pew Internet and American Life Project site for many other subjects.

deliver learning opportunities. Costa (2006) recommends that teachers post assignments in podcasts for students to listen to. After students become familiar with podcasts, they can create their own podcasts about a topic and post them for other class members to download and listen to, thus using listening to learn more about any topic. Activity 9.5 shows an assignment for listening to a podcast about microbes for middle school students.

Locating and Selecting Information

Until students understand the importance of locating information, they can't select what they should study. Knowing how information is organized can help students find information in the table of contents, index, preface, headings, footnotes, glossaries, or appendix. At the beginning of a school year, content teachers might use a textbook inventory as a class activity to help them learn about their students' proficiency in using textbooks. This activity assesses students' knowledge of the parts of a book and can be effective at any grade level from kindergarten through twelfth grade. Activity 9.6 contains some questions from a parts-of-the-book search developed to help students in a computer class become familiar with a word processing manual.

ACTIVITY 9.5 Listening to a Podcast (Middle School Biology Class)

1. Go to the NASA web site and select a 4-minute podcast about "Mars Rovers."
2. Play the podcast (either listen online or download it and listen on your podcasting device).
3. Listen as many times as you need to.
4. Write a statement that tells what this podcast is about, such as: "Mars rovers can tell us about discoveries on Mars."
5. What does the rover Spirit sound like? How was the sound made audible to human ears? (Engineers sped things up about a thousand times so we could hear it.)
6. What is a motion sensor? (A motion sensor, called an accelerometer, measures bumps and vibrations in the rocky Martian road as the rovers roam around.)
7. Why did you like listening to this podcast?

ACTIVITY 9.6 Parts-of-the-Book Search for Computer Intermediate Manual

BECOMING FAMILIAR AND COMFORTABLE WITH THE MANUAL

1. Where do you find the explanation of the special symbols used in the table of contents? How many special symbols are used in the manual?

   Page ____________

   Number of special symbols ____________

2. How many appendices does the manual contain? ____________ Which appendix explains the features bars? ____________

3. Where will you find an explanation of how to insert columns or rows into a table? Page ____________

4. Where did you look to find the page number to answer the previous question—the table of contents or the index? ____________
   Would either one work?
   Yes ____________ No ____________

5. Where do you find an explanation of the keyboard shortcuts? Page ____________

Developed by Mary L. Seward.

The danger of locating incorrect information increases exponentially with the plethora of resources on the Web, many of which are unreliable. Students must have guidance to know where to locate material for study in both paper and computer resources. Although past generations of learners remember the card catalog as their major resource for locating information, we seldom find any card catalogs today except in antique stores or in use as CD and DVD storage containers. Libraries now use online catalogs. Searching the Internet is a study skill for locating and selecting information, but the information age requires people to use new techniques. Teachers must know and share how to search and what the results of a search really mean in relation to the importance of citations and best choices. To successfully search the Internet, Henry (2006) proposes a searching system she calls SEARCH. The acronym stands for:

Chapter 10 presents an activity to demonstrate the importance of critical thinking by tracking authors of websites (the Martin Luther King activity).

Set a purpose for searching.

Employ effective search strategies.

Analyze search engine results.

Read critically and synthesize information.

Cite your sources.

How successful was your search?

Students use search engines such as Google or Yahoo! often, but these engines can be dubious sources of help. Even though the information the site presents may seem credible, it can be biased. A good alternative is **Google Scholar**, which searches scholarly journals and selected areas of the Web. Teachers can also create Google custom search engines. *Kidsclick* is a website for preschool through high school readers that is reviewed by children's librarians and searchable by grade level. For a simple way to begin a search on *Kidsclick*, see Activity 9.7.

Teachers can help themselves and their students gather information by subscribing to online services for deciphering and organizing incoming information, such as the free service InfoBeat or a pay service such as Lexis-Nexis Universe. InfoBeat offers a way to keep abreast of news without spending money, but caution must be observed because it can quickly overwhelm an email account with voluminous information.

Because ***Wikipedia***—the online encyclopedia that users can not only read but also add to—contains so many topics, *Wikipedia* URLs usually come up in the first five hits of a search! However, this does not mean Wikipedia contains the best information; it means that the word being searched for has been cited the most times on Wikipedia during the search. Most searchers use only a single-word search rather than being more specific; this brings up more resources, some of which are not as credible as those a more specific search would have found. Domain names can reveal sources and credibility. For instance, "edu" means an education-sponsored site, and "org" means a general site that may not be as scholarly.

Teachers should explain how *Wikipedia* works as soon as they realize that students are using it. Many children as early as first grade refer to Wikipedia.

Students often fall into the trap of relying on one resource that is simple to locate. This used to be the set of encyclopedias in the library or on the home bookshelf. Now it is *Wikipedia*. The "wiki" in *Wikipedia* is derived from Hawaiian for "quick." The information in *Wikipedia* may have been written by a scholar in the field—or by

ACTIVITY 9.7 *Kidsclick* and Art

Go to the *Kidsclick* website. Select "The Arts," then "Comic Books."

Now you see some websites where you can learn about different comics. How many sites are listed?

Try it out!

anyone else who wished to generate the entry. In fact, any reader can edit an entry. Although this may seem disturbing, *Wikipedia* is actually a democratic resource: Everyone can have a voice in the creation of an entry. It is a wonderful example of how technology has influenced the way we learn. *Wikipedia* can be an excellent tool for helping students learn about locating and selecting information. By looking at the history of an entry, one can determine how many times the entry has been altered and how it was altered (authors can also ask to be notified when an entry has been altered so they can delete unwanted changes to their entries). This search for changes can help students understand that "facts" can be altered or biased and that one must exercise care in accepting resources. Many educators use *Wikipedia* to demonstrate lively interaction and critical thinking at work. However, the democratic nature of *Wikipedia* is also a reason for consulting more than one resource to form one's knowledge of a subject.

Activity 9.8 encourages thoughtful reading to locate resources by starting with Wikipedia. This activity is for middle school mathematics, but it can be adapted for other grade levels and content areas as well.

For links to Web-based bookmarking, please visit the Education CourseMate website at **www.cengagebrain.com**.

Teachers of elementary-aged students may find that using Web-based bookmarks will help provide younger readers with the structure and content they need to locate information (Forbes, 2004). Web-based bookmarking lets a teacher create a list of bookmarks and store them on the Web. In this way, all sites will be previewed, so Internet safety is improved. Because so many people mistype addresses, there is no telling where a child might land on the Internet without such guidance. But with this kind of bookmarking, time on task is increased, frustration is reduced, and learning is facilitated. Services that help teachers create Web-based bookmarks make this process easy.

The old-fashioned way of saving an interesting newspaper article would have been to clip and laminate it. The new way is to locate it on the website for the newspaper and save the URL for easy access anytime. Students can be guided to scan a newspaper and locate an article they would like to save and then find it on the

ACTIVITY 9.8 Using *Wikipedia*

1. Go to *Wikipedia* and type in the word *circumference.*
2. Select the definition and go to it. What is the definition? (The circumference is the distance around a closed curve. Circumference is a kind of perimeter.)
3. Look for the tabs above the entry. Select the tab for "Discussion." What is the discussion about? What would you add to this discussion?
4. Select the tab for "Edit" the page. What is the message you receive; could this clue help you determine how credible this definition is? (The message is that anyone can edit the page, but the IP address of the editor will be shown to anyone who looks at the history of the article. By registering, one can hide the IP address from viewers—but not from the Wikipedia editor!)
5. Select the tab for "View History." What do you find here? (Many links to the edits that have been done for this definition.)
6. What have you learned about how to search for a definition? When would you use Wikipedia? When should you use more than one resource to find an answer?

newspaper's website. In the same way, students can practice locating a phone number in a paper directory and then locating it online. Teachers can enhance geography lessons by using websites with atlases, maps, and helping students "visit" remote lands via Google earth.

Previewing

Previewing may be the most important reading and study skill. Chapter 4 describes the directed reading–thinking activity (DR-TA) (Stauffer, 1969a), the classic technique that teachers can use to model correct reading processes. Fundamental to the DR-TA is previewing, a process that is important for clarifying thinking before students read textbook material. Previewing has been found to help improve comprehension and achievement in students—especially low-achieving students (O'Donnell et al, 2003; Skinner et al, 1997). Previewing activates schema, establishes purposes for reading, engages students in asking questions about text headings, and directs them to important information (Lee, 2010).

In the previewing stage, students begin selecting strategies appropriate to the depth and duration of study needed. To select proper strategies—whether note taking, underlining, or rapid reading—students must spend time clarifying their thinking about the topic. They need to ask themselves questions such as:

How interested am I in this section?

How deeply do I need to think and concentrate to learn this material?

How fast can I read this material?

What do I still need to learn about this topic?

Teachers might take students step-by-step through the previewing phase and then ask them to record how they will study the material. Will taking notes work best? Is underlining acceptable?

Just as one might size up a piece of clothing and decide whether it is too big and needs altering, a reader can size up a reading selection and realize that "mental alterations" are needed. Such assessment is the purpose of previewing. A preview builds anticipation for material that is not familiar to the reader. Previewing to clarify thinking reduces uncertainty about reading assignments, allowing students to gain confidence, read in a more relaxed manner, gain interest, and improve their attitude toward the material. In addition, previewing strategies enable students to decide how much of the material is in their own background of experience. As a result of the previewing process, learners are clearer about what they know and what they need to know. In effect, they set a purpose for reading before they begin.

When previewing a technical chapter or a report, students should examine and think about the following:

Title and subtitle: Readers need to discover the overall topic of the chapter or article. Students too often skip this step, but it is where a reader should figure out what she or he knows about the chapter as a whole and what this chapter has to do with the chapter that came before it. What will this chapter be about?

Author's name: We might ask whether the author is a recognized authority. What is the author's point of view?

Copyright: This is examined to see whether the material is current.

Introduction: Here we find out what the author intends to talk about. The main points that will be covered are usually discussed here, and sometimes objectives and goals are stated in the body of the paragraph(s) or highlighted in marginal notes.

Headings and subheadings: Identification of the topics of the sections that follow (forming these headings into questions gives purpose to the reading).

Graphs, charts, maps, tables, pictures: These are aids in understanding specific aspects of the chapter. It is important to study these because a reader can gain vital information here that is nowhere else in the reading.

Summary: Here we get an overview of what has been discussed in the reading. This is important to study in the preview to get a sense of where the entire reading is going.

Questions: Readers should examine questions as a way to review important topics covered in the chapter.

In practicing with a group or a class, the teacher assists students in deciding what they already know about the material and what they need to learn, turning what is not known into questions. Students reading fiction need to preview the title, illustrations, and introduction in order to make hypotheses about the outcome of the story. This preview heightens suspense and helps maintain interest. Most important, predicting story structure gives the reader a purpose for reading: to find out whether the predictions are correct.

Students can learn to preview by using a preview guide. Activity 9.9 is an example of such a guide, which teachers can adapt to different grade levels.

For fiction and expository material alike, it is important to preview. Doing so forces readers to do the sophisticated kind of thinking required for drawing inferences and developing interpretations. Thus students think critically about a chapter or story before reading, operating at higher levels of cognition. Interest in the reading material is usually greatly heightened by using this strategy. Unfortunately, students generally do not preview material on their own unless teachers model and provide practice in this important skill, starting at the kindergarten level and consistently practicing throughout the grades. Teachers should make students aware that they are teaching content while using the strategy of previewing. By starting with the table of contents of a textbook, teachers help students discover the theme or structure of the course material. The teacher might ask, for example, why the author chose to organize the table of contents in a particular manner.

Garber-Miller (2006) encourages the use of "playful textbook previews" that show students how to preview while having fun with textbook sales pitches and commercials, textbook picture walks, sticky note votes, and other lively ways to learn how to preview. Partner previews (Ogle & Correa-Kovtun, 2010) encourage students to help each other preview—by identifying text features such as highlighted vocabulary and subheadings—and support each other in this process.

THIEVES (Manz, 2002) is a text previewing strategy that uses a memorable acronym. It can be used for most textbooks to encourage students from grade 5 through college level to sneak in and "take as much as they can" (p. 434). Manz suggests questions for use with each component to help students make connections and predictions based on prior knowledge and clues found within the text (Activity 9.10).

ACTIVITY 9.9 Book + Chapter Preview Guide

Overview of Your Textbook

Question	Answer	Give page # where you found answer. Provide evidence or response for answer.
How many chapters are in this text?		
When was this book published? Is it up to date?		
Who do the authors thank in their acknowledgments and dedication?		
Which seems to be the easiest chapter? Why?		
Which seems to be the hardest chapter? Why?		
Look at the chapter you think is hardest and answer these questions: • How does it help you with vocabulary or technical terms? • Does it have goals or objectives or topic lists at the start? • Does it have an introduction? • Does it have margin notes? • Does it have feature boxes? • Does it have visuals? Where are they? What are they? • Does it have a summary? • Does it have questions at the end?		
Did you find any other features in the textbook chapter that could help you read critically and well?		
Select three subheadings within the chapter and write three questions to answer as you read.		
Select three words from the chapter and write possible meanings.		

Previewing can be done for any type of reading material, including a website. Activities 9.8 and 9.9 are examples of Web previews. Digital jumpstarts (Rance-Roney, 2010) can be especially helpful to struggling readers and ELL students. Teachers construct previews of the material by selecting important vocabulary and ideas from text and creating a compelling video as in a movie or *PowerPoint*. Students then can view this video as many times as necessary to develop strong preparation for the

ACTIVITY 9.10 THIEVES

T—Title

- What is the title?
- What do I already know about this topic?
- What does it have to do with the preceding chapter?
- Does it express a point of view?
- What do I think we will be reading about?

H—Headings

- What does this heading let me know I will be reading about?
- What is the topic of the paragraph beneath it?
- How can I turn this heading into a question that is likely to be answered in the actual content?

I—Introduction

- Is there an opening, perhaps italicized?
- Does the first paragraph introduce the chapter?
- What does the introduction let me know I will be reading about?
- Do I know anything about this already?

E—Every first sentence in a paragraph

- What do I think this chapter is going to be about based on the first sentence in each paragraph?

V—Visuals and vocabulary

- Are any photographs, drawings, maps, charts, or graphs included?
- What can I learn from them?
- How do the captions help me better understand the meaning?
- Is there a list of key vocabulary terms and definitions?
- Are there important words in boldface type throughout the chapter?
- Do I know what the boldfaced words mean?
- Can I tell the meaning of the boldfaced words from the sentences in which they are embedded?

E—End-of-chapter questions

- What do the questions ask?
- What information do they mark as important?
- What information do I learn from the questions?
- Let me keep in mind the end-of-chapter questions so that I may annotate my text where pertinent information is located.

S—Summary

- What do I understand and recall about the topics covered in the summary?

Adapted from Manz, 2002, A strategy for previewing textbooks: Teaching readers to become THIEVES. *The Reading Teacher, 55,* pp. 434–435.

material. A digital jumpstart preview is an especially helpful way for teachers to manage a heterogeneous class in which ELL students and struggling readers may need more preview time than others.

Following Directions

Following directions is an important study skill. After finding information for a study project, following the directions to complete the study is the next effective step. Of course, the teacher must model by providing clear directions. Students need to rely, however, on their own deep thinking about directions to make any study successful. Hubbard (2003) encourages study that includes deep strategies rather than surface ones. Consider Activity 9.8, in which students follow the directions to discover the actions behind each tab for a Wikipedia entry. The surface might be just following the directions provided in the activity, but the deep strategy involved in following the directions requires students to think about why following these directions helps them use Wikipedia now and in the future. The goal is to for students to learn how to create their own directions that can guide study successfully.

Assistance Strategies and Activities

The following strategies and activities are grounded in the assistance stage of study. But they can also be considered part of the reflection and even preparation stages of study, depending on the circumstances.

Interpreting Graphic Aids

Certainly, visual aids help one preview and prepare to study, but interpretation of those visual aids also leads a student into the assistance phase of study. Visual representations in text are graphic clues and aids designed to help readers comprehend a content textbook. Teachers say that they use visual aids 84 percent of the time when they study (Barry, 2002). It is important for teachers to teach visual representations, yet students often skip over them because they incorrectly assume that such visuals represent a "free page!" As presented in Principle 3 in Chapter 1, visual literacy is the first and most pervasive literacy (Avgerinou & Ericson; 2002; Stokes, 2002). "The fact that we are visual beings before we become linguistic beings is sometimes forgotten" (Chauvin, 2003), p. 126).

Many standardized tests assess graph, chart, and map reading, so when teachers stress reading visuals, they are directly helping students perform better on standardized tests.

Richardson and Forget (1995) illustrated the calculations that Mark Twain used in "proving" that the Mississippi River would be shortened to a length of a mile and three-quarters 742 years from the time he wrote *Life on the Mississippi.* By reading a graph that applies the formula for slope, readers can see how slope always reflects the relationship of one variable to another. Both Twain's humorous essay and the formula for slope are more interesting and clear when the graphic information is available.

Please visit the Education CourseMate website at **www.cengagebrain.com** to read the lesson Richardson and Forget (1995) propose to accompany "Cut-offs and Stephen" by Mark Twain.

If students are having particular difficulty reading visual information, teachers can use a modified textbook treasure hunt to teach the skill. Activity 9.11 shows how

ACTIVITY 9.11 An Internet Treasure Hunt for Manatee

Surf's up! Grab your brain and head for the further reaches of cyberspace. There is a lot to learn in this information age. Using the Web allows you to discover tons more than you may have ever known possible. Below is a list of questions about manatees. Surf the Internet links on this page to find answers to the questions. Don't forget to go after the monster learning wave—the big question. Have fun and avoid any watery danger.

QUESTIONS

1. Give a detailed description of a manatee (e.g., color, size, weight)
2. Is the manatee population increasing or decreasing? Why?
3. Where does the West Indian manatee live? Does it migrate?
4. Do manatees have teeth?
5. Are manatees omnivores, carnivores, or herbivores? Give an example of their diet.

THE INTERNET RESOURCES

Your teacher will show you how to do an Internet search on manatees and provide you with some Web links.

THE BIG QUESTION

How can we protect this endangered species?

Activity developed by Jody Irvin.

this procedure can help upper elementary and middle school students read about manatees while searching Internet sites on the subject. Lorenzo and Dziuban (2006) caution that digital images are easily altered to display falsehoods as fact. Cropping, enhancing, and altering images can seem to depict what is not really true. To prepare visually literate students who can look critically, Metors and Woosley (2006) suggest encouraging questions such as these: Does this image tell the truth? How representative is this image? What is the source of this image? Are we responding to emotional issues or content? Also, as a form of study, students can draw their own pictures or make their own graphic outlines that depict the meaning of their reading (Haynes, 2006).

Pictures make a textbook interesting and vital. Teachers should frequently ask students to "read" pictures in an effort to clarify their thinking about concepts in a chapter. Cartoons are specialized pictures that carry significant messages or propaganda. What meaning does the comic depicted earlier in this chapter convey to you? Irony? Pessimism? Is it a satire on studying? Activity 9.12 illustrates how a digital camera, household objects, and a computer can help children in primary grades use visuals to organize and retain information about math shapes and simple geometry.

Organizing Information

When students organize for study, they are using study systems that help them direct study and use the most effective ways to remember. Behaviors can include adoption of a particular study system and use of mnemonics. Simpson and Nist (2000) indicate that organizing strategies may be the most researched study strategies. Organizational strategies should focus on cognitive and metacognitive processing. Which of the following methods of organizing should a student select? This is personal preference based on individual study behaviors and needs, but it should be a deliberate and thoughtful choice.

UNDERLINING

Underlining is a popular study behavior for many older students (Cubuku, 2007). It helps students organize their thinking enough to begin an outline. Underlining, then, can be a first step to outlining. To begin, teachers should create "pre-underlining" reading assignments in handout materials that coincide with the textbook. Teachers need to show students how to underline relevant material. Students must learn how to underline superordinate statements rather than subordinate details. When they learn this, students will underline relatively little, but what they underline will be important. With underlining, less is more, and any time saved by underlining can be put to good use in further study of the material. Teachers also need to teach students when to use techniques other than underlining. Even when underlining in textbooks is not possible, pre-underlining is an important study strategy for students to learn.

OUTLINING

The software programs *Inspiration* and *Kidspiration* allow easy transformation of a map into an outline.

Outlining is the traditional method of organization. There is no agreement, however, on the best way to teach this skill. Outlining is an organizational tool that lets readers create for themselves a condensed presentation of a chapter that they want to understand. Outlining is particularly useful because it actively involves the reader and because the notes are not made in the textbook, which the student might not own. A well-made outline shows the relationships of main ideas, supporting details, definitions of terms, and other data to the overall topic. Mapping can be an early, unstructured form of

ACTIVITY 9.12 Using Visuals to Organize and Retain Information (First Grade Mathematics)

Have the students take pictures of household objects that show circles, rectangles, or triangles. Use digital cameras so the pictures can be downloaded to a computer. The teacher will download the pictures to the class computer and resize them to be small. Next the teacher will create a chart like the one in this activity. Then the students will open the file and select, copy, and paste pictures into the correct columns.

Circles	Rectangles	Triangles
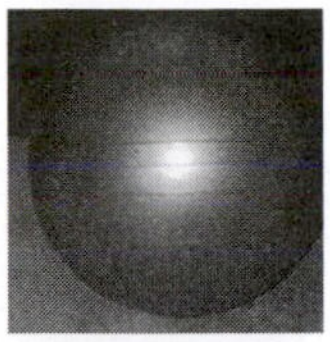 Pilates ball  Rug with a circle  Bread	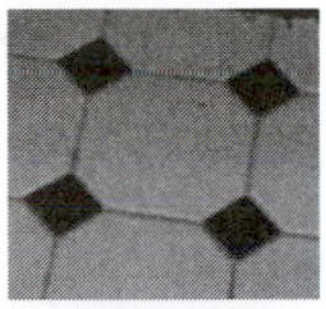 Bathroom tile  Refrigerator door + pictures	 Shoji screen  Plate

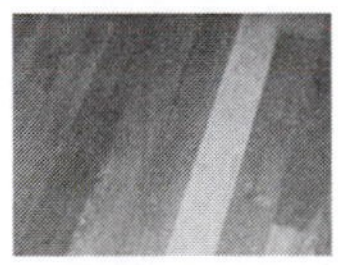

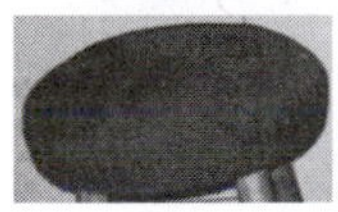

Courtesy of the author.

outlining. Outlines are valuable because they help students understand difficult texts, take notes, write papers, and give oral presentations.

Teachers can help students learn to outline by preparing outlines with key words missing. By replacing missing words or terms, even very young children can begin to learn outlining. Teachers can give students partially finished outlines to complete as they read a chapter. These can even be done on sentence strips or index cards as a

ACTIVITY 9.13 Social Studies Outline for Primary School

MAPS

- **I.** Maps and globes
  - **A.** Legend
    - **1.** Key
    - **2.** Compass rose
    - **3.** Flat
- **II.** Globes
  - **A.** Sphere

manipulative format to help young learners learn to order and organize. Outlining is a form of writing to learn. Activity 9.13 is an example from first grade social studies. The following are some features of successful outlines:

1. The material itself determines the number of headings and subheadings.
2. Each heading expresses one main idea.
3. Ideas are parallel. All ideas recorded with Roman numerals are equally important.
4. All subheadings relate to the major heading above them.
5. In a formal outline, each category has more than one heading. (Notice that the teacher does not follow stringent rules about needing a B to go with A under Globes. Outlining for purposes of personal study need not follow rules for publication.)
6. Each new level of heading is indented under the heading above it.
7. The first letter of the first word in each heading and subheading is capitalized.

An outline enables students to organize material in a hierarchical fashion. A graphic organizer also works well.

NOTE TAKING

Note taking is informal writing to be used specifically for learning and study. How can teachers encourage a focus on writing for study purposes?

Note taking, a common study skill, produces good study results. Teachers rate this skill highly for their own study, indicating that they use it during 74 percent of their study time (Barry, 2002). Research about student time spent constructing study notes showed that their notes were more effective than those provided by instructors (Crooks & Katayama, 2002). However, when middle school students were asked about their note-taking strategies, they reported understanding how to take notes but admitted that they did not practice note taking (Brown, 2005).

To help students become effective note takers:

1. Be certain students realize that the use of notes to store information is more important than the act of taking the notes.
2. Provide questions, verbal cues, and nonverbal cues while talking.
3. Project material (on the board or on the website) to be sure students will record it.

4. If talking, compensate for possible overload of information by pausing at intervals.
5. Tell students what type of test to expect so they will take the notes appropriate for that test.
6. Use handouts, especially with poor note takers, and be sure the handout provides space for student notes.

Teachers may find it helpful to give the following advice to students who will be writing notes on paper in class (Morgan et al, 1986):

Use a spiral notebook (contrary to what is often advocated). A two- or three-ring notebook with loose-leaf paper enables students to rearrange their notes and permits easy addition or subtraction of material.

Write on every other line whenever possible or when it seems logical to separate topics. This leaves room to correct errors or add points missed and makes for easier reading at review time. Content words should be recorded in full and spellings checked with a dictionary or a textbook.

Develop a shorthand system. Students should reduce frequently used words to a symbol, such as "w" for *with*. Other commonly used words should be abbreviated, such as "ex" for "example" and "intro" for "introduction."

Underline, star, or record the teacher's pet theories or concepts. Listen for key statements such as: "I particularly agree with this theory" or "You'll probably be seeing this information again." If the teacher writes terminology or math examples on the board, always record them word for word (or figure by figure). If the teacher lists or numbers remarks, such as: "Three significant facts stand out," number them in the notes.

Do not try to outline notes according to a Roman numeral system with main ideas and supporting details. No one thinks in Roman numerals. Important points may be missed if students worry too much about how they are taking the notes.

Do not disregard related discussions. Teachers frequently use questions as a teaching tool. Students should write down questions that are introduced for discussion purposes.

Ask questions when there is misunderstanding. If one student is confused by a concept or misses a point in a lecture, usually other students have missed it, too. Students should not be embarrassed to ask for clarification.

Review often and with different purposes in mind. When rereading textbook assignments, students should coordinate the chapter with their notes. Make certain main ideas from the chapter are included directly in the lecture notes. For some students, rewriting notes is a helpful memory device.

Students have an added incentive to take thorough notes when they will be able to use them during an open-note test. Phillips (2006) found that college students who were able to rely on notes during tests improved their grades on average by 4.47 points; weaker students improved even more, on average 23.79 points. Of course, students should not be able to find the answers to test questions directly in their notes; they should be required to use inference and application skills when forming their answers.

Note taking is usually somewhat messy. The process the mind uses while thinking and taking notes often resembles a webbing or mapping approach.

The role of summarizing is often embedded in note-taking activities and as part of outlining techniques. When one edits and reorganizes notes, summarizing and annotating them, deep thinking happens (Hubbard & Simpson, 2003).

The Cornell system (Pauk, 1997), is a practical approach to taking notes. Pauk's **two-column note-taking system,** or "5 R's," can be used with younger children. To use this system, students divide the page in the following way: The main heading, the notes students make for themselves, and keywords all go in the narrow left column. The students also may use the left side as their side to record topics, questions, key phrases, definitions, comments, and summaries of information from the lecturer or textbook. The wider right column is for information from the lecturer or the textbook.

The key to two-column note taking is space. Just as adolescents and even younger students need physical space, they also need intellectual space—that is, space to think. The left column provides space for students to question themselves about the big picture of the lesson and the major concepts to be learned. The system is based on the sound theory of categorization, with subordinate concepts consolidated and organized under superordinate headings. Students practice these steps (the 5 Rs):

Step 1: They *record* the information as they hear it or read it.

Step 2: They *reduce* the information by putting their abbreviated notes about it in the narrow left column.

Step 3: They *recite* the information by using their reduction notes with the recorded notes in the wider right column.

Steps 4 and 5: They *reflect on* and *review* the notes over time.

Two-column notes are often referred to by other names, such as double-entry notes or split-column notes.

The two-column system allows students great flexibility. Pairs of students can "call" the notes to each other, covering either column and asking each other what belongs in that column. Teachers can ask students to form groups at the beginning or end of class and brainstorm two or three recently covered major topics (to go in the left column). In this manner, note taking is made an integral part of all the class operations.

Activity 9.14 is an example of a two-column note-taking handout from an early elementary classroom. The teacher is discussing a story and asks students to complete the notes. Teachers can prepare such handouts and give them to students before a lecture or before students read a chapter so they can practice the two-column method. This handout uses a modified cloze procedure: Students fill in gaps as they listen

ACTIVITY 9.14 Early Elementary Two-Column Note Taking

Directions: Listen very closely as I discuss *Franklin Fibs* by Paulette Bourgeois. Fill in the missing words to complete these notes.

Main characters	Franklin, Bear, ____________, Beaver, Mom, and ____________.
Setting	Franklin's ____________.
Beginning	Bear, Hawk, and ____________ were ____________ about things they could ____________.
Middle	Franklin said he could eat ____________ flies in the ____________ of an eye.
End	Franklin did ____________ seventy-six flies, but he ate them in a ____________.
Problem	Franklin told a ____________.
Solution	Franklin told the ____________ and did something that he could brag about.

Developed by Stephanie Hunter.

ACTIVITY 9.15 Two-Column Notes: How to Boost Your Brainpower

Your brain	It is always ______________________.
	It is selective in the way it gets ______________________.
Two amino acids are important for brain function	Tyrosine is an amino acid that helps with ______________________, long-term ______________________, and feelings of being ______________________
	From tyrosine, the brain makes ______________________ and ______________________.
	Tryptophan slows ______________________ time and makes you ______________________.
	Scientists believe you can control the activity ______________________ of the mind with the foods you eat.
If you want to get tyrosine to the brain,	eat ______________________.
If you want to get tryptophan to the brain,	eat ______________________.
Protein lunches	enhance ______________________ performance.
Carbohydrates	can ______________________ thought processes of the brain. are good for helping you ______________________ can ______________________ people with seasonal affective disorder (SAD).
Fats	are important for thinking. Brain ______________________ are made largely of fat. Take ______________________ hours for fats to reach the brain and affect thinking. Saturated fats ______________________ ability to think. Polyunsaturated fats ______________________ ability to think.

to the lecture or read the chapter. In subsequent lessons, more and more notes are omitted (more blanks are used) until eventually students complete all the note taking themselves.

Activity 9.15 is an example of a two-column note-taking handout from a high school health class about brain functioning's relations to diet and eating habits.

COOPERATIVE GROUPING FOR ASSISTED STUDY

Opitz (1992) describes a strategy for emphasizing cooperative study called the cooperative reading activity (CRA). It entails locating a reading selection and breaking it into sections, having students individually read and identify important points of particular sections, and forming groups in which students who have read the same section come to an agreement on essential points. Each group, in turn, is expected to share its findings with the rest of the class. Opitz suggests the following steps for constructing a CRA:

1. Choose selections that are already divided by headings into sections roughly equal in length. A selection with an interesting introduction is helpful.
2. Count the sections of the selection and determine the number of students in each group. Generally, groups of four are ideal.
3. Prepare copies of the text you will use for the CRA. Prepare enough copies so that each group member will have a cut-and-paste version of the proper section and a card with the section heading, which will be used to assign students to groups.
4. Design a form that readers can use to record important information learned from the reading.

Knox and Anderson-Inmann (2001) studied whether note taking with laptops could enrich and support Hispanic students in mainstreamed history classrooms. When an experienced note taker took and shared notes with these students, the students understood more, received study notes, and learned how to take notes. Teachers who cannot rely on an experienced note taker might provide written notes that students can access easily via computer.

Research suggests that students first read their sections and record important concepts. When they finish reading and completing their record sheets, they get into groups, and each person reads the important points out loud from his or her record sheet. After everyone has a turn, each group lists important details using a marker on a piece of chart paper. If details are similar, students still write them on the group list. Then other details that students believe are important are added. Students must come to an agreement before a detail goes on the list. After all details are listed, students go over them again to make sure everything is clear and to locate and eliminate duplication before sharing them with the class. When the work is completed, each group in turn reads its list to the class. Students are held accountable for all of the information presented. Lists are then posted for all to see. In this manner, the groups construct cooperatively the essential meanings of the text.

Another excellent activity for teaching cooperative study can be termed *cooperative graphing*. Students work in groups to rate the importance of concepts in a chapter; the ratings appear in the form of a graph. In the second part of the lesson, students work cooperatively to justify their ratings.

Teachers can construct study guides for a cooperative graphing exercise such as the one shown in Activity 9.16. This is an excellent activity for teaching both cooperative study and graphing; it can be modified for English classes or whenever story structure is being studied by changing the "most important–least important" continuum of the graph to "most liked–least liked" to let students rate how they empathized with characters in the story.

Reflection Study Techniques

Students need to know that reflection is difficult but always rewarding. Sternberg (1991) noted that learning and retention are enhanced when students study in fairly equal distributions over time rather than in what he calls **massed study**—last-minute cramming before a test or exam. Others refer to this condition of studying over time rather than all at once as "**the spacing effect**" (Bahrick & Phelps, 1987; McIntyre & Munson, 2008; Willingham, 2002). McIntyre and Munson found by researching grades of marketing students that students practice either a methodical or a cramming approach. In the short run, on multiple-choice tests in particular, crammers did as well on tests as methodical studiers. But overall, crammers had lower grades in a course and retained much less information needed for next level courses. McIntyre and Munson recommend that instructors foster a deep level of learning versus a surface-level approach, asking fewer short-term recall type questions and requiring more critical thinking. Reflection study strategies should depend on deep thinking. Brinthaupt and Shin (2001) considered why college students crammed or procrastinated; they found differences between crammers, who waited until cramming seemed like the good and appropriate way to study, and procrastinators, who waited because other activities were more compelling than studying. Cramming is a learned behavior—if students receive a good grade by cramming, then they will continue to cram. It is probably human nature to put off studying until the last minute. Also, students form this habit because teachers do not explain to them how distributed study enhances retention.

Findings from McIntyre and Munson are very consistent with the recent literature cited in this chapter's "A Brief History of Study Skills." How one *views* study is as important as how one *does* study. When students cram, they have only a short-term solution because the brain can't hold more than about seven items in short-term memory at one time (Lehrer, 2009).

The famous Ebbinghaus (1908) findings a century ago support the need for spaced learning. Ebbinghaus postulated that tremendous amounts of information are

ACTIVITY 9.16 Cooperative Graphing Guide: Accounting (High School)

COST FACTORS THAT INFLUENCE DECISIONS

Part I. Make a graph of how important the following concepts are from most important to least important. An example is done for you.

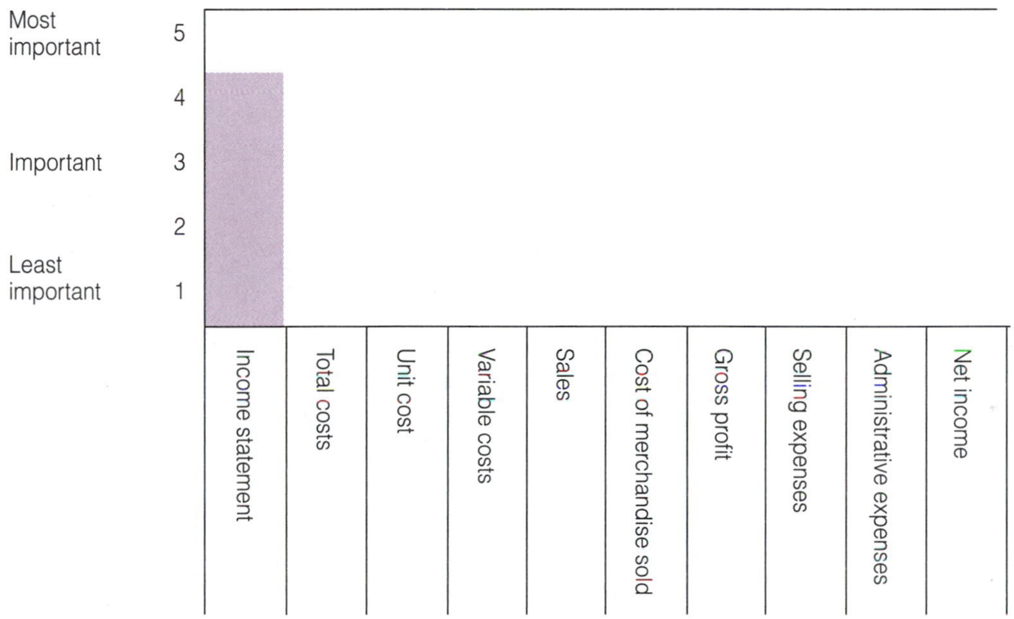

Part II. Work in small groups to justify your answers.

I gave ______ income statement ______ an importance of 5 (most important) because ______ it is the basis for other concepts. basic ______

I gave ______ an importance of ______ because

______

I gave ______ an importance of ______ because

______

I gave ______ an importance of ______ because

______

I gave ______ an importance of ______ because

______

I gave ______ an importance of ______ because

______

I gave ______ an importance of ______ because

______

I gave ______ an importance of ______ because

______

I gave ______ an importance of ______ because

______

I gave ______ an importance of ______ because

______

A study by Krulwich and Abumrad called "Willpower and the Slacker Brain" illustrates how distractions interfere with memorizing more than two digits. Please visit the Education CourseMate website at **www.cengagebrain.com** for a link to the National Public Radio podcast or search the title. Teachers could try a similar experiment with students.

Many studies have shown the benefit of mnemonics for students with learning disabilities (Thomas, Scruggs, & Mastropiere, 2003; Wolgemut, Cobb, & Alwell, 2008). Mnemonics instruction has also been effective for learning new words in foreign language classes (Cohen, 1987; Fritz, Morris, Acton, Voelkel, & Etkind, 2006) and as aids in learning Chinese and Japanese characters (Lu, Webb, Krus, & Fox, 1999).

Students who use a Mac can program notes to pop up on the computer screen to remind them to study at a certain time for a predefined period. In *Microsoft Word*, a feature is also available to remind a reader to review a certain document at a prescribed time: Select Help/Tools/Flag for follow-up.

These learning aids are especially helpful for struggling readers and diverse learners, not only to help memory but also to improve self-concept and self-image. With practice, there seems to be almost no limit to improvement in long-term memory skill.

forgotten in a short period—up to 60 or 70 percent in only a few days. He also made these important discoveries:

1. Fatigue affects one's ability to remember.
2. Earlier study and learning tend to get buried by later learning.
3. Learned images may decay over time and end up changed in meaning from what was originally perceived.
4. Memories erode, and most information (an estimated 90 percent) is forgotten over prolonged periods.

In short, forgetting is natural, and remembering is difficult. The following strategies and activities are grounded in the reflection stage of study, but they can also be considered as part of the assistance stage of study, depending on the circumstances.

Mnemonics

Fortunately, the use of **mnemonics**—devices and techniques to improve memory—can help students retain information over time. Students instructed in mnemonic strategies demonstrate improved memory when using mnemonics (Fontana, Scruggs, & Mastropiere, 2007; Irish, 2002). Mnemonics seem to work by taking the load off working memory, or short-term memory, by retrieving learning directly from long-term memory. This is completed through a single association with an existing memory code (Levin, 1993; Wang & Thomas, 1995). Not all research on the efficacy of using mnemonics has been positive, however. Hwang and Levin (2002) have found that students have trouble applying complex mnemonic strategies independently. They state that teachers must provide auxiliary support for a mnemonic strategy to be effective. Acronyms, acrostics, method of loci, and other mnemonic learning techniques are also useful study techniques, especially because forgetting is natural (remember the Ebbinghaus studies!). Mnemonics can start with children in the primary grades, providing them with a skill useful for the rest of their lives.

The most time-honored of mnemonics, an **acronym**, is a word or phrase composed entirely of letters that are cues to words we want to remember. For example, PAR is an acronym for the instructional framework that we explain in this book. Suppose a student needs to review musculoskeletal systems for a biology test and needs to remember the six boundaries of the axilla: apex, base, anterior wall, posterior wall, medial wall, and lateral wall. The initial letters are A, B, A, P, M, and L. He or she could rearrange these letters to form the acronym AB PALM. Or consider the following list of the six branches of the axillary artery: supreme thoraces, thoracromial, lateral thoracic, anterior humeral circumflex, posterior humeral circumflex, and subscapular. A student could use the initial letters S, T, L, A, P, and S to form the name of a fictitious patron saint of arteries: ST. LAPS. Here are a few examples of more common acronyms:

HOMES—The Great Lakes: Huron, Ontario, Michigan, Erie, Superior

ROY G BIV—The colors of the spectrum: red, orange, yellow, green, blue, indigo, violet

FACE—The notes represented by the spaces of the treble clef

An acrostic is a phrase or sentence in which the first letter of each word is a cue. For example, another way of remembering the boundaries of the axilla—initial letters A, B, A, P, M, and L—would be to create a phrase such as "above, below, and pretty much lost." Acrostics can be made for any area. To improve reading study skills, ask students to RELAX by doing the following:

Rest plenty

Exude enthusiasm

Laugh often

Anticipate what's coming

Xcite yourself about the reading.

To remember the nautical terms *bow, stern, cabin,* and *traveler,* a student could use this acrostic: "Big storms cause trouble."

Students can be taught to associate new words with outrageous images. For instance, to memorize the words in the left column, students can imagine the images in the right column:

WORD	IMAGE
Sweater	Sweater
Horse	A gigantic horse wearing a gigantic sweater
Surf	A huge horse surfing
Iron gate	A surfer on a high surfboard flying over an iron gate
Typewriter	Tiny iron gates spewing out of a typewriter

In this manner, one word leads to the next to make a long list of associations.

Another means of associational learning is a *peg-word system,* which associates a target word with a numbered peg word. Listed here are 10 peg words that name familiar places found at many schools:

1. Computer center
2. Guidance office
3. Cafeteria
4. Auditorium
5. Library
6. Classroom
7. Hallway
8. Principal's office
9. Nurse's clinic
10. Gymnasium

The words to be memorized—*plot, setting,* and *character*—are linked to the peg words through outrageous images. The words *plot, setting,* and *character* can be associated with one of the numbered peg words:

1. A criminal with a *plot* to blow up the *library*
2. Someone *setting* a tray down in the *cafeteria*
3. A drunken *character* sitting in the back of a *classroom* filled with disbelieving students

The peg words do not have to name places. They can be words that sound similar to or rhyme with the words to be learned. An example is the peg word *commotion* for *commodities* in an economics class or *this criminal* for *discrimination.*

Teachers might stimulate interest in using loci by suggesting that students create an electronic drawing of a loci; this also imprints the information effectively and makes it more permanent.

The method of loci (Latin for "places") improves students' ability to remember lists of unrelated objects. It also can be a sequencing task, enabling a student to remember items in a definite order. In this ancient method used by Roman orators, a person mentally walks through a house that has familiar surroundings. Cicero and other classical orators constructed "memory places" and linked sections of their speeches to architectural features. Then as orators spoke, they imagined the place where they had established the links. This process enabled them to remember huge amounts of information. By choosing 15 to 20 distinct loci—for example, the stove, the closet, the desk, or the kitchen sink—students can mentally place objects to be learned in strategic spots throughout a designated space, such as one's home. In a variation, students memorize words by placing them in strategic places in each of the six or seven rooms where they have classes each day or in various places around the school.

Students learn most effectively by using their own, rather than teacher-created, mnemonics. Go MAD (use the mnemonic-a-day technique): Students work in groups to make a mnemonic for 10 days and keep MAD logs to help them remember the accumulated mnemonics. Teachers can reward individuals or groups who create a MAD example for the most consecutive days.

Chunking large amounts of information into categories can help students remember information more readily and retrieve it faster. Activity 9.17 demonstrates how chunking might work in a middle school English class. Chunking information through categorization exercises (which can be used to review for tests) is an excellent way to help struggling readers understand text material. Chunking capitalizes on connecting prior knowledge to new knowledge, thus enhancing learning. After students gain experience with chunking, they can construct hierarchies of mnemonics to learn 15 to 50 items. Activity 9.18 provides an example from a class in home economics, where the total number of items to be learned is 14.

Middle and high school students are able to create complex hierarchies of mnemonics because they may have considerable experience using simple acronyms and acrostics. Such complex chunking is more difficult to construct, but it allows students considerable leeway in memorizing prodigious amounts of information.

ACTIVITY 9.17 Chunking (Middle School English Class)

To learn these 15 items in a language arts unit on puppetry, one might categorize:

Director	Equipment	Props	Create	Purchase
Lights	Story development	Size of puppets	Analysis	Microphone
Copyright	Budget	Sound	Stories	Spotlight

Chunking information into categories makes learning the 15 items much easier:

Scripts	**Technical**
Director	Lights
Copyright	Equipment
Story development	Props
Budget	Size of puppets
Create	Sound
Analysis	Microphone
Stories	Spotlight
Purchase	

ACTIVITY 9.18 Chunking through Categorization (Middle School)

BEING A SUCCESSFUL BABYSITTER

Acronym = JOG

(J)ob acceptance		(O)n the job		(G)etting started	
P	Parents' permission	N	No TV	P	Prompt for arrival
A	Address of family	A	Attend to task	A	Address where couple will be
D	Day and time	M	Make file of family after job	R	Reaching doctors, firefighters, etc.
M	Meet children	E	Exploring in house is out		
O	Offer fee	S	Stay awake		
M	Meet family				

SONGS AND RAPS

Another memory device that students enjoy is putting words and concepts into song. Bintz (2010) advocates "singing across the curriculum" as an instructional strategy. With song, students feel free to express themselves and use informal discourse and repetition. When they put information in a song, they have to think carefully about which ideas to use and how to express them. Learning is a natural result. A good example of this strategy is the rap song created by two economists to explain and contrast the work of John Maynard Keynes, father of the modern-day stimulus package, and Friedrich von Hayek, the intellectual founder of what is known today as the Austrian School of Economics. The resulting rap song is a delightful teaching tool and could lead to student raps on any number of content topics.

Please visit the Education CourseMate website at **www.cengagebrain.com** to find a link to a Fresh Air podcast in which the rap song authors Papola and Roberts are interviewed and sing their song.

TECH APP

Songs and Raps

Create a Mnemonic Device through Songs and Raps.

To Record And Publish: Use *PowerPoint* with Voice, Mac *Garage Band*, or *Audacity*

Time Commitment: Minimal! Can be used over & over!

To Listen: Smartphone; computer

Why Do It? Timeshifting → Anytime learning

Values: Using writing to learn; using familiar and contemporary discourse; repeated listening, learning with familiar devices; creativity

Reading Flexibly

Flexible reading is at the heart of good study habits because students have to realize when to vary their speed according to the purpose for their reading and study. Flexible reading should not be confused with *fluency*, a term that refers mainly to "reading accurately, effortlessly and quickly, with appropriate expression and meaning" (Griffith & Rasinski, 2004, p. 126). Although similar to flexibility, fluency has taken on importance in theories about learning to read and beginning reading instruction. Discussions about fluency usually include word recognition to the point of automaticity—that is, recognizing words so quickly that comprehension takes over the act of decoding. The goal is more about comprehension and expressive reading than comprehension and study. Behaviors for developing fluency have included slowing reading rates, pausing while reading to make sure meaning is obtained, looking back, skipping and going back to difficult text, rereading, and reading aloud (Walczyk & Griffith-Ross, 2007). Activities suggested for gaining fluency include readers' theater, timed readings, and partner readings (Griffith & Rasinski, 2004). Reading flexibly also includes fluency considerations, but here the focus is on reading to learn and varying one's rate for the intended study purpose.

Rate of Reading

Rate of reading is a controversial topic. One of Edmund Burke Huey's tenets in *The Psychology and Pedagogy of Reading* (1908/1968) was that children should be taught, from their first reading experiences, to read as fast as the reading material and their purpose would allow. Huey recommended speed drills to help students get information efficiently and effectively. After Huey, William S. Gray, in a 1925 review of the literature on speed of reading, endorsed rapid reading by concluding that such training could increase speed without concurrently reducing comprehension. Unfortunately, many professionals have forgotten Huey's and Gray's work, and rapid reading has fallen into disfavor as a bona fide reading skill that students should acquire. In their review of the history of study skills since the early 1900s, Richardson, Robnolt, and Rhodes (2010) noted a contradiction: They located no articles about rate of reading and speed reading; however, study skills assessments still contain a high incidence of questions about rate of reading.

Probably no area of reading is as controversial as speed reading (Carver, 1992). One problem with speed reading may be the misconception that one can read faster simply by accelerating a physical activity. The physical process of reading requires the eyes to move in a jerky pattern over the page (**saccadic eye movements**), stopping to let the brain take in information (fixations), and then moving again. These saccadic eye movements and eye fixations constitute the physical process of reading. A reader can get a headache by trying to accelerate this physical process too much. What is important is how readers manipulate the information taken in with each fixation, or as Frank Smith (1988) puts it, what goes on "between the eye and the brain" rather than from the page to the eye. This mental process requires chunking information into the largest meaningful units that one can assimilate and relating those chunks to an existing schema (chunking). We do not recommend speed reading per se, but we do advocate rapid reading or speeding up one's reading along with an emphasis on encouraging the reader to decide what he or she needs and wants to know. Although early work on this topic stressed drills and techniques to learn to read faster, it neglected emphasizing the reader's purpose. In fact, when students read extensively and with purpose, they learn to vary their rate of reading (Bell, 2001). The strategy of SCAN and RUN (Salembier, 1999) reinforces this viewpoint. Students were taught a system of study that encourages not only **s**urveying, **c**apturing visuals, **a**ttacking boldface words, and **n**oting chapter questions but also

reading and adjusting speed along with **u**sing word attack and **n**oticing when to check and reread.

CHALLENGE BOX

JaNette, the At-Risk Student

JaNette faces many challenges daily outside of school. Her grades are up and down; although she is very capable, she often does not try—and does not see much value in doing so. However, she wants to graduate from high school and maybe go to community college so she can get a good job.

SITUATION: Study at home is difficult because of many distractions; in school, she would rather hang out than study. Her grades would improve if she did study.

How can JaNette decide the most effective ways to study?

JaNette first needs to think about her study habits, attitudes, and behaviors. She would benefit from honestly assessing her study habits and skills. She should recognize that she already has good time management skills—she has been using these to survive in her home environment for all of her life. By tracking how she spends her time, she could identify small blocks of time for study, maybe at school or the library.

How can teachers help JaNette see the value of study?

She would probably appreciate "Willpower and the Slacker Brain" because this amusing podcast would allow her to practice listening skills while learning why cramming is ineffective. JaNette could discover the power of previewing through a DR-TA. Then she could practice reading a long chapter in manageable units using skimming and scanning to locate answers to questions. She would probably like to be a "THIEF"!

What would be the best ways for JaNette to approach study?

She could be part of a group jigsaw (see Chapter 6) or a Grouping Activity (such as CRA) for Study where each member reads a portion of text and shares the information as others practice note taking. The group might also use cooperative graphing to graph and show the merits of different study systems to an entire class. She can study with a group, maybe using Twitter to share information. She could use her smartphone to record and retrieve notes, and she could compose raps to help her retain information. JaNette may feel empowered to realize that she can regulate her own study; decisions about study are hers to make. However, the teacher should ensure that topics are presented in an interesting manner and homework is compelling and relevant.

Skimming and Scanning

Skimming is rapid glancing through text to find out generally what the reading is about (Jacobson, 1998). **Scanning** is rapid reading for some specific purpose—for instance, to find out where, when, or how something happened. When scanning, the reader may read an introduction or opening paragraph, a summary, and the first and last sentences of each paragraph, note material in bold print, and glance at visual aids. Unlike skimming, in which the reader glances at the whole text to get its general sense, scanning is searching for specific information, such as a word or detail. Students need much practice (beginning at an early age) to acquire these skills. Scanning can be practiced as students demonstrate how they confirmed predictions or found a word's meaning by returning to that place in the material.

Refer to Chapters 1 and 2 to refresh your memory on JaNette, the at-risk student.

Retention and Systems of Study

After a reader has skimmed and scanned, he or she should read the material carefully. Then he or she should reread the material to check difficult text; answer preview questions; and decide on ways to record, such as underlining, highlighting, or outlining. This process of rereading in different ways increases comprehension (Hedin & Conderman, 2010) and enables retention in a natural manner. Retention is necessary to enhance readers' purposes, values, and beliefs; it is not a mere accumulation of information to be regurgitated. Information is more easily retained when one wants to know it and add it to one's store of knowledge. Therefore, presenting subject matter through stimulating strategies and activities and following a framework of instruction such as PAR can facilitate student motivation to learn and study.

One of the first ways teachers can model how to study, starting in early elementary grades, is the DR-TA technique (Stauffer, 1969b). See also the explanation in Chapter 4 on DR-TA.

Providing students with several study systems and letting them select the ones that work best for them enables students to practice good study techniques and retain information. Systems of study are sometimes referred to as the best systems of learning that no one ever uses! By the fourth or fifth grade, students can be introduced to a **study system**—a systematic set of steps for studying text. Study systems are useful when students can decide for themselves which aspects of a system work best for them. If students are required to use a study system imposed by their teachers, they are unable to make an autonomous choice about something very personal—the way they prefer to study. Three study systems are presented in Table 9.1 as a comparison chart.

Teachers should model study systems in the classroom as many as 10 times before students understand and begin to use them. When study systems combine previewing, reading, reflection, and writing, students begin to perform better on tests (Alber, Nelson, & Brennan, 2002).

TABLE 9.1 Study Systems Comparison Chart

Study System	**SQ3R (Robinson, 1961)**	**PQR2ST+ (Morgan, Forget, & Antinarella, 1996)**	**SQRC (Sakta, 1999)**
Acronym stands for	**Survey** → major ideas **Question** → turn headings into questions **Read** → to answer questions **Recite** → look away from material and repeat it in your own words **Review** → study and recall	**Preview** → parts of material, such as headings, visuals, bold print **Question** → write your questions based on the preview **Read** → think in personal terms about what is read **Remember** → close text and write notes in right column **Scan** → rapidly check notes against text **Touch-Up** → add any important details **+(Plus)** → fold two-column notes and study (do within 24 hours)	**State** → activation of "before" phase **Question** → activation of "before" phase **Read** → activation of "during" phase **Conclude** → activation of "after" phase **Three phases:** **Before** = teacher introduces topic and presents a position; students write for or against the position and why and then rewrite the position as a question **During** = students find information to support or reject position and take notes **After** = class separates into two groups that argue the positions
Notations @ Study System	Five steps Lipson and Wixson (2003) call this the grandfather of study strategies; Bhat, Rapport, and Griffin (2000) generally speak of the benefits and positive results of using this approach	Seven steps Two-column notes by reader Requires cross-checking and personalization Very thorough	Four steps + three phases Works best for expository reading material Beneficial because, similar to SQ3R and PQR2 ST+, it combines key elements of cognitive learning theory and constructivist approaches

ONE-MINUTE SUMMARY

In this chapter, we have considered what it means to study, especially the need for deep thinking and student decision making. Students who most need study skills and ways they can learn them are featured. Specific definitions of study skills are provided. Through a brief history of study skills, we show that study must be self-regulated. Metacognition has changed the view of study skills from that of a set of specific steps one must follow to a set of behaviors from which a student selects based on the environment and purposes for study.

Teachers need to demonstrate study skills in a systematic manner and to emphasize them in early elementary grades through high school. As students mature and progress through school, the skills that are taught may include assessing one's study skills, creating good conditions for study, listening, locating and selecting information, following directions, interpreting visual information, organizing material for study, retaining information, being flexible, and using study systems. Teachers must convince students that study works best when spaced out rather than crammed in.

Table 9.2 summarizes the strategies discussed in this chapter and indicates where each can be introduced in the school continuum.

TABLE 9.2 Study Strategies

	K	1	2	3	4	5	6	7	8	9	10	11	12
Assessing one's study skills	■	■	■	■	■	■	■	■	■	■	■	■	■
Creating good conditions for study	■	■	■	■	■	■	■	■	■	■	■	■	■
Listening	■	■	■	■	■	■	■	■	■	■	■	■	■
Locating and selecting information			■	■	■	■	■	■	■	■	■	■	■
Following directions	■	■	■	■	■	■	■	■	■	■	■	■	■
Interpreting visual information	■	■	■	■	■	■	■	■	■	■	■	■	■
Organizing material for study				■	■	■	■	■	■	■	■	■	■
Retaining information				■	■	■	■	■	■	■	■	■	■
Being flexible					■	■	■	■	■	■	■	■	■
Using study systems					■	■	■	■	■	■	■	■	■

END-OF-CHAPTER ACTIVITIES

Assisting Comprehension

1. What new study skills have you learned about in this chapter? Can you add to your repertoire of study skills training methods after reading and studying this chapter?
2. Select a study system that you like to use. Apply it to a content material of your choice in both a paper-based and a computer-based environment. Do you use the system in the same way for both environments? If not, how does your application differ? What is most helpful to your study and retention within this study system?

Reflecting on Your Reading

1. Your content organization (e.g., National Council of Teachers of Mathethmatics, National Council of Teachers of English, National Council for the Social Studies, National Science Teachers Association, International Reading Association) has most likely developed a set of standards that identify the performance criteria relevant to classroom teachers. Standards usually delineate elements of foundational knowledge that a classroom teacher should possess. Locate and become familiar with what the organization recommends. For instance, teachers should model study strategies "enthusiastically" in the classroom and should help students use a variety of strategies independently, such as:
   - Preview selections by using pictures, diagrams, titles, and headings.
   - Set purposes for reading.
   - Read fiction and nonfiction fluently and accurately.
   - Develop notes that include important concepts, summaries, and identification of information sources.
   - Organize information on charts, maps, and graphs.
   - Skim manuals or informational sources to locate information.
2. Think about the study skills described in this chapter. How can you model these strategies in your classes?

CHAPTER 10

Technology in Today's Content Classrooms

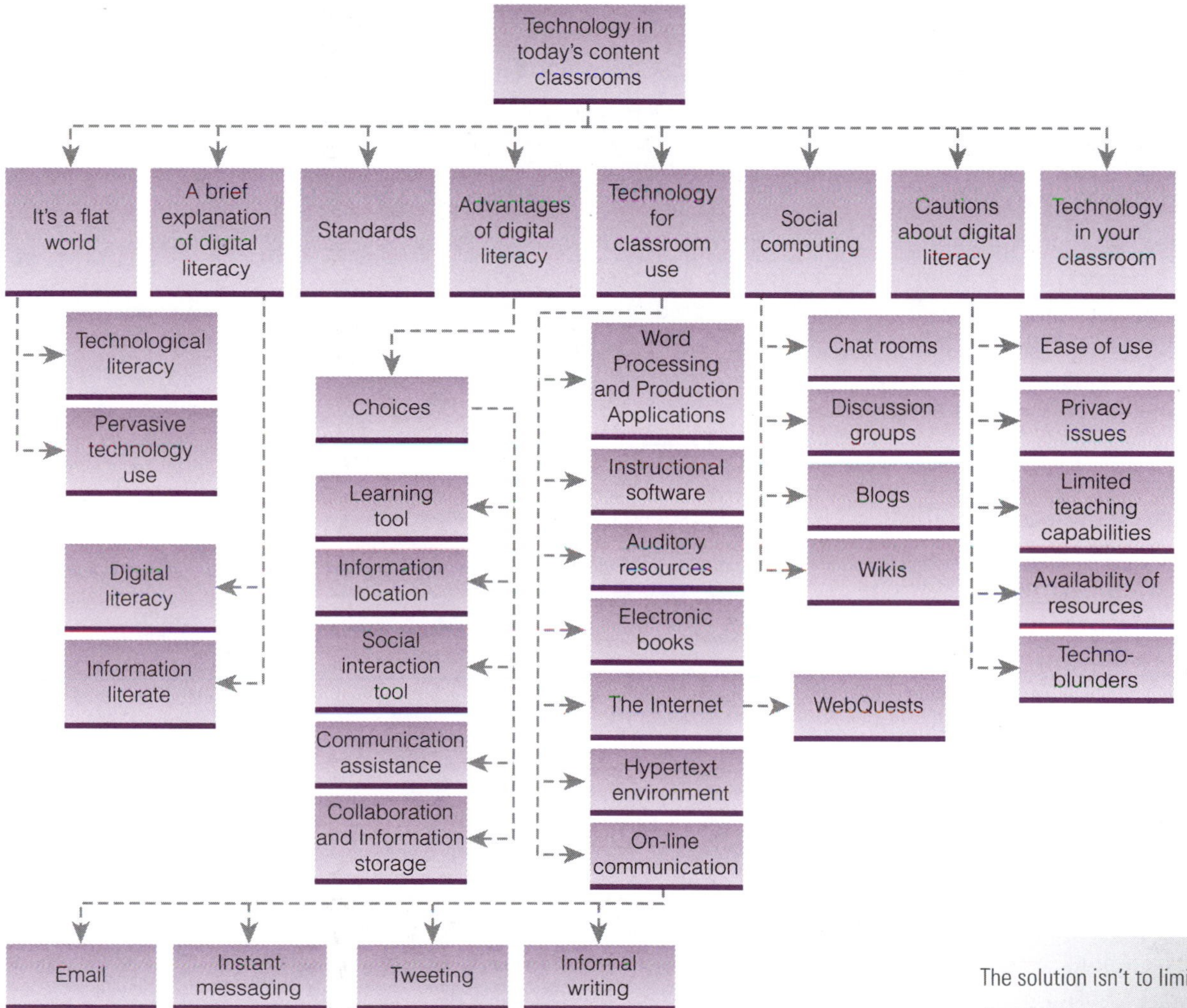

The solution isn't to limit the information you receive. Ultimately, you want to have the entire world's knowledge connected directly to your mind.

SERGEY BRIN, CO-FOUNDER GOOGLE, INC.

VOICES FROM THE CLASSROOM

Travis Macy, a ninth and tenth grade English and literature educator and winner of the International Reading Association's Grand Prize Award for Technology in Reading in 2010, is an expert at using cutting-edge, interactive technology in his classes for students with learning differences (O'Toole, 2010). Students in Macy's classes use technology to carry out projects, use a dynamic weblog, and use interactive "clicker" technology to demonstrate understanding of content. SMART Board technology is implemented fully in Denver Academy, Macy's school, to support a multimedia curriculum aimed at improving student achievement and engagement. Macy believes using multifaceted technology instructional activities with multiple entry points is beneficial for his students, allowing them to fully demonstrate what they know about course content.

Why might Mr. Macy believe that providing multiple entry points for instruction is beneficial to students in his classroom? Are there any technologies mentioned in the vignette above with which you are unfamiliar? How might a teacher learn more about the technologies that are best for meeting the needs of individual learners? As you work through the remainder of this chapter, consider which technologies might be best for adoption in your content area.

PREPARING TO READ

Following is a list of terms used in this chapter. Some may be familiar to you in a general context, but in this chapter, they may be used in unfamiliar ways. Decide how to arrange the terms in four or five groupings and give each group an appropriate label. There may be several ways to group the terms. Be ready to explain your selections. Next, using a piece of paper, make a three-column organizer with the following headings: "Terms," "Predicted Definitions," and "Chapter Definitions." Select the 10 terms with which you are least familiar, record them in your organizer, and predict how they might be defined for this chapter. As you read the chapter, verify your predictions and rewrite your definitions as necessary.

_______ technological literacy
_______ ICTs
_______ digital literacy
_______ information literate
_______ social media
_______ NETS
_______ Net savvy
_______ SNS
_______ VoIP
_______ wikis
_______ blogs
_______ podcast
_______ WebQuest
_______ hypertext
_______ synchronous
_______ avatars
_______ instant messages
_______ asynchronous
_______ e-book
_______ MUVE games
_______ e-reader
_______ listserv
_______ digital divide
_______ tweeting
_______ cloud computing

OBJECTIVES

As you read this chapter, focus your attention on the following objectives.

1. Understand the need for integrating technology and critical literacy instruction in content area classrooms.
2. Examine and consider the applicability of several activities that integrate digital literacy with content area information in kindergarten through twelfth grade classrooms.
3. Learn about technology resources used in classrooms.
4. Appreciate the benefits and challenges of using digital communication, including social media, with students.

It's a Flat World

The Voices from the Classroom quote and vignette used to start this chapter suggest that many educational opportunities present themselves because of the availability of information and new technologies in today's Internet-driven society. Sergey Brin and Larry Page, the co-founders of Google, Inc., developed their search engine to "organize the world's information and make it universally accessible and useful" (Google, 2010). Today teachers and students have tremendous access to textual, visual, and auditory information to support content area instruction. The ability to determine relevancy, analyze information critically, and embrace new technologies and tools have become essential expectations for all learners.

As initially noted by Marshall McLuhan (1962), the use of computers has had a societal impact equivalent to the Gutenberg revolution when access to the written word became broadly available. Contemporary students use both digital media and printed text to locate information, purchase goods and services and communicate in and out of the school environment (Rhodes & Robnolt, 2008). Perhaps no one has shown us the impact to the technological changes taking place better than Thomas Friedman, whose best-selling book *The World Is Flat* (2005) had to be updated in 2006 to match the pace of technological innovations. By the time this textbook is published, newer technologies will be available than are presented in this chapter. The printed page has many advantages over the electronic page, but delivery speed is not one of them! The authors will endeavor to update this book's website with current Internet resources and commentary so as to retain the best of both paper and digital text. The aim of this chapter, then, is to introduce some possibilities and help you find ways to engage readers in learning as they use the new technologies of the 21st century. Activity 10.1 provides the reader with a sense of how technology is used in the daily activities of today's "net generation" (Oblinger, 2005).

The word *technology* is derived from the Greek word *techne*, which refers to "the process by which humans modify nature to meet their wants and needs" (Katehi, Pearson, & Feder, 2000, p. 19). **Technological literacy** is "the ability to use, manage, assess, and understand technology" (International Technology Education Association, 2000, p. 9). Technologically literate people are able to understand what technology is and how it is created as well as how technology shapes and is shaped by society. Students require knowledge in using the **information communication technologies (ICTs)** needed for lifelong learning and successful employment in our global, knowledge-based society.

This chapter was significantly revised and updated by Joan A. Rhodes, Ph.D., Associate Professor in the Department of Teaching and learning, School of Education at Virginia Commonwealth University.

Travis Macy's project, *Old tricks, new look: Using technology to reach the zone of proximal development in the millennial literacy classroom*, earned him recognition as a leader in the innovative use of technology in reading education.

View the video to understand how the use of technology as a tool can assist students in critical thinking. Students must make decisions and selections for a PowerPoint presentation to demonstrate their learning.

ACTIVITY 10.1 Technology Use in the Twenty-First Century

After reading the quote below, respond to the questions on your course discussion board or in an email you send to a classmate.

> A junior at the university, Eric wakes up and peers at his PC to see how many instant messages (IMs) arrived while he slept. Several attempts to reach him are visible on the screen, along with various postings to the blog he's been following. After a quick trip to the shower, he pulls up an eclectic mix of news, weather, and sports on the home page he customized using Yahoo. He then logs on to his campus account. A reminder pops up indicating that there will be a quiz in sociology today; another reminder lets him know that a lab report needs to be e-mailed to his chemistry professor by midnight. After a few quick IMs with friends he pulls up a wiki to review progress a teammate has made on a project they're doing for their computer science class. He downloads yesterday's chemistry lecture to his laptop; he'll review it while he sits with a group of students in the student union working on other projects. After classes are over he has to go to the library because he can't find an online resource he needs for a project. He rarely goes to the library to check out books; usually he uses Google or Wikipedia. Late that night as he's working on his term paper, he switches back and forth between the paper and the Internet-based multiplayer game he's trying to win (Oblinger & Oblinger, 2005, p. 2.1).

What does Eric's day indicate about the use of technology in the lives of today's students? What literacy activities are evident in Eric's daily routine? Beginning tomorrow morning, record your use of technology for a 24-hour period. Which technology did you use most frequently? As educators of students in kindergarten through twelfth grades, which technology skills do we need to incorporate in our content area instruction to ensure that students will be successful after high school?

Access the Children's Internet Protection Act at the Education CourseMate website at **www.cengagebrain.com**. How does this act impact your school and public library? What types of instruction are provided in your school district or community related to Internet safety?

American public schools are being encouraged to incorporate instruction in the study of technology through legislation such as the Children's Internet Protection Act and by the inclusion of technology items in the National Assessment of Educational Progress in 2012 (National Center for Technology Education, 2010).

To indicate how pervasive technology has become in our culture, consider a study in which the search engine company Yahoo! participated. Researchers wanted to find out how people would respond to having no Internet access for two weeks. Barnako (2004) reports that the researchers had trouble finding participants—because almost no one was willing to give up Internet access! Of those who did participate, across all age, income, and ethnic groups, the participants recounted feelings of withdrawal, loss, frustration, and discontent. We have indeed become dependent on this global technology (Bean & Readance, 2002; Schaeffer, 2003). Brown (2000) argues that the increasing reliance of students on the Internet for information and social interactions creates an electronic community of practice where all members exchange and share knowledge. Friedman (2006) describes this as a "flattening process" in which creativity, connectivity, communication, work, and play can be instantaneous.

Prensky (2001, 2006) notes that digital natives, who have spent their entire lives in a digital environment, often encounter an education system that does not engage them in learning or ignores the knowledge they are gaining through technology use outside the classroom walls. How might you increase the use of technology used outside school within your classroom?

There continues to be a great need for practical information about integrating technology in kindergarten through twelfth grade instruction (Gambrell, 2005). Although we cannot provide a deep study of instructional technology here, we give a brief background on literacy as it applies to the digital environment, address some advantages and related challenges of using technology, discuss forms of technology that contribute to digital literacy skills, and describe applications for the content classroom.

A Brief Explanation of Digital Literacy

Contemporary students are completing their schooling in the midst of a transition from reliance on paper-based texts to digital text and therefore must have literacy skills appropriate for learning in both environments. In the past, definitions of literacy centered on individual competencies such as a "minimal ability to read and write in a designated language, as well as a mindset or way of thinking about the use of reading and writing in everyday life" (Venezky, 1995, p. 142). However, this type of definition is not sufficient for reading in multimedia, **hypertextual** environments in which students must navigate through text where linear movement is easily interrupted with opportunities for linking to other related items with the click of the mouse.

Defining the **digital literacy** needed for reading in digital environments has been challenging, with many terms proposed by researchers including "multiliteracies," which suggests that meaning making occurs in settings where written text is part of visual, audio, and spatial patterns of meaning (Cope & Kalantzis, 2000), and "new literacies," which focuses on the skills and strategies necessary to work with rapidly changing ICTs (Leu, 2002; Leu, Kinzer, Coiro, & Carrmack, 2004). The challenge in defining literacy has led researchers to focus on the emerging characteristics or skills needed for success in digital environments. Representatives at the 21st Century Literacy Summit (2005) used the following definition of literacy to guide their work:

> 21st century literacy is the set of abilities and skills where aural, visual and digital literacy overlap. These include the ability to understand the power of images and sounds, to recognize and use that power, to manipulate and transform digital media, to distribute them pervasively, and to easily adapt them to new forms (p. 2).

This definition takes into consideration the technological advances that have placed new and varied literacy demands on students while highlighting the difference between digital and technological literacies. The definition of 21st century literacy also accounts for the current blurring of the relationship of author and reader: Readers create multimedia and textual products for mass consumption and collaboratively contribute to group revisions of online written material.

The volume of information available on the Internet and the assertion of business leaders that sharing more information is good (Fletcher, 2010) can result in information overload for today's students. Expectations for readers now include being **information literate** (Henderson & Scheffler 2004)—that is, able to find and use information in any paper or electronic form—and being critically literate (Hall & Piazza, 2008)—able to analyze information to determine multiple meanings or political undertones. Visual literacy, the ability to understand information presented in pictorial or graphic forms, is also essential when working with today's multimedia materials. Visually literate students are able to use and create images with conventional and new media to communicate, make decisions, and learn (North Central Regional Education Laboratory, n.d.). Students are also expected to analyze information for relevance, accuracy, and authenticity and synthesize content from multiple sources (Castek, Coiro, Hartman, Henry, Leu, & Zawilinski, 2007).

Think about the types of literacy described in the text. How do you assist students in becoming information literate? What types of classroom activities would support your students' critical and visual literacy skills?

Although teachers may have had different experiences from their "**Net savvy**" students (Lorenzo & Dziuban, 2006) as they grew up, they cannot afford to maintain an "industrial age mindset" (Frand, 2000). To avoid a clash of cultures between educators with an industrial age mindset and students with an information age mindset, teachers must use and implement technology in their classrooms. Instruction in paper text is not enough; comprehending digital text is now essential for academic success (Castek et al, 2007).

The challenge is to discover how to seamlessly integrate technology to create academically engaging content lessons. Most teachers realize that they need to become digitally literate, and they recognize how difficult this can be. In one study (Watts-Taffe, Gwinn, Johnson, & Horn, 2003), three beginning teachers were followed for one year as they strove to incorporate technology in their classrooms. They found themselves using technology for multiple purposes, such as creating graphic organizers and gathering information with encyclopedias on CDs. The teachers found that they could integrate technology more easily as they practiced and gained confidence with it themselves. Their students became more motivated and engaged in learning as the teachers incorporated technology. By the end of their first year, these teachers had lots of ideas for what to do with technology in their next year of teaching.

Standards

Please visit the Education CourseMate website at **www.cengagebrain.com** to find a link to Project Tomorrow to find out more about its annual national research program.

The use of technology in classrooms has increased exponentially as a visit to the website of the National Center of Educational Statistics shows; the percentage of schools with Internet access increased from 35 percent in 1994 to nearly 100 percent in 2005 (Wells & Lewis, 2006). In 2006, more than one-third of twelfth grade students used the Internet to keep informed of current news and were beginning to use podcasts and blogs as a means of sharing and receiving information (Project Tomorrow, 2006). When not in school, much of adolescents' literacy happens online through participation in **social media** activities such as text messaging, creating webpages, and reading and maintaining personal blogs (Lenhart, Madden, Macgill & Smith, 2007; Williams, 2005).

The increased use of technology has made standards for instructional technology a national reality. The **National Educational Technology Standards (NETS)**, developed by the International Society for Technology in Education (ISTE), outline core technological competencies that teachers, as well as students and administrators, should meet. In fact, 90 percent of the United States has adopted or relies on the NETS in developing state technology plans (Loshert, 2003).

Although National Educational Technology Standards (NETS) have been in existence since 1998, technology skills do not appear on any state assessments as of the writing of this edition (Castek et al, 2007).

The International Reading Association and National Council of Teachers of English have set the following standard for students, thus assuming that teachers can instruct accordingly: "Students use a variety of technological and information resources (e.g., libraries, databases, computer networks, video) to gather and synthesize information and to create and communicate knowledge (p. 28)." Technology is here to stay, and we must use it effectively in content classrooms.

Advantages of Digital Literacy

Please visit the Education CourseMate website at **www.cengagebrain.com** to find a link to the National Education Technology Plan 2010.

No teacher can compete with the pace and lure of new technologies; all we can do is try to use new technologies as the medium for engaging students in the real work and joy of learning. Integrating technology tools into content area instruction offers students enhanced opportunities to become actively engaged in their learning. When focused on improving students' understanding of content material, technology can advance literacy. Technology presents choices and advantages for instruction, outlined below, that educators did not have in the past.

1. **Learning tool.** Technology is a viable means to learning—one that fascinates the Net generation. Digital literacy seems to promote learning in ways that paper cannot. The U.S. National Education Technology Plan 2010 supports a model of technology integration in which students are able to participate in engaging environments with tools that help them understand and remember content. Through the use of this model, students have access to a wider and more flexible group of learning resources and a broader group of instructors that may include teachers, parents, and other experts from outside the classroom. Learning experiences and pacing can be differentiated by using technology to personalize the educational activities used in modern classrooms (Office of Educational Technology, 2010). Ruddell (2000) encourages teachers to embrace the possibilities of technology to promote "fully engaged learners who are excited, exhilarated, and passionately involved in school" (p. 2).

View this video to see how a high school biology teacher uses technology as a tool to provide simulations that offer relevance for understanding genetic concepts.

The use of computer games can be an excellent way for students to learn problem solving skills along with content information. Gee (2010) indicated that when using games, players learn from guided experience by living in virtual worlds, making decisions and solving problems without fear of failure.

2. **Information location.** Instead of traveling to a physical library, learners can locate information by visiting virtual libraries, accessing the Internet, and searching for information by typing a query into a search engine. Voluminous records can be kept within a tiny memory drive and transported on a keychain. Technology offers an ever-expanding wealth of knowledge to be retrieved, manipulated, and shared.
3. **Social interaction tool.** The social aspect of digital literacy engages students. By using online social media tools, students have learned to share information and work collaboratively with global partners through blogs, wikis, **social networking websites (SNSs)** such as Facebook, virtual communities, and Web-based social spaces (Lenhart, Madden, & Hitlin, 2005; New Media Consortium [NMC], 2007, 2008, 2009). Social networking marks and supports the development of personal identity as students interact with others (Boyd & Ellison, 2007). This social and cultural dynamic (Luke, 2000) has the potential to shift instruction into the emotional zone, where cognition and affect can be used to full advantage in capitalizing on students' interests, along with familiarity with their own medium, in creating learning activities within this social space. By so doing, teachers invite students to use a popular way of communicating to bridge into more academic communication (Activity 10.2).

Look in Chapter 2 for more on the role of affect and cognition in the learning process. Recall Principle 3 in Chapter 1: "Literacy in the 21st century is more than the traditional communicative arts."

4. **Communication assistance.** Teachers and students can communicate from great physical distances with rapidity not dreamed of in earlier times. Through **Voice over Internet Protocol (VoIP)** services such as Vonage and Skype, educators can provide both video and audio communication opportunities at a low cost. Learners can "be there" on virtual field trips and in virtual classrooms without leaving their homes.
5. **Collaboration and information storage.** Digital text, as contrasted with paper text, is beneficial because it is easy to modify, revise, and use in collaborative workspaces such as **wikis.** It can be adapted to the reader and programmed to accept reader responses. Moving from place to place is easy in electronic text environments. Students develop organization and retrieval skills, and information is stored more efficiently within digital text.

ACTIVITY 10.2 Culture and Geography on a Social Networking Website (Middle School and High School)

Select a social network site, such as Facebook, that you belong to or would like to join. After you are logged on to the website, connect with an acquaintance by requesting that he or she become your friend. After your friend connection is established, begin a chat session. Ask your friend to share a description of and picture from a favorite holiday celebration in his or her community. Ask two additional friends to share the same information. Add the information to a notes page to compare and contrast the three responses with your own holiday celebration. Now look for information in another resource, such as a website that presents information on the customs and traditions of your friends' communities, to increase your understanding of their celebrations. Your notes page might begin in this fashion:

Christmas Holiday Celebration—Jeffrey McGadney

My family celebrates on Christmas Eve. We gather together in the middle of the day to prepare a special dinner that reminds of us of the years we spent in Germany. We spend time cooking Jaeger Schnitzel and spaetzle from scratch. Since we have such a large family, it takes several hours to finish the task. After a late lunch, we open presents from each other and talk until the little children head to bed to wait for Santa Claus.

Technology for Classroom Use

After reading through this section, consider which of the tools might be most applicable to your content area. Which of the technological tools have you already used in your classroom?

With some of these advantages of digital literacy in mind and the realization that the Net-savvy generation is here to stay, a brief overview of some contemporary technological tools and their impact on the classroom follows.

Word Processing and Other Production Applications

Many teachers know that writing is an effective means of learning. Learning logs and journals are two means of enabling students to express what they are learning and clarify difficult concepts. In today's world, journals may be written on paper, but more likely, students are posting their writing to personal **blogs**, SNSs, or classroom web pages, with access provided by the presenter to selected users. In Chapter 8, we explored the benefits of writing in the content areas more fully. In this chapter, we point out that students can write with pens or pencils, but more often, they prefer to use keyboards.

A range of word processing programs are available for classroom use, including simple free downloadable programs such as *OpenOffice*, programs bundled with computer operating systems, and sophisticated applications such as Microsoft Word. Word processing programs let users create and edit text, insert pictures and graphics, and make appealing book-like products. Software tools such as *Inspiration* allow teachers to create maps, graphic organizers, Venn diagrams, and outlines to support writing for and with students. Some software applications, such as *PowerPoint*, part of the *Microsoft Office Suite*, let users create slideshows that enhance text with audio and animation. Such software is not content specific; it provides numerous opportunities for teachers to produce subject-specific instructional materials. Hall and Strangman (2002), from the Center for Applied Special Technology, reviewed 15 studies that used graphic organizers in classrooms. Each of the studies showed some type of positive learning outcome, particularly in the areas of comprehension and vocabulary knowledge. Graphic organizers can be used across all grade levels and across content areas by comparing and contrasting concepts, mapping cause and effect, problem solving, and relating information to main ideas (Hall & Strangman, 2002).

Adding graphics to a written assignment enhances students' understanding of and interest in the content material. By using scanners, digital cameras, or video recorders with easy USB port downloading, students can place graphics and video in text to create lively visual displays to document their learning. Students can also access free sources of clip art and art within such programs as *Inspiration* and *Word* to enhance their products. Additionally, students can use audio files from applications such as *Garage Band*, *iTunes*, or *Audacity*, or video files embedded on sites such as *YouTube and TeacherTube.*

Applications such as *Dreamweaver* and *iWeb* let users create presentations that can be published on the Web. Currently, many simple programs for Web presentations are available, so a user does not have to purchase and learn advanced technology to create a website. Children are intrigued by the multisensory nature of production applications and seem to spend more time on learning when such resources are available.

Databases are a popular and efficient means of storing information. Teachers often use a database "to enter, store, update, access, and manipulate information" (Merkley, Schmidt, & Allen, 2001, p. 220). For instance, a teacher might store student information or activity ideas in a database such as *Access* (from Microsoft) or *FileMaker Pro.* Students can easily enter, store, and retrieve data about virtually any topic that can be categorized. Mathematic calculations can also be accomplished using databases such as *Excel*, another program in the *Microsoft Office Suite.*

Instructional Software

Software is delivered on CDs or over Internet downloads and typically includes supporting instructions and materials for individual and classroom use. Programs such as *Oregon Trail* and *Amazon Trail* have been around for some time and have been updated. *Leonardo the Inventor* takes learners to the Renaissance, where they experience da Vinci's ideas and inventions. Such programs simulate a situation and ask readers to make choices based on careful thinking about the information presented. Some software features a familiar text but provides multimedia, such as read-alongs and question-and-answer interaction. Students are expected to respond; their responses can be tracked to provide a score for the learner and instructor. This can be a helpful monitoring device for teachers who want to record which types of resources students use to learn about a topic and how effective those resources seem to be.

Instructional software programs can be wonderful learning resources. Software can track what users are doing, keeping records for students and teachers. As with textbooks, some are better than others. Haugland (2005) suggests that educators consider three main issues when selecting and upgrading educational software for classroom use: (1) software should integrate with the goals and standards identified for instruction, (2) violence should be avoided and (3) materials should be developmentally appropriate for the students who will be using the software.

Quirk and Schwanenflugel (2004) analyzed the motivational appeal of five popular software programs for struggling readers and found that all could have motivated students more. One study (U.S. Department of Education, 2007) found that software programs have not been very effective at improving students' test scores. How can you ensure that software selected for use in your classroom meets students' educational needs?

Recall "Approaches to Reading Electronic vs. Traditional Print" in Chapter 6. How does the information presented in this chapter on reading in software environments relate to the approaches described in Chapter 6?

Please visit the Education CourseMate website at **www.cengagebrain.com** to find a link to the Harvard *River City* project.

Fox (2003) suggests that software should always be instructionally relevant as well as student and teacher friendly. Clearly, software is not good simply because it is there; rather, it must conform to educational standards and facilitate achieving the intended instructional goals.

Instructional software should teach about content and stimulate critical thinking rather than provide only skill-and-drill or rote learning of isolated facts. One major advantage of software over Internet resources is that teachers can preview the material and be sure its content is suitable for the age group. Another advantage is that the teacher does not depend on an Internet connection, which might be unreliable or sometimes inaccessible.

How software is used makes a difference. Greenlee-Moore and Smith (1996) investigated the effects on reading comprehension when fourth grade students read either short and easy or difficult texts using either interactive software or printed text. When reading longer and more difficult narratives, the software group had higher scores. The authors speculate that students paid more attention to the text on the computer than to the text in the book. However, current researchers (Castek et al, 2007; Coiro & Dobler, 2007) suggest that the skills and strategies needed for comprehending material in online environments differ from those used in paper-text environments. Teachers must be aware of the need to provide instruction for reading digital text.

Gaming software has been gaining popularity as a support for content learning. Gaming allows students to test hypotheses and attempt challenges without fearing failure. Students are able to use critical thinking and problem solving skills to develop creative solutions to hypothetical challenges (Glazer, 2006). Increasingly, educators are seeing the benefits of **multi-use virtual environment (MUVE) games** that are able to visually simulate real geographic features of the environment. Participation in online gaming communities using **avatars**, virtual characters with human attributes, is on the rise with hundreds of thousands of teens engaging peers in sites such as Second Life (Blaisdell, 2006).

Second Life virtual worlds used in the academic community (Dede, 2007) have multiple educational purposes, including fostering a sense of community, allowing for group work, and facilitating role-playing exercises (Inman, Wright, & Hartman, 2010). Empirical evidence supports adopting the use of virtual worlds in programs such as Harvard Graduate School of Education's *River City*. Using a problem-based approach, middle school students working in three-person collaborative teams determine the cause of an epidemic in a 19th-century town. Each student controls an avatar that lives in the virtual city and uses his or her computer to resolve a simulated health crisis (Dede, 2007; Harvard University, 2007). Data from the 1,000 students who participated in the project during 2004 and 2005 indicate that after 20 sessions, students' knowledge of biology improved 32 to 35 percent (Blaisdell, 2006). Galas and Kettelhut (2006) noted that preliminary findings of a study of more than 3,000 students in fifth through twelfth grades showed that using *River City* resulted in the use of scientific inquiry and the development of skills in virtual communication and expression. Preliminary results from Ketelhut, Dede, Clarke, and Nelson (2006) indicated that student attendance improved and misbehavior decreased through use of this highly engaging activity; students were also building the virtual communication skills necessary for success in modern society. Use of this type of gaming activity changes classroom instruction from teacher-driven lecture to an interactive delivery where students construct knowledge in small group activities through problem solving and inquiry (Dede, 2007; Ketelhut et al, 2006).

Auditory Resources

The use of sound enhances student understanding and provides multiple ways for them to express knowledge. VoIP has taken telephony—voice communication over distances—to the Internet. Transmission of digitized voice data has surpassed telephone use among the Net savvy. It is now possible for a person to "call" a number that transmits a voice message to an audio file that is received at an email address. The recipient can then hear the message at leisure while checking email. Additionally, this system can be used to conduct synchronous audio and video conversations across long distances with free VoIP tools such as Skype.

TECH APP

Select Educational Applications of VoIP

- Ask students to submit book reports via a VoIP service. The teacher can listen and respond via VoIP so that the student receives a personal critique.
- Have students record via VoIP and then listen to themselves, for example to practice before an oral presentation or to make sure they have not forgotten any steps in an explanation.
- Encourage students to practice foreign language conversation and pronunciation skills with native speakers (Elia, 2006).
- Provide personal feedback to individual students.
- Post an assignment that students and parents can listen to in order to clarify directions.

Participating in cell phone conversations and listening to radio and music are popular pastimes that also can be used as educational resources. Podcasts provide excellent examples of such possibilities. The term podcast combines the "pod" from Apple's iPod device with the "cast" from the word broadcasting; audio (or video) files can be cast our for anyone to download from the Internet and listen to and/or watch. Podcasts use the Internet's Real Simple Syndication (RSS) to directly transmit files to an iPod or another MP3 player. Anyone with a reasonably well-configured computer can create an audio file. And anyone with an Internet connection and enough bandwidth can download a podcast. Since its inception in 2003, podcasting grew to include more than 10,000 different podcasts by 2005 (Hew, 2009). Podcasting continues to grow rapidly, with many teachers developing their own podcasts. Podcasts can be posted where students can easily access and listen to them as often as they are interested. Through organizations such as the International Reading Association, teachers are able to access podcasts to improve instruction. University professors also provide opportunities for teachers and students to gain personal professional development on topics of interest through iTunes U, where open access to college-level course podcasts is available.

Please visit the Education CourseMate website at **www.cengagebrain.com** to find a link to downloadable podcasts for reading and writing instruction.

Electronic Books

An electronic book (**e-book**) is a book presented on a computer or an electronic reader (**e-reader**) using digital text. E-books typically resemble traditional books but add multimedia effects and activities to support student understanding of the content (Shamir & Korat, 2006). The user's main focus is still on reading text, but the text can be augmented with hypertext links to create a nonlinear reading environment. A wide range of e-books is available, including contemporary fiction, children's literature, and nonfiction works such as *The Autobiography of Benjamin Franklin* (Franklin, 1994) and

Amazon's Kindle and Barnes & Nobles' Nook are two popular e-readers. Both offer many e-books, newspapers, and magazines at discounted prices. The portable nature of the devices and the option to take notes, bookmark, and highlight digital text on the e-reader increase their appeal as study tools.

CHALLENGE BOX

Trinka, a Student with Learning Disabilities

SITUATION: Trinka has made consistent progress during the first several months of third grade due in large part to the collaborative and cross-disciplinary instructional planning of her classroom teacher and the three reading support group educators who work with her each day. However, Trinka is still challenged by the amount of material she needs to remember in her social studies class. She loves to use the Internet and has made *YouTube* videos with her older brother at home.

How can Trinka's teachers meet her needs?

Students with learning differences benefit from opportunities for repeated encounters with information in a variety of formats. As students reconstruct information, they practice identifying main ideas in a variety of text structures and make personal connections to the text elements. Research indicates that the use of retelling also enhances students' ability to answer questions and improves overall text comprehension (Caldwell & Leslie, 2005). Trinka's teacher might also consider developing a class e-book that allows each student to contribute a slideshow page that highlights an important concept from the social studies chapter. In this inclusive activity, Trinka would be able to work with a manageable amount of content for her own contribution to the book. She would further benefit by viewing the content created by her classmates. E-books can be copied easily onto a CD or thumbdrive for viewing at home. If Trinka's teacher has a class web page, he or she may also post the class e-book so Trinka's parents have access to the material at home. Directions for e-book development are available in Activity 10.3 for this chapter.

How can teachers use technology to help Trinka retain information in social studies and other content areas?

The use of graphic organizers to structure information is an excellent way to assist Trinka in remembering important concepts and facts. The use of *Kidspiration* or *Inspiration* software to develop a mindmap of the major points of a chapter would allow Trinka to attach visual images to important labels to aid in recalling vocabulary items. *Inspiration* can even translate a student's mindmap into a traditional outline format that can be used for developing a written summary of the material presented in class.

Paganini's 24 Caprices Op. 1 (Paganini, 1820), which enables musicians to download and study sheet music that they otherwise might never see.

Electronic encyclopedias offer an interesting and efficient way to support textbooks with additional literature (Wepner, Seminoff, & Blanchard, 1995). *Compton's Interactive Encyclopedia* and *Grolier Multimedia Encyclopedia* rival the print versions for number of articles and include pictures, sound clips, and animation to support the texts. Many textbooks are published entirely on the Internet with production applications or are available on CD or by download through an e-reader for student home use. Students can read the digital text, see the same illustrations that are included in the printed textbook, and in some formats even *hear* the instructor explain points about a graph or clarify complicated directions. At given points, students can click and soar to other locations (using the hypertext feature), escaping the linear nature of a textbook for a nonlinear world.

Teachers can create electronic books to share information or capture student responses to engaging content (Rhodes & Milby, 2007). See the Challenge Box, where this process is described as a means of supporting Trinka, a student with learning disabilities. What material from your content area would be most easily adapted for use in an electronic book? How would using an electronic book support learning in your content classroom?

Please visit the Education CourseMate website at **www.cengagebrain.com** to find a link to an article that describes how to develop e-books for use in retelling stories.

The Internet

The Internet makes electronic text easily accessible and has become "the medium of the future" (Anderson-Inman, 1998). We are now in the age of "Globalization 3.0," according to Friedman (2006), during which using the Internet leads to "digitization, miniaturization, virtualization, personalization, and wireless" (p. 196). The Internet is a collection of many resource networks—an electronic library of information. Every second something new is posted for viewers to find on the Internet. A Web search engine allows a learner to find many possible resources by entering keywords, titles and authors' names. Some resources are worthless, but many can enhance learning

ACTIVITY 10.3 Creating an E-book to Reinforce Content Knowledge

Creating a class or individual e-book for use with students to reinforce concepts is a fabulous content area reading activity. E-books are easily made using slideshow presentation software such as *PowerPoint*. Select a content area topic for review or in-depth study. First, open the slideshow and select a background. Insert a text box on each page that includes the information to be shared. Then add clip art or a digital image to support the main idea and help the reader comprehend the text. Custom animation can be added to move from slide to slide. Finally, use the slide show program's record narration feature to add voice or sound effects to the e-book. Classroom e-books do not infringe on copyright law when students use their own language and illustrations to retell the content. When students add quotes from textbooks or images from websites such as *Flickr*, it is important to ensure they know how to provide appropriate credit to authors and photographers.

in content areas. Using the Internet to search for information is highly personal, but students need guidance to find the best and most completely verifiable information. Just as a reader should note the copyright date of a textbook, an Internet user should note when a website was posted and whether it has been revised (Rekrut, 1999). And just as a reader should want to know a text author's credentials, Internet users should be cautious about the sources of information they discover on the Web; learners must judge the quality and reliability of the information. Content teachers can help by suggesting and previewing possible sites in advance of sending students to surf the Internet.

The Internet is changing what it means to be literate (Castek et al, 2007; Leu, 1997):

1. Internet literacy requires new and sophisticated navigational skills.
2. Learning is endless; just as one masters a new literacy skill on the Internet, a new challenge arises.
3. The Internet requires new ways of reasoning and thinking critically.
4. Content on the Internet can be presented with multiple meanings and combinations.

These literacy challenges are part of what make the Internet appealing to students but often require teachers to provide guidance so the Internet can be used as a tool for effective learning. Teachers often find that the Internet can provide a means of extending literacy practice and proficiency (Karchmer, 2001). Students find the Internet an appealing source of information (Leu, Castek, Henry, Coiro, & McMullan, 2004) where they have opportunities to respond to literature, view authors' websites, and learn about diverse cultures.

The Internet can make it easy to consult an expert and locate engaging supplemental instructional materials. Rather than traveling to the expert, which can be expensive and reduce the size of the intended audience, students can visit the expert online. We can see him or her talking to us, listening, and responding through a video conference. Supplemental materials such as a high school posting about the short story "The Battle of Pythagorus" can enliven the study of the Pythagorean theorem. The short story was a wonderful lead-in to the math. Leu, Karchmer, and Leu (1999) provide numerous lessons in content areas that engage learners on the Internet. For example, they help learners find out about Japan by visiting "Kid's Web Japan." This site provides steps by which students can learn about Japan's climate, culture, and art.

Use the Internet to locate resources for your content area. How many resources are immediately accessible? Share your findings with your classmates.

The Internet also provides access to many libraries. Electronic journals let readers locate resources for immediate consideration. Professional development occurs online (Anderson-Inman, 1998) when current and back issues of journals are available. There is a move under way to provide open access to the knowledge created at the university level through online publication of materials in open repositories. Harvard and other universities are now mandating that researchers publish online and are creating open-source repositories for faculty work (*Library Journal*, 2008). Studies have confirmed that open access broadens readership and results in additional citations of articles (Evans & Reimer, 2009; Lawrence, 2001). This type of challenge to the status quo in educational publishing will have far-reaching impact on the availability of information and the financial arrangements between paper-based journal editors and authors.

Treasure hunts are similar to WebQuests, which focus on fact finding. Students are given a question that they answer by visiting teacher-selected sites. For both WebQuests and treasure hunts, the Internet offers numerous sites where teachers can follow directions to create and post their activities at no cost. The WebQuest model was designed in 1995 by Dr. Bernie Dodge at San Diego State University. Please visit the Education CourseMate website at **www.cengagebrain.com** to find a link to a video about using WebQuests.

WebQuests send students on a problem-solving journey to several preselected websites. The teacher poses a question and provides clues that are found within websites. WebQuests give students authentic problem-solving tasks. They guide purposeful reading and can also be used by cooperative groups of students. Teachers must carefully search each possible website to be used in a WebQuest, making sure the content is correct and suitable for the learners and that the site does not link to any questionable sites. Clues must be thoughtfully prepared. This activity is time consuming but very effective as a learning tool.

A Hypertext Environment

Hypertext supports the use of a wide variety of resources in content classrooms. On the Internet, a student can start at one location and click on a hyperlink (an icon or underlined text) to immediately link to another site where there is more information. Reinking (1997) demonstrates how hypertext works in an online and print format article as he discusses the possibilities of technology and literacy. The learner can go backward, forward, and sideways in many hierarchies. Instead of reading each line in order on each web page, the learner can branch from here to there in a nonlinear fashion. The student can click to view a footnote and then click back to the main article. Readers can check a reference without turning a page. This environment is similar to that of a learner who leaps from one idea to another, jumping between piles of information on a desk as needed to take care of several tasks. Many hypertexts are also multimodal and include hypermedia, defined as "hypertext with multiple representation forms (text, graphics, sounds, videos, etc.)" (Jonassen, 2006, p. 185). In short, Web hypertext and links create a typical learning environment.

Online Communication

The traditional view of oral communication and collaboration assumes **synchronous**, face-to-face, same time, same place encounters. Online communication, however, allows learners to collaborate in both synchronous and **asynchronous** (own time, own place) learning environments. The communication possibilities for **electronic mail (email)** within content instruction are intriguing. The most obvious is that email provides a means for teachers, parents, and students to communicate outside classroom hours. E-pals allow students from different schools—or even countries—to talk to each other about content topics.

Learners are able to contact favorite authors or content experts who have made their email addresses available. Many legislators also provide their email addresses for constituents, giving students an opportunity to write and receive quick responses as they study political issues. Several studies have been conducted to determine the effect of email correspondence on literacy skills and learning. Rekrut (1999) believes that email is the best application with which to introduce the Internet to new users because it is so simple to learn.

Students today are opting for increasing the speed with which they are able to communicate online in a synchronous manner. Informal communication using **instant messaging (IM)** and chat features simplify formal spelling and grammar. This simplification is similar to what happens to language when many more users adopt it, and complexities are lost (Nettle & Romaine, 2000). Many students are moving toward sharing quick snippets of their lives by **"tweeting"** 140-character messages through Twitter. A broader audience is able to read and respond to tweets than an IM.

Teachers can use "tweeting" to help students learn to write succinctly. Try to convey an important piece of information or concept related to your content area in only 140 characters. What other ways could "tweeting" be used to support content area learning?

Perhaps the most dramatic change in synchronous communication is the use of cell phones for sending and receiving text messages. Parents of adolescents note that their children often use text messaging more frequently than oral conversation because of the privacy it affords and its ability to allow multiple audience members to read and respond to the same text simultaneously. IMs, text messages, and tweets can also contain references that are familiar to the communicators but not to other speakers. Some might even call this communication style a type of pidgin, an abbreviated form of communication adopted to allow speakers of different languages to use a very simple language, such as for trade. Students can apply the informal language of IMs to content topics by partnering to IM about a concept and then "translate" the message into more formal report language.

Common informal writing can help boost more formal writing and communication skills. Teachers cannot ignore the power of communication through text or IM. Quick electronic communication systems are just that—quick! A recent letter to the editor, "Will Young PPL Gro Up 2 B Literate? OMG LOL! (*Richmond Times Dispatch*, May 29, 2005), captures the power of the changing forms of communication. It is up to teachers to help learners see how quick communication can be carried to a more academic level of communication. Activity 10.4 uses quick electronic communication as a way to move toward writing about content learning.

Match the common texting term with its definition.

LOL	parents looking over shoulder
BRB	talk to you later
PLOS	be right back
TTYL	laugh out loud

Social Computing

Social computing has been identified as an emerging technology to notice by both *The Pew Internet and American Life Project* and the *2007 and 2008 New Horizons Reports* (Lenhart, Madden, & Hitlin, 2005; NMC, 2007, 2008). Social computing incorporates the growing use of social media tools that let students communicate virtually through

ACTIVITY 10.4 Expanding on Electronic Messaging

As a class, read and discuss a short nonfiction selection related to your content curriculum. After discussing your subject matter, assign students to communicate a summary of the reading to a classmate using email, IM, and finally as a 140-character Twitter message. Ask students to bring a copy of the resulting conversations or responses to the next class. In class, have students share with a partner a way to expand and elaborate on the language of the messages to create an explanation of the main idea and important details of the selection. This kind of expansion of language is similar to what teachers do to help English language learners (ELLs) switch code from informal to formal language usage. Be sure to ask students which form of communication allowed them to convey the main idea most accurately.

blogs, wikis, SNS, virtual communities, and Web-based social spaces. In 2008, the two technologies highlighted as "first adoption tools" were grassroots video and collaboration webs—technologies that support sharing information and media in a community space (NMC, 2008).

YouTube, a video posting and viewing site, allows students and faculty to share in the movement to document learning in a visual format. YouTube is "cool," according to Trier (2007), who uses McLuhan's term "cool" (McLuhan, 1995) to mean a medium that is highly participative. Trier suggests several activities that help teachers use YouTube in academic settings, such as showing videos from this site to introduce a new topic and provide it with relevance for today's Net-savvy generation, assigning students to hunt for videos that illustrate a topic, or having students post their own videos after studying a topic (Activity 10.5).

Blogs can be excellent tools for ELLs because they allow students to summarize their learning daily in a written format. Please visit the Education CourseMate website at **www.cengagebrain.com** to find a link to the Technorati website for a directory of blogs. Which blogs are appropriate for ELLs in your classroom? How might you use these blogs to support the needs of diverse learners?

Blogs provide an opportunity to share information for both personal and professional interests. Read the Virginia Department of Education's Training and Technical Assistant team's *The Assistive Technology Blog*, which is available on the Education CourseMate website at **www.cengagebrain.com** to learn about how assistive technology can be used to support learners in content classrooms.

Chat rooms (Morgan & Beaumont, 2003) are found online at various locations, usually through a host Internet service provider. In chat rooms, users talk to each other about a topic of common interest. Teachers can create their own chat rooms on a school server, where their students can chat about a content topic. In chat rooms, several people can talk; the conversation can occur instantaneously or at a convenient time for users to submit their thoughts.

Discussion groups allow many people to discuss a topic either in real time or over a period of time on a website; unlike regular email, this medium does not allow real-time communication. A respondent can receive replies from several different people, all of whom can then read one another's responses. This threaded discussion offers opportunities for reflection and allows numerous visits to consider and reconsider other points of view. Knowlton and Knowlton (2001) define threaded discussion as "the **asynchronous** exchange of messages using a bulletin board or e-mail software" (p. 39). Discussion groups are an excellent vehicle for students to learn from one another and to discuss a forthcoming test or a point they do not understand. They provide a kind of online tutorial and can be an excellent resource for content instruction. Similar to chat rooms in that people talk to each other about a set topic, discussion groups are usually more formal and follow a specific thread, or thought. Chat rooms tend to be more spontaneous forms of conversation and are often very informal. Figure 10.1 shows an example of a threaded discussion board where topics to be discussed are posted. Figure 10.2 is the threaded aspect for one of the threads in Figure 10.1.

Participation in **listservs** is by subscription. People who are interested in the same topic subscribe to an information source—a listserv—much as they might

ACTIVITY 10.5 Selecting Video Material Using *YouTube*

Web 2.0 is a term used to describe the use of the Internet to create content. Think about how students can use the Internet to collaborate and generate new information. Record any questions you might have about this process. Next, find and view the video "The Machine Is Using Us!" on *YouTube*. See how many of your questions are answered during this viewing.

Explore the *YouTube* site. Locate two videos that would be appropriate to share in your content classroom. Discuss with a classmate the process you used to sort through the videos to select appropriate material with a classmate. Compare the content on *YouTube* with content on *TeacherTube*, a site geared specifically to the needs of educators. How are they similar or dissimilar?

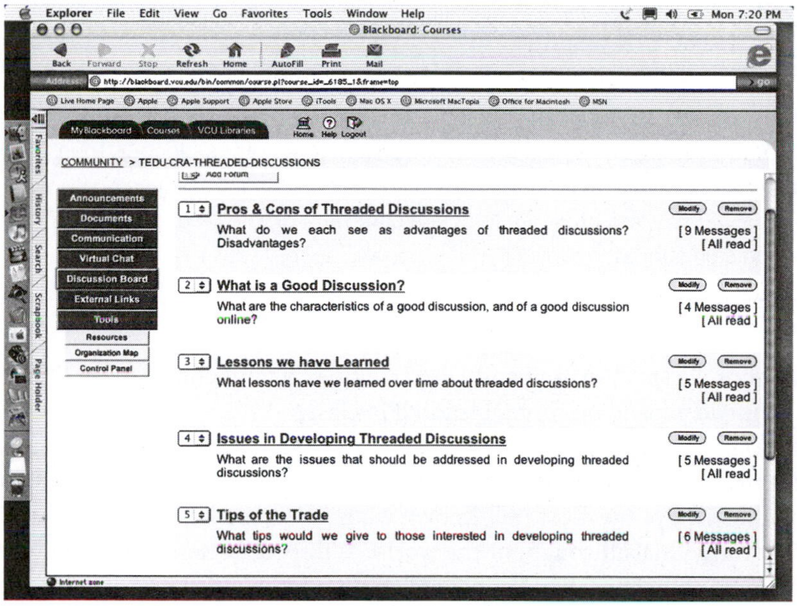

Blackboard Inc.

FIGURE 10.1

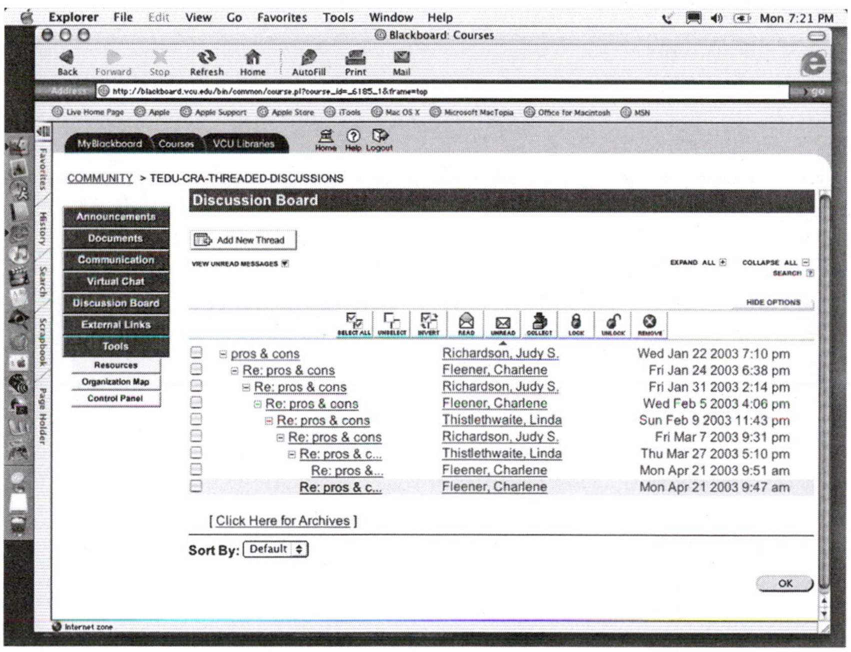

Blackboard Inc.

FIGURE 10.2

subscribe to a magazine. When someone writes a message, it is sent to everyone on the listserv by email. All of the list members can read other members' comments. Listservs are a good means of disseminating information quickly to many people who have a common interest. Teachers might subscribe to a listserv where the common topic is lesson plans for teaching grammar. When one subscriber posts his or her plan, all of the other listserv members receive it.

Another form of electronic text communication is a **blog**, which is a Web log. It is a journal on a website in which a person shares personal reflections or posts content related to a specific theme. After a blog is posted, others can visit it and add brief comments. Dieu (2004) notes that blogs work best as long-term assignments that can help

Students contribute to wikis for both personal and educational purposes. According to a recent study, university students reported using wikis for personal use (59.3%) more than for educational use (40.7%) (Nugent, Reardon, Smith, Rhodes, Zander, & Carter, 2008). How can you encourage students to use the wiki writing skills they have developed outside of class to share current class content?

ACTIVITY 10.6 Using a Blog

Ask students to read a blog about a topic you are studying. Using a blog directory can help locate appropriate blogs. Ask students to present the most important statements in the blog in the exact words of the blogger. Then ask them to restate in their own words what they read. Ask the students to compare what the blogger believes with what they know about this topic from your class. Finally, ask students to post a comment on the blog, either confirming the author's opinion or explaining their opinion about the topic.

students improve their writing and language fluency and competence. Activity 10.6 uses blogging to expand on content learned in class.

For additional information on the use of wikis and other current technologies, read the *7 Things You Should Know About* series from the EDUCAUSE Learning Initiative and the *In Plain English* series presented by CommonCraft on *YouTube*. The URLs for both resources are available on the Education CourseMate website at **www.cengagebrain.com**.

Another type of digital text in use today is the **wiki**. Wikis offer students and teachers a means for remixing information from individuals into a piece of collaborative written work. One of the most well-known wikis is Wikipedia, an online encyclopedia created by individuals throughout the world. Wikipedia offers anyone, anywhere an opportunity to contribute, revise, and edit content on the Internet, creating a growing body of collected knowledge.

These resources for digital literacy support the creation of a community of learners. Students who might not speak out in class may feel freer to communicate via email, discussion groups, blogs, and wikis. Using these tools for educational purposes allows many diverse perspectives to become available in the learning environment (Morrison, 1999).

Cautions about Digital Literacy

Students and the authors of this text agree that the advantages of technology and digital literacy outweigh their disadvantages; however, it is important to consider potential abuses and dangers as well. The series of panels about April, a teenager in the comic strip "For Better or for Worse" (from early December 2004) illustrates our first caution. April has finished her homework, which was to "write" an essay. Her mother discovers that she "wrote" it by visiting the Internet and copying and pasting from some sources there. Her mother makes her sit down with text material, including an encyclopedia; read these materials in paper format; and then write her own original essay. April mutters, "I was just told to do an essay. I wasn't told to LEARN anything."

Ease of Use

Refer to Chapter 9 for activities on electronic study skills that give teachers ideas for how to accomplish this goal.

Go to Cengage.Brain.com to find links to additional information about combating student plagiarism.

Our first caution, then, is that the ease of using digital literacy can lead to borrowing, plagiarizing, or misappropriating others' work. Thus, teachers need to be constantly vigilant to encourage careful selection of information and making the source part of new thoughts as well as incorporating information with attribution. Reviewing copyright law related to educational use of material online is a beneficial practice for educators and older students (United States Copyright Office, 2002). This problem has become so prevalent that software companies have produced programs to "catch" overquotation without appropriation; many college instructors rely on such tools to help them locate plagiarized papers. Catching students in this act is the last desperate step in "solving" the problem—and probably not the best one! Much better is teaching our students to respect others' work, to value it, and to cite it appropriately while also adding their own critical thoughts about that work to the knowledge base. When students think of themselves as adding value to what they read, they are less likely to misappropriate information.

One of the best ways to avoid plagiarism is to encourage critical thinking. However, critical thinking—sometimes challenging for teachers to fit into test-based curricula—can be even more challenging to teach in computer-based environments. For background on critical thinking in a reading-to-learn context, review Chapters 5 and 6 in this textbook. For some tips on how to encourage critical thinking in Internet environments, consider ways that the Web "turf" can be manipulated. Ream (2007) provides several helpful ideas for practicing critical thinking:

- The average user does only a single-word search and does not look beyond the first 10 items on the list that is generated.
- The ranking of a page in a search engine's results (such as Google or Yahoo!) is determined by its relevance to the searched terms and—in Google searches—also the page's popularity as measured by the number of links to that page on the Web.
- A link is like a citation in a print journal in that it refers to a preexisting other source; in doing so, it is implied that the linker is recommending that page to others.
- Relevance ranking is done when the search engine looks at the occurrence of the item being searched for within the page. (Google also considers how many pages are linked to the one you are looking up as part of their page ranking formula.)
- Search engine optimizers use various techniques so their clients' pages will be ranked higher in search results. These techniques include choosing different terms or adding more terms to the text of the page and using link farms to increase the number of links to an optimized page.
- Sponsored links in Google are highlighted across the top and along the right side. Other search engines allow companies to pay for having their pages ranked higher in search results. (Google does not allow this latter practice.)

Therefore, students need to realize that search engines do not locate infallible resources; rather, they locate the number of "hits" for the query—the number of times this site has been visited by others or its popularity with searchers. Web designers realize that a citation analysis will get their site in the first several "hits" to a query. So web page creators may try to ensure that their sites contain the terms they think you might be searching for—not necessarily the content you may need. A critical reader should think about the author's credentials, the objectivity of the site, the relevance and current nature of the site, and the quality of the presentation.

To determine whether a website contains credible information, students need to know how to conduct a web page identity check. Any site should have a history that tells who posted the site, which can give important clues to its viability; it is just a click away from the website and is a useful tool for readers. Complete Activity 10.7 to learn more about credibility checking.

Privacy Issues

Another danger on the Internet is that it is so easy to make permanent and visible to all a quick thought that should have been kept private! Some people use blogs as a way to write their personal diaries, thinking they are protected from unwanted readers by

ACTIVITY 10.7 Martin Luther King, Jr., Critical Thinking and History (Middle School and High School)

You are going to find out how to read a website critically. Select your search engine, such as Google.com, and follow these steps.

1. Find the Martin Luther King site. Type in "Martin Luther King."
   Select the site titled "Martin Luther King Jr.— A True Historical Examination."
   Scroll to the end of the page and click on the link "hosted by Stormfront."
2. Find information about the creator of the Martin Luther King site. Click that link and find answers to these questions: What is Stormfront? What do they advocate?
3. Verify information from the Martin Luther King site. Now visit at least two other websites and one paper-based resource about Dr. King.
   Then answer this question: Is the Stormfront message consistent with what you know about Dr. King? (Based on the visual aspects of the web page, we would expect that this site is posted and maintained by credible authorities, correct?)
4. Determine the credibility of the Martin Luther King site. Let's check out whether we can trust this site to give us good information.
   Copy the URL for the site; then go to a search engine such as Google.
   Type in the search box the term "easywhois."
   Select the site for Easy Who Is.
   When the Easy Who Is site appears, paste in the link you copied for "Martin Luther King Jr.—A True Historical Examination" where the box says "Enter domain." What do you find? Can you now tell if the creator of this site is biased or unbiased?

passwords. But who protects the passwords? Readership can expand without an author's knowledge when a password is shared or stolen. An email is targeted at a specific user; but when that message arrives, what the reader does with it is now in his or her control. Of course, this has always been true of paper, too, but it's a bit harder to pass along than in the electronic environment. Consider Activity 10.8 as one way to impress this message on students.

Limited Teaching Capabilities

Thomas Friedman (2006) wrote, "There comes a time when you've got to put away the Game Boy, turn off the television, shut off the iPod, and get your kids down to work" (p. 383). Is there a danger for overusing technology in the content area classroom? Which activities in your classroom are better suited for integration with technology?

Yet another caution is that technology and computers cannot teach; they can only facilitate. "It may be unreasonable to think that any innovation—technological or otherwise—would bring radical change to an institution as old, large, and as established as education" (Oppenheimer, 2003, pp. 23–24). When technology helps educators do their job better, this is a great bonus. But technology is no more a final solution to educational challenges than movies or television were. As Steve Jobs commented (1996), "You're not going to solve the problems just by putting all knowledge onto CD-ROMs. We can put a Web site in every school—none of this is bad. It's bad only if it lulls us into thinking we're doing something to solve the problem with education" (p. 102).

ACTIVITY 10.8 Communication Down the Lane: A New Version of Whisper Down the Lane

Explain what the game Whisper Down the Lane is about: In a circle, a "secret" is whispered to one person, then repeatedly whispered to the next person in the circle. By the time the "secret" comes back to the person who first shared it, the secret is usually garbled—and not at all what the sharer intended.

Play Whisper Down the Lane by giving a student a message about a topic you will be studying. Make sure the message is passed along to each other student in the room. The last recipient reports the message he or she hears aloud to the whole group.

Alternate game: Give a message to your students and ask them to share it with someone in an email. At the end of the message, ask that each person type his or her name and city and forward it to at least one other friend. Within the email include a sentence that asks each person to return the email to the original student by 9:00 PM the same day. Be sure to keep the original student's name in the carbon copy (cc) address line so the email address is still available. How many copies of this email have been forwarded? How many people will have seen this email? Where were they located? Make a comparison between playing the game in class versus in the email version:

	What Happened to the Message?	How Many People Heard or Saw the Message?
Whisper Down the Lane	The message changed.	A limited number heard the message.
Forward Down the Lane	The message did not change.	Many people read it in just one day!

Note: Always make sure the message used for this activity is appropriate to the age group you teach.

Availability of Resources

Finally, technology's globalization of communication has created a **digital divide** between those who have the resources to access and use digital literacy and those who do not. In affluent communities, schools, and homes, students and teachers may own or have access to computers at almost any time. Students in all communities should have access to technology for educational purposes in order to ensure digital equity (Attewell, 2001). Teachers and students in poorer communities may find that trying to access digital literacy creates a chasm between their students' educational progress and that of the technologically advanced. DeBell and Chapman (2003) found that students from families in poverty and those with parents who have not earned a high school credential reported accessing the Internet only at school. When children and adolescents report Internet access at only one location, 52 percent of youth from families in poverty access the Internet only at school compared with 26 percent of youth from families living above the poverty level. The role of schools in bridging the gap for students who lack access to technology at home is clearly evident and is one means of reducing the digital divide.

How can you address the digital divide if you have students from low-income families or teach in a school with limited access to technology?

To close this section, Wepner identifies several "techno-blunders" (2004) that can occur if educators assume that technology is a panacea:

- Always have a backup plan (of course, this should be true for any lesson).
- Make sure that a technological tool is easier and more effective than another way. Do not assume that students can use the technology.
- Understand that using technology takes time—it is not a quick fix.

- Use technology in creative ways—why replicate what can be done as effectively or better with paper?
- Select websites that fit the learners' skills, not because they are there!
- Beware of publisher claims (of course, this should be true for paper materials as well).
- Make sure there is a support system for the technology you plan to use.
- Make sure assistance is available.
- Make sure the technology works before starting the lesson.

Wepner, Seminoff, and Blanchard (1995) caution that teachers who understand their goals and are involved in planning for technological innovation will be more successful than those who do not understand the cautions. They encourage teachers making curricular decisions to ask the following questions:

- Where are we?
- Where do we want to be?
- How do we get there?
- How do we know we are there?

Technology in Your Classroom

What will technology resources look like in future classrooms? The NMC's yearly *Horizon Report* identifies the trends in technology use. The NMC has identified social networking, gaming, virtual worlds, grassroots video, and collaboration webs as important technologies to watch (NMC, 2006, 2007, 2008). Two of the top technologies forecasted for growth included the use of portable mobile media devices and cloud computing (NMC, 2009).

This chapter has described the use of social networking, the use of video and *YouTube* for presentations, and the use of virtual worlds and gaming to support instruction. The use of portable mobile media devices such as e-readers and smart cell phones will allow easier access to information in handheld devices; these tools have the potential to reduce the cost of reading print material. **Cloud computing** allows content to be maintained in a "cloud" of servers rather than on networks or individual hard drives. Material kept in the cloud is accessible from multiple locations through Web connections. Collaboration and joint authorship of multimedia materials is certain to remain among the technologies that students use for entertainment outside of school. Encouraging students to bring their technological skills into the classroom is essential for increasing students' technological literacy.

Teachers now need an announcement similar to that of airlines: "Please turn off all electronic devices." How can you convince your students that your class content is more interesting than their latest incoming text message? Refer to the policies regarding the use of electronic devices available on the Education CourseMate website at **www.cengagebrain.com**.

Teachers will certainly continue to use the Internet for enhancing lessons and communicating with students and parents. Continued improvements in two-way audio and video communication will continue to increase students' ability to travel virtually to other locations and further compress an already "flattened" globe. More electronic devices will be brought to classrooms and used along with or instead of books. Students and teachers are using e-readers, iPods, and cell phones for educational purposes in classrooms already (Harland, Plante, Marker, Falter, Thompson, Guilmett, & Hogan, 2010; Kervin & Vardy, 2007; Lu, 2008).

All of these possibilities can enhance content instruction and open new resources far beyond what a static, concise textbook can provide. Why should we consider technology as a resource for learning? "This is a nonquestion," according to Bruce (1998). Technology engages learners by providing motivation—a reason to learn and a need to know within a new environment. Technology engages learners by developing their contextual knowledge and showing the world in new ways. For instance, writing to friends via email creates a new and vital use for reading in a social environment (Baker, 2001), and learners can compose questions to experts in distant locations and read replies to those self-generated questions. Technology can make personal inquiry and purposeful reading and writing powerful tools.

Technology engages learners because they want to know effective strategies to find discussion groups and listservs to read what others have said about a topic, to locate websites, and to access databases. Technology can engage learners because it can provide the means to a social process: From remote locations, we can learn together.

ONE-MINUTE SUMMARY

Faced with an ever-expanding amount of information to be digested and learned in every content area subject, teachers increasingly realize that no single textbook can deliver all the concepts in, and differing viewpoints about, any unit of study. Thus, many content area teachers recognize the need to incorporate digital resources that complement textbooks and support retaining information in daily classroom instruction. This chapter presented information on how the increased use of technology resulted in a changing definition of literacy. A description of digital literacy was provided, featuring changes in culture and history that have led to standards for instructional technology. The chapter addressed technology for classroom use, including software, e-books, the possibilities of using the Internet in instruction, the use of social media, and some advantages and cautions about digital literacy. The future offers great promise for continued change with the use of mobile technologies further increasing access to content information.

END-OF-CHAPTER ACTIVITIES

Assisting Comprehension

1. Read this entire chapter online to experience a hyperlinked, electronic text environment. Keep a list of the links you select as you read. Compare your list with a classmate to determine if you "read" the same chapter.
2. Review the information presented in this chapter and the recommended articles available on the Education CourseMate website at **www.cengagebrain.com** related to defining literacy in digital environments. Which definition do you find most comprehensive? Develop your own definition of digital literacy. How does your definition compare and contrast with the definition of 21st century literacy in the *A Brief Explanation of Digital Literacy* section.
3. A list of the applications and instructional software mentioned in this chapter can be found on the Education CourseMate website at **www.cengagebrain.com** (under Chapter 10 Resources). Select and use one resource with your students or classmates. Did the use of technology support your instructional objectives?

Reflecting on Your Reading

1. Your content organization (e.g., National Council of Teachers of Math, National Council of Teachers of English, National Council for the Social Studies, National Science Teachers Association, International Reading Association) has most likely developed a set of standards that identify performance criteria relevant

to classroom teachers. Standards typically delineate elements of foundational knowledge that a classroom teacher should possess. Locate and become familiar with the organization's recommendations in the area of technology education. For instance, teachers should be able to:

- Use technology to gather information for instructional planning.
- Select technology-based information and non-print materials representing multiple levels, broad interests, and cultural and linguistic backgrounds for instruction (International Reading Association, 2003).

2. How did this chapter address these issues? How do the standards outlined by your professional organization compare with the NETS developed by the ISTE (available on the Education CourseMate website at **www.cengagebrain.com**)? How does knowledge about the technology standards support content instruction?

CHAPTER 11

Supporting Diverse Learners in Content Classrooms

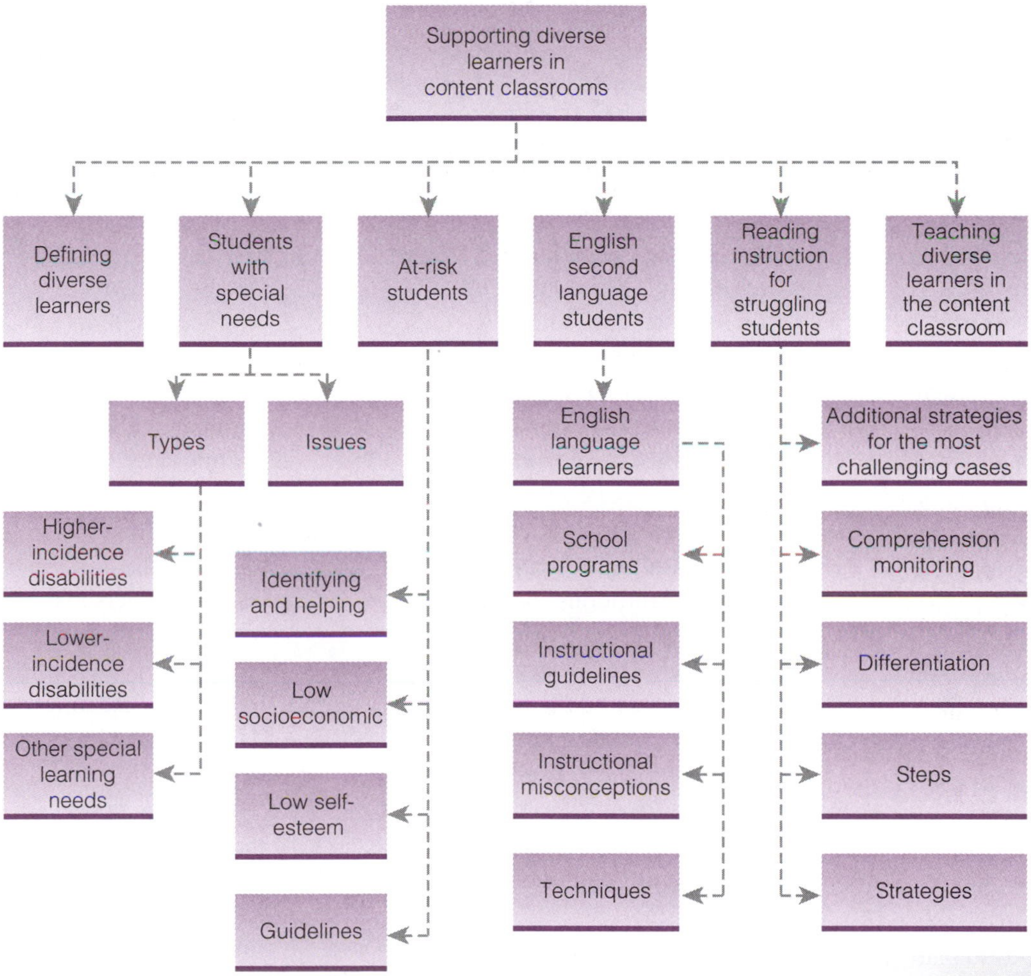

There will never be a single solution that will be a perfect fit for our diverse society. Don't wish for a unilateral answer to our educational dilemmas. Instead, we should work toward partnerships of families, communities, and educators who will enjoy the process of problem solving.

ELAINE GRIFFIN, 1995 UNITED STATES TEACHER OF THE YEAR

VOICES FROM THE CLASSROOM

Mr. Johnson was beginning his second year as a fifth grade teacher at Horseshoe Elementary. The community attracted migrant workers because there were a few large orchards on the edge of town and a poultry business. He had two new Hispanic students, Laticia and Maria, from south Texas. They each had enough knowledge of English to speak socially and understand typical day-to-day conversation but had little knowledge of the form and subtleties of academic language. The previous year Mr. Johnson had not had any English as a second language (ESL) learners in his classroom, so he was both delighted and a little apprehensive about the possibilities. He asked Mrs. Carson, a seasoned teacher, what special accommodations and considerations he should make to provide the best learning experience for these students. Mrs. Carson assured him that they just needed good instruction to help them get ready for the standards exam at the end of the year. She told him to be patient and not to expect too much from them. One or two others in the class were always willing to work with them. She advised that children of migrant workers are generally shy and don't contribute much even when asked questions directly. She suggested that he bring in special materials in May to highlight Cinco de Mayo to help them feel included. After this conversation, Mr. Johnson felt somewhat discouraged but not daunted. He knew there must be techniques and strategies he could use that would make a positive difference for these students.

Why do you think Mrs. Carson had such low expectations for these students? What, beyond "just good instruction," should Mr. Johnson consider when planning lessons? What suggestions would you give Mr. Johnson?

PREPARING TO READ

1. Answer the following statements thoughtfully and be ready to respond about your instruction for diverse students:

   ______ I know how to accommodate instructional practices in my classroom—or future classroom—for learners with a wide range of needs.

   ______ I do not (or expect I will not) encounter students with cultural or language diversity in my classroom.

   ______ I can use student interests, reading abilities, and backgrounds to plan highly successful content lessons, no matter how diverse the students might be.

2. Some of the terms that follow may be familiar to you in a general context, but in this chapter, they may be used in unfamiliar ways. Using prior knowledge, decide how you could group the terms in four or five sets and give each group an appropriate label. There may be several ways to group them, so there is no single right answer. Be ready to explain your selections. Next, using a piece of paper, make a three-column organizer with the following headings: "Terms," "Predicted Definitions," and "Chapter Definitions." Select 10 terms with which you are least familiar, record them in your organizer, and predict how they might be defined for this chapter. As you read the chapter, verify your predictions and rewrite your definitions as necessary.

   ______ diverse learners
   ______ equity pedagogy
   ______ Individuals with Disabilities Education Act (IDEA)
   ______ inclusion
   ______ response to intervention (RTI)
   ______ differentiated instruction
   ______ universal design for learning (UDL)
   ______ at-risk students
   ______ resilient students
   ______ self-efficacy
   ______ English as a second language (ESL)
   ______ immigrants
   ______ refugees
   ______ acculturating
   ______ assimilate
   ______ basic interpersonal communication skills (BICs)
   ______ cognitive academic language proficiency (CALP)
   ______ Improving America's Schools Act
   ______ cultural discontinuity
   ______ culturally responsive instruction (CRI)
   ______ English language learner (ELL)
   ______ teaching English to speakers of other languages (TESOL)
   ______ bilingual education
   ______ comprehension monitoring
   ______ language experience approach (LEA)

OBJECTIVES

As you read this chapter, focus your attention on the following purposes. You will

1. Understand and identify characteristics of students with special education needs.
2. Identify teacher-directed reading strategies for aiding students with special education needs.
3. Identify characteristics of at-risk students.
4. Describe why teachers have to discourage passive approaches to reading.
5. Identify teacher-directed reading strategies for aiding at-risk, low-socioeconomic, and low-self-esteem learners.
6. Identify and clarify common misconceptions concerning instruction for English language learners.
7. Identify culturally responsive teacher-directed reading strategies for aiding English language learners.
8. Identify teacher-directed reading strategies for aiding struggling readers.

Diverse Learners

All learners are unique. Even in classrooms that may be designated as "homogeneous"—that is, where all learners are supposed to be grouped by a like factor such as giftedness or advanced or deficient academic ability—we discover a great range of diversity. Educators often define **diverse learners** as those who might be at risk for academic failure and who need special understanding and attention. In every classroom, teachers find students who are diverse in intellectual ability, social and emotional background, language proficiency, racial background, cultural background, and physical attributes. Teachers must be prepared to deal effectively with these individual differences (Au, 1992; Carolan & Guinn, 2007; Hammerberg, 2004; Heilman & Williams, 2006). Today's classrooms are a reflection of a changing American population. Learning to appreciate and work collaboratively with students different from themselves offers rich opportunities for preparing students for living in a global society.

Current trends in the United States indicate that our population will continue to diversify. The population in the United States has experienced pattern shifts reflecting larger proportions of cultural, linguistic, and socioeconomic differences in recent years, and literacy as it relates to diversity has gained new attention (Au & Raphael, 2000; Xu, 2001). Achievement gaps between students in the mainstream population and their diverse peers remain a challenge. "A fundamental shift in teachers' knowledge, skills, and assumptions about children in high-poverty schools and students who are culturally and socioeconomically diverse is needed for the achievement gap to narrow"

(Williams, 2006, p. 11). Content area teachers must practice **equity pedagogy** (Au, 2001; Banks, 1995), striving to educate all students, no matter what their heterogeneous or diverse qualities. This often means not treating or instructing each individual in the same way—but rather with respect to their differences and needs to provide effective instruction and ultimate learning success for them all. Equity pedagogy stresses instructional opportunity for all learners. In this chapter, we discuss students with special or diverse needs, including those diagnosed and requiring accommodations under the law and gifted students; we also discuss those who need consideration because of their status as at-risk students, their cultural and linguistic differences, or their reading difficulties. We offer some strategies that can help content teachers teach diverse learners effectively.

Go to CourseMate to see a video showing how an elementary language arts teacher designs instruction that meets the needs of different types of learners. This elementary school teacher uses "task-analysis," differentiated and directed instruction, and buddy reading.

Students with Special Needs

Students with special needs are a heterogeneous group who may need special education with instructional accommodations in order to learn successfully. Special education is defined as "a specially designed and coordinated set of comprehensive, research-based instructional and assessment practices and related services to students with learning, behavioral, emotional, physical health, or sensory disabilities" (Salend, 2011, p. 7). Specifically, special education involves the following key features: individualized assessment and planning; specialized, intensive, and goal-directed instruction; research-based instructional practices; collaborative partnerships; and student performance evaluation (Heward, 2009). Today, most students with special needs receive their education in general education classrooms.

In the academic year 2007 to 2008, about 95 percent of U.S. students ages 6 to 21 served under the **Individuals with Disabilities Education Act (IDEA)** were enrolled in regular schools (U.S. Department of Education, 2010). The percentage of these students who received more than 80 percent of their school day in inclusive classrooms was increased from 32 percent in 1989 to 1990 to 57 percent in 2007 to 2008.

This section on special education was revised by Yaoying Xu, PhD, associate professor in the Department of Special Education and Disability Policy, School of Education at Virginia Commonwealth University.

Inclusion is a philosophy that values *all* students' right to receive appropriate education within the general education classroom. It recognizes that all students are able to learn and benefit from a "meaningful, challenging, and appropriate curriculum delivered within the general education classroom" (Salend, 2010, p. 7).

When students are included in general education classrooms, content teachers must understand the special education needs that their students possess and how to provide appropriate accommodations. In this section, we will introduce types of students with special needs, legal issues in special education, and evidence-based strategies for content teachers in inclusive classrooms.

Types of Students with Special Needs

Students served by IDEA are distributed among 13 disability categories. (For the specific definition of each category, see IDEA 2004, pp. 46,756–46,757.) IDEA provides special education and related services to students who are eligible under these disability areas. Each type of disability may be described as higher incidence disability or lower incidence disability based on its prevalence. In addition to these IDEA categories and definitions, other sources of classroom diversity may include culturally and linguistically diverse groups, gifted and talented groups, and at-risk groups. Students with any of these characteristics or backgrounds may need individualized accommodations to succeed at school.

STUDENTS WITH HIGHER INCIDENCE DISABILITIES

Higher incidence disabilities refer to the disabilities that are more commonly seen in schools. Individuals who have higher incidence disabilities are a diverse group with a wide range of abilities and disabilities from mild to severe in intensity. Disabilities under IDEA include the following areas: speech or language impairments, specific learning disabilities, mild or moderate intellectual disabilities, and emotional disturbance (U.S. Department of Education, 2007). Higher incidence disabilities make up more than 80 percent of the total population of students ages 6 to 21 years. In addition to these categories identified under IDEA, students with attention deficit hyperactivity disorder (ADHD) make up approximately 3 to 5 percent of the total student population (Kauffman & Landrum, 2009). Most of these students are served in general education classrooms with appropriate accommodations. These students may or may not qualify for special education and related services under IDEA.

STUDENTS WITH LOWER INCIDENCE DISABILITIES

Lower incidence disabilities refer to disabilities that are far less commonly represented in schools compared with higher incidence disabilities. Lower incidence disabilities may be present at birth or acquired later in life and may be temporary or permanent or life threatening (Mastropieri & Scruggs, 2010). Lower incidence disabilities involve a wide range of disabilities, including physical and other health impairments, autism, severe and multiple disabilities, visual impairments, and hearing impairments. Traditionally, most students with lower incidence disabilities were served in separate schools or programs. With the advances in assistive technology and creative adaptations, individuals with lower incidence disabilities can succeed in inclusive classrooms.

STUDENTS WITH OTHER SPECIAL LEARNING NEEDS

Individuals with other special learning needs may not have a diagnosed disability, but curriculum adaptations or material accommodations may be necessary to ensure the success of these students. Individuals with other special learning needs also represent a wide range of abilities, including students who are gifted and talented, students from culturally and linguistically diverse backgrounds, and students who are at risk for school failure because of environmental or biological risk factors. All of these students are served in general education classrooms; however, their unique needs may or may not be identified because these characteristics are not included in the IDEA category.

Issues in Special Education

The first special education law, Public Law (PL) 94-142, the Education of All Handicapped Children Act, was renamed as the **Individuals with Disabilities Education Act (IDEA)** in 1990. This law states that all children with disabilities will receive a free and appropriate public education in the least restrictive environment. In 1997, the Act was amended with several important new provisions to strengthen the implementation of the essential principles included in the initial Act. One of the most important new provisions added to IDEA 1997 was that the law recognized that most students with disabilities spend all or most of their school time in general education settings; it included a provision requiring that a general education teacher become a member of the team for a student's individualized education program (IEP).

The most recent reauthorization of the special education law, P.L. 108-446, the Individuals with Disabilities Education Improvement Act (IDEIA)—often referred to as IDEA 2004—was to provide more educational opportunities for students with disabilities. This new special education law seeks multiple innovative ways to improve educational results for students with disabilities. For example, IDEIA or IDEA 2004 does not require the use of discrepancy models (IQ vs. achievement) for determining specific learning disabilities (SLDs) (Harris-Murri, King, & Rostenberg, 2006). Instead, the **response to intervention (RTI)** model was proposed as an alternative approach to determining the eligibility for special education and related services.

RTI is referred to as tiered instruction, or intervention, because of its different levels of intervention. Most school districts that are using RTI have implemented a three-tier intervention process. Tier 1 refers to high-quality instructional and behavioral supports for all children in general education settings by measuring the rate of academic growth of all students in comparison to other classes in the school or district or nation. Curriculum-based measurement (CBM) would be used to determine the overall achievement level and growth in achievement for the classroom of the struggling student. Tier 1 attempts to rectify the previous difficulty in assessing the quality of past educational experiences to rule out inadequate instruction as a possible reason for underachievement (Drame & Xu, 2008). Interventions at Tier 2 are still provided within general education settings. If students are not making satisfactory performance with the more intensive, specialized intervention, they will be moved to Tier 3, which provides even more individualized intervention but is not yet special education and offers no related services. This intervention level could occur within the general education curriculum or in a setting outside the classroom that is more appropriate for individualized instruction.

Some programs have proposed an additional level, Tier 4 intervention, before a student is referred. The continuous progress monitoring that measures how adequately students respond to an intervention is particularly important in an RTI model. Instead of keeping a student in a specific tier level for a fixed period of time, most programs use the rate of progress as a means of determining whether a student should move from one tier to the next. For example, in moving a student from Tier 2 to Tier 3, instead of a 15-week fixed schedule, the student may be moved to a Tier 3 intervention after the ongoing documentation shows consistent the student's nonresponsiveness to a scientific, research-based intervention. After Tier 3, the nonresponsiveness could be the cause to suspect that a student has a disability and should be referred for a comprehensive special education evaluation.

Research has demonstrated that the use of IQ–achievement discrepancy models for determining SLD contributes to the disproportionate minority representation in special education programs (Donovan & Cross, 2002). One of the fundamental differences between the RTI and the discrepancy model is in early intervention. Unlike the discrepancy model, which is primarily an assessment system for eligibility requirement, RTI is an intervention delivery system that is provided for *all* children, regardless of their ability level. Additionally, instead of looking for within-child deficits as evidence of a disability, RTI targets a broader and more contextual analysis by considering day-to-day interpersonal and institutional factors that may impact student achievement and behavior (Harris-Murri et al, 2006).

At which tier would intervention for Trinka be referred for special services? Why do you think so? Are there any advantages or disadvantages to RTI for Trinka?

Despite the existing and potential benefits of the RTI model, various concerns about this model exist. One particular concern is related to its outcome-focused approach that could lead to systematic errors in identifying students with learning disabilities. Students with learning disabilities are a heterogeneous group with a wide range of abilities (Vaughn, Bos, & Schumm, 2011). Some high-ability students with learning disabilities may not be identified and may therefore be excluded from special education and related services. These students may achieve well within the normal range by using their intellectual strengths and coping strategies as well as support services. For example, if they respond well to an intervention by achieving at an average or above average level at Tier 1 within the large group, they are less likely to be moved to Tier 2 or 3 for more individualized intervention and thus may miss the opportunity to reach the level consistent with their abilities. On the other hand, some students who do not respond to the intervention for cultural or linguistic reasons rather than a disability may be identified inappropriately as having a learning disability at the end of the intervention process.

Please visit the Education CourseMate website at **www.cengagebrain.com** to find links for IDEA and other resources related to teaching students with learning disabilities.

Teaching Students with Special Needs in the Content Classroom

Teachers of content subjects teach students with special needs in the general education or inclusive classrooms. The goal is to provide appropriate instruction to all students (with or without disabilities) in the classroom, including students who are gifted or talented. To reach this goal, it is essential to provide effective **differentiated instruction (DI)** to meet the diverse educational needs, learning styles, and interests of all learners in the inclusive classroom. (DI) is an alternative approach to teaching and learning that allows teachers options of varying learning contents, contexts, and modes of assessment to meet the individual needs of each student (Stanford & Reeves, 2009; Thousand, Villa, & Nevin, 2007).

Universal design for learning (UDL) is one way to implement DI. UDL is a theoretical framework designed to guide the development of curricula that are flexible and supportive of all students (Dolan & Hall, 2001; Meyer & Rose, 1998; Pisha & Coyne, 2001; Rose, 2001). Within the framework of UDL, the individual needs of all children in the setting can be addressed, including students who have disabilities, students who are gifted or talented, and students who are from culturally and linguistically diverse backgrounds. All learners can use the methods, materials, and assessment. UDL helps meet the challenges of diversity by suggesting flexible instructional materials, techniques, and strategies that empower educators to meet the various individual needs within the general education curriculum. Three principles of the UDL framework guide the development of adaptable curricula: multiple means of representation, multiple means of expression, and multiple means of engagement (CAST, 2008). Instead of adapting the existing curriculum to meet the individual needs of students, UDL promotes flexible *accessibility* for diverse learners through multiple options of materials in representation, expression, and engagement.

Gifted students have unique needs that must be considered for them to reach their full potential. Please visit the Education CourseMate website at **www.cengagebrain.com** to find resources for gifted students.

Contrary to popular beliefs, gifted students also need support so that appropriate individualized instruction is provided to accommodate their unique needs. These students may not be able to identify for themselves their unique learning needs even though they may realize that the regular classroom does not meet their needs; therefore, they need guidance to reach their potential capabilities (Manning, Stanford, & Reeves, 2010). Gifted students may benefit both cognitively and affectively from working in homogeneous groups rather than cooperative groups (Feldhusen, 1989; Fiedler, Lange, & Winebrenner, 2002; Kulik & Kulik, 1990). Some experts are concerned that it is unfair to expect these students to always be the tutors taking on the role of teacher (Robinson, 2003). Boaler (2006) found that higher ability students initially complained about having to spend too much time explaining things to peers but thought about it differently over time. Students reported that their own understanding deepening through the explanations and examples they devised to help their peers. They also gained new respect for their peers because they recognized the strengths and talents of classmates as they worked on a variety

Refer to these chapters for more information:

- Brain research tells us that when learners receive information in more than one way, they process it more effectively (Chapter 2).
- A multimodal approach helps to differentiate instruction. Lankutis (2001) encourages teachers to provide instruction in more than one mode (Chapter 6).
- Using technology can be an aid to multimode presentation (Chapter 10).

Co-Writer 4000, a software program (Don Johnston, Inc.), helps students who have difficulty moving ideas from thought to print. The program "guesses" what word the student might mean to write from clues given so the student can make good writing choices: "I want to r-" might be translated as "I want to read." *L & H Kurweil 3000* is a program that scans and reads text to students. It also has study skills features.

What information in this section helps you to understand Trinka and would allow you to help students with learning disabilities in your classroom?

of projects. Many of Slavin's (1990) and Johnson and Johnson's (1974) structures are designed to work with a transmission model of instruction, letting students practice and master skills and information. Other structures are open ended and lend themselves to a transformation model, letting students solve problems and create products and ideas. Huss (2006) contends that when working with gifted students, "heterogeneous groups should be reserved for challenging, creative, open-ended, and higher-order thinking tasks" (p. 20). Teachers can gather basic information to make decisions and design solutions that provide a challenge for all the learners. "Collaborative formats that emphasize the development of higher levels of understanding and that require students to explain and justify their ideas can promote the learning of both gifted and nongifted students as they interact together" (Patrick, Bangel, Jeon, & Townsend, 2005, p. 103).

Maroney (1990) advises teachers to *tell* students exactly what is expected; *teach* by modeling; *watch* students in action to see if they understand; *coach* students who seem unsure; *remind* students frequently; and encourage them to *practice, practice, practice* to make perfect!

At-Risk Students

Recommended reading: Ma'ayan, "Erika's Stories: Literacy Solutions for a Failing Middle School Student." The article provides a very good description of an at-risk student.

At-risk students are students in danger of dropping out of school because of low achievement, usually because of educational disadvantages, low socioeconomic status (SES), or underachievement. They are often disengaged and silent in school; score low on standardized tests; and are unfulfilled, believing that they lack control of their own destiny. Ma'ayan (2010) presents such a student, Erika, who describes herself as frustrated and failing middle school. Of the many terms used to describe at-risk students, two less desirable terms are "hard to reach" and "hard to teach," which resound negatively and seem to place responsibility on the students. The designation "students who present special challenges" may come closer to expressing the challenge to teachers rather than the deficiencies of students; for the present, the term "at risk" seems to be accepted as the popular terminology.

Although poor minority children may be at greatest risk, many other students in our classrooms are also at risk of school failure. The reasons are varied: poverty, drug and alcohol abuse, crime, teen pregnancy, low self-esteem, ill health, poor school attendance, welfare dependence, and others. The concern about at-risk learners is not new; Pellicano warned in 1987 that at-risk students might become "unproductive, underdeveloped, and noncompetitive" (p. 47) in our technological and complex world. He called for a national policy agenda that "legitimates the school as a mediating structure for those who are powerless to develop their own potential" (p. 49).

Recent statistics from the National Assessment of Educational Progress (NAEP) show a troubling and continuing trend. The National Center for Education Statistics (NCES) report "Status and Trends in the Education of Racial and Ethnic Groups" (Aud, Fox, & KewalRamani, 2010) notes that fewer Hispanics, American Indians, and blacks graduated from high school than did other groups in 2003 to 2004. Forty-eight percent of public school fourth graders were eligible for free or reduced lunch in 2009, and of this group, 77 percent were Hispanics, 74 percent were blacks, 68 percent were American Indian or Alaska Natives, 34 percent were Asian or Pacific Islanders, and 29 percent were white. Although reading scores for fourth and eighth graders rose slightly between 1998 and 2009, those eligible for free or reduced lunch continue to score about 30 points lower than others.

At-risk learners manifest the poorest reading behaviors and are so fearful and negative that they often cannot be motivated, especially by threats. Psychologists tell us that when an organism is threatened, its perception narrows to the source of the threat. This may be why so many poor students "take it out" on the teacher. Feeling threatened, they do not pay attention to coursework, to commands, or to anything but how to repay the teacher for all the failure and frustration they feel. At-risk students tend to focus entirely too much on the teacher, thus developing an external locus of control. Therefore, a teacher's attitude toward students and learning can be powerful.

Refer to Chapter 2 to refresh your understanding of motivation and external locus of control. Why do you think JaNette reacts as she does to the academic world?

Identifying and Helping At-Risk Students

Attention to at-risk students can help educators focus on identifying and helping these students so they become successful learners. It is important, however, not to interpret the term "at risk" to be a prediction of failure, resulting in a negative label that perpetuates a self-fulfilling prophecy (Gambrell, 1990). In fact, studies have demonstrated that with careful attention and instruction, many "at-risk" students overcome this label to graduate from high school and attend college (Ferguson, 2000). Out-of-school-time programs (OST) sponsored by schools and offered after school or in summers can make a difference in supplementing and building success for at-risk learners (Lauer, Akiba, Wilkerson, Apthor; Snow, & Martin-Glenn, 2006).

Please visit the Education CourseMate website at **www.cengagebrain.com** to find links to websites with examples of OST.

First and foremost, teachers need to be positive and caring enough to realize that behaviors putting these students at risk cannot be changed quickly. At-risk students may have acquired bad study habits and negative thinking. There are no absolute critical periods with human beings; it is never too late to learn.

Mark Twain once said, "A habit cannot be tossed out the window. It must be coaxed down the stairs a step at a time." What do you think he meant by this?

Resilient Students

Unless students can be resilient to challenges such as difficult environmental and academic challenges, as well as stress and setbacks in education, they will face great difficulty in school (Martin, 2002). Students who are resilient can adapt successfully to such challenges despite the difficult circumstances they may face (Borman & Overman, 2004). **Resilient students** are those who, despite hardships and at-risk factors, bounce back and succeed in school (Harvey, 2007; Howard & Johnson, 2000; Patterson, 2001). These students have chosen and learned to cope and respond positively to situations that often spawn anxiety, depression, withdrawal, and underachievement. They are persistent. Research has provided evidence that positive social relationships, positive attitudes and feelings, taking responsibility for controlling personal behaviors, and feelings of competence all encourage resilience (Harvey, 2007).

Refer to Chapter 9 for more information on homework and its role in student study.

Aud, Fox, and KewalRamani (2010) note that:

- Asian students spend the most hours per week on homework (about 10 hours); if teachers can find ways to provide relevant homework and places to do it (OST), more at-risk learners might increase their time doing homework.
- Black and Hispanic students work more hours per week than others.
- The unemployment rate is higher for those who did not finish high school: 8 percent for Hispanics, 9 percent for blacks, 10 percent for American Indians

and Alaska Natives, and 10 percent of people of two or more races compared with 4 percent each for whites and Asians. Working more during school may increase the odds of earning less later.

Including students in conversations on expectations, rules, and goals can give them a sense of responsibility and respect while encouraging self-regulation. Recognizing and supporting students' talents contributes to increased feelings of confidence.

Harvey (2007) offers seven ways of promoting resilience in school settings: (1) provide a caring, supportive learning environment; (2) foster positive attitudes; (3) nurture positive emotions; (4) foster academic self-determination and feelings of competence; (5) encourage volunteerism; (6) teach peace-building skills; and (7) ensure healthy habits. (p. 12).

Teachers and administrators can encourage resilience by fostering positive teacher–student communication. Harvey (2007) emphasizes the importance of giving praise in public and criticism in private. Teachers can help students develop prosocial behaviors and attitudes of respect for peers and others by providing opportunities for cooperation, decision making, and collaborative problem solving. Listening to and allowing students time to recognize, name, and express emotions while discussing appropriate means for dealing with those emotions can validate feelings and produce positive outcomes. Cook and Kaffenberger (2003) describe an intensive counseling program for at-risk students that netted very positive results for 75 percent of the 35 middle school students enrolled in the areas of strengthening the home-school connection and academic performance. (Figure 11.1 depicts a model of factors influencing resilient students, developed by McMillan and Reed, 1994.)

This chapter could not possibly present all the characteristics and problems associated with at-risk learners. Physical and mental disabilities, substance abuse, and many other issues are beyond the scope of this textbook. However, characteristics associated with at-risk learners and school failure that are critically linked to reading to learn are relevant: low-socioeconomic environments, low self-esteem, issues concerning English language learners (ELLs), and struggles with reading. These characteristics are not independent of one another. An at-risk student who speaks English as a second language may come from a low-socioeconomic environment or have low self-esteem. Rarely is a student at risk of school failure as a result of only one of these characteristics.

Using the techniques and strategies described in this chapter will not solve all problems with at-risk students. The task is arduous and often frustrating for teachers, and no single set of strategies will solve such an overwhelming problem. However, the PAR (preparation, assistance, and reflection) Lesson Framework and the techniques explained in this text, along with much attention to the affective domain of teaching, are steps in the right direction. Certainly, studies such as Borman and Overman's (2004)

FIGURE 11.1 A Conceptual Model of Factors Influencing Resilient Students at Risk

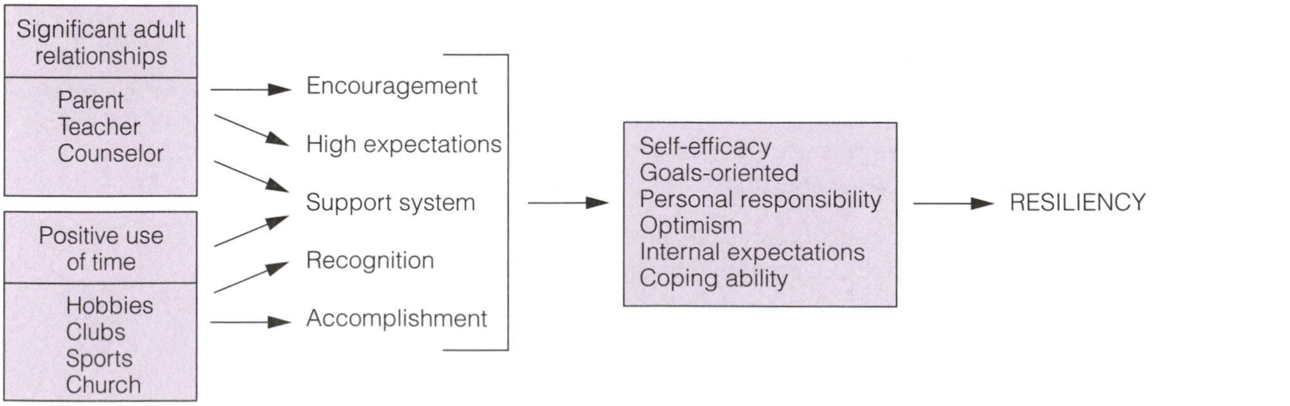

From *The Journal of At-Risk Issues,* Vol. 1, No. 2 (Fall 1994), Fig. 1, p. 32. Used with permission.

look at mathematics students who "beat the odds," and McMillan and Reed's (1994) interviews with resilient students indicate that this is true. Resilient students often do not receive the support of parents and family and look to and receive needed help from teachers or other school personnel (Lessard, Fortin, Marcotte, Potvin, & Royer, 2009). Teachers must endeavor to enable this sizable group of failing students to become successful.

Students from Low-Socioeconomic Environments

These students usually come from impoverished neighborhoods and often score poorly on standardized tests. Their families do not have much extra money for anything beyond food and basic clothing. Most of these students are interested in school and are eager to learn but lack educational or cultural exposure outside the classroom.

By all accounts, far too many students in classrooms today suffer from the effects of living in poverty. The impact of poverty on students' lives is profound, and the consequences are complex. Pogrow (2006) decries the necessity for school reform and a call to action:

> We must confront the fact that, despite a century of alternating progressive and traditional reforms and despite the unselfish and creative efforts of many in high-poverty schools and of the profession as a whole, such schools generally remain highly ineffective in terms of their ability to reduce the learning gap or to accelerate their students after the third grade (p. 233).

The conditions in poor students' surroundings put them at serious risk of school failure. Low performance, seemingly influenced by poverty, contributes to continuing literacy struggles for adolescents (Hinchman, Alvermann, Boyd, Brozo, & Vacca, 2004). The differences between low- and middle-income homes indicate that poverty leads to many fewer literacy resources for children (Neuman & Celano, 2001). "The problem of meeting students' individual needs is compounded in high-poverty schools by student mobility and absenteeism, which make it difficult for teachers to establish continuity" (Pogrow, 2006, p. 225). Their literacy is at peril (Noll & Watkins, 2003).

Please visit the Education CourseMate website at **www.cengagebrain.com** for a link to NCES, which provides an excellent website where one can view study reports and charts that summarize data.

In a now classic study, Adams (1990) reports that children raised in high-literacy homes may experience more than 1,000 hours of reading and writing activities before even arriving at school. Many students from low-socioeconomic families come from homes characterized by oral literacy rather than books, magazines, and adults who read. Although these are rich language experiences, they are not the ones many teachers assume that children possess. Schools often fail to recognize the cultural and linguistic strengths of students from an oral literacy environment. Children raised in middle or upper socioeconomic homes are often accustomed to print-rich environments characterized by literacy materials such as newspapers, library books, periodicals, and computers, as well as cultural experiences such as museums and theaters; access to such an environment may give children an advantage for negotiating the discourse expected in classroom environments. For students living in poverty, the ways of talking and responding learned in the home or community may conflict with or be a mismatch for the discourse expected in school. Not being familiar with academic discourse may require an additional layer of learning for them and may also serve as a source of tension between home and school communities (Williams, 2005, 2006). Such a disadvantage is a high-stakes proposition. As Williams points out, "Access to power and cultural capital is why academic discourses that reflect the values of the dominant culture are the foundation for most literacy pedagogy" (p. 344).

Even though communities in most parts of the country are becoming more diverse, such diversity of interactions and relationships often do not exist in settings where there are many people of color (Seidi, 2007). Smaller concentrations and less exposure to those of other cultures and socioeconomic levels may dilute or distort the differences and can create the illusion that we are all the same in how we think, act, and believe. Thus, a teacher may mistakenly expect that a student from poverty should respond to prompts, praise, admonitions, directions, and instruction in the same way as those from middle- or upper-income homes. Some may also hold preconceived notions about poor students' capacity to learn that may result in less effective instruction for them (Lazar, 2006). "A fundamental shift in teachers' knowledge, skills, and assumptions about children in high-poverty schools and students who are culturally and socioeconomically diverse is needed for the achievement gap to narrow" (Williams, 2006, p. 11).

Many students come to school with a future orientation—able to set goals and to set smaller subgoals to reach the larger goals. Some students from low-socioeconomic environments, however, have not been exposed to and therefore have not developed the traditional goal orientation associated with school achievement. These students have had little experience with the type of success in which most teachers believe. Teachers must understand that lack of goal orientation does not necessarily mean that these students are lazy; the teacher must try a variety of ways to motivate them. Behavior management techniques that require the teacher and student to establish short-range goals may help these students develop the skills necessary for successful school learning.

Instructional Guidelines for Working with Students from Low-Socioeconomic Environments

Richard Rhodes, recipient of the Pulitzer Prize and the National Book Award for his 1987 book *The Making of the Atomic Bomb,* suffered the effects of physical abuse and poverty during early adolescence. Rhodes survived with his capacity to love intact because others not only cared but also acted. He cites several teachers who helped him. Rhodes tells us: "Don't be a bystander" (1990).

The following guidelines will help teachers work with students from low-socioeconomic environments:

1. **Be sensitive to the conditions that may influence students' behavior and achievements.** Students from deprived environments tend to have poor self-concepts and low aspirational levels, to be tardy and absent frequently, to be poorly oriented to school tasks, to display hostility toward school and authorities, and to resist or reject values that are foreign to them.
2. **Be aware of the effect of poor nutrition and health on learning.** Students without sound diets and with health problems are not likely to be able to concentrate and may lack the feeling of well-being that is essential to learning. Teachers can work with families and community social service agencies to diagnose and address the diet and health care needs of students.
3. **Take action to change students' lives for the better.** Teachers should not be bystanders when they see students who suffer from the consequences of poverty.

Many resources are available so teachers can help at-risk students: social service agencies that can address the basic needs of families, including health care, shelter, nutrition, and counseling; youth agencies, such as Big Brothers and Big Sisters, that can offer enrichment programs after school, on weekends, and during summers; and adult tutors, particularly senior citizens, who can work with individual students. Timely teacher intervention can make a decisive difference.

Students with Low Self-esteem

The literature continually stresses the relationship between self-esteem and learning for at-risk students (Patterson, 2001). Lack of self-esteem manifests itself most obviously during adolescence, when students are in a state of flux, constantly searching, focusing, and reevaluating themselves. Unfortunately, by the time some students enter middle school, they have a negative self-image, viewing themselves as helpless and without control over their level of achievement. They behave in ways that cause teachers to label them unmotivated, immature, uncooperative, and even hostile. Although the behavior of these students may be inappropriate, it most likely reflects their distress at facing failure in the classroom day after day (Hinchman, Alvermann, Boyd, Brozo, & Vacca, 2004).

Motivation is related to self-esteem. Motivation has been defined as the process of initiating, directing, and sustaining behavior or as the force that causes the "arousal, selection, direction and continuation of behavior" (Biehler & Snowman, 1997, p. 399). Motivation is viewed as a drive toward competence that is sustained and augmented by the feelings of efficacy that accompany competent interaction with the environment (Connell & Ryan, 1984). Bandura (1977, 2001) popularized the term **self-efficacy**—an individual's belief in her or his own effectiveness to cope with given situations. Self-efficacy determines the degree and quality of effort and the limits of persistence of which an individual is capable. It is more than self-esteem, which is a perception of self-worth; rather, it is what one perceives about being able to achieve a goal.

Please visit the Education CourseMate website at **www.cengagebrain.com** for a link to an interesting discussion of self-efficacy, including its history, definitions, and place in social cognitive theory.

Building Positive Relationships

Brendtro, Brokenleg, and Bockern (1990, pp. 62–63) offer guidelines for building relationships that promote self-esteem, including crisis as opportunity, caring, and earning trust. Think back to Chapter 2 as you read about these characteristics.

The importance of teachers building positive relationships with at-risk students who have low self-esteem cannot be stressed too much. Caring is real concern for the life and growth of the student. *Knowledge* is genuine understanding of the students' feelings even if they are not readily apparent. *Respect* is the ability to see and appreciate students as they are. *Responsibility* means being ready to act to meet the needs of the student.

CRISIS AS OPPORTUNITY

The struggling students who are most difficult to work with are those who create trouble rather than friendships. These students are often labeled "hard to reach." If a teacher waited for such a student to warm up, he or she might wait forever. Many effective teachers have long recognized the great hidden potential of turning crisis into opportunity, as in the following story shared by a high school teacher:

> Rob entered first period class 10 minutes after the bell, looking disheveled and agitated. I asked for his late pass, and he swore and stormed from the room. I stepped into the hall to confront him about his behavior but recalled our discussion of "crisis as opportunity." I called him back and asked simply, "What's wrong, Rob?" "What's wrong!" he exclaimed. "I'm driving to school and my car gets hit. After I get through with the police, I'm late into the building and get stopped by the principal. When I tell him what happened, he tells me to get to class. Now you send me out of class!" He whirled around, starting down to the office. "Where are you going?" I asked. "To get a pass!" he replied. "That's OK, Rob. Enough has gone wrong for one day; you're welcome in class." His hostility melted in tears. After a moment, he regained his composure and thanked me, and we went back in the room. (Brendtro, Brokenleg, & Bockern, 1990, p. 62).

Literature can give teachers a good view of at-risk learners and how to care for them; examples include *Stand By Me*, the novella by Stephen King; *Teacher* by Tracy Kidder; *Lives on the Boundary* by Mike Rose; and *I Hate English* by Ellen Levine.

The teacher in this example could easily have responded in a manner that would have alienated this student. Instead, the teacher used this crisis situation as an opportunity for relationship building. When a teacher manages a crisis with sensitivity, relationship bonds become more secure.

CARING FOR ALL STUDENTS

Struggling students—students who suffer from low self-esteem, those who are withdrawn, or those from a different economic or cultural background—may not find others lining up to build relationships with them. These are the students who are sometimes ignored or rejected. These students often believe that teachers are uncaring, unfair, and ineffective. Teachers need to take affirmative action to enhance the standing of these students with their peers. Doing this requires that teachers actively focus on identifying the strengths of these at-risk students. Harvey (2007) recommends encouraging students to develop individual talents that will build feelings of competence and confidence. Talents such as dancing, illustrating, or even rock climbing can provide multifaceted benefits that may serve as a source of joy and help when dealing with stress.

Lipsitz (1995) points out that "we are not being respectful or caring when we fail to teach children to read, compute, and write; nor are we respectful or caring when we hold different expectations for children because of their race, gender, or economic status" (p. 666). It is common for children from adverse backgrounds to expect negative or apathetic responses from adults based on their past experiences. Harvey (2007) emphasizes that if we hope "to reverse this pattern, adults must deliberately, repeatedly, and genuinely communicate positive regard" (p. 11).

EARNING TRUST

Perhaps the central ingredient in building positive and effective relationships is trust. According to Brendtro, Brokenleg, and Bockern (1990), trust between a student and teacher develops over time in three predictable stages:

> *Casing:* In this stage, the student needs to "check out" the teacher. The student observes how the teacher behaves, how much power the teacher wields, and how others respond to this adult. All of these observations are crucial data to students who may view virtually all teachers and adults as threatening.
>
> *Limit testing:* During this stage, the student will "test out" interactions with the teacher. A student who distrusts a teacher's friendly manner may misbehave or provoke the teacher to determine whether this person is really different. In this situation, the teacher should take a calm but firm approach to avoid either "giving in" or confirming the student's view that this adult is really just like all the others and not to be trusted.
>
> *Predictability:* The first two stages provide a foundation for developing a more secure relationship between the student and the teacher. Consistency is important to building a trusting relationship. In such a relationship, each party—the student and the teacher—knows what to expect from the other. In some situations when trust building is difficult, it may be better for the teacher to simply acknowledge, "I know you don't feel you can trust me yet, and that's all right." It takes patience and persistence to build trust, and it is important to remember that trust begets trust.

Guidelines for Working with Students with Low Self-esteem

Improving the self-esteem of students is a major concern of most teachers but especially for teachers of at-risk students.

1. **Focus on the strengths of students with low self-esteem.** At-risk students typically have low self-esteem because they have not been successful in school. These students, however, may have had many successful experiences outside the classroom. With some discussion and probing, students often identify successful aspects of their lives that they may not have recognized before. Spend time having students recall, write about, draw, and share their past achievements. Teachers must plan instruction that allows students with low self-esteem to demonstrate their strengths.
2. **Make sure these students are given opportunities to read from materials that are within their reading proficiency level.** Students need to be successful in their reading in order to build positive self-concepts as readers. This means that the material should be familiar enough so that the student can use sense-making strategies. When readers continually have to deal with text that is too difficult, they expend their energy constructing a hazy model of meaning and do not have the opportunity to elaborate on the content or strategies needed to enhance comprehension.
3. **Provide opportunities for students to engage in cooperative learning.** As presented in Chapter 3, cooperative learning promotes higher self-esteem, greater social acceptance, more friendships, and higher achievement than competitive or individual learning activities. Cooperative learning experiences are beneficial for all students but especially for those with low self-esteem. Students can be organized into small groups that are monitored and rewarded for both individual and group accomplishments. Cooperative learning can be used in any content area, as well as for reading and writing lessons and activities. The major principle of cooperative learning is that members of a team can succeed only if all members of the group are successful. Students have a vested interest in ensuring that the other group members learn.

What information in this section helps you to understand JaNette and would allow you to help students at risk in your classroom?

As you read the information and strategies in the next few sections make notes for ideas important to remember when teaching Gustavo, our ESL student.

English as a Second Language Students

Increasing numbers of students whose first language is not English arrive in classrooms daily (National Clearinghouse for English Language Acquisition, 2010). ESL students are diverse members of our population, but they are not necessarily at risk. Unfortunately, false assumptions are sometimes made when these children have difficulty demonstrating knowledge and skills considered "normal" at the grade level in which they are placed when they are assessed using traditional assessment measures (Williams, 2006). As a result, ESL students may be inappropriately categorized, labeled, and identified for special education or alternative education. Many teachers do not understand ESL students, so this section explains several issues that may affect their school performance. First we introduce some important situations that have an impact on ESL students and their instruction.

Please visit the Education CourseMate website at **www.cengagebrain.com** to read a story about an ESL student who "beat the odds" by graduating from high school in four years rather than needing extra time to manage his new language and content requirements. Although his story is not typical, it is encouraging.

Families from other countries come to the United States for various reasons. Students who left their home countries with families who purposefully chose to move, seeking a different way of life, are **immigrants**. Other families fled their home

What is the difference between an immigrant and a refugee? How might this difference influence how or how much a student learns?

countries because of unstable and dangerous conditions in their homeland; they might not have wanted to move but left because they were no longer safe in their own countries. They are **refugees**. In either case, students might be confused and intimidated by their new surroundings, but refugees may have more challenges to overcome.

How well ESL students settle into their new environment depends on several factors. First, students should be encouraged to feel proud of and retain their cultural heritage; when they integrate by maintaining their first language and culture and integrating as necessary, they are **acculturating** to English and the new country. If they feel forced to give up or deny their traditions, they may **assimilate**—or become much similar to others in this country—but lose an important part of themselves. In the case of assimilation, students may begin to resent the forced choice and develop low self-esteem. Students who can balance between the two cultures and find positive attitudes toward both cultures will find it easier to acculturate.

What is the difference between acculturation and assimilation? How might this difference influence learning?

Stephen Krashen, an expert on language acquisition and its impact on learning English, developed a model that many ESL teachers refer to frequently. In his monitor model, Krashen (1982, 1989) argues for a balance between determinism and environmental factors as contributors to second language acquisition. His model includes five hypotheses:

1. **Any language is acquired unconsciously more than through direct learning.** The power of acquisition ought to be used more effectively in teaching ESL. For instance, less reliance on organized learning through workbooks and more reliance on learner environment are necessary components of effective ESL instruction.

2. and 3. The next two hypotheses are interrelated. **Learners monitor their learning,** but **they need sufficient time to focus on form and specific knowledge of when to apply rules.** Because these conditions are difficult to meet during most communication—which demands quick responses—explicit rule teaching and error correction slow down or impede progress. The natural order hypothesis suggests that language learners acquire language "rules" in a natural, predictable sequence rather than by direct instruction. Grammatical features evolve despite a prescribed sequence.

4. **As a logical extension, natural communication seems to provide a relaxed setting for language learning.** Learners do best when language input is comprehensible and just beyond their current level of knowledge. Krashen calls this comprehensible input "i + 1," whereby i is input and 1 is the challenge level.

5. **Socioemotional factors strongly influence language learning and may account for older learners who master a second language despite the critical age factor.** Krashen calls this the *affective filter hypothesis*; he writes that this is the single most important variable in language learning. When the filter is high, it represents a tense, highly anxious socioemotional climate, which impedes learning.

Revisit Principles 4 and 5 in Chapter 1 to refresh your memory about different versions of discourse in students' lives. Please visit the Education CourseMate website at **www.cengagebrain.com** to find a link to the journal *English for Academic Purposes*. This journal features issues about discourse and helps teachers find effective ways to communicate with ESL learners.

ESL students may learn an informal version of English before they learn an academic version. Cummins (1979, 1994, 2000) argued for a distinction between conversational language proficiency, which he labeled **basic interpersonal communication skills (BICs)**, and **cognitive academic language proficiency (CALP)**, which is more formal academic instruction. Learning English for conversational and functional purposes is less cognitively stressful and more immediately practical than is learning English for academic purposes. This notion supports Krashen's fourth hypothesis: natural communication in a relaxed setting is the best vehicle for learning English as a starting point for ESL students.

Several second language experts discuss the variable of time in language acquisition. Achieving conversational proficiency might take approximately two years, but achieving academic proficiency might take as much as five to seven years (Cummins, 1994; Thomas & Collier, 2003). Mora (2009) reports that English language learner (ELL) students need about six years to reach a level of English proficiency. Leki (1992), an established expert on ESL, wrote that time is the single most important factor in learning ESL; more recent experts echo this (Bult, Housen, Pierrard, & Van Daele, 2008; Peregoy and Boyle, 2009). Helping students make the transition from a first to a second language involves special attention to "linguistic bridges" that show the learner how the languages are similar and different (Gibbons, 2003). The process takes time.

Please visit the Education CourseMate website at **www.cengagebrain.com** to find a link to a website that discusses the amount of time required to learn a new language.

English Language Learners

Some ESL students have little difficulty learning English, perhaps because of positive acculturation, facility with academic English, previous experiences, and time to practice English; however, many have difficulty. PL 93-380 (enacted in 1974) stipulates that there be provisions for bilingual education in virtually every aspect of the educational process. This law recognizes that students with limited English proficiency (LEP) have special educational needs and requires that teachers take into account the cultural heritage into which each student was born (Harris & Smith, 1986). The Office for Civil Rights Memorandum (1991) is intended to ensure that schools comply with Title VI of the Civil Rights Act, requiring them to provide language programs so that minority students with LEP "have **meaningful** access to the schools' programs." And in 1994, PL 103-382, **Improving America's Schools Act,** reauthorized Title VII to fund initiatives and programs to meet the educational needs of culturally and linguistically diverse students. Considering these laws and with demographers continuing to predict increasing numbers of immigrant and refugee students from Central and South America, western Europe, and Asia, teachers must consider how instruction can be modified to meet the special needs of those with LEP.

Please visit the Education CourseMate website at **www.cengagebrain.com** to find a link to the "Policy Update on Schools' Obligations Toward National Origin Minority Students With Limited English Proficiency (LEP students)."

Many issues have an impact on effective instruction for ELL students. The term **cultural discontinuity** (Cholewa & West-Olatunji, 2008; Ledlow, 1992; Lovelace & Wheeler, 2006) describes the serious internal conflict brought about by a disparity between the language and the culture of the home and of the school. Both immigrants and refugees may experience a language and cultural environment in the home that differs significantly from the language and cultural environment of the school. The differences may be so pronounced that, for some students, there is serious conflict. A student may be placed in the position of having to choose between the school's or the home's language and culture. Such a choice is counterproductive to the educational development of the student. Rejection of the home background may result in a serious loss of self-esteem, and rejection of the language and culture of the school may result in a serious loss of educational opportunities (Williams, 2005, 2006). This dilemma is called *culture shock*. When learners are refugees, the rejection is compounded by a deep sense of loss and guilt about fleeing, often called survivor guilt.

Teachers should learn about the different cultures represented in their classrooms and provide instruction that encourages acceptance of native languages and cultures while facilitating the learning of English (Au, 2001; Mohr, 2004). When teachers understand cultural and language differences, they can create examples and analogies in lessons to clarify meaning for students. Such lessons build community and respect within the classroom. When teachers prepare lessons, it is important that

Please visit the Education CourseMate website at **www.cengagebrain.com** to find a link to articles by Katherine Au about CRI.

they pay attention to vocabulary, figurative language, and multiple-meaning words that may cause confusion so that appropriate background can be built. Making these considerations (among others) is **culturally responsive instruction (CRI)**:

> Successfully teaching students from culturally and linguistically diverse backgrounds—especially students from historically marginalized groups—involves more than just applying specialized teaching techniques. It demands a new way of looking at teaching that is grounded in an understanding of the role of culture and language in learning. (Villegas & Lucas, 2007, p. 29)

Please visit the Education CourseMate website at **www.cengagebrain.com** and read Nagel's (2002) article about the ABCs of the cultural and communication model.

Differences among cultures related to social style and attitudes also have implications for instruction. Past studies (Downing, 1973; Downing, Ollila, & Oliver, 1975; Heath, 1986; Schieffelin & Cochran-Smith, 1984) as well as current ones (Ma'ayan, 2010; Perry 2008) confirm that students from non–school-oriented cultures do not have the same literacy skills as students from school-oriented cultures. The value and utility of literacy in the culture, particularly in the home environment, influence the development of literacy skills (Sheets, 2005).

One model that can raise cultural awareness levels of both teachers and students within a classroom or school community is the ABCs of cultural understanding and communication, developed by Schmidt (1998) (see Activity 11.1 for an example that could be used in a social studies classroom). Everyone has a life story, and this gives us permission to thoughtfully consider and tell that story, learn about the stories of others, and discover in what ways we are alike and different. The steps of Schmidt's model are adaptable for a variety of grade levels. This type of experience helps students

ACTIVITY 11.1 Model: ABCs of Cultural Understanding and Communication for Middle or High School Social Studies

1. ***A**utobiography:* Students can talk with family members, reflect, and record events that have shaped their own life stories. They can include descriptions of personal, educational, athletic, or other accomplishments; special family, holiday, and religious traditions; successes and disappointments; and even accounts of family or ancestral milestones.
2. ***B**iography:* Students select and interview someone from a culture other than their own. Depending on the confidence and ability of the students, these interviews could be unstructured or semistructured. In small or large groups, students could brainstorm possible questions to select from, modify, or add to for an interview framework. The interview could be recorded and conducted over more than one sitting. After the interview is completed, students write a biography, including key events and important details to best describe the individual and his or her culture. The student should then give the person interviewed the opportunity to read what was written to clarify or correct misinformation or misinterpretations.
3. ***C**ross-cultural analysis and appreciation of differences:* Students consider and chart the similarities and differences between their own life stories and those of the people interviewed. This can be done independently or with the people interviewed.
4. ***C**ultural self-analysis of differences:* Students reflect on and react to the findings in the chart created in Step 3. As differences and similarities are uncovered, students think about their feelings of comfort or discomfort and examine the causes. The results can be written or simply discussed.
5. ***C**ommunication and home–school connections:* Findings and understandings resulting from previous steps can be used to modify classroom activities and communication with the home and community to build relationships and acceptance.

Adapted from Nagle's ABC model, Building cultural understanding and communication: A model in seven situations. *Reading Online, 6*(4). 2002.

better understand their own and others' cultures. Nagel (2002) found that when she paired students in the classroom, they discovered that they had much in common with their partners, as well as many interesting and admirable qualities they had not known about each other. The assignments in Activity 11.1 build awareness and appreciation of many cultures. Students learn to listen with a caring attitude and come to value new perspectives and viewpoints by seeing the world through another's eyes.

School Programs for English Language Learners

When ESL students arrive at school with some proficiency, but not fluency, in English, they are often labeled as limited English proficient (LEP) or as students with limited English proficiency (SLEP). Also, some designate these ESL students as "speakers of other languages." However, a more recent and less deficit-implying term is ELL.

Two types of programs are prevalent in American schools for ELLs: an ESL or teaching English to speakers of other languages (TESOL) approach or a bilingual approach. These programs are usually conducted by a specialist in teaching ESL. When students receive language instruction in special programs, classroom teachers should be aware of what the specialist is doing and monitor student progress to ensure that students receive adequate classroom opportunities to develop English, reading, and writing skills (Mohr, 2004).

The first type of program is ESL or **TESOL**. Instruction in English progresses from oral skills (listening and speaking) to written skills (reading and writing). The methodology emphasizes English language skills and learner-centered activities that stress meaningful communication. ESL or TESOL is somewhat similar to programs that teach English-speaking students a second language. Whereas the latter usually focus more on CALP, the former focuses on basic communication. The main goal of ESL or TESOL is to help students attain the language skills needed for success in school as quickly as possible. Most ESL and TESOL programs now include not only oral but also reading and writing skills. The goal of ESL and TESOL classes is to move students to the regular classroom as soon as possible. Many ESL and TESOL classrooms have learners from 10 or more different countries, and the only common language is English.

The second type of program is **bilingual education**, which provides instruction in both English and the native language in the same classroom. Separate instructional periods are provided, one in English and one in the students' native language. In a variation of this approach—transitional bilingual education—bilingual teachers begin instruction in the students' native language and gradually introduce English. A review of the history of bilingual education indicates that this approach can be very effective (Rothstein, 1998; Thomas & Collier, 2003). Of course, it works only when all learners speak a common language and need to learn English as their second language. Teachers must be aware of the view of the community and school system concerning bilingual education. In some communities, parents may feel strongly that their children's education should emphasize bilingual competence; in other communities, parents want their children to speak and read only in English.

Instructional Guidelines for Working with English Language Learner Students

Sheltered content instruction focuses on "teaching subject matter through the principles of second language acquisition" (Russell, 1995, p. 30). Russell advocated making sure that ELLs learn content along with learning English. The Sheltered Instruction Observation Protocol (SIOP) developed by Echevvarla, Vogt, and Short (2008) is intended to coordinate language instruction in content area teaching. SIOP is similar to PAR in that it incorporates preparation; instruction that builds background, explanation, strategies, and interaction; plus practice and review.

Go to CourseMate to view a video that can help you understand how helpless a middle school ELL student and her teacher feel, and how the teacher patiently works to find ways to help the student learn English.

When ELL students are included in regular classrooms, teachers of content subjects will also be their instructors. In consultation with the ESL teacher, they can prepare effective lessons. Bauer, Manyal, & Cook (2010) describe how to design content lessons that incorporate language.

For instance, when studying in science and learning to follow steps in an experiment, students should tune in on the words that identify sequence, such as *first*, *next*, and *then*. Mohr and Mohr (2007) recommend that teachers proactively scaffold classroom talk for ESL students to encourage language and content. Their response protocol offers specific examples and ways for building language skills within the general classroom. To avoid instructional traps when working with ELL students, teachers should keep the following guidelines in mind:

1. **ESL students should be assessed and placed in appropriate programs.** Specialists should perform this kind of assessment and communicate with content teachers. Furthermore, teachers should maximize ELL learning opportunities (Mohr, 2004).
2. **Teachers should become as knowledgeable as possible about the native cultures of students** (Bauer, Manyak, & Cook, 2010). Teachers should ask the following questions: Is a student's native culture literate? What is the common method of instruction in this native culture? Are the relatives living in the present home literate in English? Is English spoken in the home? Is reading (in any language) a part of their home activities? It is relatively easy for a teacher to determine answers to these questions by interviewing the student, parents, relatives, or other members of the culture. Using local reference sources such as community groups, libraries, and knowledgeable professionals can also provide insights about other cultures.

Culturegrams—brief descriptions of a culture—can be obtained by visiting a country's embassy website or by linking to sites we recommend on the Education CourseMate website at **www.cengagebrain.com.**

3. **Teachers should model how oral language ability precedes reading.** Students can read what they can say and understand. Accordingly, students should begin reading instruction in their native language, or they should receive instruction that focuses on language development before formal reading instruction.
4. **Whenever possible, use reading materials for instruction that reflect the backgrounds and cultures of students** by supplementing existing materials with literature about the native cultures represented in the classroom or reading aloud from books that feature minority cultures. Students can be encouraged to contribute proverbs, recipes, and stories from parents and grandparents that can be used as the basis for experience stories (see Activity 11.1).
5. **Create learning situations in which students can develop a sense of security and acceptance.** Language proficiency is developed through oral and written activities that direct students' attention to significant features of English. Students can gain fluency in English by working with proficient English-speaking peers, learning key phrases for school tasks, and reading predictable texts.

Use threaded discussion boards to facilitate practice in meaningful use of English in the content context (Bikowski & Kessler, 2002).

6. **Use thematic units** (see Chapter 6) **and literature so ELL students can explore their own identities as they learn about content** (Vann & Fairbairn, 2003; Vyas, 2004). Use group or partner work so language and content are integrated in an informal manner (Bauer, Manyak, & Cook, 2010; Ogle & Correa-Kovtun, 2010).

7. **Practice patience.** Time is the single greatest factor influencing success for ESL learners; they need time to acculturate, learn language, and apply that learning to the act of reading. Teachers need to be willing to provide ELL students enough time, to get to know them, to consult with them often, and to adapt their curricula as needed.

Instructional Misconceptions about English Language Learner Students

It is easy to fall into the trap of believing that teaching ELL students is just a matter of good teaching. Harper and de Jong (2004) explain four commonly held misconceptions:

1. **Exposure and interaction will result in English language learning.** Although daily exposure and opportunities for verbal exchange are important for language development, they are not sufficient. Social interchange with native English-speaking peers in small-group exercises is frequently reduced to one- or two-word exchanges that limit language development. Frequent practice and appropriate feedback are needed to extend and develop both language and content development.
2. **All ELL students learn English in the same way and at the same rate.** Young learners often readily develop social language skills as they work on building their understanding of more formal academic language. Learners who have well-developed academic language skills in their first languages may instead learn to read and write formal English first as they grapple with affective and sociocultural issues experienced by adolescents. The rate is as individual as it is with other skills and concepts.
3. **Good teaching for native speakers is good teaching for ELL students.** Although good research-based instructional strategies used with native speakers are important for ELL students, the demands imposed by the terms and language inherent to the subject or topic, as well as the procedures for activities and assignments, must be recognized and reconciled.
4. **Effective instruction means nonverbal support.** Although visuals and graphic organizers can be valuable tools for decreasing the language demands of instruction, care should be taken as well to use nonverbal aids as a means to encourage vocabulary and concept development.

Although strategies that work well for native English-speaking students may also work well for ELL students, teachers should give additional consideration to particular needs and instructional demands posed by language.

Techniques That Work Well with English Language Learner Students

The majority of techniques and approaches that ESL experts propose are centered around language arts, of course. These approaches use some of the strategies that we stress throughout this book, such as cooperative learning, response journals, higher level thinking skills, use of visuals to teach vocabulary and concepts, directed readings, and use of predictions in reading. As discussed in Chapter 8, writing is an excellent tool for content teachers. Cook and Gonzales (1995) suggest that ESL students be encouraged to visualize and manipulate literature they read because "second language learners need a social context for both understanding and producing English." Although such activities are not new—visualization through drawing is similar to postgraphic

ACTIVITY 11.2 Group Frame for Elementary Mathematics

Dictation from Students	Dictation from Students
We use a series of steps to solve a problem.	Usamos una serie de pasos para resolver un problema.
We can make a chart showing how we solved the problem.	Podemos hacer un esquema que nos muestra cómo resoldimos el problema.
The answer to the problem should be at the end of the chart.	La solución del problema debería estar al final del esquema.
Revised Dictation	**Revised Dictation**
A series of steps to solve a problem is called an *algorithm*.	Una serie de pasos para resolver un problema se llama un "algorithm."
The picture of this is called a *flowchart*.	El diagrama se llama un "flowchart."
Shapes of things in the flowchart tell you something.	Las formas de los pasos en el esquema te indican algo.

organizers—they encourage students to use what they already know in making connections to the new language and culture.

The group frame from the guided language experience model is recommended for reading and writing and is directly applicable to content area material (Brechtel, 1992). Using this strategy, the teacher takes dictation (pertaining to the content area) from the class and records the information on a chart. This information is used to model revising and editing for the group. The revised dictation is reproduced and used for the reading lesson. Activity 11.2 shows a group frame from an elementary mathematics lesson about flowcharts and algorithms. In this example, the teacher can begin with the child's native language (in this case, Spanish) or start with English and dictate later in the second language.

A modified anticipation guide (Activity 11.3) provides more hints or visual elements and can net very positive results. A group of 10 adult ESL students (seven men and three women) from Vietnam, Egypt, Bangladesh, China, El Salvador, Colombia, and Hong Kong, reacted to the statements shown in Activity 11.3. First the teacher presented the statements to encourage reading in English. Class members discussed their opinions based on their experiences in the United States. After discussion, a passage about an American family was read. The students were eager to volunteer information and were interested in finding out about family life in each other's cultures as well as in the United States. The teacher noted that she had fewer requests to explain the vocabulary during the reading time, and she speculated that approaching the passage with a good idea of the concepts helped the students use context clues to make sense of unfamiliar vocabulary. This activity engaged ESL students in listening, speaking, and reading in English, and it respected their various cultures.

Ogle & Correa-Kovtun (2010) suggest "Partner Reading and Content Too" (PRC2) to support ELLs as they practice literacy skills while learning content. Students should have similar reading levels, share a textbook, and use silent and oral reading as they discuss and share content. In PRC2, a lot of rereading occurs; enough time for previewing and rereading is available. The climate is friendly and comfortable for students. Ultimately, partners participate in whole class discussion.

ACTIVITY 11.3 Modified Anticipation Guide for English as a Second Language Adults

MOST MARRIAGES LAST A LONG TIME

Most students believed that marriages in the United States do not last a long time. Discussion turned to the question: "What is a long time?" The students decided it meant a lifetime. We talked about divorce in the United States and how divorce is viewed in other cultures.

WOMEN ARE EQUAL TO MEN IN THE UNITED STATES

Most students agreed that women are equal to men in the United States. After much laughter, the Vietnamese men commented that American women seem to be superior to American men because they always get to go first!

TELEVISION IS BAD FOR CHILDREN

Although the class generally disagreed with the statement, several students commented that television can be both good and bad for children. We talked about the need for parents to be selective and to monitor programs. Watching TV is one way to learn English.

WORKING MOTHERS NEGLECT THEIR CHILDREN

This statement generated the most controversy and debate among the students. The student from Egypt believed that mothers needed to be with children for long times; other students brought up the idea of quality time.

Developed by Karen Curling.

Multitext activities are especially important for ESL learners. When books are provided at many levels and on many topics, ESL learners have opportunities to select, read, reread, and practice (Ogle & Correa-Kovtun, 2010). Hadaway and Mundy (1999) share how they used picture books about science topics to create compare/contrast maps, poetry, semantic maps, and jot charts with secondary ESL students. Watching videos and movies and then discussing the content and American culture depicted in them is a good way to combine oral and written media (Pally, 1998).

Multimodal resources, as presented in Chapter 6, are especially good bridges to success for ELL students.

Rance-Roney (2010) guided her students—pre- and in-service teachers—in creating digital storytelling via iMovie. These "digital jump-starts" (p. 386) used imagery to develop prereading schema, facilitate vocabulary, and provide factual information. Thus, ELLs could read challenging text. Smythe & Neufeld (2010) report their observations of a podcast project that gave seventh graders a nontraditional way to learn content. Although success was somewhat limited when measured by traditional means, ELLs gained both language skills and content information.

What information in this section can help you to understand Gustavo and would allow you to help ESL learners in your classroom?

TECH APP

Podcasting as a Bridge to Success

To Record and Publish: *Use iMovie, PowerPoint* with *Voice*, or Mac *Garage Band* or *Audacity*

To Do: Read challenging text and report about it digitally.

Time Commitment: Unit combining several lessons; can be used over and over!

Why Do It? Timeshifting → Anytime learning

Values: Practicing language skills; using comprehension, imagery, and writing; repeated listening and learning with familiar devices; creativity

Reading Instruction for Struggling Students

Why would students invite rejection?

Proficiency in reading stands at the center of academic learning. Students who struggle in reading avoid reading at all costs. Such students read when instructed to do so but only to "get through" the assignments. Negative perspectives toward book reading and low expectations for themselves are common among these students. Vlach and Burcie (2010) explain that struggling readers "expect rejection" and even invite it. Some choose to withdraw and become "invisible," and others act out in frustration. Bad behavior and poor reading habits are difficult to break. Often, these students adopt a "poor" reader identity and a defeatist attitude that affect both in-school and out-of-school behaviors (Greenleaf & Hinchman, 2009).

The earlier work of Allington (1991) and of Pallas, Natriello, and McDill (1989) suggested that improving the teaching and learning of struggling students does not result from special remedial programs. Scripted and highly structured programs may help students learn decoding and some of the basic skills, but such programs make few or no allowances for individual needs or differences (Pitcher, Martinez, Dicembre, Fewster, & McCormick, 2010). When the focus of instruction does not go beyond decoding and literal questions, "this surface-level approach to reading does not teach students how to engage or interact with text" (Dennis, 2010, p. 284). Greenleaf and Hinchman (2009) and Pitcher et al (2010) found that the source of reading problems for struggling adolescent learners is more often related to aspects of comprehension associated with understanding specialized vocabulary, background knowledge, and the organization of texts. Deep thinking necessary for problem solving and analytical reasoning involves dynamic processes beyond formulaic drill and practice. Techniques such as those listed in Table 11.1 can change the reading patterns of many students who are experiencing difficulties. Using a think-aloud, a teacher can model, explain steps in detail, and provide clear purposes for using strategies to help students understand the importance and appropriate use of each strategy before, during, and after reading a story or text (Kamil, Borman, Dole, Kral, Salinger, & Torgesen, 2008).

Comprehension Monitoring

Please visit the Education CourseMate website at **www.cengagebrain.com** to find the website for EurekAlert. Read the article "Warm-blooded Giants of the Ancient Seas" about scientists' conclusions from the oxygen levels in reptile teeth: Similar to certain modern ocean reptiles, some ancient ocean reptiles may have had "homeothermic" capabilities. Compare the article to the Text Mapping Plus example in Activity 11.4. Would mapping help you retell the key ideas in this article?

Because they lack experience in constructing meaning, struggling learners read words passively instead of actively questioning their understanding (Walker, 1990, 2003). When readers begin to scrutinize their comprehension processes and actively evaluate and regulate them, comprehension monitoring occurs. **Comprehension monitoring** is the conscious control of one's own level of reading comprehension (Brown, 1980). Struggling learners need frequent feedback that is detailed enough to encourage in-depth thinking and risk taking (Kamil et al, 2008). Selecting materials that challenge without frustrating learners serves to help with this process and to keep them moving forward. It is well worth the effort to model how to reflect on the learning process, asking oneself: "How did I learn this? What did I do well? What do I still need to work on?" These readers just need to think about their own comprehension and learn to recognize when it falls apart. This awareness of processing allows readers to take remedial action to rectify comprehension failure.

One strategy that can assist students in thinking about their comprehension is Text Mapping Plus, a strategy developed by Lapp, Fischer, and Johnson (2010) to support students in recalling and retelling what they have read. Retelling offers a venue for reflecting on the reading and organizing the main points to explain the essence of the story, article,

TABLE 11.1 Becoming a Self-Regulating, Strategic Reader: An Incomplete List of What to Do When

Prereading	Reading	Postreading
As you select or consider a text . . .	*Now that you're in the midst of it . . .*	*Now that you have read the entire text . . .*
Consider your purpose: Consider the assigned purpose. Develop a self-selected purpose. Pose umbrella questions.	**Predict, monitor, and regulate:** Anticipate the "next move." Anticipate relationships among concepts. Ask if it is making sense. Read to confirm or reject. Adjust your reading pace. Look back in the text. Look forward in the text. Look inside your thinking.	**Deepen your sense of the text:** Pose new questions, revisit same text. Discuss or debate it with someone. Write about it. Search for its significance or impact. Reduce or summarize it. Rehearse and study it.
Consider what you bring to the text: Recall the key players. Recall the key point of view. Recall the key jargon or vocabulary. Recall key facts, concepts, and relations. Search for gaps in your understanding. Find the outer limits of your own knowledge. Create a framework (e.g., web, outline).	**Plan for gist or summary retrieval:** Attend to key vocabulary. Attend to textual and graphic cues. Attend to the author's style and angle. Select important ideas or delete trivia. Make connections within the text. Make connections outside the text. Summarize segments, if needed. Reduce the information (e.g., web). Visualize the relationships.	**Find a place in your mind for the text:** Assess it in light of original purpose. Place this author among others. Place this text among others. Extend your thinking along the same purpose or question. Develop a new purpose or question.
Consider what the text offers you: Will it support your purpose? Preview title and overall focus. Preview the table of contents, headings, subheadings. Preview pictures and graphics. Preview organizational patterns. Preview author's biography.		

Source: From O'Flanahan, J. F. & McDonell. G. M. (1990). Is practice keeping pace with research? *Reading in Virginia,* XV, 1–9. Reprinted with permission of the Virginia State Reading Association.

or other type of text. Although the format and retelling of a story may be quite familiar to students, recalling key ideas from a nonfiction selection involves understanding very different organizational structures (e.g., cause and effect, sequence of steps, time order, classification). Text Mapping Plus provides a framework for jotting down important terms and adding symbols, sketches, or clip art. The arrangement of the content words and visuals, along with connecting words for recalling relationships, provides students support when recalling the passage. Modeling, guidance, and practice are critical to the success of this strategy. Visual and directional components can help struggling students grapple with the meaning, explanation, and personal connections important for understanding the concepts to be learned. See an example of this strategy in Activity 11.4.

Ivey and Broaddus (2000) encourage teachers to "tailor the fit" of their instruction by being responsive to the needs and interests of their students. Dennis (2010) stresses the need to recognize and make use of the strengths and cultural capital struggling students bring to the classroom for designing meaningful instruction.

What information in this section helps you to understand Mark and would allow you to help struggling readers in your classroom?

Differentiation for Struggling Learners

An already full instructional schedule and high-stakes assessment pressures have teachers feeling overwhelmed by expectations and responsibilities. Teachers sometimes mistakenly assume that differentiating instruction to address various needs and learning styles means creating separate and multiple ways for teaching every concept (Carolan & Guinn, 2007). But differentiation for these students can be accomplished in small and subtle ways using student interests, cultural backgrounds, flexible grouping, visual

Please visit the Education CourseMate website at **www.cengagebrain.com** to find tips and example instructional units to help with differentiation.

ACTIVITY 11.4 Text Mapping Plus for Elementary/Middle School Science

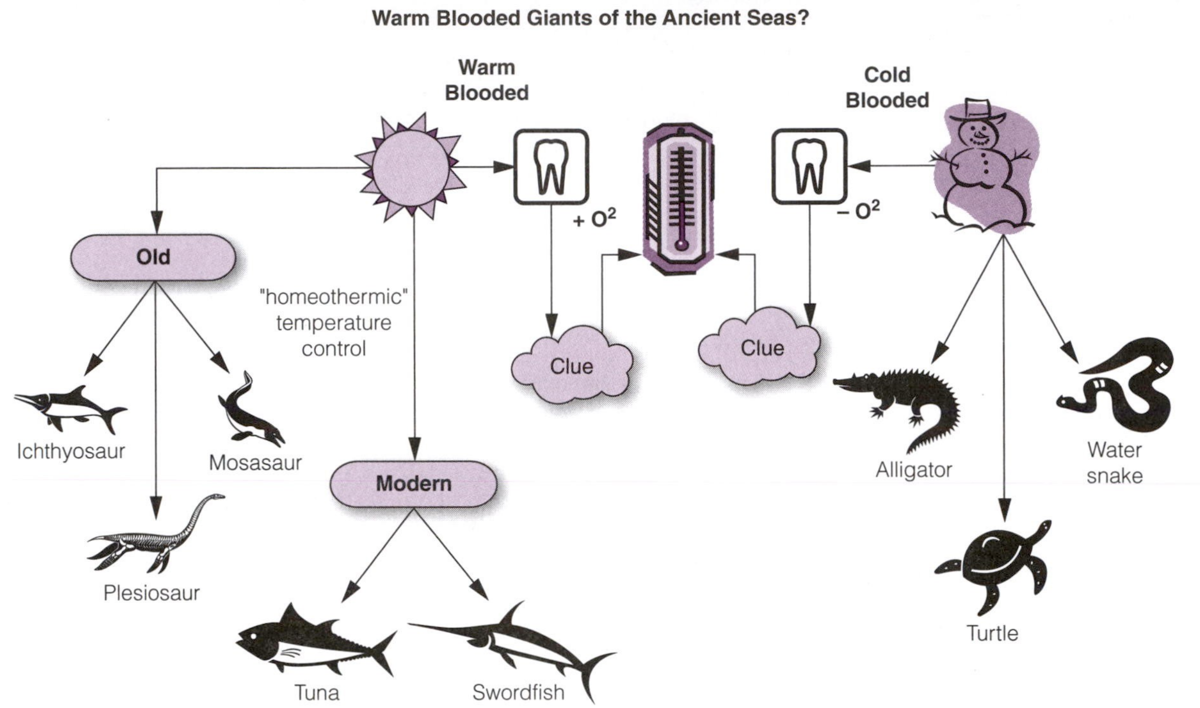

Text Map Plus based on the online article, "Warm-blooded giants of the ancient seas?" posted on the EurekAlert!: Science Reporting for KIDS! website sponsored by the American Association for the Advancement of Science.

Please visit the Education CourseMate website at **www.cengagebrain.com** to find a link to EurekAlert!

and tactile experiences, and peer discussion that fit naturally into a lesson (Kelley & Clausen-Grace, 2009). Tomlinson (2005) explains that "in effectively differentiated classrooms, teachers use a variety of graphic organizers, reading materials at different levels of complexity, direct instruction in small groups, curriculum compacting, up-front teaching of vocabulary to support reading success, and so on" (p. 10).

It is often easy to incorporate topics of student interest without sacrificing specific skills, strategy, and concept objectives. Research has shown that effective teachers create a safe environment, use consistent routines, and set high expectations for all learners (Kamil et al, 2008; Lazar, 2006; Lee & Spratley, 2010). Lee and Spratley recommend key components for successfully integrating content and literacy strategies:

1. Ensure that students understand that reading is a "meaning making" process.
2. Build in ways of helping students make sense of the text while they are actively engaged in reading.
3. Use gradual release to provide appropriate support as students gain confidence and proficiency to become independent readers.
4. Provide a variety of discipline specific readings and related activities that develop understanding of the concepts while developing strategies "good" readers use.
5. Use classroom discussion to encourage students to explain how their thinking and use of strategies helped them to understand and learn from the texts and tasks related to the discipline.

Please visit the Education CourseMate website at **www.cengagebrain.com** to find links to sites that offer interesting news stories related to various content areas.

Well-developed discussion can serve to motivate and actively engage struggling learners while positively impacting their comprehension and learning (Kamil et al, 2008). Sustained interaction that probes or explores a topic in depth elicits greater understanding than brief "question–response–move on" types of teacher–student talk. Open-ended questions that can have multiple answers followed by prompts that ask students to defend or explain their answers can reveal misunderstanding and clarify meanings. Provocative texts that can often be found on the Internet, accompanied by "I wonder" and "What if" kinds of questions, can energize and enrich topics of study in any of the disciplines. For these types of discussions to be effective with struggling readers, the environment must be one that is supportive and encourages risk taking. Students need to believe that mistakes are learning opportunities, not times for derision or "put downs."

Forgan and Mangrum (1997) remind content teachers that there are many possible causes of reading failure. They use the acronym **PLEASE** to remind teachers to consider:

1. **P**hysical factors may have caused difficulties, such as poor vision, hearing, or health at an early age.
2. **L**anguage problems or delays may cause a child to fall behind in development.
3. **E**nvironment—the home or the community—may not stress literacy or may distract from learning.
4. **A**ptitude may be over- or underestimated, causing lower or higher expectations than are fair.
5. **S**ES may influence the will to learn; interests and attitudes may conflict with learning.
6. **E**ducational factors may play a role—for example, poor educational facilities, teachers without the proper background, or lack of materials.

Use PLEASE to help guide understanding of struggling readers.

Steps for Content Teachers

To help struggling readers, the first step is for content teachers to consult the reading specialists in their schools. Yes, every school should have a reading specialist on board! According to Tatum (2004), the reading specialist should be ready to assess students who are struggling and share assessment results along with suggestions that incorporate appropriate strategies within content classrooms. Also, this specialist can assist by selecting and demonstrating curriculum materials and resources that aid content teachers. Dole (2004) suggests that reading teachers should coach teachers in how to teach reading within their subject areas.

Second, content teachers need to understand how their students view literacy. The story of Jacques (Knobel, 2001) provides a sobering illustration. Jacques declared that he was "not a pencil man" (p. 407). He used many avoidance strategies, such as fooling around to distract attention from the reading task assigned; remarking on "how boring" the assignment was; and not listening—or pretending not to listen. When teachers realize what these avoidance behaviors might be, they can counter them with relevant use of text and activities that pull these "nonpencil" students into literacy.

Third, when teaching struggling learners, content teachers need to ask hard questions and seek answers rather than abdicating responsibility. Ganske, Monroe, and Strickland (2003) pose some of these hard questions and provide brief responses. One question posed is: "Why don't students come to each grade level more prepared?" (p. 126). The answer is not easy, but the authors point out that early literacy experiences (see Chapter 1), background knowledge (see Chapter 3), choice of materials used in classrooms (see Chapter 6), and difficulty of tests (see Chapter 12) are all contributors. The next section provides some specific suggestions to address some of the needs of struggling learners.

Strategies for Struggling Readers

REQUEST

Manzo (1969) describes a questioning strategy called ReQuest that encourages students to ask informed questions. This procedure has worked and continues to work especially well in a remedial situation or with poor readers (Jones & Leahy, 2006; Whalon & Hanline, 2008). The key to this technique is that it requires students to "open up" their thinking—to question and think critically. A short selection is read, usually a paragraph, which is quite manageable for a struggling reader.

With this technique, the teacher and students first read silently a selected portion of the text (usually one or two paragraphs). The students then ask the teacher questions about what they read. The teacher must keep the book closed during this phase. When the students exhaust their questions, the teacher begins asking questions. During this phase, the students must also keep their books closed. The activity can be repeated with other paragraphs as time allows. The teacher then sets purposes for reading the remainder of the lesson, referring to the questions asked and information received during the ReQuest.

How would you adapt ReQuest for your content area?

Because Manzo (1969) had remedial readers and small groups in mind when designing ReQuest, some modifications for the content class are in order. The teacher should probably select a small but representative portion of text and not try to use ReQuest for a long period. The teacher also might want to limit the questioning time. It is likely that students' questions will be mainly literal; the teacher can then concentrate on inferences and applications. If ReQuest is used often, students will readily adapt to asking more sophisticated questions. After focusing on listening, speaking, and reading in this activity, teachers can follow the same steps using written rather than oral questions. Written questions tend to be more intricate than oral questions and thus enhance students' levels of sophistication with writing as well. The results of a sixth grade mathematics teacher using ReQuest are reported in Activity 11.5.

Ciardiello (1998) added a training model to ReQuest that encourages formal questioning. In Stage 1, divergent questions are identified; in Stage 2, divergent questions are classified; and in Stage 3, divergent questions are generated. The model enhances ReQuest by enabling struggling readers to comprehend at higher levels.

For follow-up, students received an ordered copy of the clues, which they cut apart and then pasted in correct sequence again. The teacher found that her students, often distracted, paid attention and participated enthusiastically. She thought that their understanding was greatly enhanced.

MYSTERY CLUE GAME

The mystery clue game, described in Chapter 4, is useful for helping students understand the sequential listing organizational pattern. Because this activity is particularly

ACTIVITY 11.5 ReQuest for Middle School Mathematics

ReQuest was used to introduce the chapter about integers. Students read the first two pages of the chapter and then asked the teacher questions directly pertaining to those pages. The students referred to their pages, but the teacher could not. After two minutes, the teacher had students close their books, and she asked questions. The teacher explained that even students who are often reluctant to participate joined in for this "stump the teacher" opportunity. Their engagement resulted in increased comprehension compared with previous lessons.

STUDENTS' SAMPLE QUESTIONS

What was the coldest temperature recorded in the United States? (–80°F)

What was the name of the weather station? (Prospect Creek Camp)

In what state was the weather station located? (Alaska)

How do you write a negative integer? (–4)

TEACHER'S SAMPLE QUESTIONS

What are some examples other than those on these pages where integers are used? (profit/loss; elevation . . .)

Which number is larger, 0 or –5? (0: it is farther to the right on the number line)

Describe the locations of 2 and 2 on the number line. (+2 is two units to the right of 0, and –2 is two units to the left of 0.)

Developed by Beverly Marshall.

useful for oral language development, it is important to revisit it in this chapter. The example provided in Activity 11.6 is adapted for first graders in an inner-city school. The teacher used this activity to help students recognize the sequence of steps in a science experiment about fire and air. The question they were to answer was: "Can fire burn without air?" The teacher wrote each step on a different card. When she presented the cards to the students, she said that she had "dropped them and needed to get the cards back in order." She had "found" the first card and placed it at the top of the pile. Their job was to put the rest of the cards in order. She read each card aloud, pointing to the picture and word clues. After the students reread, discussed, and sequenced the cards, they completed the experiment.

ANALOGIES

Analogies (see Chapter 3) are especially helpful to struggling readers, who often require relational (concrete, gestalt, example-oriented, relevant) rather than analytical (abstract, detail- and lecture-oriented, definitional) learning experiences (Anderson & Adams, 1992). At-risk readers might be better equipped to understand what they read after hearing analogies such as these:

> When I begin a new year of teaching mathematics, I always draw a little house on the board, starting with a foundation of bricks, and I explain that the foundation in math is being able to do the four basic operations—first with whole numbers, then with decimals, then with fractions. As we get into time, measurement, money, percents, and geometry, having a good foundation is absolutely necessary in order to do the work. So I tell my students that we cannot have any "loose bricks," or else doing multistep problems, story problems, solving for one or more unknowns, and graphing will be impossible. Students seem to appreciate the foundation analogy and can accept that doing calculations well is as important as grasping the new concept.

ACTIVITY 11.6 Mystery Clue Game for Primary Students

Use a knife to cut off the top of the pumpkin.

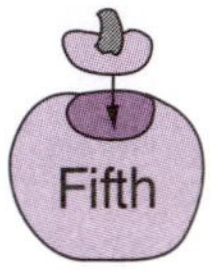

Put the top back on the pumpkin.

Put a candle inside the pumpkin.

Then

Relight the candle.

Clean the inside of the pumpkin with a spoon.

Next

Cut eyes, nose, and a mouth in the pumpkin.

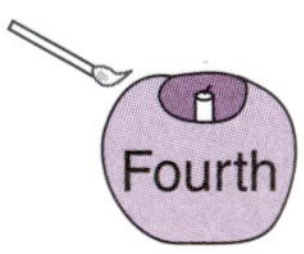

Light the candle.

Last

Put the lid back on.

Developed by Megan K. Houston.

The teaching of the new concepts must be "laid down" on a solid understanding of old concepts and the ability to apply them.

—Kerry Blum, middle school mathematics teacher

When a student does not understand new words or does not have any prior knowledge to link with new content, the student is likely to reject the new information. Deoxyribonucleic acid is a very complex molecule made up of different nucleotides linked together and is very difficult to understand. However, Watson and Crick's double helix model of DNA can be taught easily by taking the very basic approach of comparing it to something the students already know. By drawing a picture in students' minds of a circular staircase, and by describing the links of nucleotides as building blocks that can match up only in specific pairs (cytosine to guanine and adenine to thymine), the mystery of the DNA molecule dissolves.

—Diana Freeman, high school biology teacher

Additional Strategies for the Most Challenging Cases

What can the content area teacher do with a student who can barely read or who is a nonreader? The teacher can (1) pretend such a student is really not that bad a reader and do nothing, (2) get help from a reading specialist, or (3) assign extra work to help a student in this situation. Ideally, content area teachers do both (2) and (3). The reading specialist can help with basic skills while aiding the content teacher in adapting assignments for this type of student. Most of the techniques described in this book will help very poor readers and nonreaders. But the following techniques are especially important for the success of such students.

LANGUAGE EXPERIENCE APPROACH

The **language experience approach (LEA)** has been used by reading specialists for a long time (Ashton-Warner, 1959). Fisher and Frey (2003) suggest its use again as part of what they term a "gradual release model." In this model, teachers move from teacher-controlled to student-directed writing. Students dictate to a teacher or another individual their thoughts about a topic; then they copy to their own notebooks the words they have said and now see. The words next become the topic of discussion, which can also generate new words, phrases, and sentences. Next, students are encouraged to try to write just a few more sentences. In the Fisher and Frey model, students go on to interactive writing, relying on models of good writing to expand their own writing, and generating sentences. Eventually, students are able to expand their writing and move beyond the teacher's help with dictation. The model can also apply to reading. In the same way, by having struggling readers dictate their impressions about a subject and then use that dictation to talk about the subject and add to it, a very beginning reader—even in a content classroom—will have some text material to read and use for study. Landis, Umolu, and Mancha (2010) describe the use and effectiveness of the LEA for students with language and cultural differences. The strategy validates their language and perspectives while addressing the curriculum.

CONCEPT FORMATION STUDY GUIDES

The ability to create superordinate generalizations is a skill often completely lacking in reluctant readers and at-risk learners. Concept formation study guides (Thompson & Morgan, 1976) are excellent motivational tools for such readers. Such guides use a fundamental learning operation: the categorization of facts (subordinate concepts) under more inclusive, superordinate concepts. Thompson and Morgan note that "once a key concept has been acquired, we use it at different levels of abstraction, complexity, and generality, depending upon our stage of motivation" (p. 132). The function of this type of study guide is to teach the key concepts of a passage and to provide practice in applying those concepts to more complex and more general situations.

Activities 11.7 and 11.8 present two examples of concept formation study guides. The first is for elementary students, and the second is for high school social studies.

ACTIVITY 11.7 Concept Formation Study Guide For Elementary Students

I. Read the story. Put an X before each statement you think is true.

_______ **1.** A person should find out how the neighborhood feels about pets.

_______ **2.** Some small pets grow into large pets.

_______ **3.** Someone must care for your pet if you are sick.

_______ **4.** A kangaroo will not make a good pet.

_______ **5.** Do not read about a pet before you buy it.

_______ **6.** It is hard to keep a pet in a small apartment in the city.

II. Put true statements from Part I where they fit below.

Choosing a pet depends on:

Size Care Space

III. When you are finished, get together with a classmate and discuss your answers.

EMBEDDED QUESTIONS

Weir (1998) encourages the use of questions embedded in reading material to engage struggling readers. When they are confronted with questions during reading, they will be more likely to practice metacognitive strategies. Weir actually cut up reading material and inserted questions and response slots to keep students' attention while reading. Students began to make more and more elaborate responses as they answered embedded questions. Their test scores reflected increased comprehension.

Embedded questions must be carefully considered to maintain balance and variety. Reading selections found on the Internet or created by the teacher can lend themselves well to this strategy. Questions could be placed within the text, or portions of the text could be "clickable," linking students to questions. This is a fix-up activity that is best reserved for struggling readers, but the investment of time does help students become active, more proficient readers.

BEGINNER-ORIENTED TEXTS

Please visit the Education CourseMate website at **www.cengagebrain.com** to find a link to information and cautions for using graphic novels for instruction.

The texts used in content classes are too difficult for many struggling readers. Texts that are high in interest, contain fewer words per sentence and page, use less metaphoric language, and have illustrations that provide context will be more successful (Cole, 1998). Graphic novels have gained popularity, and publishers now include some selections in this genre. Media specialists can help content teachers locate these texts. Low-interest, low-readability, content-oriented books are also available from a few publishers. Most provide Lexile, as well as interest levels, to assist teachers in matching readers with appropriate texts. Activity 11.9 lists some high-interest, low-readability book series and publishers.

INTERACTIVE NOTEBOOKS

Interactive notebooks have been used for a variety of purposes but may be best known for their use in science and social studies. As Chesbro (2006) notes when discussing the value of interactive science notebooks, they "encapsulate and promote the most cutting-edge constructivist teaching strategies while simultaneously addressing standards, differentiation of instruction, literacy development, and maintenance of an

ACTIVITY 11.8 Concept Formation Study Guide for High School Social Studies

THE MOVE TO WINTER GRASSLANDS

Key Concept: Social transience

Main idea: Interactions among people and the physical and social environment that surrounds them influence how they meet the basic needs of life.

PART I

Directions: Think of a family that you know who recently moved. What reasons did this family have for moving? In the chart below, complete a list of reasons American families and Al'Azab families have for moving from one place to another.

Reasons for Moving

American Families	Bedouin Al'Azab Clan
1. Dad's new job	1. Good grasslands
2.	2.
3.	3.
4.	4.
5.	5.
6.	6.
7.	7.
8.	8.
9.	9.
10.	10.

PART II

Directions: From your list in Part I, answer the following questions:

1. Select those items under the "American" list that are related to making a living. Do the same thing for the Al'Azabs. How are the reasons different? Alike?
2. Based on the information you have organized above, make a list of the Al'Azab family's basic needs of life. Are they different from the American family's basic needs?
3. Based on the information you have organized above, define in your own words what you think *social transience* is.

ACTIVITY 11.9 Resources for High-Interest, Low-Readability Content Series

From Follet Educational Services (Follett Educational Services, 1433 Internationale Parkway, Woodridge, IL 60517-494)

Capstone You Choose: Interactive History Adventure
On the Front Line
Astonishing Headlines
Extreme Environmental Threats

From Capstone Publishers (Capstone Publishers, 151 Good Counsel Drive, PO Box 669, Mankato, MN 56002):

Graphic Science
Graphic Expeditions
Voices of War
Wild Outdoors

From High Noon Books (Academic Therapy Publications, 20 Commercial Boulevard, Novato, CA 94949)

Illustrated Classics
Great Medical Milestones
Strange (but True) Stories
Disasters Collections
Great Trials in History

The Horn Book Guide: Interactive database, reviews more than 79,000 books, searchable by level and topic (The Horn Book, Inc., 56 Roland Street, Suite 200, Boston, MA 02129).

An alternative to beginner-oriented texts is rewriting (see Chapter 3). This requires teacher time, but it tailors the text to the specific content to be taught.

Please visit the Education CourseMate website at **www.cengagebrain.com** to find links to all these publishers and sources for high-interest, low readability materials.

organized notebook as laboratory and field scientists do" (p. 31). The concept of an interactive notebook provides a great deal of flexibility for teachers to structure designs and parameters to reflect the needs and organization of the content and skills to be learned. Pages on the right side of the notebook are used for "input" or incoming information in the form of notes taken from lectures, presentations, textbook or other readings, podcasts, CDs, video clips, lab sessions, or class activities. Pages on the left are reserved for "output" in the form of student responses or connections to the information on the right. These could be charts, graphs, webs, tables, illustrations, diagrams, poems, cartoons, reflections, or the like. Entries may be written or drawn right on the page or taped in and folded to the size of the page. Interactive notebooks are in some ways quite similar to double-entry journals, except that instead of dividing a page in half, the entire left page is used for student responses and the entire right page is used for notes or information. An interactive notebook allows creativity and modification appropriate to the various needs and differences among students. Assessment can be based on rubrics and criteria provided by the teacher or decided collaboratively among students and teachers.

Teaching Diverse Learners in the Content Classroom

Horn and Tynan (2001) state that the most effective educational strategies for special education students are the same ones that help most students in regular education. This may be true, but teachers need also to understand that diverse learners often "reside" outside of a traditional academic space that relies on a print-focused model. Benson (2010) observed students over an academic year in a language arts course. She describes one student, Bud, who devised ways to circumvent print-based assignments. For instance, he started out enthusiastically on a term paper, selecting to research Guns N' Roses, but he faltered when he had to write about his findings. He needed a "third space" where he could transform an academic assignment into something closer to his own interests. She encourages teachers to find ways to use the "third space" that disaffiliated students often create for themselves; teachers can develop opportunities where students can use their expertise in the digital world—often not the teachers' expertise!—to create non-print products that demonstrate knowledge and encourage deep learning.

Some alternative ways of reaching diverse learners include:

- Multimodalilty, as discussed in Chapter 6
- Technology, as discussed in Chapter 10

ONE-MINUTE SUMMARY

This chapter has considered several groups of diverse learners: students at risk, students from low-socioeconomic environments, students with low self-esteem, students with LEP, special education students, and struggling readers. We suggested that at-risk learners can become successful, as studies of resilient students indicate. The types of intervention suggested for all diverse learners include cooperative grouping; teacher interaction and high expectations; boosting students' confidence and encouraging an internal locus of control; and interesting, systematic, and strategy-based learning. Most of the techniques presented in this textbook are appropriate with some modifications for diverse learners. Some additional strategies that are especially effective for these learners were suggested in this chapter.

The population in U.S. classrooms has changed considerably in the past decade, reflecting the increasingly diverse population of the nation. The teacher's perspective and attitudes are critical for shaping the approach and benefits of working with and teaching diverse learners. When diversity is regarded as an enrichment opportunity for all, the teacher's approach is to use those differences as instructional advantage. It may take extra effort and require myriad strategies, but all learners benefit from the respect and understanding developed in the process.

END-OF-CHAPTER ACTIVITIES

Assisting Comprehension

1. This activity could be done in an online environment in preparation for a class meeting or in its entirety during a class meeting. Using a cooperative learning jigsaw strategy, students read, share, and teach each other. Students in a base group (numbers 1–4) are given unique information about one or more types of learners. After reading the material, students meet in "expert" groups (all As together, all Bs together, and so forth) to discuss and plan how to teach the information. Students share their "expert" knowledge in their base groups, each taking a turn. In this way, the puzzle is completed. The following diagram illustrates the structure of this activity. Expert groups can be structured as follows:

   Group A: Special education students

   Group B: At-risk, resilient, low-socioeconomic, and low self-esteem students

   Group C: ESL and ELL students

   Group D: Struggling readers

Base Group 1

A	B
C	D

Base Group 2

A	B
C	D

Base Group 3

A	B
C	D

Base Group 4

A	B
C	D

2. Consider the diverse learners presented in other chapters (JaNette, Trinka, Gustavo, and Mark) and create a table to identify specific areas of need and appropriate PAR strategies that you might use for each of them. Then think of two or three students with special needs in your classroom and complete the table with information about them.

Reflecting on Your Reading

1. Read *Among Schoolchildren* by Tracy Kidder (1989), particularly the chapter titled "The Science Fair," in which Chris, the teacher, confronts Robert about his failed science project. *Supporting Struggling Readers* by Barbara Walker (2003) gives many practical instructional suggestions. Rosa Hernandez Sheets' *Diversity Pedagogy: Examining the Role of Culture in the Teaching-Learning Process* builds understanding and offers practical classroom applications. Make a table listing instructional ideas you found in these readings and match them with content or concepts you will be teaching.
2. Your content organization (e.g., National Council of Teachers of Mathematics, National Council of Teachers of English, National Council for the Social Studies, National Science Teachers Association, International Reading Association) has most likely developed a set of standards that identify the performance criteria relevant to classroom teachers. Standards usually delineate elements of foundational knowledge that a classroom teacher should possess. Locate and become familiar with what the organization recommends. For instance, teachers should:
   - Use a variety of strategies and materials, including appropriate technology applications to address the diverse learning needs and abilities of students from different cultures, languages, and backgrounds.
   - Develop a positive learning environment that encourages risk taking and holds high expectations for all learners.
3. How were these elements addressed in this chapter? How does being informed about these elements aid in content instruction?

CHAPTER 12

Assessment and Evaluation Issues

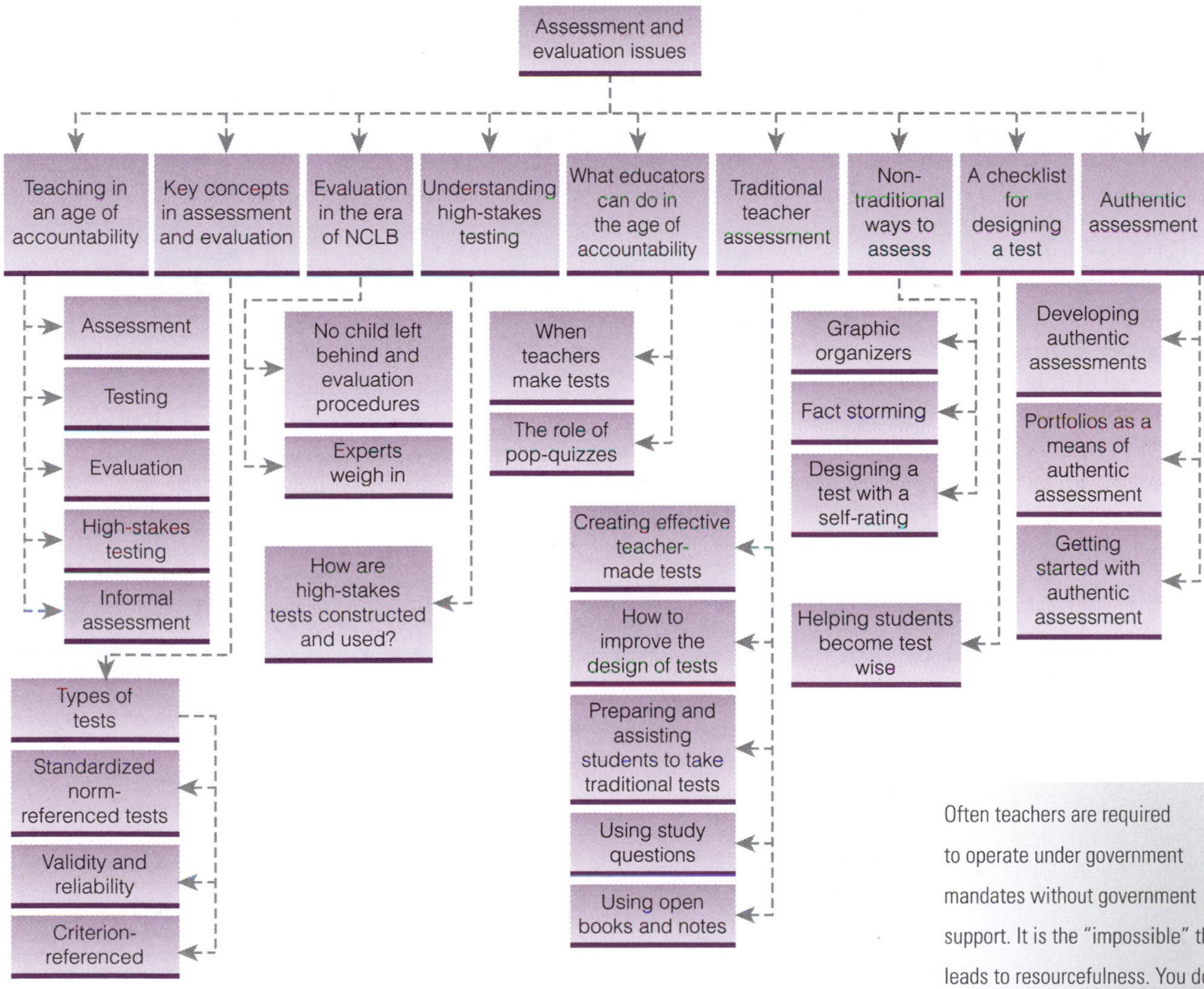

Often teachers are required to operate under government mandates without government support. It is the "impossible" that leads to resourcefulness. You do not teach for your government; you teach for your students . . . and for yourself.

MEDITATIONS FOR TEACHERS BY GREG HENRY QUINN, APRIL 15 ENTRY

VOICES FROM THE CLASSROOM

It is near the end of the school year. An entire week is being devoted to testing, and everyone is nervous. The students worry that their scores will be low and they won't pass; the teachers worry that low scores will reflect on their performance ratings; the administrators worry that their schools, districts, and states will not meet their government-mandated adequate yearly progress (AYP) goals. Teachers, parents, and students are resigned to the fact that after this week, not much real instruction will occur because "everyone knows" the year is over after tests are taken to "prove" that students learned enough.

"Everything" has already been done: Theories and workshop advice have driven instruction; children have been encouraged to get a good night's sleep and eat a healthy breakfast. As they walk into the classrooms for the testing, they receive peppermints just like students across the country. The "peppermint theory" (Aratani, 2007; Dember, Warm, & Parasuraman, 1996; Warm, Dember, & Parasuraman, 1991) indicates that focus is improved and affect is engaged when one sniffs peppermint. Even skeptical teachers are willing to give this research-based testing gimmick a try!

What is familiar to you about this scenario? What issues might trouble you about the week for testing, the anxieties created, and the stakes of the testing results? Are you surprised by the tactics used to support student success?

PREPARING TO READ

1. Before reading this chapter, read the assessment standards for classroom teachers developed by the professional organization in your field (e.g., International Reading Association, National Council of Teachers of English). How do you rate your knowledge at this point? Could you do these tasks? In which area do you need additional support?
2. Following is a list of terms used in this chapter. Some may be familiar to you in a general context, but in this chapter, they may be used in unfamiliar ways. Rate your knowledge by placing a plus sign (+) for those you are certain you know, a check mark (✓) for those you have some knowledge about, and a zero (0) for those you don't know. Be ready to locate unfamiliar vocabulary terms in the chapter and pay special attention to their meanings. Select three terms for which you wrote 0 and create a possible sentence—a sentence using the term that makes sense and reflects the meaning of the term.

_______ assessment
_______ testing
_______ evaluation
_______ high-stakes testing
_______ informal assessment
_______ standardized test
_______ norm-referenced test
_______ validity
_______ reliability
_______ criterion-referenced test
_______ NCLB
_______ Race to the Top
_______ AYP
_______ PIRLS
_______ highly qualified
_______ value-added assessment
_______ nontraditional test
_______ test-wise
_______ authentic assessment
_______ portfolio
_______ ARA

OBJECTIVES

As you read this chapter, focus your attention on the following objectives.

1. Define the term *high-stakes testing* and describe its influence on assessment.
2. Understand why the content teacher must take a large role in assessment, testing, and evaluation in today's classroom.
3. Describe traditional tests, including standardized, criterion-referenced, and teacher-made tests.
4. Understand the problems of traditional tests and review suggestions for improving them.
5. Understand how to design a test whereby students complete a self-rating of their performance.
6. Understand the importance of nontraditional testing.
7. Understand how being test-wise affects student performance on tests.
8. Learn about practical forms of authentic assessment for the content classroom.
9. Learn about the value of portfolios and how to use them for effective assessment.
10. Consider the role that technology can play in testing, test preparation and review, and digital portfolio assessment.

Teaching in an Age of Accountability

We are living in an age of accountability (Johnson & Johnson, 2002; Stewart, 2004) where standards for learning (Valencia & Wixson, 1999) are used as the basis for high-stakes testing (Afflerbach, 2002; Giambo, 2010; Kornhaber, Mishook, Edwards, & Nomi, 2006; Worthy & Hoffman, 2000), which often results in less than positive unintended consequences. Expectations for accountability, testing, and standards cut across school divisions, states, and nations and serve as a policy instrument for governments to leverage school change (Supovitz, 2009). It is no longer enough to focus on one's own content in one's own classroom. Educators recognize that all teachers must be accountable to a set of standards that permeate every classroom. For instance, the International Reading Association has prepared a set of standards for assessment, diagnosis, and evaluation specifically targeted at classroom teachers. (In Preparing to Read, you were asked to review assessment standards for the professional organization in your field before reading this chapter.) Knowing more about accountability issues is clearly becoming part of every content teacher's responsibility. Such knowledge helps teachers discuss standards for learning, evaluation, assessment, and high-stakes testing in a manner that helps all learners receive the best education and all educators provide it. This chapter presents information about assessment, testing, and evaluation as it pertains to the content teacher. Both formal and informal means of assessment are discussed, and suggestions for classroom assessments are provided.

Assessment, "the gathering of information about students from multiple measures or sources at multiple points in time" (Gottleib, 2003, p. 2), is used to make educational decisions by collecting data (Salvia & Ysseldyke, 1998). Assessment is an

This chapter was significantly revised and updated by Joan A. Rhodes, Associate Professor in the Department of Teaching and learning, School of Education at Virginia Commonwealth University.

Peppermint and other enhancements for improving test performance have been in use for quite some time. Please visit the Education CourseMate website at **www.cengagebrain.com** to find a link to a recent report about these practices.

When teachers conduct an assessment before instruction, they are determining the background knowledge of their students. Refer to Chapter 3 to review this type of practice and several other assessment procedures.

ongoing process; it can include such data as formal test scores, but classroom tests and observations are also part of the assessment process. Each time a teacher begins a new unit of instruction, assessment should occur.

Testing is a part of assessment; it is one event, or data source, from one instrument given at one point in time. Tests are a "proxy for accomplishment" (Afflerbach, 2002, p. 352) because they provide a sketch—not an entire profile—of how a general population is doing on the factors being tested. Theodore Sizer commented that tests "tend to test how one individual performs on that kind of test. It's like taking a temperature in a hospital. It's one important index, but it's only one. We're judging kids on the basis of their temperatures" (Oppenheimer, 2003, p. 282). Tests are useful in providing a point of comparison and one measure of evaluation.

Evaluation is a term usually reserved for making judgments about educational performance based on collected assessment data. Evaluation requires the educator to make a comparison of data with a standard to determine its worth or quality (Huitt, Hummel, & Kaeck, 2001). Evaluation requires a value judgment and therefore differs from assessment (the gathering of information). A test is one piece of data for an evaluation. When teachers give tests in their content areas, they use the results to evaluate student knowledge. However, teachers often use many more sources of data in evaluating student learning. When *one* instrument is used to make an educational decision, that process is labeled **high-stakes testing**. According to the American Educational Research Association, "Certain uses of achievement test results are termed 'high stakes' if they carry serious consequences for students or for educators" (2004, np). In other words, a single test is given specifically to determine how well students know content information.

Teachers are constantly assessing learners because they collect information about their students' performance regularly. In the past, such **informal assessment** was used to evaluate students and assign grades that should reflect student learning and success. However, today, informal assessment alone is not considered adequate to demonstrate student progress. Uniform assessment procedures at the state level are now required to provide evaluation of educational progress. A formal measure, usually a designated test, is selected as the way to determine whether students have learned what they "should know." Assessment and evaluation support teachers in planning appropriate instruction that meets the needs of individual students. However, because of this trend toward consistent, uniform testing with one test as the only measure of success, all teachers must take the first step toward appropriate assessment by becoming informed. Teachers must understand how to balance informal and formal means of assessment to obtain the information needed for good instructional planning and to meet educational policy demands.

Key Concepts in Assessment and Evaluation

Assessment can involve both quantitative and qualitative testing. Quantitative assessment is designed to ascribe numerical results to student performance. Several types of tests are available to assess students. Aptitude tests predict potential for learning. Diagnostic tests designate areas of strength and need. Suppose a student was not achieving and the teacher suspected that the student could do much better. An aptitude test might verify this observation and lead to an effective educational plan for that student, such as a program that challenges gifted students. Suppose a student was below grade level in reading performance but specific ways to help were not apparent. A diagnostic test could help pinpoint the areas of need. In these examples, the tests assess and the findings help the teacher evaluate the student to activate an instructional plan. Usually, guidance personnel or educational specialists administer quantitative forms of assessment, which can be informal or formal measures. The initial observations of the teacher, often including informal assessment of student class performance, inform remediation plans, and when further support is needed, are often used as a basis to begin the special education testing process.

Achievement tests are intended to show what students have achieved or learned about a specific area. Teachers create and administer informal achievement tests all the time. Most schools have participated in annual evaluations of student achievement for decades. Such evaluations have focused on creating a picture that informs us about student progress, especially in math and reading skills. One national example, cited throughout this textbook, is the National Assessment of Educational Progress (NAEP), which publishes results of nationwide testing. School systems have systematically administered tests to determine how their schools are doing, but the tests they have used—and thus the information they have gathered—have differed from state to state and even from district to district. Decisions about individual students' progress or a school's standing were seldom made from the results of such tests. Teachers of content subjects may have helped administer achievement tests in their classrooms, but in the past, the results were used to improve school-wide programs and plan for individual student's instruction. In today's content classrooms, however, teachers are expected to ensure that all children can meet achievement goals and are held accountable for each child's test results.

Students take many types of tests. What are the three types of tests discussed here? Reflect on the types of tests you have administered and taken. Which tests have had the most influence on your academic progress? How were test results used?

Standardized, Norm-Referenced Tests

Standardized tests can be norm-referenced or criterion-referenced tests. A **norm-referenced test** measures ability or achievement against an expectation (a norm or standard). The major purpose of standardized, norm-referenced tests is to evaluate the amount of information that students know about a subject. The Scholastic Aptitude Test (SAT) and the Graduate Record Examination (GRE), developed and published by Educational Testing Service (ETS), and the Stanford 10 (the 10th edition of the Stanford Achievement Test) are examples of common standardized tests. Such tests usually consist of multiple-choice or closure questions, which are readily and quickly scored by computer or scan sheets. One correct answer is expected per item. Standardized tests are used to compare the performance of groups, such as the results from one school compared with those of a school system, a system with the state, or the state with the nation. The tests are designed by a group of experts and are pilot tested on a representative sample of students. The results are studied, the test is modified, and a set of norms is developed. The norms become the basis for comparing results; hence, the term **norm-referenced test** is often used to describe standardized tests. Scores on a standardized test are given in percentiles, stanines, standard score equivalents, grade equivalents, or normal curve equivalents. Many classroom teachers follow the formats used on standardized tests as they construct classroom tests.

Not all standardized tests are equally effective for all users. Perhaps the norming groups are not representative of the particular population to be tested. Perhaps the items on the test do not reflect the content taught to the students tested or the test purports to test content that it in fact does not really test. Standardized tests, however, are subject to a system of checks that helps users make appropriate selections. These measurement concepts include validity and reliability. **Validity** is the "truthfulness" of the test—a check of whether the standardized test actually measures what it claims to measure. **Reliability** is the "consistency" of the test—whether it will produce roughly the same results if administered more than once to the same group in the same period. Reliability checks how dependable the test is. Both validity and reliability contribute to confidence in a quantitative measure. The higher the validity and reliability, the better a test is reported to be.

A school system should select the standardized test best suited to its system by asking these questions:

1. Does this test measure what has been taught?
2. Can we depend on it to give about the same results if we administer it today and tomorrow?
3. Is the norming group similar to our group of students?

Unfortunately, the decision to use a standardized test usually does not reside at the school level; it is the choice of a state or national mandate.

Criterion-Referenced Tests

Criterion-referenced tests are less formal than standardized tests, although their format is much like that of standardized tests—usually multiple-choice or closure questions. Criterion-referenced tests can be standardized, but their major purpose is not to compare one group against another, so they often are not normed. Short-answer, true/false, and other objective forms may appear as well because they are less formal. The purpose of criterion-referenced tests is to measure whether a student can perform a specific task or knows a specific body of knowledge. Thus, their purpose resembles that of classroom tests.

The criterion is the level of performance necessary to indicate that a student knows the task. The school systems are often able to decide this criterion. Thus, two schools could use the same test but set different criteria. One school might set 85 percent as a passing score, and the other might set 90 percent as passing. The level of performance on the task is the score: A score of 85 percent means that the student responded correctly to 85 percent of the items. No grade-equivalent scores, percentiles, or other scores are provided.

Because criterion-referenced tests indicate mastery of a task, they should be based on specific objectives. For example, the objective might be stated as follows: "The student will demonstrate mastery by correctly identifying 48 of 50 states and their capitals." A student who has been taught 50 states and capitals and can identify 48 on the test has demonstrated mastery of the criterion. A school system that elects to use a criterion-referenced test developed by an outside source can select an appropriate test by asking these questions:

1. Do the objectives and criteria match our objectives in this content?
2. Are enough items included to indicate whether our students have met the criteria?
3. Do the test items reflect the way in which we taught the information?

Criterion-referenced tests are not new, but their evolution into more uniform, formalized tests is. In fact, the concept of criterion mastery is what individual teachers rely on as they design tests for individual classroom use. Unfortunately, even criterion-referenced tests in today's world of testing may not be selected at the school level; this choice is often made by a state or national mandate.

Evaluation in the Era of No Child Left Behind

For many years, a perception has existed that public education in the United States is not adequate. During the last third of the 20th century, national results for fourth and eighth graders showed a decline (National Center for Educational Statistics, 2003). In 2009, the results were very similar, with only 33 percent of fourth graders and only 32 percent of eighth graders attaining a "proficient" level—a standard that test officials say represents solid academic performance (NAEP, 2009). Many experts assert that American schools are in crisis and standards have to be established as a benchmark for all students. Researchers such as Bloom (1987) and Hirsch (1987) led the charge that resulted in legislation at the federal and state levels and raised awareness of assessment and evaluation in schools. Policy-making interventions include vouchers and national testing (Godwin & Sheard, 2001). Although many experts contest the perception that public education is failing and suggest that the effects of poverty and social policies are influencing student performance (Berliner, 2009, 2001; Bracey, 1997; McQuillan, 1998; Whittington, 1991), the voices of concern have led to new federal interventions such as the No Child Left Behind (**NCLB**) Act of 2001 and government educational initiatives such as **Race to the Top**.

Information cited in Chapter 1 demonstrates why the public believes that American public education is not effective.

The NAEP, Progress in International Reading Literacy Study (PIRLS), and Programme for International Student Assessment (PISA) results allow educators to compare students' performance at the national and international levels. PISA (2006) indicated that 15-year-old Americans scored lower than the mean of 30 countries on the combined science literacy scale and mathematics literacy scale (IES, n.d.). Please visit the Education CourseMate website at **www.cengagebrain.com** to find links to the NAEP, PIRLS, and PISA results.

NCLB was incorporated in the reauthorization of the Elementary and Secondary Education Act (ESEA), which indicated an expectation of greater school accountability, as well as the use of proven research-based teaching methods. With this legislation, significant federal funds have been provided to states to ensure strong education for all students—and for teachers as well. Educators must be **highly qualified**—that is, specifically endorsed to teach the subjects they are hired to teach.

NCLB has resulted in an unprecedented increase in school accountability and testing, beyond the requirement to administer the NAEP in grades 4 and 8 in every state. A major goal of NCLB is to ensure a strong emphasis on reading instruction, especially for children in the first few grades. Some professionals argue that this emphasis takes away support for older students who need reading instruction and for those who have special needs, as described in Chapter 11 (Conley & Hinchman, 2004; Paul, 2004). NCLB funding comes with a condition: Schools must demonstrate that the education resulting from the funding has been effective. This demonstration takes place through the results of mandated testing in grades 3 through 8. Schools must show **adequate yearly progress** (**AYP**) by demonstrating at least minimal progress for every student in every school. If AYP is not met after two years, parents may move their children to other schools, and federal dollars may be taken away from low-performing schools. AYP must be based on scientific and research-based instruction and evaluation.

The NCLB Act repeats the words *scientific* or *scientifically* 115 times and the word *research* 245 times. (See pp. 240 and 436 of Oppenheimer's *The Flickering Mind.*) Why does NCLB focus on the use of scientific research? What constitutes scientific research, according to NCLB?

Many states decided, in the wake of NCLB, that all schools should use a designated test to determine mastery of content deemed important in their states. They created, or commissioned the creation of, criterion-referenced tests that match their state standards for education, or they chose a nationally recognized standardized test that they believe demonstrated such competence. The broad use of designated assessments created a situation new to many content teachers in which high-stakes tests became a greater part of their instructional considerations.

No Child Left Behind and Evaluation Procedures

In the past few years, national test scores have gone up, especially in reading (NAEP, 2007). Some people believe the improved test scores are a result of increased attention to student performance and effective teaching. Others believe that this rise in scores is the direct result of NCLB. However, the tide may be turning on NCLB. The latest Phi Delta Kappa/Gallup Poll (Bushaw & Lopez, 2010) indicates that fewer than one in four respondents believes that NCLB has helped their schools. The public has become vocal about the negative consequences of high-stakes testing on student motivation for learning, and the resulting narrowing of curriculum to meet minimum standards (Center on Educational Policy, 2008; Pierce, 2010).

Experts Weigh In

Many experts in education are quite concerned about the emphasis NCLB seems to place on the use of high-stakes tests (Paul, 2004). Now that NCLB has been in place for several years, analyses of its effectiveness are indicating that its success is, at best, uneven (Liston, Whitcomb, & Borko, 2007; Rose & Gallup, 2007). Critics wonder whether conceptual understanding can truly be assessed on tests selected to meet the goals of NCLB (Liston, Whitcomb, & Borko, 2007). Houston (2005) questions whether teachers can accommodate different learning styles with an emphasis on standardized tests without impeding the joy of learning. Uzzell (2005), a former member of the U.S. Department of Education and the U.S. House and Senate Committees on Education, also shared concerns, pointing out that schools may be reporting inaccurate and imprecise data in order to meet the provisions of NCLB. Director Bushaw and International President Fujloka of Phi Delta Kappa published a statement titled "Rethinking assessment and reforming NCLB" (Bushaw & Fujloka, 2006). They point out that although most Americans agree with the underlying purpose of NCLB, they want schools to focus on yearly student improvement rather than on a school's scores. Parent–teacher associations (PTAs) report that one in three PTA members believes that NCLB has been effective for his or her children but also that too much pressure is being placed on schools and teachers (Robelen, 2005).

Paul (2004) titled his article, "The Train Has Left: The No Child Left Behind Act Leaves Black and Latino Literacy Learners Waiting at the Station." How has NCLB impacted minority students in your school system?

One important group of experts, the Phi Delta Kappa/Gallup poll, reported that in 2006, 39 percent of those polled (up 9 percent from the 2005 poll) indicated that there was too much emphasis on testing; in 2008, the same organizations found that most people believe "examples of student work" and "teachers' observations" are more meaningful than test scores. (Bushaw & Lopez, 2010; Rose & Gallup, 2006). Rose and Gallup (2007) evaluated the data as follows: "[T]he public, despite its desire for high standards and accountability, does not approve of the strategies used in NCLB" (p. 36).

Not all of the news about NCLB is negative. On the positive side, NCLB has brought to the surface an increasing need for more standardized means of determining at least some measure of success and needed areas of improvement in instruction. NCLB has improved awareness that many diverse students need more instructional attention. This can mean those subgroups such as English language learners (ELLs) and children with learning disabilities or those who are at risk and from low-socioeconomic environments (see Chapter 11) will receive more attention from qualified teachers. Another benefit is that uniform testing will be provided so that learners and groups of learners can be consistently compared on the same measure. The concerns about NCLB by teachers, parents, superintendents, and politicians, however, will result in changes to the interpretation of the act.

The recent Commission on NCLB (2007) has recommended significant levels of support for teachers and principals, as well as accurate and fair accountability and quality student options for demonstrating competence. Criticism related to the types of standards and levels of performance required by individual states has resulted in a new government educational initiative, Race to the Top (Pierce, 2010). Competitive grant funding is available through this federal program for states that agree to educational reforms, including the tying of student performance measure results to teacher evaluation (Khadaroo, 2010). Although some states have accepted the national common standards and worked successfully with teacher unions to develop proposals for Race to the Top, other states, such as Texas, Alaska, and Virginia, have opted out of the grant competition (Abowd, 2010; Harrison, 2010). The tenets of Race to the Top are likely to be proposed as part of the reauthorization of the ESEA when it is reviewed by Congress (Harrison, 2010).

For content teachers, the emphasis on demonstrating AYP through standardized testing and the increased accountability expectations of both NCLB and Race to the Top means that *all* teachers must become involved!

Understanding High-Stakes Testing

Several professional organizations have developed position statements to assist teachers in understanding the cautions related to relying on high-stakes testing (American Psychological Association, 2001; International Reading Association, 1999; National Council of Teachers of Mathematics, 2000). Educators may wonder if high-stakes tests are appropriate measures of academic success. Today they seem to be "major influences on curriculum and instruction, on teachers and their professional development, on community–school relationships, and on levels of school funding" (Afflerbach, 2002, p. 1). Should one test be used to make decisions about performance when other indicators, or a combination of other indicators, might better reflect progress? Can a test really capture the learning that "involves complex, recursive processes of interpretation and meaning construction" (Afflerbach, 2002, p. 354)? Thornburg (2001) encourages educators to "put the pencils down" because standardized test items "decontextualize" learning. He notes that test items focus on isolated facts that are often not at all applicable in real-world knowledge.

Can tests replicate the daily tasks students will be expected to perform after graduating from high school? How do your tests prepare students for work beyond graduation?

One concern about any standardized testing is the *washback* effect of tests (Bardovi-Harlig & Dörnyei, 1998). Constant exposure makes students and teachers very familiar with the language of tests; this familiarity itself can influence test results. The adoption of state and national standards may lead to too much emphasis on testing and not enough on learning content (Berube, 2004), so students may end up learning more about how to take tests than about the content the tests purportedly assess. Another major concern is that one size truly does not fit all. Often, questions about what test to choose (such as those we have suggested) do not yield satisfactory answers for a school system; nevertheless, school systems use the tests as a measure of performance. They do so because comparisons can be made across schools, divisions, states, and nations. They also do so because demand for national testing, using the same test throughout every state, is increasing. This concern leads to the *high-stakes issue*: More educators and politicians are questioning why students should achieve a passing grade in a content class when they perform poorly on a designated test. Policy makers want the test to be the common denominator and the grade to be consistent with the test score.

How Are High-Stakes Tests Constructed and Used?

See Chapter 1 for examples of these standards within the PAR (preparation, assistance, and reflection) Lesson Framework. Please visit the Education CourseMate website at **www.cengagebrain.com** for a link to California's Standards for Reading Assessment and to the Common Core State Standards Initiative. How do the standards for your state compare?

The essential content information that students "should know" is determined by a group of experts. This group of experts may include content teachers, administrators, state education department personnel, and citizens. The "essential content knowledge" is usually written in the form of standards and competencies that all students are expected to meet.

After state standards are developed and accepted, they are used to formulate a test that students must take to demonstrate mastery of content. To meet the requirements of NCLB, such tests are given in grades 3 through 8, but many states also test mastery at the end of content courses to make sure students know specific content before graduating from high school.

If students do not demonstrate mastery of the test material, they and their teachers are held accountable. The consequences of poor scores on this one test are often disturbing. Funding for a school may be withheld by the district, state, or nation; students may not be able to pass a grade or graduate until they pass the test even if their grades in the content courses are passing; or teachers may be asked to explain why their students have "gained so little" in their classrooms. Students who do not pass a mandated test are usually required to repeat the test until they do pass it. Schools and teachers whose students consistently do not pass the test are asked to explain why and to provide remediation for failing students. Many schools have come under fire for low test scores. Because it appears that only one measure of knowledge, the designated test, is being used to judge student, school, district, or state performance, the stakes are indeed high.

What Educators Can Do in the Age of Accountability

View the video to find ways to successfully prepare students for standardized forms of assessment.

How do teachers today cope with high-stakes testing in their classrooms? Hughes (2007) wrote about how teachers at his school persisted through many principals and mandates for testing—some effective and some not so effective. They trudged on, building relationships with students, parents, and community. Their school has remained instructionally sound through it all. For a teacher voice on this topic, refer to Activity 12.1.

ACTIVITY 12.1 Coping with High-Stakes Testing in Content Classrooms

NCLB is an ironic term because so many children are left behind because their needs are not considered when it comes to testing. How is it that a child who is not on grade level for reading has to take the grade level test anyway? Yes, there is a student who reads at a first grade level in my daughter's class, and by law he must take the fourth grade test for reading. We know this student will not pass. Why put him through the frustration? Why can't a student take the test that is appropriate for him regardless of his grade level? There still would be a statistical means of showing adequate progress.

—Lori Levy

Part 1: Survey two educators in your content area, in person or by email, regarding their responses to these two questions:

1. How have teachers adapted their instruction to deal with high-stakes testing?
2. What accommodations do they make for student with disabilities and ELLs?

Part 2: Share your findings with your classmates in a live or virtual discussion.

Teachers should remember that formal testing provides valuable information; it is a part of good assessment and evaluation of instructional success. Professional organizations provide sound advice for teachers in this age of accountability through their position statements (American Psychological Association, 2001; International Reading Association, 1999; National Council of Teachers of Mathematics, 2000):

- Teachers should explain the appropriate use of tests whenever they can. Teachers can point out the importance of using multiple measures. One recommendation (of the International Reading Association position statement) is that teachers "construct rigorous classroom assessments to help outside observers gain confidence in teacher techniques" (p. 1). Such action might demonstrate to outsiders that because instructional quality is high, extreme measures of accountability (that do not really account for progress) are not necessary. Teachers need to explain to parents and policy makers that classroom assessment is important and reflects students' achievement. Teachers need to teach students about tests but not teach to a test. One school recently took a stand that it will not teach to any test (Fisher, 2004). The principal explained that teachers had been spending too much time preparing students to take the test rather than on deepening student learning and integrating art and music into the classroom. The diversity of the students in this school (77 percent English language learners) meant that more creativity rather than less was necessary. Richardson (2002) found that high school students who had experienced a humanities curriculum (focusing on the impact of history on literature, philosophy, and art) with little emphasis on a high-stakes test did as well as or better than students who had experienced concentrated test preparation.
- Teachers should understand the purpose of a test or any other means of evaluation well enough to describe it to parents, students, and other stakeholders. If an "assessment team" (Murray, 2002) consists of students, parents, teachers, and administrators, everyone can share this job, and all can be ready to help describe the how and why of assessment.
- Teachers need to practice accountability by choosing formats for assessment and evaluation that match the content being learned and making sure that the formats are as authentic and representative as possible. This includes technological formats. Informal and authentic assessment should be incorporated into instruction, as will be described in the following sections of this chapter.
- Informed teachers might argue that some of the conflicts raised by high-stakes tests result from trying to equate different sources of data meant to demonstrate different aspects of education. By consistently raising questions and balancing test results with other measures, teachers can keep the role of standardized tests in perspective for themselves—and, we hope, for administrators and the community.
- The most effective solution should be excellent instruction and multiple means of assessment that lead to solid evaluation.
- As Bushaw and Fujloka (2006) suggest, the emphasis should be on **value-added assessment** that looks at a student's growth and achievement over time. The emphasis would no longer be on comparing students with each other but on comparing a student's past achievements with newer marks of achievement.

When Teachers Make Tests

Teacher-made tests are one way of increasing accountability. Teachers should test to determine what their students have learned and still need to learn. Their tests should reflect high academic standards but be based on what was taught. Tests mark the culmination of periods of study about a content topic. Tests come in many forms—from informal observations of student learning to formal final examinations. Students' ages and the topics covered influence the type of evaluation that teachers use as part of their instructional program.

Tests should match the learning, not vice versa. Walton and Taylor (1996) created workshops to help teachers at the elementary level produce more relevant tests for the test takers that stretch their minds. Kahn (2000) found that high school English teachers tended to teach students to think critically and analyze literature but then gave tests of factual knowledge. Such inconsistencies and weak teacher-made assessments confuse students about what to learn, how to take tests, and why tests matter. Rather than giving practice with stale questions, teachers should seek ways to improve their tests, thereby eliciting the cognitive skills that are the ultimate goal of instruction. A teacher's main purpose in giving a test is to evaluate whether students have learned. Traditionally, teachers ask questions about what they have taught, and students answer them. Teachers then evaluate the answers as a gauge of how well students have learned the material. A secondary purpose is to provide test grades as one sign of progress in a report to students, parents, and administrators.

In addition, students' performance on a test should tell teachers how well they have presented content material. Overlooked in the past, this testing purpose has the greatest potential for creating an optimal classroom learning environment. If students can produce fine responses to questions, teachers may conclude not only that students are confident with the topic but also that they as teachers are presenting the content in ways that assist comprehension effectively. If students cannot produce satisfactory answers, the material may need to be retaught with different instructional strategies. Teachers, who consider tests as a way to evaluate their own instruction, as well as to evaluate students' knowledge and to assign grades, often alter their instruction and revise their tests. The result is that both teachers and students improve at their respective jobs. But changing the evaluation to match instructional practice is difficult. Teachers need support and time, as well as good reasons, to do so (Liston, Whitcomb, & Borko, 2007). The next sections of this chapter suggest several new ways of thinking about assessment and evaluation.

The Role of Pop Quizzes

Pop quizzes have often been popular with teachers. Teachers may think that pop quizzes provide a means of control over "making" students learn. They may think that such quizzes demonstrate their instructional rigor. The usual scenario for pop quizzes is to find out whether students have read an assignment. But what if students tried to read the assignment and experienced difficulty? A pop quiz may penalize students for not understanding rather than for not reading the material. Students may require assistance before being able to demonstrate learning.

Teachers must think carefully about administering a pop quiz and then design the quiz to achieve their objectives. If the objective is to promote student independence and responsibility, then the homework comprehension sheet in Activity 12.2 is appropriate. If the purpose is to "catch" students, teachers should rethink evaluating comprehension.

Nessel (1987, p. 443) comments that question-and-answer sessions that do not develop understanding "amount to a thinly disguised test, not a true exchange of ideas." Developing a conceptual understanding of a topic is difficult to do with just one homework assignment completed; discussion and thought are required. The question

"How did you know the answer was boxcar?" (Walton and Taylor, 1996) may convey the complexity that good questions and discussions require before any measure of knowledge can be made fairly. Most pop quizzes leave no room for such development. Because pop quizzes are often used more like drills, there are no follow-up prompts asking how the student arrives at an answer. Consequently, the teacher cannot tell if the question is just worded poorly or if the student did not understand the concept. Unless teachers use pop quizzes for instruction rather than for grading, they will defeat their own purposes and send an incorrect message to students; It's not important to understand the material, just to recount it!

Instead, pop quizzes should be used to evaluate what teachers can be reasonably sure has been achieved. For instance, rather than "popping" questions for a grade, a teacher could check to see whether students understand the content of the previous night's reading assignment. Recently, the use of classroom response systems (CRSs), commonly known as "clickers," to digitally poll students in real time has allowed educators to quickly determine whether students have fully understood the instruction and assignments.

Clickers promote engagement and class participation and have potential for enhancing learning and test readiness. Clickers use infrared or radiofrequency technology that transmits and records the responses students click into their remote devices. In this system, students press a clicker button to record their answer to a question, which is then transmitted wirelessly to a computer program; results are aggregated and displayed immediately by the classroom's projection system for all to view (Hu, 2008). According to EDUCAUSEConnect (2005), interaction and engagement are often limited by class size and human dynamics (a few students may dominate the conversation while most avoid interaction). Clickers, plus well-designed questions, provide an easy-to-implement mechanism for enhancing interaction. Clickers can also facilitate discipline-specific discussions, small group cooperation, and student-to-student interactions. Clicker technology enables more effective, more efficient, and more engaging education (EDUCAUSEConnect, 2005).

The EDUCAUSE Learning Initiative provides a series of concise information papers on emerging learning technologies that can be used to enhance instruction. Please visit the Education CourseMate website at **www.cengagebrain.com** to view the *7 Things You Should Know About . . .* series. Which of the emerging technologies would support instruction in your content area?

In classrooms without clicker technology, teachers can use a writing activity (e.g., the activities described in Chapter 10) to make certain that students attempt homework assignments. If understanding the homework was the problem, the students' written comments will show the teacher that the attempt was made. If students do this, they demonstrate that they tried to read for the assigned purpose. This demonstration and the student responses using a CRS will accomplish the same purpose as a pop quiz.

Middle school mathematics teacher Mary Broussard allows students to accumulate points toward their final grade by doing homework. The students are also tested, and the homework points do not outweigh the test grade. This teacher encourages students to try, knowing that they can get some credit for doing so, and she uses the class review to clear up confusion. Activity 12.2 shows a homework comprehension sheet designed by a middle school social studies teacher to indicate whether students attempted their homework and to help the teacher focus the lesson. Before assigning the reading as homework, the teacher asks the students to survey the reading and write three questions that they expect to be able to answer after completing the reading. When they arrive in class the next day, the teacher distributes this exercise. The teacher can rapidly review the responses to the homework comprehension sheet to find out who completed the assignment. Areas of student confusion as well as student interests can be ascertained. This activity serves as a check of homework and as a way to determine student background for the rest of the lesson.

ACTIVITY 12.2 Homework Comprehension Sheet (Middle School Social Studies)

Answer the following questions as completely as you can.

1. How did you study pages 192 to 194 in Social Studies?
2. What did you learn from these pages?
3. Do you see any similarities between your life and the lives of the people mentioned?
4. Were there any passages, terms, or concepts that you found difficult to understand?
5. What part of this reading did you find most interesting?
6. How do you think that you answered these questions?
7. Why do you feel the way you do?

Developed by Charles Carroll.

ACTIVITY 12.3 Proverbia (High School Latin Students)

Proverbs use English words, which are derived from Latin words. They serve as vocabulary builders and critical thinking exercises while also taking the place of pop quizzes.

Proverbium #1: Members of an avian species of identical plumage congregate.

Answer: Birds of a feather flock together.

Note: I encourage students to share the proverbia with their parents. Parents may give suggestions to their children regarding problem-solving strategies but must not give the answer.

Correct answers count + 1 toward the quiz!

Developed by Amy Nowlin.

A high school foreign language teacher uses "proverbia" to encourage students to keep up with class work. She thus accomplishes what many teachers think pop quizzes should do while showing her students that practice for their quizzes is important, interesting, and challenging. Activity 12.3 provides an example.

Traditional Teacher Assessments

Traditional test items include objective questions, essay questions, or a combination of these. Objective tests include multiple-choice, true/false, matching, and completion questions. Teachers find such items easy to grade but difficult to construct. Students sometimes label objective items as tricky, confusing, or even too easy. Essay tests require students to write about a given topic and offer a viable way to evaluate critical thinking and the applied level of comprehension. Students sometimes call essay questions confusing, too hard, or unfair. Essay formats are also labeled as subjective because teachers must spend time considering responses carefully when grading. These student complaints do not have to be the status quo. Essay questions are not subjective or difficult to grade when questions are written clearly and carefully. Objective items can measure student knowledge when revised to increase challenge and reduce confusion in interpretation.

Creating Effective Teacher-Made Tests

The single greatest problem with traditional tests is that the grades students receive often disappoint teachers. The single best solution to this problem is for teachers to stop giving tests before students complete the preparation and assistance phases of the PAR (preparation, assistance, and reflection) Lesson Framework. Yet even allowing for this solution, traditional tests have many other problems.

A few decades ago, *Captrends* (1984) reported a study of 342 teacher-made tests in a Cleveland school district. Administrators, supervisors, and teachers representing all subject areas reviewed tests from all grade levels. The reviewers found test formats that were similar to the format that we described: objective, short-answer questions. Only 2 percent of all items in the 342 tests were of the essay type. The researchers found unclear or nonexistent directions, poor legibility, and incorrect grammar. Point values for test items and sections were noticeably absent. Ambiguity in questions led to the possibility of more than one correct response or student confusion. In addition, the types of questions asked were predominantly literal. Questions at the application level of comprehension accounted for only 3 percent of the questions asked. The situation has not changed much since then (Ayers, 2001; Kahn, 2000; Rhodes, Robnolt, & McKelvey, 2004; Walton & Taylor, 1996). However, with careful analysis and revision, teacher-made tests can be effective. Consider the benefits of activities such as Activity 12.4 for improving assessment practices.

ACTIVITY 12.4 Revising Content Area Tests

Teachers should not underestimate the value of revising content area tests. The following activity provides an example of how an English teacher revised her assessment and asks the reader to review his or her own testing material.

Context: One eighth grade English teacher took a hard look at her own test and found that the primary comprehension focus was a mixture of all three levels but more literal and inferential than application. . . . "Comprehension was dependent on recall more than real learning. . . . The test was too long and looked hard. . . . I neglected to give point values or the weight of the test in the final grade" (Baxter, 1985).

The teacher's response: This teacher revised her test and summarized her satisfaction with the new version: "All in all, I feel that the best feature of my redesigned test is that it captures many concepts and is a more appealing form. . . . I feel this test allows the student to demonstrate more of his/her knowledge of the material covered in the unit by giving specific responses. . . . I feel this test will net better student response because it appears shorter, looks more appealing, and is different from usual tests I would have given in similar teaching situations before" (Baxter, 1985).

Your task: Select a teacher-made test you designed or borrow one from a colleague in your field. Evaluate the quality of the items, the written directions, and the breadth of information covered. Revise the assessment accordingly. How did you improve the test? What challenges did you encounter while rewriting?

Four problems characteristic of teacher-designed classroom tests are:

1. Teachers rely on the objective format, and factual questions dominate their tests. We infer that teachers find such items relatively easy to construct. Perhaps they think knowledge of facts is especially important to test or they rely on textbooks that bombard learners with an abundance of facts without incorporating in-depth explanation to construct their tests. Students won't learn how to think critically if they are not required to demonstrate such thinking on tests. Note how Activity 12.5 provides a check of whether students understand a third grade mathematics lesson by asking students to demonstrate learning through interpretation and application.
2. Teachers seem to have difficulty expressing themselves clearly when they write questions and construct tests. Perhaps teachers need practice in constructing good questions.
3. Teachers sometimes design tests before fully covering the content material. Students may not be ready for a test because they have not developed enough understanding of a topic. This problem might occur because teachers actually cover the content differently than intended. Teachers may need to provide more targeted assistance and may need to encourage students to take some responsibility for their own learning.
4. Some tests do not allow students to demonstrate their learning. Students need to have an active role in designing assessments that help them demonstrate what they know in relation to real-life situations. If teachers always design the tests, students have a limited role: regurgitating information for the teacher. This is why so many students quit rather than study; they don't see any point to a test that doesn't seem real to them.

ACTIVITY 12.5 Demonstrating Learning through Interpretation and Application (Third-Grade Mathematics)

SUMMING UP YOUR MEASUREMENTS

These activities are designed to determine how well you have understood the chapter on measurements. You will demonstrate your knowledge and understanding by performing the following activities.

The first activity will be done with your assigned group. The next three will be performed on your own. Be careful and have fun!

1. Read the recipe first. Make the individual assignments. With your group, make a vanilla pudding.
   - Who will read the recipe?
   - Who will assemble the cooking utensils and cups?
   - Who will mix the ingredients?
   - Who will pour the hot mixture into the cups? (Use pot holders!)
   - Who will place the cups in the pan and take them to the refrigerator?
2. Read the outdoor thermometer at three different periods of the day (morning, midday, afternoon). Record the temperature at each period.
3. Use the scales to weigh your empty lunch box, your mathematics book, and your wallet or purse. Record each weight.
4. Measure the perimeter of your desktop, your closet cubbyholes, and any other item on the classroom floor. Record each measurement.

Developed by Bessie Haskins.

How to Improve the Design of Tests

Many teachers like to use traditional tests. There is great value in what is known and experienced. By reviewing the flaws discovered in many tests, teachers can improve traditional tests immensely. Coombe and Hubly (2004) offer several suggestions for constructing classroom tests. Teachers need to test to course outcomes, prepare unambiguous items, write clear directions, and take the tests themselves! The following general guidelines will help:

A number of websites are available for supporting educators in constructing classroom based assessments. Please visit the Education CourseMate website at **www.cengagebrain.com** to view an example of this type of resource. Consider revising an assessment from your content area using this tool.

1. The content to be evaluated should be carefully selected to match not only the teachers' content goals but also those of any standards (such as of a professional organization or a state-mandated criterion-referenced test) to be met.
2. Questions on a test should reflect a balance among the three basic comprehension levels. The difficulty of questions should be related to the task required. Recall is harder than recognition; production is harder than recall. Questions with several parts are more difficult than questions with one part. Selecting is easier than generating. Teachers should try to vary their use of difficult and easy questions within a test.
3. Sometimes the answer that a student gives is unanticipated but better than the expected response. Teachers should write questions carefully to avoid ambiguity but still encourage spontaneous critical thinking.
4. The best-worded test items do not provide secondary clues to the correct answer. Teachers often give inadvertent clues to students, who spot the giveaways. For instance, students may learn that correct answers on a multiple-choice test are often keyed to choice *c* and that the longest choice is most likely to be the correct answer. Also, the stem often signals an obvious match among the multiple choices. Students realize that for both multiple-choice and true/false items, positive statements are more likely than negative statements to be correct choices. Teachers sometimes give answers away with grammatical clues.
5. When wording test items, teachers need to consider their students' language proficiency. A well-worded test that does not match the students' knowledge of language will result in poor comprehension even though the students' learning may be excellent. Make sure instructions and items are clearly written. Also, balance gender and ethnicity in creating scenarios; don't stereotype.
6. Include distractors if they will test careful reading, content understanding, and critical thinking; do *not* include them if your intention is merely to trick students.
7. Create a table to see if you accomplished your objectives after you finish writing the test:

Question	Does content tested match a standard?	Comprehension level?	Ambiguity?	Secondary clues?	Language match?	Distractors?

8. Ayers (2001) recommends, at this point of test development, that the teacher ask a colleague to review the test and provide comments. She notes that creating a good multiple-choice test takes time, but a good test can be used to generate new tests, so it ultimately saves time for the teacher—and gives students a fair opportunity for success.

Preparing and Assisting Students to Take Traditional Tests

By using the PAR Lesson Framework, teachers can fulfill much of their instructional role in readying students to take tests. We find that some other techniques also prepare and assist students in test performance. Chapter 10 describes uses for technology as a learning tool, such as using graphic organizers and databases that students can access on their own. The development of study questions can be facilitated by using both of these items. Chapter 9 on study skills also provides additional information related to this topic.

TECH APP

Using Technology as an Assessment Tool

Many technology programs assist teachers in preparing tests (for students) or performing assessment tasks (themselves).

- Consider the appeal of computer-based assessment: Individual learners can participate and receive their results quickly.
- Find Internet-based quiz or test creation programs (including one for use on an iPod): Google "test quiz creator."
- Select electronic aids for assessment, testing, and evaluation.
- Beware: Digitally administered tests have the same pitfalls as isolated tests (as opposed to several sources of assessment data).
- Beware: Sophisticated test creation programs are costly.

Using Study Questions

Teachers encourage students to use study questions in a variety of ways. The teacher can prepare a list of questions to be included on the test and distribute the list at the beginning of a unit so students can refer to it throughout the unit. A graphic organizer can be used to generate questions related to items grouped together visually by topic. Or the teacher can suggest possible test questions as instruction proceeds and then review all of the questions after completing the unit. This list can become the pool for essay test items that the teacher uses exclusively for test development. Such a technique has merit for two reasons: A test bank is acquired as the unit progresses, thus eliminating last-minute test construction, and students have a study guide that is familiar, thorough, and not intimidating. If the teacher creates questions that follow the question construction guidelines and cover representative content, the technique works well.

Some teachers tell students before testing what the specific test questions will be. This technique works better with essay questions than with objective questions.

Although many teachers hesitate to provide questions in advance, fearing that students will not study everything, this can be a wise way to prepare and assist students. In fact, students cannot study everything, and they certainly cannot remember everything for a long time. If the essential information is covered in the proposed questions, then a question list can be effective. A pool of essay questions from which the specific question for a particular test is drawn can also be provided in an electronic environment.

Having students create the questions for a test is sometimes a good technique. This option requires that students understand the content thoroughly and understand how to write good questions. An alternative for younger students and those not proficient at question construction is to have students use brainstorming to predict possible test topics and then informally generate questions. A first grader could speculate, "I think you might ask me to explain how fish breathe." Students can construct possible items for an objective test as well as an essay test, or they can review items from sample tests that the teacher provides. Teachers who encourage students to create possible test questions should include some version of the students' questions on the actual test.

A threaded discussion on a teacher's classroom website can allow students to share their possible test questions with each other. Other students can respond, and the teacher can interject as well.

Any variation on student construction of the test questions will let students practice questioning and answering, provoke critical thinking, and promote students' responsibility for their own learning. Another bonus is that students who are familiar with the teacher's way of designing a test will be less anxious about being tested. Students often experience test anxiety, and this can account for poor test response.

Using Open Books or Notes

Teachers find that allowing students to use open books or open notes—or both—lets students concentrate on producing the best response on a test and assists them in the actual test-taking process. This technique encourages good note-taking strategies and clear organization of information by promoting recognition and production rather than recall. If students take their tests in a digital environment and they cannot use notes, be sure that the computer is clean of any aids and that the medium for saving the test (e.g., flash drives, CDs) is also clean.

Teachers can use technology to demonstrate the types of questions students will encounter on a test. Electronic quizzes for practice, such as those on the website accompanying this textbook, are a means for independent practice in **test-wiseness**. The CRS, described earlier, can also be used to support students as they prepare to take traditional tests. For instance, multiple-choice or true/false problems that require careful thinking and application of knowledge can be presented to students, who respond by clicking answers on personal response devices. The compiled answers are converted into graphs that allow the teacher to understand how the students are reasoning and whether more instruction is necessary. It also allows the students to become familiar with how to think about test items with greater clarity and less nervousness. Activity 12.6 contains two such questions (and a diagram to accompany one question) that pose problems crucial to understanding introductory physics and dental hygiene. Using clicker technology makes learning the concepts enjoyable while teaching test skills.

ACTIVITY 12.6 Questions for a Classroom Response System or Clicker Activity

Two identical beakers are filled to the same level with water. One of the two glasses has ice cubes floating in it. When the ice cubes melt, in which glass is the level of the water higher?

A. The glass with the ice cubes.

B. The glass without the ice cubes.

C. It is the same in both.

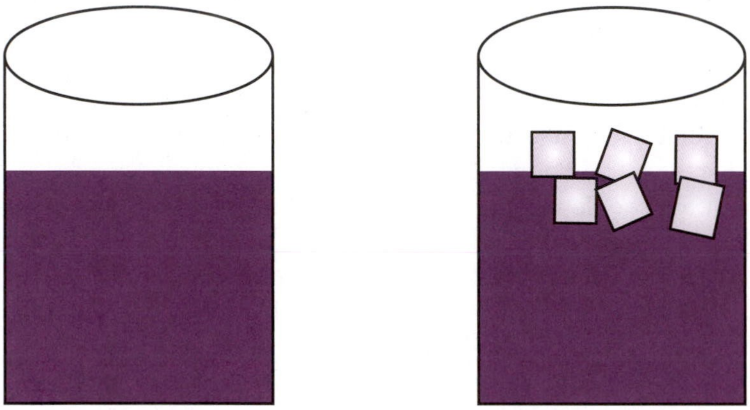

The frequency of brushing your teeth is the most important factor in the prevention of tooth decay.

A. True

B. False

Developed by Jeff Nugent.

Nontraditional Ways to Assess

Everyone appreciates variety. Teachers may be pleasantly surprised to find that students increase productivity when an evaluation looks more like the strategies that have been used for instruction rather than the same old test format. We encourage teachers to use new strategies for assessment, testing, and evaluation; even when poorly made objective tests are redesigned, they do not correlate with the type of achievement required in a world where concepts are more important than facts. We must alter our testing procedures if we want to produce critical, thoughtful readers. Creative thinkers often perform much better on tests that are nontraditional and reflect nontraditional instructional activities.

By using some of the strategies presented in this book, teachers can construct tests that contain few traditional items. The most **nontraditional test** would eliminate questioning altogether and rely on student application of knowledge. Although teachers may not wish to design an entire test with no questions, some nontraditional items might spark interest. Primary teachers are often especially attracted by nontraditional tests, and intermediate and secondary teachers may prefer adding some nontraditional items to a more traditional test. The possibilities are as numerous as the types of activities presented in this text.

The following instructional activities can be used as nontraditional test items. Teachers who have designed tests using such items report that they elicit more critical thinking from their students. Certainly, teachers will see the possibilities for designing many activities as nontraditional test items.

Graphic Organizers

Graphic organizers offer excellent possibilities for assessing student knowledge. Research (Katayama & Robinson, 2000; Kim, Vaughn, Wanzek, & Wei, 2004; Robinson & Schraw, 1994) has shown that notes and partial notes recorded as graphic organizers help students comprehend better than fully formed outlines. Students demonstrate the applied level of comprehension when they create organizers using terms they learned during the lesson. The interpretive level of comprehension is tested when the teacher asks students to explain why they positioned words in certain places on the organizer. No traditional questions are asked, yet comprehension can be evaluated and graded.

The authors feel so strongly about the value of graphic organizers that they use one to begin each chapter in this book. Chapter 3 explains the construction of graphic organizers. How might you adapt a graphic organizer you currently use for assessment purposes?

A teacher can repeat the use of graphic organizers at the end of some lessons but with gaps; readers should identify what is missing and recall where it should be placed within each organizer. This activity encourages readers to remember what they have read. Similarly, a teacher can instruct by using a graphic organizer, map, structured overview, jot chart, or any such visual aid, and then present the organizer with blanks on a test, where it becomes a nontraditional test item for eliciting responses that demonstrate knowledge of facts. Test items such as these might read as follows:

> Study the organizer I have drawn for you. It is like the one we studied in class, but in this one there are several blank spaces. Using the list of terms attached, fill in the term that fits best in each space (1 point each). Then write one sentence beside each term listed; this sentence should explain why you think the term belongs where you put it in the organizer (2 points each). Next, write an essay that includes the information in this organizer. Your first paragraph should provide four (4) details. Your last paragraph should summarize by telling what new information you have learned by reading this chapter (25 points).

Note that the directions are specific and that point values are given for each procedure. Students need to demonstrate their factual knowledge, but they must also interpret and apply information. Writing an essay is also part of this question. Because the components of the essay are defined, grading it should be simple. It is also possible to prepare a rubric for this essay:

> An "A" essay will contain three or four paragraphs that fully explain all the information on the organizer. Students not only will demonstrate factual knowledge but will also show inferences and applications. The essay will have a clear beginning and end.
>
> A "B" essay will contain two or three paragraphs that explain the information on the organizer. Students will demonstrate factual and interpretive knowledge. The essay will have a clear beginning and end.

Activities 12.7 and 12.8 demonstrate ways that graphic organizers can be used in the classroom for nontraditional assessment. Activity 12.7, designed by an eleventh grade teacher, allows students to demonstrate their ability to remember facts. When the teacher provides a list of terms that could complete the organizer as in Activity 12.8, student recall of elementary social studies information is enhanced.

ACTIVITY 12.7 High School Geometry Organizer

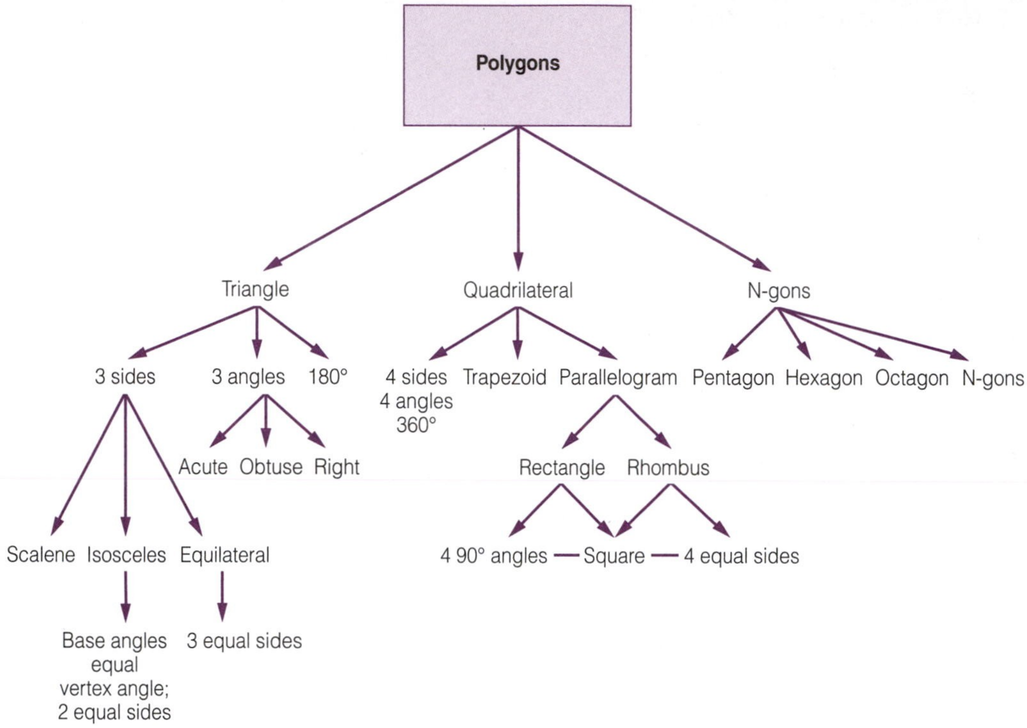

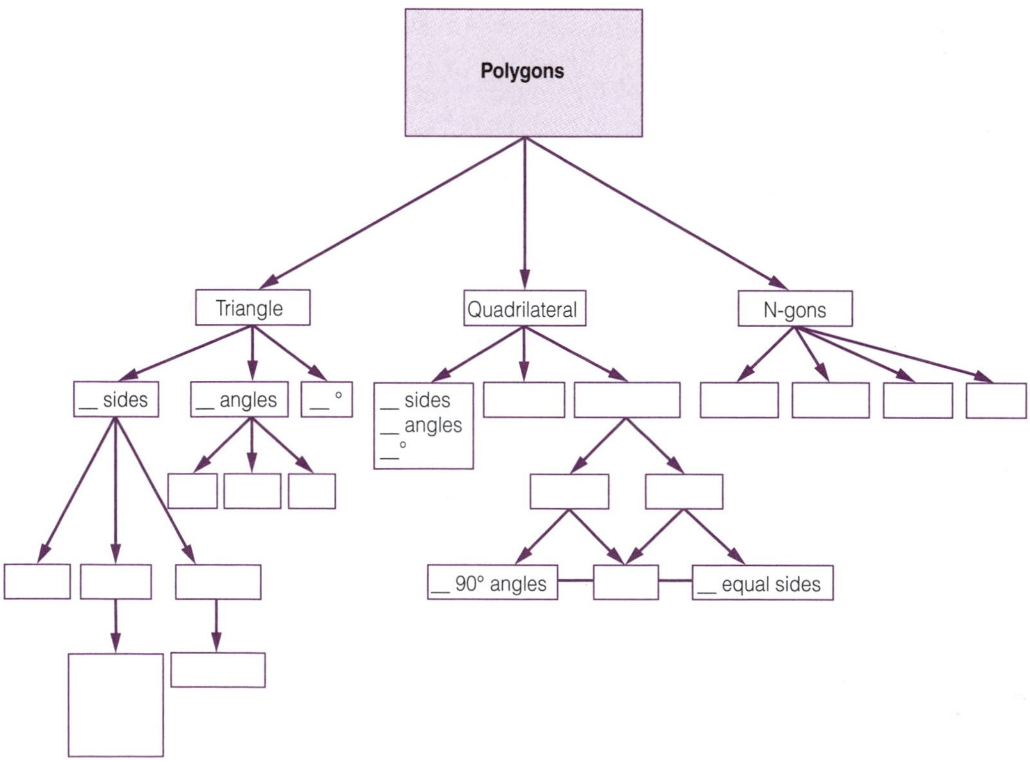

Developed by Frances Reid.

ACTIVITY 12.8 Elementary School Social Studies Organizer

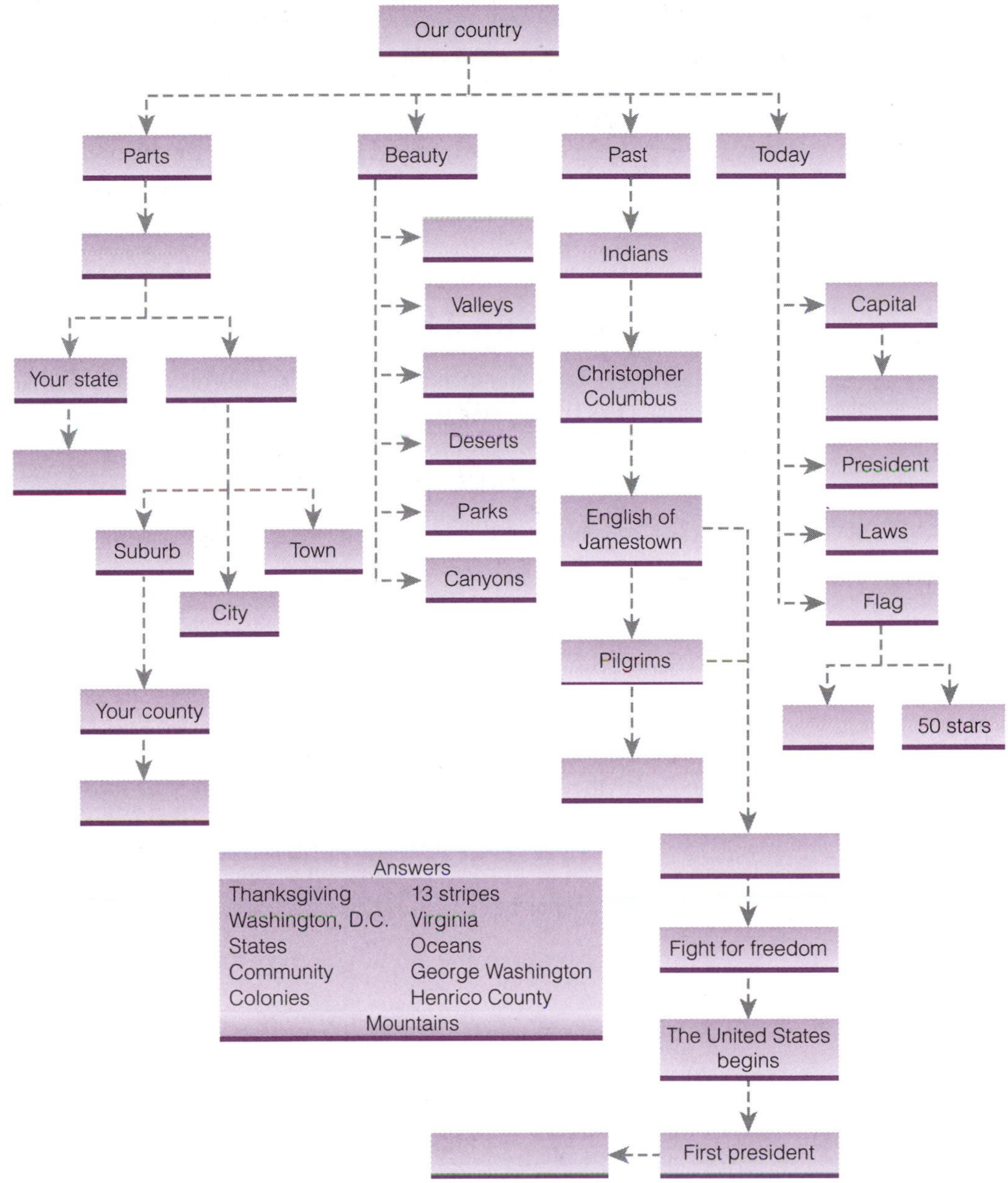

Developed by Sandra Zeller and Brenda Winston.

Factstorming

Factstorming is explained in Chapter 3 as a good preparation activity because students identify familiar terms about a topic before they study further. Students can add to the list produced by factstorming after their studying is complete; the

Refer to:
- Chapter 1 for an example of a What-I-Know Activity (WIKA)
- Chapter 4 for further explanation of WIKAs
- Chapter 5 for information on cubing, quick-writes, free-writes and student-generated questions

additions become an evaluation of new learning. If students are asked to explain each addition, they are demonstrating interpretation of information. Students demonstrate application when they categorize the already known and new information and then write an essay about this categorization. The use of factstorming as a test item is similar to the last step in a What-I-Know Activity (WIKA), but it is graded.

Other strategies discussed in this text can also be used as tests. A number of strategies for writing that are explained in Chapter 10 can be used as effective tests. Some of these are cubing, quick-writes and free-writes, and student-generated questions (also discussed in Chapter 5).

Designing a Test with a Self-Rating

Teachers can design tests that include self-ratings. This technique originated years ago when Hoffman (1983) suggested this rating technique for journal entries and Richardson (1992b) created a version for tests.

The first questions on a test might resemble these:

- How did you study for this test?
- How much did you study?
- How well do you think you will do?

The answers show how the students prepared. Before the test is returned, a second set of questions should be asked:

- Now that you have taken the test, was this test what you expected and prepared for?
- What grade do you think you will receive?

These questions can help the student take responsibility for studying and producing a good test response. The third set of questions promotes reflection. It is answered after the teacher returns and reviews the test with the students:

- Now that you have gone over your test, would you say that you studied adequately?
- Was your grade representative of your learning? Why or why not?
- What have you learned about taking tests?

Such a three-step process built into the testing procedure sends the message that the student is ultimately responsible for demonstrating learning. If teachers use the procedure often on tests, students should begin to take a more active role. Teachers will also be enlightened by students' views of studying and taking tests and can apply this information in their instruction, in their test design, and in test preparation activities with students.

One requirement for designing good tests is to use previous tests as the basis for constructing new ones. Students learn how to take an individual teacher's tests by learning that teacher's style. Teachers should learn how to design tests based on students' styles of learning as well. Did students need clearer directions? Did they use appropriate study procedures? Do they need reminders about certain test procedures?

A Checklist for Designing a Test

The following questions constitute a checklist for test construction. The checklist is useful for teachers who want to review tests that have produced unsatisfactory results.

1. **Preparation for testing.** How did you prepare the class to study for this test? If you suggested certain study strategies, are you asking questions that will capitalize on these strategies? For instance, if you suggested that students study causes and effects by using a pattern guide, are you designing test items that will call for a demonstration of causes and effects?
2. **Student self-evaluation.** Are you including a self-evaluation of test preparedness or some other way of reminding students about their responsibilities as test takers?
3. **Content verification.** Do the items on your test reflect your goals and objectives in teaching the content? Test items should test what was taught. If a major objective is that students be able to name states and their capitals, how can this test measure that objective?
4. **Inclusion.** Have you been considerate of the needs of students with diverse needs in your test design?
5. **Comprehension focus.** What is your main comprehension focus? Why? If you think factual knowledge is more important on this test than interpretation or application, can you justify this emphasis? Remember that many tests rely too much on factual questions at the expense of other levels of comprehension. Consider whether assessing knowledge at the factual level is important for this test.
6. **Levels of comprehension.** Do you require comprehension at each of the three levels? What proportion of your questions addresses each level? What is your reasoning for this division? Remember that tests imply the kind of thinking that teachers expect of their students. Have you asked your students to think broadly and deeply?
7. **Student responses.** What types of responses are you asking of students? Will they need to recognize, recall, or produce information? A good balance of responses is usually preferable to only recognition, recall, or production. More thinking is required of students when production is requested.
8. **Item phrasing.** Did you phrase your test items so that comprehension depends on the learned material rather than on experience or verbatim recall? Remember that although the preparation stage often calls for students to identify what they already know before a topic is taught, your test should find out what they have learned since then.
9. **Scoring.** Is the weight of the test in the final grade clear to students? Is the weight of each item on the test clear? Is the weight of parts of an item clear within the item?
10. **Alternative test items.** Did you consider alternatives to traditional test items, such as statements (instead of questions) or graphic organizers? Is writing an important part of your test? Why or why not?

11. **Question format.** For objective tests, what format have you selected (multiple-choice, true/false, incomplete sentences, short answers), and why? How many of each type did you include? Why?
12. **Essay design.** For essay tests, have you carefully asked for all the aspects of the answer that you are looking for? Are verbs (e.g., *describe* or *compare*) clear?
13. **Test format.** Is the wording on this test clear? Is the test uncluttered, with items well spaced? Does the test look appealing?

Helping Students Become Test-Wise

The tried-and-true acronym **SCORER** (Carmen & Adams, 1972; Lee & Allen, 1981) refers to a test-taking strategy. High SCORERs **s**chedule their time; identify **c**lue words to help answer the questions (the directions should contain them); **o**mit the hardest items, at least at first; **r**ead carefully to be sure they understand and fully answer the questions; **e**stimate what to include in their responses, perhaps by jotting down some notes or an outline; and **r**eview their responses before turning in tests. Teachers might teach SCORER to students and then insert the acronym into test directions or include it as a reminder on tests. Students could even be asked to account for how they used SCORER while completing a test. This strategy places responsibility on students to take a test wisely in an organized and comprehensive manner. SCORER can be used as part of any test design.

Consider when and how you became test-wise. Did a teacher support you in devising a plan of attack for studying material in your content area? How do you support students in successfully mastering content material for assessments?

There are other ways to teach students to become **test-wise**—that is, able to use a plan of attack regardless of specific test content. Students become used to taking tests and gain confidence as they learn how tests are designed and apply that knowledge. Being test-wise means knowing the system. When students know how to take a test, they can concentrate on answering the items. Being test-wise helps alleviate test anxiety. Panic—the "blank mind syndrome"—can be avoided.

Carter (1986) indicated that students discern the inadvertent clues teachers give in test items; this is a test-wise ability. Many teachers provide a bit of information in one question that can help students answer another question. Students who watch for these clues are SCORERs. Studies (Ritter & Idol-Mastas, 1986; Scruggs, White, & Bennion, 1986; Turner, 2009) indicate that instruction in test-wise skills can help students perform better on tests. An instructional session that reviews a list of test-taking tips is helpful, particularly with older students, in improving results on standardized tests. When a teacher wants students to improve performance on classroom tests, such test-wise instruction is best done in the content teacher's classroom with application to a particular test. Linn and Gronlund (2000) and Supon (2004) suggest that teachers follow several guidelines when preparing students for test taking. They note that teachers should suggest ways for students to study, give practice tests similar to those to be administered, teach test-taking skills, and show students how to write organized essay answers. Furthermore, teachers are urged to stress the importance of assessments for improving learning and to maintain a positive attitude to relieve student anxiety. The following list of test-taking tips indicates the kinds of suggestions that educators can give to help students become proficient test takers:

1. Be calm.
2. Read through the entire test before answering any items. Look for questions that might provide clues to other answers.
3. Plan your time. If some questions are worth more than others, spend most of your time on those that are worth the greatest number of points.

4. Answer first the questions for which you are most confident about your answers.
5. On objective tests, remember to be logical and reasonable. Consider your possible answers carefully. Look for "giveaway" words that indicate extremes (e.g., *all, none, never, always*). They probably should be avoided when you select the correct answer. On multiple-choice items, think what the answer should be; then look at the choices. Also, eliminate implausible responses by thinking carefully about each choice.
6. For essays, jot down an outline of what you intend to write before you start writing. Be sure you understand the teacher's terms: *List* means to state a series, but *describe* means to explain the items. *Compare* means to show similarities; *contrast* means to show differences. Make sure you answer all the parts of a question.

Authentic Assessment

Many authorities in education (Herman, Aschbacher, & Winters, 1992; Neisworth & Bagnato, 2004; Wiggins, 1989) have pointed to "alternative assessment" as the solution to the dilemma of traditional testing. The advice to move to such forms of assessment waned with the push for high states tests in the 2000s and the era of NCLB. But with reconsideration of how to regulate NCLB, policy makers and educators are also reconsidering alternative assessments. For instance, the National Board for Professional Teaching Standards (NBPTS, 2007) encourages using alternatives to standardized tests. One such alternative assessment is the VGLA (Virginia Grade Level Alternative, 2006), which allows students with disabilities to demonstrate their knowledge in a form other than a standardized test—usually via a portfolio. Unfortunately, this assessment is scheduled for phase out in mathematics and reading over the 2011–2013 school years. http://www.doe.virginia.gov/news/news_releases/2010/apr22.shtml

The alternative assessment movement is motivated by the belief that alternative assessment methods facilitate good teaching because assessments are part of the existing curriculum (Neisworth & Bagnato, 2004). Wood (1996) noted that traditional multiple-choice tests may not suffice in an educational climate of learning outcomes, higher order thinking skills, and integrated learning. **Authentic assessment** offers a viable solution. This term often refers to assessment that takes place in naturalistic situations that resemble the settings in which a skill or knowledge is actually used or applied. Teachers take an active role in observing student activities that demonstrate what the learners can do. Whereas *assessment* implies finding out what students already know, authentic assessment is broader in application, including informal evaluation procedures as well as determination of prior knowledge. In this section, we describe ways to use authentic assessment as a means of evaluating what students have learned.

Please visit the Education CourseMate website at **www.cengagebrain.com** to read more about the VGLA. This authentic assessment is being phased out because districts have over enrolled students with disabilities in the VBLA program. This abuse may have occurred so students can avoid taking the standardized assessment required for NCLB (Hollingsworth, 2010).

When teachers incorporate some nontraditional test items, they are moving toward authentic assessment, which is alternative, performance based, and process oriented. Traditional tests are specific measures given at specified times. Authentic assessment measures or samples student performance over time to see how student learning develops, matures, and ultimately reflects knowledge of the concepts learned in a real context. Authentic assessment is essentially a means of showing students why they are learning, as well as a means of showing educators what students have learned.

Authentic assessment emphasizes learner-centered activities that are rooted in students' lived experiences; the inclusion of such items can lead to improved instruction and greater accountability and motivation for students (Van Duinen, 2005). As Hager and Gable (1993) indicate, the increased use of observational and performance-based measures and process instruments as well as content- or course-specific instruction is essential to authentic assessment. Students can help decide what should be assessed, thus assuming an important role in demonstrating their own learning. Students enjoy creating authentic projects regardless of their age. Seitz and Bartholomew (2008) noted that using portfolios as authentic assessments allows students to become more self-directed and responsible for their own learning.

The context for authentic assessment might include observing a performance or simulation or completing a task in a real-world situation. Students will want to do well because the real-world consequences are clear. For instance, actually driving a car yields a more authentic assessment than taking a paper-and-pencil test in a driver education course. Encouraging a student to show the steps he or she followed to complete a math problem is a way of demonstrating the logical processing of information. The process of completing the task reveals as much (or more) about the student's learning as the product recorded as a test grade.

The importance of using authentic assessments was recently highlighted because of national conversation surrounding the inability of multiple choice tests used in state assessments to adequately assess 21st-century skills needed for the workplace (Tung, 2010). Janesick (2006) highlights a few of the reasons classroom teachers might adopt authentic assessment to determine student understanding of content material. Authentic assessment is fair and doesn't penalize racial or ethnic groups. It allows students to connect content knowledge to a problem that exists and asks them to construct a product or performance to demonstrate learning. Rather than emphasizing the memorization of facts, performance tasks are used for evaluation. Authentic assessment provides feedback on student learning across time, allowing students to adjust and improve as they work.

Lund (1997) has also written about the importance of using authentic assessment in every classroom. Teachers might consider the following list of characteristics provided by Lund as they construct their own authentic assessments.

1. Worthwhile tasks have meaning for the student and are designed to broadly represent a field of study.
2. The emphasis is on higher level thinking and more complex types of learning.
3. Criteria are always given in advance so students know how they will be graded.
4. Assessments are deeply embedded in the everyday workings of the curriculum so it is hard to distinguish between assessment and instruction.
5. The role of the teacher changes from dispenser of knowledge (or even antagonist) to facilitator, modeler, and ally in learning.
6. Students know that there will be a public presentation of the work that has been accomplished.
7. Students know that there will be an examination both of the processes they used in learning and of the products that resulted from the learning.

Developing Authentic Assessments

Historically, assessment practices have been under constant scrutiny to ensure that decision making is based on sound information. More than a decade ago, Tierney (1998) wrote about reforming assessment practice but noted that developing better evaluation means more than just creating new tests. He argues that we must be thoughtful about how we incorporate authentic assessment into our evaluation procedures.

Because learning is a complicated process, evaluation must consider many complex ways to represent itself. Stephens (2010) used learning logs (explained in Chapter 10) with high school biology students to encourage student reflection on their learning. We know teachers who keep gummed labels on a clipboard; as they walk around the classroom, they make anecdotal notes on these labels, which they later stick into students' folders. These notes often reveal important learning patterns when collected across time. Such notes can be kept in any content classroom; they could be particularly useful during science labs, reading or writing workshops, cooperative group work, or library work. Performance measures might include oral debates, post-graphic organizers, or even presentations developed using *PowerPoint*. Teachers can increase the authenticity of assessments in classrooms by asking students to communicate with each other as they participate in activities that reflect real purposes for reading and writing (Rhodes & Shanklin, 1991). Afflerbach (2007b) suggests that educators need to develop classroom assessments that help "identify the teachable moments for each student" and give the detail to "effectively teach to students' needs" (p. 268).

Portfolios as a Means of Authentic Assessment

Even though educators realized the value of portfolios for encouraging students to take an active role in their own learning, (Green and Smyser, 1996), portfolios were all but abandoned in the past decade. A recent edition of the *Journal of Adolescent and Adult Literacy* (Goodson, 2007) reintroduces the place of portfolios in authentic assessment, especially in digital form. A **portfolio** is a representative sampling of artifacts that demonstrates a feature or specialty about a person. It is not simply a collection but a showcase. The National Capital Language Resource Center (2009) suggests that portfolio assessment is the "systematic, longitudinal collection of student work created in response to specific, known instructional objectives and evaluated in relation to the same criteria" (Section. 2.1) *A student* might collect many samples of work, but only one artifact might be selected for inclusion in the portfolio because it demonstrates best what the student is showing about her- or himself. Teachers might consider including multimedia presentations as a part of their portfolio collection process.

In 2008, a group of high school students wrote a script and produced a video about the book *The Great Gatsby* for English class. The students and their friends viewed the video and self-evaluated their ability to accurately convey what they had read. Their understanding of characterization and plot was enhanced through this authentic task. Furthermore, the production was used two years later to support the learning of other students reading the same novel. Similarly, students and art educators participated in a digital portfolio project using digital photographs of student work and hypermedia slide shows. Participants noticed increased growth because of increased opportunities for reflection. Educators reported that students began to look at their artwork more holistically (Fitzsimmons, 2008). Teachers evaluate these student products when they measure individual works and the entire portfolio against specific criteria matched to learning objectives. Unlike traditional tests, many portfolios demonstrate growth over time.

Portfolios can be used at any grade level. Hallman (2007) used e-portfolios with preservice English educators and found that the portfolios offered potential spaces for talk about teacher identity. Irfan and Tolda (2009) found that portfolio assessment for

Teachers need to carefully consider which types of assessments will be used for student evaluation. Should observation be an assessment component? How? For how long? Under what conditions? Should learners select for themselves what will illustrate their learning?

View the video to see how portfolio assessment can be approached and managed in an elementary classroom.

Digital portfolios provide students with a space for demonstrating growth across a school year or longer. Please visit the Education CourseMate website at **www.cengagebrain.com** for links related to digital portfolios. How might you implement digital portfolios in your classroom?

The National Center for Response to Intervention outlines the following four components of Response to Intervention (RtI):

- A school-wide, multi-level instructional and behavioral system for preventing school failure
- Screening
- Progress monitoring
- Data-based decision making for instruction, movement within the multi-level system, and disability identification (in accordance with state law) (National Center on Response to Intervention, 2010)

CHALLENGE BOX

Trinka, A Student with Learning Disabilities

SITUATION: Trinka's teachers are very concerned about her ability to pass the state-mandated exams at the end of third grade. During the first semester of school, she was evaluated using multiple assessments in the school-wide RtI program. RtI allows students to obtain instructional support and intervention in a multi-leveled prevention system designed to increase student achievement. Trinka's school identifies students at risk for poor performance and adjusts the intensity and nature of interventions based on how each student responds to instructional support.

Trinka's teachers support her needs by providing small group instruction in social studies and science classes where Trinka has difficulty expressing her knowledge in writing. Mrs. Healy, the art teacher, noticed that Trinka developed an intricate sculpture that replicated a compass rose and clearly demonstrated her understanding of the directional points for maps. When compared with her written exam on the same topic, Trinka's teachers discovered a major discrepancy between her artwork and her failing exam grade.

How have teachers used assessment to support Trinka's instructional program?

Trinka's school has implemented RtI. Every couple of weeks, student performance in all content subjects is assessed for progress monitoring. Based on individual performance, Trinka is assigned to intervention groups to receive instructional support. Although Trinka is identified as a student with learning disabilities, she can participate in interventions with students enrolled in the regular education program. Trinka's response to the interventions is considered to determine whether she still needs assistance, her current level of support should be maintained, or her level of services should be increased. This systematic assessment support tailors instruction to meet Trinka's current needs.

Based on the situation described above, what types of assessment might Trinka's teachers consider in the future? What have Trinka's teachers learned about her from Mrs. Healy's observations?

Students with learning differences benefit from having multiple means of representing their understanding of concepts. Trinka's intricate sculpture demonstrated that she had internalized the directional concepts presented in her social studies classroom, but her written assessment did not. In the future, Trinka's teachers may wish to provide her with opportunities to share her knowledge through art. Her art can be annotated and collected in a portfolio to demonstrate that she has mastered concepts. This type of assessment allows Trinka to use her strengths to demonstrate her understanding.

students enrolled in a secondary school language preparatory class had significant influence on writing skills. Portfolios work well with both elementary and secondary students (Afflerbach, 2007; Chi-Cheng, 2009). Activity 12.9 is an artifact selected by a third grader to show the many facts he learned over 12 weeks while he studied animals. Activity 12.10 is a list of history books that a fourth grader included in his portfolio to show how much he had read in four weeks.

RtI programs rely heavily on formative assessment for decision making about a student's individual instructional program. For more on how assessments is used to plan instruction, please visit the Education CourseMate website at **www.cengagebrain.com** and read *Essential Components of [RTI]—A Closer Look at Response to Intervention* (National Center on Response to Intervention, 2010).

When students are involved in an authentic assessment plan from the start of the grading period, they become more active participants in the learning process. Wilcox (1997) notes that an active portfolio, in which the student, teacher, and even the parents are actively engaged in the selection and presentation process, is a "working portfolio that changes and grows with new input as it creates and generates new input" (p. 96). Students should be encouraged to develop goals for their progress during the period and indicate possible ways they can demonstrate their growth at the end of the period. Teachers, in consultation with their students, can guide students toward realistic and reasonable goals. Students then collect their own evidence of learning from the beginning of a grading period.

If portfolios are created as paper-based products, teachers should supply each student with a folder; then the teacher and students can decide together what types of work will be kept in it. At the end of a specified period, students designate which pieces of work in the folder show progress or demonstrate a particular accomplishment.

ACTIVITY 12.9 A Third-Grade Science Mini-Page

My
Fantastic
Animals

Did you know that snakes eat bats?

Did you know that the Indian Python is one of the largest snakes in the world?

The smallest snakes can fit in your hand.

Hummingbirds can fly backward and hover motionless.

This is my mini-page about animals. I wanted to include this page in my portfolio to show what I learned about animals.

ACTIVITY 12.10 A Page from a Fourth Grader's History Portfolio

Books I read in History:

Meet Martin Luther King, Jr.

Meet Maya Angelou

The Story of Harriet Tubman, Conductor of the Underground Railroad

The Story of George Washington Carver

If You Traveled on the Underground Railroad

I chose this list of books for my portfolio because I never liked to read before. I did not know very much about history, but now I have practiced reading and learned a lot too! I like to read about real people and find out about real things.

It is a good idea to keep the portfolio folders in the classroom in a storage file at all times. This ensures that papers will not be lost and provides easy access for students wishing to peruse or upgrade their portfolios. Products they select may reflect their learning much more fully over a long time than a traditional test—which captures only one moment in time.

If portfolios are created as electronic products, there are many possibilities for presentation. When portfolios are to be freely shared and open to the public, blogs might work best (Fahey, Lawrence, & Paratore, 2007). But if an element of privacy is desired, portfolio spaces can be created within course authoring tools

Refer to Chapter 7 for an explanation of blogs.

ACTIVITY 12.11 A Portfolio Window Created in Blackboard (Middle School or High School)

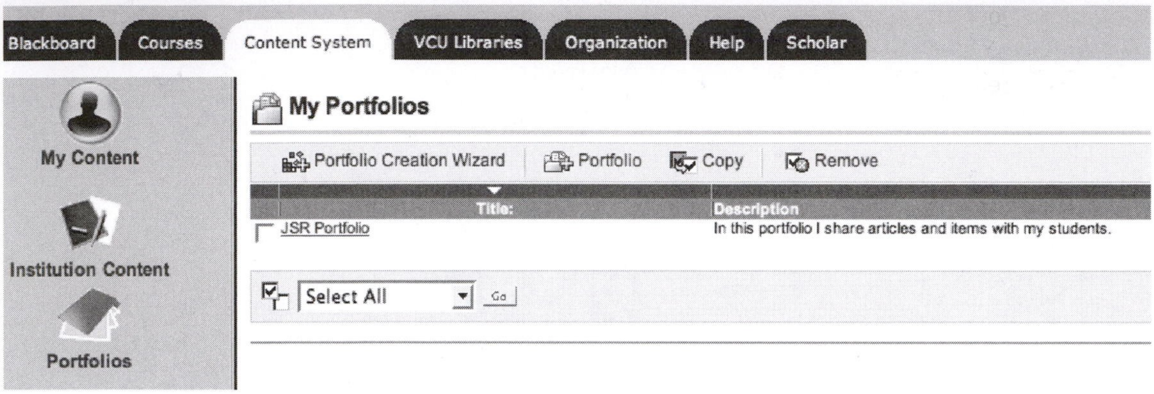

Blackboard Inc.

such as BlackBoard. Activity 12.11 is a screen capture of a portfolio window created in BlackBoard.

Portfolios should include evidence of problem-solving and communication skills. Samples for a portfolio that demonstrates writing ability could be a table of contents, a best piece, a letter, some creative writing, a personal response, a prose piece from a content area, and an on-the-spot writing sample. Samples for a portfolio that demonstrates math ability could be several best pieces, such as puzzles, a letter to the evaluator, and a collection of math work.

Here are some general guidelines for assembling a portfolio:

1. Organize with a table of contents and section divisions. Select categories to best represent progress, such as "Favorite Activities," "Activities I Did Not Like," and "What I Am Most Proud Of."
2. Include representative samples of work over time. Be sure to date the samples and make clear why they are included.
3. Annotate each sample to explain why it is included. The focus here is on individual samples, not the total progression.
4. Conclude with a reflective but brief summary that explains progress in relation to the portfolio contents: What were the goals? What was learned? How, overall, do these artifacts demonstrate this?
5. Make sure that the number of samples is representative of the depth and breadth of learning (at least one sample per week during a grading period).

A portfolio demonstrating how to solve a chemistry problem might include a diagram or mathematic calculations. What type of writing might you ask a student to do to accompany these types of problem solving examples?

What types of samples should be collected each week? What types of samples should be collected to demonstrate the achievement of course goals? Some measures of prior knowledge of topics, such as recognition pretests or anticipation guides, would provide baseline measures (see Chapters 3 and 4). For instance, pre- and post-unit attitude surveys might be the first and last pieces collected. Students can include work samples such as jot charts (explained in Chapter 4), two-column notes (explained in Chapter 8), and graphic organizers—in their portfolios. Teachers can also suggest that students save

ACTIVITY 12.12 Portfolio Requirements for English 11—First Grading Period

This portfolio will count as 25 percent of your grade. Include pieces that YOU think best represent your learning about early American history and literature.

Include at least eight pieces, one per week. Annotate each piece to explain why it represents your learning for this marking period. You may include more than one piece of the same type, but there should be some variety.

Write a summary of no more than two pages that explains how you met the objectives for this unit.

Suggestions for Selections

Completed jot chart of early American authors: their work, language style, and representative vocabulary

Quizzes

Essays—this can include any drafts that you think show your progress in writing and thinking about the topic

Three-level guides (completed and annotated)

Notes from any day's discussion

Postgraphic organizer of *The Crucible*

Favorite quotes from *The Crucible*

Maps of *The Crucible*: acts, characters

quizzes, tests, and corrections. At grading time, students should include the most representative piece and a best piece of work that represent both process activities and final products. If a student is showing that a standard has been met, the activity that demonstrates this would be included in the portfolio. For instance, John may be unable to compute a problem about fractions on the mandated test because of his learning disability, but he can tell in his own words how he would solve it and draw a picture.

Teachers need to establish the elements they expect students to demonstrate in their portfolios. Will specific knowledge be expected? Will some example of weekly progress be necessary? How will the portfolios be graded, if at all? Will they constitute the total grade or a portion of the grade? Who will read the portfolios—just the teacher and student, the parent, the principal, other students? After making the expectations clear to students, teachers need to encourage students to take ownership and make their own choices within the established parameters. It is a good idea to hold at least a midpoint conference so students can practice articulating their choices, and the teacher can guide the process. Activity 12.12 is an example of a portfolio guideline for high school English students.

Teachers can manage and analyze authentic assessment results using an electronic database and templates so each student record can be quickly updated. What would you include in a template to evaluate student performance on authentic assessments in your content area?

Getting Started with Authentic Assessment

Content area teachers can begin focusing on authentic assessment by keeping a checklist of essential developments that they want students to demonstrate. The checklist presented in Activity 12.13 can be modified as new criteria are added and then removed as students' developmental needs are met. Such a checklist can help teachers keep an ongoing record of subtle developments in the students' reading, writing, and thinking abilities.

Using a checklist is the easiest way to begin authentic assessment. The students' development—trial and error, dialogue, self-criticism—can be assessed most readily. Students can take samples over time and assist with designing the assessment and

ACTIVITY 12.13 Checklist for Assessment Observed Over the Month of ___________

★ Excellent ✓ Good × Average ♦ Lacking—needs to improve

Name	Student Self-evaluation	Decision Making	Questioning	Problem Solving	Attitude and Motivation	Inferential Thinking	Clarity of Writing
Billy	✓	★	★	✓	★	✓	×
Tanesia	×	✓	×	♦	✓	×	×
Jacob	★	✓	★	★	✓	✓	★
Cassandra	♦	♦	×	♦	✓	✓	×
Jorge	×	✓	×	×	✓	✓	♦

collecting the samples. Also, the teacher can make certain that both process and product are measured and that the targeted audiences—such as the students, their parents, and administrators—will be able to understand the samples and how they demonstrate progress in learning. Authentic assessment is the ultimate nontraditional evaluation. It is a challenge that can bring new enthusiasm to learning in every content area.

After a teacher tries a few of these ideas for nontraditional testing and authentic assessment, the next step might be to combine the data collected with the test data required by NCLB or state evaluations. Boyd-Batstone (2004) suggests that teachers can fill in gaps left by questions about what a test score means for instruction and attend to immediate classroom needs by collecting informal observations and data that match state and national standards. This approach might be described as standards-based teaching in which the standard, the test of the standard, and the classroom performance can be integrated. Boyd-Batstone calls his method **ARA** (anecdotal records assessment). Teachers can organize this data digitally by creating templates that include a list of standards along with notes describing how individual students meet each of the standards. Teachers can focus on what each learner knows and can do, but the learning is also matched to the standard and should substantiate any testing. As Boyd-Batstone writes, "A quality assessment is like a well-woven fabric" (p. 236).

ONE-MINUTE SUMMARY

Assessment and evaluation are crucial components for ensuring good instruction. In the age of accountability in the United States, content teachers must play a larger role in assessment than ever before. Federal legislation and state standards have become a prominent influence on classroom instruction. This chapter presented key concepts about testing, including the design of successful tests and the role of tests in the larger picture of assessment and evaluation. The chapter also presented viewpoints from several experts about the impact of NCLB on assessment and the continued involvement of the U.S. Department of Education through the Race to the Top educational initiative. Educators have begun to view assessment and evaluation more broadly and to select assessment methods suited to different purposes. We described teacher-made tests and authentic assessment as ways to measure whether desired learning outcomes are taking place. The chapter discussed traditional and authentic forms of evaluation, including paper-based and digital portfolios.

END-OF-CHAPTER ACTIVITIES

Assisting Comprehension

1. Select one way to introduce authentic assessment into your content classroom. Relate this assessment to a standard about which you need to instruct. How can using and recording student performance on this authentic assessment technique demonstrate student progress in achieving the standard?
2. How will you use technology to assist in formative as well as summative assessment of student progress?

Reflecting on Your Reading

1. Your content organization (e.g., National Council of Teachers of Math, National Council of Teachers of English, National Council for the Social Studies, National Science Teachers Association, International Reading Association) has most likely developed a set of standards that identifies the assessment performance criteria relevant to classroom teachers. Standards delineate the elements of assessment, diagnosis, and evaluation that a classroom teacher should possess. Teachers should be able to select and administer formal and informal assessments; analyze assessment results to evaluate student progress and develop instructional plans; recognize the variability in reading levels across different subject areas; identify students' proficiencies and difficulties; recognize the need to make referrals for appropriate services; and communicate assessment results to students, parents, and colleagues. How were these elements addressed in this chapter? How does being informed about these elements assist you as a teacher of content?
2. How have testing, assessment and evaluation changed across time? Inform yourself by reading about:
   - NCLB and Race to the Top (Please visit the Education CourseMate website at **www.cengagebrain.com** for links to these resources)
   - Your professional organization's standards for teaching and assessing important content (Google it by typing in the name of your organization)
   - A history of testing in Oppenheimer's *The Flickering Mind: The False Promise of Technology in the Classroom and How Learning Can be Saved*
3. How is the information you read similar to or different from what you find in the schools you have attended or where you currently teach?

Assessing Attitudes toward Reading

Elementary Reading Attitude Survey

Directions for Use

The Elementary Reading Attitude Survey (ERAS) provides a quick indication of student attitudes toward reading. It consists of 20 items and can be administered to an entire classroom in about 10 minutes. Each item presents a brief, simply worded statement about reading, followed by four pictures of Garfield. Each pose is designed to depict a different emotional state, ranging from very positive to very negative.

ADMINISTRATION

Begin by telling students that you wish to find out how they feel about reading. Emphasize that this is not a test and that there are no "right" answers. Encourage sincerity.

Distribute the survey forms. If you wish to monitor the attitudes of specific students, ask all students to write their names in the space at the top. Hold up a copy of the survey so that the students can see the first page. Point to the picture of Garfield at the far left of the first item. Ask the students to look at this picture on their own survey form. Discuss with them the mood Garfield seems to be in (very happy). Then move to the next picture and again discuss Garfield's mood (this time, a *little* happy). In the same way, move to the third and fourth pictures and talk about Garfield's moods—a little upset and very upset. It is helpful to point out the position of Garfield's *mouth*, especially in the middle two figures.

Explain that together you will read some statements about reading and the students should think about how they feel about each statement. They should then circle the picture of Garfield that is closest to their own feelings. (Emphasize that the students should respond according to their own feelings, not as Garfield might respond!) Read each item aloud slowly and distinctly; then read it a second time while students are thinking. Be sure to read the item *number* and to remind students of page numbers when new pages are reached.

SCORING

To score the survey, count four points for each leftmost (happiest) Garfield circled, three for each slightly smiling Garfield, two for each mildly upset Garfield, and one point for each very upset (rightmost) Garfield. Three scores for each student can be obtained: the total for the first 10 items, the total for the second 10, and a composite total.

The first half of the survey relates to attitude toward recreational reading; the second half relates to attitude toward academic aspects of reading.

INTERPRETATION

You can interpret scores in two ways. One is to note informally where the score falls in relation to the four nodes of the scale. A total score of 50, for example, would fall about midway on the scale, between the slightly happy and slightly upset figures, therefore indicating a relatively indifferent overall attitude toward reading. The other approach is more formal. It involves converting the raw scores into percentile ranks by means of Table A.1. Be sure to use the norms for the right grade level and to note the column headings (Rec = recreational reading; Aca = academic reading; Tot = total score). If you wish to determine the average percentile rank for your class, average the raw scores first; then use the table to locate the percentile rank corresponding to the raw score mean. Percentile ranks cannot be averaged directly.

Technical Aspects

THE NORMING PROJECT

To create norms for the interpretation of scores, a large-scale study was conducted in late January 1989, at which time the survey was administered to 18,138 students in grades 1 through 6. A number of steps were taken to achieve a sample that was sufficiently stratified (that is, reflective of the American population) to allow confident generalizations. Children were drawn from 95 school districts in 38 U.S. states. The number of girls exceeded by only 5 the number of boys. Ethnic distribution of the sample was also close to that of the U.S. population (*Statistical Abstract of the United States, 1989*). The proportion of blacks (9.5%) was within 3 percent of the national proportion, while the proportion of Hispanics (6.2%) was within 2 percent.

Percentile ranks at each grade for both subscales and the full scale are presented in Table A.1. These data can be used to compare individual students' scores with the national sample, and they can be interpreted like achievement test percentile ranks.

RELIABILITY

Cronbach's alpha, a statistic developed primarily to measure the internal consistency of attitude scales (Cronbach, 1957), was calculated at each grade level for both subscales and for the composite score. These coefficients ranged from .74 to .89 and are presented in Table A.2.

It is interesting that with only two exceptions, coefficients were .80 or higher. These were for the recreational subscale at grades 1 and 2. It is possible that the stability of young children's attitudes toward leisure reading grows with their decoding ability and familiarity with reading as a pastime.

Scoring Sheet

Student name ______________________________
Teacher ______________________________
Grade ______________________ Administration date ______________________

Scoring guide

4 points	Happiest Garfield
3 points	Slightly smiling Garfield
2 points	Mildly upset Garfield
1 point	Very upset Garfield

Recreational reading	Academic reading
1. ______	11. ______
2. ______	12. ______
3. ______	13. ______
4. ______	14. ______
5. ______	15. ______
6. ______	16. ______
7. ______	17. ______
8. ______	18. ______
9. ______	19. ______
10. ______	20. ______
Raw score: ______	Raw score: ______

Full scale raw score (recreational + academic): ____________

Percentile ranks		
	Recreational	
	Academic	
	Full scale	

TABLE A.1	Midyear Percentile Ranks by Grade and Scale

Raw Scr	Grade 1 Rec Aca Tot	Grade 2 Rec Aca Tot	Grade 3 Rec Aca Tot	Grade 4 Rec Aca Tot	Grade 5 Rec Aca Tot	Grade 6 Rec Aca Tot
80	99	99	99	99	99	99
79	95	96	98	99	99	99
78	93	95	97	98	99	99
77	92	94	97	98	99	99
76	90	93	96	97	98	99
75	88	92	95	96	98	99
74	86	90	94	95	97	99
73	84	88	92	94	97	98
72	82	86	91	93	96	98
71	80	84	89	91	95	97
70	78	82	86	89	94	96
69	75	79	84	88	92	95
68	72	77	81	86	91	93
67	69	74	79	83	89	92
66	66	71	76	80	87	90
65	62	69	73	78	84	88
64	59	66	70	75	82	86
63	55	63	67	72	79	84
62	52	60	64	69	76	82
61	49	57	61	66	73	79
60	46	54	58	62	70	76
59	43	51	55	59	67	73
58	40	47	51	56	64	69
57	37	45	48	53	61	66
56	34	41	44	48	57	62
55	31	38	41	45	53	58
54	28	35	38	41	50	55
53	25	32	34	38	46	52
52	22	29	31	35	42	48
51	20	26	28	32	39	44
50	18	23	25	28	36	40
49	15	20	23	26	33	37
48	13	18	20	23	29	33
47	12	15	17	20	26	30
46	10	13	15	18	23	27

(Continued)

TABLE A.1 *(Continued)*

Raw Scr	Grade 1			Grade 2			Grade 3			Grade 4			Grade 5			Grade 6		
	Rec	Aca	Tot	Rec	Aca	Tot	Rec	Aca	Tot	Rec	Aca	Tot	Rec	Aca	Tot	Rec	Aca	Tot
45			8			11			13			16			20			25
44			7			9			11			13			17			22
43			6			8			9			12			15			20
42			5			7			8			10			13			17
41			5			6			7			9			12			15
40	99	99	4	99	99	5	99	99	6	99	99	7	99	99	10	99	99	13
39	92	91	3	94	94	4	96	97	5	97	98	6	98	99	9	99	99	13
38	89	88	3	92	92	3	94	95	4	95	97	5	96	98	8	97	99	10
37	86	85	2	88	89	2	90	93	3	92	95	4	94	98	7	95	99	8
36	81	79	2	84	85	2	87	91	2	88	93	3	91	96	6	92	98	7
35	77	75	1	79	81	1	81	88	2	84	90	3	87	95	4	88	97	6
34	72	69	1	74	78	1	75	83	2	78	87	2	82	93	4	83	95	5
33	65	63	1	68	73	1	69	79	1	72	83	2	77	90	3	79	93	4
32	58	58	1	62	67	1	63	74	1	66	79	1	71	86	3	74	91	3
31	52	53	1	56	62	1	57	69	0	60	75	1	65	82	2	69	87	2
30	44	49	1	50	57	0	51	63	0	54	70	1	59	77	1	63	82	2
29	38	44	0	44	51	0	45	58	0	47	64	1	53	71	1	58	78	1
28	32	39	0	37	46	0	38	52	0	41	58	1	48	66	1	51	73	1
27	26	34	0	31	41	0	33	47	0	35	52	1	42	60	1	46	67	1
26	21	30	0	25	37	0	26	41	0	29	46	0	36	54	0	39	60	1
25	17	25	0	20	32	0	21	36	0	23	40	0	30	49	0	34	54	0
24	12	21	0	15	27	0	17	31	0	19	35	0	25	42	0	29	49	0
23	9	18	0	11	23	0	13	26	0	14	29	0	20	37	0	24	42	0
22	7	14	0	8	18	0	9	22	0	11	25	0	16	31	0	19	36	0
21	5	11	0	6	15	0	6	18	0	9	20	0	13	26	0	15	30	0
20	4	9	0	4	11	0	5	14	0	6	16	0	10	21	0	12	24	0
19		2	7		2	8		3	11		5	13		7	17		10	20
18		2	5		2	6		2	8		3	9		6	13		8	15
17		1	4		1	5		1	5		2	7		4	9		6	11
16		1	3		1	3		1	4		2	5		3	6		4	8
15		0	2		0	2		0	3		1	3		2	4		3	8
14		0	2		0	1		0	1		1	2		1	2		1	3
13		0	1		0	1		0	1		0	1		1	2		1	2
12		0	1		0	0		0	0		0	1		0	1		0	1
11		0	0		0	0		0	0		0	0		0	0		0	
10		0	0		0	0		0	0		0	0		0	0		0	0

TABLE A.2 Descriptive Statistics and Internal Consistency Measures

		Recreational Subscale				Academic Subscale				Full Scale (Total)			
Grade	N	M	SD	S_eM	Alpha[a]	M	SD	S_eM	Alpha	M	SD	S_eM	Alpha
1	2,518	31.0	5.7	2.9	.74	30.1	6.8	3.0	.81	61.0	11.4	4.1	.87
2	2,974	30.3	5.7	2.7	.78	28.8	6.7	2.9	.81	59.1	11.4	3.9	.88
3	3,151	30.0	5.6	2.5	.80	27.8	6.4	2.8	.81	57.8	10.9	3.8	.88
4	3,679	29.5	5.8	2.4	.83	26.9	6.3	2.6	.83	56.5	11.0	3.6	.89
5	3,374	28.5	6.1	2.3	.86	25.6	6.0	2.5	.82	54.1	10.8	3.6	.89
6	2,442	27.9	6.2	2.2	.87	24.7	5.8	2.5	.81	52.5	10.6	3.5	.89
All	18,138	29.5	5.9	2.5	.82	27.3	6.6	2.7	.83	56.8	11.3	3.7	.89

[a]Cronbach's alpha (Cronbach, 1951).

VALIDITY

Evidence of construct validity was gathered by several means. For the recreational subscale, students in the national norming group were asked (a) whether a public library was available to them and (b) whether they currently had a library card. Those to whom libraries were available were separated into two groups (those with and without cards), and their recreational scores were compared. Cardholders had significantly higher ($p < .001$) recreational scores ($M = 30.0$) than noncardholders ($M = 28.9$), evidence of the subscale's validity in that scores varied predictably with an outside criterion.

A second test compared students who presently had books checked out from their school library with students who did not. The comparison was limited to children whose teachers reported not requiring them to check out books. The means of the two groups varied significantly ($p < .001$), and children with books checked out scored higher ($M = 29.2$) than those who had no books checked out ($M = 27.3$).

A further test of the recreational subscale compared students who reported watching an average of less than one hour of television per night with students who reported watching more than two hours per night. The recreational mean for the low televiewing group (31.5) significantly exceeded ($p < .001$) the mean of the heavy televiewing group (28.6). Thus the amount of television watched varied inversely with children's attitudes toward recreational reading.

The validity of the academic subscale was tested by examining the relationship of scores to reading ability. Teachers categorized norm-group children as having low, average, or high overall reading ability. Mean subscale scores of the high-ability readers ($M = 27.7$) significantly exceeded the mean of low-ability readers ($M = 27.0$, $p < .001$), evidence that scores were reflective of how the students truly felt about reading for academic purposes.

The relationship between the subscales was also investigated. It was hypothesized that children's attitudes toward recreational and academic reading would be moderately but not highly correlated. Facility with reading is likely to affect these two areas similarly, resulting in similar attitude scores. Nevertheless, it is easy to imagine children inclined to read for pleasure but disenchanted with assigned reading and children academically engaged but without interest in reading outside school. The intersubscale correlation coefficient was .64, which meant that just 41 percent of the variance in one set of scores could be accounted for by the other. It is reasonable to suggest that the two subscales, while related, also reflect dissimilar factors—a desired outcome.

To tell more precisely whether the traits measured by the survey corresponded to the two subscales, factor analyses were conducted. Both used the unweighted least squares method of extraction and a varimax rotation. The first analysis permitted factors to be identified liberally (using a limit equal to the smallest eigenvalue greater than 1). Three factors were identified. Of the ten items composing the academic subscale, nine loaded predominantly on a single factor while the tenth (item 13) loaded nearly equally on all three factors. A second factor was dominated by seven items of the recreational subscale, while three of the recreational items (6, 9, and 10) loaded principally on a third factor. These items, however, did load more heavily on the second (recreational) factor than on the first (academic). A second analysis constrained the identification of factors to two. This time, with one exception, all items loaded cleanly on factors associated with the two subscales. The exception was item 13, which could have been interpreted as a recreational item and thus apparently involved a slight ambiguity. Taken together, the factor analyses produced evidence extremely supportive of the claim that the survey's two subscales reflect discrete aspects of reading attitude.

Garfield Revisited: Permission to Use the ERAS

Michael C. McKenna / Georgia Southern University
Dennis J. Kear / Wichita State University

Educators wishing to use the scale should copy and paste the legend on each page of the scale.

Since its appearance, the ERAS has grounded a number of research studies of reading attitudes, and each of these studies has contributed to an understanding of the instrument. The following sources may be useful to educators who have used the ERAS:

Allen, L., Cipielewski, J., & Stanovich, K. E. (1992). Multiple indicators of children's reading habits and attitudes: Construct validity and cognitive correlates. *Journal of Educational Psychology, 84,* 489–503.

Bromley, K., Winters, D., & Schlimmer, K. (1994). Book buddies: Creating enthusiasm for literacy learning. *The Reading Teacher, 47,* 392–399.

Grisham, D. L. (1993, December). *The integrated language arts: Curriculum enactments in whole language and traditional fourth grade classrooms.* Paper presented at the meeting of the National Reading Conference, Charleston, SC.

Kush, J. C., Watkins, M. W., McAleer, M. T., & Edwards, V. A. (1995). One-year stability of the elementary reading attitude survey. *Mid-Western Educational Researcher, 8,* 11–14.

McKenna, M. C., & Kear, D. J. (1990). Measuring attitude towards reading: A new tool for teachers. *The Reading Teacher, 43,* 626–639.

McKenna, M. C., Kear, D. J., & Ellsworth, R. A. (1995). Children's attitudes toward reading: A national survey. *Reading Research Quarterly, 30*(4), 934–956.

McKenna, M. C., Stratton, B. D., & Grindler, M. C. (1992, November). *Social desirability of children's responses to a reading attitude survey.* Paper presented at the meeting of the College Reading Association, St. Louis.

McKenna, M. C., Stratton, B. D., Grindler, M. C., & Jenkins, S. (1995). Differential effects of whole language and traditional instruction on reading attitudes. *Journal of Reading Behavior, 27,* 19–44.

Payne, D. A. (1994, April). *Two-year evaluation of a continuous progress K–3 program.* Paper presented at the meeting of the American Educational Research Association, New Orleans.

Rasinski, T. V., & Linek, W. (1993, November). *Do students in whole language classrooms like reading more than students in traditional classrooms?* Paper presented at the meeting of the College Reading Association, Richmond, VA.

Reinking, D., & Watkins, J. H. (1996). *A formative experiment investigating the use of multimedia book reviews to increase elementary students' independent reading* (Technical Report). Athens, GA: National Reading Research Center.

Stanovich, K. E. (1993). Does reading make you smarter? Literacy and the development of verbal intelligence. In H. Reese (Ed.), *Advances in child development and behavior* (Vol. 24, pp. 133–180). Gilsum, NH: Academic Press.

Whitney, P. (1994). *Influences on grade-five students' decisions to read: An exploratory study of leisure reading behavior.* Unpublished doctoral dissertation, University of British Columbia, Vancouver.

Mikulecky Behavioral Reading Attitude Measure

Norming and Validation Information*

The *Mikulecky Behavioral Reading Attitude Measure* (MBRAM) was developed to be a sound reading-attitudes measure appropriate for use with mature readers. To establish the instrument on sound theoretical foundations, all items were written with direct reference to the Hovland-Rosenberg tricomponent model of attitude and to the stages of Krathwohl's *Taxonomy of the Affective Domain.* A pool of 40 items, each of which was designed to reflect a specific Krathwohl substage, was reduced to 20 items after

*Mikulecky, L. J. *The developing, field testing, and initial norming of a secondary/adult level reading attitude measure that is behaviorally oriented and based on Krathwohl's Taxonomy of the Affective Domain.* Unpublished doctoral dissertation, University of Wisconsin–Madison, 1976.

Mikulecky Behavioral Reading Attitude Measure

Name ______________________________ Instructor's Name ______________________________

Age ____________ Sex ____________ School ______________________________

Example

You receive a book for a holiday present. You start the book, but decide to stop halfway through.

VERY UNLIKE ME 1 2 3 ④ 5 VERY LIKE ME

1. You walk into the office of a doctor or dentist and notice that there are magazines set out.

   VERY UNLIKE ME 1 2 3 4 5 VERY LIKE ME

2. People have made jokes about your reading in unusual circumstances or situations.

   VERY UNLIKE ME 1 2 3 4 5 VERY LIKE ME

3. You are in a shopping center you've been to several times when someone asks where books and magazines are sold. You are able to tell the person.

   VERY UNLIKE ME 1 2 3 4 5 VERY LIKE ME

4. You feel very uncomfortable because emergencies have kept you away from reading for a couple of days.

   VERY UNLIKE ME 1 2 3 4 5 VERY LIKE ME

5. You are waiting for a friend in an airport or supermarket and find yourself leafing through the magazines and paperback books.

   VERY UNLIKE ME 1 2 3 4 5 VERY LIKE ME

6. If a group of acquaintances would laugh at you for always being buried in a book, you'd know it's true and wouldn't mind much at all.

   VERY UNLIKE ME 1 2 3 4 5 VERY LIKE ME

7. You are tired of waiting for the dentist, so you start to page through a magazine.

   VERY UNLIKE ME 1 2 3 4 5 VERY LIKE ME

8. People who are regular readers often ask your opinion about new books.

   VERY UNLIKE ME 1 2 3 4 5 VERY LIKE ME

9. One of your first impulses is to "look it up" whenever there is something you don't know or whenever you are going to start something new.

   VERY UNLIKE ME 1 2 3 4 5 VERY LIKE ME

10. Even though you are a very busy person, there is somehow always time for reading.

    VERY UNLIKE ME 1 2 3 4 5 VERY LIKE ME

11. You've finally got some time alone in your favorite chair on a Sunday afternoon. You see something to read and decide to spend a few minutes reading just because you feel like it.

    VERY UNLIKE ME 1 2 3 4 5 VERY LIKE ME

(continued)

Mikulecky Behavioral Reading Attitude Measure (*continued*)

12. You tend to disbelieve and be a little disgusted by people who repeatedly say they don't have time to read.

    VERY UNLIKE ME 1 2 3 4 5 VERY LIKE ME

13. You find yourself giving special books to friends or relatives as gifts.

    VERY UNLIKE ME 1 2 3 4 5 VERY LIKE ME

14. At holiday time, you look in the display window of a bookstore and find yourself interested in some books and uninterested in others.

    VERY UNLIKE ME 1 2 3 4 5 VERY LIKE ME

15. Sometimes you find yourself so excited by a book you try to get friends to read it.

    VERY UNLIKE ME 1 2 3 4 5 VERY LIKE ME

16. You've just finished reading a story and settle back for a moment to enjoy and remember what you've just read.

    VERY UNLIKE ME 1 2 3 4 5 VERY LIKE ME

17. You *choose* to read nonrequired books and articles fairly regularly (a few times a week).

    VERY UNLIKE ME 1 2 3 4 5 VERY LIKE ME

18. Your friends would not be at all surprised to see you buying or borrowing a book.

    VERY UNLIKE ME 1 2 3 4 5 VERY LIKE ME

19. You have just gotten comfortably settled in a new city. Among the things you plan to do are check out the library and bookstores.

    VERY UNLIKE ME 1 2 3 4 5 VERY LIKE ME

20. You've just heard about a good book but haven't been able to find it. Even though you're tired, you look for it in one more book store.

    VERY UNLIKE ME 1 2 3 4 5 VERY LIKE ME

considering the evaluations of a panel of judges familiar with Krathwohl's taxonomy and after an item analysis that eliminated all items that correlated at $r = .600$ or less with the sum of items reflecting the Krathwohl stage appropriate to each item. The hierarchical framework hypothesized by Krathwohl was supported by an analysis of subjects' item responses using a method for Scaling a Simplex developed by Henry Kaiser (*Psychometrika,* 1962). The MBRAM hierarchy gave evidence of a .933 out of a possible 1.000 goodness-of-fit to an ideal hierarchy. This was interpreted as empirical support for the Krathwohl theoretical foundation of the MBRAM.

A graduate-level seminar on affective domain measurement helped survey and refine all items to reflect everyday reading-related behaviors, thereby establishing *face validity*. Correlations of *concurrent validity* ranging from .446 to .770 were established with such formal reading attitude measures as the Estes Scale, the Dulin-Chester Scale, and the Kennedy-Halinski Reading Attitude Measure. The MBRAM correlated more highly with the Estes Scale and the Dulin-Chester Scale than either of those measures did with the other.

To establish *construct validity,* five informal criteria for reading attitude (selfreported liking and amount of reading, teacher and classmate judgment of reading attitude, and number of books read in six months) were administered along with the MBRAM. All MBRAM correlations with these informal criteria were significant to the $p<.001$ level, and the majority of correlations ranged from .500 to .791. The MBRAM correlated significantly more highly with these informal measures than did the other, formal reading attitude measures used in the study. Analysis of variance statistically demonstrated the ability of the MBRAM to discriminate subjects of high, average, and low reading attitude as measured by the informal criteria.

The MBRAM demonstrated a test–retest reliability of .9116.

The MBRAM was administered to 1,750 subjects ranging from seventh grade through college–adult. 1,343 of the subjects were public school students selected from urban, suburban, and rural populations. These subjects were randomly sampled to create a composite, stratified Wisconsin Population Model. Norms for the MBRAM are reported for each grade level in terms of this model and also in terms of urban, suburban, and rural populations. For ease of interpretation of scores, attitude-level scoring bands are provided. No significant differences in scores of urban, suburban, or rural subjects were found from seventh to tenth grade, but rural subjects exhibited slightly higher MBRAM mean scores in the upper grades. Reading attitude scores decreased slightly in all locations with each year in school. (See Tables A.3 and A.4.)

TABLE A.3 Summary Statistics: Junior High School (Grades 7–9) and Senior High School (Grades 10–12); Urban, Suburban, and Rural Subjects, MBRAM Scores

	Urban				Suburban				Rural			
Level	*N*	Mean	Range	*S.D.*	*N*	Mean	Range	*S.D.*	*N*	Mean	Range	*S.D.*
Jr	127	55.93	27–90(63)	12.11	276	59.60	25–98(73)	14.33	182	60.81	22–92(70)	13.91
Sr	332	55.24	20–90(70)	12.51	144	58.29	24–95(71)	15.55	190	59.28	29–97(68)	15.17

Attitude Bands for Junior and Senior High School by Location

	Urban		Suburban		Rural	
Attitude Level	**Jr. High**	**Sr. High**	**Jr. High**	**Sr. High**	**Jr. High**	**Sr. High**
Above average	66–100	62–100	68–100	67–100	69–100	68–100
Average	53–65	49–61	52–67	59–66	54–68	52–67
Below average	20–52	20–48	20–51	20–59	20–53	20–51

TABLE A.4 Adult Norms: Results of Analyses of Variance and Post Hoc Scheffe Tests of Attitude toward Reading (MBRAM Score) by Each Demographic Variable

All Cases	*N*	Mean	S.D.	F-Ratio	*Post Hoc* Test of Significance
Sex					
M	118	65.02	14.15	33.58	***
F	166	74.47	13.10		
Race					
W	262	70.78	14.36	.43	Not significant
B	20	67.90	14.22		
O	2	65.50	0		
Education					
Less than high school	40	66.87	12.13	2.48	*
High school	88	68.69	15.79		
Post high school	93	71.07	14.19		
College	42	73.71	13.34		
Graduate work	22	77.09	11.13		
Family Income					
Less than 3,000	13	69.38	12.72	2.79	*
3–5,000	17	70.12	13.37		
5–10,000	39	71.69	10.76		
10–20,000	112	69.26	15.23		
Greater than 20,000	86	73.85	12.89		
No response	17	60.94	19.46		
Employment					
Full time	141	68.38	15.75	3.008	**
Part time	20	75.45	11.80		
Housewife	49	74.96	11.45		
Unemployed	9	78.67	17.33		
Student	36	67.81	11.57		
Retired	29	71.10	12.26		

*$p < .05$
**$p < .01$
***$p < .001$
From Mikulecky, Shanklin, & Caverly (1979).

Stages of Krathwohl's Taxonomy as Reflected by Mikulecky Behavioral Reading Attitude Measure Items

Stage 1 (attending) of Krathwohl's taxonomy is reflected by items 1, 3, 5, and 7 (see Table A.5). Each item provides from 1 to 5 points. A perfect score at this stage would be 4 items × 5 points, or 20 points. A student can be said to have attained a stage if he or she has 75 percent of the possible points at that stage. By interpreting items and stages, a deeper understanding of a student's reading attitude is possible.

Complete Survey Items for MARSI

We presented some items from The MARSI (Metacognitive Awareness of Reading Strategies Inventory) in Chapter 4. The following is the entire MARSI.

TABLE A.5 Stages of Krathwohl's Taxonomy as Reflected by Mikulecky Behavioral Attitude Measure Items

Krathwohl Stages	Items (1–5 Points Possible Each Item)	Criterion Score (75 Percent of Possible Points)
I. *Attending:* The individual is generally aware of reading and tolerant of it.	1, 3, 5, 7	15 pts.
II. *Responding:* The individual is willing to read under certain circumstances. He or she begins to choose and occasionally enjoy reading	11, 14, 16	11 pts.
III. *Valuing:* The individual begins to accept the worth of reading as a value to be preferred and even to extend to others.	13, 15, 17 18, 19, 20	23 pts.
IV. *Organization:* For the individual, reading is part of an organized value system and is so habitual that it is almost "instinctive."	9, 10, 12	11 pts.
V. *Characterization:* For the individual, reading is so much a part of life that both the reader and others see reading as crucial to this person	2, 4, 6, 8	15 pts.

TABLE A.6 From Mokhtari, K., & Reichard, C. A. (2002). Assessing students' metacognitive awareness of reading strategies. *Journal of Educational Psychology, 94*(2), 249–259. Used with permission.

All items graded on a 1 to 5 Lickert Scale:

1. I never or almost never do this.
2. I do this only occasionally.
3. I sometimes do this (about 50 percent of the time).
4. I usually do this.
5. I always or almost always do this.

_______ **1.** I have a purpose in mind when I read.

_______ **2.** I take notes while reading to help me understand what I read.

_______ **3.** I think about what I know to help me understand what I read.

_______ **4.** I preview the text to see what it is about before I read it.

_______ **5.** When text becomes difficult, I read aloud to help me understand what I read.

_______ **6.** I summarize what I read to help me reflect on important information in text.

_______ **7.** I think about whether the content of the text fits my reading purpose.

_______ **8.** I read slowly but carefully to make sure I understand what I am reading.

_______ **9.** I discuss what I read with others to check my understanding.

_______ **10.** I skim the text first by noting characteristics like length and organization.

_______ **11.** I try to get back on track when I lose concentration.

_______ **12.** I underline or circle information in the text to help me remember it.

_______ **13.** I adjust my reading speed according to what I am reading.

_______ **14.** I decide what to read closely and what to ignore.

_______ **15.** I use reference materials such as dictionaries to help me understand what I read.

_______ **16.** When text becomes difficult, I pay closer attention to what I am reading.

_______ **17.** I use tables, figures, and pictures in text to increase my understanding.

_______ **18.** I stop from time to time and think about what I am reading.

_______ **19.** I use context clues to help me better understand what I am reading.

_______ **20.** I paraphrase (restate ideas in my own words) to better understand what I read.

_______ **21.** I try to picture or visualize information to help remember what I read.

_______ **22.** I use typographical aids like boldface and italics to identify new information.

_______ **23.** I critically analyze and evaluate the information presented in the text.

_______ **24.** I go back and forth in the text to find relationships among ideas in it.

_______ **25.** I check my understanding when I come across conflicting information.

_______ **26.** I try to guess what material is about when I read.

_______ **27.** When text becomes difficult, I reread to increase my understanding.

_______ **28.** I ask myself questions I like to have answered in the text.

_______ **29.** I check to see if my guesses about the text are right or wrong.

_______ **30.** I try to guess the meaning of unknown words or phrases.

From Mokhtari, Kouider, & Reichard, Carla A. (2002). Assessing students' metacognitive awareness of reading strategies. Journal of Educational Psychology, 94(2), pp. 249–259. Used with permission.

Readability Information

The Fry Readability Graph

Edward Fry developed the Fry readability graph in the 1960s for African teachers who taught English as a second language. In 1977, Fry revised the graph to include explanations, directions, and an extension to the 17th grade level. The Fry graph offers a quantifiable way to measure text difficulty.

To use this graph, teachers select at least three 100-word passages from different parts of the material (see direction 1 in the list that follows). For each 100-word passage, two counts are made: the number of syllables and the number of sentences (directions 2 and 3). The three counts of syllables are added and then averaged; the three counts of sentences are added and then averaged (direction 4). The teacher next locates the average for the number of syllables across the top of the graph and the average for the number of sentences along the side of the graph. The point at which these two averages intersect is the readability score. The point will fall within a fanlike, numbered segment on the graph; this number corresponds to the grade-level score. Fry says to count all words, including proper nouns, initials, and numerals (direction 1), and he defines *word* as well as *syllable* (directions 6 and 7). If a point falls in a gray area, the score is unreliable and should be recalculated by using additional 100-word passages.

Expanded Directions for Working the Fry Readability Graph

1. Randomly select three (3) sample passages and count out exactly 100 words each, beginning with the beginning of a sentence. Count proper nouns, initializations, and numerals.
2. Count the number of sentences in the 100 words, estimating the length of the fraction of the last sentence to the nearest tenth.
3. Count the total number of syllables in the 100-word passage. If you don't have a hand counter available, an easy way is to simply put a mark above every syllable over one in each word; then when you get to the end of the passage, count the number of marks and add 100. Small calculators can also be used as counters by pushing the numeral 1 and then pushing the + sign for each word or syllable when counting.
4. Enter the graph with the *average* sentence length and the *average* number of syllables; plot the dot where the two lines intersect. The area where the dot is plotted will give you the approximate grade level.

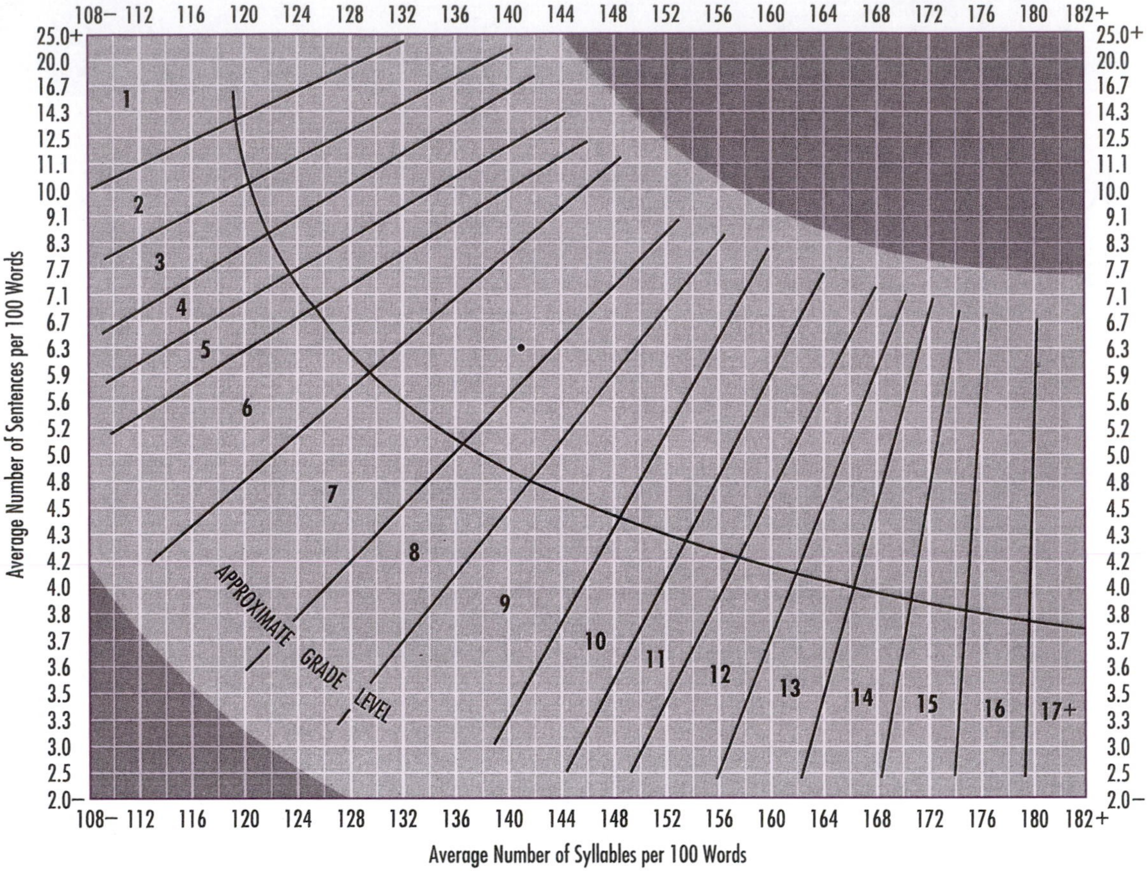

5. If a great deal of variability is found in syllable count or sentence count, putting more samples into the average is desirable.
6. A *word* is defined as a group of symbols with a space on either side; thus *Joe, IRA, 1945,* and *&* are each one word.
7. A *syllable* is defined as a phonetic syllable. Generally there are as many syllables as vowel sounds. For example, *stopped* is one syllable and *wanted* is two syllables. When counting syllables for numerals and initializations, count one syllable for each symbol. For example, *1945* is four syllables, *IRA* is three syllables, and *&* is one syllable.

Using the Fry Graph for Short Selections

The Procedure

The Fry graph can be used with selections of fewer than 100 words if some conversions are made (Forgan & Mangrum, 1985). This technique will be useful to teachers of primary grades, where material is partly visual and partly verbal, or for teachers using newspaper or magazine articles to supplement instruction. It also can help teachers measure the difficulty of word problems in math or of essay questions on tests. The

If the number of words in the selection is:	Multiply the number of syllables and sentences by:
30	3.3
40	2.5
50	2.0
60	1.67
70	1.43
80	1.25
90	1.1

From *Teaching Content Area Reading Skills,* 3rd ed., by Harry W. Forgan and Charles T. Mangrum II, copyright © 1985. Merrill Publishing Co., Columbus, OH. Used with permission.

FIGURE B.1

Conversion Chart for Fry's Graph for Selections with Fewer Than 100 Words

material should contain fewer than 100 words; if the material contains at least 100 words, then the Fry graph can be applied. To use this short-selection version, a teacher should do the following:

1. Count the total number of words.
2. Round *down* to the nearest 10.
3. Refer to the conversion chart (Figure B.1), and identify the conversion number corresponding to the rounded number.
4. Count the number of syllables and sentences in the rounded-down number of words (see steps 1 and 2).
5. Multiply the number of syllables by the number on the conversion chart; multiply the number of sentences by the number on the conversion chart.
6. Plot the final numbers on the regular Fry graph.

Using the SMOG Formula

McLaughlin (1969) named his readability formula SMOG as a tribute to another formula—the FOG—and after his birthplace, London, where "smog first appeared" (p. 641). Some have said that SMOG stands for the Simple Measure of Gobbledygook! Although its name is very lighthearted, this formula is a serious solution to the problem of measuring the readability of material that students may have to read on their own.

The SMOG formula is very easy to compute. However, the teacher needs to use a calculator that computes square roots or have a table of square roots handy. To use the SMOG formula, follow these steps:

1. Count three sets of 10 sentences (a total of 30 sentences).
2. Count all words of three or more syllables.
3. Take this number, and determine the nearest perfect square root.
4. Add 3 to this square root.
5. The final number is the readability level.

Differences between the Fry Graph and the SMOG Formula

The differences between the Fry graph and the SMOG formula are important to note. Each formula is based on a different premise, so the readability scores must be read differently. The Fry formula measures the readability of material used in an instructional setting. Because the teacher will explain the difficult words and sentences, the score is based on students' understanding of 65 to 75 percent of the material at a given grade level. The SMOG formula is intended to measure the readability of material that a teacher will not be teaching. Perhaps it is material that the teacher has suggested a student use independently. Because the teacher will not be explaining the difficult words and sentences, the score is based on students' understanding of 90 to 100 percent of the material. If a Fry and a SMOG were calculated on the same material, the Fry score would probably be lower. Table B.1 illustrates the basic differences between these two popular measures of readability.

Constructing Cloze for Determining Background Knowledge

Grades K to 3

Directions for constructing a cloze test to determine a readers' comprehension in kindergarten through third grade:

1. Select a passage of about 125 words.
2. Leave the first sentence intact.
3. Consistently delete every 10th word thereafter until a total of 10 deletions occurs. Make all blanks uniform in length.
4. Leave the last sentence intact or include the remainder of the paragraph to give the passage continuity.
5. Make a key of the exact words that have been deleted.

TABLE B.1 A Comparison of the Fry Graph and the SMOG Readability Formula

Readability Measure	Provides Readability Score for	Teacher Will Be Assisting Instruction?	Student Is Expected to Comprehend	Readability Score May Be	Apply This Formula When
Fry	Instructional reading settings	Yes	65–75% of material	Lower*	Teacher will instruct the group using the material being measured.
SMOG	Independent settings	No	90–100% of material	Higher*	Student will be reading the measured material on her or his own, as in report writing, homework, etc.

*As measured on the same passage.

6. Write directions that stress the purpose of the activity—to determine prior knowledge, not to test them. Explain that they are to fill each blank with the word they think the author might have used. Make certain you familiarize your students with the topic to be covered in the cloze. Remember that it is your job to get real scores from the students, not inflated or deflated ones. Therefore, it is important to "warm them" to the task to get the most accurate picture you can.
7. For each student, count the number of correct responses and multiply by 10 (if 10 blanks were used, or the number of blanks used) to express a percentage.

Grades 4 to 12

Directions for constructing a cloze test for use with students in the fourth through twelfth grades:

1. Select a passage of 250 to 300 words.
2. Leave the first sentence intact.
3. Consistently delete every fifth word thereafter until there are 50 deletions. Make all blanks uniform in length.
4. Leave the last sentence intact or include the remainder of the paragraph to give the passage continuity.
5. Make a key of the exact words that have been deleted.
6. Write directions for your students. Go over the directions and discuss the topic with your students before they perform the cloze.
7. For each student, count the number of correct responses and multiply by 2 (if 50 blanks were used) to express a percentage.

For *both* kindergarten through grade 3 and grades 4 to 12 cloze constructions, use these scores to determine whether students will (1) be independent in reading the passage, (2) simply be able to understand the passage, or (3) be frustrated in their reading. A score of 60 percent or higher indicates the independent level; a score between 40 and 60 percent indicates the instructional level. The material is suitable for teaching students with those scores. A score of less than 40 percent indicates the frustration level; the material may be too hard for students achieving such a low score. It may be helpful to list your students under each of these three levels, as follows:

Independent (scores above 60%)	**Instructional (scores 40% to 60%)**	**Frustration (scores below 40%)**
Material is easy	Material is suitable	Material is too difficult
(list students)	(list students)	(list students)

References

Abbott, R. D., Berninger, V. W., & Fayol, M. (2010). Longitudinal relationships of levels of language in writing and between writing and reading in grades 1 to 7. *Journal of Educational Psychology, 102*(2), 281–298.

Abowd, P. (2010, January 28). Race to the top: Unions asked to play ball for education dollars. *LaborNotes*. Retrieved August 12, 2010, from http://labornotes.org/blogs/2010/01/race-top-unions-asked-play-ball-education-dollars.

Abrami, P. C., Chambers, B., d'Apollonia, S., Farrell, M., & DeSimone, C. (1992). Group outcome: The relationship between group learning outcome, attributional style, academic achievement, and self-concept. *Contemporary Educational Psychology, 17,* 201–210.

Adams, M. J. (1990). *Beginning to read: Thinking and learning about print.* Cambridge, MA: MIT Press.

Adler, M. J. (1994). *Socrates: Art, the arts, and the great ideas.* New York: Simon and Schuster.

Afflerbach, P. (1987). How are main idea statements constructed? Watch the experts. *Journal of Reading, 30,* 512–518.

Afflerbach, P. (2002). The road to folly and redemption: Perspectives on the legitimacy of high-stakes testing. *Reading Research Quarterly, 37*(3), 348–360.

Afflerbach, P. (2007). Portfolio assessment. In *Understanding and using reading assessment K–12* (pp. 72–92). Newark, DE: International Reading Association.

Afflerbach, P. (2007b). Best practices in literacy assessment. In L. B. Gambrell, L. M. Morrow & M. Pressley (Eds.), *Best practices in literacy instruction.* New York: Guilford Press.

Agbenyega, S., & Jiggetts, J. (1999). Minority children and their overrepresentation in special education. *Education, 119*(4), 619–628.

Aguiar, L., & Brady, S. (1991). Vocabulary acquisition and reading ability. *Reading and Writing: An Interdisciplinary Journal, 3*(3), 413–425.

Ajayi, L. (2009). English as a second language learners' exploration of multimodal texts in a junior high school. *Journal of Adolescent & Adult Literacy, 52*(7), 585–595.

Alber, S. R., Nelson, J. S., & Brennan, K. B. (2002). A comparative analysis of two homework study methods on elementary and secondary school students' acquisition and maintenance of social studies content. *Education & Treatment of Children, 25*(2), 172–197.

Albright, J. (2001). The logic of our failures in literacy practices and teaching. *Journal of Adolescent & Adult Literacy, 44,* 644–658.

Alexander, P. A., & Jetton, T. L. (2000). Learning from text: A multidimensional and developmental perspective. In M. L. Kamil, P. B. Mosenthal, P. D. Pearson, & R. Barr (Eds.), *Handbook of Reading Research* (Vol. 3, pp. 285–310). Mahwah, NJ: Erlbaum.

Alexander, P. A., & Judy, J. E. (1998). The interaction of domain-specific and strategic knowledge in academic performance. *Review of Educational Research, 58,* 375–404.

Alexander, P. A., & Murphy, P. K. (1998). *The research base for APA's learner-centered psychological principles.* Washington, DC: American Psychological Association.

Alfassi, M., Weiss, I., Lifshitz, H. (2009). The efficacy of reciprocal teaching in fostering the reading literacy of students with intellectual disabilities. *European Journal of Special Needs Education, 24*(3), 291–305.

Ali, A. (2004). Applying constructivism in a traditional environment. *Academic Exchange Quarterly, 8*(1), 71–76.

Al khawaldeh, S., & Alolaimat, A. (2010). The contribution of conceptual change texts accompanied by concept mapping to eleventh-grade students understanding of cellular respiration concepts. *Journal of Science and Technology, 19*(2), 115–125.

Allan, J., & Clarke, K. (2007). Nurturing supportive learning environments in higher education through the teaching of study skills: To embed or not to embed? *International Journal of Teaching and Leaning in Higher Education, 19*(1), 64–76.

Allen, R., Brown, K., & Yatvin, J. (1986). *Learning language through communication: A functional approach.* Belmont, CA: Wadsworth.

Allington, R. L. (1991). How policy and regulation influence instruction for at-risk learners: Or why poor readers rarely comprehend well and probably never will. In L. Idol & B. F. Jones (Eds.), *Educational values and cognitive instruction: Implications for reform* (pp. 277–299). Hillsdale, NJ: Erlbaum.

Alvarez, M. C., & Rodriguez, W. J. (1995). Explorers of the universe: A pilot case study. In *Generations of literacy, seventeenth yearbook of the College Reading Association* (pp. 221–236). Commerce, TX: East Texas State University.

Alvermann, D. (1999). Modes of inquiry into studying engaged reading. In J. Guthrie & D. Alvermann (Eds.), *Engaged reading: Processes, practices, and policy implications* (pp. 134–149). New York: Teachers College Press.

Alvermann, D. E., O'Brien, D. G., & Dillon, D. R. (1990). What teachers do when they say they're having discussions of content reading assignments: A qualitative analysis. *Reading Research Quarterly, 25,* 296–321.

American Educational Research Association. (2004). *AERA position statement on high-stakes testing in pre-K–12 education.* Retrieved September 12, 2010, from http://www.aera.net/policyandprograms/?id=378.

American Psychological Association. (2001). Appropriate use of high-stakes testing in our nation's schools. *APA Online.* Retrieved September 7, 2004, from http://www.apa.org/pubs/info/brochures/testing.aspx.

American School Counseling Association. (2000). *Study skills survey.* Alexandria, VA: Author.

Ammons, R. I. (1987). *Trade books in the content areas.* Tempe, AZ: Jan V.

Anderson, J., & Adams, M. (1992, Spring). Acknowledging the learning styles of diverse student populations: Implications for instructional design. In L. L. B. Border & N. Van Note Chism (Eds.), *Teaching for Diversity, 49,* 21–33.

Anderson, R. C., & Pearson, P. D. (1984). A schematheoretic view of basic processes in reading comprehension. In P. D. Pearson (Ed.), *Handbook of reading research* (pp. 255–291). New York: Longman.

Anderson-Inman, L. (1998a). Electronic journals in technology and literacy: Professional development online. *Journal of Adolescent & Adult Literacy, 41*(15), 400–405.

Anderson-Inman, L. (1998b). Electronic text: Literacy medium of the future. *Journal of Adolescent & Adult Literacy, 41*(8), 678–682.

Anderson-Inman, L. (1999, July–Sept). Computer-based solutions for secondary students with learning disabilities: Emerging issues. *Reading and Writing Quarterly: Overcoming Learning Difficulties, 15*(3), 239–249.

Anderson-Inman, L., Knox-Quinn, C., Szymanski, M. (1999). Computer-supported studying: Stories of successful transition to postsecondary education. *Career Development for Exceptional Individuals, 22*(2), 185–212.

Anderson-Inman, L., & Zeitz, L. (1993). Computer-based concept mapping: Active studying for active learners. *The Computing Teacher, 21*(1), 6–10.

Anstey, M., & Bull, G. (2006). *Teaching and learning multiliteracies: Changing times, changing literacies.* Newark, DE: International Reading Association.

Antari, L. (2007, March 20). The power of peppermint is put to the test. *The Washington Post.* Retrieved August 12, 2010, from http://www.washingtonpost.com/wp-dyn/content/article/2007/03/19/AR2007031901624.html.

Applebee, A. N. (1981). *Writing in the secondary school.* Urbana, IL: National Council of Teachers of English.

Applefield, J. M., Huber, R, I., & Moallem, M. (2000). Constructivism in theory and practice: Toward a better understanding. *High School Journal, 84*(2), 35.

Aratani, L. (2007). The power of peppermint is put to the test. The Washington Post, 3-20-2007. Retrieved 4-19-2011: http://www.washingtonpost.com/wp-dyn/content/article/2007/03/19/AR2007031901624.html?nav=emailpage

Ariail, M., & Albright, L. K. (2006). A survey of teachers' read-aloud practices in middle schools. *Reading Research and Instruction, 45*(2), 69–89.

Arlin, P. K. (1984). *Arlin test of formal reasoning.* East Aurora, NY: Slosson Educational Publications.

Armbruster, B. (1992). Content reading in RT: The last two decades. *The Reading Teacher, 46,* 166–167.

Armbruster, B., & Anderson, T. (1984). *Producing "considerate" expository text: Or easy reading is damned hard writing* (Reading Education Report No. 36). Champaign, IL: University of Illinois, Center for the Study of Reading.

Aronson, E. (1978). *The jigsaw classroom.* Beverly Hills, CA: Sage.

Ashby-Davis, C. (1985). Cloze and comprehension: A qualitative analysis of critique. *Journal of Reading, 28,* 585–593.

Ashton-Warner, S. (1959). *Spinster.* New York: Simon & Schuster.

Ashworth, M. (1992). *First step on the longer path: Becoming an ESL teacher.* Markham, Ontario: Pippin.

Atkinson, R. C. (1975). Mnemotechnics in second language learning. *American Psychologist, 30,* 821–828.

Atkinson, T. S., Matusevich, M.N., & Huber, L. (2009). Making Science Trade Book Choices for Elementary Classrooms. *The Reading Teacher, 62*(6), 484–497.

Attewell, P. (2001, July). Comment: The first and second digital divides. *Sociology of Education, 74*(3),252–259. Retrieved July 16, 2007, from http://www.jstor.org/view/00380407/di020079/02p0121f/0.

Atwater, R., & Atwater, F. (1988). *Mr. Popper's penguins.* Boston: Little, Brown and Co.

Atwell, N. (1987). *In the middle: Writing, reading, and learning with adolescents.* Portsmouth, NH: Heinemann.

Atwell, N. (1989). *Coming to know: Writing to learn in the intermediate grades.* Portsmouth, NH: Heinemann.

Au, K. H. (1992). *Literary instruction in multicultural settings.* Fort Worth, TX: Harcourt Brace Jovanovich.

Au, K. H. (1998). Social constructivism and the school literacy learning of students of diverse backgrounds. *Journal of Literacy Research, 30,* 297–331.

Au, K. H. (2001). Culturally responsive instruction as a dimension of new literacies. *Reading Online, 5*(1). Retrieved December 7, 2004, from http://www.readingonline.org/newliteracies/lit_index.asp?HREF=/newliteracies/xu/index.html.

Au, K. H., & Raphael, T. E. (2000). Equity and literacy in the next millennium. *Reading Research Quarterly, 35,* 171–188.

Aud, S., Hussar, W., Planty, M., Snyder, T., Bianco, K., et al. (2010). The Condition of Education. National Center for Education Statistics. Washington, DC: U.S. Department of Education.

Aud, S., Fox, M. A., & KewalRamani, A. (2010). Status and trends in the education of racial and ethnic groups. National Center for Education Statistics. Retrieved July 30, 2010, from http://nces.ed.gov/pubsearch/pubsinfo.asp?pubid=2010015.

August, D. & T. Shanahan (Eds.), Developing literacy in second-language learners: Report of the National Literacy Panel on Language Minority Children and Youth. Mahwah, NJ: Erlbaum.

Aurandt, P. (1983). *Destiny.* New York: Bantam Books.

Austen, J. (2008). *Sense and sensibility.* Oxford: Oneworld Classics.

Ausubel, D. (1960). The use of advance organizers in learning and retention of meaningful verbal material. *Journal of Educational Psychology, 51,* 267–272.

Ausubel, D. (1963). *The psychology of meaningful verbal learning.* New York: Grune and Stratton.

Ausubel, D. (1968). *Educational psychology: A cognitive view.* New York: Holt, Rinehart and Winston.

Avgerinou, M., & Ericson, J. (2002). A review of the concept of visual literacy. *British Journal of Educational Technology, 28*(4), 280–291.

Ayers, J., & Miller, M. (2009). Informing adolescent literacy policy and practice: Lessons learned from the Striving Readers Program. Washington, DC: Alliance for Excellent Education, ERIC: ED 506790.

Ayers, S. F. (2001). Developing quality multiple-choice tests for physical education. *The Journal of Physical Education, Recreation & Dance, 72*(16), 23–30.

Bader, L. (1987). *Textbook analysis chart: Reading, writing, speaking, listening, and critical thinking in content area subjects.* Unpublished manuscript. East Lansing, MI: Michigan State University.

Baerwoald, T. J., & Fraser, C. (1992). *World geography.* New Jersey: Prentice-Hall.

Bahrick, H. P., & Phelps, E. (1987). Retention of Spanish vocabulary over 8 years. *Journal of Experimental Psychology: Learning, Memory & Cognition, 13*(2), 344–349.

Baker, E. A. (2001). The nature of literacy in a technology-rich, fourth grade classroom. *Reading Research and Instruction, 40,* 159–184.

Baker, J., Luo, Y., & Hung, Y. (2007). Helping daunted low level adult EFL learners get a fresh start with a literature ladder. *Asian EFL Journal, 9*(4), 254–279.

Baker, S. K., Simmons, D. C., & Kame'enui, E. J. (1998). Vocabulary acquisition: Research bases. In D. C. Simmons & E. J. Kame'enui (Eds.), *What reading research tells us about children with diverse learning needs* (pp. 183–218). Mahwah, NJ: Erlbaum.

Ball, D. L., & Cohen, D. K. (1999). Developing practice, developing practitioners: Toward a practice-based theory of professional education. In L. Darling-Hammond & G. Sykes (Eds.), *Teaching as the learning profession: Handbook of policy and practice* (pp. 3–32). San Francisco: Jossey-Bass.

Bandura, A. (1977). Self-efficacy: Toward a unifying theory of behavioral change. *Psychological Review, 84,* 191–215.

Bandura, A. (1986). *Social foundations of thought and action: A social-cognitive theory.* Upper Saddle River, NJ: Prentice-Hall.

Bandura, A. (Ed.). (1995). *Self-efficacy in changing societies.* New York: Cambridge University Press. Bandura, A. (1997). *Self-efficacy: The exercise of control.* New York: W. H. Freeman.

Bandura, A. (2001), Social cognitive theory: An agentic perspective. Annual Review of Psychology 52, 1–26.

Bangert-Drowns, R. L. (1993). The word processor as an instructional tool: A meta-analysis of word processing in writing instruction. *Review of Educational Research, 63*(1), 69–93.

Bangert-Drowns, R. L., Hurley, M. M., & Wilkinson, B. (2004). The effects of school-based writing-to-learn interventions on academic achievement: A meta-analysis. *Review of Educational Research, 74,* 29–58.

Banks, J. A. (1995). Multicultural education: Historical development, dimensions, and practice. In J. A. Banks & C. A. M. Banks (Eds.), *Handbook of research on multi-cultural education* (pp. 3–24). New York: Macmillan.

Bardovi-Harlig, K., & Dornyei, Z. (1998). Do language learners recognize pragmatic variations? *TESOL Quarterly, 32*(2), 233–259.

Barnako, F. (2004). Life without the Net is unbearable. Retrieved September 23, 2004, from http://cbs.marketwatch. com/news/archivedStory.asp?archive=true&dist=ArchiveSplash&siteid=mktw&guid=%7BB0361CD7%2D6B85%2D4808%2D860B%2D9EE55739D9BE%7D&returnURL=%2Fnews%2Fstory%2Easp%3Fguid%3D%7BB0361CD7% 2D6B85%2D4808%2D860B%2D9EE55739D9BE%7D%26siteid%3Dmktw%26dist%3Dnbc%26archive%3Dtrue%26param%3Darchive%26garden%3D%26minisite%3D.

Barnett, J. E. (2000). Self-regulated reading and test preparation among college students. *Journal of College Reading and Learning, 31*(1), 42–61.

Barry, A. (2002). Reading strategies teachers say they use. *Journal of Adolescent and Adult Literacy, 46*(2), 132–141.

Barry, C. (2010). From great texts to great thinking. *Educational Leadership, 67*(6), 42–46.

Bartlett, F. C. (1932). *Remembering.* Cambridge: Cambridge University Press.

Barton, J. (1995). Conducting effective classroom discussions. *Journal of Reading, 38,* 346–350.

Bauer, E. B., Manyak, P. C., & Cook, C. (2010, February). Supporting content learning for English learners. The Reading Teacher, 63(5), 430–432.

Baumann, J., Edwards, E., Font, G., Tereshinski, C., Kame'enui, E., & Olejnik, S. (2002). Teaching morphemic and contextual analysis to fifth-grade students. *Reading Research Quarterly, 37,* 150–176.

Baumann, J. F. (2005). Vocabulary comprehension relationships. In B. Maloch, J. V. Hoffman, D. L. Schallert, C. M. Fairbanks, & J. Worthy (Eds.), *54th yearbook of the National Reading Conference* (pp. 117–131). Oak Creek, WI: National Reading Conference.

Baumann, J. F., Edwards, E. C., Boland, E. M., Olejnik, S., & Kame'enui, E. J. (2003). Vocabulary tricks: Effects of instruction in morphology and context on fifth-grade students' ability to derive and infer word meanings. *American Educational Research Journal, 40,* 447–494.

Baxter, J. (1985). *Designing a test.* Unpublished paper, submitted in partial fulfillment of course requirements for Reading in the Content Areas. Richmond, VA: Virginia Commonwealth University.

Beach, R., Anson, C., Breuch, L. K., & Swiss, T. (2009). *Teaching writing using blogs, wikis, and other digital tools.* Norwood, MA: Christopher-Gordon Publishers, Inc.

Bean, T. W. (1988). Organizing and retaining information by thinking like an author. In S. Glazer, L. Searfoss, & L. Gentile (Eds.), *Reexamining reading diagnosis* (pp. 103–127). Newark, DE: International Reading Association.

Bean, T. W. (2001). An update on reading in the content areas: Social constructivist dimensions. *Reading Online, 5*(5). Retrieved December 7, 2004, from http://www.readingonline.org/articles/art_index.asp?HREF=handbook/bean/index.html.

Bean, T. W., & Readance, J. E. (2002). Adolescent literacy: Charting a course for successful futures as lifelong learners. *Reading Research and Instruction, 41*(3), 203–210.

Bean, T. W., & Steenwyk, F. L. (1984). The effect of three forms of summarization instruction on sixth graders' summary writing and comprehension. *Journal of Reading Behavior, 16,* 297–306.

Beane, J. (1990). *A middle school curriculum: From rhetoric to reality.* Columbus, OH: National Middle School Association.

Beck, I. L., & McKeown, M. B. (2007). Increasing young low-income children's oral vocabulary repertoires through rich and focused instruction. *The Elementary School Journal, 107*(3), 251–271.

Beck, I. L., & McKeown, M. G. (1988, August–September). Toward meaningful accounts in history texts for young learners. *Educational Researcher, 17*(6), 31–39.

Beck, I. L., McKeown, M. G., & Kucan, L. (2002). *Bringing words to life: Robust vocabulary development.* New York: Guilford Press.

Beck, I. L., McKeown, M. G., Sinatra, G. M., & Loxterman, J. A. (1991). Revising social studies text from a text processing perspective: Evidence of improved comprehensibility. *Reading Research Quarterly, 26,* 251–276.

Beers, T. (1987). Schema-theoretic models of reading: Humanizing the machine. *Reading Research Quarterly, 22*(3), 369–377.

Belfiore, P. J., Auld, R., & Lee, D. L. (2005). The disconnect of poor-urban education; Equal access and a pedagogy of risk taking. *Psychology in the Schools, 42,* 855–863.

Bell, T. (2001). Extensive reading: Speed and comprehension. *The Reading Matrix, 1*(1). Retrieved March 14, 2007, from http://www.readingmatrix.com/articles/bell/article.pdf.

Belzer, S., Miller, M., & Hoemake, S. (2003). Concepts in biology: A supplemental study skills course designed to improve introductory students' skills for learning biology. *The American Biology Teacher, 65*(1), 30–40.

Bembenuttty, H. (2009). The last word: An interview with Lyn Corno—the ingredients for making a self-regulated scholar. *Journal of Advanced Academics, 21*(1), 142–156.

Benson, S. (2010). "I don't know if that'd be English or not": Third pace theory and literacy instruction. *Journal of Adolescent and Adult Literacy, 53*(7), 555–563.

Bereiter, C., & Scardamalia, M. (1987). An attainable version of high literacy: Approaches to teaching higher-order skills in reading and writing. *Curriculum Inquiry, 17*(1), 9–30.

Bergenske, M. D. (1987). The missing link in narrative story mapping. *The Reading Teacher, 41,* 333–335.

Berlak, H. (1992). The need for a new science of assessment. In H. Berlak, F. M. Newmann, E. Adams, et al. (Eds.), *Toward a new science of educational testing and assessment.* New York: State University of New York Press.

Berliner, D. C. (2008). Why rising test scores may not equal increased student learning, Dissent UpFront/Online Argument and Commentary. Retrieved May 28, 2010, from: http://dissentmagazine.org/online.php?id=156.

Berliner, D. C. (2001). Mythology and the American system of education. In K. Ryan & J. M. Cooper (Eds.), *Kaleidoscope: Readings in education* (pp. 106–115). Boston: Houghton Mifflin.

Berliner, D. (2009). Are teachers responsible for low achievement by poor students? *Kappa Delta Pi Record, 46*(1), 18–21.

Berninger, V. W., & Winn, W. D. (2006). Implications of advancements in brain research and technology for writing development, writing instruction, and educational evolution. In C. A. MacArthur, S. Graham, & J. Fitzgerald (Eds.), *Handbook of writing instruction* (pp. 96–114). New York: Guilford Press.

Berube, C. T. (2004). Are standards preventing good teaching? *The Clearing House, 77*(6), 264–267.

Beyer, B. K. (1983). Common sense about teaching thinking skills. *Educational Leadership, 41,* 44–49.

Bezemer, J., & Kress, G. (2008). Writing in multimodal texts: A social semiotic account of designs for learning. *Written Communication, 25*(2), 166–195.

Bhat, P., Rapport, M. J., & Griffin, C. C. (2000). A legal perspective on the use of specific learning methods for students with learning disabilities. *Learning Disabilities Quarterly, 23*(4), 283–297.

Bieger, E. M. (1995). Promoting multicultural education through a literature-based approach. *The Reading Teacher, 49,* 308–311.

Biehler, R., & Snowman, J. (1997). *Psychology applied to teaching.* (8th ed.). Boston: Houghton Mifflin. Retrieved April 7, 2008, from http://college.hmco.com/education/pbl/tc/motivate.html#motivation.

Biemiller, A. (2001). Teaching vocabulary. *American Educator,* 143–148.

Biemiller, A., & Boote, C. (2006). An effective method for building meaning vocabulary in primary grades. *Journal of Educational Psychology, 98*(1), 44–62.

Bikowski, D., & Kessler, G. (2002). Making the most of discussion boards in the ESL classroom. *TESOL Journal, 11*(3), 27–30.

Bintz, W. P. (2010). Singing across the curriculum. *The Reading Teacher, 63*(8), 683–686.

Bintz, W., & Williams, L. (2005). Questioning techniques of fifth and sixth grade reading teachers. *Middle School Journal, 37*(1):45–52.

Bintz, W. P., & Shelton, K. S. (2004). Using written conversation in middle school: Lessons from a teacher researcher project. *Journal of Adolescent & Adult Literacy, 47,* 492–507.

Blachowicz, C., & Ogle, D. (2001). *Reading comprehension: Strategies for independent learners.* New York: Guilford.

Blachowicz, C. L. Z., & Fisher, P. (2000). Vocabulary instruction. In M. Kamil, P. Mosenthal, P. D. Pearson, & R. Barr (Eds.), *Handbook of reading research* (Vol. III, pp. 503–523). Mahwah, NJ: Erlbaum.

Blachowicz, C. L. Z., & Fisher, P. (2004). Vocabulary lessons. *Educational Leadership, 61*(6), 66–69.

Blachowicz, C. L. Z., & Fisher, P. (2008). Attentional vocabulary instruction: Read-alouds, word play, and other motivating strategies for fostering informal word learning. In A. E. Farstrup & S. J. Samuels, (Eds.), *What research has to say about vocabulary instruction* (pp. 32–55). Newark, DE: International Reading Association.

Blachowicz, C. L. Z., & Fisher, P. J. L. (2006). *Teaching vocabulary in all classrooms* (3rd ed.). Upper Saddle River, NJ: Pearson Education.

Blachowicz, C. L. Z., Fisher, P. J. L., Ogle, D., & Watts-Taffe, S. (2006). Vocabulary: Questions from the classroom. *Reading Research Quarterly, 41*(4), 524–539.

Blai, B. (1993). A study guide for students. *The Clearing House, 67*(2), 98–103.

Blaisdell, M. (2006, September). All the right muves: The use of computer simulations that appeal to students' love of video games has shown compelling educational benefits (educational gaming). Technological Horizons in Education Journal, 28. Retrieved January 31, 2007, from http://find.galegroup.com.proxy.library.vcu.edu/itx/infomark.do?&contentSet=IAC-Documents&type=retrieve&tabID=T002&prodId=ITOF&docId=A153517450&source=gale&srcprod=ITOF&userGroupName=viva_vcu&version=1.0.

Blasingame, J., & Bushman, J. H. (2005). *Teaching writing in middle and secondary schools.* Upper Saddle River, NJ: Pearson Education.

Block, C. C. (2004). *Teaching comprehension: The comprehension process approach.* Boston: Allyn & Bacon.

Block, C. C., & Israel, S. E. (2004). The ABCs of performing highly effective think-alouds: Effective think-alouds can build students' comprehension decoding, vocabulary, and fluency. *The Reading Teacher, 58*(2), 154–168.

Blume, J. (1991, 1972). *Tales of a fourth grade nothing.* New York: Dell.

Blumenfeld, P. C., Marx, R., Soloway, E., & Krajcik, J. (1997). Learning with peers: From small group cooperation to collaborative communities. *Educational Researcher, 25,* 37–40.

Boaler, J. (2006). Promoting respectful learning. *Educational Leadership, 63*(5), 74–78.

Boling, E., Castek, J., Zawilinski, L., Barton, K., & Nierlich, T. (2008). Collaborative literacy: Blogs and internet projects. *The Reading Teacher, 61*(6), 504–506.

Borko, H., & Putnam, R. T. (1996). Learning to teach. In D. C. Berliner & R. C. Calfee (Eds.), *Handbook of educational psychology* (pp. 673–708). New York: Macmillan.

Borman, G. D., & Overman, L. T. (2004). Academic resilience in mathematics among poor and minority students. *The Elementary School Journal, 104*(3), 177–197.

Bormouth, J. R. (1969). *Development of a readability analysis.* (Final Report, Project No. 7-0052, Contract No. OEC-3-7-070052-0326). Washington, DC: USOE, Bureau of Research, U.S. Department of Health, Education, and Welfare.

Bormouth, J. R. (1975). Literacy in the classroom. In W. D. Page (Ed.), *Help for the reading teacher: New directions in research* (pp. 60–90). Urbana, IL: National Conference on Research in English and ERIC/RCS Clearinghouse.

Bos, C. S., & Anders, P. L. (1990). Effects of interactive vocabulary instruction on the vocabulary learning and reading comprehension of junior-high learning disabilities students. *Learning Disabilities Quarterly, 13*(1), 31–42.

Bos, C. S., & Vaughn, S. (2002). *Strategies for teaching students with learning and behavior problems* (5th ed.). Boston: Allyn & Bacon.

Bottomley, D. M., Truscott, D. M., Marimak, B. A., Henk, W. A., & Melnick, S. A. (1999). An affective comparison of whole language, literature-based, and basal reader literacy instruction. *Journal of Research and Instruction, 38*(2), 115–130.

Boyd, D.M., & Ellison, N. B. (2007). Social network sites: Definition, history, and scholarship. *Journal of Computer-Mediated Communication, 13*(1), article 11. Retrieved from http://jcmc.indiana.edu/vol13/issue1/boyd.ellison.html.

Boyd, W. L. (2004, February). Relaunching the *American Journal of Education* in "interesting times." *The American Journal of Education, 110,* 105–107.

Boyd-Batstone, P. (2004). Focused anecdotal records assessment: A tool for standards-based, authentic assessment. *The Reading Teacher, 58*(3), 230–239.

Boyer, T. L. (2006). Writing to learn in social studies. *The Social Studies, 97*(4), 158–160. Retrieved from http://web.ebscohost.com.proxy.library.vcu.edu/ehost/pdfviewer/pdfviewer?vid=2&hid=15&sid=4a3d55f9-351f-464c-b10a-a9b09e5d5060%40sessionmgr4.

Brabham, E. G., & Villaume, S. K. (2002). Vocabulary instruction: Concerns and visions. (Questions and answers). *The Reading Teacher, 56,* 264–269.

Bracey, G. (1992). The condition of public education. *Phi Delta Kappan, 74,* 104–117.

Bracey, G. (1997). *Setting the record straight: Responses to misconceptions about public education in the United States.* Alexandria, VA: Association for Supervision and Curriculum Development.

Bradbury, R. (1983, July). Goodbye grandma. *Reader's Digest, 23,* 139–142.

Bravo, M. A., & Cervetti, G. N. (2008). Teaching vocabulary through text and experience in content areas. In A. E. Farstrup & S. J. Samuels, (Eds.), *What research has to say about vocabulary instruction* (pp. 130–149). Newark, DE: International Reading Association.

Brechtel, M. (1992). *Bringing the whole together: An integrated whole-language approach for the multilingual classroom.* San Diego: Dominie Press.

Brendtro, L. K., Brokenleg, M., & Bockern, S. V. (1990). *Reclaiming youth at risk: Our hope for the future.* Bloomington, IN: National Educational Service.

Bright, R. (1995). *Writing instruction in the intermediate grades: What is said, what is done, what is understood.* Newark, DE: International Reading Association.

Brindley, R., & Schneider, J. J. (2002). Writing instruction or destruction: Lessons to be learned from fourth-grade teachers' perspectives on teaching writing. *Journal of Teacher Education, 53,* 328–341.

Brinthaupt, T. M., & Shin, C. M. (2001). The relationship of academic cramming to flow experience. *College Student Journal, 35*(3), 457–472.

Britton, B. K., & Tesser, A. (1991). Effects of time-management practices on college grades. *Journal of Educational Psychology, 83,* 405–410.

Bromley, K. (1993). *Journaling: Engagements in reading, writing, and thinking.* New York: Scholastic.

Brooks, J. G., & Brooks, M. G. (1993). *The case of constructivist classrooms.* Alexandria, VA: Association for Supervision and Curriculum Development.

Brown, A. L. (1980). Metacognitive development and reading. In R. J. Spiro, B. Bruce, & W. F. Brewer (Eds.), *Theoretical issues in reading comprehension* (pp. 453–481). Hillsdale, NJ: Erlbaum.

Brown, A. L., Campione, J. C., & Day, J. D. (1981). Learning to learn: On training students to learn from texts. *Educational Researcher, 10,* 14–21.

Brown, A. L., & Day, J. D. (1983). Macrorules for summarizing texts: The development of expertise. *Child Development, 48,* 1–8.

Brown, J., Phillips, L., & Stephens, E. (1992). *Toward literacy: Theory and applications for teaching writing in the content areas.* Belmont, CA: Wadsworth.

Brown, J., & Stephens, E. (1995). *Teaching young adult literature.* Belmont, CA: Wadsworth.

Brown, J. S. (2000). Growing up digital: How the Web changes work, education, and the ways people learn. *Change,* March/April, 11–20.

Brown, R. (2005). Seventh-graders' self-regulatory note-taking from text: Perceptions, preferences, and practices. *Reading Research and Instruction, 44*(4), 1–26.

Bruce, B. (1998). Dewey and technology. *Journal of Adolescent & Adult Literacy, 42*(3), 222–226.

Brozo, W. G., & Flynt, E. S. (2008). Motivating students to read in the content classroom: Six evidence-based principles. *The Reading Teacher, 62*(2), 172–174.

Brunwin, B. (Ed.). (1989). *The Bucktrout swamp.* Written by first- to sixth-grade students at Greenbriar Elementary School, Chesapeake, VA.

Bryant, D. P., Goodwin, M., Bryant, B. R., & Higgins, K. (2003). Vocabulary instruction for students with learning disabilities: A review of the research. *Learning Disability Quarterly, 26,* 117–128.

Bryant, D. P., Vaughn, S., Linan-Thompson, S., Ugel, N., Hamff, A., & Hougen, M. (2000). Reading outcomes for students with and without reading disabilities in general education middle-school content area classes. *Learning Disabilities Quarterly, 23*(3), 24–38.

Bryant, J. A. R. (1984). Textbook treasure hunt. *Journal of Reading, 27,* 547–548.

Budig, G. A. (2006). Writing: A necessary tool. *Phi Delta Kappan, 87,* 663.

Buehl, D. (2009). Story impressions. In *Classroom strategies for interactive learning* (3rd ed., pp. 162–165). Newark, DE: International Reading Association.

Bult, B., Housen, A., Pierrard, M. & Van Daele, S. (2008). Investigating lexical proficiency development over time—the case of Dutch-speaking learners of French in Brussels. *Journal of French Language Studies, 18*(3), 277–298.

Burns, M. (1975). *The I hate mathematics! book.* New York: Little Brown and Co.

Burns, O. A. (1993). *Cold Sassy Tree.* New York: Delta Trade Paperbacks.

Bushaw, W. J., & Fujloka, J. (2006, February 22). *Education Week.* Retrieved June 2007 from http://www.pdkintl.org/newsroom/publicst/0602advt_ew.htm.

Bushaw, W. J., & McNee, J. A. (2009). Americans speak out: Are educators and policy makers listening? The 41st Annual Phi Delta Kappa/Gallup Poll of the public's attitudes toward the public schools. *Phi Delta Kappan, 9,* 9–23.

Bushaw, W. J., & Lopez, S. J. (2010, September). A time for change: The 42nd Annual Phi Delta Kappa/Gallup Poll of the public's attitudes toward the public schools. *Phi Delta Kappan, 92*(11), 9–26.

Butler, G., & McManus, F. (1998). *Psychology: A very short introduction.* Oxford: Oxford University Press.

Byrnes, J. P. (1995). Domain specificity and the logic of using general ability as an independent variable or covariable. *Merrill-Palmer Quarterly, 41,* 1–24.

Cadenhead, K. (1987). Reading level: A metaphor that shapes practice. *Phi Delta Kappan, 68,* 436–441.

Caldwell, J. S., & Leslie, L. (2005). *Intervention strategies to follow informal reading inventory assessment: So what do I do now?* Boston: Pearson Education.

Calfee, R. C. (1987). *The role of text structure in acquiring knowledge: Final report to the U. S. Department of Education* (Federal Program No. 122B). Palo Alto, CA: Stanford University, Text Analysis Project.

Callison, D. (2003). Concept mapping. *School Library Media Activities Monthly, 17*(10), 30–32.

Calkins, L. M. (1994). *The art of teaching writing* (2nd ed.). Portsmouth, NH: Heinemann.

Calkins, L. (1986). *The art of teaching writing.* Portsmouth, NH: Heinemann.

Cantrell, S. C. (2002). Promoting talk: A framework for reading discussions in teacher education courses: Using reading discussion groups with preservice teachers leads to greater comprehension and engagement. *Journal of Adolescent & Adult Literacy, 45*(7), 642–652.

Cardoso, S. (Ed.). (2003). *Brain and mind: Electronic magazine and neuroscience.* Retrieved from http://www.epub.org.br/cm/n05/mente/estados_i.htm.

Carico, K. M., & Logan, D. (2004). A generation in cyberspace: Engaging readers through online discussions. *Language Arts, 81*(4), 293–302.

Carney, J. J., Anderson, D., Blackburn, C., & Blessing, D. (1984). Preteaching vocabulary and the comprehension of social studies materials by elementary school children. *Social Education, 48*(3), 195–196.

Carmen, R., & Adams, W. (1972). *Study skills: A student's guide to survival.* New York: Wiley.

Carolan, J., & Guinn, A. (2007). Differentiation: Lessons from master teachers. *Educational Leadership, 64*(5), 44–47.

Carr, E., & Ogle, D. (1987). KWL plus: A strategy for comprehension and summarization. *Journal of Reading, 30,* 626–631.

Carr, E., & Wixson, K. K. (1986). Guidelines for evaluating vocabulary instruction. *Journal of Reading, 29,* 588–595.

Carter, K. (1986). Test-wiseness for teachers and students. *Educational Measurement: Issues and Practices, 5,* 20–23.

Carver, R. P. (1990). *Reading rate: A review of research and theory.* New York: Academic Press.

Carver, R. P. (1992). Reading rate: Theory, research, and practical applications. *Journal of Reading, 36*(2), 84–95.

Carver, R. P. (1994). Percentage of unknown vocabulary words in text as a function of the relative difficulty of the text: Implications for instruction. *Journal of Reading Behavior, 25*(4), 413–437.

Cassidy, J., Valadez, C. M., Garrett, S. D., & Barrera IV, E.S. (2010). What's hot, what's not for 2010. *Journal of Adolescent & Adult Literacy, 53*(6), 448–456.

Castek, J., Coiro, J., Hartman, Henry, L., Leu, D., Zawilinski, L. (2007). Thinking about our future as researchers: New literacies, new challenges, and new opportunities. In M. B. Sampson, F. Falk-Ross, M. F. Foote & P. E. Linder (Eds.), Multiple literacies in the 21st century: The twenty-eighth yearbook. (pp. 31–50). Readyville, TN: The College Reading Association. Retrieved July 28, 2010, from http://web.ebscohost.com.proxy.library.vcu.edu/ehost/pdfviewer/pdfviewer?vid=10&hid=10&sid=5256c220-7663-4133-b187-7362570e0e9e%40sessionmgr13.

Center for Applied Special Technology (2008). *Universal design for learning (UDL) guidelines 1.0.* Retrieved July 25, 2010, from http://www.udlcenter.org/aboutudl/udlguidelines.

Center on Educational Policy. (2008, February). A closer look at changes for specific subjects. *Instructional Time in Elementary Schools.* Washington, DC: Center on Educational Policy. Retrieved August 12, 2010, from http://www.cep-dc.org/document/docWindow.cfm?fuseaction=document.viewDocument&documentid=234&documentFormatId=4589.

Chall, J. (1958). *Readability: An appraisal of research and application.* Columbus: Ohio State University, Bureau of Educational Research.

Chall, J. (1983). *Stages of reading development.* New York: McGraw-Hill.

Chamberlain, C.J. (2005). Literacy and technology: A world of ideas. In R.A. Karchmer, M.H. Mallette, J. Kara-Soteriou, & D.J. Leu, Jr. (Eds.), *Innovative approaches to literacy education: Using the Internet to support new literacies* (pp. 44–64). Newark, DE: International Reading Association.

Chang, I. (1991). *A separate battle: Women and the Civil War.* New York: Lodestar Books/Dutton.

Chang, M. (2010). Effects of self monitoring on web-based language learner's performance and motivation. *CALICO Journal, 27*(2), 298–310.

Chase, A. C., & Dufflemeyer, F. A. (1990). VOCAB-LIT: Integrating vocabulary study and literature study. *Journal of Reading, 34*(3), 188–193.

Chauvin, R. A. (2003).Visual or media literacy, *Journal of Visual Literacy, 23*(2), 119–128. Retrieved May 28, 2010, from http://webcache.googleusercontent.com/search?q=cache%3ACMb6vCQqnvsJ%3Awww.ohio.edu%2Fvisualliteracy%2FJVL_ISSUE_ARCHIVES%2FJVL23%282%29%2FJVL23%282%29_pp.119-128.pdf+visual+literacy+%2B+Sinatra&hl=en&gl=us.

Chesbro, R. (2006). Using interactive science notebooks for inquiry-based science. *Science Scope, 29*(7), 30–34.

Chi, F. (1995). ESL readers and a focus on intertextuality. *Journal of Reading, 38,* 638–644.

Chi-Cheng, C. (2009). Self-evaluated effects of web-based portfolio assessment system for various student motivation levels. *Journal of Educational Computing Research, 41*(4), 391–405.

Childress, H. (1998). Seventeen reasons why football is better than high school. Retrieved November 26, 2004, from http://www.pdkintl.org/kappan/kchi9804.htm.

Chinn, C. A., & Anderson, R. C. (1998). The structure of discussions that promote reasoning. *Teachers College Record, 100,* 315–368.

Chinn, C. A., Anderson, R. C., & Waggoner, M. A. (2001). Patterns of discourse in two kinds of literature discussion. *Reading Research Quarterly, 36*(4), 378–411.

Choate, J. S., & Rakes, T. A. (1987). The structured listening activity: A model for improving listening comprehension. *The Reading Teacher, 41,* 194–200.

Choi, I., Land, S., & Turgeon, A. (2008). Instructor modeling and online guidance for peer questioning during online discussion. *Journal of Educational Technology Systems, 36,* 255–275.

Cholewa, B., & West-Olatunji, C. (2008). Exploring the relationship among cultural discontinuity, psychological distress, and academic outcomes with low-income, culturally diverse students. *Professional School Counseling*, 10962409, *12*(1), 54–61.

Christensen, T. A. (2002). *Supporting struggling writers in the elementary school.* Newark, DE: International Reading Association.

Ciardello, A. V. (1998). Did you ask a good question today? Alternative cognitive and metacognitive strategies. *Journal of Adolescent & Adult Literacy, 42*(3), 210–219.

Ciardiello, A. V. (2004). Democracy's young heroes: An instructional model of critical literacy practices. *The Reading Teacher, 58,* 138–147.

Cisneros, S. (2009). *The house on Mango Street.* New York: Vintage Contemporaries.

Clark, D. (1999). Critical reflection. Retrieved November 22, 2003, from http://www.nwlink.com/~donclark/hrd/development/reflection.html.

Cleary, B. (1982). *Ralph S. Mouse.* New York: William Morrow.

Cochran-Smith, M. (1991). Word processing and writing in elementary classrooms: A critical review of related literature. *Review of Educational Research, 61*(1), 107–155.

Cohen, A. D. (1987). The use of verbal and imagery mnemonics in second-language vocabulary learning. *Studies in Second Language Acquisition, 9,* 43–61.

Cohen, M. R., Cooney, T. M., Hawthorne, C., McCormack, A. J., Pasachoff, J. M., Pasachoff, N., Rhines, K. L., & Siesnick, I. L. (1991). *Discover science.* Glenview, IL: Scott, Foresman.

Coiro, J. (2003). Reading comprehension on the Internet: Expanding our understanding of comprehension to encompass new literacies. *The Reading Teacher, 56,* 458–464.

Coiro, J., & Dobler, E. (2007). Exploring the online reading comprehension strategies used by sixth-grade skilled readers to search for and locate information on the Internet. *Reading Research Quarterly, 42(2),* 214–257.

Cole, A. D. (1998). Beginner-oriented texts in literature-based classrooms: The segue for a few struggling readers. *The Reading Teacher, 51*(6), 488–501.

Cole, R., Raffier, L. M., Rogan, P., & Schleicher, L. (1998). Interactive group journals: Learning as a dialogue among learners. *TESOL Quarterly, 32*(3), 556–568.

Cole, R. P., & Goetz, V. W. (2000). Epistemological beliefs of underprepared college students. *Journal of College Reading and Learning, 31*(1), 60–70.

College Board, Touchtone Applied Science Associates. (1986). *Degrees of reading power.* New York: College Board.

Colwell, C. G., Mangano, N. G., Childs, D., & Case, D. (1986). Cognitive, affective, and behavioral differences between students receiving instruction using alternative lesson formats. Kansas City, MO: *Proceedings of the National Reading and Language Arts Conference.*

Commission on No Child Left Behind. (2007). Commissioner Messina Gives Remarks at Annual State School Board Conference. Retrieved June 14, 2007, from http://www.aspeninstitute.org/site/c.huLWJeMRKpH/b.938015/k.40DA/Commission_on_ No_Child_Left_Behind.htm.

Compton-Lilly, C. (2010, May). Learning about Mason: A Collaborative lesson with a struggling reader. The Reading Teacher, *63*(8), 698–700.

Conley, M. W., & Hinchman, K. A. (2004). No Child Left Behind: What it means for U.S. adolescents and what we can do about it. *Journal of Adolescent & Adult Literacy, 48*(1), 42–48.

Connell, J. P., & Ryan, R. M. (1984). A developmental theory of motivation in the classroom. *Teacher Education Quarterly, 11,* 64–77.

Conner, J. (2003). Instructional reading strategy: Anticipation guides. Retrieved from http://www.indiana.edu/~1517/anticipation_guides.htm.

Cook, J. B., & Kaffenberger, C. J. (2003). Solution shop: A solution-focused counseling and study skills program for middle school. *Professional School Counseling, 7*(2), 116–123.

Cook, L., & Gonzales, P. (1995). Zones of contact: Using literature with second language learners. *Reading Today, 12,* 27.

Coombe, C. A., & Hubley, N. J. (2004). *Fundamentals of language assessment.* Presentation and booklet, TESOL conference, Long Beach, CA.

Cooper, J., & Kiger, N. (2003). *Literacy: Helping children construct literacy.* Boston: Houghton Mifflin.

Cooter, R. B. (1990, October/November). Learners with special needs. *Reading Today,* 28.

Cooter, R. B., & Chilcoat, G. W. (1991). Content-focused melodrama: Dramatic renderings of historical text. *Journal of Reading, 34,* 274–277.

Cooter, R. B., Joseph, D., & Flynt, E. (1986). Eliminating the literal pursuit in reading comprehension. *Journal of Clinical Reading, 2,* 9–11.

Cooter, R. B., Jr. (1994). Assessing affective and conative factors in reading. *Reading Psychology, 15*(2), 77–90.

Cope, B., & Kalantzis, M. (2000). Introduction: Multiliteracies: The beginning of an idea. In B. Cope & M. Kalantzis (Eds.), *Multiliteracies: Literacy learning and the design of social futures.* London: Routledge.

Corcoran, C. A., & Mamalakis, A. (2009). Fifth grade students' perceptions of reading motivation techniques. *Reading Improvement, 46*(3), 137–142.

Cordova, R. A., & Matthiesen, A. L. (2010). Reading, writing, and mapping our worlds into being: Shared teacher inquiries into whose literacies count. *The Reading Teacher, 63*(6), 452–463.

Costa, C. (2006). My adventure in Podland. *Essential Teacher, 3*(4), 38–41.

Covey, S. (1990). *Seven habits of highly effective people* New York: Simon and Schuster.

Cowan, G., & Cowan, E. (1980). *Writing.* New York: Wiley.

Cox, J., & Wiebe, J. (1984). Measuring reading vocabulary and concepts in mathematics in the primary grades. *Reading Teacher, 37,* 402–410.

Cox, W. E., & Matthews, F. L. (2001). Blacks are more likely to be placed in special education. *Black Issues in Higher Education, 18*(3), 22.

Coxhead, A. (2000). A new academic word list. *TESOL Quarterly, 34*(2), 213–238.

Crapse, L. (1995). Helping students construct meaning through their own questions. *Journal of Reading, 38*(5), 389–390.

Credé. M., &. Kuncel, N. R. (2008). Study habits, skills, and attitudes: The third pillar supporting collegiate academic performance. *Perspectives on Psychological Science, 3*(6), 425–453.

Cronbach, L. J. (1951). Coefficient alpha and the internal structure of tests. *Psychometrika, 16,* 297–334.

Cronbach, L. J. (1957). *Psychological tests and personnel decisions.* Urbana, IL: University of Illinois Press.

Cronin, H., Meadows, D., & Sinatra, R. (1990). Integrating computers, reading, and writing across the curriculum. *Educational Leadership, 48,* 57–62.

Crooks, S. M., & Katayama, A. D. (2002). Effects of online notetaking format on the comprehension of electronic text. *Research in the Schools, 9,* 22–23.

Cruse, A. (2007). Teaching and learning: An ethnographic, sociolinguistic analysis of the teacher's role in the construction of knowledge in a small group directed reading thinking activity. *Dissertation Abstracts International, A: The Humanities and Social Sciences, 68*(3), 929.

Crystal, D. (2004). *The stories of English.* New York: Penguin Books.

Cubukcu, F. (2007). Cross-cultural differences in learning strategies and study skills. *Porta Linguarum, 8*(June), 99–116. Retrieved from http://www.ugr.es/~portalin/articulos/PL_numero8/6-FERYAL.pdf.

Culham, R. (2003). *6+1 traits of writing: The complete guide grades 3 and up.* New York: Scholastic Professional Books.

Cullinan, B. E., Karrer, M. K., & Pillar, A. M. (1981). *Literature and the child.* New York: Harcourt Brace and Jovanovich.

Cummins, J. (1979). Linguistic interdependence and the educational development of bilingual children. *Review of Educational Research, 49,* 222–251.

Cummins, J. (1994). The acquisition of English as a second language. In K. Spangenberg-Urbschadt & R. Pritchard (Eds.), *Kids come in all languages.* Newark, DE: International Reading Association.

Cummins, J. (2000). *Language, power and pedagogy: Bilingual children in the crossfire.* Clevedon, UK: Multilingual Matters.

Cunningham, A. E., & Stanovich, K. E. (1998). What reading does for the mind. *American Educator, 22*(1, 2), 8–15.

Cunningham, J. W. (1982). Generating interactions between schemata and text. In J. A. Niles & L. A. Harris (Eds.), *New inquiries in reading research and instruction: Thirty-first yearbook of the National Reading Conference* (pp. 42–47). Rochester, NY: National Reading Conference.

Cunningham, P. (1995). *Phonics they use.* New York: Harper Collins.

Cunningham, P. (2006). What if they can say the words but don't know what they mean? *The Reading Teacher, 59*(7), 708–711.

Cunningham, P., & Stanovich, K. E. (1997). Early reading acquisition and its relation to reading experience and ability 10 years later. *Developmental Psychology, 33,* 934–945.

Cunningham, R., & Shablak, S. (1975). Selective reading guide-o-rama: The content teacher's best friend. *Journal of Reading, 18,* 380–382.

Currie, H. (1990). Making texts more readable. *British Journal of Special Education, 17,* 137–139.

Curtis, M. E., & Longo, A. M. (2001). Teaching vocabulary to adolescents to improve comprehension. *Reading Online, 5*(4). Retrieved from http://www.readingonline.org/articles/art_index.asp?HREF=curtis/index.html.

Cushman, K. (1996). *The midwife's apprentice.* New York: HarperTrophy.

Dahlman, A., & Rilling, S. (2001). Integrating technologies and tasks in an EFL distance learning course in Finland. *TESOL Journal, 10*(1), 4–8.

Daisey, P. (2010). Secondary preservice teachers remember their favorite reading experiences: insights and implications for content area instruction. *Journal of Adolescent and Adult Literacy, 53*(8), 678–687.

Dale, E. (1965). Vocabulary measurement: Techniques and major findings. *Elementary English, 42,* 395–401.

Dale, E., & Chall, J. (1948). A formula for predicting readability. *Educational Research Bulletin, 27,* 11–20, 37–54.

Dale, E., & O'Rourke, J. (1976). *The living word vocabulary.* Elgin, IL: Dome.

Dale, E., O'Rourke, J., & Bamman, H. (1971). *Techniques of teaching vocabulary.* Palo Alto, CA: Field Educational Publications.

Dana, C., & Rodriguez, M. (1992). TOAST: A system to study vocabulary. *Reading Research and Instruction, 31*(4), 78–84.

Daniels, H. (1994). *Literature circles: Voice and choice in the student-centered classroom.* Portsmouth, NH: Heinemann.

Danziger, P. (1995). *Amber brown is not a Crayon.* New York: Scholastic.

Davey, B. (1983). Think aloud: Modeling the cognitive processes of reading comprehension. *Journal of Reading, 27,* 44–47.

Davidowitz, B., & Schreiber, B. (2008). Facilitating adjustment to higher education. South African Journal of *Higher Education,* 22(1), 191–206.

Davis, B. (1985). *The long surrender.* New York: Random House.

Davis, F. B. (1968). Research in comprehension in reading. *Reading Research Quarterly, 3*(4), 499–545.

Davis, F. B. (1944). Fundamental factors of comprehension in reading. *Psychometrika, 9*(3), 185–197.

Davis, J. (1997). *Mapping the mind: The secrets of the human brain and how it works.* Secaucus, NJ: Carol Publishing Group.

Davis, S., & Winek, J. (1989). Improving expository writing by increasing background knowledge. *Journal of Reading, 33,* 178–181.

Davis, W. C. (1985). *Touched by fire: A photographic portrait of the Civil War.* Boston: Little, Brown and Co. Davis, W. C. (1990). *Diary of a Confederate soldier.* Columbia, SC: University of South Carolina Press.

Davison, D., & Pearce, D. (1988a). Using writing activities to reinforce mathematics instruction. *Arithmetic Teacher, 35,* 42–45.

Day, B., & Anderson, J. (1992). Assessing the challenges ahead. *Delta Kappa Gamma Bulletin, 58*(4), 5–10.

Deal, D. (1998). Portfolios, learning logs, and eulogies: Using expressive writing in a science methods course. In E. G. Sturtevant, J. A. Dugan, P. Linder, & W. M. Linek (Eds.), *Literacy and community: Twentieth yearbook of the College Reading Association* (pp. 243–256). Commerce, TX: Texas A & M Press.

DeBell, M., & Chapman, C. (2003). *Computer and Internet Use by Children and Adolescents in 2001* (NCES 2004–014). Retrieved July 13, 2007, from http://nces.ed.gov/programs/quarterly/vol_5/5_4/2_1.asp.

De Bono, E. (1976). *Teaching thinking.* London: Temple Smith.

Dechant, E. (1970). *Improving the teaching of reading.* Englewood Cliffs, NJ: Prentice-Hall.

Dede, C. (2007, January 23). *Emerging educational technologies and neomillennial learning styles.* Presentation at the annual meeting of Educause Learning Initiative, Atlanta, GA.

Deen, M. Y., Bailey, S. J., & Parker, L. (2001). *Life skills evaluation system.* Wenatchee, WA: Washington State University Cooperative Extension.

Dehaene, S. (2009). *Reading in the brain.* New York: Viking.

Delgardo, B. (2001). Interpretations of constructivism and consequences for computer assisted learning. *British Journal of Educational Technology, 32*(2), 183–194.

Dember, W. M., Warm, J. S., & Parasuraman, R. (1996). Olfactory stimulation and sustained attention. In A. Gilbert (Ed.), *Compendium of olfactory research* (pp. 39–46). New York: Olfactory Research Fund, Ltd.

Derby, T. (1987). Reading instruction and course-related materials for vocational high school students. *Journal of Reading, 30,* 308–316.

Demetriou, H., & Wilson, E. (2010). *Improving Schools. 13*(54), 54–69.

Demski, J. (2009). Free at last. *T.H.E. Journal, 36*(6), 39–44.

Dennis, D. V. (2010). "I'm not stupid": How assessment drives (in)appropriate reading instruction. *Journal of Adolescent & Adult Literacy, 53*(4), 283–290.

Deshler, D. D., & Schumaker, J. B. (1988). An instructional model for teaching students how to learn. In J. L. Graden, J. E. Zins, & M. J. Curtis (Eds.), *Alternative educational delivery systems: Enhancing instructional options for all students* (pp. 391–411). Washington, DC: National Association of School Psychologists.

Devault, R., & Joseph, L. M. (2004). Repeated readings combined with word boxes phonics technique increases fluency levels of high school students with severe reading delays. *Preventing School Failure, 49*(1), 22–28.

DeVoogd, G. (2006). Question authority. *School Library Journal, 52*(4), 48–52.

Dewey, J. (1933). *How we think.* Boston: Heath.

Diamond, M., & Hopson, J. (1998). *Magic trees of the mind: How to motivate your child's intelligence, creativity, and healthy emotions from birth through adolescence.* New York: Penguin Putnam.

DiCecco, V. M., & Gleason, M. M. (2002). Using graphic organizers to attain relational knowledge from expository text. *Journal of Learning Disabilities, 35*(4), 306–321.

Dickson, R. (2002). Creating joy: Adolescents writing poetry with young children. *Voices from the Middle, 10*(2), 38–42.

Dieu, B. (2004). BLOGs for language learning. *The Essential Teacher, 1*(4), 28–30.

Dillon, J. T. (1983). *Teaching and the art of questioning.* Bloomington, IN: Phi Beta Kappa Educational Foundation. Fastback No. 194.

Dixon, F., Cassady, J., Cross, T., & Williams, D. (2005). Effects of technology on critical thinking and essay writing among gifted adolescents. *Journal of Secondary Gifted Education, 16*(4), 180–190.

Dolan, R. P., & Hall, T. E., (2001). Universal Design for Learning: Implications for large-scale assessment. *IDA Perspectives, 27*(4), 22–25.

Dole, S. (2000). The implications of the risk and resilience literature for gifted students with learning disabilities. *Roeper Review, 23*(2), 91.

Donovan, S., & Cross, C. (Eds.). (2002). *Minority students in special and gifted education.* Washington, DC: National Academic Press.

Dove, M. K. (1998). The textbook in education. *Delta Kappa Gamma Bulletin, 64*(3), 24–30.

Downing, J. (1973). *Comparative reading.* New York: Macmillan.

Downing, J., Ollila, L., & Oliver, P. (1975). Cultural differences in children's concepts of reading and writing. *British Journal of Educational Psychology, 45,* 312–316.

Drame, E., & Xu, Y. (2008). Examining sociocultural factors in response to intervention models. *Childhood Education, 85*(1), 26–32.

Drevno, G. E., Kimball, J. W., Possi, M. K., Howard, W. L., Gardner, R., & Barbetta, P. M. (1994). Effects of active student response during error correction on the acquisition, maintenance, and generalization of science vocabulary by elementary students: A systematic replication. *Journal of Applied Behavior Analysis, 27*(1), 179–180.

Drum, P. (1985). Retention of text information by grade, ability, and study. *Discourse Processes, 8,* 21–51.

Duffelmeyer, F. A., & Baum, D. D. (1992). The extended anticipation guide revisited. *Journal of Reading, 35,* 654–656.

Duffy, G. G., & Hoffman, J. V. (1999). In pursuit of an illusion: The flawed search for a perfect method. *The Reading Teacher, 53,* 10–16.

Duke, N. (2003). Information text? The research says, "Yes!" In L. Hoyt, M. Mooney, & B. Parkes (Eds.), *Exploring informational texts: From theory to practice* (pp. 2–7). Portsmouth, NH: Heinemann.

Duke, N., & Pearson, P. D. (2002). Effective practices for developing reading comprehension. In A. E. Farstrup & S. J. Samuels (Eds.), *What research has to say about reading instruction* (3rd ed,. pp. 205–242). Newark, DE: International Reading Association.

Duke, N. K. (2000). 3.6 minutes per day: The scarcity of informational texts in first grade. *Reading Research Quarterly, 35,* 202–224.

Duke, N. K., Purcell-Gates, V., Hall, L. A., & Tower, C. (2006). Authentic literacy activities for developing comprehension and writing. *The Reading Teacher, 60,* 344–355.

Dunn, M., Bonner, B., & Huske, L. (2007). *Developing a systems process for improving instruction in vocabulary: Lessons learned.* Alexandria, VA: Association of Supervision and Curriculum Development.

Dunston, P. J. (1992). A critique of graphic organizer research. *Reading Research and Instruction, 31,* 57–65.

Durkin, D. (1979). What classroom observations reveal about reading comprehension. *Reading Research Quarterly, 14,* 481–533.

Durkin, D. (1981). Reading comprehension instruction in five basal reading series. *Reading Research Quarterly, 16,* 515–544.

Durkin, D. (1984). Is there a match between what elementary teachers do and what basal reader manuals recommend? *The Reading Teacher, 37,* 734–744.

Duvdevany, I., & Rimmerman, A. (1996). Individuals with work-related disabilities: Locus of control, attitudes toward work, and cooperation with the rehabilitation worker. *Journal of Applied Rehabilitation Counseling, 27*(2), 30–35.

Dzaldov, B. S., & Peterson, S. (2005). Book leveling and readers. *The Reading Teacher, 59,* 222–229.

Eanet, M., & Manzo, A. V. (1976). REAP—a strategy for improving reading/writing/study skills. *Journal of Reading, 19,* 647–652.

Earle, R., & Barron, R. F. (1973). An approach for teaching vocabulary in content subjects. In H. L. Herber & R. F. Barron (Eds.), *Research in reading in the content areas: Second year report* (pp. 84–100). Syracuse, NY: Syracuse University, Reading and Language Arts Center.

Ebbinghaus, H. (1908/1973). *Abriss der psychologie* (M. Meyer, Trans. and Ed.). New York: Arno Press. EDUCAUSEConnect (May, 2005). 7 Things you should know about clickers. Retrieved June 2007 from http://connect.educause.edu/library/abstract/7ThingsYouShouldKnow/39379?time=1182561758.

Echevarria, J. Vogt, M. E., & Short, D. (2008). *Making content comprehensible for English Language learners: The SIOP model.* Boston: Pearson/Allyn & Bacon.

Edmunds, K. M., & Bauserman, K. L. (2006). What teachers can learn about reading motivation through conversations with children. *The Reading Teacher, 59*(5), 414–424.

Edwards, E. C., Font, G., Baumann, J. F., & Boland, E. (2004). Unlocking word meanings: Strategies and guidelines for teaching morphemic and contextual analysis. In J. F. Baumann & E. B. Kame'enui (Eds.), *Vocabulary instruction: Research to practice* (pp. 159–176). New York: Guilford Press.

Egan, M. (1999). Reflections on effective use of graphic organizers. *Journal of Adolescent & Adult Literacy, 42*(8), 641–645.

Elia, A. (2006, December). Language learning in tandem via Skype. *Reading Matrix: An International Online Journal,* 6(3), 269–280.

El-Koumy, A. (2006). The effects of the Directed Reading-Thinking Activity on EFL students' referential and inferential comprehension. Retrieved from http://www.eric.ed.gov/PDFS/ED502645.pdf

Elder, L., & Paul, R. (2009). Critical thinking: Strategies for improving student learning, part 111. *Journal of Developmental Education, 32*(3), 40.

Eldredge, J. L. (1990). Learning and study strategies inventory—high school version. *Journal of Reading, 34*(2), 146–149.

Elley, W. B. (1992). *How in the world do students read?* The Hague, The Netherlands: International Association for the Evaluation of Educational Achievement.

Elliot, L., Foster, S., & Stinson, M. (2002). Student study habits using notes from a speech-to-text support service. *Exceptional Children, 69*(1), 25–41.

Erickson, B. (1996). Read-alouds reluctant readers relish. *Journal of Adolescent & Adult Literacy, 40*(3), 217–221.

Erten, I., & Karakas, M. (2007). Understanding the divergent influences of reading activities on the comprehension of short stories. *The Reading Matrix: An International Online Journal, 7*(3), 113–133.

Evans, J. A., & Reimer, J. (2009, February). Open access and global participation in science. *Science*, 323(5917), 1025. Retrieved February 25, 2009, from http://www.sciencemag.org/cgi/content/abstract/323/5917/1025.

Eveland, W. P., & Dunwoody, S. (2002). An investigation of elaboration and selective scanning as mediators of learning from the Web versus print. *Journal of Broadcasting and Electronic Media, 46*(1), 34–54.

Fahey, K., Lawrence, J., & Paratore, J. (2007). Using electronic portfolios to make learning public. *Journal of Adolescent and Adult Literacy, 50*(9), 460–471.

Farley, W. (1941). *The black stallion.* New York: Random House.

Farstrup, A. E., & Samuels, S. J. (2008). *What research has to say about vocabulary instruction.* Newark, DE: International Reading Association.

Feldhusen, J. (1989). Synthesis of research on gifted youth. *Educational Leadership, 46*(6), 6–11.

Ferguson, D. B. (2000). Reexamining at-risk. *Curriculum Administrator, 36*(6), 79–90.

Fiedler E., Lange, R., & Winebrenner, S. (2002). In search of reality: Unraveling the myths about tracking, ability grouping, and the gifted. *Roeper Review, 24,* 108–111.

Fillmore, L. W. (1981). Cultural perspectives on second language learning. *TESL Reporter, 14,* 23–31.

Finkbeiner, C., & Koplin, C. (2002, October). A cooperative approach for facilitating intercultural education. *Reading Online, 6*(3). Retrieved June 3, 2007, from http://www.readingonline.org/newliteracies/lit_index.asp?HREF=finkbeiner/index.html.

Fisher, C. W., & Berliner, D. (Eds.). (1985). *Perspectives on instructional time.* New York: Longman.

Fisher, D., Flood, J., Lapp, D., & Frey, N. (2004). Interactive read-alouds: Is there a common set of implementation practices? *The Reading Teacher, 58*(1), 8–17.

Fisher, D., & Frey, N. (2003). Writing instruction for struggling adolescent writers: A gradual release model. *Journal of Adolescent & Adult Literacy, 46*(5), 395–405.

Fisher, D., & Frey, N. (2008). *Improving adolescent literacy: Content area strategies at work.* Upper Saddle River, NJ: Merrill Prentice Hall.

Fisher, M. (2004, October 12). Falls Church school won't teach to the test. *The Washington Post,* B1.

Fisher, M. (2010). Unplugged: Eight reporters attempt to quit the Internets. *The Washington Post.* Retrieved May 29, 2010, from http://www.washingtonpost.com/wp-srv/metro/story-lab/unplugged.html.

Fitzsimmons, D. (2008). Digital portfolios in visual arts classrooms. *Art Education, 61*(5), 47–53.

Flanagan, K., & Greenwood, S. C. (2007). Effective content vocabulary instruction in the middle: Matching students, purposes, words, and strategies. *Journal of Adolescent & Adult Literacy, 51*(3), 226–238.

Fleener, C., Hager, J., Morgan, R. F., & Childress, M. (2000). *The integration of conation, cognition, affect, and social environment in literacy development.* In P. Linder, W. M. Linek, E. G. Sturtevant, & J. Dugan (Eds.), *Literacy at a new horizon: Twenty-second yearbook of the College Reading Association* (pp. 88–98). Commerce, TX: Texas A & M University.

Fleming, C. B., Harachi, T. W., Cortes, R. C., Abbott, R D., & Catalano, R. F. (2004). Level and change in reading scores and attention problems during elementary school as predictors of problem behavior in middle school. *Journal of Emotional and Behavioral Disorders, 12*(3), 130–144.

Flesch, R. (1949). *The art of readable writing.* New York: Harper and Row.

Fletcher, D. (2010, May 31). Facebook: Friends without borders. *Time, 175*(21), 32–38.

Florida Coalition for Assessment Reform, Inc. (FCAR) (n.d.). *About FCAR.* Retrieved September 12, 2010, from http://web.archive.org/web/20080622120356/www.fcarweb.org/about_fcar.htm.

Fontana, J. L., Scruggs, T., & Mastropiere, M. A, (2007). Mnemonic strategy instruction in inclusive secondary social studies classes. *Remedial and Special Education, 28*(6), 345–355.

Forbes, L. S. (2004). Using Web-based bookmarks in K–8 settings: Linking the Internet to instruction. *The Reading Teacher, 58*(2), 148–153.

Forgan, H. W., & Mangrum, C. T. (1985, 1997). *Teaching content area reading skills.* Columbus, OH: Merrill.

Forget, M. A. (2004). *MAX teaching with reading and writing: Classroom activities for helping students learn new subject matter while acquiring literacy skills.* Victoria, BC: Trafford Publishing.

Fox, B. J. (2003). Teachers' evaluations of word identification software: Implications for literacy methods courses. In M. B. Sampson, P. E. Linder, J. R. Dugan, & B. Brancato (Eds.), *Celebrating the freedom of literacy: The twenty-fifth yearbook of the College Reading Association.* Commerce, TX: Texas A & M University.

Francis, M. A., & Simpson, M. L. (2003). Using theory, our intuitions, and a research study to enhance students' vocabulary knowledge. *Journal of Adolescent & Adult Literacy, 47*(1), 66–78.

Francis-Smythe, J. A., & Robertson, I. T. (1999). On the relationship between time management and time estimation. *British Journal of Psychology, 90*(3), 333–334.

Frand, J. L. (2000). The information-age mindset. *Education Review, 35*(5), 15–24.

Franklin, B. (1994). *The autobiography of Benjamin Franklin.* Kindle Version. Retrieved August 11, 2010, from http://www.amazon.com/Autobiography-Benjamin-Franklin-book/dp/B000JMLMXI/ref=sr_1_4?ie=UTF8&m=AG56TWVU5XWC2&s=digital-text&qid=1281525655&sr=1-4.

Friedman, T. L. (2006). *The world is flat.* New York: Farrar, Straus & Giroux.

Friend, R. (2001). Teaching summarization as a content area reading strategy. *Journal of Adolescent and Adult Literacy, 44*(4), 320–329.

Fritz, C. O., Morris, P. E., Acton, M., Voelkel, A. R., & Etkind, R. (2006). Comparing and combining retrieval practice and the keyword mnemonic for foreign vocabulary learning. *Applied Cognitive Psychology, 21*(4), 499–526.

Fry, E. (1968). The readability graph validated at primary levels. *The Reading Teacher, 3,* 534–538.

Fry, E. (1977). Fry's readability graph: Clarifications, validity, and extension to level 17. *Journal of Reading, 21,* 242–252.

Fry, E. (1987). The varied uses of readability measurement today. *Journal of Reading, 30,* 338–343.

Fry, E. (1989). Reading formulas—maligned but valid. *Journal of Reading, 32,* 292–297.

Fry, E. (1990). A readability formula for short passages. *Journal of Reading, 33,* 594–597.

Frymier, A. B., & Schulman, G. (1995). "What's in it for me?" Increasing content relevance to enhance students' motivation. *Communication Education, 44,* 40–50.

Fulwiler, T. (1987). *Teaching with writing.* Portsmouth, NH: Boynton/Cook.

Gagne, R. (1974). Educational technology and the learning process. *Educational Researcher, 3,* 3–8.

Gainer, J. S. (2010). Critical media literacy in middle school: Exploring the politics of representation. *Journal of Adolescent & Adult Literacy, 53*(5), 364–373d.

Galas, C., & Ketelhut, D. J. (2006). River City, the MUVE. *Learning and Leading with Technology, 33*(7), 31–32.

Galeman, D. (1995). *Emotional intelligence: Why it can matter more than IQ.* New York: Bantam.

Gallagher, J. M. (1995). Pairing adolescent fiction with books from the canon. *Journal of Adolescent & Adult Literacy, 39,* 8–14.

Gallo, A. M. (2003). Assessing the affective domain. *The Journal of Physical Education, Recreation & Dance, 74*(4), 44–49.

Gambrell, L.B. (2004). Shifts in the conversation: Teacher-led, peer-led, and computer-mediated discussions. *The Reading Teacher, 58,* 212–215.

Gambrell, L. B. (1995). Motivation matters. In *Generations of literacy: Seventeenth yearbook of the College Reading Association* (pp. 2–24). Commerce, TX: East Texas State University.

Gambrell, L. B., & Almasi, J. F. (1996). *Lively discussions: Fostering engaged reading.* Newark, DE: International Reading Association.

Ganske, K., Monroe, J. K., & Strickland, D. S. (2003). Questions teachers ask about struggling readers and writers. *Journal of Adolescent & Adult Literacy, 57*(2), 118–128.

Garber-Miller, K. (2006). Playful textbook previews: Letting go of familiar mustache monologues. *Journal of Adolescent and Adult Literacy, 50*(4), 284–288.

Gardner, J. E., & Wissick, C. A. (2002). Enhancing cooperative learning using the World Wide Web: Tools and strategies that integrate technology for students with mild disabilities. *Journal of Special Education Technology, 17,* 27–38.

Gardner, J. E., Wissick, C. A., Schweder, W., & Canter, L. S. (2003). Enhancing interdisciplinary instruction in general and special education: Thematic units and technology. *Remedial and Special Education, 24*(3), 161–173.

Garner, R., & Gillingham, M. (1987). Students' knowledge of text structure. *Journal of Reading Behavior, 29,* 247–259.

Garner, R., Hare, V. C., Alexander, P., Haynes, J., & Winograd, P. (1984). Inducing use of a text look-back strategy among unsuccessful readers. *American Educational Research Journal, 21,* 789–798.

Garner, R., Macready, G. B., & Wagoner, S. (1985). Reader's acquisition of the components of the text-lookback strategy. *Journal of Educational Psychology, 76,* 300–309.

Garrison, W. B. (1992). *Civil War trivia and fact book.* Nashville, TN: Rutledge Hill Press.

Gates, H. L., Jr. (1995). *On honoring blackness. American Enterprise* 6(5), 49.

Gebhard, A. (1983). Teaching writing in reading and the content areas. *Journal of Reading, 27,* 207–211.

Gee, J. P. (2000). Teenagers in new times: A new literacy studies perspective. *Journal of Adolescent and Adult Literacy, 43*(5), 412–420.

Gee, J. P. (2001). Literacy discourse and linguistics: Introduction. In E. Cushman, M. Rose, B. Kroll, & E. R. Kitgen (Eds.), *Literacy: A critical sourcebook* (pp. 525–544). Boston: Bedford/St. Martin's.

Gee, J. P. (2010). Video games: What they can teach us about audience engagement. *Nieman Reports, 64*(2), 52–54.

Gee, R. W. (1999). Encouraging ESL students to read. *TESOL Journal, 8*(1), 3–7.

George, J.C.(1971). *All upon a stone.* New York: Crowell.

Gere, A. (1985). *Roots in the sawdust: Writing to learn across the disciplines.* Urbana, IL: National Council of Teachers of English.

Gersten, B. F., & Tlusty, N. (1998). Creating international contexts for cultural communication: Video exchange projects in the EFL/ESL classroom. *TESOL Journal, 7*(6), 11–16.

Gettinger, M., & Seibert, J. K. (2002). Contributions of study skills to academic competence. *School Psychology Review, 31*(3), 350–366.

Gholar, C. R., & Riggs, E. G. (2004). *Connecting with students' will to succeed: The power of conation.* Glenview, IL: Pearson Education.

Giambo, D. A. (2010, Spring). High-stakes testing, high school graduation, and limited English proficient students: A case study. American Secondary Education, *38*(2), 44–56.

Gibbons, P. (2003). Mediating language learning: Teacher interaction with ESL students in a content-based classroom. *TESOL Quarterly, 37*(2), 247–273.

Gillett, J. W., & Temple, C. (1983). *Understanding reading problems: Assessment and instruction.* Boston: Little, Brown.

Gillies, R. M., & Ashman, A. F. (1998). Behavior and interactions of children in cooperative groups in lower and middle elementary grades. *Journal of Educational Psychology, 90*(4), 746–757.

Gillies, R. M., & Boyle, M. (2006). Ten Australian elementary teachers' discourse and reported pedagogical practices during cooperative learning. *The Elementary School Journal, 106*(5), 429–452.

Glazer, S., Searfoss, L. & Gentile, L (Eds.), Reexamining reading diagnosis (pp. 103–127). Newark, DE: International Reading Association.

Glatthaar, J. T. (1990). *Forged in battle: The Civil War alliance of black soldiers and white officers.* New York: Free Press.

Glaubman, R., Glaubman, H., & Ofir, L. (1997). Effects of self-directed learning, story comprehension, and self-questioning in kindergarten. *Journal of Educational Research, 90,* 361–374.

Glynn, S. M. (1997). *Learning from science text: Role of an elaborate analogy.* College Park, MD: National Reading Research Center.

Godwin, K., & Sheard, W. (2001). Education reform and the politics of 2000. *Publius: The Journal of Federalism, 31*(3), 11–129.

Goett, A., & Foot, K. E. (2000). Cultivating student research and study skills in Web-based learning environments. *Journal of Geography in Higher Education, 24*(1), 92–99.

Gold, P. C. (1981). The directed listening–language experience approach. *Journal of Reading, 25,* 138–141.

Goldberg, A., Russell, M., & Cook, A. (2003). The effect of computers on student writing: A meta-analysis of studies from 1992 to 2002. *Journal of Technology, Learning, and Assessment, 2*(1). Retrieved November 26, 2004, from http://www.bc.edu/research/intasc/jtla/journal/v2n1.shtml.

Goldman, S., & Rakestraw, J. (2000). Structural aspects of constructing meaning from text. In M. Kamil, P. Mosenthal, P. D. Pearson, & R. Barr (Eds.), *Handbook of reading research* (Vol. 3, pp. 311–335). Mahwah, NJ: Erlbaum.

Goodson, F. T. (2007). The electronic portfolio: Shaping an emerging genre. *Journal of Adolescent and Adult Literacy, 50*(9), 432–434.

Google. (2010). *Corporate information: Company overview.* Retrieved July 28, 2010, from http://www.google.com/corporate/index.html.

Gottlieb, M. (2003). *Large scale assessment of English language learners.* Alexandria, VA: TESOL.

Grady, M. P. (1990). *Whole brain education.* Bloomington, IN: Phi Delta Kappa Educational Foundation.

Graham, S., & Perin, D. (2007). *Writing next: Effective strategies to improve writing of adolescents in middle and high schools—a report to Carnegie Corporation of New York.* Washington, DC: Alliance for Excellent Education.

Graves, D. (1994). *A fresh look at writing.* Portsmouth, NH: Heinemann.

Graves, D., Prenn, M., & Cooke, C. (1985). The coming attraction: Previewing short stories. *Journal of Reading, 28,* 594–598.

Graves, M. F. (1985). *A word is a word . . . or is it?* New York: Scholastic.

Graves, M. F. (2000). A vocabulary program to complement and bolster a middle-grade comprehension program. In B. M. Taylor, M. F. Graves, & P. van den Broek (Eds.), *Reading for meaning: Fostering comprehension in the middle grades* (pp. 116–135). New York: Teachers College Press.

Graves, M. F. (2004). Teaching prefixes: As good as it gets? In J. F. Baumann & E. B. Kame'enui (Eds.), *Vocabulary instruction: Research to practice* (pp. 81–99). New York: Guilford Press.

Graves, M. F. (2006a). Building a comprehensive vocabulary program. *The New England Reading Association Journal, 42*(2), 1–7.

Graves, M. F. (2006b). *The vocabulary book: Learning and instruction.* New York: Teachers College Press, International Reading Association, National Council of Teachers of English.

Graves, M. F. (2008). Instruction on individual words: One size does not fit all. In A. E. Farstrup & S. J. Samuels (Eds.), *What research has to say about vocabulary instruction* (pp. 56–79). Newark, DE: International Reading Association.

Graves, M. F. (2009). *Teaching individual words: One size does not fit all.* New York: Teachers College Press.

Gray, F. E., Emerson, L., & MacKay, B. (2005). Meeting the demands of the workplace: Science students and writing skills. *Journal of Science Education and Technology, 14*(4), 425–435.

Gray, W. (1925). *Summary of investigations related to reading* (Supplementary Educational Monographs No. 28). Chicago: University of Chicago Press.

Gray, W. (1960). The major aspects of reading. In H. Robinson (Ed.), *Development of reading abilities* (Supplementary Educational Monographs No. 90). Chicago: University of Chicago Press.

Gray, W. S. (1937). The nature and organization of basic instruction in reading. In G. M. Whipple (Ed.), *The teaching of reading: A second report* (thirty-eighth yearbook of the National Society for the Study of Education, Part I). Bloomington, IL: Public School Publishing Company.

Green, F. E. (1999). Brain and learning research: Implications for meeting the needs of diverse learners. *Education, 119*(4), 682–687.

Green, J. F., & Smyser, S. O. (1996). *The teacher portfolio: A strategy for professional development and evaluation.* Lancaster, PA: Technomic Publishing.

Green, S. K., & Gredler, M. E. (2002). A review and analysis of constructivism for school-based practice. *School Psychology Review, 31*(1), 53–71.

Greenleaf, C. L., & Hinchman, K. (2009). Reimagining our inexperienced adolescent readers: From struggling, striving, marginalized, and reluctant to thriving. *Journal of Adolescent & Adult Literacy, 53*(1), 4–13.

Greenlee-Moore, M., & Smith, L. (1996). Interactive computer software: The effects on young children's reading achievement. *Reading Psychology: An International Quarterly, 17,* 43–64.

Gregory, A. E., & Chaill, M. (2010). Kindergarteners can do it too! Comprehension strategies for early readers. The Reading Teacher, *63*(6), 515–520.

Griffith, L. W., & Rasinski, T. V. (2004). A focus on fluency: How one teacher incorporated fluency with her reading curriculum. *The Reading Teacher, 58*(2), 126–137.

Groenke, S. L., & Puckett, R. (2006). Becoming environmentally literate citizens. *The Science Teacher, 73*(8), 22–27.

Groff, P. (1981). Direct instruction versus incidental learning of reading vocabulary. *Reading Horizons, 21*(4), 262–265.

Guillaume, A. M. (1998). Learning with text in the primary grades. *The Reading Teacher, 51*(6), 476–486.

Gunderson, L., & Siegel, L. S. (2001). The evils of the use of IQ tests to define learning disabilities in first and second language learners. *The Reading Teacher, 55*(1), 48–55.

Gusak, F. J. (1967). Teacher questioning and reading. *The Reading Teacher, 21,* 227–234.

Guthrie, J. (2000). Contexts for engagement and motivation in reading. In M. L. Kamil, P. B. Mosenthal, P. D. Pearson, & R. Barr (Eds.), *Handbook of reading research* (Vol. III, pp. 403–422). Retrieved October 1, 2004, from http://www.readingonline.org/articles/handbook/guthrie/index.html.

Guthrie, J. T. (2004, May 1). *CORI: Classroom practices promoting engagement and achievement in comprehension.* Keynote address presented at the International Reading Association Reading Research 2004 conference, Reno, Nevada.

Guthrie, J. T., Burnam, N., Caplan, R. I., & Seifert, M. (1974). The maze technique to assess and monitor reading comprehension. *The Reading Teacher, 28,*161–168.

Guthrie, J. T., Hoa, L. W., Wigfield, A., Tonks, S. M., Perencevich, K. C. (2006). From spark to fire: Can situational reading interest lead to long-term reading motivation? *Reading Research and Instruction, 45*(2), 91–117.

Guthrie, J. T., Wigfield, A., & Perencevich, K. C. (Eds.). (2004). *Motivating reading comprehension: Concept-oriented reading instruction.* Mahwah, NJ: Erlbaum.

Guzzetti, B. (1990). Enhancing comprehension through trade books in high school English classes. *Journal of Reading, 33,* 411–413.

Guzzetti, B., Hynd, C. R., Skeels, S. A., & Williams, W. O. (1995). Improving physics texts: Students speak out. *Journal of Reading, 38,* 656–663.

Guzzetti, B., Kowalinski, B. J., & McGowan, T. (1992). Using a literature-based approach to teaching social studies. *Journal of Reading, 36,* 114–122.

Guzzetti, B., Snyder, T., & Glass, G. (1992). Promoting conceptual change in science: Can texts be used effectively? *Journal of Reading, 35,* 642–649.

Hadaway, N., & Mundy, J. (1999). Children's informational picture books visit a secondary ESL classroom. *Journal of Adolescent & Adult Literacy, 42*(6), 464–475.

Hager, J. M., & Gable, R. A. (1993). Content reading assessment: A rethinking of methodology. *The Clearing House, 66,* 269–272.

Haggard, M. R. (1986). The vocabulary self-collection strategy: Using student interest and world knowledge to enhance vocabulary growth. *Journal of Reading, 29,* 634–642.

Halberstam, M. (2009). Reciprocal teaching: The effects on reading comprehension of third grade students. *Dissertation Abstracts International, A: The Humanities and Social Sciences, 69,* 10.

Haley, A. N., & Watson, D. C. (2000). In-school literacy extension: Beyond in-school suspension. *Journal of Adolescent & Adult Literacy, 43*(7), 654–661.

Hall, L. A. (2007). Understanding the silence: Struggling readers discuss decisions about reading expository text. *The Journal of Educational Research, 100,* 3, 132–141.

Hall, L. A., & Piazza, S.V. (2008, September). Critically reading texts: What students do and how teachers can help. *The Reading Teacher, 62*(1), 32–41.

Hall, T., & Strangman, N. (2002). *Graphic organizers.* Wakefield, MA: National Center on Accessing the General Curriculum. Retrieved from http://www.cast.org/publications/ncac/ncac_go.html.

Hall-Quest, A. L. (1916). *Supervised study.* New York: Macmillan.

Halladay, M. A. K. (1994). *An introduction to functional grammar* (2nd ed.). London: Edward Arnold.

Hallman, H.L. (2007, March). Negotiating teacher identity: Exploring the use of electronic teaching portfolios with preservice English teachers. Journal of Adolescent & Adult Literacy, 50(6), 474–485. Retrieved September 12, 2010, from http://www.reading.org/Publish.aspx?page=/publications/journals/jaal/v50/i6/abstracts/jaal-50-6-hallman.html&mode=redirect.

Hamachek, D. E. (1975). *Behavior dynamics in teaching, learning, and growth.* Boston: Allyn & Bacon.

Hammerberg, D. D. (2004). Comprehension instruction for socioculturally diverse classrooms: A review of what we know. *The Reading Teacher, 57*(7), 648–658.

Hancock, D. (2004). Cooperative learning and peer orientation effects on motivation and achievement. *Journal of Educational Research, 97*(3), 159–167.

Hand, D. (2006). Adolescent literacies: Reading, thinking, writing. *Knowledge Quest, 35,* 40–43.

Hanna, T. (2009). Effects of nonfiction guided interactive reading-alouds and think-alouds on fourth grader's depth of content area science vocabulary knowledge and comprehension. *Dissertation Abstracts International, A: The Humanities and Social Sciences, 69*(8), 3090.

Hansen, J. (1981). The effects of inference training and practice on young children's comprehension. *Reading Research Quarterly, 16,* 391–417.

Hansen, J., & Pearson, D. (1983). An instructional study: Improving the inferential comprehension of fourth grade good and poor readers. *Journal of Educational Psychology, 75,* 821–829.

Hapgood, S., & Palincsar, A. S. (2006/2007). Where literacy and science intersect. *Educational Leadership, 64,* 56–60.

Harland, P., Plante, A., Marker, J., Falter, C., Thompson, K., Guilmett, K., & Hogan, M. (2010, June). The high school book club—now with Kindles!, *Teacher Librarian, 37*(5), 57–59.

Harper, C., & de Jong, E. (2004). Misconceptions about teaching English language learners. *Journal of Adolescent & Adult Literacy, 46,* 152–162.

Harris, K., & Graham, S. (1985). Improving learning disabled students' composition skills: Self-control strategy training. *Learning Disability Quarterly, 8,* 27–36.

Harris, T. L., & Hodges, R. E. (1995). *The literacy dictionary: The vocabulary of reading and writing.* Newark, DE: International Reading Association.

Harris, L. A., & Smith, C. B. (1986). *Reading instruction: Diagnostic teaching in the classroom.* New York: Macmillan.

Harris-Murri, N., King, K., & Rostenberg, D. (2006). Reducing disproportionate minority representation in special education programs for students with emotional disturbances: Toward a culturally responsive response to intervention model. *Education and Treatment of Children, 29*(4), 779–799.

Harrison, D. (2010, June 9). States and schools: A race against time. *Stateline.* Retrieved August 14, 2010, from http://www.stateline.org/live/details/story?contentId=490279.

Hart, B., & Risley, T. R. (2003). The early catastrophe: The 30 million word gap by age 3. *American Educator, 27*(1), 4–9.

Hart, L. (1975). *How the brain works.* New York: Basic Books.

Harvard University. (2004–2007). *The River City project: A multi-user virtual environment for learning scientific inquiry and 21st century skills.* Retrieved January 30, 2007, from muve.gse.harvard.edu/rivercityproject/index.html.

Harvey, S., & Goudvsi, A. (2000). *Strategies that work: Teaching comprehension to enhance understanding.* York, ME: Stenhouse.

Harvey, V. S. (2007). Schoolwide methods for fostering resiliency. *Principal Leadership, 7*(5), 10–14.

Hattie, J., Biggs, J., & Purdie, N. (1996). Effects of learning skills interventions on student learning: A meta-analysis. *Review of Educational Research, 66,* 99–136.

Haugland, S. (2006). Selecting or upgrading software and websites in the classroom. *Early Childhood Education Journal, 32*(5), 329–341.

Hayes, H., Stahl, N., & Simpson, M. (1991). Language, meaning, and knowledge: Empowering developmental students to participate in the academic community. *Reading Research and Instruction, 30*(3), 89–100.

Haynes, J. (2006). DSL—Digital as a second language. *Essential Teacher, 3*(4), 6–7.

Heath, S. B. (1986). Critical factors in literacy development. In S. de Castell, A. Luke, & K. Egan (Eds.), *Literacy, society, and schooling: A reader* (pp. 209–229). New York: Cambridge University Press.

Hedin, L.R., & Conderman, G. (2010, April). Teaching students to comprehend informational text through rereading. *The Reading Teacher, 63*(7), 556–565.

Heilman, A. W., Blair, T. R., & Rupley, W. H. (1986, 1994). *Principles and practices of teaching reading.* Columbus, OH: Merrill.

Heller, M. (1986). How do you know what you know? Metacognitive modeling in the content areas. *Journal of Reading, 29,* 415–422.

Helman, L. (2008). English words needed: Creating research-based vocabulary instruction for English learners. In A. E. Farstrup & S. J. Samuels, (Eds.), *What research has to say about vocabulary instruction* (pp. 211–237). Newark, DE: International Reading Association.

Helsel, L., & Greenberg, D. (2007). Helping struggling writers succeed: A self-regulated strategy instruction program. *Reading Teacher, 60*(8), 752–760.

Hemmingway, E. (1996, 1952). *The old man and the sea.* New York: Scribner.

Henderson, M. V., & Scheffler, A. J. (2004). New literacies, standards, and teacher education. *Education, 124*(2), 390–395.

Henk, W. A., & Helfeldt, J. P. (1987). How to develop independence in following written directions. *Journal of Reading, 30,* 602–607.

Henry, G. H. (1974). *Teach reading as concept development: Emphasis on affective thinking.* Newark, DE: International Reading Association.

Henry, L. A. (2006). SEARCHing for an answer: The critical role of new literacies while reading on the Internet. *The Reading Teacher, 59*(7), 614–627.

Herber, H. (1978). *Teaching reading in the content areas* (2nd ed.). Englewood Cliffs, NJ: Prentice-Hall.

Herber, H. (1987). Foreword. In D. Alvermann, D. Moore, & M. Conley (Eds.), *Research within reach: Secondary school reading.* Newark, DE: International Reading Association.

Herman, J. L., Aschbacher, P. R., & Winters, L. W. (1992). *A practical guide to alternative assessment.* Alexandria, VA: Association for Supervision and Curriculum Development.

Hew, K.F. (2009). Use of audio podcast in K-12 and higher education: A review of research topics and methodologies. *Education Tech Research Development, 57,* 333–357.

Heward, W. L. (2009). *Exceptional children: An introduction to special education* (9th ed.). Upper Saddle River, NJ: Merrill/Pearson Education.

Hiebert, E. H. (1999). Text matters in learning to read. *The Reading Teacher, 52*(6), 552–566.

Hiebert, E. H., & Lubliner, S. (2008). The nature, learning, and instruction of general academic vocabulary. In A. E. Farstrup & S. J. Samuels, (Eds.), *What research has to say about vocabulary instruction* (pp. 106–129). Newark, DE: International Reading Association.

Higgins, B., Miller, M., & Wegmann, S. (2006/2007). Teaching to the test. . .not! Balancing best practice and testing requirements in writing. *The Reading Teacher, 60,* 310–319.

Hill, W., & Erwin, R. (1984). The readability of content textbooks used in middle and junior high schools. *Reading Psychology, 5,* 105–117.

Hillocks, G., Jr. (2002). *The testing trap: How state writing assessments control learning.* New York: Teachers College Press.

Hinchman, K. A., Alvermann, D. E., Boyd, F. B., Brozo, W. G., & Vacca, R. T. (2004). Supporting older students' in-and-out-of-school literacies. *Journal of Adolescent & Adult Literacy, 47*(4), 304–310.

Hirsch, E. D. (1987). *Cultural literacy.* Boston: Houghton Mifflin.

Hittleman, D. R. (1978). Readability, readability formulas, and cloze: Selecting instructional materials. *Journal of Reading, 22,* 117–122.

Hmelo, C. E., Nagarajan, A., & Day, R. S. (2000). Effects of high and low prior knowledge on construction of a joint problem space. *The Journal of Experimental Education, 69*(1), 36.

Hoffman, J. (1992). Critical reading/thinking across the curriculum: Using I-charts to support learning. *Language Arts, 69,* 121–127.

Hoffman, S. (1983). Using student journals to teach study skills. *Journal of Reading, 26,* 344–347.

Hogan, K., Nastasi, B. K., & Pressley, M. (2000). Discourse patterns and collaborative scientific reasoning in peer and teacher-guided discussions. *Cognitive Instruction, 17,* 379–432.

Holiday, W. G. (1983). Overprompting science students using adjunct study questions. *Journal of Research in Science Teaching, 20,* 195–201.

Hollingsworth, B. (2010, February 23). Jack dale slapdown: Virginia legislators curb VGLA abuse. The Washington Examiner. Retrieved August 15, 2010, from http://www.washingtonexaminer.com/opinion/blogs/SharpSticks/

Jack-Dale-slapdown-Virginia-legislators-curb-VGLA-abuse-85052402.html.

Holmes, B., & Roser, N. (1987). Five ways to assess readers' prior knowledge. *The Reading Teacher, 40,* 646–649.

Holschuh, J. P. (2000). Do as I say, not as I do: High, average, and low-performing students' strategy use in biology. *Journal of College Reading and Learning, 31*(1), 94–132.

Honebein, P. C. (1996). Seven goals for the design of constructivist learning environments. In B. G. Wilson (Ed.). *Constructivist learning environments: Case studies in instructional design* (pp. 11–24). Englewood Cliffs, NJ: Educational Technology Publications.

Horn, W. F., & Tynan, D. (2001). Revamping special education. *The Public Interest,144,* 36–42.

Hornberger, T. R., & Whitford, E. V. (1983). Students' suggestions: Teach us study skills! *Journal of Reading, 27,* 71.

Houston, G. (2004). *How writing works: Imposing organizational structure within the writing process.* Boston: Pearson Education.

Houston, P. D. (2005). NCLB: Dreams and nightmares. *Phi Delta Kappan, 86*(6), 469–471.

Howard S., & Johnson, B. (2000). What makes the difference? Children and teachers talk about resilient outcomes for children "at risk." *Educational Studies, 26,* 321–337.

Howes, E. V., Hamilton, G. W., & Zaskoda, D. (2003). Linking science and literature through technology: Thinking about interdisciplinary inquiry in middle school. *Journal of Adolescent & Adult Literacy, 46,* 484–504.

Howland, J. (1995). Attentive reading in the age of canon clamor. *English Journal, 84,* 35–38.

Hu, W. (2008, January 28). Students click, and a quiz becomes a game. *The New York Times*, p. 1.

Hubbard, B. P., & Simpson, M. (2003). Developing self-regulated learners: Putting theory into practice. *Reading Research and Instruction, 42*(4), 62–89.

Huber, J. (2004). A closer look at SQ3R. *Reading Improvement, 41*(2), 108–113.

Huck, C., Hepler, S., & Hickman, J. (1987). *Children's literature in the elementary school.* Fort Worth, TX: Holt, Rinehart and Winston.

Huey, E. (1908/1968). *The psychology and pedagogy of reading.* Cambridge, MA: MIT Press.

Hughes, J. (2007). Rotting principals, persistent teachers. *Essential Teacher, 4*(2), 7–8.

Huitt, W., Hummel, J., & Kaeck, D. (2001). Assessment, measurement, evaluation, and research. *Educational Psychology Interactive.* Valdosta, GA: Valdosta State University. Retrieved August 12, 2010, from http://www.edpsycinteractive.org/topics/intro/sciknow.html.

Hunsader, P. D. (2004). Mathematics trade books: Establishing their value and assessing their quality. *The Reading Teacher, 57*(7), 618–629.

Hunter, K. (2006). A textbook case. *T.H.E. Journal, 33*(15), 48–50.

Hurd, P. (1970). *New directions in teaching secondary school science.* Chicago: Rand-McNally.

Huss, J. A. (2006). Gifted education and cooperative learning: A miss or a match? *Gifted Child Today, 29*(4), 19–23.

Hwang, Y., & Levin, J. (2002). Examination of middle school students' independent use of a complex mnemonic system. *The Journal of Experimental Education, 7*(1), 25–39.

Hynd, C. (1999.) Teaching students to think critically using multiple texts in history. *Journal of Adolescent & Adult Literacy, 42*(6), 428–436.

Inman, C. Wright, V.H., & Hartman, J. A. (2010). Use of second life in K-12 and higher education: A review of research. *Journal of Interactive Online Learning, 9(1),* 44–63.

Inan, F., Lowther, D., Ross, S., & Strahl, D. (2010).Pattern of classroom activities during students' use of computers: Relations between instructional strategies and computer applications. *Teaching and Teacher Education: An International Journal of Research and Studies, 26*(3), 540–546.

Individuals with Disabilities Education Improvement Act of 2004, 20 U.S.C. § 1400 et seq. (2004). (Reauthorization of the Individuals with Disabilities Education Act of 1990).

Individuals with Disabilities Education Improvement Act of 2004, Pub. L. 108–466.

Inspiration Software. (2000). *Kidspiration* (computer software). Portland, OR: Author.

Inspiration Software. (2002). *Inspiration 7.0* (computer software). Portland, OR: Author.

Interactive Tdc. (1993). *A survey of western art.* Manhattan Beach, CA: Author.

International Reading Association. (2003). *Standards for reading professionals.* Newark, DE: Author, Professional Standards and Ethics Committee.

International Technology Education Association. (2000). *Standards for technological literacy: Content for the study of technology.* Retrieved July 27, 2010, from http://www.iteaconnect.org/TAA/PDFs/xstnd.pdf.

Irfan, Y., & Tolga, E. (2009). The effects of portfolio assessment on reading, listening and writing skills of secondary school prep class students. *Journal of International Social Research, 2*(9), 526–538.

Irish, C. (2002). Using peg- and keyword mnemonics and computer-assisted instruction to enhance basic multiplication performance in elementary students with learning and cognitive disabilities. *Journal of Special Education Technology, 17*(4), 29–40.

Irvin, J. L. (1990). *Vocabulary knowledge: Guidelines for instruction. What research says to the teacher.* Washington, DC: National Education Association.

Irvin, J. L., Buehl, D. R., & Klemp, R. M. (2007). *Reading and the high school student: Strategies to enhance literacy* (2nd ed.). Boston: Pearson Education.

Irvin, J. L., Buehl, D. R., & Radcliffe, B. J. (2007). *Strategies to enhance literacy and learning in middle school content area classrooms* (3rd ed.). Boston: Pearson Education.

Ivey, G., & Broaddus, K. (2001). "Just plain reading": A survey of what makes students want to read in middle school classrooms. *Reading Research Quarterly, 36*(4), 350–377. Retrieved from http://www.jstor.org.proxy.library.vcu.edu/stable/pdfplus/748056.pdf.

Ivey, G., & Broaddus, K. (2000). Tailoring the fit: Reading instruction and middle school readers. *The Reading Teacher, 54*(1), 68–78.

Iwicki, A. L. (1992). Vocabulary connections. *The Reading Teacher, 45,* 736.

Izard, J. (2005). Overview of test construction. In K. N. Ross (Ed.), *Quantitative research methods in educational planning.* Paris: International Institute for Educational Planning/UNESCO. Retrieved September 12, 2010, from http://www.iiep.unesco.org/fileadmin/user_upload/Cap_Dev_Training/Training_Materials/Quality/Qu_Mod6.pdf.

Jackson, F. R., & Cunningham, J. (1994). Investigating secondary content teachers and preservice teachers' conceptions of study strategy instruction. *Reading Research and Instruction, 34,* 11–135.

Jacobson, J. M. (1998). *Content area reading: Integration with the language arts.* Albany, NY: Doman.

Jaimes, J. (2005). Critical thinking, reflective writing: Learning? *Academic Exchange Quarterly, 9*(1), 192–197.

Janesick,V. (2006). Issues related to assessment. In *Authentic assessment primer* (pp. 75–87). New York: Peter Lang Publishing.

Jenkins, C., & Lawler, D. (1990). Questioning strategies in content area reading: One teacher's example. *Reading Improvement, 27,* 133–138.

Jensen, E. (1998). *Teaching with the brain in mind.* Alexandria, VA: Association for Supervision and Curriculum Development.

Jetton, T. L., & Alexander, P. A. (2000). Learning from text: A multidimensional and developmental perspective. In M. L. Kamil, P. B. Mosenthal, P. D. Pearson, & R. Barr (Eds.), *Handbook of reading research* (Vol. III.). Retrieved September 7, 2004, from http://www.reading online.org/articles/handbook/jetton/index.html.

Jewitt, C. (2008). Multimodality and literacy in school classrooms. *Review of Research in Education, 32,* 241–267.

Jitendra, A. K., Edwards, L. L., Sacks, G., & Jacobson, L. A. (2004). What research says about vocabulary instruction for students with learning disabilities. *Exceptional Children, 70,* 299–322.

Johnson, D. (2002, October). Web watch: Poetry workshop. *Reading Online, 6*(3). Retrieved December 12, 2004, from http://www.readingonline.org/electronic/elec_index.asp?HREF=webwatch/poetry/index.html.

Johnson, D., & Johnson, B. (2002, August/September). The unfairness of uniformity. *Reading Today, 20,* 18.

Johnson, D. D. (2001). *Vocabulary in the elementary and middle school.* Boston: Allyn & Bacon.

Johnson, D. W., & Johnson, R. T. (1974). Instructional goal structure: Cooperative, competitive, or individualistic. *Review of Educational Research, 44,* 213–240.

Johnson, D. W., & Johnson, R. T. (2003). *Joining together Group theory and group skills.* New York: A and B Publishing.

Johnson, D. W., Johnson, R. T., & Stanne, M. B. (2000). Cooperative learning methods: A meta-analysis. Retrieved June 24, 2007, from http://www.co-operation.org/pages/cl-methods.html.

Jones, C. H., Slate, J. R., & Marini, I. (1995). Locus of control, social interdependence, academic preparation, age, study time, and the study skills of college students. *Research in the Schools, 2,* 55–62.

Jones, F. R., Morgan, R. F., & Tonelson, S. W. (1992). *The psychology of human development* (3rd ed.). Dubuque, IA: Kendall/Hunt.

Jones, H. J., Coombs, W. T., & McKinney, C. W. (1994). A themed literature unit versus a textbook: A comparison of the effects on content acquisition and attitudes in elementary social studies. *Reading Research and Instruction, 34,* 85–96.

Jones, J., & Leahy, S. (2006). Developing strategic readers. *Science and Children, 44*(3), 30–34.

Jonassen, D. H. (2006). *Modeling with technology: Mindtools for conceptual change* (3rd ed.). Upper Saddle River, NJ: Pearson Education, Inc.

Joseph, B. (2008). Beyond the textbook: Studying Roswell in the social studies classroom. *The Social Studies, 99*(3), 132–134.

Juel, C., & Deffes, R. (2004). Making words stick. *Educational Leadership, 61*(6), 30–34.

Juel, C., Hebard, H., Haubner, J. P., & Moran, M. (2010). Reading through a disciplinary lens. *Educational Leadership, 67*(6), 12–17.

Juster, N. (1961). *The phantom tollbooth.* New York: Random House.

Kagan, S. (1994). *Cooperative learning.* San Clemente, CA: Resources for Teachers, Inc.

Kahn, E. A. (2000). A case study of assessment in a grade 10 English course. *The Journal of Educational Research, 93*(5), 276–286.

Kaiser, Henry F. (1962). Scaling a simplex. *Psychometrika, 27*(2), 155–162.

Kamil, M. L., Borman, G. D., Dole, J., Kral, C. C., Salinger, T., & Torgesen, J. (2008). *Improving adolescent literacy: Effective classroom and intervention practices: A practice Guide* (NCEE#2008-4027). Washington, DC: National Center for Education Evaluation and Regional Assistance Institute of Education Sciences, U.S. Department of Education. Retrieved from http://ies.ed.gov/ncee/wwc.

Kamil, M. L., & Hiebert, E. H. (2005). The teaching and learning of vocabulary: Perspectives and persistent issues. In E. H. Hiebert & M. L. Kamil (Eds.), *Teaching and learning vocabulary: Bringing research to practice* (pp. 1–23). Mahwah, NJ: Erlbaum.

Kane, B. (1984). *Remarks made at the regional meeting on reading across the curriculum.* Richmond, VA: Reading to Learn in Virginia, Capital Consortium.

Kapinus, B. (1986). *Ready reading readiness.* Baltimore: Maryland State Department of Education.

Kaplan, D., Rupley, W., Sparks, J., & Holcomb, A. (2007). Comparing traditional journal writing with journal writing shared over E-mail list serves as tools for facilitating reflective thinking: A study of preservice teachers. *Journal of Literacy Research, 39*(3), 357–387.

Karabenick, S. A. (1998). Help seeking as a strategic resource. In S. A. Karabenick (Ed.), *Strategic help seeking: Implications for learning and teaching* (pp. 1–11). Mahwah, NJ: Erlbaum.

Karchmer, R. (2001). The journey ahead: Thirteen teachers report how the Internet influences literacy and literacy instruction in their K–12 classrooms. *Reading Research Quarterly, 36*(4), 442–466.

Karlin, R. (1977). *Teaching reading in the high school.* Indianapolis: Bobbs-Merrill.

Katayama, A. D., & Robinson, D. H. (2000). Getting students "partially" involved in note-taking using graphic organizers. *Journal of Experimental Education, 68*(2), 119.

Katehi, L., Pearson, G., & Feder, M. (Eds.). (2000). *Engineering in K-12 education: Understanding the status and improving the prospects* . Washington, DC: The National Academies Press. Retrieved July 27, 2010, from http://books.nap.edu/openbook.php?record_id=12635&page=18.

Katz, I., Kaplan, A., & Gueta, G. (2010). Students' needs, teachers' support and motivation for doing homework: A cross-sectional study. *The Journal of Experimental Education, 78,* 246–267.

Kauffman, J. M., & Landrum, T. (2009). *Characteristics of emotional and behavioral disorders of children and youth* (9th ed.). Upper Saddle River, NJ: Merrill/Pearson.

Kellogg, R. (1972). Listening. In P. Lamb (Ed.), *Guiding children's language learning* (pp. 141–170). Dubuque, IA: William C. Brown.

Kelly, M. J., & Clausen-Grace, N. (2009). Facilitating engagement by differentiating independent reading. *The Reading Teacher, 63*(4), 313–318.

Kenner, C. (2004). *Becoming biliterate: Young children learning different writing systems.* Stoke-on-Trent, UK: Trentham.

Kerr, J. (2009, 1971). *When Hitler stole pink rabbit.* New York: Puffin Books.

Kervin, L., & Vardy, J. (2007). Look who's talking: Incorporating iPods in the classroom. *Screen Education, 48,* 58–64.

Ketelhut, D. J., Dede, C., Clarke, J., & Nelson, B. (2006). *A multi-user virtual environment for building higher order inquiry skills in science.* Paper presented at the annual meeting of the American Educational Research Association, San Francisco. Retrieved January 30, 2007, from http://muve.gse.harvard.edu/rivercityproject/documents/rivercitysympinq1.pdf.

Khadaroo, S.T. (2010, July 29). Obama refuses to budge on Race to the Top education reforms. *The Christian Science Monitor,* n.p. Retrieved August 12, 2010, from http://proxy.library.vcu.edu/login?url=http://search.ebscohost.com/login.aspx?direct=true&AuthType=ip,url,cookie,uid&db=a9h&AN=52576973&site=ehost-live&scope=site.

Kibby, M. W. (1995). The organization and teaching of things and the words that signify them. *Journal of Adolescent & Adult Literacy, 39,* 208–223.

Kieffer, M. J., & Lesaux, N. K. (2007). Breaking down words to build meaning: Morphology, vocabulary, and reading comprehension in the urban classroom. *The Reading Teacher, 61,* 134–144.

Kim, A., Vaughn, S., Wanzek, J., & Wei, S. (2004, March). Graphic organizers and their effects on the reading comprehension of students with LD: A synthesis of research. *Journal of Learning Disabilities, 37*(2), 105–118. Retrieved August 14, 2010, from http://ldx.sagepub.com/content/37/2/105.abstract.

Kinder, D., Bursuck, B., & Epstein, M. (1992). An evaluation of history textbooks. *Journal of Special Education, 25,* 472–491.

King, S. (1982). *"The body" in different seasons.* New York: Penguin Books.

King, S. (2002). *On writing: A memoir of the craft.* New York: Pocket Books.

Kinniburgh, L., & Shaw, E. (2009). Using question-answer relationships to build: Reading comprehension in science. *Science Activities: Classroom Projects and Curriculum Ideas, 45*(4), 19–28.

Kintch, W., & Van Dijk, T. (1978). Toward a model of text comprehension and production. *Psychological Review, 85,* 363–394.

Kinzer, C.K. (2005). The intersection of schools, communities, and technology: Recognizing children's use of new literacies. In R. A. Karchmer, M. H. Mallette, J. Kara-Soteriou, & D. J. Leu, Jr., *Innovative approaches to literacy education: Using the Internet to support new literacies* (pp. 65–82). Newark, DE: International Reading Association.

Kirkpatrick, L., & Klein, P. (2009). Planning text structure as a way to improve students' writing from sources in the compare-contrast genre. *Learning and Instruction, 19*(4), 309–321.

Kist, W. (2000). Beginning to create the new literacy classroom: What does the new literacy look like? *Journal of Adolescent and Adult Literacy, 43,* 710–718.

Kitsantas, A. (2002). Test preparation and performance: A self-regulatory analysis. *The Journal of Experimental Education, 70*(2), 101–114.

Kleiner, A., & Lewis, L. (2003). *Internet access in U. S. public schools and classrooms: 1994–2002.* Washington, DC: National Center for Educational Statistics. Retrieved December 14, 2004, from http://nces.ed.gov.

Kletzein, S. B. (1991). Strategy use by good and poor comprehenders reading expository text of differing reading levels. *Reading Research Quarterly, 26,* 67–86.

Klingner, J. K., & Vaughn, S. (1996). Reciprocal teaching of reading comprehension strategies for students with learning disabilities who use English as a second language. *The Elementary School Journal, 96,* 275–292.

Klingner, J. K., & Vaughn, S. (1999). Promoting reading comprehension, content learning, and English acquisition through collaborative strategic reading. *The Reading Teacher, 52*(7), 738–747.

Knickerbocker, J. L., & Rycik, J. A. (2006). Reexamining literature study in the middle grades: A critical response framework. *American Secondary Education, 34*(3), 43–56.

Knipper, K. J., & Duggan, T. J. (2006). Writing to learn across the curriculum: Tools for comprehension in content area classes. *The Reading Teacher, 59,* 462–470.

Knowles, M. S. (1975). *Self-directed learning: A guide for learners and teachers.* New York: Association Press.

Knowles, M. S. (1980). *The modern practice of adult education: From pedagogy to andragogy.* New York: Cambridge Books.

Knowlton, D. S., & Knowlton, H. M. (2001). The context and content of online discussions: Making cyberdiscussions viable for the secondary school curriculum. *American Secondary Education, 29*(4), 38–52.

Knox, C., & Anderson-Inman, L. (2001). Migrant ESL high school students succeed using networked laptops. *Learning and Leading with Technology, 28*(5), 18–28.

Koeze, S. (1990). The dictionary game. *Reading Teacher, 43,* 613.

Kolic-Vehovec, S., & Bajanski, I. (2007). Comprehension monitoring and reading comprehension in bilingual students. *Journal of Research in Reading, 30*(2), 198–211.

Kolic-Vehovec, S., & Bajanski, I. (2006). Metacognitive strategies and reading comprehension in elementary-school students. *European Journal of Psychology of Education, 21*(4), 439–451.

Konigsburg, E. L. (2002). *From the mixed up files of Mrs. Basil E. Frankweiler.* New York: Atheneum Books for Young Readers.

Kornhaber, M., Mishook, J., Edwards, M., & Nomi, T. (2006). Testing's influence on the arts: Some unexpected findings from Virginia. *KEDI Journal of Educational Policy, 3*(1), 45–67.

Kowalski, P., & Taylor, A. K. (2004). Ability and critical thinking as predictors of change in students' psychological misconceptions. *Journal of Instructional Psychology, 31*(4), 297–304.

Kowalski, T. (1995). Chasing the wolves from the schoolhouse door. *Phi Delta Kappan, 76,* 486–489.

Kozen, A. A., Murray, R. K., & Windell, I. (2006). Increasing all students' chance to achieve: Using and adapting anticipation guides with middle school learners. *Intervention in School & Clinic, 4*(4), 195–201.

Krashen, S. (1982). *Principles and practices in second language acquisition.* New York: Pergamon Press.

Krashen, S. (1989). *Language acquisition and language education.* Englewood Cliffs, NJ: Prentice-Hall.

Krathwohl, D. R., Bloom, B. S., & Masia, B. B. (1964). *Taxonomy of educational objectives: Handbook II: Affective domain.* New York: David McKay.

Kropiewnicki, M. (2006). Comprehending comprehension: Training pre-service teachers in reading comprehension strategies. *The Reading Professor, 28*(1), 20–24.

Kruse, M. (2009, December 27). Looking for a name for the past 10 years? It was the search decade. *St. Petersburg Times.* Retrieved July 28, 2010, from http://www.tampabay.com/news/humaninterest/looking-for-a-name-for-the-past-10-years-it-was-the-search-decade/1061069.

Kulik, J. A., & Kulik, C. C. (1990). Ability grouping and gifted students. In N. Colangelo & G. A. Davis (Eds.), *Handbook of gifted education* (pp. 178–196). Boston: Allyn & Bacon.

Laing, S. P., & Kamhi, A. G. (2002). The use of think-aloud protocols to compare inferencing abilities in average and below-average readers. *Journal of Learning Disabilities, 35*(5), 436–448.

L'Allier, S., & Elish-Piper, L. (2007). "Walking the walk" with teacher education candidates: Strategies for promoting active engagement with assigned readings. *Journal of Adolescent and Adult Literacy, 50*(5), 338–353.

Lambiotte, J. G., & Dansereau, D. F. (1992). Effects of knowledge maps and prior knowledge on recall of science lecture content. *The Journal of Experimental Education, 60,* 189–201.

Landis, D, Umolu, J., & Mancha, S. (2010). The power of language experience for cross-cultural reading and writing. *The Reading Teacher, 63*(7), 580–289.

Langer, J. (1981). From theory to practice: A prereading plan. *Journal of Reading, 25,* 152–156.

Langer, J. (2001). Beating the odds: Teaching middle and high school students to read and write well. *American Educational Research Journal, 38,* 837–880.

Langer, J. A. (1986). Learning through writing: Study skills in the content areas. *Journal of Reading, 29,* 5, 400–406.

Lankutis, T. (2001). Reaching the struggling reader. *Technology and Learning, 21*(10), 24–30.

Lapp, D., Fisher, D., & Johnson, K. (2010). Real time teaching: Text mapping plus: Improving comprehension through supported retellings. *Journal of Adolescent & Adult Literacy, 53*(5), 423–426.

Larson, C., & Dansereau, D. (1986). Cooperative learning in dyads. *Journal of Reading, 29,* 516–520.

Last, D. A., O'Donnell, A., & Kelly, A. E. (2001). The effects of prior knowledge and goal strength on the use of hypertext. *Journal of Educational Multimedia and Hypermedia, 10,* 1, 3.

Latendresse, C. (2004). Literature circles: Meeting reading standards, making personal connections, and appreciating other interpretations. *Middle School Journal, 35*(3), 13–20.

Lauber, P. (1995). *Who eats what? Food chains and food webs.* New York: Harper Collins.

Lauer, P. A., Akiba, M., Wilkerson, S. B., Apthorp, H. S., Snow, D., & Martin-Glenn, M. L. (2006). Out-of-school-time programs: A meta-analysis of effects for at-risk students. *Review of Educational Research, 76*(2), 275–313.

Law, C., & Kaufhold, J. (2009). An analysis of the use of critical thinking skills in reading and language arts instruction. *Reading Improvement, 46*(1), 29–34.

Lawless, K. A., Brown, S. W., Mills, R., & Mayall, H. J. (2003). Knowledge, interest, recall and navigation: A look at hypertext processing. *Journal of Literacy Research, 35*(3), 911–934.

Lawrence, M. (2007). A cultural classroom library. *Science and Children, 45*(3), 34–36.

Lawrence, S. (2001). *Online or invisible?* Retrieved February 26, 2009, from http://citeseer.ist.psu.edu/online-nature01.

Lawrence, S., Robinowitz, R., & Perna, H. (2009). Reading instruction in secondary English language arts classrooms. *Literacy Research and Instruction, 48*(1), 39–64.

Lazar, A. (2006). Literacy teachers making a difference in urban schools: A context-specific look at effective literacy teaching. *Journal of Reading Education, 32,* 13–21.

Lederer, J. M. (2000). Reciprocal teaching of social studies in inclusive elementary classrooms. *Journal of Learning Disabilities, 33*(1), 91.

Lederer, R. (1987). *Anguished English.* New York: Dell/Bantam Doubleday.

Ledlow, S. (1992). Is cultural discontinuity an adequate explanation for dropping out? *Journal of American Indian Education, 31*(3). Retrieved August 12, 2010, from http://jaie.asu.edu/v31/V31S3cul.htm.

Lee, A. (2010, February). A way of understanding the world of science informational books. *The Reading Teacher, 63*(5), 424–428.

Lee, C. D., & Spratley, A. (2010). *Reading in the disciplines: The challenge of adolescent literacy.* New York: Carnegie Corporation of New York.

Lee, P., & Allen, G. (1981). *Training junior high LD students to use a test-taking strategy* (Eric Document No. ED 217 649). Washington, DC: Bureau of Education for the Handicapped.

Lehrer, J. (2010). The human brain: How we decide (YouTube video). Retrieved September 1, 2010, from: http://www.youtube.com/watch?v=N2iJF2I94pg.

Lehrer, J. (2009). *How we decide.* New York: Houghton-Mifflin.

Leki, I. (2001). "A narrow thinking system": Nonnative English-speaking students in group projects across the curriculum. *TESOL Quarterly, 35*(1), 39–67.

Lemke, J. L. (2004). The literacies of science. In E. W. Saul (Ed.), *Crossing borders in literacy and science instruction* (pp. 33–47). Newark, DE: International Reading Association and Arlington, VA: NSTA Press.

Lemkuhl, M. (2002, May). Pen-pal letters: The cross-curricular experience. *The Reading Teacher, 55*(8), 720–722. Retrieved December 12, 2004, from http://www.readingonline.org/electronic/elec_index.asp? HREF=/electronic/RWT/lemkuhl/index.html.

Lenhart, A., Madden, M., & Hitlin, P. (2005). Teens and technology: Youth are leading the transition to a fully wired and mobile nation. *Pew Internet & American Life Project.* Washington, DC: American Institutes of Research.

Lenhart, A., Madden, M., Macgill, A., & Smith, A. (2007). Teens and social media. *Pew Internet & American Life Project.* Washington, DC: American Institutes of Research.

Lennon, C., & Burdick, H. (2004). *The lexile framework as an approach for reading measurement and success.* Durham, NC: MetaMetrics, Inc.

Leno, L. C., & Dougherty, L. A. (2007). Using direct instruction to teach content vocabulary. *Science Scope, 31*(1), 63–66.

Lent, R. (2006). In the company of critical thinkers. *Educational Leadership, 64*(2), 68–72.

Lenz, B. K., Ellis, E. S., & Scanlon, D. (1996). *Teaching learning strategies to adolescents and adults with learning disabilities.* Austin, TX: Pro-Ed.

Leonard, J., & McElroy, K. (2000). What one middle school teacher learned about cooperative learning. *Journal of Research in Childhood Education, 14*(2), 239.

Lesaux, N. K., Kieffer, M. J., Faller, S. E., & Kelley, J. G. (2010). The effectiveness and ease of implementation of an academic vocabulary intervention for linguistically diverse students in urban middle schools. *Reading Research Quarterly, 45*(2), 196–228.

Lesesne, T. S. (2001). Timing: The right book at the right moment. *Voices from the Middle, 9,* 68–72.

Lessard, A., Fortin, L., Marcotte, D., Potvin, P., & Royer, E. (2009). Why did they not drop out? Narratives from resilient students. *The Prevention Researcher, 16*(3), 21–24.

Lester, J. H., & Cheek, E. H., Jr. (1998). The "real" experts address the textbook issues. *Journal of Adolescent & Adult Literacy, 41*(4), 282–291.

Leu, D. J., Jr. (1997). Caity's question: Literacy as deixis on the Internet. *The Reading Teacher, 51*(1), 62–67.

Leu, D. J., Jr. (2000). Literacy and technology: Deictic consequences for literacy education in an information age. In M. L. Kamil, P. B. Mosenthal, P. D. Pearson, & R. Barr (Eds.), *Handbook of reading research* (Vol. III, pp. 743–770). Mahwah, NJ: Erlbaum.

Leu, D.J., Jr. (2002). The new literacies: Research on reading instruction with the internet. In A.E. Farstrup, & S.J. Samuels (Eds.), *What research has to say about reading instruction* (3rd ed., pp. 310–336). Newark, DE: International Reading Association.

Leu, D. J., Castek, J., Henry, L. A., Coiro, J., & McMullan, M. (2004). The lessons that children teach us: Integrating children's reading and the new literacies of the Internet. *The Reading Teacher, 57*(5), 496–504.

Leu, D. J., Jr., Kinzer, C. K., Coiro. J., Cammack, D. (2004). Toward a theory of new literacies emerging from the Internet and other information and communication technologies. In R. B. Ruddell & N. Unrau (Eds.). *Theoretical models and processes of reading* (5th ed., pp. 1569–1611). Newark, DE: International Reading Association. Retrieved October 15, 2005, from http://www.readingonline.org/newliteracies/lit_index.asp?HREF=/newliteracies/leu.

Leu, D. J., Jr., Karchmer, R., & Leu, D. D. (1999). Exploring literacy on the Internet. *The Reading Teacher, 52*(6), 636–642.

Leu, D. J., Jr., Kinzer, C. K., Coiro, J., & Cammack, D. W. (2004). Toward a theory of new literacies emerging from the Internet and other communication technologies. In R. Ruddell & N. Unrau (Eds.), *Theoretical models and processes of reading* (5th ed., pp. 1570–1613). Newark: DE: International Reading Association.

Leu, D. J., Jr., & Leu, D. D. (1999). *Teaching with the Internet: Lesson from the classroom.* Norwood, MA: Christopher Gordon.

Levin, J. R. (1993). Mnemonic strategies and classroom learning: A 20-year report card. *Elementary School Journal, 94,* 235–244.

Levin, J. R., Levin, M. E., Glassman, L. D., & Nordwall, M. B. (1992). Mnemonic vocabulary instruction: Additional effectiveness evidence. *Contemporary Educational Psychology, 17,* 156–174.

Levine, E. (1995). *I hate English!* New York: Scholastic.

Lewis, C., & Fabos, B. (2005). Instant messaging, literacies, and social identities. *RRQ, 40*(4), 470–501.

Liaw, S. (2004). Consideration for developing constructivist Web-based learning. *International Journal of Instructional Media, 3*(3), 309–322.

Library Journal. (2008, February). *A shot heard 'round the academic world: Harvard FAS mandates open access.* Retrieved February 27, 2009, from http://www.libraryjournal.com/info/CA6532658.html#news1.

Lin, L. M., Zabrucky, K., & Moore, D. (1997). The relations among interest, self-assessment comprehension, and comprehension performance in young adults. *Reading Research and Instruction, 36*(2), 127–139.

Lindfors, J. W. (1980). *Children's language and learning.* Englewood Cliffs, NJ: Prentice-Hall.

Linn, R., Baker, E., & Dunbar, S. (1991). Complex, performance-based assessment: Expectations and validation criteria. *Educational Researcher, 20*(8), 15–21.

Linn, R. L., & Gronlund, N. E. (2000). *Measurement and assessment in teaching* (8th ed.). Upper Saddle River, NJ: Merrill.

Lipsitz, J. (1995). Why we should care about caring. *Ph Delta Kappan, 76,* 665–666.

Lipson, M. Y., & Wixson, K. K. (2003). *Assessment and instruction of reading and writing disability* (3rd ed.). New York: Longman.

Liston, D., Whitcomb, J., & Borko, H. (2007). NCLB and scientifically based research. *The Journal of Teacher Education, 58*(2), 99–107.

Liu, P., Chen, C., & Chang, Y. (2010). Effects of a computer-assisted concept mapping learning strategy on EFL college students' English reading comprehension. *Computers and Education, 54*(2), 436–445.

Lizama, J. A. (2010). Strong education in Vietnam key to success of graduating Tucker High senior. *Richmond Times-Dispatch.* Retrieved from http://www2.timesdispatch.com/rtd/news/local/education/article/GRAD14_20100613-222007/351000.

Loschert, K. (2003). High-tech teaching. *Tomorrow's Teachers, 9,* 2–5.

Lotan, R. (2003). Group-worthy tasks. *Educational Leadership, 60,* 6.

Lorenzo, G., & Dziuban, C. (2006). Ensuring the Net generation is net savvy. *EDUcause Learning Initiative.* Retrieved from http://www.educause.edu/LibraryDetailPage/666?ID=ELI3006.

Lovelace, S., & Wheeler, T. R. (2006). Cultural discontinuity between home and school language socialization patterns: implications for teachers. *Education, 127*(2), 303–309.

Lowery, L. F. (1998). *The biological basis for thinking and learning* [monograph]. Berkeley, CA: Lawrence Hall of Science.

Lowry, L. (1989). *Number the stars.* Boston: Houghton Mifflin.

Lu, M. (2008, December). Effectiveness of vocabulary learning via mobile phone. *Journal of Computer Assisted Learning, 24*(6), 515–525.

Lu, M., Webb, J. M., Krus, D. J., & Fox, L. S. (1999). Using order analytic instructional hierarchies of mnemonics to facilitate learning Chinese and Japanese Kanji characters. *The Journal of Experimental Education, 67*(4), 293.

Luke, A. (2000). New literacies in teacher education. *Journal of Adolescent and Adult Literacy, 43*(5), 424–435.

Lund, J. (1997). Authentic assessment: Its development and applications. *JOPERD—The Journal of Physical Education, Recreation, and Dance, 68*(7), 25.

Lynch-Brown, C., & Tomlinson, C. M. (1993). *Essentials of children's literature.* Boston: Allyn & Bacon.

Macan, H. T., Shahani, C., Dipboye, R. L., & Phillips, A. P. (1990). College students' time management: Correlations with academic performance and stress. *Journal of Educational Psychology, 82,* 760–768.

Maatta, D. Dobb, F., & Ostlund, K. (2006). Strategies for teaching science to English learners. In A. K. Fathman & D. T. Crowther (Eds.), *Science for English language learners: K-12 classroom strategies* (pp. 37–59). Arlington, VA: National Science Teachers Association Press.

Ma'ayan, H. D. (2010). Erika's stories: Literacy solutions for a failing middle school student. *Journal of Adolescent and Adult Literacy, 53*(8), 646–654.

MacDonald, J. (1986). Self-generated questions and reading recall: Does training help? *Contemporary Educational Psychology, 11,* 290–304.

Macdonald, J., Heap, N., & Mason, R. (2001). "Have I learnt it?" Evaluating skills for resource-based study using electronic resources. *British Journal of Educational Technology, 32*(4), 419–433.

Madrid, L. D., Canas, M., & Ortega-Medina, M. (2007). Effects of team competition versus team cooperation in classwide peer tutoring. *Journal of Educational Research, 100*(3), 155–160.

Mahler, W. R. (1995). Practice what you preach. *The Reading Teacher, 48,* 414–415.

Manning, S., Stanford, B., & Reeves, S. (2010). Valuing the advanced learner: Differentiating up. *The Clearing House, 83,* 145–149.

Manyak, P. C., & Bauer, E. B. (2009). English vocabulary instruction for English learners. *The Reading Teacher, 63*(2), 174–176.

Manz, S. L. (2002). A strategy for previewing textbooks: Teaching readers to become THIEVES. *The Reading Teacher, 55,* 434–435.

Manzo, A. V. (1969). The ReQuest procedure. *Journal of Reading, 11,* 123–126.

Manzo, A. V. (1975). The guided reading procedure. *Journal of Reading, 18,* 287–291.

Manzo, A.V. (1983). Subjective approach to vocabulary acquisition (or, ". . . I think my brother is arboreal!"). *Reading Psychology, 3*(2), 155–160.

Manzo, A. V., Manzo, U. C., & Thomas, M. M. (2006). Rationale for systematic vocabulary development: Antidote for state mandates. *Journal of Adolescent & Adult Literacy, 49*(7), 610–619.

Manzo, K. (2001, December 12). Schools stress writing for the test. *Education Week on the Web.* Retrieved March 31, 2007, from http://www.edweek.org/ew/newstorycfm?slug=15write.h21.

Manzo, U. C., & Manzo, A. V. (2008). Teaching vocabulary-learning strategies: Word consciousness, word connection, and word prediction. In A. E. Farstrup & S. J. Samuels, (Eds.), *What research has to say about vocabulary instruction* (pp. 80–105). Newark, DE: International Reading Association.

Marashio, P. (1995). Designing questions to help students peel back the layers of a text. *Interdisciplinary Humanities, 12*(1), 27–31.

Marcell, B., DeCleene, J., & Juettner, M. (2010, May). Caution! Hard hat area! Comprehension under construction: Cementing a foundation of comprehension strategy usage that carries over to independent practice. The Reading Teacher, *63*(8), 687–691.

Maria, K., & Junge, K. (1993). *A comparison of fifth graders' comprehension and retention of scientific information using a science textbook and an informal storybook.* Paper presented at the annual meeting of the National Reading Conference, Charleston, SC.

Maria, K., & MacGinitie, W. (1987). Learning from texts that refute the readers' prior knowledge. *Reading Research and Instruction, 26,* 222.

Marinek, B.A., & Gambrell, L.B. (2010). Reading motivation: Exploring the elementary gender gap. *Literacy Research and Instruction, 49*(2), 129–141.

Marks, L. I., (1998). Deconstructing locus of control: Implications for practitioners. *Journal of Counseling and Development, 76,* 251–260.

Maroney, S. A. (1990). Step by step. *Instructor, 110*(2), 101–102.

Marshall, J., & Klein, A. (2009). Lessons in social action: Equipping and inspiring students to improve their world. *Social Studies, 100*(5), 218–221.

Martin, A. (2002). Motivation and academic resilience: Developing a model for student enhancement. *Australian Journal of Education, 46*(1), 34–49.

Martin, N., D'Arcy, P., Newton, B., & Parker, R. (1976). *Writing and learning across the curriculum.* Montclair, NJ: Boynton/Cook.

Martin, S. H., & Martin, M. A. (2001). Using literature response activities to build strategic reading for students with reading difficulties. *Reading Improvement, 38*(2), 85–94.

Massey, D. D., & Heafner, T. L. (2004). Promoting reading comprehension in social studies. *Journal of Adolescent & Adult Literacy, 48*(1), 26–40.

Mastropieri, M. A., Scruggs, T. E., Mantzicopoulos, P. Y., Sturgeon, A., Goodwin, L., & Chung, S. (1998). "A place where living things affect and depend upon each other": Qualitative and quantitative outcomes associated with inclusive science teaching. *Science Education, 82,* 163–179.

Mastropieri, M. A., & Scruggs, T. E. (2010). *The inclusive classroom: Strategies for effective differentiated instruction* (4th ed.). Upper Saddle River, NJ: Merrill/Pearson Education.

Maxwell, R. (1996). *Writing across the curriculum in the middle and high schools.* Boston: Allyn & Bacon.

McBride, J. P. (1994). Study habits of Isaac Newton. *Education, 114*(3), 461–464.

McCombs, B. L. (1986). The role of the self-system in self-regulated learning. *Contemporary Educational Psychology, 11,* 314–332.

McCrindle, A. R., & Christensen, C. A. (1995). The impact of learning journals on metacognitive and cognitive processes and learning performance. *Learning and Instruction, 5,* 167–185.

McDermott, M. (2010). More than writing-to-learn: Using multimodal writing tasks in science classrooms. *The Science Teacher, 77*(1), 32–36. Retrieved from http://web.ebscohost.com.proxy.library.vcu.edu/ehost/pdfviewer/pdfviewer?vid=3&hid=15&sid=076d9357-e196-4523-a7fa-3fa28a910405%40sessionmgr13.

McDonald, S., & Stevenson, R. J. (1998). Effects of text structure and prior knowledge of the learner on navigation in hypertext. *Human Factors, 40*(1), 18–28.

McGinley, W.J., & Denner, P.R. (1987). Story impressions: A prereading/writing activity. *Journal of Reading, 31*(3), 248–253.

McGivern, J. E., & Levin, J. R. (1983). The keyword method and children's vocabulary learning: An interaction with vocabulary knowledge. *Contemporary Educational Psychology, 8*(1), 46–54.

McInnes, A., Humphries, T., Hogg-Johnson, S., & Tannock, R. (2003). Listening comprehension and working memory are impaired in attention-deficit hyperactivity disorder irrespective of language impairment. *Journal of Abnormal Child Psychology, 31*(4), 427–444.

McIntyre, S. H., & Munson, J. M. (2008). Exploring cramming: Student behaviors, beliefs, and learning retention in the Principles of Marketing course. Journal of Marketing Education. Retrieved from http://jmd.sagepub.com/content/30/3/226.

McKeachie, W. J. (2002). *McKeachie's teaching tips: Strategies, research, and theory for college and university teachers* (11th ed.). Boston: Houghton Mifflin.

McKenna, M. C., & Kear, D. J. (1990). Measuring attitude toward reading: A new tool for teachers. *The Reading Teacher, 43,* 626–639.

McKenna, M. C., Labbo, L. D., Reinking, D., & Zucker, T. A. (2007). Effective uses of technology in literacy instruction. In L. B. Gambrell, L. M. Morrow, & M. Pressley (Eds.), *Best Practices in Literacy Instruction* (3rd ed., pp. 344–372). New York: The Guilford Press.

McKeown, M. G., & Beck, I. L.(1988). Learning vocabulary: Different ways for different goals. *Remedial and Special Education, 9*(1), 42–52.

McKeown, M. G., & Beck, I. L. (2003). Taking advantage of read-alouds to help children make sense of decontextualized language. In A. van Kleeck, S. A. Stahl, & E. B. Bauer (Eds.), *On reading books to children* (pp. 159–176). Mahwah, NJ: Erlbaum.

McKeown, M. G., & Beck, I. L. (2004). Direct and rich vocabulary instruction. In J. F. Baumann & E. J. Kame'enui (Eds.), *Vocabulary instruction: Research to practice* (pp. 13–27). New York: Guilford.

McKeown, M. G., Bede, I. L., & Worthy, J. (1992). *Engaging students with text.* Paper presented at the annual meeting of the National Reading Association Conference, San Antonio, TX.

McLaughlin, H. (1969). SMOG grading—a new readability formula. *Journal of Reading, 12,* 639–646.

McLaughlin, M., & DeVoogd, G. (2004). Critical literacy as comprehension: Expanding reader response. *Journal of Adolescent & Adult Literacy, 48,* 52–62.

McLuhan, M. (1962). *The Gutenberg galaxy: The making of typographic man.* Toronto: University of Toronto Press.

McLuhan, M. (1995). *Understanding media: The extensions of man.* New York: Routledge.

McMaster, K. N., & Fuchs, D. (2002). Effects of cooperative learning on the academic achievement of students with learning disabilities: An update of Tateyama-Sbuezej's review. *Learning Disabilities Research and Practice, 17,* 107–117.

McMaster, K. N., & Fuchs, D. (2005, Spring). Cooperative learning for students with disabilities. *Current Practice Alerts, 11.* Retrieved from http://www.teachingld.org/pdf/alert11.pdf.

McMillan, J. H., & Reed, D. F. (1994). Resilient at-risk students: Students' views about why they succeed. *Journal of At-Risk Issues, 1,* 27–33.

McMurry, F. M. (1909). *How to study, and teaching how to study.* Boston: Houghton Mifflin.

McQuillan, J. (1998). *The literacy crisis: False claims, real solutions.* Portsmouth, NH: Heinemann.

McTighe, J., & Lyman, F. T. (1988). Cueing thinking in the classroom: The promise of theory embedded tools. *Educational Leadership, 45*(7), 18–24.

McWilliams, L., & Rakes, T. (1979). *The content inventories.* Dubuque, IA: Kendall/Hunt.

Mealey, D., & Konopak, B. (1990). Content area vocabulary instruction: Is preteaching worth the effort? *Reading: Exploration and Discovery, 13*(1), 39–42.

Medo, M. A., & Ryder, R. J. (1993). The effects of vocabulary instruction on readers' ability to make causal connections. *Reading Research and Instruction, 33*(2), 119–134.

Meller, W., Richardson, D., & Hatch, J. (2009). Using read-alouds with critical literacy literature in K-3 classrooms. *Young Children, 64*(6), 76–78.

Meloth, M. S., & Deering, P. D. (1992). Effects of two cooperative conditions on peer-group discussions, reading comprehension, and metacognition. *Contemporary Educational Psychology, 17,* 175–193.

Memory, D. M. (1990). Teaching technical vocabulary: Before, during, or after reading assignment? *Journal of Reading Behavior, 22,* 39–53.

Meneghetti, C., DeBern, R., & Cornold, C. (2007). Strategic knowledge and consistency in students with good and poor study skills. *European Journal of Cognitive Psychology, 19*(4), 628–649.

Menke, D. J., & Pressley, M. (1994). Elaborative interrogation: Using "why" questions to enhance the learning from text. *Journal of Reading, 37*(8), 642–645.

Merkley, D. J., Schmidt, D. A., & Allen, G. (2001). Addressing the English language arts technology standard in a secondary reading methodology course. *Journal of Adolescent & Adult Literacy, 45*(3), 220–231.

Merriam-Webster's Online Dictionary. (n.d.). *Study.* Retrieved February 17, 2007, from http://www.m-w.com/dictionary/study.

Mesmer, H. A. E. (2010). Textual scaffolds for developing fluency in beginning readers: Accuracy and reading rate in qualitatively leveled and decodable text. *Literacy Research and Instruction, 49*(1), 20–39.

Mesmer, H. A. E. (2005). Text accessibility and the struggling reader. *Reading and Writing Quarterly, 21,* 1–5.

Mesmer, H. A. E., & Hutchins, E. J. (2002). Using QARs with charts and graphs. *The Reading Teacher, 56,* 21–27.

Metcalfe, S. (2005, January 1). Preparing at-risk alternative school students for high-stake testing success. Addressing the question: "What happens to student learning when selected organizational and study skills strategies are taught to students with behavioral and clinical needs in an alternative high school setting in preparation for standardized high-stakes testing (MCAS)?" *Boston College Dissertations and Theses.* Paper AA13173673. Retrieved from http://escholarship.bc.edu/dissertations/AAI3173673.

Metors, S. E., & Woosley, K. (2006). Visual literacy: An institutional imperative. *EDUCAUSE Review, 41*(3), 80. Retrieved March 13, 2006, from http://www.educause.edu/LibraryDetailPage/666?ID=ERM0638.

Metzger, M. (1989). *Voices from the Civil War.* New York: Crowell.

Mevarech, Z. R. (1999). Effects of metacognitive training embedded in cooperative settings on mathematical problem solving. *Journal of Educational Research, 92*(4), 195.

Meyer, A., & Rose, D. H., (1998). *Learning to read in the computer age.* Cambridge, MA: Brookline Books.

Meyer, B. J. F. (2003). Text coherence and readability. *Topics in Language Disorders, 23,* 204–224.

Meyer, B. J. F., Brandt, D. M., & Bluth, G. J. (1980). Use of top-level structure in text: Key for reading comprehension of ninth grade students. *Reading Research Quarterly, 16,* 72–103.

Meyer, K. (2010). A collaborative approach to reading workshop in the middle years. *Reading Teacher, 63*(6), 501–507.

Meyer, K. E. (2010). A critical literacy perspective for teaching and learning social studies. *Reading Teacher, 63*(6), 486–494.

Mikulecky, L., Shanklin, N., & Caverly, D. (1979). Mikulecky behavioral reading attitude measure. In *Adult reading habits, attitudes, and motivations: A cross-sectional study.* Bloomington, IN: Indiana University, School of Education.

Miller, L., Straits, W., Kucan, L., Trathen, W., & Dass, M. (2007). Using literature circle roles for enhanced science vocabulary understanding. *Journal of Science Teacher Education, 18,* 29–43.

Milligan, J. H. (2007). The efficacy of a strengths-based study skills and strategies program for students on academic probation. Dissertation. Retrieved July 7, 2010, from http://gateway.proquest.com/openurl%3furl_ver=Z39.88-2004%26res_dat=xri:pqdiss%26rft_val_fmt=info:ofi/fmt:kev:mtx:dissertation%26rft_dat=xri:pqdiss:3269708.

Miyake, N., & Norman, D. (1979). To ask a question, one must know enough to know what is not known. *Journal of Verbal Learning and Verbal Behavior, 18,* 357–364.

Moats, L. C. (2001). When older students can't read. *Educational Leadership, 58*(6), 36–40.

Mohr, K. A. J. (2004). English as an accelerated language: A call to action for reading teachers. *The Reading Teacher, 58*(1), 18–26.

Mohr, K. A. J., & Mohr, E. S. (2007). Extending English language learners' classroom interactions using the response protocol. *The Reading Teacher, 60,* 440–450.

Moje, E. B. (2000). What will classrooms and schools look like in the new millennium? *Reading Research Quarterly, 35,* 128–134.

Moje, E. B. (2002). Reframing adolescent literacy research for new times: Studying youth as a resource. *Reading Research and Instruction, 41*(3), 211–228.

Moje, E. B. (2008). Foregrounding the disciplines in secondary literacy teaching and learning: A call for change. *Journal of Adolescent and Adult Literacy, 52*(2), 96–107.

Moje, E. B., Ciechanowski, K. M., Kramer, K., Ellis, L., Carrillo, R., & Collazo, T. (2004). Working toward the third space in content area literacy: An examination of everyday funds of knowledge and discourse. *Reading Research Quarterly, 39*, 38–70.

Mokhtari, K., & Reichard, C. A. (2002). Assessing students' metacognitive awareness of reading strategies. *Journal of Educational Psychology, 94*(2), 249–259.

Molden, K. (2007). Critical literacy, the right answer for the reading classroom: Strategies to move beyond comprehension for reading improvement. *Reading Improvement, 44*(1), 50–56.

Montague, M., & Applegate, B. (2000). Middle school students' perceptions, persistence, and performance in mathematical problem solving. *Learning Disabilities Quarterly, 23*(3), 215–228.

Montelongo, J., Herter, R. J., Ansaldo, R., & Hatter, N. (2010). A lesson cycle for teaching expository reading and writing. *Journal of Adolescent and Adult Literacy, 53*(8), 656–666.

Moore, D., & Arthur, S. V. (1981). Possible sentences. In E. K. Dishner, T. W. Bean, & J. E. Readance (Eds.), *Reading in the content areas: Improving classroom instruction.* Dubuque, IA: Kendall/Hunt.

Moore, D., & Murphy, A. (1987). Selection of materials. In D. Alvermann, D. Moore, & M. Conley (Eds.), *Research within reach: Secondary school reading* (pp. 94–108). Newark, DE: International Reading Association.

Moore, D. W., Readance, J. E., & Rickelman, R. J. (1983). An historical exploration of content area reading instruction. *Reading Research Quarterly, XVIII*, 419–438.

Moore, J. C., & Surber, J. R. (1992). Effects of context and keyword methods on second language vocabulary acquisition. *Contemporary Educational Psychology, 17*, 286–292.

Mora, J. K. (2009). From the ballot box to the classroom. *Educational Leadership, 66*(7), 14–19.

Morgan, B., & Smith, R. D. (2008). A wiki for classroom writing. *The Reading Teacher, 62*(1), 80–82.

Morgan, R., & Culver, V. (1978). Locus of control and reading achievement: Applications for the classroom. *Journal of Reading, 21*, 403–408.

Morgan, R., Otto, A., & Thompson, G. (1976). A study of the readability and comprehension of selected eighth grade social studies textbooks. *Perceptual and Motor Skills, 43*, 594.

Morgan, R. F., Meeks, J. W., Schollaert, A., & Paul, J. (1986). *Critical reading/thinking skills for the college student.* Dubuque, IA: Kendall/Hunt.

Morgan, W., & Beaumont, G. (2003). A dialogic approach to argumentation: Using a chat room to develop early adolescent students' argumentative writing. *Journal of Adolescent & Adult Literacy, 47*(2), 146–157.

Morrison, J. L. (1999). The role of technology in education today and tomorrow: An interview with Kenneth Green. *On The Horizon, 7*(1), 1–4.

Morrison, T. G., Jacobs, J. S., & Swinyard, W. R. (1999). Do teachers who read personally use recommended literacy practices in their classrooms? *Reading Research and Instruction, 38*(2), 81–100.

Morrison, V., & Wlodarczyk, L. (2009). Revisiting read aloud: Instructional strategies that encourage students' engagement with texts. *Reading Teacher, 63*(2), 110–118.

Mosenthal, P. B., & Kirsch, I. S. (1998). A new measure for assessing document complexity: The PMOSE/IKIRSCH document readability formula. *Journal of Adolescent & Adult Literacy, 41*(8), 638–657.

Moss, B., & Hendershot, J. (2002). Exploring sixth graders' selection of nonfiction trade books. *The Reading Teacher, 56*, 6–17.

Moss, J. (1990). *Focus units in literature: A handbook for elementary school teachers* (2nd ed.). Urbana, IL: National Council of Teachers of English.

Muller-Kalthoff, T., & Moller, J. (2003). The effects of graphical overviews, prior knowledge, and self-concept on hypertext disorientation and learning achievement. *Journal of Educational Multimedia and Hypermedia, 12*(2), 117–135.

Murray, D. (1982). *Learning by teaching.* Montclair, NJ: Boynton/Cook.

Murray, J. (2002). Creating placement tests. *ESL Magazine Online.* Retrieved November 26, 2004, from http://eslmag.com/modules.php?name=News&file= article&sid=30.

Myer, K., & Kelley, M. L. (2007). Improving Homework in adolescents with attention-deficit/hyperactivity disorder: Self vs. Parent monitoring of homework behavior and study skills. *Child and Family Behavior Therapy, 29*(4), 25–42.

Myers, J. W. (1984). *Writing to learn across the curriculum.* Bloomington, IN: Phi Delta Kappa.

Myers, P. M., & Savage, T. (2005). Enhancing student comprehension of social studies material. *The Social Studies, 96*(1), 18–23.

Myers, P. (1998). Passion for poetry. *Journal of Adolescent & Adult Literacy, 41*(4), 262–271.

Nagel, G. K. (2002, November). Building cultural understanding and communication: A model in seven situations. *Reading Online, 6*(4). Retrieved June 3, 2007, from http://www.readingonline.org/newliteracies/lit_index.asp?HREF=nagel/index.html.

Nagy, W., Herman, P., & Anderson, R. C. (1985). Learning words from context. *Reading Research Quarterly, 20,* 233–253.

Nagy, W., & Scott, J. A. (2000). Vocabulary processes. In M. Kamil, P. Mosenthal, P. D. Pearson, & R. Barr (Eds.), *Handbook of reading research* (Vol. III, pp. 269–284). Mahwah, NJ: Erlbaum.

Nagy, W., & Stahl, S. (2000). *Promoting vocabulary development.* Austin: Texas Education Agency.

Nagy, W. E. (1988). *Teaching vocabulary to improve reading comprehension.* Newark, DE: International Reading Association.

Nagy, W. E., Garcia, G. E., Durgnuoglu, A. Y., & Hancin-Bhatt, B. (1993). Spanish-English bilingual students' use of cognates in English reading. *Journal of Reading Behavior, 25*(3), 241–259.

Nash, R. (1997). *NTC's dictionary of Spanish cognates.* Lincolnwood, IL: NTC Publishing.

National Assessment of Educational Statistics. (2010). *Digest of Educational Statistics, 2009.* (NCES 2010-013), Chapter 2. Retrieved September 9, 28-2010, from http://nces.ed.gov/programs/digest/d09/ch_2.asp.

National Board for Professional Teaching Standards Assessment. (2007). Retrieved June 2007, from http://www.nbpts.org/help_and_faqs/assessment.

National Capital Language Resource Center. (2009). *Portfolio assessment in the foreign language classroom.* Retrieved August 15, 2010, from http://www.nclrc.org/portfolio/modules.html.

National Center for Education Statistics. (1996). *Reading literacy in the United States: Findings from the IEA reading literacy study.* Washington, DC: U.S. Department of Education.

National Center for Education Statistics. (1999). *Digest of educational statistics, 1998.* Washington, DC: U.S. Department of Education.

National Center for Educational Statistics. (2003). The NAEP reading achievement levels. *The nation's report card, 2003.* Retrieved from http://nces.ed.gov/nationsreportcard/reading/achieveall.asp#grade12.

National Center for Education Statistics. (2004). Learner outcomes: Academic outcomes: Indicator 10: Writing performance of students in grades 4, 8, and 12. *The condition of education.* Retrieved November 27, 2004, from http://nces.ed.gov/programs/coe/2004/section2/indicator10.asp.

National Center for Educational Statistics. (n.d.). *Programme for international assessment.* Retrieved August 13, 2010, from http://nces.ed.gov/surveys/pisa/pisa2006highlights.asp.

National Center for Fair and Open Testing (n.d.). *K-12 testing.* Retrieved September 12, 2010, from http://www.fairtest.org/k-12.

National Center on Response to Intervention. (2010, April). *Essential components of RTI- A closer look at response to intervention.* Washington, DC: U.S. Department of Education. Retrieved August 15, 2010, from http://www.rti4success.org/images/stories/pdfs/rtiessentialcomponents_051310.pdf.

National Center for Technology Literacy. (2010). *Technological literacy takes shape: Engineering education expands.* Retrieved July 27, 2010, from http://www.mos.org/nctl/docs/MOS_NCTL_Literacy.pdf.

National Clearinghouse for Bilingual Education. (2002). *Rate of LEP growth in the United States.* Retrieved September 9, 2004, from http://www.ncbe.gwu.edu.

National Clearing House for English Language Acquisition. (2010). Retrieved from http://www.ncela.gwu.edu.

National Commission on Excellence in Education. (1983). *A nation at risk: The imperative report to the nation and the secretary of education.* Washington, DC: U.S. Government Printing Office.

National Council of Teachers of Mathematics. (2000). *High-stakes testing.* Reston, VA: Author. Retrieved September 9, 2004, from http://www.nctm.org/position_statements/highstakes.htm.

National Education Association. (2002). *National Education Association 2002 instructional materials survey.* Retrieved June 24, 2007, from http://www.publishers.org/SchoolDiv/research/research_02/NEA2002InstrMatReport.pdf.

National Education Association. (2003). *Status of the American public school teacher 2000–2001.* Washington, DC: Author.

National Institute of Child Health and Human Development. (2000). *Report of the National Reading Panel. Teaching children to read: An evidence-based assessment of the scientific research literature on reading and its implications for reading instruction* (NIH Publication No. 00-4769). Washington, DC: U.S. Government Printing Office.

Neisworth, J. T. & Bagnato, S. J. (2004). The mismeasure of young children: The authentic assessment alternative, *Infants and Young Children, 17*(3), 198–212.

Nessel, D. (1987). Reading comprehension: Asking the right questions. *Phi Delta Kappan, 68,* 442–445.

Nettle, D., & Romaine, S. (2000). *Vanishing voices: The extinction of the world's languages.* New York: Oxford University Press.

Neufeld, P. (2005). Comprehension instruction in content area classes. *The Reading Teacher, 59*(4), 302–313.

Neuman, S. B., & Celano, D. (2001). Access to print in low-income and middle-income communities: An ecological study of four neighborhoods. *Reading Research Quarterly, 36*(1), 8–26.

Neuschwander, C. (1997). Sir Cumference and the First Round Table: A Math Adventure, illustrated by Wayne Geehan, Charlesbridge (Watertown, MA).

Newman, J. M. (2000). Following the yellow brick road. *Phi Delta Kappan, 81,* 774–779.

The New Media Consortium. (2006). *The horizon report—2006 edition.* Retrieved September 7, 2009, from http://www.nmc.org/pdf/2006_Horizon_Report.pdf.

The New Media Consortium. (2007). *The horizon report—2007 edition.* Retrieved September 3, 2009, from http://net.educause.edu/ir/library/pdf/CSD4781.pdf.

The New Media Consortium. (2008). *The horizon report—2008 edition.* Retrieved September 3, 2009, from http://www.nmc.org/pdf/2008-Horizon-Report.pdf.

The New Media Consortium. (2009). *The horizon report—2009 edition.* Retrieved September 3, 2009, from http://wp.nmc.org/horizon2009.

Nichols, W. D., & Rupley, W. H. (2004). Matching instructional design with vocabulary instruction. *Reading Horizons, 45*(1), 55–71.

Nist-Olejnik, S. L., & Holschuh, J. P. (2009). *College success strategies.* New York: Pearson Education.

Noll, E., & Watkins, R. (2003). The impact of homelessness on children's literacy experiences. *The Reading Teacher, 57*(4), 362–371.

North Central Regional Educational Laboratory. (2005). *NCREL quick key 10: Using student engagement to improve adolescent literacy.* Retrieved June 25, 2010, from http://www.ncrel.org/litweb/adolescent/qkey10/qkey10.pdf.

North Central Regional Education Laboratory (n.d.). *21st century skills: Visual literacy.* Washington, DC: Learning Point Associates. Retrieved July 15, 2007, from http://www.ncrel.org/engauge/skills/vislit.htm.

Nugent, J. S., Reardon, R. M., Smith, F. G., Rhodes, J. A., Zander, M. J., & Carter, T., (2008). Exploring faculty learning communities: Building connections among teaching, learning, and technology, *Journal of Teaching and Learning in Higher Education, 20*(1), 51–58.

Nuthall, G. (1999). The way students learn: Acquiring knowledge from an integrated science and social studies unit. *Elementary School Journal, 99*(4), 303.

Oblinger D. G. (2005). Learners, learning and technology. *Educause Review,* Sept/Oct 69–75. Retrieved July 30, 2010, from http://www.educause.edu/educatingthenetgen.

Oblinger, D. G., & Oblinger, J. L. (2005). Is it age or IT: First steps toward understanding the net generation in D. G. Oblinger & J. L. Oblinger (Eds.), Educating the net generation (pp. 2.1–2.20). Retrieved July 27, 2010, from http://net.educause.edu/ir/library/pdf/pub7101b.pdf.

O'Brien, R. (1971). *Mrs. Frisby and the rats of NIMH.* New York: Atheneum.

O'Dell, S. (1987). *The serpent never sleeps.* New York: Ballantine.

O'Donnell, P., Weber, K. P., & McLaughlin, T. F. (2003). Improving correct and error rate and reading comprehension using key words and previewing: A case report with a language minority student. *Education & Treatment of Children, 26*(3), 237–255.

Office of Educational Technology. (2010). *What 21st century learning should look like.* Transforming American education: Learning powered by technology: Draft national education technology plan 2010. U.S. Department of Education Retrieved July 30, 2010, from http://www.ed.gov/technology/netp-2010/what-21st-century-learning-should-look-like.

Ogle, D. (1986). KWL: A teaching model that develops active reading of expository text. *The Reading Teacher, 39,* 564–570.

Ogle, D. (1992). KWL in action: Secondary teachers find applications that work. In E. K. Dishner, T. W. Bean, J. E. Readance, & D. W. Moore (Eds.), *Reading in the content areas: Improving classroom instruction* (3rd ed., pp. 270–281). Dubuque, IA: Kendall/Hunt.

Ogle, D., & Correa-Kovtun, A. (2010). Supporting English-Language learners and struggling readers in content literacy with the "partner reading and content, too" routine. The Reading Teacher, *63*(7), 532–542.

Olson, C. B. (2007). The reading/writing connection: Strategies for teaching learning in the secondary classroom (2nd ed.). Boston: Pearson Education.

Olson, M. R., & Truxaw, M. P. (2009). Preservice science and mathematics teachers and discursive metaknowledge of text. *Journal of Adolescent & Adult Literacy, 52*(5), 422–431.

Onwuegbuzie, A. J., Slate, J. R., & Schwartz, R. A. (2001). Role of study skills in graduate-level educational research courses. *The Journal of Educational Research, 94*(4), 238–248.

Opitz, M. (1992). The cooperative reading activity: An alternative to ability grouping. *The Reading Teacher, 45,* 736–738.

Opitz, M. F., & Rasinski, T. V. (2008). *Good-bye round robin: 25 effective oral reading strategies* (Updated ed.). Portsmouth, NH: Heinemann.

Oster, L. (2001). Using the think-aloud for reading instruction. *The Reading Teacher, 55,* 65–69.

O'Toole, B. (2010, May 5). Denver academy teacher receives top prize from international reading association. *The Denver Post.* Retrieved July 30, 2010, from http://www.denver.yourhub.com/Denver/Stories/News/...Story~786581.aspx.

Ozkan, H. H. (2010). Cooperative learning technique through internet based education: A model proposal. *Education, 30*(3), 499–508.

Ozura, Y., Dempsey, K., & McNamara, D. (2009). Prior knowledge, reading skill, and text cohesion in the comprehension of science texts. *Learning and Instruction, 19*(3), 228–242.

Padak, N. (2006). What's in a word? Teaching vocabulary from the inside out. *The New England Reading Association Journal, 42*(2), 8–11.

Padak, N., Newton, E., Rasinski, T., & Newton, R. M. (2008). Getting to the root of word study: Teaching Latin and Greek word roots in elementary and middle grades. In A. E. Farstrup & S. J. Samuels (Eds.), *What research has to say about vocabulary instruction* (pp. 6–31). Newark, DE: International Reading Association.

Padmala, S., & Pessoa, L.,(2010). Interactions between cognition and motivation during response inhibition. *Neuropsychologia, 48*(2), 558–565.

Paganini, N. (1820). *Paganini's 24 caprices op. 1.* Retrieved August 11, 2010, from http://ebooks.ebookmall.com/title/paganini-24-caprices-for-violin-op1-paganini-vilnitis-ebooks.htm.

Page, B. (1987). From passive receivers to active learners in English. In J. Self (Ed.), *Plain talk about learning and writing across the curriculum* (pp. 37–50). Richmond, VA: Virginia Department of Education.

Palincsar, A. S., & Brown, A. L. (1986). Interactive teaching to promote independent learning from text. *The Reading Teacher, 39,* 771–777.

Pallas, A. M., Natriello, G., & McDill, E. L. (1989). Changing nature of the disadvantaged population: Current dimensions and future trends. *Educational Researcher, 18,* 16–22.

Pally, M. (1998). Film studies drive literacy development for ESL university students. *Journal of Adolescent & Adult Literacy, 41*(8), 620–628.

Palmer, P. J. (1998). *The courage to teach.* San Francisco: Jossey-Bass.

Palmer, R. G., & Stewart, R. A. (2003). Nonfiction trade book use in primary grades. *The Reading Teacher, 57,* 38–48.

Palmer, R. G., & Stewart, R. A. (2005). Models for using nonfiction in the primary grades. *The Reading Teacher, 58,* 426–434.

Palombo, R. (2000). Brain based learning. *Training & Development, 54*(7), 21–35.

Pappas, C. (1991). Fostering full access to literacy by including information books. *Language Arts, 68,* 449–462.

Pappas, C. C. (1993). Is narrative "primary"? Some insights from kindergartners' pretend readings of stories and information books. *Journal of Reading Behavior, 25,* 97–129.

Paquette, K. R. (2009). Integrating the 6+1 writing traits model with cross-age tutoring: An investigation of elementary students' writing development. *Literacy Research and Instruction, 48*(1), 28–38.

Paris, S. G. (1986). Teaching children to guide their reading and learning. In T. E. Raphael & R. Reynolds (Eds.), *Context of literacy* (pp. 115–130). New York: Longman.

Paris, S. G., Lipson, M. Y., & Wixson, K. K. (1983). Becoming a strategic reader. *Contemporary Educational Psychology, 8,* 393–396.

Paris, S. G., & Oka, E. R. (1989). Strategies for comprehending text and coping with reading difficulties. *Learning Disability Quarterly, 12,* 32–42.

Parker, M., & Hurry, J. (2007). Teachers' use of questioning and modeling comprehension skills in primary classrooms. *Educational Review, 59*(3), 299–314.

Patrick, H., Bangel, N. J., Jeon, K., & Townsend, M. A. R. (2005). Reconsidering the issue of cooperative learning with gifted students. *Journal for the Education of the Gifted, 29,* 90–108.

Patrick, H., Ryan, A., & Kaplan, A. (2007). Early adolescents' perceptions of the classroom social environment, motivational beliefs, and engagement. *Journal of Educational Psychology, 99,* 83–98.

Patterson, J. H. (2001, Spring). Raising resilience in classrooms and homes. *Childhood Education, 77*(3), 180.

Pauk, W. (1997). *How to study in college* (6th ed.). Boston: Houghton Mifflin.

Paul, D. G. (2004). The train has left: The No Child Left Behind Act leaves black and Latino literacy learners waiting at the station. *Journal of Adolescent & Adult Literacy, 47*(8), 647–656.

Paulsen, G. (1990). *Canyons.* New York: Delacorte Press.

Pearce, D. (1983). Guidelines for the use and evaluation of writing in content classrooms. *Journal of Reading, 17,* 212–218.

Pearce, D. (1987). Group writing activities: A useful strategy for content teachers. *Middle School Journal, 18,* 24–25.

Pearce, D., & Bader, L. (1984). Writing in content area classrooms. *Reading World, 23,* 234–241.

Pearson, P. D. (1985). Changing the face of reading comprehension. *The Reading Teacher, 38,* 724–738.

Pearson, P. D., & Santa, C. M. (1995). Students as researchers of their own learning. *Journal of Reading, 38,* 462–469.

Pearson, P. D., & Tierney, R. (1983). In search of a model of instructional research in reading. In S. Paris, G. Okon, & H. Stevenson (Eds.), *Learning and motivation in the classroom.* Hillsdale, NJ: Erlbaum.

Pellicano, R. (1987). At-risk: A view of "social advantage." *Educational Leadership, 44,* 47–50.

Peregoy, S., & Boyle, O. (1997; 2009). *Reading, writing, and learning in ESL: A resource book for K–12 teachers.* White Plains, NY: Longman.

Perry, K. H. (2008). "Look, you have to sign": Literacy practices among Sudanese refugee families. *Dissertation Abstracts International Section A: Humanities and Social Sciences, 68*(9-A), 3770.

Peterson, S. E., & Miller, J. A. (2004). Comparing the quality of students' experiences during cooperative learning and large-group instruction. *Journal of Educational Research, 97*(3), 123–134.

Phillips, G. Using open-book tests to strengthen the study skills of community-college biology students. *Journal of Adolescent & Adult Literacy, 49*(7), 574–582.

Piaget, J. (1963). *The origin of intelligence in children.* New York: Norton.

Pierce, D. (2010, February 14). Duncan offers guiding principles for rewriting NCLB. *eSchool News.* Retrieved August 13, 2010, from http://www.eschoolnews.com/2010/02/14/duncan-offers-guiding-principles-for-rewriting-nclb.

Pierce, M. E., & Fontaine, L. M. (2009). Designing vocabulary instruction in mathematics. *The Reading Teacher, 63*(3), 239–243.

Pilonieta, P. (2010). Instruction of research-based comprehension strategies in Basal Reading programs. *Reading Psychology, 31*(2) 150–175.

Pink, D. (2005). *A whole new mind: Moving from the information age to the conceptual age.* New York: Riverhead Publishing.

Pisha, B., & Coyne, P., (2001). Smart from the start: the promise of universal design for learning. *Remedial and Special Education, 22*(4), 197–203.

Pitcher, B., & Fang, Z. (2007). Can we trust text levels? An examination of their readability and quality from a linguistic perspective. *Literacy, 41*(1), 43–51. Retrieved from http://web.ebscohost.com.proxy.library.vcu.edu/ehost/pdfviewer/pdfviewer?vid=2&hid=107&sid=dbe9c2f3-2b44-4e79-8126-4ef15df481e4%40sessionmgr114.

Pitcher, S. M., Albright, L. K., DeLaney, C.J., Walker, N. T., Seunarinesingh, K., Mogge, S., Headley, K. N., Ridgeway, V. G., Peck, S., Hunt, R., & Dunston, P. J. (2007). Assessing adolescents' motivation to read. *Journal of Adolescent and Adult Literacy, 50*(5), 378–396.

Pitcher, S. M., Martinez, G., Dicembre, E. A., Fewster, D., & McCormick, M. K. (2010). The literacy needs of adolescents in their own words. *Journal of Adolescent and Adult Literacy, 53*(8), 636–644.

Pittleman, S. D., Heimlich, J. E., Berglund, R. L., & French, M. P. (1991). *Semantic feature analysis.* Newark, DE: International Reading Association.

Planty, M., Hussar, W., Snyder, T., Kena, G., KewalRamani, A., Kemp, J., Bianco, K., & Dinkes, R. (2009). *The condition of education 2009* (NCES 2009-081). Washington, DC: National Center for Education Statistics, Institute of Education Sciences, U.S. Department of Education. Retrieved June 17, 2010, from http://nces.ed.gov/pubs2009/2009081.pdf.

Pogrow, S. (2006). Restructuring high-poverty elementary schools for success: A description of the hi-perform school design. *Phi Delta Kappan, 88,* 223–229.

Polacco, P. (1998). *Chicken Sunday.* New York: PaperStar.

Prensky, M. (2001)). Digital natives, digital immigrants. *On the Horizon, 9*(5), 1–6. Retrieved January 25, 2007, from http://www.marcprensky.com/writing/Prensky%20-%20Digital%20Natives,%20Digital%20Immigrants%20-%20Part1.pdf.

Prensky, M. (2006, September/October). "Enrage me or engage me": What today's learner's demand. *EDUCAUSE.* Retrieved July 28, 2010, from http://www.educause.edu/ir/library/pdf/erm0553.pdf.

Pressler, M. W. (2006, October 11). The handwriting is on the wall. *The Washington Post,* A 01.

Pressley, M. (2002a). Comprehension strategies instruction: A turn-of-the-century status report. In C. C. Block & M. Pressley (Eds.), *Comprehension instruction: Research-based best practices* (pp. 11–27). New York: Guilford.

Pressley, M. (2002b). *Reading instruction that works: The case for balanced teaching* (2nd ed.). New York: Guilford.

Pressley, M. (2002c, September). Comprehension instruction: What makes sense now, what might make sense soon. *Reading Online, 5*(2). Retrieved July 30, 2004, from http://www.readingonline.org/articles/art_index.asp?HREF=/articles/handbook/pressley/index.htm.

Pressley, M., & Afflerbach, P. (1995). *Verbal reports of reading: The nature of constructively responsive reading*. Hillsdale, NJ: Erlbaum.

Pressley, M., & Schneider, W. (1997). *Introduction to memory development during childhood and adolescence*. Mahwah, NJ: Erlbaum.

Pressley, M., Wharton-McDonald, R., Hampson, J., & Echevarria, M. (1998). The nature of literacy instruction in ten fourth and fifth grade classrooms in up-state New York. *Scientific Studies in Reading, 2,* 159–191.

Proctor, B. E., Prevatt, F. F., Adams, K. S., Reaser, A., & Perscher, Y. (2006). Study skills profiles of normal-achieving and academically struggling college students. *Journal of College Student Development, 47*(1), 37–51.

Project Tomorrow. (2006). Our voices, our future: Student and teacher views on science, technology & education. National Report on NetDay's 2005 SpeakUp Event. Retrieved January 24, 2007, from http://www.netday.org/speakup/pdfs/SpeakUpReport_05.pdf.

Pulido, D. (2004, September). The effect of cultural familiarity on incidental vocabulary acquisition through reading. *The Reading Matrix, 4*(2). Retrieved April 1, 2004, from http://www.readingmatrix.com/articles/pulido/article.pdf.

Purcell-Gates, V., Degener, S. C., Jacobson, E., & Soler, M. (2002). Impact of authentic adult literacy instruction on adult literacy practices. *Reading Research Quarterly, 37,* 70–92.

Purcell-Gates, V., Duke, N. K., & Martineau, J. A. (2007). Learning to read and write genre-specific text: Roles of authentic experience and explicit teaching. *Reading Research Quarterly, 42,* 8–45.

Purdie, N., & Hattie, J. (1999). The relationship between study skills and learning outcomes: A meta-analysis. *Australian Journal of Education, 43*(1), 72.

Purkey, W. W., & Novak, J. M. (1984). *Inviting school success: A self-concept approach to teaching and learning* (2nd ed.). Belmont, CA: Wadsworth.

Purmensky, K. (2006). Weblogs transform service-learning reflection. *Academic Exchange Quarterly, 10*(1), 3–5.

Purves, A. C., & Bech, R. (1972). *Literature and the reader: Research in response to literature, reading interests, and the teaching of literature*. Urbana, IL: National Council of Teachers of English.

Putnam, S. M., & Kingsley, T. (2009). The atoms family: Using podcasts to enhance the development of science vocabulary. *The Reading Teacher, 63*(2), 100–108.

Quirk, M. P., & Schwanenflugel, P. J. (2004). Do supplemental remedial reading programs address the motivational issues of struggling readers? An analysis of five popular programs. *Reading Research and Instruction, 43*(3), 1–19.

Rainie, L., & Madden, M. (2005). Podcasting catches on. Pew Internet and American Life Project. Retrieved March 11, 2007, from http://www.pewinternet.org/PPF/r/194/report_display.asp.

Rakes, G. C., Rakes, T. A., & Smith, L. J. (1995). Using visuals to enhance secondary students' reading comprehension of expository texts. *Journal of Adolescent & Adult Literacy, 39,* 46–54.

Ralph, J., Keller, D., & Crouse, J. (1994). How effective are American schools? *Phi Delta Kappan, 76,* 144–150.

Rance-Roney, J. (2010, February). Jump-starting language and schema for English-language learners: Teacher-composed digital jumpstarts for academic reading. *Journal of Adolescent & Adult Literacy, 53*(5), 386–395.

Raphael, T. (1984). Teaching learners about sources of information for answering comprehension questions. *Journal of Reading, 27,* 303–311.

Raphael, T. E., & Au, K. H. (2005). QAR: Enhancing comprehension and test taking across grades and content areas. *The Reading Teacher, 59*(3), 206–221.

Raphael, T. E., Florio-Ruane, S., & George, M. (2004). Book club plus: Organising your literacy curriculum to bring students to high levels of literacy. *Australian Journal of Language & Literacy, 27*(3), 198–216.

Rasinski, T., & Padak, N. (2009). Write soon! *The Reading Teacher, 62*(7), 618–620.

Ray, K. W., & Cleaveland, L. B. (2004). *About the authors: Writing workshop with our youngest writers*. Portsmouth, NH: Heinemann.

Ray, K. W., & Glover, M. (2008). *Already ready: Nurturing writers in preschool and kindergarten*. Portsmouth, NH: Heinemann.

Read, S. (2005). First and second graders writing informational text. *The Reading Teacher, 59,* 36–44.

Readance, J. E., Bean, T. W., & Baldwin, R. S. (1981).*Content area reading: An integrated approach.* Dubuque, IA: Kendall/Hunt.

Ream, D. (2007, June). Personal e-mail communication.

Reinking, D. (1997). Me and my hypertext: A multiple regression analysis of technology and literacy. *The Reading Teacher, 50*(8), 626–643.

Reinking, D., & Wu, J. H. (1990). Reexamining the research on television and reading. *Reading Research and Instruction, 29,* 30–43.

Reynolds, R. E., Sinatra, G. M., & Jetton, T. L. (1996).Views of knowledge acquisition and representation: A continuum from experience centered to mind centered. *Educational Psychologist, 21,* 93–104.

Rhodes, J. A., & Milby, T. M. (2007). Teacher-created electronic books: Integrating technology to support readers with disabilities. *The Reading Teacher, 61*(3), 255–259.

Rhodes, J. A., & Robnolt, V. J. (2008). Digital literacies in the classroom. In L. Christenbury, R. Bomer, & P. Smagorinsky (Eds.), *Handbook of adolescent literacy research* (pp. 153–169). New York: Guilford Press.

Rhodes, J. A., Robnolt, V. J., & McKelvey, S. (2004). *Alignment of classroom assessments with the Virginia Standards of Learning (SOL).* Richmond, VA: Metropolitan Educational Research Consortium. Retrieved September 10, 2006, from http://64.233.161.104/u/vcu?q=cache:5mz0mbhpjYMJ:www.soe.vcu.edu/merc/Alignmnt%2520Stdy%2520Rhodes%2520%26%2520Robnolt1.doc+Alignment+of+classroom+assessments&hl=en&gl=us&ct=clnk&cd=1&ie=UTF-8.

Rhodes, J. A., Robnolt, V. J., & Richardson, J. S. (2005).Study skills in the electronic age. In P. Linder, M. B. Sampson, J. A. R. Dugan, & B. Brancato (Eds.), *The College Reading Association yearbook* (pp. 221–235). Logan, UT: College Reading Association.

Rhodes, L. K., & Shanklin, N. (1991). *Windows into literacy: Assessing learners K–8.* Portsmouth, NH: Heinemann.

Rhodes, R. (1990, October 14). Don't be a bystander. *Parade,* 4–7.

Rice, G. E. (1992, April). *The need for explanations in graphic organizer research.* Paper presented at the annual meeting of the American Educational Research Association, San Francisco.

Richardson, J. (1991). Developing responsibility in English classes: Three activities. *Journal of the Virginia College Reading Educators, 11,* 8–19.

Richardson, J. (1992a). Generating inquiry-oriented projects from teachers. In A. Frager & J. Miller (Eds.), *Using inquiry in reading teacher education* (pp. 24–29). Kent, OH: Kent State University, College Reading Association.

Richardson, J. (1992b). Taking responsibility for taking tests. In N. Padak & T. Rasinski (Eds.), *Literacy research and practice: Foundations for the year 2000* (pp. 209–215). Kent, OH: Kent State University, College Reading Association.

Richardson, J. S. (1994). Great read-alouds for prospective teachers and secondary students. *Journal of Reading, 38,* 98–103.

Richardson, J. S. (1995a). Three ways to keep a middle school student in the "reading habit." *Affective Reading Education, 14,* 5–7.

Richardson, J. S. (1995b). A read-aloud for cultural diversity. *Journal of Adolescent & Adult Literacy, 39,* 160–162.

Richardson, J. S. (1997). *An English teacher's survival guide.* Toronto, Canada: Pippin.

Richardson, J. S. (2000a). *Read it aloud! Using literature in secondary content classrooms.* Newark, DE: International Reading Association.

Richardson, J. S. (2000b). *Voices of adolescents and strategies for change.* Paper presented at the World Congress on Reading, Aukland, New Zealand.

Richardson, J. S. (2002). *Forum on adolescent literacy:* Reading is drudgery. Paper presented at the World Congress on Reading, Edinburgh, Scotland.

Richardson, J. S. (2004, July/August). Content area literacy lessons go high tech. *Reading Online, 8*(1). Retrieved July 10, 2004, from http://www.reading online.org/articles/art_index.asp?HREF=richardson/index.html online.

Richardson, J. S., Fleener, C. E., & Thistlethwaite, L. (2005). Using threaded discussions to learn about threaded discussions. In J. R. Dugan, P. Linder, M. B. Sampson, B. Brancato, & L. Elish-Piper (Eds.), *Celebrating the power of literacy* (pp. 439–461). Commerce, TX: Texas A&M University, College Reading Association.

Richardson, J. S., & Forget, M. A. (1995). A read-aloud for algebra and geography classrooms. *Journal of Adolescent & Adult Literacy, 39,* 322–326.

Richardson, J. S., & Morgan, R. F. (1991). Crossing bridges by connecting meaning. *Texas Affect in Reading Journal, 34*(1).

Richardson, J. S., & Morgan, R. F. (1997). *Reading to learn in the content areas.* Belmont, CA: Wadsworth ITP.

Richardson, J. S., Rhodes, J. A., & Robnolt, V. J. (2004, October 30). *Electronic study skills: What do the new study skills look like?* Paper presented at the College Reading Association, Delray Beach, FL.

Richardson, J. S., Robnolt, V. J., & Rhodes, J. A. (2007, November 3). A history of study skills: Not hot, but not forgotten. Paper presented at the College Reading Association, Salt Lake City, UT.

Richardson, J. S., Robnolt, V. J., & Rhodes, J. A. (2010). A history of study skills: Not hot, but not forgotten. *Reading Improvement, 46,* 4.

Rifkin, J. (1987). *Time wars.* New York: Henry Holt.

Rifkin, J. (2002). *The hydrogen economy.* New York: Tarcher/Putnam.

Riggs, E. G., & Gholar, C. R. (2009). *Strategies that promote student engagement: Unleashing the desire to learn* (2nd ed.). Thousand Oaks, CA: Corwin Press.

Ritter, S., & Idol-Mastas, L. (1986). Teaching middle school students to use a test-taking strategy. *Journal of Educational Research, 79,* 350–357.

Robelen, E. (2005, February 23). PTA members are split on NCLB's effectiveness. *Education Week, 24,* 2(4), 30.

Robertson, J. I. (1992). *Civil War: America becomes one nation.* New York: Knopf.

Robinson, A. (2003). Cooperative learning and high ability students. In N. Colangelo & G. Davis (Eds.), *Handbook of gifted education* (3rd ed., pp. 282–292). Boston: Allyn & Bacon.

Robinson, D. H. (1998). Graphic organizers as aids to text learning. *Reading Research and Instruction, 37*(2), 85–105.

Robinson, D. H., & Schraw, G. (1994). Computational efficiency through visual argument: Do graphic organizers communicate relations in text too effectively? *Contemporary Educational Psychology, 19,* 399–415.

Robinson, F. P. (1961). *Effective study* (rev. ed.). New York: Harper and Row.

Rogers, D. B. (1984). Assessing study skills. *Journal of Reading, 27,* 346–354.

Rohrbeck, C. A., Ginsburg-Block, M. D., Fantuzzo, J. W., &Miller, T. R. (2003). Peer-assisted learning interventions with elementary school students: A meta-analytic review. *Journal of Educational Psychology, 95,* 240–257.

Romance, N. R., & Vitale, M. R. (1997). *Knowledge representation systems: Basis for the design of instruction for undergraduate course curriculum.* Paper presented at the Eighth National Conference on College Teaching and Learning, Jacksonville, FL.

Romance, N. R., & Vitale, M. R. (1999). Concept mapping as a tool for learning. *College Teaching, 47*(2), 74.

Rose, D. (2001). Universal design for learning: Deriving guiding principles from networks that learn. *Journal of Special Education Technology, 16*(2), 66–67.

Rose, L. C., & Gallup, A. M. (2006). The 38th Annual Phi Delta Kappa/Gallup Poll of the public's attitudes toward the public schools. *Phi Delta Kappan, 88,* 41–53.

Rose, L. C., & Gallup, A. M. (2007). The 39th Annual Phi Delta Kappa/Gallup Poll of the public's attitudes toward the public schools. *Phi Delta Kappan, 89*(1), 33–51.

Rose, M. C. (1999). Don't stop now. *Instructor, 108*(8), 28.

Roser, N. L., & Keehn, S. (2002). Fostering thought, talk, and inquiry: Linking literature and social studies. *The Reading Teacher, 55,* 416–426.

Rotter, J. B. (1966). Generalized expectancies for internal versus external control of reinforcement. *Psychological Monographs: General and Applied, 80*(1), 1–28.

Routeman, R. (2004). *Writing essentials: Raising expectations and results while simplifying teaching.* Portsmouth, NH: Heinemann.

Ruddell, M. R. (2000, July). Dot.com lessons worth learning: Student engagement, literacy, and project-based learning. *Reading Online, 4*(1). Retrieved September 7, 2004, from http://www.readingonline.org/articles/ruddell/.

Rudestam, K. E., & Schoenholtz-Read, J. (2002).Overview: The coming of age of adult online education. In K. E. Rudestam & J. Schoenholtz-Read (Eds.), *Handbook of online learning* (pp. 3–29). Thousand Oaks, CA: Sage.

Rumelhart, D. E. (1980). Schemata: The building blocks of cognition. In R. J. Spiro, B. C. Bruce, & W. F. Brewer (Eds.), *Theoretical issues in reading comprehension* (pp. 33–58). Hillsdale, NJ: Erlbaum.

Rupley, W. H., & Slough, S. (2010). Building prior knowledge and vocabulary in science in the intermediate grades: Creating hooks for learning. *Literacy Research and Instruction, 49*(2), 99–112.

Russell, M. (1999.) Testing on computers: A follow-up study comparing performance on computer and on paper. *Education Policy Analysis Archives, 7,* 20, EJ588928. Washington, DC: ERIC.

Russell, M., & Abrams, L. (2004). Instructional uses of computers for writing: The effect of state testing programs. *Teachers College Record, 196,* 1332–1357.

Russell, S. (1995). Sheltered content instruction for second language learners. *Reading Today, 13,* 30.

Ryder, R. J., & Graves, M. F. (1994). Vocabulary instruction presented prior to reading in two basal readers. *Elementary School Journal, 95*(2), 139–153.

Sachar, L. (2002). *Holes.* New York: Farrar, Straus and Giroux.

Sadoski, M., Paivio, A., & Goetz, E. T. (1991). A critique of schema theory in reading and a dual coding alternative. *Reading Research Quarterly, 26*(4), 463–484.

Saenz, L. M., & Fuchs, L. S. (2002). Examining the reading difficulty of secondary students with learning disabilities: Expository versus narrative text. *Remedial and Special Education, 21,* 31–41.

Sakta, C. G. (1999). SQCR: A strategy for guiding reading and higher level thinking. *Journal of Adolescent & Adult Literacy, 42*(4), 265–269.

Salahu-Din, D., Persky, H., & Miller, J. (2008). *The Nation's Report Card: Writing 2007* (NCES 2008–468). Washington, DC: National Center for Education Statistics, Institute of Education Sciences, U.S. Department of Education. Retrieved from http://nces.ed.gov/nationsreportcard/pdf/main2007/2008468.pdf.

Salcedo, J. B. (2009). Inviting students and teachers to connect. *Language Arts, 86*(6), 440–448.

Salembier, G. B. (1999). SCAN and RUN: A reading comprehension strategy that works. *Journal of Adolescent & Adult Literacy, 42*(5), 386–401.

Salend, S. J. (2011). *Creating inclusive classrooms: Effective and reflective practices.* Boston: Pearson.

Salinger, J. D. (2001, 1951). *The catcher in the rye.* Boston: Little Brown.

Salvia, J., & Ysseldyke, J. (1998). *Assessment* (7th ed.). Boston: Houghton Mifflin.

Sanacore, J. (1998). Promoting the lifelong love of reading. *Journal of Adolescent & Adult Literacy, 41*(5), 392–396.

Sandmann, A., & Gruhler, D. (2007). Reading is thinking: Connecting readers to text through literature circles. *International Journal of Learning, 13*(10), 105–114.

Scarborough, H. A. (Ed.). (2001). *Writing across the curriculum in secondary classrooms: Teaching from a diverse perspective.* Upper Saddle River, NJ: Pearson Education.

Scarborough, H. S. (1998). Early identification of children at risk for reading disabilities: Phonological awareness and some other promising predictors. In B. K. Shapiro, P. J. Accardo, & A. J. Capute (Eds.), *Specific reading disability: A view of the spectrum* (pp. 75–119). Timonium, MD: York Press.

Schaeffer, R. K. (2003). Globalization and technology. *Phi Kappa Phi Forum, 83*(4), 30–33.

Schmar-Dobler, E. (2003). Reading on the Internet: The link between literacy and technology. *Journal of Adolescent and Adult Literacy, 47(1),* 80–85.

Section Editorial Desk, *The New York Times.* (2010, July 31). The fight over education in Washington. *The New York Times,* 18.

Shamir, A., & Korat, O. (2006). How to select CD-ROM storybooks for young children: The teacher's role. *The Reading Teacher, 59*(6), 532–544.

Shermis, S. (1999). Reflective thought, critical thinking. *Eric Digest.* Retrieved November 30, 2003, from http://www.ericfacility.net/databases/ERIC_Digests/ed436007.html.

Schieffelin, B. B., & Cochran-Smith, M. (1984). Learning to read culturally: Literacy before schooling. In H. Goelman, A. Oberg, & F. Smith (Eds.), *Awakening to literacy* (pp. 3–23). Portsmouth, NH: Heinemann.

Schisler, R., Joseph, L., Konrad, M., & Alber-Morgan, S. (2010). Comparison of the effectiveness and efficiency of oral and written retellings and passage review as strategies for comprehending text. *Psychology in the Schools, 47*(2), 135–152.

Schmidt, P. R. (1995). Working and playing with others: Cultural conflict in a kindergarten literacy program. *The Reading Teacher, 48,* 404–412.

Schmidt, P. R. (1998). The ABC's of cultural understanding and communication. *Equity and Excellence in Education, 31*(2), 28–38.

Schmoker, M. (2007). Radically redefining literacy instruction: An immense opportunity. *Phi Delta Kappan, 88,* 488–493.

Schnotz, W., & Kürschner, C. (2008). External and internal representations in the acquisition and use of knowledge: visualization effects on mental model construction. *Instructional Science, 36,* 175.

Schoenbach, R., Greenleaf, C. L., Cziko, C., & Hurwitz, L. (1999). *Reading for understanding.* San Francisco: Jossey-Bass.

Schumann, J. (1978). Second language acquisition: The pidginization hypothesis. In E. Hatch (Ed.), *Second language acquisition.* Rowley, MA: Newbury House.

Schumm, J. (1992). Content area textbooks: How tough are they? *Journal of Reading, 36,* 47.

Schumm, J., Mangrum, C., Gordon, J., & Doucette, M. (1992). The effect of topic knowledge on the predicted test questions of developmental college readers. *Reading Research and Instruction, 31,* 11–23.

Schumm, J., & Vaughn, S. (1991). Making adaptations for mainstreamed students: General education teachers' perspectives. *Remedial and Special Education, 12*(4), 18–27.

Schwartz, D. M. (1999). *If you hopped like a frog.* New York: Scholastic Press.

Schwartz, R. M., & Raphael, T. E. (1985). Concept of definition: A key to improving students' vocabulary. *Journal of Reading, 39,* 198–205.

Scieszka, J. (1995). *The math curse.* New York: Penguin Books.

Scott, J. A., Jamieson-Noel, D., & Asselin, M. (2003). Vocabulary instruction throughout the day in twenty-three Canadian upper-elementary classrooms. *The Elementary School Journal, 103*(3), 269–288.

Scruggs, T., Mastropieri, M. A., Brigham, F. J., & Sullivan, G. S. (1992). Effects of mnemonic reconstructions on the spatial learning of adolescents with learning disabilities. *Learning Disability Quarterly, 15*(3), 154–167.

Scruggs, T., White, K., & Bennion, K. (1986). Teaching test-taking skills to elementary students: A meta-analysis. *Elementary School Journal, 87,* 69–82.

Sebasta, S. (1997). Hot literacy topics of the past. *Journal of Adolescent and Adult Literacy, 40*(6), 500.

Sedita, J. (1999). Helping your child with organization and study skills. Retrieved July 15, 2010, from http://www.ldonline.org/article/5884.

Seidi, B. (2007). Working with communities to explore and personalize culturally relevant pedagogies. *Journal of Teacher Education, 58,* 168–183.

Seitz, H., & Bartholomew, C. (2008). Powerful portfolios for Young Children. *Early Childhood Educational Journal, 36,* 63–68.

Self, J. (1987). The picture of writing to learn. In J. Self (Ed.), *Plain talk about learning and writing across the curriculum* (pp. 9–20). Richmond, VA: Virginia State Department of Education.

Shanahan, T. (1997). Reading–writing relationships, thematic units, inquiry learning . . . in pursuit of effective integrated literacy instruction. *The Reading Teacher, 51*(1), 12–19.

Shanahan, T., & Beck, I. L. (2006). Effective literacy teaching for English-language learners. In D. August & T. Shanahan (Eds.), *Developing literacy in second-language learners: Report of the National Literacy Panel on Language Minority Children and Youth* (pp. 415–488). Mahwah, NJ: Erlbaum.

Shanahan, T., Robinson, B., & Schneider, M. (1995). Avoiding some of the pitfalls of thematic units. *The Reading Teacher, 48,* 718–719.

Shannon, D. (1999). *David goes to school.* New York: The Blue SkyPress, Scholastic Books.

Shapiro, A. M. (1999). The relationship between prior knowledge and interactive overviews during hyper-media-aided learning. *Journal of Educational Computing Research, 20,* 143–167.

Sheets, R. H. (2005). *Diversity pedagogy: Examining the role of culture in the teaching-learning process.* Boston: Pearson Education.

Sherry, L., Cronje, J., Rauscher, W., & Obermeyer, G. (2005). Mediated conversations and the affective domain: Two case studies. *International Journal of E-Learning, 4*(2), 177–191.

Short, K. (1997). *Reading as a way of knowing.* York, ME: Stenhouse.

Sideridis, G. D., Mouzaki, A., Simos, P., & Protopapas, A. (2006). Classification of students with reading comprehension difficulties: The roles of motivation, affect, and psychopathology. *Learning Disabilities Quarterly, 29*(3), 159–181.

Siedow, M. D., & Hasselbring, T. S. (1984). Adaptability of text readability to increase comprehension of reading disability students. *Reading Improvement, 21,* 276–279.

Siegle, D. (2004). The merging of literacy and technology in the twenty-first century: A bonus for gifted children. *Gifted Child Today, 27*(2), 32–36.

Silva, P. U., Meagher, M. E., Valenzuela, M., & Crenshaw, S. W. (1996). E-mail: Real-life classroom experiences with foreign languages. *Learning and Leading with Technology, 23*(5), 10–12.

Simon, K. (1993). Alternative assessment: Can real-world skills be tested? *The Link, 12,* 1–7.

Simon, S. (2003). *The Moon.* NY: Simon & Schuster Children's Publishing.

Simmons, M. (2006). Effective study skills for post-secondary education. *College Quarterly, 9*(2). Retrieved from http://eric.ed.gov/ERICWebPortal/search/detailmini.jsp?_nfpb=true&_&ERICExtSearch_SearchValue_0=EJ835405&ERICExtSearch_SearchType_0=no&accno=EJ835405.

Simpson, M. L. (1987). Alternative formats for evaluating content area vocabulary understanding. *Journal of Reading, 30,* 20–27.

Simpson, M. L., & Nist, S. (2000). An update on strategic learning: It's more than textbook reading strategies. *Journal of Adolescent and Adult Literacy, 43*(6), 528–541.

Silverstein, S. (1996). *Falling up.* New York: HarperCollins.

Sinatra, R. (1986). *Visual literacy connections to thinking, reading, and writing.* Springfield, IL: Charles C. Thomas.

Singer, H., & Bean, T. (1988). Three models for helping teachers to help students learn from text. In S. J. Samuels and P. D. Pearson (Eds.), *Changing school reading programs* (pp. 161–183). Newark, DE: International Reading Association.

Singer, H., & Donlan, D. (1985). *Reading and learning from text.* Hillsdale, NJ: Erlbaum.

Skarakis-Doyle, E., & Dempsey, L. (2008). The detection and monitoring of comprehension errors by preschool children with and without language impairment. *Journal of Speech, Language, and Hearing Research, 51*(5), 1227–1243.

Skinner, C. H., Cooper, L., & Cole, C. L. (1997). The effects of oral presentation rates on reading performance. *Journal of Applied Behavior Analysis, 30,* 331–334.

Slaouti, D. (2002). The World Wide Web for academic purposes: Old study skills for new? *English for Specific Purposes, 21*(2), 105–124.

Slavin, R. E. (1980). Cooperative learning. *Review of Educational Research, 50,* 315–342.

Slavin, R. E. (1990). Cooperative learning and the gifted: Who benefits? *Journal for the Education of the Gifted, 14,* 28–30.

Slavin, R. E. (1991). Synthesis of research on cooperative learning. *Educational Leadership, 48,* 71–82.

Slavin, R. E. (1995). *Cooperative learning* (2nd ed.). Boston: Allyn & Bacon.

Slavin, R. E. (1996). Research on cooperative learning and achievement: What we know, what we need to know. *Contemporary Educational Psychology, 21,* 43–69.

Slavin, R. E. (2000). *Educational psychology: Theory and practice* (6th ed.). Boston: Allyn & Bacon.

Slavin, R. E. (2001). Cooperative learning and the cooperative school. In K. Ryan & J. M. Cooper (Eds.), *Kaleidoscope: Readings in education* (9th ed.). Boston: Houghton Mifflin.

Smith, D. J. (1992). Common ground: The connection between reader response and textbook reading. *Journal of Reading, 35*(8), 630–635.

Smith, F. (1973). *Psycholinguistics and reading.* New York: Holt, Rinehart and Winston.

Smith, F. (1988). *Understanding reading: A psycholinguistic analysis of reading and learning to read* (4th ed.). Hillsdale, NJ: Erlbaum.

Smith, F. (1989). Overselling literacy. *Phi Delta Kappan, 70,* 352–359.

Smith, F. (1994). *Understanding reading: A psycholinguistic analysis of reading and learning to read* (5th ed.). Hillsdale, NJ: Erlbaum.

Smith, J. B. (1983). "Pique": A group dictionary assignment. *Exercise-Exchange, 29*(1), 35.

Smith, M. C. (1990). A longitudinal investigation of reading attitude development from childhood to adulthood. *Journal of Educational Research, 83,* 215–219.

Smith, N. B. (1965). *American reading instruction.* Newark, DE: International Reading Association.

Smith, S., & Bean, R. (1980). The guided writing procedure: Integrating content reading and writing improvement. *Reading World, 19,* 290–294.

Smuin, S. (1978). *Turn-ons.* Belmont, CA: Fearon Pitman.

Snow, C. E., Burns, M. S., & Griffin, P. (Eds.). (1998). *Preventing reading difficulties in young children.* Washington, DC: National Academy Press.

Snow, C. E. (2002). *Reading for understanding. Toward an R&D program in reading comprehension.* Santa Monica, CA: RAND.

Smythe, S., & Neufeld, P. (2010, March). "Podcast time": Negotiating digital literacies and communities of learning in a middle years ELL classroom. *Journal of Adolescent & Adult Literacy, 53*(6), 488–496.

Soares, L., & Wood, K. (2010, March). A critical literacy perspective for teaching and learning social studies. *The Reading Teacher, 63*(6), 486–494.

Sobrol, D. T. (1997). Improving learning skills: A self-help group approach, *Higher Education, 33,* 39–50.

Sommers, C. H. (2000). *The war against boys: How misguided feminism is harming our young men.* New York: Simon and Schuster.

Sousa, D. (2005). *How the brain learns to read.* Thousand Oaks, CA: Corwin Press.

Spache, G. (1953). A new readability formula for primary grade reading materials. *Elementary School Journal, 53,* 410–413.

Spandel, V. (2009). *Creating writers through 6-Trait writing: Assessment and instruction* (5th ed.). New York: Pearson Education.

Spector, P. E., & O'Connell, B. J. (1994). The contribution of personality traits, negative affectivity, locus of control, and type A to the subsequent reports of job stressors and job strains. *Journal of Occupational and Organizational Psychology, 67,* 1–12.

Speigel, D. (1998). Silver bullets, babies, and bath water: Literature response groups in a balanced literacy program. *The Reading Teacher, 52,* 114–124.

Spence, L. K. (2010). Generous reading: Seeing students through their writing. *The Reading Teacher, 63*(8), 634–542.

Sporer, N., Brunstein, J., & Kieschke, U. (2009). Improving students' reading comprehension skills: Effects of strategy instruction and reciprocal teaching. *Learning and Instruction, 19*(3), 272–286.

Stahl, K. (2008). The effects of three instructional methods on the reading comprehension and content acquisition of novice readers. *Journal of Literacy Research, 40*(3), 359–393.

Stahl, S. (1983). Differential word knowledge and reading comprehension. *Journal of Reading Behavior, 15,* 33–50.

Stahl, S. A. (1999). *Vocabulary development.* Cambridge, MA: Brookline.

Stahl, S. A., Hynd, C. R., Britton, B. K., McNish, M. M., & Bosquet, D. (1996). What happens when students read multiple source documents in history? *Reading Research Quarterly, 31,* 430–456.

Stahl, S. A., & Shiel, T. G. (1999). *Teaching meaning vocabulary: Productive approaches for poor readers. Read all about it! Readings to inform the profession.* Sacramento: California State Board of Education.

Stanford, B., & Reeves, S. (2009). Making it happen: Using differentiated instruction, retrofit framework, and universal design for learning. *TEACHING Exceptional Children Plus, 5*(6). Retrieved July 30, 2010, from http://escholarship.bc.edu/education/tecplus/vol5/iss6/art4.

Statistical abstract of the United States—1989. Prepared by the chief of the Bureau of Statistics, Treasury Department. Washington, DC: U.S. Government Printing Office.

Stauffer, R. G. (1969a). *Directing reading maturity as a cognitive process.* New York: Harper and Row.

Stauffer, R. G. (1969b). *Teaching reading as a thinking process.* New York: Harper and Row.

Steen, P. (1991). Book diaries: Connecting free reading with instruction, home and school, and kids with books. *The Reading Teacher, 45,* 330–333.

Stefl-Mabry, J. (1998). Designing a Web-based reading course. *Journal of Adolescent & Adult Education, 41*(7), 556–571.

Steinman, L. (2002). A Touch of . . . class!: Considering the cloze. *The Canadian Modern Language Review, 59*(2), 291–302.

Stephens, K., & Winterbottom, M. (2010). Using a learning log to support students' learning in biology lessons. *Journal of Biological Education, 44*(2), 72–80.

Sternberg, R. J. (1985, November). Teaching critical thinking, Part 1: Are we making critical mistakes? *Phi Delta Kappan,67*(3), 194–198.

Sternberg, R. J. (1991). Are we reading too much into reading comprehension tests? *Journal of Reading, 34,* 540–545.

Sternberg, R. J. (1994). Answering questions and questioning answers. *Phi Delta Kappan, 76,* 136–138.

Sternberg, R. J. (1997). What does it mean to be smart? *Educational Leadership, 5,* 20–24.

Sternberg, R. J., & Baron, J. B. (1985). A statewide approach to measuring critical thinking skills. *Educational Leadership, 43,* 40–43.

Stewart, M. T. (2004). Early literacy instruction in the climate of No Child Left Behind. *The Reading Teacher, 57*(8), 732–743.

Stien, D., & Beed, P. L. (2004). Bridging the gap between fiction and nonfiction in the circle setting: Reading circles can be a valuable tool for engaging students with nonfiction texts. *The Reading Teacher, 57*(6), 510–519.

Stokes, S. (2002). Visual Literacy in teaching and learning: A literature perspective, *Electronic Journal of the Integration o f Technology in Education.* Retrieved May 28, 2010, from http://ejite.isu.edu/Volume1No1/Stokes.html.

Straits, W., & Nichols, S. (2006). Literature circles for science. *Science and Children, 44*(3), 52–55.

Strang, R. (1928). Another attempt to teach how to study. *School and Society, 28,* 461–466.

Strang, R. (1937). The improvement of reading in high school. *Teachers College Record, 39,* 197–206.

Strang, R. (1962). Progress in the teaching of reading in high school and college. *The Reading Teacher, 16,* 170–177.

Strauss, V. (2003). Start early with study skills instruction. *Curriculum Review, 42*(8), 3.

Street, C., & Stang, K. K. (2009). In what ways do teacher education courses change teachers' self confidence as writers? *Teacher Education Quarterly, 36*(3), 75–94. Retrieved from http://www.eric.ed.gov/PDFS/EJ858724.pdf.

Strong, M. (1995). Socratic practice as an organizing principle. *Paideia Next Century, 4,* 5–6.

Strong, M. (2000). Students lack needed study skills. *USA Today, 128*(2659), 15.

Sturtevant, E. G., & Kim, G. S. (2010). Literacy motivation and school/non-school literacies among students enrolled in a middle-school ESOL program. *Literacy research and instruction, 49*(1), 68–85.

Sturtevant, E. G., & Linek, W. M. (2003). The instructional beliefs and decisions of middle and secondary teachers who successfully blend literacy and content. *Reading Research and Instruction, 4*(3), 74–90.

Sullo, B. (2007). *Activating the desire to learn.* Alexandria, VA: Association for Supervision & Curriculum Development.

Summers, J. J. (2006). Effects of collaborative learning in math on sixth graders' individual goal orientation from a socioconstructivist perspective. *The Elementary School Journal, 106*(3), 273–291.

Supon, V. (2004). Implementing strategies to assist test-anxious students. *Journal of Instructional Psychology, 31*(4), 292–296.

Supovitz, J. (2009, May). Can high stakes testing leverage educational improvement? Prospects from the last decade of testing and accountability reform. *Journal of Educational Change*, 10(2/3), 211–227.

Suraya, A., Tarmizi, R. A., Nor, S., Abu, R., Ismail, H., Wan, Z. W. A., Abu Bakar, K., & Hamzah, R. (2007). *International Journal of Learning, 13*(10), 41–55.

Swafford, J. (1995). "I wish all my groups were like this one": Facilitating peer interaction during group work. *Journal of Reading, 38,* 626–631.

Sweeny, S. M. (2007). Reading for technology savvy students: Utilizing choice of multi-modal texts to engage students in content literacy. *The New England Reading Association Journal, 43*(1), 15–22.

Sylwester, R. (1994, October). How emotions affect learning. *Educational Leadership, 52*(2), 60–68.

Sylwester, R. (1995). *A celebration of neurons: An educator's guide to the human brain.* Alexandria, VA: Association for Supervision and Curriculum Development.

Tatum, A. W. (2004). A road map for reading specialists entering schools without exemplary reading programs: Seven quick lessons. *The Reading Teacher, 58*(1), 28–39.

Taylor, B. M., Pressley, M., & Pearson, P. D. (2002). Research supported characteristics of teachers and schools that promote reading achievement. In B. M. Taylor & P. D. Pearson (Eds.), *Teaching reading* (pp. 361–374). Mahwah, NJ: Erlbaum.

Taylor, M. (1997). *Roll of thunder, hear my cry.* New York: Puffin Books.

Taylor, W. (1953). Cloze procedure: A new tool for measuring readability. *Journalism Quarterly, 30,* 415–433.

Tchudi, S. J., & Tchudi, S. N. (1999). *The English language arts handbook* (2nd ed.). Portsmouth, NH: Heinemann.

Tekmen, E. A., & Daloglu, A. (2006). An investigation of incidental vocabulary acquisition and relation to learner proficiency level and word frequency. *Foreign Language Annals, 39*(3), 220–243.

Thomas, W., & Collier, V. (2003). A national study of school effectiveness for language minority students' long term academic achievement. Research report, Santa Cruz, CA and Washington, DC: Center for Research on Education, Diversity and Excellence and Center for Applied Linguistics.

Tompkins, G. (2002). Struggling readers are struggling writers too. *Reading and Writing Quarterly, 18*(2), 175–193.

Thompson, G., & Morgan, R. (1976). The use of concept formation study guides for social studies reading materials. *Reading Horizons, 7,* 132–136.

Thompson, M. (2008). Multimodal teaching and learning: Creating spaces for content teachers. *Journal of Adolescent and Adult Literacy, 52*(2), 144–153 .

Thornburg, D. D. (2001, May/June). Pencils down! How decontextualized standardized testing can destroy education. *MultiMedia Schools.* Retrieved April 2007 from http://www.infotoday.com/MMSchools/may01/dcon0105.htm.

Thousand, J. S., Villa, R. A., & Nevin, A. I. (2007). *Differentiating instruction: Collaborating planning and teaching for universally designed learning.* Thousand Oaks, CA: Corwin Press.

Thurstone, L. L. (1946). A note on a reanalysis of Davis's reading tests. *Psychometrika, 11,* 185–188.

Tierney, R. J. (1998). Literacy assessment reform: Shifting beliefs, principled possibilities, and emerging practice. *The Reading Teacher, 51*(5), 374–390.

Toch, T. (1984, March 7). Bell calls on education to push publishers for better materials. *Education Week,* 11.

Todd, C. J. (1995). The semester project: The power and pleasures of individualized study. *English Journal, 84,* 73–76.

Tolkien, J. R. R. (2001). *The hobbit.* Boston: Houghton Mifflin Co.

Tomlinson, C. A. (2005). Traveling the road to differentiation in staff development. *Journal of Staff Development, 26*(4), 8–12.

Tonjes, M. J., & Zintz, M. V. (1981). *Teaching reading/thinking study skills in content classrooms.* Dubuque, IA: William Brown Co.

Torgensen, J., & Licht, B. (1983). The learning disabled child as an inactive learner: Retrospect and prospects. In J. McKinney & L. Feagans (Eds.), *Current topics in learning disabilities* (Vol. 1, pp. 3–31). Norwood, NJ: Ablex.

Tracy, B., Reid, R., & Graham, S. (2009). Teaching young students strategies for planning and drafting stories: The impact of self-regulated strategy development. *Journal of Educational Research, 102*(5), 323–331. Retrieved from http://web.ebscohost.com.proxy.library.vcu.edu/ehost/pdfviewer/pdfviewer?vid=6&hid=6&sid=bad412ab-dab3-4f60-8f23-1b86c39bb078%40sessionmgr10.

Trier, J. (2007). "Cool" engagements with YouTube: Part two. *Journal of Adolescent and Adult Literacy, 50*(7), 598–603.

Trueman, M., & Hartley, J. (1996). A comparison between the time-management skills and academic performance of mature and traditional-entry university students. *Higher Education, 32*(2), 199–215.

Tung, R. (2010, January). *Including performance assessments in accountability systems: A review of scale up efforts.* Boston: Center for Collaborative Education.

Turbill, J. (2002, February). The four ages of reading philosophy and pedagogy: A framework for examining theory and practice. *Reading Online, 5*(6). Retrieved December 10, 2004, from http://www.reading online.org/international/inter_index.asp?HREF= turbill4/index.html.

Turner, S. (2009). Ethical and appropriate high-stakes test preparation in middle school: Five methods that matter. *Middle School Journal, 41*(1), 36–45.

Tyner, K. (1998). *Literacy in a digital world: Teaching and learning in the age of information.* Mahwah, NJ: Erlbaum.

United States Copyright Office. (2002). *Copyright law of the United States of America and related laws contained in title 17 of the United States Code Circular 92.* Retrieved April 12, 2006, from http://www.copyright.gov/title17/92chap1.html.

Unsworth, L. (1999). Developing critical understanding of the specialized language of school science and history texts: A functional grammatical perspective. *Journal of Adolescent & Adult Education, 42*(7), 508–521.

Ur, P., & Wright, A. (1992). *Five-minute activities: A resource book of short activities.* New York: Cambridge University Press.

U.S. Department of Education. (1993). *The condition of education 1993.* Washington, DC: Author.

U.S. Department of Education. (2007). *To assure the free appropriate public education of all children with disabilities: Twenty-seventh annual report to Congress on the implementation of the Individuals with Disabilities Education Act.* Washington, DC: Author.

U.S. Department of Education, National Center for Education Statistics. (2006). *The Condition of Education 2006* (NCES 2006–071). Washington, DC: U.S. Government Printing Office.

U.S. Department of Education, National Center for Education Statistics. (2007). *The Condition of Education 2007* (NCES 2007-064). Washington, DC: U.S. Government Printing Office.

U.S. Department of Education, National Center for Education Statistics. (2010). *Digest of Education Statistics, 2009* (NCES 2010-013).

Uzzell, L. (2005, September). Cheat sheets. *American Spectator, 36*(7), 26–30.

Vacca, R. T. (2002). From efficient decoders to strategic readers. *Educational Leadership, 60*(3), 6–11.

Valencia, S. W., & Wixson, K. K. (1999, April 1). *Policy-oriented research on literacy standards and assessment.* CIERA Report No. 3-004. Ann Arbor, MI: Center for the Improvement of Early Reading Achievement.

Valeri-Gold, M. (1987). Previewing: A directed reading–thinking activity. *Reading Horizons, 27,* 123–126.

Van Blerkom, D. L., Van Blerkom, M. L., & Bertsch, S. (2006). Study strategies and generative learning: What works? *Journal of College Reading and Learning, 37*(1), 7–19.

Van der Heuval, G. (1988). *Crowns of thorns and glory: Mary Todd Lincoln and Varina Howell Davis, the two first ladies of the Civil War.* New York: Dutton.

Van der Schoot, M., Vasbinder, A., Horsley, T., Reijntjes, A., & Van Lieshout, E. (2009). *Journal of Educational Psychology, 101*(1), 21–36.

Vanderventer, N. (1979, Winter). RAFT: A process to structure prewriting. *Highway One: A Canadian Journal of Language Experience, 26.*

Vandiver, F. E. (1992). *Blood brothers: A short history of the Civil War.* College Station, TX: Texas A&M Press.

Van Duinen, D. (2005). Authentic Assessment: Praxis with Power. The Twelfth International Conference on Learning, University of Granada. Retrieved 4–19–2011 from: http://l05.cgpublisher.com/proposals/251/index_html

Van Horn, R. (1999). The electronic classroom and video conferencing. *Phi Delta Kappan, 80*(5), 411–412.

Van Leeuwen, C. A., & Gabriel, M. A. (2007). Beginning to write with word processing: Integrating writing process and technology in a primary classroom. *The Reading Teacher, 60,* 420–429.

Vann, R. J., & Fairbairn, S. B. (2003). Linking our worlds: A collaborative academic literacy project. *TESOL Journal, 12*(3), 11–16.

Van Sertima, T. (1976). *The African presence in ancient America: They came before Columbus.* New York: Random House.

Vaughan, C. L. (1990). Knitting writing: The double-entry journal. In N. Atwell (Ed.), *Coming to know: Writing to learn in the intermediate grades* (pp. 69–75). Portsmouth, NH: Heinemann.

Vaughan, J., & Estes, T. (1986). *Reading and reasoning beyond the primary grades.* Boston: Allyn & Bacon.

Vaughn, S., & Fuchs, L. (2003). Redefining learning disabilities as inadequate response to instruction: The promise and potential problems. *Learning Disabilities Research & Practice, 18,* 137–146.

Vaughn, S., Bos, C. S., & Schumm, J. S. (2011). *Teaching students who are exceptional, diverse, and at risk in the general education classroom* (5th ed.). Boston: Allyn & Bacon.

Van Valkenburg, J., & Holden, L. K. (2004). Teaching methods in the affective domain. *Radiologic Technology, 75*(5), 347–355.

Vasquez, V. (2010). Critical literacy isn't just for books anymore. *The Reading Teacher, 63*(7), 614–161.

Veatch, J. (1968). *How to teach reading with children's books.* New York: Citation Press.

Venezky, R. L. (1995). Literacy. In T. L. Harris & R. E. Hodges (Eds.), *The literacy dictionary: The vocabulary of reading and writing* (p. 142). Newark, DE: International Reading Association.

Verdugo, R. R. (2007). English language learners: Key issues. *Education and Urban Society, 39,* 167–193.

Verkoeijen, P., Rikers, R., & Schmidt, H. G. (2005). The effects of prior knowledge on study-time allocation and free recall: Investigating the discrepancy reduction model. *The Journal of Psychology, 139*(1), 67–80.

Vermette, P. (1994). The right start for cooperative learning. *High School Journal, 77,* 255–260.

Vermette, P., Foote, C., Bird, C., Mesibov, D., Harris-Ewing, S., & Battaglia, C. (2001). Understanding constructivism: A primer for parents and school board members. *Education, 122*(1), 87–94.

Vermette, P., Harper, L., & DiMillo, S. (2004). Cooperative and collaborative learning with 4–8 year olds: How does research support teachers' practice? *Journal of Instructional Psychology, 31*(2), 130–135.

Verplaeste, L. S. (1998). How content teachers interact with English language learners. *TESOL Journal, 7*(5), 24–28.

Villaune, S. K. (2000). The necessity of uncertainty: A case study of language arts reform. *Journal of Teacher Education, 51*(1), 18.

Villano, T. L. (2005). Should social studies textbooks become history? A look at alternative methods to activate schema in the intermediate classroom. *The Reading Teacher, 59,* 122–130.

Villegas, A. M., & Lucas, T. (2007). The culturally responsive teacher. *Educational Leadership, 64,* 28–33.

Viorst, J. (1978). *Alexander who used to be rich last Sunday.* New York: Atheneum.

Virginia Department of Education. (2006). *Virginia grade level alternative procedural manual.* Retrieved June 2007 from Web site: http://www.pen.k12.va.us/go/VDOE.

Vlach, S., & Burcie, J. (2010). Narratives of the struggling reader. *The Reading Teacher, 63*(6), 522–525.

Von Glaserfeld, E. (1996). Introduction: Aspects of constructivism. In C. T. Fosnot (Ed.), *Constructivism: Theory, perspectives, and practice* (pp. 3–7). New York: Teachers College Press.

Vyas, S. (2004). Exploring bicultural identities of Asian high school students through the analytic window of a literature club. *Journal of Adolescent & Adult Literacy, 48*(1), 12–23.

Vygotsky, L. (1978a). Interaction between learning and development. In M. Cole, V. John-Steiner, S. Scribner, & E. Souberman (Eds.), *Mind in society: The development of higher psychological process* (pp. 79–91). Cambridge, MA: Harvard University Press.

Vygotsky, L. (1978b). The prehistory of written language. In M. Cole, V. John-Steiner, S. Scribner, & E. Souberman (Eds.), *Mind in society: The development of higher psychological process* (pp. 105–119). Cambridge, MA: Harvard University Press.

Vygotsky, L. S. (1962). *Thought and language.* Cambridge, MA: MIT Press.

Wade, S. E., & Adams, R. B. (1990). Effects of importance and interest on recall of biographical text. *Journal of Reading Behavior, 22,* 331–353.

Waggoner, M., Chinn, C., Yi, H., & Anderson, R. C. (1995). Collaborative reasoning about stories. *Language Arts, 72,* 582–589.

Wagner, J. O. (1995). Using the Internet in vocational education. *ERIC Digest No. 160* (ERIC Document Reproduction Service No. ED. 385–777).

Walberg, H. J., & Tsai, S. (1985). Correlates of reading achievement and attitude: A national assessment study. *Journal of Educational Research, 78,* 159–167.

Walczyk, J. J., & Griffith-Ross, D. A. (2007). How important is reading skill fluency for comprehension? *The Reading Teacher, 60*(6), 560–569.

Walker, B. (1992). *Supporting struggling readers.* Markham, Toronto, Ontario: Pippin Publishing Company.

Walker, B. (2003). *Supporting struggling readers* (2nd ed.). Toronto, Ontario: Pippin Publishing Company.

Walker, S., & Masterman, L. (2006). Learning Designs and the Development of Study Skills: Reuse and Community Perspectives. In R. Philip, A. Voerman & J. Dalziel (Eds.), *Proceedings of the First International LAMS Conference 2006: Designing the Future of Learning* (pp. 89–98). 6–8 December 2006, Sydney: LAMS Foundation.

Wallace, C. S., Hand, B., & Yand, E. (2004). The science writing heuristic: Using writing as a tool for learning in the laboratory. In W. S. Saul (Ed.), *Crossing borders in literacy and science instruction: Perspectives on theory and practice* (pp. 355–368). Newark, DE: International Reading Association.

Wallace, R. A. (1975). *Biology: The world of life.* Santa Monica, CA: Goodyear.

Walpole, P. (1987). Yes, writing in math. In J. Self (Ed.), *Plain talk about learning and writing across the curriculum* (pp. 51–59). Richmond, VA: Virginia State Department of Education.

Walpole, S. (1999). Changing texts, changing thinking: Comprehension demands of new science textbooks. *The Reading Teacher, 52*(4), 358–369.

Walpole, S., Hayes, L., & Robnolt, V. J. (2006). Matching second graders to text: The utility of a group-administered comprehension measure. *Reading Research and Instruction, 46*(1), 1–22.

Walton, S., & Taylor, K. (1996). How did you know the answer was boxcar? *Educational Leadership, 54*(4), 38–40.

Wang, A. Y., & Thomas, M. H. (1995). The effects of key words on long-term retention: Help or hindrance? *Journal of Educational Psychology, 87,* 468–475.

Wang, J. H., & Guthrie, J. T. (2004). Modeling the effects of intrinsic motivation, extrinsic motivation, amount of reading, and past reading achievement on text comprehension between U.S. and Chinese students. *Reading Research Quarterly, 39*(2), 162–184.

Warm, J. S., Dember, W. M., & Parasuraman, R. (1991). Effects of olfactory stimulation on performance and stress in a visual sustained attention task. *Journal of the Society of Cosmetic Chemists, 42,* 199–210.

Waters, M., & Waters, A. (1992). Study skills and study competence: Getting the priorities right. *ELT Journal, 46*(3), 264–273.

Watts-Taffe, S., Gwinn, C. B., Johnson, J. R., & Horn, M. L. (2003). Preparing preservice teachers to integrate technology with the elementary literacy program. *The Reading Teacher, 57*(2), 130–138.

Weaver, C. (1994). *Reading processes and practice.* Portsmouth, NH: Heinemann.

Weinstein, C. E. (1987). Fostering learning autonomy through the use of learning strategies. *Journal of Reading, 30,* 590–595.

Weinstein, C. E., & Mayer, R. E. (1986). The teaching of learning strategies. In M. C. Wittrock (Ed.), *Handbook of research on teaching* (pp. 315–327). New York: Macmillan.

Weinstein, C. E., Zimmerman, S. A., & Palmer, D. R. (1988). Assessing learning strategies: The design and development of the LASSI. In C. E. Weinstein, P. A. Alexander, & E. T. Goetz (Eds.), *Learning and study strategies: Issues in assessment, instruction, and evaluation* (pp. 25–39). New York: Academic Press.

Weir, C. (1998). Using embedded questions to jumpstart metacognition in middle school readers. *Journal of Adolescent & Adult Literacy, 41*(6), 458–467.

Weiss, R. P. (2000). Brain based learning. *Training and Development, 54*(7), 21–27.

Wells, H. G. (1988). *The war of the worlds.* New York: Bantam Classics.

Wells, J., & Lewis, L. (2006). *Internet Access in U.S. Public Schools and Classrooms: 1994–2005* (NCES 2007-020). Washington, DC: U.S. Department of Education, National Center for Education Statistics. Retrieved July 30, 2010, from http://nces.ed.gov/pubs2007/2007020.pdf.

Wepner, S. B. (1995). Using technology for literacy instruction. In S. B. Wepner, J. T. Feeley, & D. S. Strickland (Eds.), *The administration and supervision of reading programs.* New York: Teachers College Press.

Wepner, S. B. (2004). Technology run amok: The top ten technoblunders. *Reading Online, 7*(6). Retrieved December 10, 2004, from http://www.readingonline.org/electronic/elec_index.asp?HREF=wepner2/index.html.

Wepner, S. B., Seminoff, N. E., & Blanchard, J. (1995). Navigating learning with electronic encyclopedias. *Reading Today, 12,* 28.

West, M. (1953). *A general service list of English words.* London: Longman, Green.

Westby, C. (2008). What are lexiles? *Word of Mouth, 19*(4), 9–10.

Whalon, K., & Hanline, M. F. (2008). Effects of a reciprocal questioning intervention on the question generation and responding of children with autism spectrum disorder. *Education and Training in Developmental Disabilities, 43*(3), 367–387.

White, E. B. (1951). Calculating machine. In *The second tree from the corner* (pp. 165–167). New York: Harper and Row.

White, T. G., Sowell, J., & Yanagihara, A. (1989). Teaching elementary students to use word-part clues. *The Reading Teacher, 42,* 302–308.

Whitehead, D. (1994). Teaching literacy and learning strategies through a modified guided silent reading procedure. *Journal of Reading, 38,* 24–30.

Whittington, D. (1991). What have 17-year-olds known in the past? *American Educational Research Journal, 28,* 759–783.

Widmer, T. (ed), (2006). *American Speeches: Political oratory from the Revolution to the Civil War.* New York, NY: Literary Classics of the United States, The Library of America.

Wiggins, G. (1989). A true test: Toward more authentic and equitable assessment. *Phi Delta Kappan, 70,* 703–713.

Wigginton, E. (1986). *Sometimes a shining moment: The Foxfire experiences.* New York: Anchor/Doubleday.

Wilcox, B. L. (1997). Writing portfolios: Active vs. passive. *English Journal, 86*(6), 34–37.

Wiley, J., Griffin, T. D., & Thiede, K. W. (2005). Putting the comprehension in metacomprehension. *Journal of General Psychology, 132*(4), 408–429.

Wilfong, L. G. (2009). Textmasters: Bringing literature circles to textbook reading across the curriculum. *Journal of Adolescent & Adult Literacy, 53*(2), 164–171.

Wilkinson, L. C., & Silliman, E. R. (2001, February). Classroom language and literacy learning. *Reading Online, 4*(7). Retrieved November 11, 2004, from http://www.readingonline.org/articles/art_index.asp? HREF=/articles/handbook/wilkinson/index.html.

Will, M. (1984). *Bridges from school to working life: OSERS programming for the transition of youth with disabilities.* Washington, DC: U.S. Department of Education, Office of Special Education and Rehabilitative Services.

Williams, B. (2006). Lessons along the cultural spectrum. *Journal of Staff Development, 27*(4), 10–14.

Williams, B.T. (2005). Leading double lives: Literacy and technology in and out of school. *Journal of Adolescent and Adult Literacy, 48(8),* 702–706.

Williams, B. T. (2005/2006). Home and away: The tensions of community, literacy, and identity. *Journal of Adolescent & Adult Literacy, 48,* 342–347.

Williams, J., Stafford, K., Louer, K., Hall, K., & Pollini, S. (2009). Embedding reading comprehension training in content-area instruction. *Journal of Educational Psychology, 101*(1), 1–20.

Willingham, D. T. (2002). Allocating study time: Massed versus distributed practice. *American Educator, 26*(2), 37–39.

Willis, J. (2009). What brain research suggests for teaching reading strategies. *The Educational Forum, 73,* 333–346.

Wilson, A. A. (2008). Moving beyond the page in content area literacy: Comprehension instruction for multimodal texts in science. *The Reading Teacher, 62*(2), 153–156.

Winne, P. H., & Perry, N. E. (2000). Measuring self-regulated learning. In M. Boekaerts, P. Pintrich, & M. Zeidner (Eds.), *Handbook of self-regulation* (pp. 531–566). New York: Academic Press.

Winograd, P. (1984). Strategic difficulties in summarizing texts. *Reading Research Quarterly, 19,* 404–425.

Wise, H. A. (1939). *Motion pictures as an aid in teaching American history.* New Haven, CT: Yale University Press.

Wolf, G. (1996, February). Steve Jobs: The next great thing. *Wired,* 102–163.

Wolfe, D., & Antinarella, J. (1997). *Deciding to lead: The English teacher as reformer.* Portsmouth, NH: Heinemann.

Wolfe, D., & Reising, R. (1983). *Writing for learning in the content areas.* Portland, ME: J. Weston Walch.

Wolfe, P. (2001). *Brain matters: Translating research into classroom practice.* Alexandria, VA: Association for Supervision and Curriculum Development.

Wolfe, P., & Brandt, R. (1998). What do we know from brain research? *Educational Leadership, 56*(3), 8–13.

Wolgemuth, J. R.; Cobb, R. B. & Alwell, M. (2008). The Effects of Mnemonic Interventions on Academic Outcomes. *Learning Disabilities Research & Practice, 23*(1), 1–10.

Wollman-Bonilla, J. (1991). *Response journals.* New York: Scholastic.

Wood, K. D. (1987). Fostering cooperative learning in middle and secondary level classrooms. *Journal of Reading, 31,* 10–18.

Wood, K. D. (1992). Fostering collaborative reading and writing experiences in mathematics. *Journal of Reading, 36,* 96–103.

Wood, K. D., Lapp, D., & Flood, J. (1992). *Guiding readers through text: A review of study guides.* Newark, DE: International Reading Association.

Wood, T. M. (1996). Evaluation and testing: The road less traveled. In S. J. Silverman and C. D. Ennis (Eds.), *Student learning in physical education: Applying research to enhance instruction* (pp. 199–219). Champaign, IL: Human Kinetics.

Woodring, M. N., & Flemming, C. W. (1935). *Directing study of high school pupils.* New York: Columbia University Teacher's College.

Woolf, V. (1967; c. 1966). *Collected essays.* New York: Harcourt, Brace and World.

Worthy, J., & Broaddus, K. (2002). Fluency beyond the primary grades: From group performance to silent, independent reading. *The Reading Teacher, 55*(4), 334–343.

Worthy, J., & Hoffman, J. V. (2000). Critical questions—the press to test. *The Reading Teacher, 53*(7), 596–598.

Wray, D. (1994). Text and authorship. *The Reading Teacher, 48*(1), 52–57.

Wray, D., & Lewis, M. (1998). An approach to factual writing. *Reading Online.* Retrieved December 12, 2004, from http://www.readingonline.org/articles/art_index.asp?HREF=writing/index.html.

The writing report card: Writing achievement in American schools (1987). Princeton, NJ: National Assessment of Educational Progress and the Educational Testing Center.

Wright-Frierson, V. (1998). An Island Scrapbook: Dawn to dusk on a barrier island. NY: Simon & Schuster.

Xu, S. H. (2001, July/August). Exploring diversity issues in teacher education. *Reading Online, 5*(1). Retrieved June 3, 2007, from http://www.readingonline.org/newliteracies/lit_index.asp?HREF=action/xu/index.html.

Yager, S., Yager, R. & Lim, G. (2006). The Advantages of an STS Approach Over a Typical Textbook Dominated Approach in Middle School Science. *School Science and Mathematics, 106*(5), 248–260.

Yang, Y., Yeh, H., & Wong, W. (2010). The influence of social interaction on meaning construction in a virtual community. *British Journal of Educational Technology, 41*(2), 287-306.

Yanowitz, K. L. (2001). Using analogies to improve elementary school students' inferential reasoning about scientific concepts. *School Science and Mathematics, 101*(3), 133.

Yeager, D. (1991). *The whole language companion.* Glenview, IL: Goodyear.

Yell, M. M. (2002). Putting gel pen to paper. *Educational Leadership, 60*(3), 63–66.

Yochum, N. (1991). Children's learning from informational text: The relationship between prior knowledge and text structure. *Journal of Reading Behavior, 23,* 87–108.

Yolen, J. (Ed.). (1986). *Favorite folktales from around the world.* New York: Pantheon Books.

Yoon, J. (2002). Three decades of sustained silent reading: A meta-analytic review of the effects of SSR on attitude toward reading. *Reading Improvement, 39*(4), 186–196.

Yopp, R. H., & Yopp, H. K. (2010). *Literature-based reading activities* (5th ed.). New York: Allyn & Bacon.

Young, D. B., & Ley, K. (2000). Developmental students don't know what they don't know. Part I: Self-regulation. *Journal of College Reading and Learning, 31*(1), 54–62.

Young, J. P., & Brozo, W. G. (2001). Boys will be boys, or will they? Literacy and masculinities. *Reading Research Quarterly, 36*(3), 316–325.

Yovanoff, P., Duesbery, L., Alonzo, J., & Tindal, G. (2005). Grade-level invariance of a theoretical causal structure predicting reading comprehension with vocabulary and oral reading fluency. *Educational Measurement: Issues and Practice,* 4–12.

Yurick, A. L., Robinson, P. D., Cartledge, G., Lo, Y., & Evans, T. L. (2006). Using peer-mediated repeated readings as a fluency-building activity for urban learners. *Education & Treatment of Children, 29*(3), 469–507.

Zakaluk, B., & Klassen, M. (1992). Enhancing the performance of a high school student labeled learning disabled. *Journal of Reading, 36,* 4–9.

Zawilinski, L. (2009). HOT blogging: A framework for blogging to promote higher order thinking. *The Reading Teacher, 62*(8), 650–661.

Zhang, Z., & Schumm, J. S. (2000). Exploring effects of the keyword method on limited English proficient students' vocabulary recall and comprehension. *Reading Research and Instruction, 39*(3), 202–221.

Zimmerman, B. J., & Schunk, D. H. (2001). *Self-regulated learning and academic achievement.* Mahwah, NJ: Erlbaum.

Zucker, T., Justice, L., Piasta, S., & Kaderavek, P. (2010). Preschool teachers' literal and inferential questions and children's responses during whole-class shared reading. *Early Childhood Research Quarterly, 25*(1), 65–83.

Activity Contributors

Dawn Watson and Walter Richards: PAR Diagram, p. 15

Alex Seeley, Richmond, VA: Examples for primary social studies lesson (pp. 16) and Activity 1.4

Laura Tenembaum, Richmond, VA: Example for fifth grade art & poetry (pp. 18) and Activity 1.5

Michael Tewksbury, Richmond, VA: Examples for middle school mathematics (pp. 20)

Stephanie Plott: Examples for tenth grade biology (pp. 20) and Activities 1.6 & 1.7

Meredith Young, Activity 2.11, pp. 47

Sandra M. Robinson, Barnedia Morris Durrah & Gail S. Running Hawk, Activity 2.12, pp. 48

Jeannette Rosenberg: Activity 3.1, p. 57

Grace Hamlin: Example of incorrect knowledge, p. 60

Laura Hoffmeister, Activity 3.5, p. 65

Travis Sturgill: Activity 3.8, p. 68

Dr. Mark Forget: Activity 3.11, p. 72

Dr. Mark Forget: Activity 3.13, p. 74

Kathy Feltus, Activity 3.16, p. 76

Dr. Mark Forget: Activity 4.4, p. 90

Laura Clevinger: Activity 4.7, p. 96

Serena Marshall, Activity 4.11, p. 99

Nancy S. Smith, Activity 4.13, p. 104

Shante D. Asprey, Activity 5.7, p. 128

Marvette Darby: Activity 6.6, p. 161

Terry Bryce: Activity 7.2, p. 179

Brian Littman: Activity 7.4, p. 181

Tara Furges: Activity 7.5, p. 182

Audra Jones: Activity 7.6, p. 184

Suzanne McDaniel: Activity 7.7, p. 183

Heather Hemstreet: Activity 7.10, p. 192

Wendy Barcroft: Activity 7.11, p. 194

Kim Blowe: Activity 7.13, p. 196

Colleen Kean: Activity 7.15, p. 202

Ed Toscano: Activity 7.17, p. 204

Barbara Wood: Activities 7.18, 7.19, 7.20, pp. 205, 206, 207

Mary Fagerland: Activity 7.21, p. 208

Bessie Haskins: Activity 7.22, p. 209

Kathryn Davis: Activity 8.1, p. 224

Dr. Mark Forget: Activity 8.2, p. 227

Andrew Pettit: Figure 8.3, p. 220

Dr. Mark Forget: Activity 8.4, p. 230

Susan W. Hamlin: Activity 8.5, p. 231

Terry Bryce: Activity 8.7, p. 236

Jon Morgan: Activity 8.11, p. 239

Frances Lively: Activity 8.13, pp. 242

Dianne Duncan: Activity 8.17, pp. 248

Mary L. Seward: Activity 9.6, p. 268

Jody Irvin: Activity 9.11, p. 275

Stephanie Hunter, Activity 9.14, 280

Karen Curling: Activity 11.3, p. 339

Beverly Marshall: Activity 11.5, p. 345

Megan K. Houston: Activity 11.6, p. 346

Kerry Blum: Math analogy, p. 346

Diana Freeman: Biology analogy, p. 346

Lori Levy: Activity 12.1, p. 362

Mary Broussard: A homework strategy, p. 365

Charles Carroll: Activity 12.2, p. 366

Amy Nowlin: Activity 12.3, p. 366

Jane Baxter: Activity 12.4, p. 367

Bessie Haskins: Activity 12.5, p. 368

Dr. Jeff Nugent: Activity 12.6, p. 372

Frances Reid: Activity 12.7, p. 374

Sandra Zeller and Brenda Winston: Activity 12.8, p. 375

Author Index

Abbott, R. D., 219
Abowd, P., 361
Abrami, P. C., 119
Abrams, L., 224, 225
Acton, M., 284
Adams, K. S., 257, 260
Adams, M., 345
Adams, M. J., 327
Adams, R. B., 58
Adams, W., 378
Afflerbach, P., 258, 355, 356, 361, 381, 382
Aguiar, L., 189
Ajayi, L., 139
Akiba, M., 325
Alban, T., 81
Alber, S. R., 290
Alber-Morgan, S., 125
Albright, L. K., 140
Alexander, P. A., 54, 137
Allan, J., 256, 260
Allen, G., 301, 378
Allington, R. L., 340
Alvarez, M. C., 143
Alvermann, D. E., 100, 327, 329
Anders, P. L., 180
Anderson, D., 193
Anderson, J., 345
Anderson, R. C., 56
Anderson, T., 148
Anderson-Inman, L., 258, 259, 281, 304, 306
Ansaldo, R., 222
Anson, C., 218
Anstey, M., 136, 137, 139, 162
Antinarella, J., 290
Applefield, J. M., 259
Applegate, B., 112
Apthorp, H. S., 325
Aratani, L., 354
Ariail, M., 140
Arlin, P. K., 114
Armbruster, B., 148, 180
Aronson, E., 164
Arthur, S. V., 182
Aschbacher, P. R., 379
Ashby-Davis, C., 158
Ashman, A. F., 119
Ashton-Warner, S., 347
Asselin, M., 172, 173, 176
Atkinson, R. C., 138, 139, 144, 200
Attewell, P., 313
Atwell, N., 240
Au, K. H., 319, 333
Aud, S., 53, 324, 325
August, D., 175
Ausubel, D., 177
Avgerinou, M., 275
Ayers, S. F., 367, 370

Bader, L., 149, 222
Bagnato, 379
Bahrick, H. P., 282
Bailey, S. J., 116
Bajanski, I., 110
Baker, E. A., 315
Baker, J., 109
Baker, S. K., 177
Ball, D. L., 54
Bandura, A., 329
Bangel, N. J., 324
Bangert-Drowns, R. L., 215, 219, 225, 245
Banks, J. A., 320
Bardovi-Harlig, K., 361
Barnako, F., 296
Barnett, J. E., 11, 12, 258
Baron, J. B., 111
Barrera IV, E. S. 257
Barry, A., 275, 278
Barry, C., 141
Bartlett, F. C., 56
Barton, J., 100
Barton, K., 218
Bauer, E. B., 170, 336
Baum, D. D., 128
Baumann, J. F., 185, 187, 188
Bauserman, K.L., 53
Beach, R., 218
Bean, R., 241
Bean, T. W., 244, 296

Beaumont, G., 308
Bech, R., 30
Beck, I. L., 65, 148, 169, 170, 174, 175, 178, 179
Bede, I. L., 53
Beers, T., 57
Bell, T., 288
Belzer, S., 260
Bembenutty, H., 265
Bennion, K., 378
Benson, S., 351
Bereiter, C., 257
Berglund, R. L., 193
Berliner, D., 4, 5, 359
Berninger, V. W., 214, 219
Bertsch, S., 130
Berube, C., 5, 361
Beyer, B. K., 111
Bezemer, J., 148
Bhat, P., 290
Bianco, J., 53
Bieger, E. M., 142
Biehler, R., 329
Biemiller, A., 173, 174, 175
Biggs, J., 258
Bikowski, D., 336
Bintz, W. P., 219, 232, 287
Blachowitz, C. L. Z., 123, 169, 173, 176, 177, 185, 187, 192
Blackburn, C., 193
Blai, B., 256
Blaisdell, M., 302
Blanchard, J., 304, 314
Blessing, D., 193
Block, C. C., 131
Bloom, A., 359
Blume, J., 154
Blumenfeld, P. C., 116
Boaler, J., 116, 323
Bockern, S. V., 329, 330
Boland, E., 185, 187, 188
Boling, E., 218
Bonner, B., 169
Boote, C., 175
Borko, H., 55, 360, 364
Borman, G. D., 325, 326, 340
Bormouth, J. R., 157
Bos, C. S., 180, 322
Bosquet, D., 258
Bottomley, D. M., 34
Boyd, D.M., 299
Boyd, F. B., 327, 329
Boyd, W., 5
Boyd-Batstone, P., 386
Boyer, T. L., 215
Boyle, M., 110, 120
Boyle, O., 333
Brabham, E.G., 174
Bracey, G., 4, 359
Brady, S., 189
Brandt, R., 40
Bravo, M. A., 169
Brechtel, M., 338
Brendtro, L. K., 329, 330
Brennan, K. B., 290
Breuch, L. K., 218
Brigham, F. J., 183
Brindley, R., 216
Brinthaupt, T. M., 282
Britton, B. K., 258, 263
Broaddus, K., 53, 60, 341
Brokenleg, M., 329, 330
Brooks, J. G., 85
Brooks, M. G., 85
Brown, A. L., 126, 250, 340
Brown, J., 58, 215, 228, 245, 296
Brown, R., 278
Brown, S. W., 54
Brozo, W. G., 59, 327, 329
Bruce, B., 315
Brunwin, B., 243
Bryant, B. R., 172, 176
Bryant, D. P., 68, 172, 176
Budig, G. A., 214
Buehl, D. R., 62, 63, 127
Bull, G., 136, 137, 139, 162
Bult, B., 333
Burcie, J., 340
Burdick, H., 153
Burnam, N., 161
Burns, M. S., 55, 169
Bushaw, W. J, 360, 363
Butler, G., 57
Byrnes, J. P., 53

Cadenhead, K., 155
Cahill, M., 256
Calfee, R. C., 143
Calkins, L., 219, 223
Callison, D., 69
Cammack, D. W., 136, 258, 297
Campione, J. C., 250
Canas, M., 116
Cantrell, S. C., 55
Caplan, R. I., 161
Cardoso, S., 29
Carmen, R., 378
Carney, J., 193
Carolan, J., 319, 342
Carr, E., 64, 177
Carrillo, R., 258
Carter, K., 378
Carter, T., 309
Cartledge, G., 125
Carver, R. P., 177, 288
Cassady, J., 114

Cassidy, J., 257
Castek, J., 218, 297, 298, 302, 305
Caverly, D., 31
Celano, D., 327
Cervetti, G. N., 169
Chall, J., 152
Chamberlain, C.J., 225
Chambers, B., 119
Chapman, C., 313
Chase, A. C., 198
Cheek, E. H., 58, 148
Chesbro, R., 348
Chi-Cheng, C., 382
Chilcoat, G. W., 243
Chinn, C. A., 93
Choi, I., 54
Cholewa, B., 333
Christensen, C. A., 108, 232
Ciardiello, A. V., 344
Ciechanowski, K. M., 258
Clark, D., 111
Clarke, J., 302
Clark, K., 111, 260
Clausen-Grace, N., 342
Cleary, B., 222
Cleaveland, L. B., 216, 219
Cobb, R., 284
Cochran-Smith, M., 225, 334, 245
Cohen, A. D., 284
Cohen, D. K., 54
Coiro, J., 53, 54, 136, 258, 297, 302, 305
Cole, C. L., 266
Cole, R. P., 258
Collazo, T., 258
Collier, V., 333, 335
Colwell, C. G., 91
Conderman, G., 290
Conley, M., 359
Connell, J. P., 329
Conner, J., 71
Cook, A., 225, 245
Cook, C., 336
Cook, J. B., 326
Cook, L., 337
Cooke, C., 68
Coombe, C. A., 369
Cooper, J., 223
Cooper, L., 266
Cooter, R. B., 243
Cope, B., 297
Corcoran, C. A., 142
Cordova, R. A., 163
Corno, L., 265
Cornold, C., 256
Correa-Kovtun, A., 256, 272, 336, 338, 339
Costa, C., 268
Cowan, G., 226
Cowan, E., 226
Coxhead, A., 169
Coyne, P., 323
Crede, M., 257
Crenshaw, S. W., 225
Cronin, H., 245
Cronje, J., 30
Crooks, S. M., 278
Cross, C., 322
Cross, T., 114
Crystal, D., 111
Cubukcu, F., 255, 256, 260, 276
Culham, R., 223, 245
Cummins, J., 332, 333
Cunningham, A. E., 174, 177
Cunningham, J., 260
Cunningham, J. W., 126, 244
Cunningham, P., 188
Currie, H., 64
Cziko, C., 81

Dale, E., 152, 171
Daloglu, A., 175
Dana, C., 197
Daniels, H., 144, 145
Dansereau, D., 69, 124
d'Apollonia, S., 119
Dass, M., 144, 146
Davey, B., 131
Davidowitz, B., 263
Davis, F. B., 169, 170
Davis, J., 214
Davison, D., 229, 247
Day, J. D., 126, 250
Day, R. S., 54
Deal, D., 233
DeBell, M., 313
DeBern, R., 256
deBono, E., 12
Dechant, E., 256
DeCleene, J., 255, 256
Dede, C., 302
Deen, M. Y., 116
Deering, P. D., 119
Degener, S. C., 53, 216, 230
de Jong, E., 337
Dember, W., 354
Demski, J., 138,
Denner, P. R., 62
Dennis, D. V., 340, 341
Deshler, D. D., 189
DeSimone, C., 119
Devault, R., 125
Devoogd, G., 115
Dewey, J., 109,
DiCecco, V. M., 68
Dicembre, E. A., 340

Dickson, R., 235
Dieu, B., 309
Dillon, D. R., 100
Dillon, J. T., 100
DiMillo, S., 119
Dinkes, R., 53
Dixon, F., 114
Dobler, E., 53, 54, 302
Dolan, R. P., 323
Dole, S., 343
Dole, J., 340
Donovan, S., 322
Dornyei, Z., 361
Doucette, M., 58
Dougherty, L. A., 198
Douglass, F., 122
Dove, M. K., 137
Downing, J., 334
Drame, E., 322
Drevno, G. E., 177
Drum, P., 58
Duffelmeyer, F. A., 128, 198
Duffy, G. G., 110
Duggan, T. J., 214, 222, 223
Duke, N., 114, 143, 216, 217, 230
Dunbar, S., 315
Dunn, M., 169
Dunston, P. J., 180
Dunwoody, S., 259
Durgnuoglu, A. Y., 170
Duvdevany, I., 42
Dzaldov, B. S., 147
Dziuban, C., 276, 297

Eanet, M., 234
Ebbinghaus, H., 156, 282, 284
Echevarria, M., 336
Edmunds, K. M., 53
Edwards, E. C., 185, 187, 188
Edwards, L. L., 172, 173, 176
Edwards, M., 355
Egan, M., 180
Eldredge, J. L., 260
Elish-Piper, L., 123
Elliott, L., 260
Ellis, E. S., 255
Ellis, L., 258
Ellison, N. B., 299
Emerson, L., 214
Erickson, B., 140
Ericson, J., 275
Erten, I., 119
Estes, T., 227
Etkind, R., 284
Evans, J. A., 306
Evans, T. L., 125
Eveland, W. P., 259
Fahey, K., 383
Fairbairn, S. B., 336
Faller, S. E., 170
Falter, C., 314
Fang, Z., 56
Fantuzzo, J. W., 116
Farrell, M., 119
Farstrup, A. E., 169
Faulkner, W., 152
Fayol, M., 219
Feder, M., 295
Feldhusen, J., 323
Ferguson, D., 325
Fewster, D., 340
Fiedler, E., 323
Fisher, C. W., 349
Fisher, D., 141, 340, 347
Fisher, M., 363
Fisher, P., 169, 173, 176, 177, 185, 187, 192
Fitzsimmons, D., 381
Flanagan, K., 178, 179
Fleener, C. E., 36
Flemming, C. W., 257
Fletcher, D., 297
Fletcher, R., 216
Flood, J., 141,
Florio-Ruane, S., 144
Flynt, E. S., 59
Font, G., 185, 188
Fontaine, L. M., 171
Fontana, J. L., 284
Foot, K. E., 258
Forbes, L. S., 270
Forgan, H. W., 343
Forget, M. A., 69, 109, 275, 290
Fortin, L., 327
Foster, S., 260
Fox, B. J., 301
Fox, L. S., 284
Fox, M. A., 53, 324, 325
Francis, M. A., 176
Francis-Smythe, J. A., 263
Frand, J., 297
Franklin, B., 303
French, M. P., 193
Frey, N., 141, 347
Friedman, T. L., 295, 296, 304, 312
Friend, R., 126
Fritz, C. O., 284
Frost, H., 146
Fry, E., 153
Frymier, A. B., 258
Fuchs, L. S., 116, 248
Fujloka, J., 360, 363

Gable, R. A., 379
Gabriel, M. A., 225

Gainer, J. S., 162
Galas, C., 302
Gallagher, J. M., 58
Gallo, A. M., 37
Gallup, A. M., 360
Gambrell, L. B., 53, 142, 296, 325
Ganski, K., 343
Garber-Miller, K., 272
Garcia, G. E., 170
Garner, R., 125
Garrett, S. D., 257
Gebhard, A., 230
Gee, J. P., 8, 255, 299
George, M., 144
Gere, A., 235
Gettinger, M., 255, 259
Gholar, C. R., 39
Giambo, D. A., 355
Gibbons, P., 333
Gillett, J. W., 196
Gillies, R. M., 110, 119, 120
Ginsburg-Block, M. D., 116
Glasser, W., 36
Glassman, L. D., 183, 200
Glaubman, H., 232
Glaubman, R., 232
Gleason, M. M., 68
Glover, M., 216, 219
Glynn, S. M., 75
Godwin, K., 359
Goett, A., 258
Goetz, E. T., 57
Goetz, V. W., 258
Gold, P. C., 14
Goldberg, A., 225, 245
Gonzales, P., 337
Goodson, F. T., 381
Goodwin, M., 172, 176
Gordon, J., 58
Gottlieb, M., 355
Goudvis, A., 122, 143
Graham, S., 214, 219, 249
Graves, D., 68
Graves, M. F., 169, 171, 173, 175, 176, 177, 178, 179, 183, 185, 188
Gray, F. E., 214
Gray, W. S., 257, 288
Gredler, M. E., 86
Green, J. F., 381
Green, S. K., 86
Greenberg, D., 249
Greenleaf, C. L., 81, 340
Greenlee-Moore, M., 302
Greenwood, S. C., 178, 179
Gregory, A.E., 256
Griffin, C. C., 290
Griffin, T. D., 110, 169
Griffith, L. W., 288
Griffith-Ross, D. A., 288
Groenke, S. L., 240
Gronlund, N., 378
Gruhler, D., 144
Gueta, G., 265
Guillaume, A. M., 138
Guilmett, K., 314
Guinn, A., 319, 342
Guthrie, J., T., 137, 144, 161
Guzzetti, B., 143
Gwinn, C. B., 298

Hadaway, N., 339
Hager, J. M., 379
Haggard, M. R., 198
Hall, L. A., 217, 297
Hall, T., 301
Hall, T. E., 323
Halladay, M. A. K., 147
Hallman, H.L., 381
Hall-Quest, A. L., 257
Hammerberg, D., 319
Hamilton, G. W., 235
Hancin-Bhatt, B., 170
Hancock, D., 117
Hand, D., 249
Hanline, M. F., 344
Hanna, T., 131
Hansen, J., 100
Harland, P., 314
Harper, C., 337
Harper, L., 119
Harris, K., 249, 255
Harris, L. A., 333
Harris, T. L., 59, 156, 261, 333
Harris-Murri, N., 322
Harrison, D., 361
Hart, B., 175
Hartman, J. A., 297, 302
Hartley, J., 263
Harvey, S., 122, 143
Harvey, V. S., 325, 326, 330
Hasselbring, T. S., 64
Hatch, J., 115
Hatter, N., 222
Hattie, J., 258, 259, 260
Haubner, J., 139
Haugland, S., 301
Hayes, H., 6
Hayes, L., 56, 155
Haynes, J., 276
Heafner, T. L., 108
Heap, N., 258
Heath, S. B., 334
Hebard, H., 139
Hedin, L. R., 290

Heilman, A. W., 319
Heimlich, J. E., 193
Heller, M., 63
Helman, L., 170
Helsel, L., 249
Hemingway, E., 153
Henderson, M. V., 259, 297
Henry, G. H., 177
Henry, L. A., 269, 297, 305
Herber, H., 11, 14
Herman, J. L., 379
Herter, R. J., 222
Hew, K.F., 303
Heward, W. L., 320
Hiebert, E. H., 169, 170, 175
Higgins, B., 216
Higgins, K., 172, 176
Hinchman, K. A., 327, 329, 340, 355
Hirsch, E. D., 359
Hitlin, P., 299, 307
Hmelo, C. E., 54
Hoa, L. W., 144
Hodges, R. E., 59, 255
Hoemake, S., 260
Hoffman, J. V., 110, 355
Hoffman, S., 376
Hogan, K., 54
Hogan, M., 314
Holden, L. K., 30, 35
Hollingsworth, B., 379
Holschuh, J. P., 258, 263
Horn, M. L., 298
Horn, W. F., 351
Housen, A., 333
Houston, G., 214, 360
Howard, S., 325
Howes, E. V., 235
Hu, W., 365
Hubbard, B. P., 260, 274, 280
Huber, J., 138, 139, 144
Huber, R. I., 259
Hubley, N. J., 369
Huey, E. B., 257, 288
Hughes, J., 362
Huitt, W., 356
Hummel, J., 356
Hung, Y., 109
Hunsader, P. D., 144
Hunter, K., 138
Hurd, P., 138
Hurley, M. M., 215, 219
Hurwitz, L., 81
Huske, L., 169
Huss, J. A., 324
Hussar, W., 53
Hwang, Y., 284
Hynd, C., 111, 258

Idol-Mastas, L., 378
Inman, C., 302
Irfan, Y., 381
Irish, C., 284
Irvin, J. L., 127, 173
Israel, S. E., 131
Ivey, G., 53, 341

Jackson, F. R., 260
Jacobson, E., 53, 216, 230
Jacobson, J. M., 289
Jacobson, L. A., 172, 173, 176
Jaimes, J., 111
Jamieson-Noel, D., 172, 173, 176
Janesick,V., 380
Jenkins, C., 101
Jeon, K., 324
Jetton, T. L., 54, 137
Jewitt, C., 139
Jitendra, A. K., 172, 173, 176
Johnson & Johnson (1987), 119
Johnson, B., 325, 355
Johnson, D., 355
Johnson, D. W., 116, 324
Johnson, J. R., 298
Johnson, K., 340
Johnson, R. T., 116, 324
Jonassen, D. H., 306
Jones, C. H., 260
Jones, F. R., 43
Jones, J., 344
Joseph, B., 144
Joseph, L. M., 125
Judy, J. E., 54
Juel, C., 139
Juettner, M., 255, 256
Junge, K., 53

Kaeck, D., 356
Kaffenberger, C. J., 326
Kagan, S., 117, 123, 125, 164
Kahn, E. A., 364, 367
Kalantzis, M., 297
Kame'enui, E. J., 177, 187
Kamhi, A. G., 131
Kamil, M. L., 175, 340, 342, 343
Kapinus, B., 120
Kaplan, A., 265
Kaplan, D., 123
Karakas, M., 119
Karchmer, R., 305
Karlin, R., 260
Katayama, A. D., 278, 373
Katehi, L., 295
Katz, I., 265
Kaufhold, J., 111
Kauffman, J. M., 321

Kear, D. J., 31
Keehn, S., 116, 119
Kelley, J. G., 170
Kelley, M. L., 256
Kellogg, R., 6
Kelly, A. E., 54
Kelly, M. J., 342
Kemp, A., 53
Kena, G., 53
Kenner, C., 139
Kerr, M. M., 153
Kervin, L., 314
Kessler, G., 336
Ketelhut, D. J., 302
KewalRamani, A., 53, 324, 325
Khadaroo, S. T., 361
Kidder, T., 330
Kieffer, M. J., 170, 188
Kiger, N., 223
Kim, A., 373
Kim, G. S., 53
King, K., 322
King, S., 109, 330
Kingsley, T., 190
Kintch, W., 244, 250
Kinzer, C. K., 136, 225, 258, 297
Kirsch, I. S., 152
Kist, W., 258
Kitsantas, A., 258
Klassen, M., 250
Klein, A., 115
Kleiner, A., 5
Klemp, R. M., 127
Knickerbocker, J. L., 115
Knipper, K. J., 214, 222, 223
Knobel, M., 343
Knowles, M. S., 257
Knowlton, D. S., 308
Knowlton, H. M., 308
Knox, C., 281
Knox-Quinn, C., 259
Koeze, S., 193
Kolic-Vehovec, S., 110
Konigsburg, E. L., 154
Konopak, B., 193
Konrad, M., 124
Korat, O., 303
Kornhaber, M., 355
Kowalinski, B. J., 143
Kowalski, P., 111
Kowalski, T., 142
Kozen, A. A., 71
Krajcik, J., 116
Kral, C. C., 340
Kramer, K., 258
Krashen, S., 332
Kress, G., 148
Kropiewnicki, M., 82
Krus, D. J., 284
Kucan, L., 144, 146, 174
Kulik, C., 323
Kulik, J., 323
Kuncel, N. R., 257
Kurschner, C., 56

Labbo, L. D., 215
Laing, S. P., 131
L'Allier, S., 123
Lambiotte, J. G., 69
Land, S., 54
Landis, D., 347
Landrum, T., 321
Lange, R., 323
Langer, J., 74
Lankutis, T., 323
Lantendresse, C., 144
Lapp, D., 141, 340
Larson, C., 124
Last, D. A., 54
Lauer, P. A., 325
Law, C., 111
Lawler, D., 101
Lawless, K. A., 54
Lawrence, J., 383
Lawrence, M., 207
Lawrence, S., 306
Lazar, A., 328, 342
Leahy, S., 344
Lederer, R., 149
Ledlow, S., 333
Lee, A., 271
Lee, C. D., 342
Lee, P., 378
Lehrer, J., 255, 282
Leki, I., 118, 333
Lenhart, A., 298, 299, 307
Lennon, C., 153
Leno, L. C., 198
Lent, R., 162
Lenz, B. K., 255
Leonard, J., 116
Lesaux, N. K., 169, 170, 188
Lesesne, T. S., 140
Lessard, A., 327
Lester, J. H., 58, 148
Leu, D. D., 305
Leu, D. J., 136, 258, 297, 305
Levine, E., 59, 330
Levin, M. E., 183, 200
Levin, J. R., 183, 200, 284
Lewis, C., 5
Lewis, L., 298
Ley, K., 258
Liaw, S., 86

Licht, B., 249
Lim, G., 139
Lin, L., 58
Linn, R., 315, 378
Lipsitz, J., 330
Lipson, M. Y., 290
Liston, D., 360, 364
Lo, Y., 125
Lopez, S. J., 360
Lorenzo, G., 276, 297
Loschert, K., 298
Lotan, R., 119
Lovelace, S., 333
Lu, M., 284
Lubliner, S., 169, 170
Lucas, T., 334
Luke, A., 299
Lund, J., 380
Luo, Y., 109
Lyman, F. T., 127

Ma'ayan, H. D., 256, 324, 334
Macan, H. T., 263
MacDonald, J., 130, 258
Macgill, A., 298
MacGinitie, W., 60
Madden, M., 298, 299, 307
Madrid, L. D., 116
Mahler, W. R., 143
Mamalakis, A., 142
Mancha, S., 347
Mangrum, C. T., 58, 343
Manning, S., 323
Manyak, P. C., 170, 336
Manz, S. L., 272
Manzo, A. V., 170, 173, 198, 234, 344
Manzo, K., 216
Manzo, U. C., 170, 173
Marashio, P., 100
Marcell, B., 255, 256
Marcotte, D., 327
Maria, K., 53, 60
Marinek, B. A., 53
Marini, I., 260
Marker, J., 314
Maroney, S. A., 324
Marshall, J., 115
Martin, A., 325
Martin, M. A., 41
Martin, S. H., 41
Martineau, J. A., 216, 230
Martinez, G., 340
Martin-Glenn, M. L., 325
Marx, R., 116
Mason, R., 258
Massey, D. D., 108
Masterman, L., 260
Mastropieri, M. A., 116, 183, 284, 321
Matthiesen, A. L., 163
Matusevich, M. N., 138, 139, 144
Mayall, H. J., 54
Mayer, R. E., 219
McBride, J. P., 257
McCormick, M. K., 340
McCrindle, A. R., 232
McDermott, M., 215
McDill, E. L., 340
McDonald, S., 53, 54
McElroy, K., 116
McGinley, W. J., 62
McGivern, J. E., 200
McGowan, T., 143
McIntyre, S. H., 282
MacKay, B., 214
McKeachie, W. J., 117
McKelvey, S., 367
McKenna, M. C., 215
McKeown, M. G., 53, 148, 169, 170, 174, 175, 178, 179
McLaughlin, H., 154
McLaughlin, M., 115
McLaughlin, T. F., 266
McLuhan, M., 295, 308
McManus, F., 57
McMaster, K. N., 116
McMillan, J. H., 326, 327
McMullan, M., 305
McMurry, F. M., 256
McNish, M. M., 258
McQuillan, J., 359
McTighe, J., 127
Meadows, D., 245
Meagher, M. E., 225
Mealey, D., 193
Medo, M. A., 193
Meeks, J. W., 59
Meller, W., 115
Meloth, M. S., 119
Memory, D., 193
Meneghetti, C., 256
Merkley, D. J., 301
Mesmer, H. A. E., 56
Metcalfe, S., 256
Metors, S. E., 276
Meyer, A., 323
Meyer, B. J. F., 64
Meyer, K., 115
Mikulecky, L., 31
Milby, T. M., 304
Miller, L., 144, 146
Miller, J., 215
Miller, J. A., 116
Miller, M., 216, 260
Miller, T. R., 116
Milligan, J., 256

Mills, R., 54
Mishook, J., 355
Miyake, N., 54
Moallem, M., 259
Moats, L. C., 172, 176
Mohr, E. S., 336
Mohr, K. A. J., 333, 335, 336
Moje, E. B., 111, 255, 258
Mokhtari, K., 82, 83
Molden, K., 115
Moller, J., 54
Monroe, J. K., 343
Montague, M., 112
Montelongo, J., 222
Moore, D. W., 58, 182, 256, 257
Moore, J. C., 183
Mora, J. K., 333
Moran, M., 139
Morgan, R. F., 59, 279, 290, 347
Morgan, W., 308
Morris, P. E., 284
Morrison, J. L., 310
Morrison, T. G., 10
Mosenthal, P. B., 152
Mouzaki, A., 82
Muller-Kalthoff, T., 54
Mundy, J., 339
Munson, J. M., 282
Murphy, P. K., 54
Murray, J., 363
Murray, R. K., 71
Myer, K., 256
Myers, J. 138, 139

Nagarajan, A., 54
Nagel, G. K., 335
Nagy, W. E., 170, 171, 173, 176, 187
Nash, R., 170
Nastasi, B. K., 54
Natriello, G., 340
Neisworth, J. T., 379
Nelson, B., 302
Nelson, J. S., 290
Nessel, D., 364
Nettle, D., 307
Neufeld, P., 339
Neuman, S. B., 327
Neuschwander, C., 62
Nevin, A. I., 323
Newton, E., 187
Newton, R. M., 187
Nichols, S., 144, 145
Nierlich, T., 218
Nist, S., 258, 276
Nist-Olejnik, S. L., 263
Noll, E., 327
Nomi, T., 355
Nordwall, M. B., 183, 200
Norman, D., 54
Nugent, J. S., 309
Nuthall, G., 56

Obermeyer, G., 296
Oblinger, D. G., 295, 296
O'Brien, D. G., 100
O'Brien, R., 141
O'Connell, B. J., 42
O'Donnell, A., 54
O'Donnell, P., 266, 271
Ofir, L., 232
Ogle, D., 63, 64, 123, 173, 185, 256, 272, 336, 338, 339
Olejnik, S., 187
Oliver, P., 334
Ollila, L., 334
Olson, M. R., 54, 55, 136, 163
Onwuegbuzie, A. J., 260
Opitz, M., 60, 281
Oppenheimer, T., 110, 312, 356
Ortega-Medina, M., 116
Oster, L., 131
Overman, L. T., 325, 326
Ozkan, H. H., 163

Padak, N., 175, 187, 234
Pallas, A. M., 340
Pally, M., 339
Palmer, D. R., 260
Palmer, R. G., 140, 143
Palombo, R., 39
Pappas, C., 143
Paquette, K. R., 223
Parasuraman, R., 354
Paratore, J., 383
Parker, L., 116
Patrick, H., 142, 324
Patterson, J. H., 325, 328
Pauk, W., 280
Paul, D. G., 359, 360
Paul, J., 59
Paivio, A., 57
Pearce, D., 222, 229, 247
Pearson, D., 100
Pearson, G., 295
Pearson, P. D., 56, 114
Pellicano, R., 324
Peregoy, S., 333
Perencevich, K. C., 144
Perin, D., 214
Perry, N. E., 110, 334
Perscher, Y., 257, 260
Persky, H., 215
Peterson, S., 147
Peterson, S. E., 116

Phelps, E., 282
Phillips, L., 215, 228, 279, 245
Piaget, J., 86
Piazza, S.V., 297
Pierce, D., 360, 361
Pierce, M. E., 171
Pierrard, M., 333
Pink, D., 39
Pisha, B., 323
Pitcher, B., 56
Pitcher, S. M., 53, 340
Pittleman, S. D., 193
Plante, A., 314
Planty, M., 53
Pogrow, S., 327
Potvin, P., 327
Prenn, M., 68
Prensky, M., 296
Pressley, M., 54, 169, 258
Prevatt, F. F., 257, 260
Proctor, B. E., 257, 260
Protopapas, A., 82
Puckett, R., 240
Pulido, D., 175
Purcell-Gates, V., 53, 216, 217, 230
Purdie, N., 258, 259, 260
Purkey, W. W., 34, 35
Purmensky, K., 108
Purves, A. C., 30
Putnam, R. T., 55
Putnam, S. M., 190

Quirk, M. P., 302

Rakes, G. C., 69
Rakes, T. A., 69
Rance-Roney, J., 273, 339
Raphael, T. E., 144, 181, 319
Rapport, M. J., 290
Rasinski, T. V., 60, 187, 234, 288
Rauscher, W., 30
Ray, K. W., 216, 219
Read, S., 222
Readance, J. E., 256, 257, 296
Ream, D., 311
Reardon, R. M., 309
Reaser, A., 257, 260
Reed, D. F., 326, 327
Reeves, S., 323
Reichard, C. A., 82, 83
Reid, R., 219
Reimer, J., 306
Reinking, D., 215, 259, 306
Rekrut, M. D., 305, 307
Reynolds, R. E., 54
Rhodes, J. A., 257, 261, 288, 295, 304, 309, 367
Rhodes, L. K., 381
Rhodes, R., 328
Rice, G. E., 180
Richardson, D., 115
Richardson, J. S., 125, 136, 140, 141, 144, 232, 257, 261, 264, 275, 288, 363, 376
Rickelman, R. J., 256, 257
Rifkin, J., 118
Riggs, E. G., 36
Rikers, R., 54
Rimmerman, A., 42
Risley, T. R., 175
Ritter, S., 378
Robelen, E., 360
Robertson, I. T., 263
Robinson, A., 323
Robinson, D. H., 69, 373
Robinson, F. P., 290
Robinson, P. D., 125
Robnolt, V. J., 56, 155, 257, 261, 288, 295, 367
Rodriguez, M., 197
Rodriguez, W. J., 143
Rogers, D. B., 256, 260, 261
Rohrbeck, C. A., 116
Romaine, S., 307
Rose, D. H., 323
Rose, M., 330
Rose, L. C., 360
Roser, N., 116, 119
Rostenberg, D., 322
Rothstein, R., 335
Royer, E., 327
Ruddell, M. R., 299
Rumelhart, D. E., 56
Rupley, W. H., 58
Russell, M., 224, 225, 245
Russell, S., 335
Ryan, R. M., 329
Rycik, J. A., 115
Ryder, R. J., 173, 193

Sacks, G., 172, 173, 176
Sadoski, M., 57
Saenz, L. M., 248
Sakta, C. G., 290
Salahu-Din, D., 215
Salcedo, J. B., 234
Salembier, G. B., 288
Salend, S. J., 320
Salinger, J. D., 154
Salinger, T., 340
Salvia, J., 355
Samuels, S. J., 169
Sanacore, J., 240
Sandmann, A., 144
Savage, T., 138, 139
Scanlon, D., 255
Scardamalia, M., 257

Schaeffer, R. K., 296
Scheffler, A. J., 259, 297
Schieffelin, B. B., 334
Schisler, R., 125
Schmar-Dobler, E., 53, 54
Schmidt, D. A., 301
Schmidt, H. G., 54
Schmidt, P. R., 334
Schmoker, M., 214
Schneider, J. J., 216
Schnotz, W., 56
Schoenbach, R., 81
Schollaert, A., 59
Schraw, G., 373
Schreiber, B., 263
Schulman, G., 258
Schumaker, J. B., 189
Schumm, J. S, 58, 200, 322
Schunk, D. H., 110
Schwanenflugel, P. J., 302
Schwartz, R. A., 260
Schwartz, R. M., 181
Scott, J. A., 171, 172, 173, 176
Scruggs, T. E., 183, 284, 321, 378
Sebasta, S., 257
Sedita, J., 255, 256
Seibert, J. K., 255, 259
Seidi, B., 328
Seifert, M., 161
Seitz, H., 380
Seminoff, N. E., 304, 314
Shamir, A., 303
Shanahan, T., 175
Shanklin, N., 31, 381
Shapiro, A. M., 69
Sheard, W., 359
Sheets, R. H., 334
Shelton, K. S., 219, 232
Shermis, S., 109
Sherry, L., 30
Shiel, T. G., 173
Shinn, C. M., 282
Short, D. 336
Sideridis, G. D., 82
Siedow, M. D., 64
Silva, P. U., 225
Simmons, D. C., 177, 256, 257, 260
Simos, P., 82
Simpson, M., 260, 280
Simpson, M. L., 173, 174, 176, 258, 276
Sinatra, G. M., 54
Sinatra, R., 245
Singer, H., 14
Skinner, C. H., 266, 271
Slaouti, D., 258
Slate, J. R., 260
Slavin, R. E., 116, 164, 324
Slough, S., 58
Smith, A., 298
Smith, C. B., 333
Smith, D. J., 148, 258
Smith, F., 288
Smith, F. G., 309
Smith, L., 302
Smith, L. J., 69
Smith, M. C., 30
Smith, N. B., 6
Smith, S., 241
Smuin, S., 94
Smyser, S. O., 381
Smythe, S., 339
Snowman, J., 329
Snow, C. E., 169, 177
Snow, D., 325
Snyder, T., 53
Soares, L., 163, 256, 260
Sobrol, D. T., 259
Soler, M., 53, 216, 230
Soloway, E., 116
Sousa, D., 57
Sowell, J., 188
Spache, G., 152
Spandel, V., 245
Spector, P. E., 42
Spratley, A., 342
Stahl, S. A., 171, 173, 187, 258
Stanford, B., 323
Stang, K. K., 215
Stanne, M. B., 116
Stanovich, K. E., 174, 177
Stauffer, R. G., 271, 290
Steenwyk, F. L., 244
Steinman, L., 160
Stephens, E., 58, 215, 228, 245
Stephens, K., 381
Sternberg, R. J., 59, 111, 282
Stevenson, R. J., 53, 54
Stewart, M. T., 355
Stewart, R. A., 140, 143
Stinson, M., 260
Stokes, S., 275
Straits, W., 144, 145, 146
Strang, R., 126, 257
Strangman, N., 301
Strauss, V., 256
Street, C., 215
Strickland, D. S., 343
Strong, M., 35
Sturtevant, E., 53
Sullivan, G. S., 183
Summers, J. J., 110
Supon, V., 378
Supovitz, J., 355
Suraya, A., 263

Surber, J. R., 183
Swafford, J., 119
Sweeny, S. M., 136
Swinyard, W. R., 10
Swiss, T., 218
Sylwester, R., 39
Szymanski, M., 259

Tatum, A., 343
Taylor, A. K., 111
Taylor, B. M., 100
Taylor, K., 364, 365, 367
Taylor, W., 156, 157
Tchudi, S. J., 216
Tchudi, S. N., 216
Tekmen, E. A., 175
Temple, C., 196
Tesser, A., 263
Thiede, K. W., 110
Thistlethwaite, L., 86
Thomas, M. H., 284
Thomas, M. M., 170
Thomas, W., 333, 335
Thompson, G., 347
Thompson, K., 314
Thompson, M., 55, 146
Thornburg, D. D., 361
Thousand, J. S., 323
Thurstone, L. L., 170
Tierney, R., 380
Toch, T., 149
Tolga, E., 381
Tomlinson, C. M., 342
Tompkins, G., 109
Tonelson, S. W., 43
Tonjes, M. J., 249
Tonks, S. M., 144
Torgenson, J., 249, 340
Tower, C., 217
Townsend, M. A. R., 324
Tracy, B., 219
Trathen, W., 144, 146
Trier, J., 308
Trueman, M., 263
Truxaw, M. P., 54, 55, 136, 163
Tung, R., 380
Turbill, J., 258
Turgeon, A., 54
Turner, S., 378
Twain, M., 275
Tynan, D., 351
Tyner, K., 136

Umolu, J., 347
Unsworth, L., 147
Ur, P., 209
Uzzell, L., 360

Vacca, R. T, 215, 327, 329
Valadez, C. M., 257
Valencia, S., 355
Valenzuela, M., 225
Van Blerkom, D. L., 130
Van Blerkom, M. L., 130
Van Daele, S., 333
Van der Schoot, 110
Vanderventer, M., 240
Van Dijk, T., 244, 250
Van Duinen, D., 379
Van Leeuwen, C. A., 225
Vann, R. J., 336
Van Valkenburg, J., 30, 35
Vardy, J., 314
Vasquez, V., 162
Vaughan, C. L., 232
Vaughan, J., 227
Vaughn, S., 322, 373
Veatch, J., 149
Venezky, R. L., 296
Verkoeijen, P., 54
Vermette, P., 119
Villa, R. A., 323
Villano, T. L., 138, 140
Villaune, S. K., 110, 174
Villegas, A. M., 334
Vitale, M. R., 83
Vlach, S., 340
Voelkel, A. R., 284
Vogt, M., 336
Von Glaserfeld, E., 222
Von Secker, C., 81
Vyas, S., 336
Vygotsky, L., 216, 232

Wade, S. E., 58
Waggoner, M. A., 93
Walczyk, J. J., 288
Walker, B., 260, 340
Walpole, S., 56, 148, 155
Walton, S., 364, 365, 367
Wang, A. Y., 284
Wang, J. H., 284
Wanzek, J., 373
Warm, J. S., 354
Waters, A., 258
Waters, M., 258
Watkins, R., 327
Watts-Taffe, S., 173, 185, 298
Weaver, C., 86
Webb, J. M., 284
Weber, K. P., 266
Wegmann, S., 216
Wei, S., 373
Weinstein, C. E., 118, 125, 219, 260
Weir, C., 348

Weiss, R. P., 39
Wells, J., 298
Wepner, S. B., 304, 313, 314
West, M., 169
West-Olatunji, C., 333
Westby, C., 154
Whalon, K., 344
Wharton-McDonald, R., 82
Wheeler, T. R., 333
White, E. B., 155
White, K., 378
White, T. G., 188
Whitehead, D., 228
Whitcomb, J., 360, 364
Whittington, D., 359
Wigfield, A., 144
Wiggins, G., 379
Wigginton, E., 231
Wilcox, B. L., 382
Wiley, J., 110
Wilkerson, S. B., 325
Wilkinson, B., 215, 219
Williams, B. T., 225, 298, 319, 320, 327, 328, 331, 333
Williams, D., 114
Willingham, D. T., 282
Wilson, A. A., 136
Windell, I., 71
Winebrenner, S., 169, 323
Winn, W. D., 214
Winne, P. H., 110
Winograd, P., 250
Winters, L. W., 379
Wixson, K. K., 177, 290, 355
Wolfe, D., 30
Wolfe, P., 30, 40
Wolgemuth, J., 284
Wong, W., 116
Wood, K. D., 125, 163, 256, 260
Wood, T. M., 379
Woodring, M. N., 257
Woolf, V., 66
Woosley, K., 276
Worthy, J., 53, 60, 355
Wray, D., 162
Wright, A., 209
Wright, V. H., 302
Wright-Frierson, V., 143

Xu, S. H., 319
Xu, Y., 322

Yager, R., 139
Yager, S., 139
Yanagihara, A., 188
Yang, Y., 116
Yanowitz, K. L., 75
Yeager, D., 243
Yeh, H., 116
Yell, M. M., 244
Yi, H., 93
Yoon, J., 34
Yopp, H. K., 71
Yopp, R. H., 71
Young, D. B., 258
Young, J. P., 41
Yurick, A. L., 125
Ysseldyke, J., 355

Zabrucky, K., 58
Zakaluk, B., 250
Zander, M. J., 309
Zaragoza, N., 249
Zaskoda, Z., 235
Zawilinski, L., 218, 225, 297
Zhang, Z., 200
Zimmerman, B. J., 110
Zimmerman, S. A., 260
Zintz, M. V., 249
Zucker, T. A., 215

Subject Index

ABCs of cultural understanding and communication, 334
ABOUT/POINT activity, 128, 129
Academic discourse, 327
Academic vocabulary, 169
Academic Word List (AWL), 169
Access, 301
Accountability, 355, 362, 363, 364
Acculturation, 332
Achievement tests, 357
Acronym, 170, 284
Acrostic, 284
ADD, 41
ADHD, 256, 321
Adequate yearly progress (AYP), 354, 359
Adjunct strategies, 83
Advance organizer, 68
Affect, 299
Affective bonds, 34
Affective domain, 29, 31, 37, 43, 48, 326
Affective environment, 40
Affective filter hypothesis, 332
Affix Animals, 189
Affixes, 18
Age of multiliteracies, 258, 259
Alternative assessment, 379
American Library Association, 139
American Psychological Association, 361, 363
American School Counseling Association, 260
Among Schoolchildren, 352
Analogies, 75–77, 345
Analogy/example (pattern of organization), 93
Analysis (pattern of organization), 93
Analytical reading, 115
Anecdotal records assessment (ARA), 386
Annotations, 234
Anticipation guide, 71–73, 126
Antonyms, 176, 185, 186
Applied learning, 97
Apprehension, 81
Aptitude tests, 356
Arbitration, 119
Assessment, 56, 156, 158, 216, 223, 240, 241, 260, 355, 366, 367, 372, 386
Assessment instruments, 34
Assessments of study skills, 261
Assimilation, 332
Assistance, 20
Assistance phase/step of study, 15, 16, 21, 69, 81, 230, 239, 241, 244, 266, 275
Assumptive teaching, 6, 11, 12
Asynchronous, 163, 306, 308
At-risk learners, 43, 112, 256, 325
At-risk readers, 248–250, 345
At-risk students, 43, 289, 324
Attention deficit hyperactivity disorder (ADHD), 256, 321
Attention deficit disorder (ADD), 41
Attitude, 30
Attitude survey, 32
Attributes of good readers, 114
Audacity, 301
Authentic assessment, 379–386
Authenticity rating scale, 217
Authentic literacy, 217
Authentic texts, 82
Authentic writing, 216, 218
Autobiography of Benjamin Franklin, The, 303
Autonomous learners/learning, 12, 14, 109
Automony, 255
Avatar, 302
AYP, 354, 359

Background knowledge, 59, 157, 158
Bader textbook analysis, 149
Barriers to comprehension and learning, 147
Basic Interpersonal Communication skills (BICs), 332
Beginner-oriented text, 348
Behavior management techniques, 328
Bell, T., 149
BICs, 332
Bilingual approach, 335
Bilingual education, 333
Bingo, 200, 204, 206, 207
Biopoem, 235
BlackBoard, 384
Blog (Web log), 163, 218, 225, 298, 300, 308, 309
Book club, 144
Bound morpheme, 168
Boys and literacy, 41

Brain-based learning, 40
Brain-based learning theory, 39
Brain-based teaching, 39
Brain research, 214
Brainstorming, 73, 112, 119, 120, 173, 371
Brain writing, 228
Building positive relationships, 329, 330
Building background, 157

C3B4Me, 243
"Calculating Machine," 155
CALP, 332, 335
Captrends, 367
Caring for all students, 330
Cartoons, 276
Casing, 330
Catcher in the Rye, The, 154
Categorization, 195
Categorization of facts, 347
Causal relationships, 95
Cause and effect (pattern of organization), 93, 95
Cause/effect chart, 17
CBM, 322
Center on Educational Policy, 360
Charts, 327, 339, 350
Chat rooms, 308
Checklist, 149, 156, 223
Children's Internet Protection Act, 296
Chunking, 286–288
Cinquain, 237, 238
Civil Rights Act, 333
Clarification, 93
Class log/notebook, 232
Classroom response system (CRS), 365, 371
Clicker, 71, 365, 371
Closed word sort, 196
Cloze, 156–161
Cloze passage, 156, 157
Cloze procedure, 156–161
Cloud computing, 314
Code switching, 8
Cognition, 299
Cognitive Academic Language Proficiency (CALP), 332, 335
Cognitive development, 30
Cognitive dissonance, 58, 59, 61
Cognitive processing, 136
Cognitive strategies, 219
Coherence, 138, 148, 149
Collaboration, 116, 319, 320, 324, 326
Collaborative reasoning, 93, 94
Collaboration techniques, 119
Collaborative writing, 218, 243
Commission on No Child Left Behind, 360
Commitment, 118
Communicative arts, 6, 7, 8, 64, 70
Compare/contrast maps, 339
Comparison and contrast (pattern of organization), 93, 95
Comprehensible input, 332
Comprehension, 58, 64, 71, 143, 147, 156, 169, 173, 180, 196, 197, 222, 227, 230, 231
Comprehension monitoring, 109, 110, 219, 340
Comprehension strategies, 82
Computer games, 299
Computers as writing tools, 224, 225
Conation, 36, 43
Conative aspects of human behavior, 36
Conative factors, 37, 40, 49
Conative variables, 36
Concept-formation study guides, 347
Concept map/mapping, 68, 95, 183
Conceptual base of understanding, 177
Conceptual density, 138, 165
Condition of Education 2009, The, 53
Condition of Education 2010, The, 53
Consensus, 119, 196
Consistent routine, 342
Constructivism, 85–86, 259
Constructivist teaching strategies, 348
Constructivist theory of learning, 85, 86, 90, 106
Content-area literature circles, 144
Content-focused drama, 243
Content-specific vocabulary, 169
Context clue discovery, 185
Context clues, 185, 186, 187, 197
Contextual analysis, 187, 188
Contextual knowledge, 173
Conversational language proficiency, 332, 333
Cooperative graphing, 282
Cooperative group/grouping, 267
Cooperative learning, 116–119, 127, 163, 331
Cooperative learning teams, 119
Cooperative reading activity (CRA), 281
Cooperative study, 109
Cornell system, 280
CRA, 281
Cramming, 282
Creative thinkers, 372
CRI, 334
Crisis as opportunity, 329
Criteria, 78, 147, 156, 158
Criterion-referenced test, 358, 359
Critical annotation, 234
Critical literacy, 115, 139, 162
Critical reading, 11
Critical thinking, 71, 94, 111, 112, 114, 136, 164, 234, 295, 311, 369
CRS, 365, 371
Cubing, 226–228
Cultural context, 136
Cultural discontinuity, 333
Cultural fairy tales, myths, and legends, 141
Culturally responsive instruction (CRI), 334
Culturegrams, 336
Culture shock, 333
Curriculum-based management (CBM), 322

Database, 139, 298, 301
Decision making, 112, 114, 119, 126
Deep strategies, 274
Deep thinking, 141, 282, 340
Definitions, 186, 192
Dependent learners, 12
Derivational suffixes, 188
Designing a test, 369, 377
Diagnostic test, 356, 357
Dialogue journal, 234
Dictionary, 185, 190, 192
Dictionary game, 193
Differentiated instruction, 323
Differentiation of instruction, 45
Digital divide, 313
Digital images, 276
Digital jumpstarts, 273, 339
Digital jumpstart preview, 274
Digital literacy, 296–300, 310, 313, 315
Digital text, 295, 297, 298, 299, 302, 303, 304, 310
Direct explanations, 186
Direct instruction, 215, 342
Directed listening technique, 266
Directed Reading-Thinking Activity (DR-TA), 13, 87–90, 92, 103, 197, 271, 290
Disability, 320–323
Discourse, 110, 255
Discourse analysis, 93
Discrepancy model, 322
Discussion group, 142, 164, 308
DISSECT, 189
Divergent-thinking questions, 101
Diverse learners, 319
Double-entry journal, 123, 232, 350
Dreamweaver, 301
DR-TA, 13, 87–90, 103, 197, 271, 290
Dumbed-down text, 149

e-book, 303
Editing, 225, 226, 231, 240, 243, 245, 246
Education of All Handicapped Children Act, 321
EDU-CAUSEConnect, 365
Electronic book (e-book), 303
Electronic journal, 306
Electronic literacy, 313
Electronic mail (e-mail), 136, 142, 224, 303, 306
Electronic media, 136
Electronic text, 162, 299, 304
Elementary and Secondary Education Act (ESEA), 359
Elementary Reading Attitude Survey (ERAS), 31
ELL, 53, 56, 59, 66, 135, 156, 178, 273, 308, 326, 333, 335, 336, 338, 339, 360
e-mail, 136, 142, 224, 303, 306
Embedded questions, 348
Emergent literacy, 219
English as a second language (ESL), 55, 124, 335
English for academic purposes, 332
English language learner (ELL), 53, 256, 273, 308, 326, 333, 335, 337, 339
Equity pedagogy, 320
Enriched environment, 39, 40
Environment, 142
Equity pedagogy, 320
ESL, 55, 333, 335
ESL students, 139, 331–333, 337, 339
ESL/TESOL approach, 335
Evaluation, 222, 356, 359, 386
Excel, 301
Extended anticipation guide, 128
External locus of control, 42, 325

Fact and opinion, 115
Factstorming, 73, 74, 228, 375, 376
Filemaker Pro, 301
First step to note taking, 266
First-person summary, 238
5 R's, 280
Fixations, 288
Fix-up activity, 348
Fix-up strategies, 105, 106
Flash card, 131
Flesch-Kincaid readability formula, 154, 155
Flesch Reading Ease Formula, 155
Flexible reading, 287
Fluency, 287
Fluent reader/reading, 81, 140
Following directions, 274
Four-column organizer for word mastery, 198
Four-level framework, 142, 178
Foxfire books, 231
Framework, 12, 14, 16, 20
Free morpheme, 168
Free ride, 117
Free-write, 229
From the Mixed Up Files of Mrs. Basil E. Frankweiler, 154
Frustration-level score, 157
Fry Readability Formula, 66, 153, 154
Fry readability graph, 153
Fry Short Formula, 156
Future orientation, 328

Garage Band, 301
GATOR technique, 43
General Service List (GSL), 169
Geopoem, 236
Gifted and talented, 321
Gifted students, 265
GIST, 244
Global coherence, 148
Globalization, 313
Go Mad, 286
Globalization, 304, 313
Good readers, 342
Google Scholar, 269

Gradual release model, 347
Graphic aids, 255, 260, 275
Graphic organizer, 7, 22, 64, 68–70, 95, 144, 180, 298, 300, 301, 304, 342, 373
Graphic representation, 71
Graphs, 260, 272
Great Gatsby, The, 381
Group-and-label technique, 112
Group decision making, 112
Group frame, 338
Groups, 116
Group summarizations, 126
Group work, 35, 117
Group-worthy task, 119
GRP, 91, 92
Guided Language Experience model, 338
Guided reading procedure (GRP), 91, 92
Guided writing procedure, 241
Guide-o-rama, 101, 102

Habit of reading, 41
Hard to reach, 329
Harvard University, 302
Heuristic annotation, 234
Higher incidence disability, 320
Higher-level questioning bookmark, 89, 90, 101
Higher-level thinking, 90, 100, 201, 223
Higher-order questions, 87, 89
Higher-order thinking skills, 85, 136
High literacy, 258
High-literacy homes, 327
Highly qualified, 359
High-stakes assessment, 341
High-stakes issue, 361
High-stakes proposition, 327
High-stakes testing, 5, 356, 361, 362, 379
History as Story, 249
Homework, 138, 265, 365
House of the Seven Gables, The, 58
How We Decide, 255
Hypertext, 54, 259, 297, 303, 306

i + l, 332
IDEA, 320, 321
IDEA 2004, 321
IDEIA, 321
Identity kits, 8
IEP, 321
Imaging through key words, 200, 201
Immigrants, 331, 333
Improving America's Schools Act, 333
Incidental vocabulary development, 174
Inclusion, 320
Inclusive, 323
Incomplete thinking, 12
Inconsiderate discourse, 147, 148
Independent carryover, 255
Independent learners, 12
Independent-level reading, 154
Independent-level score, 157
Individualized education program (IEP), 321
Individuals with Disabilities Education Act (IDEA), 320, 321
Individuals with Disabilities Education Improvement Act (IDEIA), 321
Inferences, 186
Inferential learning, 97
Inferential questions, 100
Inflectional suffixes, 188
InfoBeat, 269
Informal assessment, 356
Information Age, 5, 136
Informational text, 222, 249
Informational text writing, 222
Information communication technologies (ICTs), 295
Information-processing model, 259
Information literacy, 259, 297
Inquiry, 226
Inspiration, 17, 83, 181, 189, 259, 300
Instant message (IM), 307
Instructional cloze, 159, 160
Instructional-level score, 157
Instructional setting, 154
Instructional software programs, 301
Intentional vocabulary development, 176
Intention annotation, 234
Interactive learning, 83
Interactive notebook, 348, 350
Interactive reading, 162
Internal-external journal, 42
Internal locus of control, 42, 43
International Reading Association, 78, 139, 298, 303, 361, 363
International Society for Technology in Education (ISTE), 298
International Technology Education Association, 295
Internet, 136, 142, 163, 177, 231, 296, 298, 299, 301–306
Internet treasure hunt, 275
Intervention delivery system, 322
Invented spellings, 222
Inventive spelling, 219
IQ-achievement discrepancy model, 322
iTunes, 301

Jigsaw, 164
Jobs, Steve, 312
Jot chart, 98–99, 191, 384
Journals, 222, 232, 234
Jumpstart, 126
Juxtapositioning, 115

Keesha's House, 146
Keypal, 225
Key-word strategy, 200

Kidsclick, 269
Kidspiration, 181, 189
K-W-L activity, 63
K-W-L Plus, 64

Language acquisition, 332
Language arts, 6
Language Experience Approach (LEA), 347
LASSI, 260
LEA, 347
Learning and Study Strategies Inventory (LASSI), 260
Learning disabilities, 41, 173, 176, 177, 248, 249, 304, 360
Learning goals, 54
Learning log, 232
LEP, 333, 335
Lesson framework, 14
Leveled texts, 147
Lexile Framework, 152, 153, 154, 348
Lexile scores, 154
Lexis-Nexis universe, 269
Life on the Mississippi, 275
Limbic system, 255
Limerick, 241
Limited English proficiency (LEP), 333, 335
Limit testing, 330
Linguistic bridges, 333
Linguistic context, 136
Listening, 266
Listening guides, 266
Listserv, 308, 309
Literacy tool, 10, 13
Literal comprehension, 100
Literal learning, 97
Literature-based approach, 34
Literature circle, 144, 145, 146
Local coherence, 148
Local discourses, 8
Locating and selecting information, 262, 268, 269, 270, 291
Locus of control, 42, 43
Long-term memory, 56
Low-achieving students, 83
Lower incidence disability, 320, 321
Low self-esteem, 329, 331
Low socioeconomic environment, 327, 328, 360
Low socioeconomic status (SES), 175, 324
Low SES students, 175

MAD, 286
Magic square, 202
Making connections strategy, 122
Maps/mapping, 83, 180, 300
Marginal gloss, 101, 102, 105
Marginalization, 256
Mark Twain, 275
MARSI, 82, 83, 260
Martin Luther King activity, 312
Massed study, 282
Matching reader with text, 55
Mature readers, 82
Maze, 156, 161, 162
Metacognition, 255, 258, 259
Metacognitive Awareness of Reading Strategies Inventory (MARSI), 82–83, 260
Metacognitive comprehension-monitoring strategies, 219
Metacognitive processing, 5, 276
Metacognitive strategies, 219
Metaphor of reading level, 155
Method of loci, 286
Microsoft *Office Suite*, 301
Microsoft *Word*, 300
Mikulecky Behavioral Reading Attitude Measure (MBRAM), 31, 32
Mnemonic-a-day technique, 286
Mnemonic device, 183, 200
Mnemonics, 201, 276
Mnemonic strategies, 201
Modeling, 10, 215
Modified anticipation guide, 338
Monitor model, 332
Morpheme, 173, 188, 189
Morphemic analysis, 187, 188
Morphology, 185, 187
Motivation, 30, 82, 329
Motivation annotation, 234
Mrs. Frisby and the Rats of NIMH, 141
Multicultural literature, 142, 143
Multimodal platform, 136
Multimodal literature circles, 146
Multimodal methods, 165
Multimodal resources, 339
Multimodal text, 137, 139, 162
Multiple resources, 139, 147
Multitext, 139
Multi-use virtual environment games, 302
Mystery clue game, 94, 95, 344

National Assessment of Educational Progress (NAEP), 4, 53, 324, 357, 359
National Board for Professional Teaching Standards (NBTS), 379
National Capital Language Resource Center, 381
National Center for Educational Statistics (NCES), 4, 298, 324, 359
National Center for Technology Education, 296
National Center on Response to Intervention, 381
National Clearinghouse for English Language Acquisition, 331
National Council for the Social Studies, 139
National Council of Teachers of English (NCTE), 78, 110, 298
National Council of Teachers of Mathematics, 78, 139, 361, 363
National Educational Technology Standards (NETS), 298
National Education Association (NEA), 138
National Institute of Child Health and Human Development, 169, 175
National Literacy Panel on Language Minority Children and Youth, 175

National Reading Panel (NRP), 169
National Science Teachers Association, 78, 139
National standards, 14
National Writing Project, 215
Natural order hypothesis, 332
NCES, 4, 324
NCLB, 5, 359, 360
Neocortex, 255
Net generation, 295, 299
Net savvy, 297, 303
Net savvy generation, 300, 308
New literacies, 5, 8, 136, 258, 259
New London Group, 136
New Media Consortium (NMC), 299
No Child Left Behind Act (NCLB), 5, 359, 360
Nonauthentic writing tasks, 217
Nonreader, 347
Nontraditional tests, 372, 373, 379, 386
Norming, 357, 358
Norm-referenced tests, 357
North Central Regional Educational Laboratory (NCREL), 137, 297
Notations, 122
Note taking, 267, 276, 280
Not listening, 343
Numbered heads together, 118, 123

Objective test, 366, 372, 378, 379
Odd word out, 207, 209
Office for Civil Rights Memorandum, 333
Office of Educational Technology, 299
Old Man and the Sea, The, 154
On-demand writing, 216
On-line communication, 306
Open notes, 371
OpenOffice, 300
Open-note test, 279
Open word sort, 197
Oral literacy, 327
Oral reading proficiency, 266
Organizational formations of text, 93
Organizational (jot) chart, 21, 22
Organizational strategies, 219, 276
Organizational structures, 94
OST, 325
Outlines/outlining, 276–278
Out-of-school discourse, 10
Out-of-school-time program (OST), 325

Paganini, 304
Paired reading, 118, 124, 125
Paired-word sentence generation, 174
Paralysis by analysis, 255
Parent-Teacher Association (PTA), 360
PAR Lesson Framework, 12, 14, 15, 16, 18, 25, 45, 64, 66, 70, 71, 81, 87, 90, 108, 137, 177, 178, 197, 201, 210, 211, 226, 251, 260, 265, 326, 370
Partner Reading and Content Too (PRC2), 338
Passive learners, 249
Pattern guides, 95
Patterns of organization, 95
Peer editing, 245, 246
Peers, 175
Peer Think-Aloud Game, 131, 132
Peg-word system, 285
Peppermint theory, 354
Perspective cubing, 228
Phi Delta Kappa/Gallup Poll, 4, 30, 360
Pictures, 272, 276
PIES, 117
Piquing Students' Interest, 192
Plagiarism, 258, 310
PL 93–380, 333
PL 94–141, 321
PL 103–382, 333
PL 108–446, 321
PLEASE, 343
Podcast, 162, 164, 190, 191, 201, 218, 267, 268, 298, 303, 339
Poetry, 235–238
Polysemous words, 172
Polysemy, 171
Pop quizzes, 364–366
Portfolio, 381–385
Positive classroom climate, 31, 35, 49
Positive relationships, 329
Positron emission tomography (PET), 214
Possible sentences, 182
Post-graphic organizer, 22, 118, 120, 121, 143, 194, 195, 337
Postreading reflective strategies, 108
Powerpoint, 164
PQR2ST+, 290
PRC2, 338
Predictability, 330
Prediction, 87, 93, 232
Prediction guide, 73, 74
Prefixes, 188
Prelearning concept check, 61
Prelearning concept guide, 21
PreP, 74, 75
Preparation, 18, 19, 21, 216, 266
Preparation phase/step, 15, 16, 53, 69, 81, 226, 241, 266
Preparing learners, 137
Preparation strategy, 66, 74, 77
Pre-underlining, 276
Preview guide, 272, 273
Previewing, 271–273
Prewriting phase, 223, 226, 242, 243, 245
Prewriting, 223, 224, 225, 241
Primer, 6
Prior knowledge, 52–60, 69, 73, 74, 75, 77, 83, 156, 157, 241, 379
Problem-solving, 54, 73, 112, 144, 299
Process writing, 216, 223, 250
Products of writing, 214, 215, 222, 223, 251
Project-based learning, 45

Project Tomorrow, 298
PTA, 360
Public Law 93–380, 333
Public Law 94–142, 321
Public Law 103–382, 333
Public Law 108–446, 321
Purkey's four levels, 34

QAR, 80, 101, 102
Quantitative assessment, 356
Question annotation, 234
Question/answer relationship (QAR), 80, 101, 102
Question-generated discussion, 100
Questioning, 43, 82, 85, 93, 100, 101, 105
Questions, 82, 86, 87, 89, 93, 100, 101
Quick-write, 229

Race to the Top, 359, 361
RAFT technique, 240
Rallytable, 118, 123
Ralph S. Mouse, 222
Random cloze, 156
Rapid reading, 288, 289
Rate of reading, 288
Rational cloze, 159
Readability, 64, 66, 147, 149, 156
Readability formula, 147, 149, 152, 153, 155, 156
Read-along, 139, 140
Read-aloud, 115, 131, 139, 140, 141
Reading as transmission, 258
Reading as transaction, 258
Reading flexibly, 256, 287, 288
Reading-writing connection, 219
Ready reading reference bookmark, 120
Real Simple Syndication (RSS), 303
REAP annotation system, 234
Reciprocal teaching, 93
Reflection, 20, 22, 82, 84, 87, 193, 198, 241
Reflection guide, 126
Reflection phase/step, 15, 16, 69, 71, 90, 108, 110, 128, 194, 226, 240, 244
Reflective learning, 110, 133
Reflective reading, 67
Reflective study technique, 132
Reflective thinking, 64, 127
Reflective thought, 108
Reflective writing, 241
Refugees, 332, 333
Reliability, 358
Remedial readers, 344
Repeated readings, 125
ReQuest procedure, 344
Rereading, 126
Resilient students, 325, 326, 327
Response to intervention (RTI), 322
Retention, 290
Revising, revision, 66, 67
Rewriting, 64–67
Rewriting text, 64–67
Role playing, 125
Root word, 173, 187, 189, 190
RSS, 303
Rubric, 223, 245
Rule of thumb, 149, 152

Saccadic eye movements, 288
Scaffolding, 110, 175, 336
SCAN and RUN, 288
Scanning, 197, 289
Schema, schemata, 56, 58, 69, 111, 140, 173, 244
Schema theory, 56, 57
SCORER, 378
SEARCH, 269
Search engine optimizer, 311
See What I Found, 237
Segments of text, 87, 93
Self-assessment, 35, 56
Self-directed learning, 380
Self-efficacy, 42, 329
Self-esteem, 245, 329, 333
Self-evaluation logs, 263
Self-inventories, 179
Self-ratings, 376
Self-regulated learners, 109
Self-Regulated Strategy Development model, 219
Self-regulated study skills, 260
Self-regulation, 219, 258, 259, 260
Semantic clues, 185
Semantic feature analysis, 193, 194
Semantic map, 68, 180, 181, 189
Sequential or chronological order, 93
SES (socioeconomic status), 138, 175
Sheltered content instruction, 335
Sheltered Instruction Observation Protocol (SIOP), 336
Short statements, 244
Short-term memory, 56
Signal words, 186
6+1 TRAIT model, 223, 245
SIOP, 336
Situated cognition, 258
Skimming, 197, 289
Skype, 164, 299
SLEP, 335
Smart phone, 41
SMOG readability formula, 153, 154
SNS, 299, 300, 308
Social computing, 307
Social media, 298
Social networking website (SNS), 299, 300
Socioemotional factors, 332
Songs and raps, 287
Sound and the Fury, The, 152
Space to think, 280

Special education, 320, 321, 322, 331, 351
Special education students, 351
Specific learning disability (SLD), 322
Spacing effect, 282
Speed drill, 288
Speed reading, 197, 288
Spider map, 181
SQ3R, 290
SQRC, 290
Standard English, 8, 10
Standardized test, 170, 215, 357, 359, 361
Standards, 78, 298, 361
Standards for learning, 5, 26
Story impressions, 62
Story mapping, 68, 146
Story web, 68
Strategic assistance, 81
Strategic instruction, 13, 94, 106
Strategy, 13, 30
Strategy repertoire, 105, 108
Striving readers, 11, 105
Structural analysis, 187, 188
Structure of text, 93
Struggling adolescent learner, 249, 340
Struggling reader, 68, 93, 103, 106, 138, 140, 176, 177, 201, 248–250, 273, 343
Struggling student, 139, 340
Student-centered approach to learning, 5
Student-generated questions, 101, 106, 130, 229
Student self-reflection, 261
Students with limited English proficiency (SLEP), 335
Students with special needs, 320, 323, 333
Study behaviors, 255, 256, 259, 276, 288
Study distracters, 261
Study questions, 370
Study skills, 255–292
Study strategy, 276
Study system, 290
Study tactics, 259
Subjective Approach to Vocabulary (SAV), 198
Subordinate, 83, 84
Suffixes, 188
Summarizing, 93, 250
Summary annotation, 234
Summary writing, 244, 250
Superordinate, 84
Survivor guilt, 333
Sustained interaction, 343
Synonym, 157, 159, 176, 185, 186
Synchronous, 163, 306, 307
Systems of study, 290

Tales of a Fourth-Grade Nothing, 154
Taxonomy, 101
Teacher-made tests, 367, 368
TeacherTube, 301
TeachQuest, 101
Teaching English to speakers of other languages (TESOL), 335
Techno-blunders, 313
Technology, 136, 148, 293–316, 371
Technological literacy, 13, 295, 314
Telephony, 303
Television, 174, 312
Temporary spellings, 222
TESOL, 335
Testing, 356, 367–369
Test-taking skills, 378
Test-taking tips, 378
Test-wise, 371, 378
Textbook analysis chart, 149, 150
Textbooks, 136–138, 146–148, 157
Textbook treasure hunt, 275
Texting, 136
Text lookback, 125, 126
Text Mapping Plus, 340, 341
Textmasters, 146
Text structure, 64, 94
Textual coherence, 138, 148
Thematic units, 336
Thesaurus, 185, 193
Thesis annotation, 234
THIEVES, 272
Think-aloud, 130, 131, 132, 133, 340
Think-pair-share, 118, 127, 128
ThinkQuest, 86
Third space, 451
Threaded discussion, 86, 142, 308, 371
3+ level study guide, 97–98
Three-level study guide, 97
Three-step interview, 118, 125, 164
Three-tier intervention process, 322
Time, 337
Time in language acquisition, 333
Time management, 263, 265
Time shifting in learning, 267
Title VI, Civil Rights Act, 333
Title VII, Civil Rights Act, 333
TOAST study system, 197
To Kill a Mockingbird, 58
Touchstone Discussion Project, 141
Trade books, 138, 143, 144
Traditional test, 365, 366, 369–372, 377, 379, 381, 383
Transaction, 258
Transitional bilingual education, 335
Transmission, 258
Transmission model of instruction, 324
Treasure hunts, 306
Tree diagram, 68, 69
Trust, 330
tWeb, 301
Tweeting, 307
21st Century Literary Summit, 297
Twitter, 307
Two-column note-taking system, 280

Two-finger thinking, 12
Typographic aids, 255

UDL, 323
Underachievement, 324
Underlining, 276
Universal design for learning (UDL), 323
U.S. Department of Education, 302, 321
Using literature in the content classroom, 143

Validity, 357
Value-added assessment, 363
Venn diagram, 144, 300
Virginia Grade Level Alternative (VGLA), 379
Visual aids, 69, 275, 337, 341, 373
Visualization, 337
Visual literacy, 7, 13, 68, 275, 297
Vocab-lit strategy, 198
Vocabulary bingo, 200, 204
Vocabulary connections, 181, 183
Vocabulary deficit, 189
Vocabulary illustrations, 200–203
Vocabulary list, 191, 198
Vocabulary podcast, 190, 191
Vocabulary rule strategy, 188
Vocabulary self-collection strategy (VSS), 198
Voice over Internet Protocol (VoIP), 299, 303
Vonage, 299
VSS, 198

Warm-up writing, 229
Washback effect, 361
Web-based learning, 86, 163
Web-based reading and study, 259
Web log (blog), 309
Web page, 300, 304, 306, 311
Web page identity check, 311
WebQuest, 86, 306
What I Know Activity (WIKA), 19, 20, 64, 89, 103, 376
When Hitler Stole Pink Rabbit, 153
WIKA, 19, 20, 64, 89, 103, 376
Wiki, 218, 225, 269, 299, 308, 310
Wikipedia, 138, 269
Woolf, Virginia, 66, 67
Word analogies, 201
Word attack paradigm, 189
Word bubble, 207
Word consciousness, 176, 183, 210
Word families, 187
Word inquiry, 200, 210
Word inventories, 179
Word knowledge, 170, 171, 174
Word map, 181
Word play, 174
Word processing, 300
Word sort, 176, 189, 196
World Is Flat, The, 295
Write-alouds, 223
Writing, importance of, 214
Writing as a product, 222, 223
Writing as a process, 223
Writing for at-risk and struggling readers, 248–250
Written conversation, 232
Written preview, 13, 68
Writing process, 222, 226, 240, 251
Writing prompts, 226
Writing to learn, 212–252

YouTube, 301, 308

PAR Cross-Reference Guide

	SCIENCE	MATH	SOCIAL STUDIES
Primary	Activity 2.9, p. 44 Activity 3.12, p. 73 Activity 4.5, p. 91 Activity 4.12, p. 103 Activity 6.6, p. 161 Activity 7.17. p. 204 Activity 8.1, p. 224 Activity 8.10, p. 237 Activity 8.14, p. 244 Activity 11.6, p. 346 Activity 12.9, p. 383	Activity 3.16, p. 76 Activity 7.12, p. 195 Activity 7.22, p. 209 Activity 9.12, p. 277 Activity 12.5, p. 368	PAR example lesson, pp. 16–18 Activity 2.12, p. 48 Activity 5.2, p. 113 Activity 9.13, p.278
Intermediate	Activity 3.9, p. 69 Activity 4.9, p. 97 Activity 5.3, p. 121 Activity 5.9, p. 130 Activity 5.10, p. 130 Activity 7.7, p. 184 Activity 8.5, p. 231 Activity 8.8, p. 236 Activity 9.11, p. 275 Activity 11.4, p. 342	Activity 4.14, p. 105 Example Brainwriting, #4, p. 228 Activity 11.2, p. 338 Activity 11.5, p. 345	Activity 3.2, p. 61 Activity 3.10, p. 70 Activity 3.14, p. 74 Activity 6.3, p. 158 Activity 12.8, p. 375 Activity 12.10, p. 383
Middle	Activity 3. 4, p. 63 Activity 6.2, p. 145 Activity 6.5, p. 160 Activity 7.13, p. 196 Activity 8.11, p. 239 Activity 9.5, p. 268 Activity 9.15, p. 281 Activity 11.4, p. 342 Activity 12.6, p. 372	PAR example lesson, pp. 19–20 Activity 3.1, p. 57 Activity 3.3, p. 62 Activity 4.11, p. 99 Activity 7.21, p. 207	Activity 2.11, p. 46 Activity 6.1, p. 141 Activity 6.7, p. 165 Activity 7.1, p. 174 Activity 8.9, p. 237 Activity 10.2, p. 300 Activity 10.7, p. 311 Activity 11.1, p. 334 Activity 12.2, p. 366
Secondary	PAR example lesson, pp. 20–22 Activity 3.6, p. 66 Activity 4.13, p. 104 Activity 6.2, p. 145 Activity 7.11, p. 194 Activity 7.14, p. 199 Activity 8.6, p. 233 Activity 8.12, p. 241 Activity 9.4, p. 266 Analogy Example, pp. 346–7	Activity 3.13, p. 74 Activity 8.2, p. 227 Activity 9.8, p. 270 Activity 9.16, p. 283 Analogy Example, p. 346 Activity 12.7, p. 374	Activity 2.11, p. 46 Activity 3.8, p. 68 Analogy example, p. 75 Activity 5.4, p. 122 Activity 5.5, p. 123 Activity 5.7, p. 128 Activity 5.11, p. 132 Activity 6.1, p. 141 Activity 8.4, p. 230 Activity 10.2, p. 300 Activity 10.7, p. 311 Activity 11.1, p. 334 Activity 11.8, p. 349